ROCKDETECTOR

A-Z *of*

BLACK METAL

GARRY SHARPE-YOUNG

www.rockdetector.com

CHERRY
RED BOOKS

This edition published in Great Britain
in 2001 by Cherry Red Books Ltd.,
Unit 17, 1st Floor, Elysium Gate West,
126–128 New King's Road,
London SW6 4LZ

All you need to know about the author:
Born: Münchengladbach 1964
Raised: On Judas Priest
Status: Decade of wedlock
Raising: Kerr, Krystan, Kjaric
Hair: By Vikernes

Artwork by Axis Europe Plc.
Printed and bound in Great Britain by
Biddles Ltd., Guildford and King's Lynn.
Cover Design by Jim Phelan at Wolf Graphics Tel: 020 8299 2342

Thanks: Michael Langbein, Martin Wickler (Nuclear Blast), Jose Montemayor
(Necropolis), DJ (Modern Invasion Music), Dana Duffey, Johan Heidegger,
Olly Hahn.

ISBN 1–901447–30–8

Introduction
Black Metal

Black Metal started the day Terry 'Geezer' Butler put down his Dennis Wheatley novel, or came out of the cinema after having witnessed a Boris Karloff movie, whichever legend you prefer to subscribe to. In the same manner as the apple dropping on Sir Isaac Newton's head or Archimedes' bathwater overflowing into the street, a great idea had been born. An inspired Butler wrote some suitably devilish lyrics, gave them to a former skinhead convict named Ozzy Osbourne and a guitarist called Tony Iommi who had recently chopped of the ends of his fingers. Black Sabbath was a union that on paper did not seem promising. Years later I recall being in a dressing room backstage with Tony Iommi in 1987 when I asked the question 'How many albums have you sold?' As luck would have it a press officer from Vertigo Records supplied the less than enthusiastic answer "47 million up to now". Tony stroked his moustache and replied "I must talk to my accountant". Black Metal would not exist without the colossal impact made upon rock 'n' roll by Black Sabbath. However, in spite of the obvious and undeniable lineage, the Birmingham veterans and the Black Metal usurpers are poles apart.

The genre is stereotypically typified by inhuman vocals; solid walls of guitars built upon riffs designed to be as unmelodic as possible and production values that are so primitive they have been perversely defined a desired sound. One factor where it is a required prerequisite to excel in is drumming. It must be faster than anything else, 'blast beats' of such frightening velocity that only recognized heroes such as Slayer's Dave Lombardo and Mayhem's Hellhammer can accomplish these feats with ease.

The above description could be applied to what is termed as 'pure' Black Metal. It does of course have many, many offshoots and derivatives some so far removed from the parent, the casual onlooker would be hard pressed to place the differing strands of music in the same camp.

Although rooted in Black Sabbath the family tree that eventually burst it's spores into the beast that is Black Metal, would over time wend it's way through the decades into ever-extreme variants. Of course parallel to Black Sabbath was Led Zeppelin, a band that took the cult of the myth to whole new unexplored areas and exploited it to unparalleled financial gain. Indeed, if anyone should be held up as the archetype and mentor it should be guitarist Jimmy Page- a man whose fascination with such figures as Aleister Crowley inspired legends that placed Led Zeppelin onto a pedestal of cult worship unrivalled even today. Although Zeppelin's combined musical talents were astounding, it was the mystique surrounding them that truly marks their presence. However, whereas Page was the master of the unsaid and the mysterious, the acts of today forego any subtlety of illusion and simply ram it down your throat.

Throughout the 80's Heavy Metal bands played the Devil as the bogeyman using references and imagery to play up their 'bad' image. The multi-platinum brummies Judas Priest found it hard going to escape the connotations of their title but did markedly change the climate musically, inspiring newer acts to play ever faster and heavier. Without ever really mentioning the Devil by name, Judas Priest littered their mid 70's albums with enough pointers alongside their more sci-fi leanings to draw in hordes of enthralled teenagers. In 1978 Judas Priest excelled with the furious 'Exciter', probably the first track to probe the almost sound barrier breaking velocities achieved by groups today.

Iron Maiden took Priest's heaviness into the commercial mainstream and even made a sizeable dent in the charts with a song whose chorus ran "666-the number of the beast". Other acts around the same time were testing the occult as a potential point of recognition such as Angelwitch, Mercyful Fate, Witchfynde, Hell, Witchfinder General, Demon and Venom.

It was to be Newcastle's Venom that would break free from the constraints of the NWOBHM movement. British fans on the whole simply could not see the attraction, being put off by the trio's basic approach. Scorn was poured onto Venom by other bands and musicians yet their single mindedness and tenacity pulled them through to achieve a cult-like status. Spurned at home, Venom established themselves in Europe and their legacy can probably be felt in more than half of the bands in this book.

Scandinavia's Bathory delivered the same message and Mercyful Fate allied esoterica with accomplished musicianship and a vocal style unprecedented. In America the previously peaceful Bay Area of San Francisco was shattered by the arrival of Metallica and Thrash Metal. Metallica, Megadeth, Exodus and Metal Church took the traditions of Heavy Metal and took the genre into a new league that was heavier and faster. Lyrically the themes were familiar until Slayer arrived on the scene.

It was these acts that directly motivated the Black Metal elite of today-Mayhem, Emperor and Darkthrone. In their wake swiftly came the hungry young pretenders Marduk, Satyricon, Immortal, Cradle Of Filth and Dimmu Borgir. The floodgates then opened…

Researching Black Metal lineages and histories I must admit is a constant source of fascination. The rules of engagement change as Rock music spans the decades. From 70's Rock stars wishing to hide the reality of their age we now have a situation where teenagers are wishing to disguise their identities with a plethora of pseudonyms. One has to guess whether these nom de guerres are in place to convey the necessary mythical spirit of their endeavours or if they hold only entertainment value.

Black Metal bands also manifest their chosen artistic territories by placing themselves in character not only verbally but visually. The adoption of corpsepaint by Mayhem triggered legions of ghostly white apparitions to stalk the stages of the world. Undoubtedly rooted in the exploits of 70's American Glam stars Kiss, corpsepaint has almost become de rigueur and a marker of a 'true' Black Metal band. Gene Simmons of Kiss, in the manner of the circus clown tradition has patented his facepaint, has been known to fire off heavy legal threats to other musicians employing similar visages. Most notable of these was Mercyful Fate singer King Diamond who was forced by law to alter his facial design. With the advent of Black Metal it seems that Simmons' lawyers have been overwhelmed or simply given it up as an impossible task.

The artistic chasm between the twee comic fantasy persona of Kiss and

Black Metal was bridged by Celtic Frost. This Swiss act was lambasted by traditional quarters for being basic and naive but held in reverence by the new generation spawned with 80's Thrash as adventurous, daring and more commonly avant-garde. Celtic Frost's image was one where bandleader Thomas Gabriel Fischer became 'Tom. G. Warrior' bedecked with unique H.R. Giger designed jewelry and a visage smeared ashen white. Judas Priest with their leather and studs look had opened the doors for numerous followers in the field of Heavy Metal but it was Celtic Frost's eccentricity that provided the next step. Celtic Frost, in the same manner of Venom, inspired many to pick up an instrument realizing that a lack of Ritchie Blackmore prowess on the guitar or the vocal chords of Ronnie James Dio did not preclude them from making records.

Corpsepaint is not the only device used to achieve an air of malevolence. Band photographs have musicians almost universally clad in black with anonymity achieved by some by appearing merely as shadowy silhouettes in mist-laden conifer forests. At the opposite end the ancient warrior creed comes to the surface with chainmail, plaited Norse beards and instruments of war. So rooted are these images that any band willing to forego the accessories is automatically assumed to be attempting to break free of the pack.

Besides the adoption of pseudonyms and disguise there is another obstacle placed in the path of a researcher and that is one fed by the workings of the movement as a whole. Black Metal is reliant on hatred and perceived strength of character and will and the vengeance portrayed to the outside world is more often than not turned swiftly within when a person is deemed to have betrayed the loyalty of others. Biographies of Black Metal bands rarely acknowledge erstwhile members or wish them a bon voyage. The usual course of action is to write off departing musicians as "worthless individuals", "weak scum", "pathetic losers" or worse. No wonder they don't use their real names.

As extreme as Black Metal undoubtedly is, it does have its operating parameters. At one end are the bands that make use of satanic imagery and ancient lore for commercial purpose first and foremost. By far the greater proportion of groups will readily admit to either an interest in Satanism and paganism or using the music to promote their own beliefs whether that be in the form of global hatred or nostalgic folklore. Plumbing the depths of Black Metal leads one into areas of extremes never before touched upon by any previous musical trend.

This is the overriding difference between Black Metal and Heavy Metal. During the 80's, high profile murders and suicides were 'linked' to Metal bands such as Judas Priest, AC/DC and Ozzy Osbourne. Prosecution lawyers would attempt to convince the outside world that somehow song lyrics and alleged backward messages had influenced or played a part in a death. Now the judges do not even have to attempt to bridge the gap of incitement because the band members themselves have either committed suicide or have killed another human being.

Of course murder and suicide, tragic for all concerned as they are, remain the rarest of events with accompanying newsprint acreage out of all proportion. More than 99% of Black Metal bands do not kill and a greater percentage than 99% of Black Metal musicians do not take their own lives. When this does happen though, one has to wonder whether the events would have occurred at the hands of the same person if they happened not to have been drawn to the beckoning flame of Black Metal.

Another vein that runs strongly throughout Black Metal is one that I am sure would have its originator turning in his grave. Little did J.R.R. Tolkein know when he penned his fantasy bedtime stories they would inspire legions of Satanic bands. The images and characters of the 'Lord Of The Rings' trilogy abound in the landscapes of Black Metal. So entrenched is this source of creativity that even the most notorious of acts such as Burzum have dabbled with Tolkein. It is indeed a strange panorama that has been created where mythical Norse creatures such as trolls and valkyries mix with the fallen angels and demons of revelations and the childhood caricatures of Mordor and Gorgoroth.

The most disturbing prevalence in Black Metal today is outright racial hatred. There are bands in this book that propagate such views and I had considered long and hard as to whether to include them or not. There is a school of thought that believes denying such views any publicity is the best policy. However, like it or not, these bands do exist and cannot be ignored. Indeed, to deny the existence of an act as influential as Burzum would be plainly ridiculous.

It would be easy to overstate the use of right-wing imagery prevalent in Black Metal. That said it certainly cannot be ignored either. My only advice to the reader is tread carefully.

Indeed, the overriding memory I have of watching Cradle Of Filth perform live at the Wacken festival in Germany is sadly not that of the band, impressed though I was, but of a sizeable gang of young kids who, when they weren't giving Dani the finger were locked into an autonomic Hitler salute. Where are we now that a band happy enough to proclaim 'Jesus is a c**t' on merchandise and are forthrightly and overtly Satanic in their approach to their life and art are then turned upon as being somehow false? Yet this is the current state of Black Metal. Becoming successful is considered by many within the scene to be selling out. Cradle Of Filth and Dimmu Borgir (probably amongst the newer crop, the only acts generating any serious fiscal return) are deemed to be posers, weak and worse. Black Metal, just as with any movement, is ridden with conflicting standpoints. There are Muslim Black Metal bands, there are even Black Metal groups based in Israel. Topping the lot are Christian 'Unblack' acts who for all intents and purposes look like, sound like and employ the imagery of Black Metal whilst hidden in the unpenetrable vocal growls and distortions are the proclamations of Jesus Christ.

Side projects abound in Black Metal and this is a relatively new phenomenon. In the past Rock musicians have stuck doggedly to their guns extolling a messianic total belief in their band. To guest on another artists recording was considered a newsworthy event. Nowadays the average Swedish musician will have at least one other diversion and sometimes as many as a handful spread into varying genres. A guitarist for example may be an active member of a high profile Black Metal outfit whilst playing bass for a Death Metal band and drumming for a Pop band. Yes, many more musicians than the fans would warrant are paying their way with acts as unblack as they could possibly be.

Traffic operates in both directions too with more mainstream artists 'secretly' involved in Black Metal projects such as former Anthrax man Dan Lilker in Hemlock and Pantera's Phil Anselmo in Viking Crown.

A favourite extra curricular activity in recent years has been the almost obligatory ambient hobby. Usually simplistic almost entirely keyboard based fantasy landscapes themed around mournful dirges and laments of purer times. Whilst Burzum has been forced by authority to pursue this direction many other bands appear to consider the genre a rightful passion to be explored. Taken out of context and with packaging stripped away these pieces of music would be hard pressed to fit the mould of Black Metal but are nonetheless valuable pointers to the future expansion of the genre.

The established practice of collecting does not appear to have got its grips into Black Metal as yet. Possibly because memories are too young, too raw as yet. However, the collecting market will wake up to this vista of musical wealth fairly soon. Black Metal has everything the collector requires, being populated by many extremely rare and limited edition releases.

So a decade in, where does Black Metal go from here? The forerunners are already pushing the boundaries to find an avenue that leads to longevity. Ultimately Darwinian laws of evolution will come to pass and out of all the bands listed in this book a mere handful will prosper. Mayhem have already suffered at their own hands with their own 'Cold Lake' and it will be interesting to see where they go next. The realization that Black Metal, just as any other art form, can only prosper with a sound financial footing is sinking in. Some would say in this case that the predilection for side projects is nothing more than a cynical hedging of bets. That said, if the followers of the devil can't be callous in this regard who can?

Black Metal will undoubtedly grow, it will shed its scales on many occasions and transform itself into a new beast many times over. Although betting on the future is generally unwise there is one piece of inside knowledge I am prepared to pass on to you as a good tip. There will be an updated version of this book sooner than you think.

Garry Sharpe-Young

ABAZAGORATH
(Wayne, NJ, USA)
Line-Up: Nyarlathotep (vocals / bass), Morgul (guitar), Cythrall (guitar), Crom (drums)

Cited by many as being New Jersey's premier Black Metal outfit. The corpse paint bedecked act was created by former NO RESTRAINTS frontman Nyarlathotep in 1995 in union with erstwhile SEDITION drummer Warhead, ex TASTE OF FEAR guitarist Cythrall and second guitarist Morgul.

ABAZAGORATH issued a self financed three track EP in 1996 'Channeling The Ethereal Moon' which elicited strong response. However, line up changes ensued with Morgul making way for Mithras and Warhead opting to found his own vehicle WARHEAD.

ABAZAGORATH pulled in former MEATSHITS and INFESTER drummer Crom and guitarist Mithras. Keyboards were in the hands of EVOKEN's Dario Derna. ABAZAGORATH's debut album 'Tenebrarum Cadent Exsurgemus' received unanimously strong reviews. In 1999 Morgul usurped his replacement Mithras.

ABAZAGORATH have supported the likes of VITAL REMAINS, SUMMON and SUFFOCATION. Members of ABAZAGORATH also operate in EVOKEN guitarist Nick Orlando's side act FUNEBRERUM.

Singles/EPs:
Rites Of The Black Herald / Night Realm / Ghosts Of The Moonlight Mist, Ancient Music (1996) ('Channeling The Ethereal Moon' EP)

Albums:
TENEBRARUM CADENT EXSURGEMUS, Elegy ER01 (1997) Calling The Spirits Of The Dead / For All Eternity / The Choice That Crawls Beyond The Stars / Bestial Moans / The Wolves Of Armageddon / Ghosts Of The Moonlight Mist / The October Storms / Tenebrarum Cadent Exsurgemus / Les Fleurs Du Mal / Rites Of The Black Herald / Night Of The Cloven Hoof / The Gates To The Spirit Kingdom / Void Of Satanic Darkness

ABBADON (HOLLAND)

Black Metal group ABBADON has undergone various transformations thoughout their career to date. The band started out in 1996 billed as SYMPLY DEATH being a trio of guitarist Sander, bassist / vocalist Bas and drummer Gijs. A name change to CONTRA MALICE ensued prior to bolstering the line up with erstwhile ENCHAINED guitarist Frank de Groot.

As the band evolved into ABBADON for their debut demo recordings 'Into The Twilight Kingdom' Daniel Classens was drafted on keyboards.

ABBADON INCARNATE
(IRELAND)
Line-Up: Steve Mather (vocals / guitar), Bill (guitar), Cory Sloan (bass), Olan Parkingson (drums)

Irish Black Death Metal with uncompromising anti- Christian lyrics previously known as BEREAVED under which guise the act issued two demos. Evolved into ABBADON INCARNATE with the 1995 demo 'Demons Come'. However, with a dearth of inspiration in their native land the band was put on ice for nearly a year.

Reassembling ABBADON INCARNATE released a 1996 two track session featuring 'Rancid Filth' and 'Nihilist' which provoked the attention of French label Seasons Of Mist. Their debut album 'The Last Supper' was recorded in Finland but mastered by renowned Death Metal guitarist JAMES MURPHY in Florida. Frontman Steve Mather later joined GEASA for their 'Angel's Cry' album, also on Season Of Mist.

Albums:
THE LAST SUPPER, Seasons Of Mist (1999)
Nihilist / I Hate / The Sharing Of Thoughts With Death / Temple Of Rancid Filth / Vermithrax / Vile Pleasures Of Transfiguration / Raping Ground / When The Demons Come / Manhead / Forced Osculam Infame

ABDULLAH (Richfield, OH, USA)
Line-Up: Jeff Shirilla (vocals / drums), Alan Seibert (guitar)

The Doom Black duo of Jeff Shirilla and Alan Siebert titled their project after the author of the renowned occult treatise 'Necromonicon' Abdulah Alhazad. Despite not employing a bass player and recording on primitive 4 track ABDULLAH nevertheless engineered a near crushing sound.

Albums:
ABDULLAH, People Like You (2000)
The Path To Enlightenment / Conundrum / Earths Answer / Visions Of The Daughters Of Time / Now Is The Winter / Lucifer In Starlight / The Black Ones / Awakening The Colossus / Proverbs Of Hell / Journey To The Orange Island / Lotus Eaters
SNAKE LORE, Rage Of Achilles (2000)

ABETTOR OF SATAN (INDONESIA)
Line-Up: Black Warrior (vocals), Imblessed Dagoth (guitar), Nyarlhatothep (bass), Beelzebub (drums)

Initially known as BORISROWO upon their formation with a line up of vocalist Essa Holopainen, guitarist Imam, bassist Yulianto and drummer Iswanto. The quartet became ABETTOR OF SATAN with the recruitment of vocalist Bisma and bassist Putra Pande. The band included a track 'Voice From The Darkside' on the 'Surabaya Underground' compilation album.
Iswanto would bail out in favour of Koko in November 1997.

ABHORER (SINGAPORE)
Line-Up: Crucifer (vocals), Exorcist (guitar), Imprecator (bass), Dagoth (drums)

Black Metal band from Singapore date from 1988. The following year saw the 'Rumpus Of The Undead' demo followed by a split album shared with NECROPHILE.

Singles/EPs:
Upheaval Of Blasphemy, Shivadarshana (1994) (7" single)

Albums:
ABHORER, Decapitated (1991) (Split album with NECROPHILE)
ZYGOTICAL SABBATORY ANABAPT, Shivadarshana (1996)
Invoking Rana Sahib, Satyrical Goat Of Mendes / Concubinal Celibatic Myrmidonian Whores / Abandonment Of Chastity / Hymeneal Altar Of Messianic Salacitation / Phlegethonic Sybaratical Demimonde / Dom Abaddoniel Abysstic Demonolatry / Zygotical Sabbatory Anabapt / Expiration Of Seraphic Patriarch / Saith... Empyrean Sabaoth Of Azarak

ABIGAIL (JAPAN)
Line-Up: Yasuyuki (vocals / bass), Yasunori (guitar), Youhei (drums)
Black Metal trio ABIGAIL dub themselves 'The most evil band in Japan'. The act dates back to their first demo recordings of 1992. However, founder members guitarist Yasunori and drummer Youhei decamped the following year leaving frontman Yasuyuki to soldier on alone. Undaunted Yasuyuki cut the 'Descending From A Black Sky' EP for Dutch label H.S.B. as a solo effort.
The 1995 album 'Abigail', released by the Colombian Warmaster label in only 700 copies, was a split affair shared with Dutch act FUNERAL WINDS.
Both Yasunori and Youhei returned in February 1995 to record the 'Intercourse And Lust' album, their first for Australian label Modern Invasion.
In 1999 both Yasunori and Youhei forged an alliance with SIGH members Mirai and Shinichi to create a Black Thrash Metal project CUTTHROAT.

Singles/EPs:
Descending From A Blackened Sky, H.S.B. (1993) (7" single)
Confound Eternal, Of God's Disgrace (1996) (7" single)

Albums:
ABIGAIL, Warmaster (1995) (Split album with FUNERAL WINDS)
INTERCOURSE AND LUST, Modern Invasion (1996)
A Witch Named Aspilcuetta / Confound Eternal / The Crown Dealer / Attack With Spell / Strength Of Other World / The Bonehunter / Mephistopholes / Intercourse And Lust / Hail Yazuka
TOGETHER WE SUMMON THE DARK, Cacophonous (1997)

ABIGOR (AUSTRIA)

Black Metal exponents ABIGOR originated with a line up of T.T., P.K. and vocalist Runa. With this incarnation ABIGOR cut four demos starting with 1993's 'Ash Nazg' and 'Lux Devicta Est' then 1994's 'Moon Rise' before Runa departed. The albums utilized the temporary services of the vocalist from the SUMMONING.
ABIGOR and AMESTIGON members founded the Chaos Metal project HEIDENREICH during 1998.
The 2000 'In Memory...' EP features covers of SLAYER's 'Crionics' and KREATOR's 'Terrible Certainty'. However, the initial three track release

was banned due to its graphic sleeve photograph depicting a disembowelment. The EP was reissued with fresh cover artwork and two extra songs.

Singles/EPs:
The Prophecy / Bloodsoaked Overture / Remembering Pagan Origins / The Rising Of Our Tribe / Medieval Echoes / Emptiness / Menchenfeind / Untamed Devastation / ...To The Final Strike / Battlefield Orphans / The Soft And Last Sleep / Severance / Langsam Verhallte des Lebens Schmerz, Napalm NPR 008 (1995) ('Orkblut - The Retaliation' EP)
Terrible Certainty / Crionics / Shadowlord, Napalm (2000) ('In Memory' EP. Withdrawn Banned Cover)
Terrible Certainty / Crionics / Shadowlord / Crimson Horizons / Verwustung, Napalm (2000) ('In Memory' EP)

Albums:
VERWUSTUNG: INVOKE THE DARK AGE, Napalm SPV 084-07962CD (1994)
Universe Of Black Divine / Kingdom Of Darkness / Beneath A Steel Sky / Eye To Eye At Armageddon / In Sin / My Soft Vision In Blood / Weeping Midwintertears / A Spell Of Dark And Evil
NACHTHYMNEN (FROM THE TWILIGHT KINGDOM), Napalm SPV 084-23832 CD (1995)
Unleashed Axe-Age / Scars In The Landscape Of God / Reborn Through The Gates Of Three Moons / Dornen / As Astral Images Darken Reality / The Dark Kiss / I Face The Eternal Winter / Revealed Secrets Of Whispering Moon / A Frozen Soul In Wintershadow
OPUS IV, Napalm SPV 084-27302 CD (1996)
Crimson Horizons And Ashen Skies / Eerie Constellation / Mirages For The Eyes Of The Blind / A Breath From Worlds Beyond / The Elder God My Dragon Magic / Dimensions Of Thy Unforgiven Sins Part 1 / Dimensions Of Thy Unforgiven Sins Part. 2 / Spektral Schattenlichter
APOKALYPSE, Napalm NPR027 (1997)
Celestial / Verwustung / Ein hauch von kaälte / Hyperwelt / Tu Es Diaboli Juna / Ublique Daemon
SUPREME IMMORTAL ART, Napalm NPR040 (1998)
Satan In Me / Supreme Immortal Art / Soil Of Souls / Eclipse My Heart, Crown Me King / The Spirit Of Venus / Blood And Soil / Magic Glass Moment /

Exhausted Remnants
ORIGO REGIUM 1993-1994, (1998)
Filii Septemtrionum / Kingdom Of Darkness / Eye To Eye At Armageddon / Animae Totae / My Soft Vision In Blood / Abysmal Scorn / Shadowlord / Midwinters Obliteration
CHANNELING THE QUINTESSENCE OF SATAN, Napalm NPR062 (1999)
Dawn Of Human Dust / Pandemonic Rebalation / Equilibrium Pass By / Wildfire And Desire / Utopia Consumed / Demons Vortex / Towards Beyond / Pandora's Miasmic Breath

ABOMINATOR (AUSTRALIA)
Line-Up: Damon Bloodstorm (vocals / bass), Undertaker (guitar), Volcano (drums)

ABOMINATOR was created by Damon Bloodstorm of BESTIAL WARLUST. The band also includes drummer Volcano, a previous member of DESTROYER 666. ABOMINATOR heralded their coming with the 1995 'Barbarian War Metal' demo. A 1997 split album shared with MORNALAND followed in 1997.

ABOMINATOR

Albums:
ABOMINATOR, Path To Enlightenment (1997) (Split album with MORNALAND)
DAMNATIONS PROPHECY, Necropolis NR031 (1999)

3

Intro- Filthy Spirit Antichrist / Debauchery (The Sinners Hammer) / Damnation's Prophecy / Intro- War Worship / Activate The Anarchus / The Conqueror Possessed / Unholy Consecration / Ode To Morbid Pleasures / Luciferian Path To Destruction / Sepulchral Vomit- Outro

ABORYM (ITALY)

Line-Up: Attila Csihar (vocals), Sethlans Larva Shaytan (guitar), Nisrok S. Sathanas (guitar), Malfeit Fabban (guitar), D. Belevedere (drums)

Notorious Italian Black Metal band ABOYRM have tightened their grip on infamy by including vocalist Attila Csihar of MAYHEM and TORMENTOR repute. ABORYM came into being during 1991 created by bassist Malfeit Fabban, guitarist Alex N. and drummer D. Belevedere. A demo session 'Worshipping Damned Souls' was issued prior to the group being put on ice as Fabban pursued other interests with FUNERAL ORATION, appearing on their debut album, and DEVIATE LADIES.
Fabban regrouped recording a second ABORYM demo 'Antichristian Nuclear Sabbath' with new faces guitarist Sethlans Larva Shaytan and vocalist Yorga S.M. A deal was then struck with Scarlet Records for the 'Kali Yuga Bizarre' album which saw Attila Csihar as guest vocalist. The band also added second guitarist Nisrok S. Sathanas of SATANIKK TERRORISTS.
Following the album release Yorga S.M. opted out and Csihar offered to front the band on a permanent basis.

Albums:
KALI YUGA BIZARRE, Scarlet (1999) Wehrmacht Kali Ma / Horrenda Peccata Christi / Hellraiser / Roma Divina Veds / Darka Mysteria / Tantra Bizarre / Come Thou Long Expected Jesus / Metal Stricken Terror Action / The First Four Trumpets
FIRE WALK WITH US, Scarlet (2000)

ABROGATION (GERMANY)

Line-Up: Frank, Rainer, Poldi

Magdeburg Black Metal crew ABROGATION emerged with the 1994 demo 'Screams Of Soul'.

Albums:
HANDWERK DES TODES, Abrogation (1999)

ABRUPTUM (SWEDEN)

Line- Up: It (vocals / guitar / bass), Evil (drums)

Strictly a duo comprising of OPTHALIMIA founder It and MARDUK member Evil (real name Morgan Hakansson), APRUPTUM are an extreme Satanic Death Metal band, what ABRUPTUM lack in song structure they make up for with a tendency to be rather heavy on unnerving screams and avante garde rhythms and noises. And the band's reputation is almost enhanced with tales that mainman It (real name Tony Särkää) is alleged to be one of the prime movers behind the Satanic Black Circle movement.
It created a side project band, VONDUR ("Evil"), in 1993 purely as a solo outing. An album, Stridsyfirlysing', featuring former ABRUPTUM vocalist All was released in 1995. Quite unbelievably the first 666 copies of the CD came with a free (and genuine) razorblade, the artwork proclaiming 'kill yourself"!
An album of early ABRUPTUM demos, plus solo material from Evil, was released in 1995 on Hellspawn records titled 'Evil Genius'. The 1996 album title translates as "The Audial Essence Of Pure Black Evil".
Of interest is the fact that the band's second album consists solely of one hour long song!!
Both OPTHALIMIA and VONDUR are both going concerns to date.

Singles/EPs:
Hopstes Orco Hostium Legiones Dis Manibus Pacis Ruptores Ultioni / Animum, Mentum Alcis, Inventum Largitionibus / Hostes Ad Dimicandum, Commotis Exita Sacris Thyias, Psychoslaughter PS003 (1991)

Albums:
OBSCURITATEM ADVOCO AMPLECTEREME, Deathlike Silence ANTIMOSH004 (1993) Obscuritatem Advoco Amplectere Me (Part I) / Obscuritatem Advoco Amplectere Me (Part II)
IN UMBRA MALICIA EAMBULABO IN AETERNUM IN TRIUMPHO TENEBRAUM, Deathlike Silence ANTI-MOSH 009 (1994) In Umbra Maliciae Ambulabo In Acternum In Triumpho Tenebraum
EVIL GENIUS, Hellspawn HELL002 (1995)

4

Honores Vultus Mutares Ex Neris Campi / Aerge Facere Alci / Jecudiv Fulminis Tecis / Calibus Frontem Tumev Acidus Abcessus / Corpus In As Trahere Abincere / Bis Semina Dies Horn Dea Membra Corpora / Feci Factum Sanguine Gladios Made Fieri Factus / Tortus Torquero Colla Tumentes / Tyrannum Bellux Eventus Alci Axco Sivium Vitae Carthaginis Integra / Hostes Arco Hostium Legiones Dis Manibus Pacio Ruptores Ultioni / Aututum, Meutem Alcis Juventutem Largitionibus, Hostes Ad Dimicandum, Commotis Exita Sacris Thyias **VI SONIS VERIS NIGRAE MALIIAES,** Fullmoon (1996)
Vi Sonis Veris Nigrae Maliiaes
DE PROFUNDIS MORS VAS COUSUMET, Regain BLOOD 006 (2000)
De Profundis Mors Vas Cousumet / Dödsapparaten / Massdöd
IN ICTU OCULI, Regain BLOOD 011 (2001)

ABSENT SILENCE (FINLAND)

Albums:
DAWN OF A NEW MOURNING, No Colours NC 018CD (1998)

ABSU (TX, USA)
Line-Up: Proscriptor McGovern (vocals / drums), Shaftiel (guitar), Equitant (bass)

Self styled 'Ancestral occult metal' act ABSU, titled after the ancient Sumerian word for the abyss, revel in a vocalist cum drummer Proscriptor McGovern (ne 'Emperor Proscriptor Magikus') who claims direct lineage to the Scottish clans and frequently wears a kilt to bolster his assertions. The band, although placed firmly in the Black Metal marketplace, have attempted to place themselves as a "Dark Occult Metal" band rather than Black Metal.
The unit began life as the 1989 band DOLMEN founded by Shaftiel and Lord Equitant Infernian. By 1991 this act had evolved into ABSU releasing a single 'Immortal Sorcery' and demo session 'Return To The Ancients'
The EP 'Temples Of Offal' was recorded in late 1991. However, early members guitarist Gary Lindholmm and drummer Daniel Benbow opted out. Fresh blood was found from the disintegration of the band MAGUS and Emperor Proscriptor McGovern and Daviel Athron Mystica

duly joined the fold in time for the debut album 'Barathrum: V.I.T.R.I.O.L.', the subtitle being Latin for "visiting the insides of the earth". A second guitarist was duly added in Black Massith but shortly after Mystica left the fold necessitating Equitant to cover both bass and guitar.
ABSU pulled in erstwhile GOREAPHOBIA vocalist Mezzadurus for touring purposes.
Mezzadurus convened a side project act titled BLOODSTORM releasing the 1997 album 'The Atlantean Wardragon' in 1997. Equitant operates an electronic solo project EQUITANT issuing the 1994 demo 'Great Lands Of Minas Ithul (City Of Isildur)'. Proscriptor has a side act titled MELECHESH.
Procriptor has also performed live as drummer for JUDAS ISCARIOT and even finds time to engage his talents as a member of Mediaeval act MOONROOT alongside Mike Riddick of THE SOIL BLEEDS BLACK.
The membership of ABSU are also engaged in the act EQUIMANTHORN having released two albums to date.

ABSU - Poscriptor McGovern.
Photo : Martin Wickler

Singles/EPs:
Immortal Sorcery / Sumerian Sands (The Silence) / Disembodied, Gothic (1991) ('Temples Of Offal' EP)
...And Shineth Unto The Gold Cometh... / Akheri Goiti- Akhera Beiti (One Black Opalith For Tomorrow),

Osmose Productions (1995) (7" single)
V.I.T.R.I.O.L. / Hallstatt / Manannan / Never Blow Out The Eastern Candle, Osmose Productions OPCD 070 (1998) ('In The Eyes Of Ioldanach' EP)

<u>Albums:</u>
BARATHRUM: VISITA INTERIORA TERRAE RECTIFICANDO INVENIES OCCULTUL LAPIDEM, Osmose Productions OPCD020 (1995)
An Involution Of Thorns / Descent To Acheron (Evolving Into The Progression Of Woe) / An Equinox Of Fathomless Disheartenment / The Thrice Is Greatest To Ninnigal / Infinite And Profane Thrones / Fantasizing To The Third Of · The Pagan Vision (Qouth The Sky, Nevermore Act III) / The Evolution Of Horns
THE SUN OF TIPHARETH, Osmose Productions OPCD029 (1996)
Apzu / Feis Mor Tin Na N'Og (Across The North Sea To Visnech) / Cyntefyn's Fountain / A Quest For The 77th Novel / Our Lust For The Lunar Plains (Nox Luna Industris) / The Coming Of War / The Sun Of Tiphareth
THE THIRD STORM OF CYTHRAUL, Osmose Productions (1997)
Prelusion To Cythraul (...And Shineth Unto The Gold Cometh...) / Highland Tyrant Attack / A Magician's Lapis Lazuli / Sword And Leather / The Winter Zephyr (... Within Kingdoms Of Mist) / Morbid Scream / Customs Of Tasseomancy / Intelligence Towards The Crown / Of Celtic Fire, We Are Born (Terminus... In The Eyes Of Ioldanach) / Akheri Goiti- Akhera Beiti (One Black Opalith For Tomorrow

ABSURD (GERMANY)
Line-Up: Hendrik Albert Möbus, Sebastian Schauscheill, Andreas K.

A notorious teenage German Black Metal band created in Sonderhausen during 1992. Guitarist Sebastian Schauscheill was known at this stage under the pseudonym of 'Werwolf Dark Mark Doom'. ABSURD marked their presence with a demo 'Death From The Forest' beginning negotiations for a record deal with Euryonymous' label Deathlike Silence. However, in April of 1993 the teenage group were convicted of collectively killing an associate, the 14 year old Sandro Beyer, by strangulation and stabbing.
A 1994 demo 'Out Of The Dungeon' and

1995's demo 'Thuringian Pagan Madness' followed. This cassette featured the murder victim Sandro Beyer's tombstone as its cover art.
Whilst in prison Hendrik Möbus contributed lyrics for other Black Metal acts including ABIGOR, GRAVELAND, THA-NORR, WOLFSBURG, FUNERAL WINDS and LIAR OF GOLGOTHA. Möbus was sentenced to 14 years but would be paroled in August of 1998 setting up the Darker Than Black Productions record label. However, this label was soon closed down by the authorities and in the summer of the following year Möbus was sentenced to a further 8 month term of imprisonmernt for publicly using the Seig Heil salute.
Australian band ABYSSIC HATE would also cover ABSURD's 'The Victory Is Ours' on their 1998 'Eternal Damnation' album and Dutch act WELTER would cover 'Mourning Soul' on their 'The Elder Land' album.
In August of 2000 Möbus was arrested once more. Travelling in America Möbus was picked up in Hillsboro, West Virginia on an international arrest warrant for violating his parole on two counts of · mocking the victim of the earlier murder and the Sieg Heil offence. There are unsubstantiated rumours that Möbus fell foul of intended business partners in America and was subjected to a vicious hammer attack.
The 'Facta Luquuntur' album was limited to 500 hand numbered copies. Möbus is also working on a BURZUM tribute album.

<u>Singles/EPs:</u>
Totenburg, (199-) (7" single)

<u>Albums:</u>
FACTA LUQUUNTUR, No Colours (1996)
Werwolf / The Gates Of Heaven / Pesttanz / Eternal Winter / Deep Dark Forest / First Winter Of Bloodred Snow / Mourning Soul / Dreaming Of Love / Wartend In Einsamkeit / Der Sieg Ist Unser
ASGARDSREI, (199-)
Intro / Asgardsrei / Crux Gammata / Germania Uber Alles / Sonnenritter

ABSURDUS (FINLAND)
Line-Up: Aki Martin Kauppi (vocals / guitar), Juha Moilanen (guitar), Taneli Nyholm (bass), Matti Roiha (drums)

Black Thrash act founded by school

7

friends vocalist / guitarist Aki Martin Kauppi, guitarist Juha Moilanen, bass player Taneli Nyholm and drummer Matti Roiha. During 1996 both Taneli and Roiha would deputize for RAVENSFALL (later CRYHAVOC) but would return to ABSURDUS for recording of the 'No Heaven In Sight' album.

Released on the British Candlelight label 'No Heaven In Sight' included a version of MOTÖRHEAD's seminal 'Bomber'.

A second album was planned but ABSURDUS opted for a more basic Rock n' Roll approach and were dropped by their label. ABSURDUS would later evolve into PANDEMONIUM OUTCASTS with all members adopting the revised names of guitarist J. 'Aki' Boa (also 'Snake'), bassist Daniel Rock (also 'Daniel Stuka' and 'Serpent') and drummer Matt C. (also 'Dragon').

Bassist Taneli Nyholm (as 'Daniel Stuka') would join BABYLON WHORES in late 1999.

Albums:
NO HEAVEN IN SIGHT, Candlelight CANDLE024CD (1998)
Ad Absurdum (One Hell Of An Introduction) / On The Way To Hell / Devil's Ride / My Kingdom / You're Below Everything / Concord In Diablo / Joyreaper / Pure Pleasure / Blood Drive / Life Is Agony / Bomber

ABYSMAL (NORWAY)
Line-Up: Endre Begby (vocals / bass), Jan Svedson (guitar), Ken-Arve Nilsen (guitar), Pal Halvorsen (drums)

Norwegian's ABYSMAL debuted with the demo 'Nebulistic Obscurity' in 1991. Although they recorded their debut album, 'The Pillorian Age', for a Greek record label, upon completion the label went bust. The album was thus picked up by Italian label Obscure Plasma Rex.

The band was hit by further complications when the decision was taken to dispense with the services of guitarist Ken-Arve Nilsen upon the record's completion. Following the album's release in 1994 frontman Endre Begby was to later join CARPATHIAN FULL MOON.

Albums:
THE PILLORIAN AGE, Avantgarde AV007 (1994)
Hymn XIV: The Pillorian Age / Hymn X: Velvet Pilloria / Hymn XI: Temptation And Undoing / Hymn VIII: Four Ravens Flew /

Hymn XIII: The Sleeping Antarct / Hymn XV: Thunder In The Gallow's Land / Hymn XVI: Out Of My Flesh

ABYSMAL FALL
(East Rochester, NY, USA)
Line-Up: Lord Iscariot (vocals / drums), Mourn (guitar), Krist (bass)

ABYSMALL FALL announced their arrival with the less than subtly titled 'Spit In The Face Of Christ' demo in 1999. Former bass player Wrath would make way for Krist.

ABYSMAL FALL also bide their time with Grind oufit IMPLEMENTS OF HELL.

Albums:
BORNE AGAINST, Arcadia Productions ARC002 (2000)

THE ABYSS (SWEDEN)
Line- Up: Mikael Hedlund (vocals / guitar), Lars Szoke (guitar), Peter Tägtgren (bass / drums)

THE ABYSS is the side project of HYPOCRISY members Peter Tägtgren, Mikael Hedlund and Lars Szöke. The album features a version of HELLHAMMER's 'Massacra' track. Bassist / drummer Tägtgren still fronts the ever more successful HYPOCRISY is now a member of ALGAION and issues solo projects as PAIN.

Albums:.
THE OTHER SIDE, Nuclear Blast NB126-2 (1995)
Marutukku / Tjänare At Besten / Psycomantum / Massacra / Mörkrets Vandring / Sorgens Dai / Slukad / Förintelsens Tid Aro Kommen.
SUMMON THE BEAST, Nuclear Blast NB 209-2 (1996)
Satan's Majestic Empire / Blessed With The Wrath Of Evil / Damned / Summon The Beast / The Hymn / Cursed / Feasting The Remains Of Heaven / The Arrival

ABYSSIC HATE (AUSTRALIA)

ABYSSIC HATE, purveyors of old school Black Metal shared their first release, a split record 'United By Heathen Blood', with Norwegians DET HEDENSKE FOLK. The band, actually a one-man concern utilizing session guitarist Brad Johnston, bowed in with the 1994 demo 'Cleansing Of An Ancient Race'. The

1995 'Depression' tape followed before an instrumental 1996 cassette 'Life Is A Pain In The Neck'.
The 1998 album 'Eternal Damnation' album, limited to 500 copies, included a cover version of 'The Victory Is Ours' by German act ABSURD.

Albums:
UNITED BY HEATHEN BLOOD, Bloodless Creation (1997) (Split album with DET HEDENSKE FOLK)
For An Unknown Place / Cleansing Of An Ancient Race / Land Of Impenetrable Darkness / Damned For Eternity / Tarrasque / Bloodletting
ETERNAL DAMNATION, No Colours (1998)
Eternal Damnation / Knight Of The Living Dead / Human Despair / attack! / The Blood War / The Victory Is Ours
SUICIDAL EMOTIONS, No Colours (2000)
Depression Part I / Betrayed / Depression Part II / Despondency

ABYSSOS (SWEDEN)
Line-Up: Rehn (vocals / guitar), Meidal (bass), Andreas Söderlund (drums)

ABYSSOS are a Sundsvall based vampiric Black Death Metal band. A demo in 1996 'Wherever Witches Might Fly' marked their arrival and secured a deal with the British Cacophonous label. They issued their debut album during 1997.

Albums:
TOGETHER WE SUMMON THE DARK, Cacophonous (1997)
We Hail Thy Entrance / Misty Autumn Dance / Banquet In The Dark- Black Friday / Lord Of The Sombre Reborn / In Fear They Left The World Unseen / As The Sky Turns Black Again- Love Eternal / Together We Summon The Dark / I've Watched The Moon Grow Old / Through The Gloom And Into The Fire
FHINSTHANIAN NIGHTBREED, Cacophonous NIHIL33 CD (1999)
Masquerade In The Flames / Finally I Kissed The Pale Horse / Where Angels Fear To Tread / She Only Flies At Night / Worthless For Sale? / Fhinsthanian Nightbreed / Queen Covered In Black / wherever The Witches Might Fly / Firebreathing Whore

A CANOROUS QUINTET (SWEDEN)

Line-Up: Marten Hansen (vocals), Linus Nibrant (guitar), Lei Pignon (guitar), Jesper Löfgren (bass), Fredrik Andersson (drums)

Formed in 1991 A CANOROUS QUINTET, a brutal Death / Black Metal act, released their 'The Time Of Autumn' demo having undergone a multitude of line-up changes up to that point.
Guitarist Leo Pignon later forged a similar Black Metal outfit NIDEN DIV. 187 with members of DAWN and THY PRIMORDIAL releasing two albums 'Towards Judgement' and 'Impergium' on Necropolis Records. Drummer Fredrik Andersson is better known for his role in premier Swedish Black Metal band MARDUK. Andersson also boasts credits with AMON AMARTH and ALLEGIANCE. Vocalist Morten Hansen guested on OCTOBER TIDE's 1999 album 'Grey Dawn'.

Singles/EPs:
Through Endless Illusions / The Joy Of Sorrow / When Happiness Dies / Strangeland, Chaos CD 02 (1994) ('As Tears' EP)

Albums:
SILENCE OF THE WORLD BEYOND, No Fashion NFR 019 (1996)
Silence Of The World Beyond / Naked With Open Eyes / Spellbound / The Orchid's Sleep / The Black Spiral / The Last Journey / In The Twilight Of Fear / Burning, Emotionless / Dream Reality
THE ONLY PURE HATE, No Fashion NFR028 (1998)
Selfdeceiver (The Purest Of Hate) / Embryo Of Lies / Red / The Void / Everbleed / The Complete Emptiness / Retaliation / Realm Of Rain / The Storm / Land Of The Lost

ACCURSED (WI, USA)

Albums:
MEDITATIONS AMONG THE TOMBS, Visceral Displeased (1995)

ACHERON (AUSTRALIA)
Line-Up: Simon Dower (vocals), David Abbott (guitar), Tim Aldridge (guitar), Justin Wornes (bass), Jason Dutton (drums)

Melbourne Death Metal act forged in 1988 by guitarist David Abbott. The band issued a single in 1991 on French label Corpsegrinder Records prior to Abbott

9

and drummer Jason Dutton leaving.
Pulling in substitute guitarist Mark Schilby and drummer Ewan Harriott the band switched titles to ABRAMELIN in order to avoid confusion with the American ACHERON.
ABRAMELIN bowed in with 1994's 'Transgression From Acheron' mini album.

Singles/EPs:
Deprived Of Afterlife / Death Of Millions, Corpsegrinder (1991)

ACHERON (Chicago, IL, USA)
Line-Up: Wade Laszlos (vocals / guitar), Mark Belliel (bass), Tom Croxton (drums)

Founded in 1986. ACHERON frontman Wade Laszlo would decamp in 1991 following the debut 'Prophecies Unholy' to create THE UNHOLY. Soon ACHERON personnel bassist Mark Belliel and drummer Tom Croxton would jump ship to THE UNHOLY.
Whilst remaining loyal to THE UNHOLY Croxton joined IMPALER in 1998 and has a side project KREPITUS.

Albums:
PROPHECIES UNHOLY, (1990)
THE PAIN DOMINION, (199-)

ACHERON (Tampa, FL, USA)
Line-Up: Vincent Crowley (vocals / guitar), Michael Estes (guitar), Reverend Peter Gilmore (keyboards), Tony Laureano (drums)

Death metal musically but with clear Satanic overtones in the lyrics ACHERON are perhaps one of the more genuine of the American exponents of black metal. Mentor and frontman Vincent Crowley is the founder of the irreligious underground movement 'Order of the evil eye' whilst renowned Church of Satan priest Reverend Peter Gilmore adds keyboards and contributes lyrically.
ACHERON marked their arrival with the live 1989 demo tape 'Messe Noir'. These recordings would later see a 1995 release on 7" single format by Reaper Records limited suitably to 666 copies.
Ex MORBID ANGEL, INCUBUS and NOCTURNUS drummer Mike Browning has also appeared with ACHERON on their 'Hail Victory' album alongside Crowley and guitarists Tony Blakk and Vincent Breeding.
The B side to the 1998 single

'Necromanteion Communion' featured a cover version of BATHORY's 'Raise The Dead'.
Guitarist Michael Estes busied himself with a side project act BURNING INSIDE assembled by renowned ICED EARTH, DEMONS & WIZARDS, DEATH and CONTROL DENIED drummer Richard Christy and BLACK WITCHERY guitarist Steve Childers.
Drummer Tony Laureano sessioned for AURORA BOREALIS and MALEVOLENT CREATION. By 2000 he was a member of Dutch act GOD DETHRONED. Another former member, keyboard player Adina Blaze, would join LILITU.
Crowley created WOLFEN SOCIETY with DARK FUNERAL guitarist Lord Ahriman and Jeff Gruslin of VITAL REMAINS in 2000.

Singles/EPs:
Alla Xul / One With Darkness, Gutted (1992) (7" single)
Messe Noir, Reaper (1995) (7" single)
Necromanteion Communion / Raise The Dead, (1998) (7" single)

Albums:
RITES OF THE BLACK MASS, Turbo 007 (1992)
Intro / Prayer Of Hell / Intro / Unholy Praises / Intro / Cursed Nazarene / Intro / The Enochian Key / Intro/ Let Us Depart / Intro / To Thee We Confess/ Intro / Thou Art Lord / Intro / Ave Satanas / Intro / Summoning The Master / Intro / One With Darkness
HAIL VICTORY, Metal Merchant (1993)
Unholy Praises / Seven Deadly Sins / Satanic Erotica / Prayer Of Hell / 666 / God Is Dead / Alla Xul / One With Darkness
SATANIC VICTORY, Turbo (1994)
Unholy Praises / Seven Deadly Sins / Satanic Erotica / Prayer Of Hell / 666 / God Is Dead
LEX TALIONIS, Turbo (1994)
Legions Of Hatred / Enter Thy Coven / Slaughterisation For Satan / Voices Within / Purification Day / Inner Beasts / The Entity / I.N.R.I. (False Prophet) / Lex Talionis March (outro)
ANTI GOD- ANTI CHRIST, Moribund (1997)
Fuck The Ways Of Christ / Shemhamforash (The Ultimate Blasphemy) / Blessed By Damnation / Baptism For Devlyn Alexandra / Total War
LEX TALIONIS-SATANIC VICTORY,

Blackened BLACK006CD (1997)
Legions Of Hatred / Enter Thy Coven / Slaughterisation For Satan / Voices Within / Purification Day / Inner Beasts / The Entity / I.N.R.I. (False Prophet) / Lex Talionis March (outro) / Unholy Praises / Seven Deadly Sins / Satanic Erotica / Prayer Of Hell / 666 / God Is Dead

ACRON (ITALY)
Line-Up: Grey (vocals), Mirko Placido (guitar), Davide (guitar), Luca (keyboards)

ACRON guitarist Mirko Placido would later join the Black Doom outfit MORNINGRISE. His tenure lasted a mere three months.

Albums:
LABYRINTH OF FEARS, Elevate ER2007 (1998)
Dislocated / Sons Of Sterility / The Last Candle's Burning / Backward Flowing Time / Obsession / Crown Of Thorns / Unenlightened / The End Of Fears

ACROSTICHON (HOLLAND)
Line-Up: Corinne (vocals / bass), Richard (guitar), Jos (guitar), Serge (drums)

Formed in 1989 by the trio of Corinne, Richard and Jos, this Dutch Black Metal outfit soon added drummer Serge to the cause and by the end of 1990 could be found opening for CARCASS, followed by gigs with MORBID ANGEL, DEATH and SODOM.
The American independent label Seraphic Decay signed the quartet, although the group's debut album was produced by Colin Richardson against their will.

Albums:
ENGRAVED IN BLACK, Modern Primitive PRIM2CD (1993)
Immolation Of The Agnostic / Walker Of Worlds / Dehumanised / Mentally Deficient / Lost Remembrance / Zombies / Havoc / Relics / Engraved In Black
SENTENCED, (1995)

ACTUS (HUNGARY)

ACTUS ('Archaic Cultural Tradition United In A Society') are a highly regarded Black folkloric outfit employing elements of mediaeval and ambient sounds. The 'Sacro Sanctum' album is a live tenth anniversary celebration.

Albums:
A WAY TO THE EMPIRE OF STRENGTH AND ORDER, (1996)
Spiritual Heritage / Cataclysm / Decay / The Mirror / Ceremony / The Decay Of The Body Is The Birth Of Another One / Apocalypse / Tabula Rasa / The Spring / A Way To The Empire Of Strength And Order
SACRO SANCTUM, Cthulu (1997)
Introduction- Rome / Spiritual Imperialism / A Haaku / Babel Pit / A Song Against The Armies Of Luther, Milton And Others / Total Mobilisation / Riding The Tiger / Introduction To The Science Of Death / Solipimus Absolutus / Affirmation Of Philosophia Perennis / A Hymn Of Nemesis
AGAIN AND AGAIN-REVELATION, (1998)
Again And Again / Revelation
DAS UNBENENNARE, (199-)
Die Lehre Der Zyklen / Anatma / Vond Der Ubergeschichtelichen Ebere Sturzen Wir Stets In Die Geschichte, Aber Des Ubergeschichtliche Ist Auch Hier Anwesend / Das Unbenennare / Solipsismus Magicus / Der Ewigliche Akt Des Prinzips / Botschaft Aus Hyperborea / Die Lehre Der Zyklen / Lila

AD INFERNA (FRANCE)
Line-Up: Sadneth (vocals), V. Orias A. (guitar / bass), As-Mody (keyboards), N. Aboriim (drums)

Previously known as DE PROFUNDIS. The debut album includes guest contributions from OBSIDIAN GATE members Marcus and Marco together with Teemu of FURTHEST SHORE.
The band lost vocalist Sadneth to MACHIEVEL in 2001.

Albums:
AD INFERNA, Skaldic Art (2000)

ADORIOR (UK)
Line-Up: Melissa (vocals), Tony (guitar), Chris (bass),

Back to basics Black Metal fronted by vocalist Melissa. Norwegian label Head Not Found broke their vow of only signing native acts with ADORIOR.
A previous bass player Chris Hastings would join the London based New Zealanders DEMONIAC.

Albums:
LIKE CUTTING THE SLEEPING, Head

Not Found HNF044 (2000)
Destroyer / Isegrim / Beyond The Distant Blue / Legends Breath / Rain Sisters / The Essence Of My Dreams / The Scarlet Hordes Of Autumn / The Judgement Of Serpents And Mirrors

ADORNED BROOD (GERMANY)
Line-Up: Teotobod Frost (vocals / guitar), Pagan (guitar), Widar (guitar), Ingeborg Anna (flute), Flajar (drums)

Dating back to 1993 Pagan Metal act ADORNED BROOD have had a troubled history spanning three albums. The band was convened by drummer Ariovist (strangely named after a well known historical German coward) and guitarist Oberon. Shortly after Teotobod Frost was drafted on bass for the debut 'Phobos-Deimus' demo.
Second guitar duties were handed over to Pagan as Teotobod Frost switched to lead vocals and guitar for the sophomore demo session 'Wapen' prior to Ingeborg Anna being enlisted on flute.
The inclusion of flute set ADORNED BROOD apart from the crowd and a deal was soon struck with Folter Records for the first album 'Hiltia', the title being elder German for "War".
A label switch to Atmosfear Records witnessed not only a second album 'Wigand' (translated as "Warrior") but the departure of Oberon in exchange for Widar. Founder member Ariovist also left the fold being superseded by Flajar.

Albums:
HILTIA, Folter (1996)
Intro / For Honour And Land / Hiltia / Unehrenhaftes Feindesblut / Furor Teutonics / Donerhamer / Undisclosed Treasures Of The Mortal / Adora / Kissing The Heathen Amulet / Die Rede Des Erhabenen / Outro
WIGAND, Atmosfear (1997)
Völuspa / The Way Of The Sword / Spiritual Weaponry / Wapen / The Oath / Wigand / Zeichen Von Zauberkraft / Lord Dvalin
ASGARD, Moonstorm (2000)
Intro / A God Called Time / Asgard / Black Beasts / Twilight In Midgard / Pride Was My Desire / The Ambush / Magic Nights / Mighty Swords / Arrival / Die Wiederkehr

ADRAMELCH (FINLAND)
Line-Up: Jarkko Rantanen (vocals), Jani Aho (guitar), Mikko Aarnio (bass), Seppo Taatila (drums)

Formed by Jani Aho (bass) Jusi Tainio (drums) and Jarkko Rantanen (vocals / guitar) in 1991, ADRAMELCH sought out a vocalist and second guitarist to join the founding trio and came up with Tuomas Ala-Nissila and Erik Parviainen respectively, Rantanen switching to drums after Tainio departed.
The band recorded the 'Grip Of Darkness' demo (featuring new bassist Mikko Aarnio) that led to a deal with the French Adipocere label.
Following the release of the 'Spring Of Recovery' single and a show with DEMILICH, BEHERIT and CRYPT OF KERBEROS in 1993, Seppo Taatila (ex DEMIGOD) joined and contributed to the recording of 'The Fall' demo. The band then featured on a compilation released by the Spanish label Repulse with the track 'Heroes In Godly Blaze'.
The liaison with the Spaniards led to a two album deal with Repulse, the first fruits of which was the commercial release on CD of 'The Fall' tape.
ADRAMELCH were to lose bassist Aarnio after the 'Psychotasia' album and also added the ex vocalist of DEMIGOD towards the end of 1996.

Singles/EPs:
Spring Of Recovery, Adipocere (1993)

Albums:
THE FALL, Repulse RPS 006 MCD (1995)
As The Gods Succumbed / Heroes In Godly Blaze / Seance Of Shamans / The Fall Of Tiamat
PSYCHOTASIA, Repulse RPS 015 CD (1996)
Heroes In Godly Blaze / Psychostasia / Seance Of Shamans / The Book Of The Worm / Thoth (Lord Of Holy Words) / Mythic Descendant / As The Gods Succumbed / Across The Gray Waters
PURE BLACK DOOM, Severe (2000)

ADVERSAM (ITALY)
Line-Up: Alter Eho (vocals / bass), Boaz (guitar), Essylit (keyboards), Algor (drums)

Black Metal from Turin. ADVERSAM made their entrance with the 1997 demo tape 'The Black Diamond Gates'.

Albums:
ANIMADVERTE, Scarlet (1999)

Miasma Demon / Monument Of A Legend / Awaiting / The Path / N.O.D. / Geisterfalle / Hypertemple / Lucifer, Crowned, Avenger And Conqueror

AEBA (GERMANY)

Line-Up: Isegrim (vocals / guitar), Schattensturm (vocals / guitar), Exul Caeli (bass), Daemonia (keyboards), Nidhögg (drums)

Northern German Black Metal crew began life inn 1992 titled ETERNAL SUFFER. Founder members were guitarists Isegrim (then known as 'Occultum Nocturnus') and Schattensturm (then 'Funeral Wisdom Of The Elder Wintermoon'). In 1994 the duo pulled in drummer Nidhögg ('Viking Lord') and evolved into AEBA. A further recruitment of bassist Exul Caeli took place in time for the 1995 demo 'Rising'. AEBA would later augment their sound with female keyboard player Daemonia. Nidhögg departed in July 2000.

Albums: ·
IM SCHATTENREICH, Last Episode (1998)
Rising Black Dominion / Gotiesmord / Dragonstorm / Ewigkeit- Gedanken Einen Misanthropischen Steele / Revenge- The Strength Beyond The Light / Superiority Is The Gift Of Hate / Zerfall
FLAMMENMANI FEST, Last Episode (1999)
Until The Darkness (Intro) / Seelenfrost / Winds Of The Dusk / Shadow Of God's Creation / Todeschaß (Of War And Darkness) / Inimicissimus / The Dark Manifestation / ... Never Ends (Outro)
THE RISING, Last Episode (1999)
The Rising Of Astaroth, Eurydome, Bael and Amduscias / Into The Infernal Dark Abyss / Inimicissimus 1995 / In Sorrow / Vom Schwarzen Blut / The Rising / Last Rites (Outro)

AEON (GREECE)

Greek Black Metal act AEON issued the 'Requiem Aeternum' and 'Crypts Of The Unlight' demos. Not to be confused with the Croatian Death Metal AEON that released the 1996 album 'Ephemeral'.

Albums:
MYSTIC PATH OF THE UNDERWORLD,
Dark Side (1996)

AETURNUS (NORWAY)

Line-Up: Ares (vocals / guitar), Radek (guitar), Morrigan (bass), Vrolok (drums)

Bergen based AETURNUS rank as one of the more individualistic acts among the higher echelons of the Norwegian Black Metal scene. During the formative years of AETURNUS frontman Ares would deputize live for IMMORTAL and also included himself among the ranks of arch Black Metal outfit GORGOROTH. Drummer Vrolok, having appeared on THY GRIEF's 'A Frozen Realm' demo, also sessioned for GORGOROTH.
The band first emerged with an EP 'Dark Sorcery' issued on the Czech label View Beyond. This release secured a contract with the noted Dutch Hammerheart concern for a debut album 'Beyond The Wandering Moon'. Touring as promotion found AETURNUS on the road in Europe alongside HADES and HELHEIM with a further tour as guests to EMPEROR and LIMBONIC ART.
In 1999 AETURNUS augmented their sound by drafting Polish guitarist Radek for the 'Shadows Of Old' album. European touring had AETURNUS on a billing with CANNIBAL CORPSE and MARDUK.
Morrigan would contribute keyboards to the 1998 OBTAINED ENSLAVEMENT album 'Soulblight'.
Not to be confused with the Christian Thrash Metal AETURNUS that issued the 'From Blackest Darkness' album.

Singles/EPs:
Black Dust / Victory / Raven And Blood / Nordlys, View Beyond (1996) ('Dark Sorcery' EP)

Albums:
BEYOND THE WANDERING MOON,
Hammerheart (1997)
Under The Blade Of The Dead / Sworn Revenge / White Realm / Sentinels Of Darkness / Embraced / Vivid / Waiting For The Storms / Winter Tale / To Enter The Realm Of Legend / Celtic Harp Solo (The Last Feast)
AND SO THE NIGHT BECAME...,
Hammerheart (1998)
There's No Wine Like Bloods Crimson / As I March / Warrior Of The Crescent Moon / Blodsverging / When The Shadow Falls / Ild Dans / And So The Night Became / Fyrndeheimer / Dark Rage / Fire And Wind / In The Darkest Circles Of Time

SHADOWS OF OLD, Hammerheart
(2000)
Under The Eternal Blackened Sky /
Descent To The Underworld / Dark Rage
/ Resurrection / The Summoning Of
Shadows / Death's Golden Truth
Revealed / Cuchulain / Prophecy Of The
Elder Reign / The Sunset's Glory
BURNING THE SHROUD,
Hammerheart (2001)
Burning The Shroud / Midnatt Storm /
Raven And Blood ('99 version) / To Enter
The Realm Of Legend (Live) / The
Summoning Of Shadows (Live) /
Cuchulain (Live) / Dark Rage (7"
version) / Fire And Wind / In The Darkest
Circles Of Time
ASCENSION OF TERROR,
Hammerheart (2001)

AGALLOCH (USA)
Line-Up: J. Haugh, S. Breyer,
L. Anderson (guitar), J. William (bass)

AGALLOCH was born out of the
disintegration of the 1995 band
AEOLACHRYMAE. In 1996 AGALLOCH,
as a duo of J. Haugh and S. Breyer with
second guitarist L. Anderson, issued the
'From Which Of This Oak' demo.

Albums:
PALE FOLKLORE, The End TE010
(1999)
She Painted Fire Across The Skyline /
The Misshapen Steed / Hallways Of
Enchanted Ebony / Dead Winter Days /
As Embers Dress The Sky / The
Melancholy Spirit

AGARTHI (ITALY)
Line-Up: Vanth (vocals), Avenir (guitar),
Adonai (keyboards), Michele Ercolano
(drums)

Black Metal band AGARTHI debuted with
the 1996 demo tape 'Beginnings' on
Entropy Productions. Vocalist Vanth and
keyboard player Adonai would join
FIURACH whilst AGARTHI's bassist
would team up with DOOMSWORD
rebilled as 'Dark Omen' and guitarist
Avenir enrolled himself into DEMON'S
GATE. Drummer Michele Ercolano would
become a member of Doom band
MORNINGRISE.

Albums:
AT THE BURNING HORIZON, Red
Stream (1997)
The Burning Horizon / And Cursed Will

Be The Sun / In Manu Maligni / Black
Triangle Sovereigns

AGATHODAIMON (GERMANY)
Line-Up: Vlad (vocals), Akaias (vocals),
Sathonys (guitar), Hyperion (guitar),
Marko T. (bass), Christine (keyboards),
Matthias (drums).

AGATHODAIMON was founded in late
1995 by the duo of guitarist Sathonys and
drummer Matthias. The band was
actually brought up to strength with the
results of advertising for suitable like
minded musicians. This search pulled in
bassist Marko and the Rumanian vocalist/
keyboard player Vlad. A later recruit was
second guitarist Hyperion.
Both Sathonys and Matthias were also
active members of NOCTE OBDUCTA
having issued two albums to date.
AGATHODAIMON got off to a flying start
when the debut demo 'Carpe Noctem'
received glowing reviews in the major
German Metal magazines. Successive
gigs alongside DESASTER, ANCIENT
CEREMONY and IMPENDING DOOM
illicited strong record company interest. A
national tour with ABLAZE MY SORROW
and BESEECH cemented this reputation
further with Century Media Records who
co-financed the acts next demo session
'Near Dark'. However, protracted
negotiations saw AGATHODAIMON slip
out of Century Media's hands as the
group signed to rivals Nuclear Blast.
Prior to recording the inaugural album
'Blacken The Angel' Vlad was detained
on a home visit to his native Rumania.
Having left the country when under
Ceaucescu's reign Vlad was deemed to
have broken the emigration laws.
Without their vocalist AGATHODAIMON
were forced into pulling in a substitute for
recording. Akaias of ASARU took the lead
vocal role and NOCTE OBDUCTA's
Vampellens aided on keyboards.
Although unable to contribute in the
studio Vlad did include his ambient piece
'Contemplation Song' which was mailed
to the band on DAT format.
AGATHODAIMON busied themselves on
the festival circuit to promote the release
and undertook numerous tours together
with DIMMU BORGIR, BENEDICTION,
DISMEMBER and HYPOCRISY. When
the dust had settled it was revealed that
'Blacken The Angel' had become the
highest selling German Black Metal
album to date.
Resolving to re-incorporate Vlad into the
band AGATHODAIMON recorded their

AGATHODAIMON

sophomore effort 'Higher Art Of Rebellion' in Rumania. Along with Vlad the band utilized Akaias once more as well as 'clean' vocalist Byron. Keyboards were now with Christine.

AGATHODAIMON headlined above GRAVEWORM and SIEBENBURGEN before putting in festival appearances at the Wacken, Windo Rock and Wave Gotik events. Meantime Sathonys severed his links with NOCTE OBDUCTA to concentrate fullly on AGATHODAIMON. AGATHODAIMON are presently occupied on a third album provisionally titled 'Architectura Apocalipsei'.

Vlad also operates the Black Ambient act RA (previously DRUSUS) releasing the albums 'Geniu Pustiu' and 'Sinnocence'.

Albums:
BLACKEN THE ANGEL, Nuclear Blast (1998)
Tristetea Vehementa / Banner Of Blasphemy / Near Dark / Ill Of An Imaginary Guilt / Die Nacht de Unwesers / Contemplation Song / Stintit Cu Rova Suferintii / Stingher- Alone / After Dark / Ribbons- Requiem
HIGHER ART OF REBELLION, Nuclear

Blast NB 422-2 (1999)
Ne Cheama Pamintul / Tongue Of Thorns / A Death In It's Plenitude / When She's Mute / Glasul Artei Viitoare / Novus Ordo Seclorum / Body Of Clay / Back Into The Shadows / Les Posedes / Neovampirism / Heaven's Coffin

AGATUS (GREECE)

Black Metal band AGATUS issued the 1993 demo 'Night Of Dark Ages' and the 1994 follow up 'Black Moon'. The 'Dawn Of Martyrdom' album also saw a release on No Colours Records with extra tracks from the first demo.

AGATUS mentor Eskarth The Dark One, now resident in Adelaide, Australia, also operates ZEMIAL.

Singles/EPs:
Rites Of Metamorphosis, Order Of Death Productions (1996) (7" single)

Albums:
DAWN OF MARTYRDOM, Hypervorea (1996)
Under The Spell Of The Dragon / Demon Of The Great Kingdom /

15

Emerge... Through My Diabolic Possession / Black Moon's Blood / When The Macabre Dance Begins / Spirits From The Depths Of Earth / Memories Of The Cold Ages / Force Of Desecration / King Of The Forest / Nostalgia

AGHAST (NORWAY)

A solo project of EMPEROR member Samoth's girlfriend Nebel. AGHAST offered dark, Gothic Rock on the 1995 released debut album. In 1997 Nebel formulated a further vehicle for her endeavours titled HAGALAZ' RUNEDANCE under her real name of Andrea M. Haugen.

Albums:
HEXERI IM ZWEILICHT DER FINSTERNIS, Cold Meat Industry CMI 33 (1995)
Enthrall / Sacrifice / Enter The Hall Of Ice / Call From The Grave / Totentanz / The Darkest Desire / Das Irrlicht / Ende

AGRESSOR (FRANCE)

Line-Up: Alex Colin-Tocquaine (vocals / guitar), Thierry (bass), Laurent (drums)

Antibes Black Thrash Metal trio that recorded their first demo in November 1986, AGRESSOR released a couple more demos and played dates with APOCALYPSE and LIVING DEATH. The band signed to Black Mark for one album, subtly titled 'Satan's Sodomy', graced with an album cover showing the immediate after effects of buggery with the devil!
AGRESSOR's line-up at this juncture was as a trio of vocalist / guitarist Alex Colin-Tocquaine, bassist J.M. Libeer and drummer Jean Luc Falsini. This incarnation recorded the first two demos 'Merciless Onslaught' and 'Satan's Sodomy'.
Things swiftly changed for the group when AGRESSOR added new drummer Thierry and ex HELLRAISER bassist Laurent in 1988.
The group then signed to Noise, recording 'Neverending Destiny', after which both new men split leaving Alex Colin-Tocquaine to soldier on alone! Thierry joined LOUDBLAST.
Undaunted, Alex put together a brand new line-up of his band, thus the 1992 version of AGRESSOR (which recorded the 'Towards Beyond' album) consisted of

Colin-Tocquaine, ex OUTBURST guitarist Patrick Gibelin, ex OUTBURST bassist Joël Guigon and ex DEATHPOWER drummer Stephan Gwegwam.
Gibelin had quit by the time AGRESSOR returned to the studio to cut the ensuing 'Symposium Of Rebirth' album, his place being taken by new guitarist Manu Ragot.
The TERRORISER cover track 'After World Obliteration', incidentally, features a guest vocal performance from NAPALM DEATH's Barney Greenaway.
The 2000 incarnation of AGRESSOR saw Colin-Tocquaine and Guigor joined by guitarist Adramelch and drummer Gorgor.

Albums:
LICENSED TO THRASH, New Wave 024 (1987) (Split LP with LOUDBLAST)
Satan's Sodomy / Brainstorm / Bloodfeast / Uncontrolled Desire / Black Church / It's Pandemonium
SATAN'S SODOMY, Black Mark BMCD 36 (1987)
Satan's Sodomy / Brainstorm / Blood Feast / Uncontrolled Desire / Black Church / It's Pandemonium
NEVERENDING DESTINY, Black Mark (1990)
Paralytic Disease / The Unknown Spell / Element Decay / Voices From Below / Blood Feast / Neverending Destiny / Prince Of Fire / Dark Power / The Arrival / Brainstorm / Bloody Corps
TOWARDS BEYOND, Black Mark BMCD 23 (1992)
Intro / Primeval Transubtantion / The Fortress / Positionic Showering / Antediluvian / Epileptic Alra / Hyaldid / The Crypt / Future Past- Eldest Things / Turkish March
SYMPOSIUM OF REBIRTH, Black Mark BMCD 55 (1994)
Barabas / Rebirth / Negative Zone / Apocalyptic Prophecies / Erga Meam Salutem / Overloaded / Theology / Civilization / Wheel Of Pain / Abhuman Dreadnought / Torture / Dor Fin-I-Guinar / After World Obliteration
MEDIEVAL RITES, Season Of Mist (2000)
Mediaeval Rites / Bloodshed / The Woodguy Vs. The Black Beast / The Sorcerer / (I Am The) Spirit Of Evil / Wandering Soul / Tye-Melane Helda / God From The Sky / Welcome home (King Diamond) / On Dolinde / Burial Desecration / Tribal Dance / At Night

16

AIMOPTYSI (GREECE)

Line-Up: John Zaminos (vocals), Alekos Bafitis (guitar), Phillip Bouramis (bass),

AIMOPTYSI embarked upon their chosen path with the demos 'Horizon' and 'Dark Aimoloth'. The band employed a drum machine for their 'Searching The Myths Of The Past' debut. The record includes guest guitar by Tassos Spiliotopoulos of FLAMES.

Albums:
SEARCHING THE MYTHS OF THE PAST, DR Productions (2000)

AIN SOPH (ITALY)

AIN SOPH have been a going concern for nearly two decades. A genuine underground act AIN SOPH merge occult and apocalyptic themes with ritualistic and industrial music that spans tribal to ambient sounds. AIN SOPH have been hugely influential in inspiring many of the better known Black Metal ambient offshoots.

Although originally released in 1990 the 'Ain Soph' album was reissued in 1999 by British label Elfenblut Records.

Singles/EPs:
Baltikum / , Misty Circles (1995) (Split 7" single with CIRCUS JOY)

Albums:
AIN SOPH I, Misty Circles (1984)
AIN SOPH II, Misty Circles (1985)
KSHATRYA, (1988)
Decimus Gradus / Monsalvet / I.A.O. / Kshatriya / Stella Maris
AURORA, Cthulu (1992)
Tutti A Cosa! / Ramayama / Pistolet Automatique / Uomin Perduti / Rubayyat / White Guard / Liberte Ou Mort / Legionnare En Algiers / Vent / Le Depart / Tempi Duri / Gli Amarti Tristi / Io E Te / Cuore Nero
ARS REGIA, Nekrophile (1992)
SIMULACRA, (1998) (Split album with SIGILLUM)
AIN SOPH, Elfenblut (1999)

AKERBELTZ (BRAZIL)

Line-Up: Ron Seth (vocals), S. Wildhagen (guitar), Alex Verdilak (guitar), M. Midgard (bass), Gorgon (drums)

AKERBELTZ are openly and unashamedly inspired by CELTIC FROST. The band emerged with the demos 'Dominus Infernus Vobiscum' and

'Songs With The Devil'.

Albums:
THERION RISING, Cogumelo COG039 (1999)
Intro / Diabolical Triumph / Ancient Witchcraft / Pagan Rituals / Rising Pantheon / Adversary / Cult To Baphomet / Evocations / Occult Ceremonial Towers / Satanas Age / Through Lost Centuries / Supreme Regency Of Satanas / Epilogue

AKERBELTZ (SPAIN)

Albums:
A WAVE OF DARKNESS, Millenium Metal Music MMM004 (2000)
Burial Of The Hyperborean Witch / Conspiracy / Fire (The Punishment Of Lilith) / Infernu Coerveca / Doomed / Black Anni's Bower / Burn In Hell
TABELLAE DEFIXIONUM, Millenium Metal Music MMM005 (2001)
The Guardian Tightly Rooted / Nocturnal Ride / The Forest Is My Haunt / The Green Eyes / Tabellae Defixionum / Akerhell

AKERCOCKE (UK)

Line-Up: Jason Mendonca (vocals), David Gray (drums)

London Black Metallers that include ex members of SALEM ORCHID. The debut album 'Rape Of The Bastard Nazarene' has been hailed as a classic of the genre although it did encounter problems with the printers who refused to manufacture the album sleeve due to it's apparent depiction of a nun's anus!

Female backing vocals on the album came courtesy of Tracy Warwick and Nicola Kemp.

Albums:
RAPE OF THE BASTARD NAZARENE, Goat Of Mendes (1999)
Hell / Nadja / The Goat / Marguerite And Gretchen / Sephiroth Rising / Zulieka / Conjuration / Il Giurdino Di Monte Oliveto Maggione / Justine

AKHENATON (FRANCE)

A solo project of Lord Vincent Akhenaton, AKHENATON, is named after the allegedly female Egyptian pharaoh that usurped the pantheon of Gods in favour of monotheistic worship of Aten.

AKHENATON was previously known as

DAEMONIUM and would figure in AMAYON. Latterly Akhenaton, under the revised title of Seigneuer V. Sandragon became a pivotal member of WINDS OF SIRIUS for the 'Beyond All Temples And Myths' album.

Albums:
DIVINE SYMPHONIES, Adipocere AR 030 CD (1995)
Act I - Raising (Intro) / Act II - Unutterable Verity / Act III - Remissions - The Sign Of Herou / Act IV - In The Circle Of Wizards - Ritual / Act V - Chase With The Shadows / Act VI - Cross The Styx (Dance With The Souls) / Act VII - The Kingdom Of Wisdom / Act VIII - At The Gates Of Obscurity / Act IX - Final Battle (Against Your Dark Side) / Act X - Pharao (The Karma Of The Hierophante)

ALASTOR (COSTA RICA)
Line-Up: Abrahkkan (vocals), Baphomet (guitar), Glaciabolous (bass), Javier (drums)

Albums:
THE HOWLING CREATION OF NIGHT, Alastor (2000)
Odio / Poetry For Thy Glory / My Fields Are Mighty / Through A Valley Of Night Souls / Where No Light Can Reach / Sanguinary Embryo / Ridin' Thy Darklands / The Infinity Of Luciferian Wings / Beyond My Unconscious Deep / Quimera

ALGAION (SWEDEN)
Line-Up: Marten Björkmann (vocals), Mathias Kamijo (guitar / bass / keyboards), Fredrik Söderlund (drums)

ALGAION is essentially a two man Black Metal project started by ex ABEMAL members Mathias Kamijo and Marten Björkman in 1993. First product was a two track demo which led to the inclusion of the track 'Kratos' on a 1994 Fullmoon compilation CD.
The band's debut album 'Oimai Algeiou' was recorded at Peter Tägtgren of HYPOCRISY and THE ABYSS' studios with Fredrik Söderlund of OCTINIMOS programming keyboards and drums and Nattfurhst of SORHIN on backing vocals. ALGAION's second record, 'General Enmity', featured Tägtgren in place of Söderlund on drums.
Kamijo joined Tägtgren's project band THE ABYSS in 1996 and also toured

America as part of HYPOCRISY.
Kamijo also operates in VERGELMER operating under a pseudonym for the 1997 album 'Light The Black Flame'.

Singles/EPs:
Vox Clementis / Throughout Times / See What Is To Come / Cupidus Imperii, Wounded Love (1996) ('Vox Clementis' EP)

Albums:
OIMAI ALGEIOU, Fullmoon FMP 002-1 (1995)
Venenum Homininitis (Intro) / Natrics Educati / Heosphoros / In Aede Dolorium / On The Reach Of Zaphonia / Kratos / The Last Delusion
GENERAL ENMITY, Wounded Love (1997)
Inductio / General Enmity / No Will Without Fire / Unstained Progress / Nature Red In Tooth And Claw / An Impending Disaster / Marigold Hold The Sceptre / Lies Of Human Value / The Angel Of Deceit / Indifferent Beyond Misanthropy / It's Darker In The Present / The Root Of Inhumanity- Conclusion

ALGAZANTH (FINLAND)
Line-Up: Thasmorg (vocals / bass), Veilroth (guitar), A. Somonen (keyboards), Gorath Moonthrone (drums)

ALGAZANTH featured bassist Dreminoc on their 1996 demo 'Behind The Frozen Forest'. With his departure frontman Thasmorg took over the role.

Albums:
THY AEONS ENVENOMED SANITY, Woodcut (1999)
Introduction- The Broken Talon / The Unbounded Wrath / My Sombreness Surmounted / On A Stormgrey Vision / He Awaits… / Towards The Tempting Infinity / Ensnared In Moonshades / When The Spirits Dare In Grief / The Thorns Cry Blood

ALGOL (NORWAY)
Line-Up: Thomas Andresen (vocals / guitar), Kjell-Ivar Andersen (guitar), Glenn Spitz (bass), Pat Solli (drums)

Albums:
ENTERING THE WOODS OF ENCHANTMENT, Effigy EFFY 004 CD (1996)
Entering The Woods Of Enchantment /

I'm The King / Eternal / Mysterious Pentagram / Remember / Sacrifice / Autumn Void / Crime Impossible / Witch Trial / Long Cold Frost / Priests Are Laughing / Dreams (Under A Full Moon) / Last Thoughts

ALKAID (ITALY)

Milan based ALKAID are a project offshoot of BLESSED BE THE WOODS.

ALLEGIENCE (SWEDEN)
Line-Up: Bogge Svenson (vocals / guitar), Pära (guitar), Micke (bass), Fredrik Andersson (drums)

ALLEGIENCE, a now highly regarded act founded in 1989, ply old style trad Thrash on their debut demo 'Sick World'. The band had got decidedly more brutal by second attempt the aptly named 'Eternal Hate'. The band shifted direction undergoing a radical line up shuffle to emerge as out and out Black Metal merchants on their third tape 'Odin Äge Er Alle'. A fourth stab at the demo scene with 1994's 'Hafdingadrapa' pursued more Viking Metal leanings.
Members of ALLEGIENCE also have an interest in MARDUK sharing drummer Fredrik Andersson and Bogge Svensson.

Albums:
HYMN TILLHANGAGUD, No Fashion NFR 014 (1996)
Höfdingadrapa / De Nordiska Lagren / The Third Raven / Himmelen Rämnar / Den Krisnes Död / The March Of Warlike Damned / Stridsärd / Spjutsängen
BLODÖRNSOFFER, No Fashion NFR021 (1997)
Intag / Med Svärd I Hand / Likbal / En Svunnen Tid / Heimdal / Yggrasil / Korpen Skall Leda Oss / Blodörnsoffer / Blot / Uttag
VREDE, No Fashion NFR028 (1998)
Na Skall Du Do Vite Krist / Sorn Drogens Hart Med Doden / I Stjarnornas Skugga / Hrodvittners Rike / Baldersbalet / Nordens Fader / Hedna Stad Hymn Till Nordens Hjaltar / Skymning

AL SIRET (POLAND)

Albums:
SIGNA TEMPORI, Metalstorm (1999)

ALSVARTR (SWEDEN)
Line-Up: Ravensvart (vocals), Tristhan (guitar), Mjødulv (guitar), Ard (bass), Vivandre (keyboards), Valdr (drums)

ALSVARTR comprise of vocalist / guitarist Ravensvart (Jan Steinar Myrvoll), guitarist Mjødulv (Tommy Nikkolaisen), bass player Ard (Stian Bakkehaug), keyboard player Vivandre (Christer Pedersen) and drummer Valdr (Kjetil Dahlen).
Both Valdr and Mjødulv are active members of another band NEBULAR MYSTIC.
ALSVARTR hit domestic turbulence in May of 1999 when Ravensvart exited. Replacement was erstwhile MACTÄTUS, BELGMØRK and LYCANTROPY man Per Erik Flatin with former INTUITION man Lars Fredriksen, rechristened 'Tristhan', on second guitar. However, by September Flatin was out and Ravensvart resumed his position.
Vivandre deputized for OLD MAN'S CHILD in May of 2000 for their European tour. Not content with this extra activity the keyboard player also signed up with APOSTASY. Vidvandre would also join VINTERSORG for touring purposes in late 2000.

Singles/EPs:
Et Hedensk Land / As Ravens Fly / Blood Revenge / Viking Feud, (2000) ('Et Hedensk Land' EP)

Albums:
LIVE IN EIDSVOLL, (1999)
Et Hedensk Land / Alsvartr / Fire In The Sky / As Ravens Fly / Battle Ground / Forever Owned Is Only The Lost / Blood Revenge / United / Taakevandring / Home Of Gods / Evighetens Kall / As I Die

ALTAR (HOLLAND)
Line-Up: Edwin Kelder (vocals), Bert Huisjes (guitar), Marcel Van Haaff (guitar), Nils Vos (bass), Marco Arends (drums)

ALTAR released a 1992 demo titled 'And God Created Satan To Blame For His Mistakes'.
The second album features ex MANDATOR guitarist Marcel Verdermen.

Albums:
YOUTH AGAINST CHRIST, Massacre MASS CD 056 (1994)
Throne Of Fire / Jesus Is Dead! / Divorced From God / Hypochristianity /

Forced Imprudence / Psycho Damn / Cross The Bridge Of False Prophecies / Cauterize The Church Council
EGO ART, Displeased D00046 (1996)
Eidelon / I Take / Ego Art / C.C.C. / Truly Untrue / Pathetic Priest / Destructive Selection / Egoverment / Follow Me / Tonight This Country Will Die
IN THE NAME OF THE FATHER,
Displeased (2000)
Holy Mask / Spunk / God Damn You / In The Name Of The Father / I Spit Black Bile On You / Hate Scenario / Pro Jagd / Walhalla Express / In Our Dominion

ALTAR (SWEDEN)
Line-Up: Magnus Karlsson (vocals / bass), Jimmy Lundmark (guitar), Fredrik Johansson (drums)

ALTAR also had drummer Per Karlsson in the ranks for a period. Karlsson would later join SUFFER then in 1996 SERPENT.

Albums:
EX OBLIVIONE, Drowned Products DC013 (1993) (Split LP with CARTILAGE)
Nothing Human / Lifeless Passion / Decapitated (New version) / Daymare / A Message From The Grave / Ex Oblivione / Severed On The Attic / No Flesh...

AMDUSCIAS (JAPAN)

Albums:
AMDUSCIAS, Blackened BLACK009CD (1998)
The Dragon Domination / The Cursed Destiny / Hell On Earth / Dominion Of Darkness / Sacrifices Within Me / Blood From Your Heart

AMEN CORNER (BRAZIL)

Singles/EPs:
The Final Celebration, Cogumelo (1992) (7" single)

Albums:
FALL, ASCENSION, DOMINATION,
Cogumelo (1992)
JACHOL VE TEHILA, Cogumelo (1994)
THE FINAL CELEBRATION, Cogumelo (1995)

AMESTIGON (AUSTRIA)
Line-Up: Thurisaz, Krim, Tharen

An Austrian band formed by ex ABIGOR singer Rune Tharen marked their inception with the 'Mysterious Realms' demo. This Black Metal outfit released a split album with ANGIZIA in 1996.
AMESTIGON guitarist Jörg Lanz would session on Tharen's project band DOMINION 3's 2000 album 'The Hand And The Sword'.

Albums:
AMESTIGON, Napalm (1996) (Split LP with. ANGIZIA)
Challerian's Fall / Samhain / Mysterious Realms / Stormlord
HOLLENTANZ, Napalm (1998)
Höllentanz / Rattenfänger / The Gates To A Red Moon / Atmosfear

AMETHYST (HOLLAND)
Line-Up: Serge (vocals), Natasja (vocals), Ayhan (guitar), Alex (guitar), Bjorn (bass), Jochem (drums)

Black Metal with female vocals and strong Gothic overtones. AMETHYST started life as a school band in 1996. Drummer Jochem is also a member of POSTMORTEM FABULAE.
AMETHYST underwent numerous line up changes before the self financed 'Dea Noctilucae' release losing drummer Norbert and keyboard player Michael in 1999.

Albums:
DEA NOCTILUCAE, Amethyst (2000)
Withering Soul / Of Damnation In Reprise / Mistress Of Gorgon / Fear / Last Touch / My Land Beyond

AMOEN GOETH (CZECH REPUBLIC)
Line-Up: Dr. Fe (vocals), Lada Larva Krupica (guitars / keyboards), Karel I. Bosak (drums)

Czech Black Metal band arrived in 1990 with the demo 'Realm Of Evil'. Further demo sessions ensued prior to the release of a cassette live album 'Alive In Hell' during 1995.
The 1995 album includes a version of CELTIC FROST's 'Into The Crypts Of Rays'.

Albums:
ALIVE IN HELL- LIVE, (1995) (Cassette release)
CALL THE MASTER, Nazgul's Eyrie Productions NEP008CD (1995)

Sign Of The Pentagram (Znameni Pentagramu) / Christian Pigs (Nabozne Svine) / Circle Of Death (Kolobeh Smrti) / On The Grave (Na Hrobe) / Steeve Ryder / Splattercore Movie / Into The Crypts Of Rays / Call The Master (Volejte Pana)
THE WORSHIP, Nazgul's Eyrie Productions (1997)

AMON (CZECH REPUBLIC)

AMON feature ex members of ROOT.

Albums:
IN THE SHADE OF DEATH, (2000)

AMON (SWITZERLAND)

Albums:
THE SHINING TROPEZOHEDRON, (1992)
Full Moon / The Shining Trapezohedron / Circle Of Slavery / Legions Rise / Infernal Realm / Vanish Into The Void / Book Of The Dead
SHEMHAMFORASH, Witchhunt (1996)
Into The Black Order / The Diatribe / Sumerian Death Call / Das Tierdrama / Words Of Warning / The Morning Of Black Magic / Dethroned Sophistas / Destructive Organism / Lucifer Dwells Within / Eternal Darkness And Winter Storms / Lost Souls / So It Is Done

AMON AMARTH (SWEDEN)
Line-Up: Johan (vocals), Hansson (guitar), Olli (guitar), Ted (bass), Nico (drums)

Hailing from Tumba, a suburb of Stockholm, AMON AMARTH trace their roots back to 1992. The unit's first available recording to have been 1993's 'Thor's Rise' demo though this was withheld and it was to be a full year before second demo 'The Arrival Of Fimbul Winter' made it onto the tape trading scene leading to a deal with Singapore based label Pulverized Records.
Following the release of debut 'Sorrow Throughout The Nine Worlds' drummer Nico opted out to be replaced by Martin Lopez.
AMON AMARTH's sophomore release was produced by HYPOCRISY's Peter Tägtgren.
AMON AMARTH, supported by PURGATORY, undertook a tour of Germany in December 2000.

Singles/EPs:
Burning Creation / The Arrival Of The Fimbul Winter / Without Fear, (1994) ("The Arrival Of The Fimbul Winter' EP)

Albums:
SORROW THROUGHOUT THE NINE WORLDS, Pulverized ASH001 MCD (1996)
Sorrow Throughout The Nine Worlds / The Arrival Of The Fimbul Winter / Burning Creation / The Mighty Doors Of The Speargod's Hall / Under The Graveclouded Winter Sky
ONCE SENT FROM THE GOLDEN HALL, Metal Blade 3984-14133-2 (1998)
Ride For Vengeance / The Dragon's Flight Across The Waves / Without Fear / Victorious March / Friends Of The Suncross / Abandoned / Amon Amarth / Once Sent From The Golden Hall
THE AVENGER, Metal Blade (2000)
Bleed For Ancient Gods / The Last With Pagan Blood / North Sea Storm / Avenger / God, His Son And Holy Whore / Metal Wrath / Legend Of A Banished Man / Thor Arise
THE CRUSHER, Metal Blade (2001)
Bastards Of A Lying Breed / Masters Of War / The Sound Of Eight Hooves / Risen From The Sea 2000 / As Long As The Raven Flies / A Fury Divine / Annihilation Of Hammerfest / The Fall Through Ginnungagap / Releasing Surtur's Fire

AMORTIS (AUSTRIA)
Line-Up: Chris, Peter, Martin, Simon (bass), Lukas (drums)

AMORTIS previously worked under the title PENETRALIA. Retitling themselves the band opened proceedings with the demo 'A Kiss From The Dusk'.

Albums:
SUMMONED BY ASTRAL FIRES, Last Episode (2000)
Centuries Of Enslavement / A Dream Of Dancing Shadows / Dark Visions By Candlelight / Mortus Animae / Like Ravens In The Nightsky / In The Spell Of Midnights Grace / Storm Of Pagan Fire / Summoned By Astral Fire

AMSVARTNER (SWEDEN)
Line-Up: Marcus Johansson (vocals), Jonathon Holmgren (guitar), Daniel Nygaard (guitar), Albin Johansson (bass), Alfred Johansson (drums)

Ulmea's AMSVARTNER debuted in 1995 with two demos 'Amsvartner' and 'Underneath The Thousand Years Gate'. The band are fronted by vocalist Marcus Johansson, his younger twin brothers Alfred and Albin supply the rhythm section.
Although the 1997 debut album 'The Trollish Mirror' displays clear Black Metal leanings it's follow up 'Dreams' found the band in more traditional Heavy Metal territory.
Following the release of 'Dreams' guitarist Daniel Nygaard quit. AMSVARTNER pulled in replacement Kalle Lundin although his tenure was brief.
Marcus Johansson also fronts Black Metal band DISORGE.

Albums:
THE TROLLISH MIRROR, Blackend BLACK 005CD (1997)
The Trollish Mirror / Underneath The Thousand Year Gate / Memories Of Faded Kingdoms / The Wilderness Of Mind
DREAMS, Blackend (1999)

ANACONDA (GERMANY)
Line-Up: Alex Kössl (vocals), Andreas 'Crazy' Opel (guitar), Henning 'Gig' Kölbl (guitar), Olle Becher (bass), Thomas 'Bondo' Drechsel (drums)

Having recorded three demos and one self financed album with ANACONDA, bassist Olle Becher quit and has not yet been replaced.

Albums:
THE LATTICE WINDOW, Anaconda (1996)
No More Gods / Gonepteryx / Rhamni / Black Cross / My Own World / The Lattice Window / Time Of Eternity / Devastation / Burning Shame / Faith The Fear

ANATOMY (AUSTRALIA)
Line-Up: Marty (vocals), Hippyslayer (guitar), Machen (guitar), J.A. (bass), Wazarah (drums)

Australian Black Death Metal band ANATOMY bowed in with the 1991 'Dark Religion' demo following it up with 1992's session 'Those Whose Eyes Are Black'.
ANATOMY's 2000 album 'The Witches Of Duthomir' included their take on POSSESSED's 'The Exorcist'. The band would later enroll former BESTIAL

WARLUST drummer Markus Hellcunt.

Albums:
TWISTING DEPTHS OF HORROR, Dark Oceans (1994)
For A Darkened Soul / Twisting Depths Of Horror / A Scream Of Seven / Burial Of Armenia / Nucleus Eclipse Torn Abyss / arrogance Within Humanity
WHERE ANGELS DIE, Destruktive Kommandöh DSTK7662-2CD (1996)
Last Pleasures For Those Of The Apocalypse Of Hate / Under The Wings / Armagedoom / Forbidden Realms / The Call For Doom / Where Angels Die / The Frozen Darkness
THE WITCHES OF DUTHOMIR, Bleed (2000)

ANCIENT (NORWAY)
Line-Up: Aphazel (vocals / guitar), Deadly Kristen (vocals), Dhilorz (bass), Jesus Christ (keyboards), Krigse (drums)

Black Metal outfit ANCIENT was initially formed as a solo project by Aphazel in late 1992. In 1993 the group added drummer / vocalist Thorg and performed a handful of Norwegian gigs with MOLESTED's bass player on loan.
ANCIENT's first official, three track demo featured 'Eerily Howling Winds', 'Trumps Of An Arc-Angel' and 'Det Glemte Riket'. The latter song was also featured on the Metal Blade Records compilation album 'Metal Massacre XII'. The tape sold over 700 copies and gained the band a deal with Listenable Records in France. At this juncture Thorg changed his stage name to Grimm. Further gigs followed, this time utilizing the services of ASMODEUS's bassist.
With the release of the 'Trolltar' EP, Grimm left the band and in came American Lord Kaiaphas, previously known as Lord Vlad Luciferion whilst a member of the bands THOKK and GRAND BELIAL'S KEY. The band also added drummer Kjetil.
ANCIENT's second album features guest female vocals from Kimberley Goss of Chicago's AVERNUS as the band now became almost entirely American. However, Goss joined Norwegians DIMMU BORGIR on loan for their European tour but cemented this into a permanent relationship later that same year. Goss would of course later found Power Metal band SINERGY.
1997's 'Mad Grandiose Bloodfiends' (recorded in the American state of

Virginia) includes a cover of MERCYFUL FATE's 'Black Funeral'. By now, ANCIENT were effectively a duo of Aphazel and Kaiaphas, but recorded together with New Orleans native Erichte on female vocals and the blasphemously named Jesus Christ (!) on guitar and other stringed instruments. Confusion followed the band into 1998 as ANCIENT imploded yet again. Out went Kaiaphas and in came bassist Tony and Jesus Christ moved over onto keyboards. By 1999 ANCIENT comprised of Aphazel on lead vocals and guitar, bassist Dhilorz, vocalist Deadly Kristen, keyboard player Jesus Christ and drummer Krigse. Aphazel and Deadly Kristen also busied themselves with the extra curricular Gothic ambient project DREAMLIKE HORROR.

Singles/EPs:
Det Clemte Riket / Huldradans, Listenable (1994)
Trolltaar / Nattens Skjonnhet / Tjellets Hemmelighet, Damnation 3 (1996) (CD single)
Trolltaar / Nattens Skjonnhet / Tjellets Hemmelighet / Eerie Howling Winds, Damnation 3 (1996) (12" single)

Albums:
SVARTALAVHEIM, Listenable POSH006 (1995)
Svartavheim / Trumps On An Arch-Angel / Huldradans / The Call Of The Absu Deep / Det Glemte Riket / Paa Evig Vandring / Ved Trollt Jern / Eerily Howling Winds / Likferd
THE CAINIAN CHRONICLE, Metal Blade 3984-14110-2 (1996)
Ponderous Moonlighting / The Curse / Lilith's Embrace / Disiplines Of Caine / Zillah And The Crone / At The Infernal Portal / Cry Of Mariamne / Prophecy Of Gehenna / Song Of Kaiaphas / Exu / The Pagan Cycle / Homage To Pan
MAD GRANDIOSE BLOODFIENDS, Metal Blade 3984-14143-2 (1997)
Malkavian Twilight / A Mad Blood Scenario / The Draining / Um Gonho Psycodelico / Sleeping Princess Of The Arges / Her Northern Majesty / Blackeyes / The Emerald Tablet / Willowthewisp / Neptune / 5 / Hecate, My Love And Lust / Vampirize Natasha / Black Funeral
DET GLEMTE RIKET, Hammerheart (1999)
Trolltaar / Nattens Skjonn Het / Eeirily Howling Winds / Det Glemte Riket / Huldra Dans / Pan Evig Vandring /

Fjellets Hermnee Lighet / Algul / Sweet Leaf
THE HALLS OF ETERNITY, Metal Blade (1999)
Cast Into The Unfathomed Depths / Born In Flames / The Battle Of The Ancient Warriors / A Woeful Summoning / Cosmic Exile / Spiritual Supremacy / The Heritage / I, Madman / From Behind Comes The Sword / The Halls Of Eternity / Arrival
GOD LOVES THE DEAD, Metal Blade (2001)

ANCIENT CEREMONY (GERMANY)
Line-Up: Christian Anderle (vocals), F.J. Krebs (guitar), Dirk Wirz (guitar), Frank Somin (bass), Stefan Müller (keyboards), Christoph Mertes (drums)

A Melodic Black Death Metal band with Gothic influences. ANCIENT CEREMONY's first recordings resulted in the 1993 demo 'Where Serpents Reign'. The first self-produced mini CD recorded by the band appeared in 1995, with a full album arriving in 1997.

Singles/EPs:
Forsaken Gardens (Intro) / Cemetery Visions / The God And The Idol / Choir Of Immortal Queens / An Ode To The Moon, Ancient Ceremony (1995) ('Cemetery Visions' EP)

Albums:
UNDER MOONLIGHT WE KISS, Cacophonous (1997)
Eternal Goddess / Her Ivory Slumber / Shadows Of The Undead / Vampyre's Birth / Thy Beauty In Candlelight / Veil Of Desire / Secrets Of Blackened Sky / Dulcet Seduction / Angel's Bloody Tears / New Eden Embraces / Pale Nocturnal Majesty / Under Moonlight We Kiss
FALLEN ANGELS SYMPHONY, Cacophonous NIHIL 32CD (1999)
Death In Desire's Masquerade / Bride's Ghostly Grace / Black Roses On Her Grave / Devil's Paradise / The Tragedy Of Forsaken Angels / Amidst Crimson Stars / Babylon Ascends / Symphoni Satani / Vampyresque Wedding Night
SYNAGOGA DIABOLICA, Alister (2000)

ANCIENT RITES (BELGIUM)
Line-Up: Gunther Theys (vocals / bass), Bart Vandereycken (guitar), Walter Van Cortenberg (drums)

Formed in 1989, ANCIENT RITES have fast become one of the leading Belgian Black Metal acts.

The group's initial line-up comprised of vocalist/bassist Gunther Theys, guitarists Johan and Phillip and drummer Stefan. This concoction released the 'Dark Ritual' demo.

A year on, however, and ANCIENT RITES was forced to make changes. Firstly, band roadie Walter Van Cortenberg replaced drummer Stefan and then tragedy struck later in the same year when, in August, guitarist Phillip was killed in a car crash. The band enlisted guitarist Bart Vandereycken but soon after Johan departed leaving ANCIENT RITES as a single guitar band.

In 1992 the outfit recorded the self financed 'Evil Prevails' EP with second guitarist Pascal. However, Pascal 's tenure was brief and soon ANCIENT RITES were a trio once more.

Recording became quite prolific as the band added a track for Tessa Records' 'Detonation' compilation album as well as recording tracks for a Colombian split album on Warmaster Records. ANCIENT RITES also joined forces with Greek act THOU ART LORD for a split 7" single.

This activity was followed by intensive gigging across Europe, including dates in Greece with ROTTING CHRIST. A further track was included on a split EP on Molten Lava Records and the band finally released their first full length album, 'The Diabolic Serenades', on After Dark Records in early 1994.

During 1995 ANCIENT RITES toured Europe in with CRADLE OF FILTH and have since cut a split EP with fellow Belgians ENTHRONED.

1998's 'Fatherland' had Theys and Van Cortenberg joined by guitarists Erik Sprooten and Jan 'Orkki' Yrlund.

Singles/EPs:
Götterdammerung / Longing For The Ancient Kingdom / Obscurity Reigns (Fields Of Flanders) / Evil Prevails / Black Plague, Fallen Angel (1992) ('Evil Prevails' EP)
From Beyond The Grave II, Molon Lave (1993) (Split single with THOU ART LORD)
Split, Warmaster (1993) (12" split single with UNCANNY)
Longing For The Ancient Kingdom II, After Dark (1995) (Split single with ENTHRONED)

Albums:
ANCIENT RITES, Warmaster (1992) (Split LP)
THE DIABOLIC SERENADES, Mascot M 7018-2 (1994)
(Intro) Infant Sacrifices To Baalberith / Crucifixion Justified (Roman Supremach) / Satanic Rejoice / Obscurity Reigns (Fields Of Flanders) / Death Messiah / Land Of Frost And Despair / Ussyrian Empire / Longing For The Ancient Kingdom / Morbid Glory (Gilles De Rais 1404-1440) / Ritual Slayings (Goat Worship Pure) / Evil Prevails / Last Rites / Echoes Of Meloncholy (Outro) / From Beyond The Grave II
BLASFEMIA ETERNAL, Mascot M7017-2 (1996)
Blasfemia Eternal / Total Misanthropia / Garden Of Delights (Eva) / Quest For Blood (Le Vampire) / Blood Of Christ (Mohammed Wept) / Epebos Ai Nia / (Het Verdronken Land Van) Sacftinge / Shades Of Eternal Battlefields (Our Empire Fell) / Vae Victis / Fallen Angel
FATHERLAND, Mascot M 7035 2 (1998)
Avondland / Mother Europe / Aris / Fatherland / Season's Change (Solstice) / 13th Of December 1307 / Dying In A Moment Of Splendor / Rise And Fall (Anno Satana) / The Seducer / Cain
THE FIRST DECADE 1989-1999, Mascot (2000)
From Beyond The Grave (1990 demo) / Infant Sacrifices To Baalberith / Death Messiah / Longing For The Ancient Kingdom / Land Of Frost And Despair / Evil Prevails / Last Rites- Echoes Of Melanchoy / Total Misantropia / Blood Of Christ (Mohammed Wept) / Fallen Angel (Outro) / (Het Verdronken Land Van) Saftinge / Quest For Blood (Le Vampire) / Avondland / Mother Europe / Aris / Seasons Change / Fatherland / Cain

THE ANCIENTS REBIRTH (SWEDEN)

Thurzhagalz Trathathn (vocals / bass), Angerboder (guitar), Sayittarius (drums)

THE ANCIENTS REBIRTH second outing, the 'Damnated Hell's Arrival' EP, included a cover of KREATOR's seminal 'Flag Of Hate'. Guitarist Angerboder would join cult act PAGAN RITES during late 2000.

Singles/EPs:
Damnated Hell's Arrival / Times To Come Are Frozen / Flag Of Hate /

24

Armageddonish Execution, Necropolis NR023 (1998) ('Damnated Hell's Arrival' EP)

Albums:
DRAIN THE PORTAL IN BLOOD, Necromantik Gallery Productions (1996)
Oceans Of Blood Over Paradise / Haunt To Guard / I Blod Skall Syndaren Vakna / Reformation Divine / Den Svarta Gudomlighheten / Laughter Of The Funeral / Mörker Och Hat... / As He Rides The Nocturnal Skies / Velvet Claws / The Ancient Rebirth

ANCIENT SUMMONING
(GERMANY)

Singles/EPs:
Blazes Unto The Darklands, (1996) (7" single)

ANCIENT WARGOD
(GERMANY)
Line-Up: Shadow (guitar), Farago (guitar)

A Black Metal act with a chaotic history leading up to the debut album 'As Darkness Rises'. Indeed, besides the ructions in the band's line up ANCIENT WARGOD has been through no less than four title changes.
The band was created as MORPHEUS in late 1990 with a line up of guitarists Shadow and Farago, vocalist Rasewerk and drummer A. Huerni. The following year Huerni bailed out and Shadow deputized on drums. This incarnation of the band was dealt a major blow though when Rasewerk also decamped. 1992 had Shadow on lead vocals with Farago on guitar, a returning Huerni on drums, Shaitan The Interfector on bass and second guitarist Short. This union was to retitle themselves DARK IMPLORE.
Both Short and Huerni would leave forcing Shadow back onto the drums as the band name evolved yet again to WARGOD. As the decision was made to draft vocalist Akinakes the group became ANCIENT WARGOD issuing the 'In A Blackened Sky demo'. Shadow was able to manouevere back to guitar as drummer Bileeam was enlisted but Shadow was then forced to undertake his military service.
October 1998 witnessed the departure of both Dirk Schneider and Farago.

Albums:
WHEN DARKNESS RISES, (1997)
Ars Nigra / When Darkness Rises / Time Of The Emperor / Uncertainty / In The Shadows Of Hell / Ancient Wargod / Insane / Immortality

ANCIENT WISDOM
(SWEDEN)
Line-Up: Marcus Norman (vocals / guitar), Andreas Nilsson (guitar), Fredrik Jacobsson (bass), Jens Ryden (keyboards)

Previously known simply as ANCIENT the band became ANCIENT WISDOM in 1993. ANCIENT WISDOM's Marcus 'Vargher' Norman also fronts BEWITCHED. Both Norman and bass guitarist Fredrik Jacobsson were previously with THRONE OF AHAZ.
For live work the band added NOCTURNAL RITES drummer Ulf Andersson. Guitarist Andreas Nilsson and Jens Ryden also play in NAGLFAR.
In 2000 Norman founded a Gothic flavoured side project HAYAFOTH in collusion with NAGLFAR's Morgan Hansson.
ANCIENT WISDOM's 2000 album 'And The Physical Shape Of Light Bled' includes a cover of NWoBHM outfit DEMON's 'Day Of The Demon'.

Albums:
FOR THE SNOW COVERED THE NORTHLAND, Avantgarde AV0015 (1996)
A Hymn To The Northern Empire / In The Land Of The Crimson Moon / They Gather Where Snow Falls Forever / Through Rivers Of The Eternal Blackness / The Journey Of The Ancients / No Tears At His Funeral / Forest Of Summoned Spirits / A Raven's Reflection Of The Ancient Northland
THE CALLING, Avantgarde AV 020 (1997)
The Awakening Of The Ancient Serpents / The Calling Of Nocturnal Demons / As The Twelve Legions Of Angels Died / In The Profane Domain Of The Frostbeast / Spiritual Forces Of Evil In The Heavenly Realms / And To The Depths They Descended / At The Stone Of Ancient Wisdom / Of Darkness Spawned Into eternity / Through The Mist Of Dusk They Arose And Clad The Sky With Fire
AND THE PHYSICAL SHAPE OF LIGHT BLED, Avantgarde (2000)
Preludium Lucifer, Aieth Gadol Leolam /

And The Physical Shape Of Light Bled / With His Triumph Came Fire / Interludium The Fall Of Man / As The Morningstar Shineth / The Serpents Blessing / Postludium His Creation Reversed / The Spell

AND OCEANS (FINLAND)

Line-Up: K-2T4-S (vocals), Neptune (guitar), De Monde (guitar), Gaunt (bass), Anzhaar (keyboards), Grief (drums)

AND OCEANS debuted with a brace of demos in 1995's 'Wave' and 1997's 'Mare Liberum'. The act had originated from the 1989 Death Metal band FESTERDAY which centred upon vocalist K-2T4-S and guitarist Neptune. Augmenting their line up with second guitarist De Monde and Mr. Oos the group evolved into AND OCEANS in 1995.

BLACK DAWN's keyboard player Anzhaar and drummer Grief plugged the gap. AND OCEANS adventurous debut album 'The Dynamic Gallery Of Thoughts' was to include lyrics in no less than four languages namely Finnish, Swedish, English and French. The cover artwork was executed by erstwhile AT THE GATES man Alf Svensson. However, after recording Mr. Oos decamped and Gaunt of ROTTEN SOUND took his position.

The 1998 album 'War Vol. 1: Vs. Bloodthorn' sees AND OCEANS covering tracks by WW III, G.G.F.H. and BLOODTHORN.

Grief also performs with ENOCHIAN CRESCENT.

Albums:
THE DYNAMIC GALLERY OF THOUGHTS, (1998)
Trollfan / The Room Of Thousand Arts / Som Öppna Böcker / Je Te connais beau masque / Microbotic Fiends- Ur Åldrig Saga Och Sång / Samtal Med Tankar- Halo Of Worlds / September (Når Hjärtat Blöder) / Kärsimyksien Vaalent Kädet
WAR VOL. 1: VS. BLOODTHORN, Season Of Mist SOM011 (1998)
…Ja Kylmä Vesi Nuolee Oksaa / 100 Metres Final / Flesh / Breeding The Evil Inside / Spite / The End Offensive / Dead Men Don't Rape / Kävsimyksia Vaalent Kädet
THE SYMMETRY OF 1, THE CIRCLE OF 0, Season Of Mist SOM016 (1999)
Mechanic Hippie / Aquarium Of Children- Ajatusten Merenpinta / The Black

Vagabond And The Swan With Two Heads / Sålipsism / Baby Blue Doll- Merry Go Mind / Åcid Sex And Marble Teeth (You-Phoria) / I Wish I Was Pregnant / Stained / Injected With Silence / Cacophonous Ballet / Higher Levels Of Microbotic Fields / Playground / Mental Trolliß / Molecules / Spasms / Chess

ANDRAS (GERMANY)

Line-Up: In Earth (vocals), Count Damien Nightsky (guitar), Black Abyss (bass), Shadow (drums)

Black Metal act ANDRAS include EMINENZ bassist Black Abyss. ANDRAS first emerged with the 1995 demos 'The True Darkness' and 'Das Schwert Unserer Ahnen'.

2000 found ANDRAS splitting down the middle with guitarist Count Damien Nightsky and Black Abyss staying the course and new members In Earth on vocals and drummer Shadow entering the fold.

Albums:
DIE RÜCKEHR DER DUNKLEN KRIEGER, Last Epitaph (1997)
Wenn die Sterne Fallen / Nacht des Todes / Die Erste Schlacht / The True Darkness / Das Licht ist Nun Erloschen / Vollkommene Einsamkeit / Die Verboten / Funeral March / Diabolical Christening / Vor Sehr Langer Zeit / Armageddon / Die Letzt Schlacht
SWORD OF REVENGE, Last Episode (1998)
Andras / Listen To The Cry Of The Banshee / Banished In Hell / Conquering The Iron Steeper / Kingdom Of Mourning Souls / Graveyard Of Souls / Reaching For The Throne / Black Wings Of Death / Spirituality / Burning Graves Of Dunwich / Fleish und Blut / Damnation / Sword Of Revenge / Chalice Of Dragons Blood / Outro
QUEST OF DELIVERANCE, Last Episode LEP059CD (2000)

ANGEL CORPSE (USA)

Line-Up: Pete Helmkamp (vocals / bass), Gene Palubicki (guitar), Tony Laureano (drums)

ANGEL CORPSE were founded in late 1995 by guitarist Gene Palubicki and vocalist / bassist Pete Helmkamp. The duo pulled in drummer John Longstreth for a 1995 demo 'Goats To Azazael' which secured a deal with the French Black

Metal label Osmose Productions.
ANGEL CORPSE's debut album 'Hammer Of The Gods' secured favourable reviews and the band drafted second guitarist Bill Taylor for live work supporting IMPALED NAZARENE in Europe.
These dates delivered the 'Nuclear Hell' EP recorded live in France. A further EP 'Wolflust' ensued as ANGEL CORPSE put in a showing at the Milwaukee Metalfest.
Second album 'Exterminate' was issued in February 1998 with former ACHERON and AURORA BOREALIS drummer Tony Laureano. ANGEL CORPSE got to grips with touring again with their inclusion on the touring European festival roster for 'No Mercy II' alongside CANNIBAL CORPSE, OBITUARY, MARDUK, GOD DETHRONED and IMMORTAL. With these shows complete ANGEL CORPSE hooked up with IMMORTAL again for a further 25 European dates. Back in America the band went straight back onto the road guesting for CANNIBAL CORPSE for a further 55 dates.
The act's third album 'The Inexorable' was promoted with American shows with support from INCANTATION and KRISIUN kicking off in January 1999.
ANGEL CORPSE added Chuck Keller, previously with ORDER FROM CHAOS. The band cut their version of 'Eat Me Alive' for the 1999 JUDAS PRIEST tribute album 'Hell Bent For Metal' and issued a split EP with MATIRE.
ANGEL CORPSE disbanded in 2000.

Singles/EPs:
Nuclear Hell EP, Osmose Productions (1997)
Wolflust EP, Osmose Productions (1997)

Albums:
ANGELCORPSE, Osmose Productions (1997)
Consecrated / Envenomed / When Abyss Winds Return / Lord Of The Funeral Pyre / Black Solstice / The Scapegoat / Soulflayer / Perversia Enthroned / Sodomy Curse
HAMMER OF THE GODS, Osmose Productions (1996)
Consecration / Envenomed / When Abyss Winds Return / Lords Of The Funeral Pyre / Black Solstice / The Scapegoat / Soulflayer / Perversion Enthroned / Sodomy Curse

EXTERMINATE, Osmose Productions (1998)
Christhammer / Wartorn / Into The Storm Of Steel / Phallelujah / Reap The Whirlwind / That Which Lies Upon / Embrace / Sons Of Vengeance
THE INEXORABLE, Olympic (1999)
Stormgods Unbound / Smoldering In Exile / Reaver / Wolflust / As Predator To Prey / Solar Wills / Begotten (through Blood And Flame) / The Fall Of The Idols Of Flesh

ANGEL DEATH (ITALY)

An Italian Black Metal act.

Singles/EPs:
Gore Blood Of War, Hard Blast (1994)
Angeldeath, Hard Blast (1995)

ANGELRUST (USA)
Line-Up: Andrew D'Cagna (vocals / guitar), Frank Gordon (bass), Tim Markle (drums)

ANGELRUST was created in October 1999 as a union of MOONTHRONE mentor Andrew D'Cagna and bass player Frank Gordon of Death Metal band MASTICATED ENTRAILS.

Albums:
ARCANE, Froizen Music (2000)

ANGIZIA (AUSTRIA)
Line-Up: Engelke, Henning, H. Agricola, Szinonem

A mixture between Black Metal and Folklore, the German speaking ANZIGIA debuted with a split album with AMESTIGON in 1996.

Albums:
ANGIZIA, Napalm (1996) (Split LP with AMESTIGON)
Die Hymnen Eines Baches / Herbstegende / Der Stechlin
DIE KEMENATEN SCHARLACHROTER LICHTER, Napalm NPR 026 (1997)
Kapiel I: Szenichter Monolog- Das rote Gold des Kerzenwaches / Kapitel II: Der kirschgarten oder Memobren an die Stirn der Kindeszeit / Kapitel III: Halbe Wahrheit, Schemeglanz und Totenlichter / Kapitel IV: Ein Sängerleben- Welch winderbarer Nachtgesang? / Kapitel V: Schellenklingeln. Vom kurzen Leben fast verschein gruner trauben

27

DAS TAGE BUCH DER HANNA ANIKEN, Napalm NRR034 (1997)
Kapitel I / Kapitel II / Kapitel III / Kapitel IV / Kapitel V / Kapitel VI / Kapitel VII
DAS SCHACHBRETT DES TROMMELBUBEN ZACHARIAS, Black Rose BRP112 (1999)
Pique Dome und Rachmaninov 1904 / Ich bin ein Bewohner de S.W. Diagramms / Der Kinderzar / Schlitternfahrt mit einer Lodenpuppe / Ungeliebter Kammerfrieden / Der Essayist / 2 Millionen Rubel / Das Bauenendsprel

ANNO DAEMONICUS
(Greene, ME, USA)
Line-Up: Amaymon (vocals / guitar), Xevilion (guitar), Elric Daemon Warrior (bass), Skaliskasaga (keyboards), Necresis (drums)

Maine's ANNO DAEMONICUS, created in 1995, are an industrious enterprise releasing self financed albums. Band members have operated under evolving pseudonyms with guitarist Xevilion being previously titled Evilee and keyboard player Skaliskasaga bizarrely as 'Glockenspiel'.
The live album 'Live At The Legion' is now extremely scarce. ANNO DAEMONICUS contributed their version of 'Waiting For Darkness' to an OZZY OSBOURNE tribute album on Dwell Records.
Former drummer Danochar made way for Necresis.

Singles/EPs:
Obscurity In The Ancient Oaks / To Encounter The Woodland Spirits, Anno Daemonicus (2000) (7" single)

Albums:
ANNO DAEMONICUS, Anno Daemonicus (1999)
The Moonstone / Blood Priest / Guardians Of The Blacklands Unite / An Ode To The Demons Of The Earth / Demon March / Epoch Of Darkness Grandeur / Chaos Overshadows The Valkyrian Castle / At Leisure In The Unspawning Dawn / Last Horizon
LIVE AT THE LEGION, Anno Daemonicus (1999)
Epoch Of Darkness Grandeur / Journey Past Falcon Ridge / At Leisure In The Unspawning Dawn / Guardians Of The Blacklands Unite / Dragonstorm, A Wizard's Myth / An Ode To The Demons Of The Earth / Waiting For Darkness / To Encounter The Woodland Spirits / Chaos Overshadows The Valkyrian Castle

ANOREXIA NERVOSA (FRANCE)
Line-Up: Hreidmarr (vocals), Stefan Bayle (guitar), Pier Couquet (bass), Neb Xort (keyboards), Nilcas Vant (drums)

Developed initially as NECROMANCIA in 1991, following a batch of gigs NECROMANCIA cut their first demo, 'Garden Of Delight', in December 1993 and proceeded to tour with the likes of NIGHTFALL and SUPERATION.
Due to the confusion within the Black Metal genre of so many bands using the 'Necro' prefix the band adopted a name change to ANOREXIA NERVOSA in mid 1995 and recorded a further demo cassette, 'Nihil Nagativium'. Further gigs included stints with CRADLE OF FILTH and ENSLAVED. By now the band's individual style, dubbed 'Nihilistic Metal', was setting them apart from the general pack.
The 'Exile' album has ANOREXIA NERVOSA attempting to strech their creative wings within the confines of Black Metal citing Dadaist Tristan Tzara as influence for the band's supposed "formulated chaos".
Vocalist Stephane Gerbaud and guitarist Marc Zebe would leave to be replaced by singer Hreidmarr and keyboard player Neb Xort.
The 'Drudenhaus' album boasts guest guitatwork from AGRESSOR's Alex.

Albums:
EXILE, Seasons Of Mist SOM004 (1997)
Prologue: To Exclude From The Cycle Of Generations, Cycle I: Delusive Complexion / Sequence I: Spiritu Fornicationis, Action I: Distressing Amnios / Sequence II: Say The World That Fall In The Sky, Action II: Gnostic Wails / Sequence III: The Unveiled Mirror, Action III: Other Wails / Sequence IV: Divert The Necessities Of The Body / Cycle II Burning Tongue / Sequence I: Against The Sail, Action I: Vertebrae Embryo / Sequence II: Faith, Action II: Discordant Effects Of Suicides / Sequence III: Acclaim New Master, Action III: Slave / Sequence IV: First Tasting Of Faecal Matter / Cycle III: Man Machine: Sequence I: Some Miracles Of Entrails, Action I: Unshowed / Sequence II: Spirit Of The Valley, Action II: Enclose / Sequence III: Flesh Goes Out Without Grace / Epilogue: Running Out Of

Mental Fluids
SODOMIZING THE ARCDEANGEL,
Osmose Productions (1999)
Divine White Light Of A Cuming
Decadence / Blood And Latex Terrortech
War / Exreted Communion Under Khaos
Zero / A Caress, Flesh And Vomited
Romance
DRUDENHAUS, Osmose Productions
(2000)
A Doleful Night In Thelema / The
Drudenhaus Anthem / God Bless The
Hustler / Enter The Church Of
Fornication / Tragedia Dekadencia /
Divine White Light Of A Cuming
Decadence / Dirge Requiem For My
Sister Whore / Das ist Zum Erschiessen
Schon / The Red Archromance

ANPHISBENAM (BRAZIL)
Line-Up: André Marqus (guitar), Ricardo
Lopez (guitar), Cézar De Cesaro (bass),

Singles/EPs:
Rise Supreme / Prophecy Of Chaos /
Portal Of Insanity / Blind Guidance,
(199-) ('Initaites The Horrendous' EP)

ANTAEUS (FRANCE)
Line-Up: Mk. M (vocals), Set (guitar),
Thorgon (guitar), Sagoth (bass), Storm
(drums)

A truly extreme Black Metal act.
ANTAEUS was originally born as a side
project of TRAGOS ADEIN involving
vocalist Mk. M, BLUT AUS NORD bassist
'A' and guitarist Piat Antaeus. 'A' would
soon bail out before any recordings had
been struck as ANTAEUS enlisted bassist
Black Priest and drummer Storm. For live
appearances Lord Tenebro Maleficium of
MANTAR was seconded.
Strife within the ranks came to a head
after a show with IMPALED NAZARENE
when namesake Antaeus departed. Twin
guitarists Set and Oliver were enrolled for
shows with THUS DEFILED. However,
Oliver opted out and a new bassist
Phillipe was inducted.
The 2000 album 'Cut Your Flesh And
Worship Satan' found surviving veterans
Mk. M and Storm in collusion with
guitarists Set and Thorgon with bassist
Sagoth.
Singles/EPs:
Inner War / Seventh Ceremony, Spikecult
(199-)
Albums:
ANTAEUS, (199-) (Split album with

ETERNAL MAJESTY)
Intro / Devotee / Those With No Eyes /
Bleeding Blasphemy / Whenever I'll Lay
**CUT YOUR FLESH AND WORSHIP
SATAN**, Baphomet BAPH2113 CD (2000)
Inner War / Seventh Ceremony /
Devotee / Those With No Eyes /
Specimen 23 / Bleeding Blasphemy /
Nihil Locus / Daemon

ANTESTOR (NORWAY)
Line-Up: Martyr (vocals), Vemod (guitar),
Gard (bass), Armoth (drums)

Theatric Norwegian Black Metal crew
involving singer Martyr (real name Kjetil
Molnes), bassist Gard (Vegard Undal)
and drummer Armoth (Svein Sander).
Although first assembled in 1990
ANTESTOR broke up for a year in 1991.
The band regrouped in 1993 for the demo
'Despair'. Following this session guitarist
Erkrbisp (real name Stig Rolfsen) joined
the fold for recording of a projected debut
album entitled 'Martyrium'. However,
once recorded the album was shelved
and by late 1996 Erkibisp had opted out.
Former ANTESTOR members vocalist
Ronny Hansen and keyboard player
Morten Sigmund Magerøy are both active
members of the Christian "unblack" band
VAAKEVANDRING. ANTESTOR guitarist
Vemod (Lars Stokstad) also performs live
with VAKEVANDRING.

Albums:
THE RETURN OF THE BLACK DEATH,
Cacophonous NIHIL 30CD (1998)
Vinterferden / A Sovereign Fortress /
Svartedauens Gjenkomst / Sorg / The
Bridge Of Death / Gamelandt / Kilden-Lik
En Endelos Elv / Kongsblod / Battlefield
/ Ancient Prophecy / Ildnatten
MARTYRIUM, Morphine (1999)
Spiritual Disease / Materialistic Lie /
Depressed / Searching / Innermost Fear
/ Under The Sun / Thoughts / Martyrium
/ Merry Land

ANTHROPOLATRI
(GERMANY / UKRAINE)
Line-Up: Rodogast (vocals / guitar),
Vogneslav (guitar), Karpath (bass),
Saturious (keyboards)

Slavonic War Metal band
ANTHROPOLATRI came into being when
Radogast, ex frontman for Death Metal
band GRIM LAMENT, travelled to the
Ukraine from Germany to assist
NOKTURNAL MORTUM with

ANTAEUS

songwriting. Whilst there a relationship was struck up with another Death Metal musician Vogneslar of FATAL EPITAPH. Joining forces the duo, together with keyboard player Saturious and bass ist Karpath of NOKTURNAL MORTUM founded ANTHROPOLATRI. The debut album of 1998 'Vozradujsja, Zemlja!' was followed by 1999's 'V Svete Kostrov'. Both these albums were issued on cassette, the latter by the Latvian label Beverina Productions. ANTHROPOLATRI's third album, their first on CD, was released oby the French Chanteluop Creations concern. By this time the band was down to a duo of Rodogast and Vogneslav. However, Rodogast would later quit making ANTHROPOLATRI's future uncertain.

Albums:
VOZRADUJSJA, ZEMLJA!, Terroraiser (1998)
Slava Slavjanskoj Zemke! / Skazanie Staroj Eli / Vozradujsja, Zemlja! / Vody Kljuchevoj Iz Rodniha Ispej / Tam, Pid Ljivsjkym Zamkorn / Ognennys Veter
V SVETE KOSTROV, Beverina Productions (1999)
Karpatskij Duk / Lesa Svjatiboga / V Svete Kostrov / Kro K Nam S Mechjom Pridjot… / Slavjanskjkoe Bratstvo / Voskhod Solntsa / A Kostry Gorjat
SJATOSLAV'S WISH, Chanteluop Creations (2000)
Vstanjmo Brattja! / Volja- Tse Mechi / Vedy Nas, Knjazke! / Volhu Ratjmyr Ta Otaman Ugonjaj / Sich Za Orianu / Chara Vischyj / Misjachne Sjajvo

ANTI CHRIST (GERMAN)

Following a run of demos starting with 'Ghoul Metal- Spread His Glory' Black Metal band ANTI CHRIST issued a split 12" single shared with VASSAGO.

Singles/EPs:
Hail War, Total War Productions (1997) (Split single with VASSAGO)

ANWYL (KS, USA)
Line-Up: Ok (vocals), Kron (guitar), Necro (bass), Mikai (drums)

Kansas Black Metal act ANWYL emerged with the 1998 demo 'Enshroud Us In Darkness' followed by the 'Forgotten Paths' session. Bassist Necro quit the band in 2000.

Albums:
GORGORUS AURA, Twelfth Planet (2001)

APHRODISIAC (NORWAY)

An Industrial noise project of Svein Egil Hatlevik of FLEURETY and DØDHEIMSGARD together with members of VED BUENS ENDE.

Albums:
NONSENSE CHAMBER, Elfenblut (1998)

DIE APOKALPTISCHEN REITER (GERMANY)
Line-Up: Eumel (vocals / guitar), Volkmar (bass), Pest (keyboards), Skeleton (drums)

Singles/EPs:
Dance With Me / Prince Of Ignorance / Dschingis Khan Human End (Part II), (1998) ('Dschingis Khan' EP)

Albums:
SOFT AND STRONGER, Ars Metalli (1997)
Iron Fist / The Almighty / Execute / Downfall / Instinct / Vader / Metal Will never Die / Dostulata / Eye Of A Rose / Slaves Of Hate / To Live Is To Die / Enslaved / Human End
ALLEGRO BARBARO, Ars Metalli (1999)
The Last Hope Burned Down To Dust / Sometimes / Perfect Without Mercy / The March Of Revenge / Game Of Violence / Heavy Metal / Dance With Me / The Fire / The Naked Beauty / No Question / Smell Of Death / revelation / Total Human End
ALL YOU NEED IS LOVE, Ars Metalli (2000)
Licked By The Tongues Of Pride / Unter Der Arsche / Erhalle Meine Seele / Gone / Regret / reitermania / Hate / Peace Of Mind / Geopfert / Rausch / Die Schönheit Der Sklaverei / … Vom Ende Der Welt

APOLLYON (DENMARK)
Line-Up: Vrykolatious (vocals), Archdemon Diabolos (guitar), HR. Alfast (bass), Sorgh (drums)

Founded in 1992 as a duo of guitarist Archdemon Diabolos and Lord Worros. This pair cut the demo 'Creation Of Evil Thought' prior to Worros decamping. APOLLYON was put on ice intil 1994 when Diabolos teamed up with drummer

Sorgh and bassist Korihor to resurrect the band. For a time APOLLYON employed DENIAL OF GOD guitarist Azter. Both he and Korihor would make their exit before recording of the album 'Diaboli Gratia'.
All of APOLLYON operate under another band name of BRANDPEST releasing the 1998 single 'I Fandens Vold Of Magt'. Diabolos and Vrykolatious also operate another Black Metal band entitled MALA FIDE.

Albums:
DIABOLI GRATIA, Full Moon Productions (199-)
Viamala / When Coldness Wraps This Suffering Clay / Darkness / Memento Mori / Offalaceum Hominum Spem

APOLLYON SUN (SWITZERLAND)
Line-Up: Thomas Gabriel Fischer (vocals / guitar), Erol Unala (guitar), Dany Zingg (bass), Roger Muller (keyboards), Marky Edelmann (drums),

After a lengthy hiatus former CELTIC FROST mentor Thomas Gabriel Fischer (previously known as Tom G. Warrior) announced his new project APOLLYON SUN during 1998, debuting with a startling mini album 'God Leaves And Dies' and backed by heavyweight management of Sanctuary.
Drummer Mark Edelmann is in fact former CORONER man Marquis Marky now sensibly using his real name.

Albums:
GOD LEAVES AND DIES, Mayan MYNCD1 (1998)
God Leaves / Reefer Boy / The Cane / Concrete Satan / Bedlam And Blind
THE NEXT LEVEL OF PROVOCATION, Sanctuary (2000)

APOSENTO (SPAIN)

Albums:
WELCOME TO DARKNESS, Walkiria (1997)

ARALLU (ISRAEL)

Solo project of one Butchered, also live bass player for MELECHESH.
Albums:
THE WAR ON THE WAILING WALL, The End (2000)
Arallu's Warriors / Sword Of Death / Morbid Shadow / Warriors Of Hell / Mesopotamian Genie / Barbaric

Bloodshed / Satanic Birth In Jerusalem / Messenger Of Evil word / My Hell / Satan's War / Kill The Traitor

ARATHORN (GERMANY)
Line-Up: A.K., Gericke, Skoell

ARATHORN's Skoell contributed as session player for NOX INTEMPESTA. It is believed that the two bands have even stronger links with Tyrann and Mordra Coldstone of NOX INTEMPESTA also being members of ARATHORN.

Albums:
NIEMALS KRÖNEDER ALS WAS EINST WAR, Folter (1997)
In Specrtren Pulsiervender Todesrinning / O Ultima Privire Asurpa Luptei Din Tinuturile Transilnies (An Armageddonish View Over The Landscape Of Transilvania) / Die Inthronisation (Der Koenig erwartet euch…) / Die Hyme Des Winters Zorn

ARCANA (ITALY)

Singles/EPs:
Cantar De Procella (The Opening Of The Wound) / The Dreams Made Of Sand / Emperor Of The Sun, Cold Meat Industry CMI 52 (1997) ('Lizabeth' EP)
Eclipse Of The Soul / Love Eternal / Hymn Of Absolute Deceit, Cold Meat Industry (1999) ('Izabel' EP)

Albums:
DARK AGE OF REASON, Cold Meat Industry CMI 43 (1996) (Limited edition of 1000)
Our God Weeps / Angel Of Sorrow / Source Of Light / The Calm Before The Storm / Dark Age Of Reason / Like Statues In The Garden Of Dreaming / The Oath / … For My Love / Serenity / The Song Of Mourning
CANTAR DE PROCELLA, Cold Meat Industry (1997)
The Opening Of The Wound / Chant Of The Awakening / The Song Of Solitude (The Cry Of Isolde) / Void Of Silence / Cantar De Procella / Aeterna Doloris / The Song Of Preparation / God Of The Winds / The Dreams Made Of Sand / Gathering Of The Storm / La Sale De Profundis / The Tree Within

ARCANE SUN (IRELAND)
Line-Up: Paul Kearns (vocals), Feargal (guitar / bass / keyboards), Mark (drums)

Black Metal From Ireland recording for the Italian Ars Metalli label. Guitarist Feargal deputies as second live guitarist for PRIMORDIAL.

Albums:
ARCANE SUN, Ars Metalli ARSCD 006 (1999)

ARCHAEAN HARMONY (MALTA)
Line-Up: Darkmortem, Lord Trebor, Adriel

Maltese Black Metal act ARCHAEAN HARMONY first engaged with the 1998 demo 'Resentment Of An Evanesce Aeon'. The band's original guitarist Adramelch departed in 1999 to be superceded by Adriel.
One wonders if member Lord Trebor has a sweet tooth!

Albums:
NIHILITY MUNDANE SOUL, Solemn Music (2000)
Nihility Mundane Soul, eschatology Bereft... L'Apostasy / Metabolism Under The Ascending Moon Part I / Metabolism Under The Ascending Moon Part II / Venery Dreams

ARCHANGEL (ITALY)
Line-Up: Vam Kama Ocean Archangel (vocals / keyboards), Blackie (guitars), The Vicar (guitar), Lucy-Guge (bass), Wewo (drums)

ARCKANUM

Singles/EPs:
Tao, (1996)

Albums:
IN TEARS THE ANGEL FALLS, (1996)
Overture No. 1, Op. 2 / You Kill Yourself / Faith In The Fate / Dark Love / The Swans Cry Of Its Lake Of Pain / Bleeding Heart / Straight To Hell / Devil As A Lover / Christ In Chains / Awakening / L.S.D. (Love Of Siddharta Dies)
NATURAL BORN MESSIAH, Lucretia LU 98027-2 (1998)
Karma Rider / They Kneel Me Down / Awakening / Christ In Chains / Tantronic
INCARNATE IN A NEW REBEL IDOL, Cyper Shamen (2000)
The Pose / Natural Born Messiah / Karma Rider / Paradise In Cyber Space / I.N.R.I. / Shotstraighoheart / They Kneel Me Down / Aliens, Angels And 51 / 33 / Electric Dreams / Inside Eyes Of Stars

ARCHGOAT (FINLAND)

Extreme Death Black Metal outfit ARCHGOAT issued the 'Jesus Spawn' and 'Penis Perversor' demos prior to the controversially titled 1994 12" single.

Singles/EPs:
Angelcunt: Tales Of Desecration, Necropolis (1994) (12" single)

ARCKANUM (SWEDEN)

ARCKANUM is the solo project of ex GROTESQUE and SORHIN member Shamaatae. Additional musicians upon the band's formation in 1992 were guitarist Loke Svarteld and vocalist Sataros. By the 1994 demo 'Trulen' ('The Trolls'), ARCKANUM was purely Shamaatae on his own.

Albums:
FRAN MARDER ('FROM THE FOREST'), Necropolis NR008 (1996)
Hvila Pa Tronan Min / Be Alder Haerskande Viesande Natur / Svinna / Kununger Af Baen Diupeste Natur / Gava Fran Trulen / Fran Marder / Baerghet / Trulmaelder / Kolin Vaeruld
KOSTOGNER, Warmageddon 6665 (1996)
Skoghens Minnen Voekks / Yvir Min Diupe Marder / Opegardr Del. II / Poen Sum Fran Griften Ganogr / Et Sorghetog / Gamall Uvermark / Oper Trulhoyghda Del. III / Gangar For Raban Vinder / Bedrovelse / Ir Bister Ensaminhet Jogh

Ugla / Groemelse Ok Voe / Kri Til Dodha Daghi
KAMPEN, (1997)
Kamps Tekn / Frana / Tronan Yvir Usand Landskaps Mark / Pa Gruvstiigher Vandrum / Minir Natz Fughlir / Trulfylket Raz Ok Os / Da Gruvsttiigher Vandrum / Naer Ok Fler / Skipu Vidit Dunkel / Paer Vindanir Dualies

ARCTURUS (NORWAY)
Line-Up: Garm (vocals), Samoth (guitar), Sverd (keyboards), Hellhammer (drums)

ARCTURUS was put together as a side project in 1989 by members of MORTEM. The 1991 single, 'My Angel', features MAYHEM's Hellhammer, keyboard player / guitarist Sverd and MORTEM bassist Marius Vold on vocals.
Shortly after, ARCTURUS were put on ice, as both Sverd and Hellhammer busied themselves with EMPEROR, but the band persevered and evolved to comprise of BORKNAGER and ULVER's Garm (naming himself after the Norse dog guardian of Hell. His real name is Kristoffer Rygg) on vocals, ULVER bassist Garm and Samoth from EMPEROR on guitar. The 'Constellation' album was a limited edition of 500 copies.
In 1994 Samoth was interned, found guilty of his part in the Norwegian church burning episode and was replaced by Carl August Tidemann from Progressive Rock act TRITONUS. ARCTURUS also added a second guitarist in the form of Skoll from ULVER and VED BUENS ENDE.
The 1997 album saw VED BUENS ENDE and BORKNAGER man Simen Hestnaes contributing alongside Garm, as well as new face guitarist Aismal (real name Knut Magne Valle), another with ULVER connections.
Sverd helped assemble Black Metal 'Supergroup' COVENANT with Hellhammer and DIMMU BORGIR's Nagash for the 'Nexus Polaris' album but quit shortly after.
Garm set up Jester Records and busies himself as a producer under the pseudonym Vargnatt Inc. Garm has also produced BORKNAGER under the title Fiery G. Maelstrom and ARCTURUS as G. Wolf.
As well as the ARCTURUS remix album 'Disguised Masters' (which includes contributions from WHEN's Lars Pedersen) 1999 found Garm also making his presence felt on ULVER's 'Themes From William Blakes's The Marriage Of

Heaven And Hell'.
During 2000 Hestnaes joined DIMMU BORGIR as bassist. The same year found Sverd guesting on FLEURETY's 'Department Of Apocalyptic Affairs'. Not wishing to be left out Tidemann established the high profile project WINDS in collaboration with drummer Hellhammer of MAYHEM and KOVENANT and vocalist Lars Eric Si of SENSA ANIMA.
Early ARCTURUS member Marius Vold would turn up again in 1999 as a member of the all star act SUSPERIA.

Singles/EPs:
My Angel, Putrefaction (1991) (Limited to 500 copies)

Albums:
CONSTELLATION, Nocturnal Art Productions ECLIPSE003 (1995) (Limited to 500 copies)
ASPERA HIEMS SYMFONIA (COLD WINTER SYMPHONIES), Ancient Lore Creations ALCP001 (1996)
To Those Who Dwellest In The Night / Wintry Grey / Whence And Whither Goest The Wind / Raudt Og Svart / The Bodkin And The Quitus (... To Reach The Stars) / Du Nordavind / Fall Of Man / Naar Kulda tar (Frostnettenes Prolog)
LA MASQUERADE INFERNALE, Misanthropy / Music For Nations (1997)
Master Of Disguise / Ad Astra / The Chaos Path / La Masquerade Infernale / Alone / The Throne Of Tragedy / Painting My Horror / Of Nails And Sinners
DISGUISED MASTERS, Jester (1999)
Preludium / Deception Genesis / Du Nordavind / Interludium / Alone (Intellecto Valle Darktrip) / The Throne Of Tragedy (Phantom F.X. Jungle remix) / La Masquerade Infernale (Valle Hellhammer Reconstruction) / Master Of Siguise (Phantom F.X. remix with Gangstafication by S.C.N.) / Painting My Horror (G. Wolf Levitation mix) / Ad Astra (The Magenta Experience) / Postludium- Ad Astra

ARGAR (SPAIN)

ARGAR drummer Katu Marus also has credits with GORTHAUR, BEHEADED LAMB and ASGAROTH.
Albums:
THE FLAME OF DARK CREATION, Arise (1998)
CWN ANNWN, Millenium Metal Music MMM006 (2001)
Reborn In Utterdarkness (Part II0 /

Millenium Funerarium / Bloodtears Fall From Heaven / Twin Of Evil / Cwn Annwn / Blood Black In The Funeral Winds / She, Lady Of The Abyss / Travel To Kadath / Pure Hate Black

ARGENTUM (MEXICO)

Black Metal band ARGENTUM issued two demos prior to their 1996 'Ad Interitum Funebrarum' album namely 1993's 'Master Misericordine' and the follow up session 'Exothaetnium'.

Albums:
AD INTERITUM FUNEBARUM, Full Moon Productions (1996)
Enter An Encysted Hibernation / Asstrum Argentum / La Sorella Di Satana / The Serpent's Lament / Horta Funebra (Including Penuria) / Mortus Infradaemoni / Spheram De Tenebras / Ad Posthumum / Pax Moriendi / Horta Funebra Revise

ARGHOSLENT (Oakton, VA, USA)
Line-Up: Zach (vocals), Alexander (guitar), Mertaugh (guitar), Thorn (bass), Stauffer (drums)

ARGHOSLENT comprises of erstwhile TWISTED TOWER DIRE and GRAND BELIAL'S KEY members. An out and out Black Metal band ARGHOSLENT have been shunned by the more mainstream media due to their outspoken right wing views. Indeed, the band has expressed the view that album sales could have been greater had it not been for a Jewish conspiracy! It is observations such as this that have put the band beyond the pale.
The origins of the band can be traced back to the 80's act GENOCIDE which included guitarist Alexander and bassist Thorn. This duo subsequently forged the Speed Metal band ASTYXIA in 1989 prior to drafting former ULTERIOR MOTIVES drummer Stauffer. A further name change to POGROM occurred then to ARGHOSLENT with the induction of vocalist Gravedigger.
Demos included 1991's 'Entity', 1992' 'Bastard Son Of A Thousand Whores' and 1994's 'Imperial Clans' before the departure of Gravedigger. New singer Zach took the reins for a 1996 session 'Arsenal Of Glory'.
Although second guitarist Mertaugh would break away upfront of recording the inaugural album 'Gallopping Through The Battle Ruins' he would return. The 1996 demo was issued on CD in 2000

including tracks from 'Imperial Clans'.

Singles/EPs:
Troops Of Unfeigned Might EP, Horror HOR005 (1997)

Albums:
GALLOPING THROUGH THE BATTLE RUINS, Wood Nymph (1998)
Defile The Angelic / The Banners Of Castile / The Entity / Prayers Upon Deaf Ears / The Imperial Clans / Ten Lost Tribes / Incursions / Fall Of The Melanic Breeds / Rape Of A Slave / Transpolar Combat
ARSENAL OF GLORY, Sempiternal Productions (2000)
Rape Of A Slave / Of Spears And Horns / Hymns Of Conquest / Branding The Peon / Arsenal Of Glory / The Negress / Wergiuld / The Imperial Clans / The Nexxus Of Chaos / A Somber Warcry

ARKANGEL

Albums:
PRAYERS UPON DEAF EARS, Released Power (1998)
Within The Walls Of Babylon / One Standard, One Ethic / Built Upon The Graves / In The Embrace Of Truth / Day Of The Apocalypse / Evilization
DEAD MAN WALKING, (2000)
From Heaven We Fall / Written In Black / Harbinger Of Doom / day Of Apocalypse / Behind The Face Of Death / Twenty One, Twenty Three / The Darkest Crime / In The Embrace Of Truth / Fearful Eyes / Nameless Track

ARKHON INFAUSTUS (FRANCE)
Line-Up: D. Deviant (guitar / vocals), 666 Torturer (bass), Hellblaster (drums)

Singles/EPs:
Dead Cunt Maniac EP, Spikekult (199-) (7" single)
Invocation Of The War God / Machiavellian Knights / Excelsi Domini Inferni, (1999) ('In Sperma Infernum' EP)

Albums:
HELL INJECTION, Osmose Productions (2001)
Brethren Of Flesh / Dominator Xtasy / Dead Cunt Maniac / The Ominous Circle / The Silent Voices Of Perversion / The Whorehouse Coven / Hokus Demons / The Ineffable King Of Hell / The Black Sukkubus Whores

ARKONA (POLAND)
Line-Up: Messiah (vocals), Pitzer (guitar), Khorzon (guitar / bass), T. Lewinski (keyboards), Sylvian (drums)

Black Metal band ARKONA had their two 1994 demo sessions 'Bogowie Zaponienia' and 'An Eternal Curse Of The Pagan Godz' combined for the 1997 Folter released CD.

Albums:
IMPERIUM, Astral Wings ERNBLISS006 (1996)
Skrajna Nienawise Egoistyeej Egzysteneji / Epidemia Kozezarowania I Redza Duchowa / Razon Los Lo Eien / Fesienne Eienie Ezekajace Ra Kolejna Heinkarnacje / W Seieklose Ktora Radehodzi / Bluje Ra Iwa Marnose Bsie! / Poganda Dia Wrogow Imperium Wszeehmocy
AN ETERNAL CURSE OF THE PAGAN GODZ, Folter (1997)
Nieporazumienie W Bezsensie Istnienia / Gwalt Wlasnego Pozadania / Przyszly Zdrajca Chrzescijanskiej Masy / Szalencza Pogon Za Bezwstydna Rozkosza / Kres Ludzkiej / Doskonalosci Obezwladniony Proznoscia / Najprostrza Martwica Zgubnej Niemocy / From The Depths Of Hell- Fire Into The Infinites War / Only True Belief / Long Hard Winter / In The Shadow Of Dying Willows / Under The Arms Of Lucipher / Frostwind From The Land Of Immortal Hatred / Barbarian Fire On The Whirlwind Hills / An Eternal Curse Of The Pagan Godz / The Infinited War
IMPERFECT PRODUCT, (199-)
SK1D Jesterrn / Warsaw Ghetto / Raw Power / Romantika / Niu Pagan Era / Global Virus / Przypadek Na Stagi / I'm, Fuckin' Pop Star / Black Sun / 25 Infinity / Techno Error / Bonus Song

ARS MORTIS (GERMANY)
Line-Up: Tom (vocals), William Grden (guitar), Gregory Brandl (guitar), Danny (bass), Uwe Pötke (drums)

ARS MORTIS include former FEROX guitarist William Grden and ex NECROMORPH guitarist Gregory Brandl.
Albums:
ERITIS SICUT MORTIS, Ars Mortis (2000)
Rotten, Cold And Dead / Vom Wahn des Seins / The Helpless Creature / Five Minutes Before… / Suicide / Black Visions / Simpliness Of Desire / My New World / Arsmortis

ARSON (NJ, USA)

Singles/EPs:
Less Perfect Than Death, Resurrection A.D. (2000)

Albums:
WORDS WRITTEN IN BLOOD, Resurrection AD (2000)
Words Written In Blood / Myth / Severed / I Lost All / Avoid The Sun

ARTHEMESIA (FINLAND)
Line-Up: Valtias Mustatuuli (vocals), Routa Salomeri (guitar / keyboards), Arbaal Mäenpää (guitar), Mor Voryon (bass), Mor Vethor (drums)

Originally titled CELESTIAL AGONY upon their formation in 1995 by vocalist Valtias Mustatuuli and guitarist Routa Salomeri. As ARETHEMESIA the band issued an inaugural demo utilizing the services of keyboard player Misery and ENISIFERUM drummer Oliver Fokin. A second tape in 1998, 'The Archaic Dreamer', saw a stable line up including guitarist Arbaal Mäenpää, bass player Mor Voryon and drummer Mor Vethor.
The band's convictions led to them self financing the recording of the first album 'Devs Iratus' ('Wrathful God'). Numerous session musicians were employed including Kaapro of CRY HAVOC.

Albums:
DEVS IRATUS, Native North (2000)
Blade Circle / Universal Black / The Breeze Of Grief / Draconis Infernus / Ancestor Of Magick / Lifemocker / Heaven Ablaze / Celebration Of The Heaven Lost / Whore Of The Satan's Night

ART INFERNO (ITALY)

Wagnerian Metal Italian trio previously titled JOURNEY THROUGH DARK under which name they released the album 'Screams Of Sirens'.

Albums:
ABYSSUS ABYSSUM INVOCAT, Scarlet SC 012-2 (2000)
Praeludium: A Porte Inferi / The Dark Rising / Through the Infernal Spheres / Bring Me Where They're Burning /

Orgiastic Dance Of Pan / Interludium: Sigillum Luciferi / Blood Of Eternal Love / Crying Mirrors / Be Silence My Ossians / Postludium: In Fornacem Ignis Aeterni

ASGARD (HOLLAND)
Line-Up: Rene Tholen (vocals), Appie Van Der Lei (guitar), Catrinus Horna (guitar), Peter Visscher (bass), Harry Graver (drums)

Albums:
IN THE ANCIENT DAYS, Noise (1986)
Before The Morning / High Society / Witches Brew / Possessed By Evil / Hounds Of Hell / Screaming Knight / Granadinas / Metal Tonight

ASGAROTH (SPAIN)
Line-Up: Lord Lupus (vocals / bass), Mythral (guitar), Katu-Marus (drums)

A Spanish Black Metal band centred upon originator Lord Lupus. Founded in 1994 ASGAROTH would later enroll erstwhile NOSTROMO guitarist Mythral and session drummer J. Muriana of ANGEL OF SUFFERING for the mini album 'The Quest For Eldenhor'.
Following the debut drummer Katu-Marus, a veteran of GORTHAUR and BEHEADED LAMB, joined the band.

Albums:
THE QUEST FOR ELDENHOR, New Gotia Requim (1996)
TRAPPED IN THE DEPTHS OF EVE, New Gotia (1998)
ABSENCE SPELLS BEYOND, (1999)
Strengthened Are The Stems Of Nasturtium / Sinking Trails Of Wisdom / Absence Spells Beyond / Epitaph… / Cry The Way We Greet Our Fates / Victorious Men On Earth / Omens (Presagios) / A Call In The Winds / The Dark Force / Last Battle (Tower Of Doom) / Lost In Natura / The Choirs Of The Elemental Dieties / Prelude In Dusk / Placious Echoes At Darkwoods You Greet… Silvering Moon Between My Shadows / Outroduction

ASHES (SWEDEN)
Line-Up: Jonas (vocals / bass), Andreas (guitar), Mourning (guitar), Mikael (drums)
Albums:
DEATH HAS MADE IT'S CALL, (199-)
AND THE ANGELS WEPT, Necropolis (1998)
Betrayed / Son Of Mourning / Eternal Feelings / Nothing / And The Angels

Wept / To The Bone

ASHES YOU LEAVE (CROATIA)
Line-Up: Dunja Radetic (vocals / flute), Kristijan Nilic (vocals), Breislav Poje (guitar), Neven Mendrila (guitar), Gordan Gencic (bass), Vladimir Krytuija (keyboards), Marta Batinic (violin),

Ambient Black Doom act ASHES YOU LEAVE were previously known as ICON. The group adopted the new title with the demo 'The Kingdom Before The Lies'. Members of ASHES YOU LEAVE united with personnel from fellow Black act CASTRUM to create a new 2000 act NELDOROTH.

Albums:
THE PASSAGE BACK TO LIFE, Effigy (1997)
Salva Me / The Passage Back To Life / Thorn Of The Dead Flower / Drowning In My Dreams / Lay Down Alone / White Chains / Tears
DESPERATE EXISTENCE, Morbid (1999)
A Wish / Never Again Alone In The Dark / Desperate Existence / Et Vidi Solem Evanere / Momentary Eclipse Of Hate / Searching For Artificial Happiness / Shadow Of Someone Else's Being / Outro
THE INHERITANCE OF SIN AND SHAME, Morbid (2000)
Tin Horns / Your Divinity / Shepherd's Song / Miles Of Worn Out Days / When Withered Flowers / And Thus You Poured Like Heaven Wept / The Inheritance Of Sin And Shame / Amber Star

AS IN AGONY YOU CRY (ITALY)

A Bologna based melodic Black Metal band with strong medieval overtones. AS IN AGONY YOU CRY issued the 1997 demo 'Christian Blood Stains The Battlefield'.

ASMODEUS (AUSTRIA)
Line-Up: Desdemon (vocals / bass), Tyr (guitar), Lestat (guitar), Ashark (drums)

Not to be confused with the Czech Hard Rock band. Austria's ASMODEUS began life in 1994 originally titled DIABOLUS. The album 'Supreme Surrender' was recorded with now departed members Hart and Dargoth.

Albums:
SUPREME SURRENDER, (1998)
Conscientious Offender / Dark Redeemer / When Darkness Bans Reality / Asmolei / Casket Garden / The Ritual

ASMODIS (GERMANY)
Line-Up: Korea Kahl (vocals), Oscar Juan Le Rocque (guitar), Fusel Wool (guitar), Janus Van Doom (bass), Slaughter Ed Crowley (drums)

ASMODIS's initial 1985 line-up utilized drummer Slaughter Ed Crowley as lead vocalist. However, the band were to add singer Korea Kahl in 1989 and finally released their first demo, 'Visitors From Beyond The Grave', in 1992.
Rumoured to include former members of EROSION.

Albums:
FAHR ZUR HÖLLE, PFLEISCHMÜTZE, Asmodis (1993)

ASMOROD (FRANCE)

Black Ambient landscapes from Nicolas D. Faure. The man also functions with KURO-TOKAGE ('Black Lizard') and LES AMANTS MAUDITS ('The Cursed Lovers') issuing a split cassette with EPHEL DUATH.

Albums:
INVOLUTION TOWARD CHTONIAN DEPTHS, Solistitium SOL013 (1997)
Poison- Transcenance / De Cantico Funebri / For A Fainter Bright High (Fragile Salicee Sous Un Terne Suaire) / Through Oceanic Calls / Ia! Ia! Cthulu Fhtagn! / Subplutonary Incubation I / Subplutonary Incubation II / Chtonian Transcubtiantation: Lorsqu'ils Rient Mais Ne Sourient Plus
DERELICT, Tesco (1999)
Suspended Motion / Vaporscreen / Glass No Kamen II: Vitreous Structures / Anaesthetic Season / Glass No Kamen I: Collapse

AS PROPHECIES (BRAZIL)

Singles/EPs:
Igna Hatura Renovalue Integra, Heavy Metal Rock (199-) (7" single)
AS SAHAR (SINGAPORE)
Line-Up: Barchiel (vocals / guitar), Hanael (bass), Iblyss (drums)

AS SAHAR started out as a straight

Thrash Metal trio during the mid 80's with founder members vocalist / guitarist Barchiel and bassist Hanael joined by drummer Uriel. At this stage AS SAHAR were a covers act.
The band dissolved but reformed a few years later opting for a new Black Metal direction, evident on their 1995 demo 'Santau'.
A further demo 'Meditas Embun Pagi' was recorded and subsequently released as a cassette EP by Nebiula Productions. However, following these sessions Uriel jumped ship. His replacement was former ABHORRER and IMPIETY man Iblyss.
Sales of the previous cassette were strong enough to warrant recording of the debut album 'Phenomistik'. A split album with HAYAGRIVA kept up the momentum prior to the departure of Iblyiss.
Barchiel and Hanael persevered as a duo changing tack once again into Gothic Electrinica for the 'Baku Karmi' album.

Albums:
PHENOMISTIK, Shivadarshana (1997)
Nadayage (Ashore) / Depressive Monsoon / Silomanial Dansecration / Tinggam / Sinfonie Jimbalang / Fandeyian Okultika Hymnology / Meditas Embun Pagi / Foleraftty Melo-Harvest / Nadaynde (Adrift)
BEYOND FIRMAMENT, Memories (1998) (Split Album With HAYAGRIVA)
Berwahi (Dalem Tuntut) / As Sahar / Wijaya Kesuma Buat Susuhunanan / My Hymns, In The East
EKSTASI TEKSTONIS, Nebiula Productions (1999)
Tuju Tuju Opus / Tinggam / Meditasti Embun Pagi / Folkerafty Melo-Harvest / Silumamial Dansecration / Santau Tuju Angin / Stroll In Kafan / Meditation Embun Pagi / My Hymns, In The East / Fandeyian Okultika Hymnology / Sinfonie Jimbalang / Repressive / Nadayaga II (Adrift)
BAKU KARMI, Nebiula Productions (2000)

ASSAMALLA (ESTONIA)
Line-Up: Erki Hirv (vocals), Andre Picken (guitar), Veigo Peetsalv (bass), Kaarit Kiibus (keyboards), Indrek Talts (drums)

Founded in 1996 ASSAMALLA at first included Janek Feodorov in the ranks. In 1998 the band pulled in guitarist Meelis Vappir and drummer Hanno Kilbus for the demo 'Taamait Töustet Toonetarmu'.
Following the release of ASSAMALLA's

38

debut album, shared with fellow Estonians KALM, both Vappir and Kilbus made their exit.

Albums:
I GAVESEKS MÄLESTAMA MÖLSTERUD, Guano GR002CD (1999) (Split album with KALM)
Mälestus Langenud Tähtedele / Kivesse Raituna / Vaikusest Vaevatud (Meire Hing Ei Hävi) / ... Kes Kahkunud Üksteise Südameist

ASTAROTH (AUSTRIA)
Line-Up: Beserker (vocals), Nemesis Styx (guitar), Myr (bass)

Although ASTAROTH were a trio centred upon mentor Nemesis Styx with vocalist Beserker and ESTATIC FEAR and THIRDMOON bassist Myr for the 1999 album 'Violent Soundtrack Martyrium' the band has seen numerous personnel.
Previous albums have included ELYMAS guitarist Chaos, SEPTIC CEMETARY, THIRDMOON and ESTATIC FEAR drummer Astaroth Magus Milan Pejak, bassist Sanguis and keyboard player Sasathys.

Albums:
CHRISTENFEIND, CCP 100156-2 (1995)
Astaroth / Onward To Destroy / Beyond Forgotten Times / Pagan Rites / In Mediaeval Winterstorms
SKLAVENGOTT, CCP 100171-2 (1997)
Iscariots Kiss / For Those We Hate / Revelation Of A New Dimension / Sklavengott / Kyrie Astaroth Eleison / Rape The Shining Stars In The Sky / Christenfiend / We Princes Of Darkness / Symphony For A Requiem / Black Decade
VIOLENT SOUNDTRACK MARTYRIUM, CCP 100195-2 (1999)
O.M.D. (Open Maneuvers In The Dark) / In Memoriam- Heavenly Creatures / Enter The Darkside Of Eden / Invisible In Heaven / The Millenium (Embodiment Forsaken) / Resistance (The Rebellion) / Members Of The Black Empire (Finishing Move)
ANNUS SUPREMIS, CCP 1002 16-2 (2000)

ASTARTE (GREECE)
Line-Up: Kinthia (vocals / guitar), Nemesis (guitar), Tristessa (bass), Alvar (drums)
All Female Black Metal band founded by former VORPHALACK bassist Tristessa. The group was originally titled LILITH and released a 1997 demo 'Dancing In The Dark Lakes Of Evil' under that name.
The 2000 album 'Rise From Within' was produced by Magus Wampyr Daoloth of NECROMANTIA.

Albums:
DOOMED DARK YEARS, Black Lotus (1998)
Passage To Eternity / Voyage Of Eternal Life / Thorns Of Charon Part I / Doomed Dark Years / Thorns Of Charon Part II / Thorns Of Charon Part III / Empress Of The Shadow Land / The Rise Of Metropolis
RISE FROM WITHIN, Black Lotus, BLRCD 016 (2000)
Furious Animosity / Rise From Within I (Mystical Provocation) / Rise From Within II (Selenium Erring) / Naked Hands / Genesis / Liquid Myth / Non Existent Equilibrium / Rise From Within III

ASTHAROTH (POLAND)
Line-Up: Blake (vocals), Kerr Homme (guitar), Drill (bass), Davy (drums)

A Polish Black Metal quartet.

Albums:
GLOOMY EXPERIMENTS, Metal Master MET 124 (1990)
Gloomy Experiments / Speed Of Light / Obsession / Tool Of Crime / Amnesia / Mirror's World / Good Night My Dear / Insomnia / My Difference

ASTRAL (CZECH REPUBLIC)
Line-Up: Maestro (vocals), Martin Sammael (guitar / bass / keyboards)

Albums:
MAGIA AEON, Leviathan (1997)
FILICETUM LUNARE, Last Episode CD 5 7065 20 561 (2000)

ATANATOS (GERMANY)
Line-Up: Jan G. (vocals / guitar), Rene Gropp (guitar), Bianka (keyboards), Jan K, Gropp (bass), Timur (drums)

ATANATOS was founded by the sibling duo of the Gropp brothers guitarist Rene and bassist Jan. The first fruits of their labour was the 'Quem Pastores Laudavere' demo tape, limited to 200 copies.
Keyboard player Bianka joined the band for the second demo 'Ancient Blood'.

Shortly after ATANATOS were committed to their first commercial release sharing a split CD with BEHERIT. The band shared a further split outing with IMPENDING DOOM.

The 1997 album 'The Oath Of Revenge' sees a cover version of SODOM's 'Outbreak Of Evil'. Touring in 2000 found ATANATOS on the road in Europe with RAGNAROK and SIEBENBURGEN.

Albums:
ASSAULT OF HEATHEN FORCES, Last Epitaph LEP 015 (1996)
Prelude- Under The Black Sky / Whore Of Revelation / Behind The Darkest Moods / Journey Through The Spiritual Past / Eternal Escape- Under The Black Sky
THE OATH OF REVENGE, Last Episode 007302-2 LEP (1997)
The Oath / Infernal Dreamquest / Return Of The Witch / Doomed To Death / Worshipper Of A Weak Lord / Armageddon (Time Of Prophecy) / Dark Age / Realm Under The Rising Moon

ATARAXIA (ITALY)
Line-Up: Francesca Nicoli (vocals / flute), Vittorio Vandelli (guitar), Giovanni Pagliani (keyboards)

Not to be confused with the Japanese act of the same name, the Italian Black Metal act ATARAXIA play an eclectic mix of Progressive, Gothic and Classic styles. Adventurously, the band delivers lyrics sung in Latin, English, French and Italian. The track 'La Nouva Mergherita' is an Italian version of the KATE BUSH hit 'Wuthering Heights'.

ATARAXIA vocalist Francesca Nicoli also lends her vocals to MONUMENTUM for their 'In Absentia Christi' album.

Singles/EPs:
In Amoris Mortisque, Apollyon EFA 12165 (1995) (10" Split single with ENGELSSTAUB)

Albums:
SIMPHONIA SINE NOMINE, Apollyon EFA 12172 (1994)
Preludio / Entrata Solemne / Canzona / Onno Corale / Fuga Trionfale / Preghiera / Marcia Cerimoniade / Elevazione / Pastorale / Ode Vespertilia
AD PERPETUAM REI MEMORIUM, Apollyon EFA 12153 (1994) (1994)
Prophetia / Anno Domini MDVLVI / Aigues Mortes / Tu Es La Force Du Silence / Flee Et Fabian / Nosce Te

Ipsum / Zweistimmenstäuschung / Torquemada / Bleumarine / Vitrage / Aquarello / Emeraude
LA MALEDICTION D'ONDINE, Apollyon EFA 12172 (1994)
Medusa / Sybil / Flora / Blanche / Annabel Lee / Astimelusa / June / Lubia / Ligeia / Ophile / Lucretia / Zela (The City Is The Sea) / Lucrecia / Ondine
THE MOON SANG ON THE APRIL CHAIR / RED DEEP DIRGES OF A NOVEMBER MOON, Apollyon EFA 12162 (1995)
A Face To Paint Tulips / Verdigis Wounds / The Tale Of The Crying Fireflies / Colouring Nocturnal Lemons / Rocking Chair Of Dreams / Satis Vixi / Lady Lazarus / Spiritus Ad Vindictum
CONCERTO No. 6: BAROQUE PLAISANTERIE, Apollyon 96029 EFA 12175-2 (1996)
Part 1: Larghetto, Passaggio Lustrale / Romanza, Scarletminded Echoes / Toccata Per Chitarra, The Winds Of Carminio / Notturno, Belle Rose Porporine / Gagliarda, Astore Serotina / Madrigale, Ticket To Ride / Arioso, La Bourgeoise Et La Noble / Gavotta, Maybe-O'-The Leaves / Forlane, Bleaumarine / Carrousel, Dulcamara / Coda, I'm The Wind / Part II: (Live) Siciliana, Lei Morra / Gavotta, Maybe-O'-The Leaves / Romanza, Scarletminded Echoes / Canticle, Wide White Wave
IL FANTASMA DELL OPERA, Avantgarde AV018 (1996)
E' Je Fantasma? (Part I) - Is It The Phantom? (Chapter One)/ E' Je Fantasma ? (Part Two) - Is It The Phantom (Chapter Two) / La Nouva Margherita (The New Marguerite) / Je Palco N5 (The Box N5 - Chapter 5) / Le Violino Incanto (The Enchanted Violin- Chapter 6) / Faust Im Ma Sala Maldetta (Faust In A Cursed Hell- Chapter 8) / Ae Ballo Mascherato (To The Bal Masque- Chapter 13) / La Liiza Ai Apollo (Apollo's Lyre- Chapter 13) / Je Signore Delle Botole (The Lord Of The Trap-Doors- Chapter 14) / Nei Sotenanei Dell Opera (In The Opera's Vaults- Chapter 21) / Le Ore Rpsa Di Mazendezay (The Pink Hours Of Manzeneran- Chapter 25) / Fine Degli Amor' Del Mostro (End Of The Monster's Lovers- Chapter 28)

ATMAN (SPAIN)

An underproduced Black Metal band with female vocals. ATMAN include ex members of MORTAL MUTILATION.

Albums:

LIKE PURE UNAWAITED MAGIC, New Gotia Requiem (1966)
On My Existence / Some Impressions From The Kingdom Of Plenitude / Beautiful Or Beautyless / Poetry And Passion (The Illuminations Of The Aura) / Personification Of The Feeling / Remembrances Of A Moment / A World Without You, Imagination / An Epilogue, A Farewell

ATROX (NORWAY)
Line-Up: Monika (vocals / keyboards), Eivind (guitar), Rune (guitar), Tom (bass), Tor Arne (drums)

Atmospheric self styled 'Schizo' Metallers ATROX, although not strictly within the genre confines, possess many links to other Black Metal acts. The act was founded in 1988 as SUFFOCATION comprising of guitarists Skei and Gundar Dragsten (later of GODSEND), bassist Sven, drummer Knarr and vocalist Gersa. The group evolved into ATROX during 1990 issuing the demos 'Mind Shadows' and 1993's 'Dead Leaves'. The same year found ENTROPY NOVA guitarist Tomas taking over the drum stool from Knarr- later of BLOODTHORN, a position taken the following year by Larry. Both Skei and Sven would also decamp, the former making his name with MANES. Drafted in were I FEAR guitarists Rune and Dagga, vocalist Monika (sister of 3RD AND THE MORTAL's Ann-Marie) and GODSEND bassist Tommy.
1997 also found ATROX contributing a version of HAWKWIND's 'Golden Void Part II' to a local compilation album. After the release of the debut album Gersa departed leaving Monika as sole vocalist.
 ATROX underwent a traumatic line up change in October of 1999 when a disagreement over musical direction forced the exit of Larry, Dagga and Tommy. MIST ENTICER members drummer Tor Arne and bassist Tom filled the role of rhythm section.
Monika, her sister Ann-Marie and Rune also operate the side project TACTILE. Eivind divides his time with MANES.
Not to be confused with either the American ATROX or the Swedish Thrash Metal ATROX that issued the 1992 single 'Land Of Silence'.

Singles/EPs:
Silence The Echoes, Danza Ipnotica (1997)

Albums:

MESMERISED, Head Not Found (1997)
Intro / Steeped In Misery As I Am / Wave / The Ocean / A Minds Escape / Flower Meadow / The Air Shed Tears / Hinc Illac La Crimac
CONTENTUM, Seasons Of Mist (2000)
Sultry Air / Unsummoned / Lizard Dance / Parta Rei / Gather In Me No More / Ignoramus / Letters To earth / Serenity / Homage / What Crawls Underneath / Torture / Outro

ATRYXION (SWEDEN)

Black Metal from ex MITHOTYN members.

Albums:
THE FALL OF ORDEXION, Avantgarde (2000)

AURA NOIR (NORWAY)
Line-Up: Apollyon, Blasphemer, Aggressor (drums)

AURA NOIR is a side project of Carl 'Agressor' Michael Eide from ULVER, CADAVER INC. and VED BUENS ENDE in partnership with DØDHEIMSGARD's Ole 'Apollyon' Jorgen and MAYHEM's Blasphemer.
As 'Aggressor' Carl Michael Eide is also a member of INFERNÖ having debuted with the 1996 album 'Utter Hell'. The man has also deputized for DIMMU BORGIR's Tjodalv whilst the latter was on paternity leave from his band.
Eide guested on FLEURETY's 2000 album 'Department Of Apocalyptic Affairs' and has sessioned for WHITE WILLOW. Apollyon also has links with LAMENTED SOULS.

Albums:
DREAMS LIKE DESERTS, Hot HR002 (1996)
The Rape / Forlorn Blessings To The Dreamking / Angel Ripper / Snake / Mirage
BLACK THRASH ATTACK, Malicious (1997)
Sons Of Hades / Conqueror / Caged Wrath / Wretched Face Of Evil / Black Thrash Attack / The Pest / The One Who Smite / Eternally Your Shadow / Destructor / Fighting For Hell
DEEP TRACTS OF HELL, Malicious (1999)
Deep Tracts Of Hell / Released Damnation / Swarm Of Vultures / Blood

Unity / Slasher / Purification Of Hell / The Spiral Scar / The Beautiful, Darkest Path / Brohl Of Oblivion
INCREASED DAMNATION, Hammerheart (2001)
The Mirage / Towers Of Limbs And Fever / Released Damnation / Broth Of Oblivion / Swarms Of Vultures / The One Who Smite / Wretched Face Of Evil / Fighting For Hell / The Rape / Forlorn Blessing To The Dreamking / Dreams Like Deserts / Angel Ripper / Snake / Mirage / Towers Of Limbs And Fever

AURORA (DENMARK)
Line-Up: Claus Frøland (vocals),

Albums:
DEVOTION, Serious Entertainment (2000)

AURORA BOREALIS
(Atlanta, GA, USA)
Line-Up: Ron Vento (vocals / guitar), Jason Ian-Vaughn Eckart (bass), Derek Roddy (drums)

Essentially a one man project of former LESTREGUS NOSFERATUS man Ron Vento. AURORA BORALIS first employed ACHERON and ANGEL CORPSE drummer Tony Laureano for the 'Mansions Of Eternity' album. By the time of 'Praise The Archaic- Lights Embrace' bassist Jason Ian-Vaughn Eckart and MALEVOLENT CREATION drummer Derek Roddy were employed.
The band is prolific on the tribute scene having cut 'After Forever' for the BLACK SABBATH tribute 'Hell Rules', Altar Of Sacrifice' for the SLAYER homage 'Gateway To Hell', JUDAS PRIEST's 'Metal Meltdown' for the 'Hell Bent For Metal' opus and 'We Rock' for the DIO collection 'Awaken The Demon'.

Albums:
MANSIONS OF ETERNITY, (199-)
Crowned With Embalment / Weighing Of The Heart / Valley Of The Kings / Slave To The Grave / Sixteenth Charm
PRAISE THE ARCHAIC- LIGHTS EMBRACE, (199-)
Offerings Of Jade And Blood / A Gaze Into Everdark / In The Depths Of A Labyrinth / Aggressive Dynasty / War Of The Rings / For Your Comprehension / Constellation Embellished With Chaos / Calm Before The Storm
NORTHERN LIGHTS, (199-)
Thrice Told / Enter The Halls / Images In

The Nightsky / Draco / Sky Dweller / Hydrah / Dream God / Distant

AURVANDIR (NORWAY)
Line-Up: Hravn (vocals), Silve Kristiansen (vocals), Lord Incubbuz (guitar), Naltav (drums)

AURVANDIR, who dub themselves "Viking Saga Metal", was an early port of call for latter day 122 STAB WOUNDS and FORLORN bassist Alvarin. The band was founded in 1995 by Hravn and drummer Naltav as LOTHLORIEN.
By 1996 AURVANDIR had been joined by vocalist Hati and bassist Alvarin. MAJESTIC men Stelferd and Taakeheimen on loan for their debut gig. The group would then enroll former AMIDST THE LEAFS and A WINTER WITHIN guitar player Lord Incubbuz as the group name changed again to EIDOLON.
A name change to AURVANDIR in 1997 saw the addition of MAJESTIC and MYRIADS bassist Telal and vocalist Silve Kristiansen. However, Telal's stay was short and he left to concentrate on his other acts.

AUTUMN BLAZE (GERMANY)
Line-Up: Eldron (vocals / guitar), Arisjel, Schwadorf (drums)

AUTUMN BLAZE is led by two members of PARAGON OF BEAUTY in Eldron and Arisjel. Eldron also goes under the name of Monesol.

Singles/EPs:
Every Silent Moment I Weep, Prophecy (1998)

Albums:
DÄMMER ELBEN TRAGÖDIE, Prophecy (1999)
BLEAK, Prophecy Productions (2000)
Someone's Pictures / I Shiver / Scared / Bleak / So Close Yet So Far / Bruderseele / The Wind And The Broken Girl / Thoughts By A Weary Man's Side / … And We Fall

AUTUMN VERSES (FINLAND)
Line-Up: T. Sitomaniemi, E. Lahdenperä

AUTUMN VERSES would record a further two projected albums for release post the 'Tunes Of Disconsolation' debut. However, the recordings were shelved only to be combined for issue as the 'Sinners Rebellion' under the acts new name of DEAD BEGINNERS.

Albums:
TUNES OF DISCONSOLATION, Solistitium SOL021 (1997)
The Uncreation / Dark Harbours / As Amongst The Wolves / There Upon Sanctimonious / Through The Fields Of Disease / Harvest Moon Shades: I) Prologue, ii) Harvest Moon Shadows, iii) Epilogue / The October Hand / Autumn Verses

AUZHIA (MEXICO)

Black Metal band AUZHIA took the unusual step of sharing their 1996 'Ancient Blasphemies' demo with another act XIBALBIA.

Albums:
DARK EMPERORS, Storm (1996)
Into The War / Shadows Of The Forest / Black Prayer / Immortal Spirit / Dark Emperors / Empire / Screams Of Darkness / Auzhia

AVATAR (BELGIUM)
Line-Up: Daemas (vocals), Occulta (guitar), Anjelen (bass), Izarothas (keyboards), Azagdaimon (drums)

A Black Metal act incited by drummer Azagdaimon, AVATAR first emerged with the 600 run 'The Emperors Of The Night' demo. Vocalist Daemas quit forcing Occulta to both play guitar and sing. Switching Anjelen to guitar as well AVATAR pulled in female bassist Hyberia just prior to inking no less than two record deals with Belgian companies Wood Nymph Records and Shiver Records.
AVATAR has shared stages in Europe with CRADLE OF FILTH, IN THE WOODS and DIMMU BORGIR.

Albums:
...MEMORIAN DRACONIS, Shiver (1996)
Memorium Draconis / Mists Of Evil / A Most Excellent Charm In Solemn Endurance / The Eternal Nothingness / Seduced By Necromancy / Emperors Of The Night / Sands Of Sheol / Hymn To The Ancient Ones / Star Castle / Outro-The Mines Of Moria
A LAND BEYOND A GREAT VAST FOREST SURROUNDED BY MAJESTIC MOUNTAINS, (1998)

AVENGER (CZECH REPUBLIC)
Line-Up: Honza Hapák (vocals / bass / drums), Petr 'Rámus' Mécak (guitar), Premek Sima (guitar), Mila Sladek (keyboards)

Renowned Black Metal act AVENGER issued a string of demos including 1993's 'Eternal Voices Of Hell' and 1994's 'Minster Of Madness'.
The 'Shadows Of The Damned' album was released on cassette in the Czech Republic by the band's own Rámus Records. It was later re-released on CD by Breath Of Night, the label owned by Akhenaten of JUDAS ISCARIOT.

Albums:
SHADOWS OF THE DAMNED, Breath Of Night, (1998)
FALL OF DEVOTION, WRATH AND BLASPHEMY, Breath Of Night (1999)
Behind The Gates / The Captives Of The Nightshide / Call Of Battle / In Chains / Evil, Hate, War / Darkness / Banished From Paradise / Pope Crucified / Opus 666 / Intro- Inferno / Ashes To Ashes, Dust To Dust / Without Fire / Before Death / The Last Man / Desolate Land

AVERNUS (Chicago, IL, USA)
Line-Up: Rick McCoy (vocals), James Genenz (guitar), Brian Whited (bass), Jeff Joseph (keyboards), Bill Hamning (drums)

Chicago Doom Metal act dating to 1993 that would give vocalist Kimberly Goss to Norway's ANCIENT and latterly her own Power Metal band SINERGY.
AVERNUS debuted with the 1993 demo tape 'A Delicate Tracery Of Red' followed by a further session 'Sadness'. Further exposure was gained with the inclusion of the track 'Godlessness' on the Metal Blade 'Metal Massacre 12' compilation. A third demo outing 'A Farewell To Eden' led to the first AVERNUS album 'Of The Fallen' for Olympic Records.
Drummer Bill Hamning deputized for ELECTRIC HELLFIRE CLUB's 2000 American dates. Recently AVERNUS added ex EVE OF MOURNING guitarist Scott.
Albums:
OF THE FALLEN, Olympic (1997)
Blood Gathers Frost / If I Could Exist / By Loves Will… Chaos / Renaissance / Ghost / Thousand Spirits / Beautiful Black Heart / Still Warm Ashes
WHERE THE SLEEPING SHADOWS LIE, Cursed Productions (2000)

An Endless Sea Of Evening / The Faustian Heart / Anaesthesia / Ashes Of Adoration / Godlessness / Dreamburn / Disappear / Silver And Black / For Every Waking Moment / Downpour

AVERSE SEFIRA (Austin, TX, USA)
Line-Up: Sanguine Asmodel Nocturne (vocals / guitar), Wrath Satherial Diabolus (bass), The Carcass (drums)

Highly rated Texan Black Metal band AVERSE SEFIRA, named after the Q'Aballahistic battling angels, are centred upon the erstwhile underground radio DJs frontman Sanguine Asmodel Nocturne (real name Sam Spoor) and bassist Wrath Satherial Diabolus (real name Jeff Tandy). Other musicians aiding on the albums include His Wolfiness E'Er Daarkening.
Live work has seen AVERSE SEFIRA utilizing NIGHT CONQUERS DAY's drummer.

Albums:
BLASPHOMET SIN ABSENT, (199-)
Flight From A Stagnant Land / Wind Witch / Arrival / Rifte Between Two Worlds / The Induction / Winter Of My Bliss / Siege
HOMECOMING'S MARCH, Arrogare (1999)
Hymns To The Scourge Of Heaven / For We Have Always Been / Sentinel's Plight / Pax Dei / Above The Firmaments Of Wrath / Ad Infinitum / Homecoming's March
BATTLE'S CLARION, Lost Disciple (2000)

AVIRGUS (AUSTRALIA)
Line-Up: Judy Chiara (vocals),

Singles/EPs:
The Final Wish / As Ivy Groweth Green / Desolate / Flesh, Warhead (1998)

AZAGHAL (FINLAND)
Line-Up: Varrjoherra (vocals), Narqath (guitar), Kalma (drums)

Borne out of Narqath and Kalma's 1995 act BELFEGOR Black Metal act AZAGHAL has witnessed turbulent times since their inception. BELFEGOR issued the demo 'The Ancient Gods Of Evil' before drummer Varjoherra joined the fold as the band renamed itself NARGOVENTOR in 1997. During the interim Narqath had demoed with WOLFHEART, VALOR, SVARTALFHEIM

and WITH HATE I BURN.
The band members switched roles under a further new banner of AZAGHAL as Varjoherra took over vocals, Narqath bass and Kalma drums. A split album with MUSTAN KUUN LAPSET was recorded for 2000 release and a further split affair with French act BEHEADED LAMB also emerged.
Narqath, besides VALOR, also operates HIN ONDE issuing the album 'Songs Of Battle'.

Albums:
KRISTINUSKO LIEKEISSÄ, (199-)
Saatanan Valtakunta / Kuilujen Herrat / Demonolatria / Murskaame Kasvot Juutalaisten Kunikaan / Kuukma Kristukselle / Kristinusko Liekeissä / Countess Bathory
MUSTAMAA, (199-)
Kuolema Kristukselle / Ruumisarkkojen Kavalkadi / Kuilusen Herrat / Murskaame Kasvot Juutalaisten Kunikaan / Yhtä Yön Kanssa / Mustamaa / De Vermis Mysteriis / Kuunvalo Kilvissamme
DEATHKULT MMDCLXVI, Millenium Metal Music MMM003 (2000)
Satanic Warfare / In The Name Of Satan / Saataanan Valtakunta / Kuilujen Herrat / Demonolatria / Kurastuli / Murskaamme Kasbot Juutalaisten Kunninkaan / Kristinusko Liekeissä / Sielunvihollinen / Inhimillisyyden Tuollapuolen
SUICIDE ANTHEMS, Millenium Metal Music MMM006 (2001)
…Ja Ma Näykimme Luita / Demonic Energy / Käärme Ja Avain / Suicide Anthem 2001 / Kill Yourself

AZAG-THOTH (SWITZERLAND)
Line-Up: The Conjurer (vocals), The Evilized One (guitar), The Ghost (guitar), The Darkified Oric (bass), The Unknown One (drums)

Swiss Black Metal act.

Albums:
REIGN SUPREME, Witchunt WIHU9623 (1996)
Reign Supreme / Sumerian Hymn / Hellfire / The Fire God / Day Of Wrath / Damnation / Evil Sorcerers / Invoke The Power

AZAZEL (FINLAND)

Albums:
THE NIGHT OF SATANICHIA, (1997)
Mediaeval Journey / The Glow Of Golder

Fullmoon / Longing For Dark Winterforest / Sussubus Seduce Me / The Night Of Sataanichia / Mediaeval Gathering

AZAZEL (ISRAEL)

Line-Up: Asaf Enav (guitar), Alex Schuster (guitar), Guy Levy (bass), Evil Haim (keyboards), Barak Zait (drums)

Israeli band AZAZEL was upon their formation inspired by Norwegian Black Metal but have evolved with a more refined almost Swedish approach with time. The band debuted with the demo 'Altar Of Sand' which included vocalist Ilia Berkowitz.

AZAZEL 's keyboard position would change hands from Gal Schuster to Roy Amar and latterly Evil Haim. For the album 'Ride Through The Horizon' guitarist Asaf Enav took the lead vocal role. Eyal Glotman guested on lead guitar.

AZAZEL recently drafted guitarist Alex Schuster.

Albums:
RIDE THROUGH THE HORIZON, (2000)
Eternal Quest Of Vengeance / Kings Nocturnal Feast / A Blaze Of Light Through Vast Forests / Call Upon Immortal Flame / Ride To The Horizon / Valhalla (Farewell To The Viking Lands) / Amaymon: King Of The East Ruler Of 26 Legions Of Spirits / E'L Te'Horn Ha' Hashecha

AZAZEL (FL, USA)

Line-Up: Xul (vocals / guitar), Xaphan (bass), Beleth (drums)

Florida's AZAZEL would retitle themselves KULT OF AZAZEL following their 'Entering Erebus' demo in order to avoid confusion with their Finnish counterparts.

AZAZEL (NC, USA)

Line-Up: Paul (vocals), Nick (guitar), Dennis (guitar), Chris (bass), Steve (drums)

Albums:
MUSIC FOR THE RITUAL CHAMBER, Tribunal (2000)
Into The Black Flames / Habitual Murderer / Where Shadows Weep For Men / Episode Of Clarity / The Damned Lie Well

AZMODAN (GERMANY)

Solo Black Metal outing of Lord Azmodan. In 2001 the man founded a Death Metal project MY DARKEST HATE along with members of SACRED STEEL and PRIMAL FEAR.

Albums:
EVIL OBSCURITY, Iron Glory IG 1002 (1998)
The Arrival / Hellbound / Evil Obscurity / A Bestia / Remember Them / Once They Were Warriors / Signum Vitiosum Dance
OF ANGELS AND DEMONS, Iron Glory 5 1006 20 561 (1999)
Of Angels And Demons / The Lords Of Sin / Princess Of Blood / Dark Tides Rising / Vampyr Romance / In Ancient Days / Subtle Essays On Curiosity

AZTEC (ISRAEL)

Albums:
LOSS OF OUR FINAL PRIDE, Raven Music (2000)
Ceremonial Death / Abused In The Future / Wolf's Dirge / A Place Of Evil Born / The Aztec / Twisted Misconception / Even Unlight / Until The Holocaust / To Die By The Sword / Prologue

AZURE (SWEDEN)

Line-Up: Amorth Bredlave (vocals / guitar), Enormous (bass), Velvet (drums)

AZURE date to 1995 with the inaugural line up of frontman Amorth Bredlave, bassist Enormous and drummer Velvet. A series of demo tapes ensued the third release 'Dark And Mysterious' seeing the departure of Enormous.

Fourth demo 'The Erocian' saw session guitarist Fredrik Pernros involved. The recordings would later be issued as a limited edition EP by Penthesia Records. Velvet decamped upfront of a deal with Solistitium Records. The resulting EP 'A Vicious Age Lasting' had former NAGLFAR and present day EMBRACING drummer Mattias Holmgren in the studio. Vocalist Amorth Bredlave (Robban Kanto) would session for CENTINEX in 2000.

Singles/EPs:
The Erocian EP, Penthesia (199-)

Albums:
MOONLIGHT LEGEND, Solistitium SOL024 (1998)
Prologue / The Eroican / … And The Prophecy Is Him / Selene- The Nocturnal

Goddess Of Luna / Embraced By Flames
/ A Romance In Darkest Harmony / Clair
Du Lune / Tears Of The Aged Mother /
Crowned By Divine Fire (Epilogue)

BABYLON WHORES
(FINLAND)
Line-Up: Ike Vil (vocals / keyboards), Antti Litmanen (guitar), Ewo Meichem (guitar), Jake Babylon (bass), Kouta (drums)

Noted exponents of "Death Rock" BABYLON WHORES mix a heady brew of Gothic Rock, 80's Thrash and Black Metal in a unique combination that has set the band apart from the pack.
The band's debut single 'Devil's Meat' released on their own Sugar Cult label saw the group comprising of vocalist Ike Vil, guitarists Jussi Konittinen and Ewo Meichem, bassist M. Ways and drummer Pete Liha. Follow up 'Sloane 313' saw the bass player's job going to the suitably titled Jake Babylon. Further changes were afoot for BABYLON WHORES third release 'Trismegistos' with guitarist Antti Litmanen taking Konittinen's position and Kouta coming in on drums.
In late 1999 Babylon Jake bailed out to found a new act DEATH FIX and was replaced by Taneli Nyholm of ABSURDUS, CRYHAVOC and PANDEMONIUM OUTCASTS. Nyholm also goes under the pseudonyms of 'Serpent', 'Daniel Rock' and 'Daniel Stuka'.
BABYLON WHORES toured America in 2000 as guests to KING DIAMOND.

Singles/EPs:
Cool / Third Eye / East Of Earth, Sugar Cult SUGAR 666 (1994) ('Devil's Meat' 7" single)
Of Blowjobs And Cocktails / Cold Hummingbird / Babylon Astronaut / Silver Apples, Sugar Cult SUGAR 667 (1995) ('Sloane 313' EP)
Love Under Will / Hellboy / Speed Doll / Beyond The Sun / Trismegistos, Sugar Cult SUGAR 668 (1996) ('Trismegistos' EP)
Errata Stigmata / Errata Stigmata (Version) / Fey (Version) Sol Niger (Video), Necropolis NR067 CD (2000)

Albums:
COLD HEAVEN, Heroine-Music For Nations MFN 226 (1997)
Deviltry / Omega Therion / Beyond The Sun / Metatron / Enchirdion For A Common Man / In Arcadia Ego / Babylon Astronaut / Flesh Of A Swine / Cold Heaven
DEGGAEL, Spinefarm SPI62CD (1998)
Dog Star A / Sol Niger / Somniferum / Omega Therion (V2) / Emerald Green / Deggael: A Rat's God
KING FEAR, Necropolis (2000)
Errata Stigmata / Radio Werewolf / Hand Of Glory / Veritas / Skeleton Farm / To Behold The Suns / Exit Eden / Sol Niger / Fey / King Fear- Song Of The Damned

BAL-SAGOTH (UK)
Line-Up: Bryon (vocals), Chris (guitar), Jason Porter (bass), Leon (keyboards), Jonny (keyboards / drums)

A Dark, Black Metal band, during March 1997 bassist Jason Porter was ousted by the recruitment of Alastair McLatchy. BAL SAGOTH supported EMPEROR in Britain the same year.
BAL SAGOTH's keyboard player Jonny Maudling found himself on loan to MY

BAL SAGOTH
Photo : Nuclear Blast

DYING BRIDE for European touring during 1999. The band signed to Nuclear Blast during 1999.

Albums:
A BLACK MOON BROODS OVER LEMURIA, Cacophonous NIHIL 4CD (1995)
Hatheg Kla / Dreaming Of Atlantean Spires / Spellcraft And Moonfire (Beyond The Citadel Of Frosts) / A Black Moons Broods Over Lemuria / Enthroned In The Temple Of The Serpent Kings / Shadows 'neath The Black Pyramid / Witch-Storm / The Ravening / Into The Silent Chambers Of The Sapphirean Throne (Sagas From The Untedelivian Scrolls) / Valley Of Silent Paths
STARFIRE BURNING OVER THE ICE VEILED THRONE OF ULTIMA THULE, Cacophonous NIHIL 18 CD (1996)
Black Dragons Soar Above The Mountain Of Shadows (Epilogue) / To Dethrone The Witch-Queen Of Mytos K'unn (The Legend Of The Battle Of Blackhelm Vale) / As The Vortex Illumines The Crystalline Walls Of Kor-Avul-Thaa / Starfire Burning Upon The Ice - Veiled Throne Of Ultima Thule / Journey To The Isle Of Sists (Over The Moonless Depths Of Night-Dark Seas) / The Splendour Of A Thousand Swords Gleaming Beneath The Blazon Of The Hyperborean Empire / Ad Lo, When The Imperium Marches Against Gul-Kothoth, Then Dark Sorceries Shall Enshroud The Citadel Of The Obsidian Crown / Summoning The Guardians Of The Astral Gate / In The Raven-Hunted Forests Of Darkenhold, Where Shadows Reign And The Hues Of Sunlight Never Dance / At The Altar Of The Dreaming Gods (Epilogue)
BATTLE MAGIC, Cacophonous NIHIL (1998)
Battle Magic / Naked Steel (The Warrior's Saga) / A Tale From The Deep Woods / Return To The Praesidium Of Ys / Crystal Shards / The Dark Liege Of Chaos Is Unleashed At The Ensorcelled Shrine Of A'Zura-Kai (The Splendour Of A Thousand Swords Gleaming Beneath The Blazon Of The Hyperborean Empire Part II) / When Rides The Scion Of The Storms / Blood Slakes The Sand At The Circus Maximus / Thwarted By The Dark (Blade Of The Vampyre Hunter) / And Atlantis Falls
THE POWER COSMIC, Nuclear Blast NB 421-2 (1999)
The Awakening Of The Stars / The Voyagers Beneath The Mare Imbrium / The Empyreal Lexicon / Of Carnage And A Gathering Of Wolves / Callisto Rising / The Scourge Of The Fourth Celestial Host / Behold, The Armies Of War Descend Screaming From The Heavens! / The Thirteen Cryptical Prophecies Of Mu
ATLANTIS ASCENDANT, Nuclear Blast NB 584-2 (2001)

BALTAK (MACEDONIA)

Albums:
MACEDONIAN DARKNESS AND EVIL, (1996)
Svetot Umira- Mekedoncite Se Borat / U Miram Sega / So Umrenite Odam / Me Sakopwa / Wampir / Odam Doly So Himi / Svetot Placy Sa Meine / Makedonzite Se Tepat / Me Kolat
THE LOST CITY, (1997)
Dead / Burning In Fire / My Time Has Come / In Battle / World War / I Will Return / Black Magic / The Lost City / Sacrifice
KING OF TWO WORLDS, (2000)
Pharao Of Egypt / Macedonia Will return / My Kingdom / King Of Two Worlds / Son Of Zeus Ammon / Alexander War Horse / Macedonian Phalanx / A King Was Born / Stench Of Death- reaking The Heavens

BARATHRUM (FINLAND)
Line-Up: Demonos Sova (vocals), Sulphar (guitar), Infernus (bass), Pimea (drums)

Black Metal band BARATHRUM, originally titled DARKFEAST, first surfaced with the 1990 tape 'Darkfeast'. A further effort 'Witchmaster' followed in 1991 with 1992's 'Battlecry' and 1993's 'Sactissime Colere Satanas' building their reputation.
Upgraded to a quartet by adding guitarist Sulphar for 1996's 'Eerie' album. In 1997 Infernus departed and Demonos took his position on bass. The new member would also busy himself as a member of WIZZARD.
With the collapse of their label, the German Nazgûl's Eyrie Productions concern, BARATHRUM toured Finland on a package billing with BABYLON WHORES, WIZZARD and HORNA during late 1997. A demo session entitled 'Devilry' soon secured a new deal with renowned Finnish label Spinefarm.
A major split in the ranks saw Sulphar and Pimea decamping to join erstwhile member Infernus in THE URN. New faces in the BARATHRUM camp were guitarist

Anathemalignant, bassist G'Thaur and drummer Natasett. However, by the time of recording the 'Sataana' album Demonos and G'Thaur had been joined by Beast Dominator on drums, THY SERPENT guitarist Somnium and second guitarist Warlord. For the subsequent tour Anathemalignent made his return ousting Warlord and Nuklear Tormentor took the bass role. MOONSORROW's keyboard player Trollhorn also sessioned.

Somnium and Beast Dominator would upon their departure found the Troll inspired Black Metal 'Oommpah' band FINNTROLL.

Members of BARATHRUM allied themselves with their cohorts in THY SERPENT to found SHAPE OF DESPAIR issuing the 'Shades Of...' album in 2000.

Recently BARATHRUM's vacant drum stool was occupied by the sticksman from WALTARI.

Demonos Sova also has a side outfit suitably titled DEMONOS.

<u>Albums:</u>
HAILSTORM, Nazgûl's Eyrie Productions NEP006CD (1995)
Deep From The Depths / In Darkness I Fly / Pure Flame Crown / Highest Beast / Lord Of South And Fire / Spears Of Sodom / Marks On My Skin / Battlecry / Gate To Jetblack Desires / Slavery And Delusion / Inferno Winds / Hailstorm
EERIE, Nazgûl's Eyrie Productions NEP010CD (1996)
Sähttän Juoiggus / Moon Calls / Wanderer In The Night / Vampire / Nocturnal Dance / Eerie / The Twilight / Black Goat / Dagger, Seal, Vengeance / Justice Of The Shining Steel / Bleeding Sky / Victory Feast / Ravens
INFERNAL, Nazgûl's Eyrie Productions NEP15CD (1997)
The Night Of The Demon Lord / The Blasphemer / Warmetal / Deliver A Battle / Death Is Saviour / Leaving The March Of The Mortals / Deadmarch / Ethereal Guest / Immortal Warrior / Demon Est Deus Inversus / Infernal
LEGIONS OF PERKELE, Spinefarm SPI57CD (1998)
Revenge By Magick / Angelburner / Dark Sorceress (Autumn Siege) / Last Day In Heaven / Necromantical Ritual / The Force Of Evil / SaLuBeLe / Legions Of Perkele
SATAANA, Spinefarm (1999)
Introitus- Satanick Alert / Dark Sorceress 2 (Winter Siege) / Boundless Arts / Beltane / Helluva Agitator / Melancholy,

Infinity, Agony / Regret Of Damnation / Contess Erszebeth Nadasdy / Sacriligeum / Sataana
OKKULT, Spinefarm (2000)
Magic In Atmosphere / The Darkness Has Landed / Bride Of Lucifer / Virgin Blood Spiller / Halfheart / I Am Very Possessed / Land Of Tears / Whores Of Hades / Devilish Sign / Fatal Bite

BATHORY (SWEDEN)
Line-Up: Quorthon (vocals / guitar), Kothaar (bass), Vvornth (drums)

A one man Extreme Metal project based around the enigmatic Quorthon (previously known as 'Ace Shot'), who was at one time rumoured to be the son of Black Mark label boss Borje Forsberg. With BATHORY Quorthon prides himself on overblown epic chunks of Metal that has attracted a loyal fan base.

BATHORY came to attention of the masses via the tracks 'The Return Of Darkness And Evil' and 'Sacrafice' that were both featured on the 'Scandinavian Metal Attack' compilation album of 1984. BATHORY was actually created a year before by Black Spade on vocals and guitar, bassist Hanoi and drummer Vans (real name Jonas Akerlund). The band toyed with various band names including NOSFERATU, MEPHISTO, ELIZABETH BATHORY and COUNTESS BATHORY before settling on BATHORY. For the 'Scandinavian Metal Attack' album Black Spade retitled himself Ace Shoot and later Quorthon.

BATHORY performed only a handful of gigs before resolving never to perform again in a deliberate intention to compound the mystique surrounding the act. An early bass player was DRILLER KILLER's Cliff. Carsten Nielsen, drummer for Danes ARTILLERY, was offered a position in BATHORY during 1985 but declined. The band nearly relented in 1986 when a European tour with CELTIC FROST and DESTRUCTION was planned. Despite Witchhunter of SODOM rehearsing with the band the touring plans were scrapped.

The rhythm section of Kothaar and Vvornth appeared on 1988's 'Blood Fire Death'.

Quorthon issued a solo album, simply titled 'Album' (Black Mark 666-9), during 1993. For reasons best known to himself Quorthon consistently refuses to take the BATHORY experience out on tour.

1995's 'Octagon' suffered a setback at the last minute before release. It was deemed that lyrics to two tracks 'Resolution Greed' and 'Genocide' were too extreme hence a cover version of the KISS classic 'Deuce' was included instead. The missing two tracks were later issued on the 'Jubileum Volume III' compilation.

A BATHORY record entitled 'Raise The Dead' was planned for release through Music For Nations, but this proposed record never appeared.

BATHORY are without doubt highly influential in the Scandinavian Black Metal scene with many later artists offering cover versions in homage.

In 1997 various Greek Black Metal acts including KAWIR, EXHUMATION and DEVISER contributed to the 'Hellas Salutes The Vikings' tribute effort. A more substantial album came the following year featuring heavyweight names such as MARDUK, GEHENNAH, DARK FUNERAL, EMPEROR, NECROPHOBIC and SATYRICON titled 'In Conspiracy With Satan'.

Singles/EPs:
The Sword / The Lake, The Woodman, Black Mark (1988) (Promotion)
Twilight Of The Gods / Under The Runes / Hammerheart, Black Mark BM CD666P (1991) (Promotion release)

Albums:
BATHORY, Tyfon / Black Mark BMCD 666-1(1984)
Hades / Reaper / Necromancy / Sacrifice / In Conspiracy With Satan /
Armageddon / Raise The Dead / War
THE RETURN, Tyfon / Black Mark BMCD 666-2 (1985)
Possessed / The Rite Of Darkness / Reap Of Evil / Son Of The Damned / Sadist / The Return... / Revelation Of Doom / Total Destruction / Born For Burning / The Wind Of Mayhem / Bestial Lust (Bitch)
UNDER THE SIGN OF THE BLACK MARK, Black Mark BMCD 666-3 (1986)
Nocturnal Obedience / Massacre / Woman Of Dark Desires / Call From The Grave / Equimothorn / Enter The Eternal Fire / Chariots Of Fire / 13 Candles / Of Doom..
BLOOD FIRE DEATH, Black Mark 666-4 (1988)
Oden's Ride Over Nordland / A Fine Day To Die / The Golden Walls Of Heaven / Pace 'Till Death / Holocaust / For All Those Who Died / Dies Irae / Blood Fire Death
HAMMERHEART, Black Mark BMCD

666-5 (1990)
Shores In Flames / Valhalla / Baptized In Fire And Blood / Father To Son / Song To Hall Up High / Home Of Once Brave / One Rode To Asa Bay
TWILIGHT OF THE GODS, Black Mark BMLP666-6 (1991)
Prologue-Twilight Of The Gods-Epilogue / Through Blood By Thunder / Blood And Iron / Under The Runes / To Enter Your Mountain / Bond Of Blood / Hammerheart
JUBILEUM VOLUME 1, Black Mark BMCD 666-7 (1992)
Rider At The Gate Of Dawn / Crawl To Your Cross / Sacrifice / Dies Irae / Through Blood By Thunder / You Don't Move Me (I Don't Give A Fuck) / Odens Ride Over Nordland / A Fine Day To Die / War / Enter The Eternal Fire / Song To Hall Up High / Sadist / Under The Runes / Equimanthorn / Blood Fire Death
JUBILEUM VOLUME II, Black Mark 666-8 (1993)
The Return Of The Darkness And Evil / Burnin' Leather / One Rode To Asa Bay / The Golden Walls Of Heaven / Call From The Grave / Die In Fire / Shores In Flames / Possessed / Raise The Dead / Total Destruction / Bond Of Blood / Twilight Of The Gods
REQUIEM, Black Mark 666-10 (1994)
Requiem / Crosstitution / Necroticus / War Machine / Blood And Soul / Pax Vobiscum / Suffocate / Distinguish To Kill / Apocalypse
OCTAGON, Black Mark 666-11 (1995)
Immaculate Pinetreeroad / Born To Die / Psychpath / Sociopath / Grey / Century / 33 Something / War Supply / Schizianity / A Judgement Of Posterity / Deuce
BLOOD ON ICE, Black Mark BMCD666-12 (1996)
Intro / Blood On Ice / Man Of Iron / One Eyed Old Man / The Sword / The Stallion / The Wodwoman / The Lake / Gods Of Thunder Of Wind And Of Rain / The Ravens / The Revenge Of Blood On Ice

BATTLELUST (SWEDEN)
Line-Up: Micke Grankvist (vocals), Markus Terramäki (guitar), Baron De Samedi (guitar / bass / drums)

BATTLELUST was created by NECROMICON member Baron De Samedi originally titled ONDSKA ("Evil"). By 1996 Samedi had left NECROMICON and, after a brief spell as a member of GATES OF ISHTAR, together with Lucichrist (Patrick Tonkvist) of EVERDAWN and resumed activies with ONDSKA. Before long a name change to

BATTLESTORM was adopted for a demo 'The Eclipse Of The Dying Sun'. A track 'The Acheron' was submitted to the Fullmoon compilation album 'A Tribute To Hell'. However, Lucichrist would leave to be replaced by Haris Agic. Agic was out of the picture by the time of recording of the debut album 'Of Battle And Ancient Warcraft'. Samedi had now been joined by SATARIEL singer Micke Grankvist and DARKEST SEASON guitarist Markus Terramäki.

Albums:
OF BATTLE AND ANCIENT WARCRAFT, Hammerheart (1998)
Armageddon Arrives / Retrobution / Angel Fire / Forever Laid In Chains / The Sword Of Death / Darkened Descendants / Of Battle And Ancient Warcraft / The Dawn Of The Black Hearts / With The Blackstorms I Came / Snow And Ice Demonmight

BEFORE GOD (St. Paul, MN, USA)
Line-Up: Adam (vocals), Wayne (guitar), Ed (guitar), Rick (bass), Mike (drums)

Albums:
WOLVES AMONGST THE SHEEP, Sub Zero (1998)
Summoning Of our Ancestors / No Allegiance / Wolves Amongst The Sheep / Rebirth Of The Pagan Man / Bountiful Life / Lions- Whips / Mark Of The Damned / Charge / Minneapolis Burns / Defiance

BEHEADED LAMB (SPAIN)

BEHEADED LAMB drummer Katu Marus is much in demand boasting stints with ARGAR, ASGAROTH and GORTHAUR.

Albums:
DARK BLASPHEMOUS MOON,
Millenium Metal Music MMM006 (2001) (Split album with AZAGHAL)
Nihilocollegats / Across The River / To The Hall Of The Horned Masters / Beheaded Lamb

BEHEMOTH (POLAND)
Line-Up: Nergal (vocals / guitar / bass), Frost (guitar), Baal Ravenlock (drums)

Black Metal act BEHEMOTH arrived with the 1991 demo 'Endless Damnation'. Further tapes 'The Return Of The Northern Moon' and 'From The Pagan Vastlands' would later be committed to CD.

BEHEMOTH's Les and Nergal also formed part of the group DAMNATION that released the 'Rebel Souls' album in 1996 on Malicious Records. On the first album S.K. played bass and Czarek Morawski played keyboards. The album featured a cover of a MAYHEM track.
1996's 'Grom' found guitarist Frost replaced by the enigmatic Les. Drummer Ravenlock forged HELL-BORN as a side project with DAMNATION / BEHEMOTH guitarist Les issuing an eponymous album in 1996.
BEHEMOTH toured Europe in December 2000 as part of an almighty Death Metal package that included ENSLAVED, MORBID ANGEL, THE CROWN, HYPNOS and DYING FETUS.

Albums:
FROM THE PAGAN VASTLANDS,
Nazgûl's Eyrie Productions NEP002 (1994)
From Honredlands To Lindesfarne / Thy Winter Kingdom / Summoning (Of The Ancient Ones) / The Dance Of The Pagan Flames / Blackvisions Of The Almighty / Fields Of Haar-Megiddo / Deathcrush
AND THE FORESTS DREAM ETERNALLY, Entropy Productions DE101MCD (1995)
Transylvanian Forest / Moonspell Rites / Sventevith (Storming Near The Baltic) / Pure Evil And Hate / Forgotten Empire Of Dark Witchcraft
SVENTEVITH (STORMING NEAR THE BALTIC), Pagan Moon CD001 (1995)
Chant Of The Eastern Lands / The Touch Of Nya / From The Pagan Vastlands / Hidden In A Fog / Ancient / Entering The Fantasian Soul / Forgotten Cult Of Aldaron / Wolves Guard My Coffin / Hell Dwells In Ice / Transylvanian Forest / Sventevith (Storming Near The Baltic)
GROM, Solistitium, SOL005 (1996)
Intro / The Dark Forest (Cast Me Your Spell) / Spellcraft And Heathendoom / Dragon's Lair (Cosmic Flames And Four Barbaric Seasons) / Lasy Pomorza / Rising Proudly Towards The Sky / Thou Shalt Forever Win / Grom
BEWITCHING THE POMMERANIA,
Solistitium (1997)
PANDEMONIC INCANTATIONS,
Solistitium SOL 020 (1997)
Diableria / The Thousand Plagues I witness / Satan's Sword (I Have Become) / In Thy Pandemaeternum / Driven By The Five Winged Star / The Past Is Like A Funeral / The Entrance To

The Spheres Of Mars / Chwaka
Mordercom Wojciechan (997-1997
Dziesiec Wiekow Hanby)
**THE RETURN OF THE NORTHERN
MOON**, Last Epitaph (1997)
... Of My Worship / Summoning The
Ancient Gods / Dark Triumph /
Monumentum / Rise Of The Black Storm
Devil / Aggressor / Dark Triumph (1994
version) / Cursed Angel Of Doom
SATANICA, (1999)
Decade Of Therion / Lam / Ceremony Of
Shiva / Of Sephirotic Transformation And
Carnality / Sermon To The Hypocrites /
Star Spawn / The Alchemist's Dream /
Chant For Eschaton 2000
THELEMA 6 INC, Avantgarde (2000)
Anti Kristian Phenomenon / The Act Of
Rebellion / Inflamed By Rage / Natural
Born Philosopher / Christians To The
Lions / Inauguration Of Scorpio Done / In
The Garden Of Dispersion / The Universe
Illumination / Hello To My Demons / Vivm
Sabbati / The Youth Manifesto

BEHERIT (FINLAND)
Line-Up: Nuclear Holocausto Vengeance
(vocals / guitar), Black Jesus (bass),
Necroperbersor (drums)

Finnish Black Metal band. BEHERIT first
released the 1990 demos '7th
Blasphemy' and 'Demonomancy'. The
following year BEHERIT shared a split 7"
single with DEATH YELL.
BEHERIT ventured into what could be
loosely termed Black Ambient sounds for
their 1994 'H418 OV 21.C' album.

Singles/EPs:
Dawn Of Satan's Millenium, Turbo
Music (1991) (7" picture disc single)
Werewolf, Semen And Blood / , Turbo
Music (1991) (Split single with DEATH
YELL)
Messe Des Morts, Necropolis (1994) (7"
single)

Albums:
OATH OF BLACK BLOOD, Turbo Music
(1992)
Intro / Metal Of Death / The Oath Of Black
Blood / Grave Desecration / Witchcraft /
Goat Worship / Demonomacy / Black
Mass Prayer / Beast Of Damnation / Hail
Satanhas / Dawn Of Satan's Millennium
DRAWING DOWN THE MOON,
Spinefarm (1994)
Intro (Tirehab) / Salomon's Gate /
Nocturnal Evil / Sadomatic Rites / Black
Arts / The Gate Of Nanna / Nuclear Girl /

Unholy Pagan Fire / Down There...
/Summerlands / Werewolf, Semen And
Blood / Thou Angel Of The Gods / Lord
Of Shadows And Goldenwood
H 418 OV 21.C, Spinefarm SPI 19CD
(1995)
The Gate Of Inanna / Tribal Death /
Emotional Ecstasy / Fish / 21st Century
Paradise (Part II) / Mystik Force / Spirit
Of The God Of Fire / Escape
ELECTRIC DOOM SYNTHESIS,
Spinefarm SPI 28 (1996)
Ambush / We Worship / Dead Inside /
Beyond Vision / Deep Night 23rd Drawing
Down The Moon / Sense / Temple
WERWOLF, SEMEN AND BLOOD,
(1997)
Werwolf, Semen And Blood / Black Mass
prayer / Beast Of Damnation / Hail
Satanas / Dawn Of Satan's Millenium

BELENOS (FRANCE)

Albums:
NOTRE AMOUR ETERNELLE, (1997)
Le Deuge / Notre Amour Eternal / Pries
Encore / Reveries / Etrange Dorceuer /
Le Visage De La Solitude / Adorable
Mepris

BELIAL (FINLAND)
Line-Up: Jarno Antilla (vocals / guitar),
Jani Lehytosaari (bass), Reima
Kellokoski (drums)

BELIAL date to April 1991 and the demo
'The God Of The Pits' brought them to the
attention of the Metal Underground.
At this stage the group comprised of
vocalist Jarno Koskinen, guitarists Jarno
Antilla and Jukka Valppu, bassist Jani
Lehtosaari and drummer Reima
Kellokoski. However, Jukka Valppu quit to
form MYTHOS in 1992.
The band's earliest recordings proved to
be so popular on the tape trading circuit
that BELIAL's initial demos were later
pressed and issued by Moribund
Records.
Having participated in the recording of the
'Wisdom Of Darkness' and 'Never Again'
albums, frontman Koskinen left to form
ETERNITIES. And, having replaced him
with new singer Jarno Antilla, BELIAL
was rocked by a further departure in early
1996 when bassist Jani Lehotosaari
joined IMPALED NAZARENE.

Singles/EPs:
The Invocation / Voices Beyond /
Deceased / For Them / Piece By Piece

52

(Remix), Moribund DEAD 05 (1993) ('The Gods Of The Pit II (Paragon Below) EP) **The Gods Of The Pit II**, Moribund DEAD 05 (1993) (7" single limited edition of 1,000)
After Taste, BMTHOMP Records SHIT-1 (1994) (Limited edition of 500)
After Taste 1 1/2, E-REC 91994) (Limited edition of 50)

Albums:
WISDOM OF DARKNESS, Lethal LRC002 (1992)
Intro-The Invocation / Of Servant Of Belial / Lost Souls / Rise Of Hecate / Hypocrisy Of The God's Sons / Voices Beyond
NEVER AGAIN, Lethal LRC 666 (1993)
Firestorm / The Red One / Dragons Kiss / Swan Song / As Above So Below / The Sun / About Love / Pain-Flood / Clouds / Desires / On You
3, Witchunt WIHU 9418 (1995)
Other Channel / Mr. Blue Sky High / I Want You To Die / The End / Exit / You / Holes And Boots / One Way In And Out On Valium / Nautilus / Saturnus / One Day / Sina Inhotat Minua Rakkaani / Hate Song

BELKETRE (FRANCE)

French Black Metal band BELKETRE were the centre of rumours that the entire band had committed group suicide. These stories turned out to be false.
The band's 'March To The Black Holocaust' album was a shared effort with fellow unholy Frenchmen VLAD TEPES.

Albums:
MARCH TO THE BLACK HOLOCAUST, Embassy Productions (1995) (Split album with VLAD TEPES)
Guilty / A Day Will Dawn / Hate / Last Sigh Of God / Night Of Sadness / Despair / Those Of Our Blood / If We Had…

BELLA BESTIA (SPAIN)

Albums:
LISTA PAVA MALOR, (1986)

BELMEZ (GERMANY)

The solo project of ex EMINENZ member Karsten Breitung, BELMEZ was rather strangely named after a Spanish village where, in 1972, one Maria Gomez Pereira saw faces on the floor of her house; the property had been built over a graveyard.
BELMEZ' records are unusual for the Black Metal scene as all lyrics are sung in German.
Breitung later sang on MORTAL DISCIPLINE's 'Child Of Retribution' album.

Albums:
BERSERKER, Napalm Records SPV 084-07962 (1995)
Und Liese Rieselt Der Wind... / Berserker / Meine Kraft / Medusa / Spaziergang Mit Pestmaske / Lautloser Gigant / Wurmland / Villa Hildebrandt / Lippen Auf Verwestem Fleisch
SIECHTUM, Napalm SPV 08423892(1996)
Belmez / Und Süss Setzt Ein Das Leiden… / Morella / Spiritische Sitzung / Bizarro / Violine Mit Knochenkopf / Wirkliche Erfüllog / Die Kriechenden Särge Von Barbados / Seichtum / Hort Das Sterbens / Schwerter Axte Lanzen
WUNDGRIND, (1998)

BELPHEGOR (AUSTRIA)
Line-Up: Sigurd (guitar), Marius (bass)

Infamous Black Metal act BELPHEGOR engaged with the 1991 demo 'Krucifixion'. A further tape emerged in 1992 titled 'Bloodbath In Paradise' upfront of the 'Obscure And Deep' EP.
Last Episode Records re-released BELPHEGOR's debut album 'The Last Supper' in 1999 with extra tracks culled from the EP.

Singles/EPs:
Obscure And Deep EP, Perverted Taste (1994)

Albums:
THE LAST SUPPER, Lethal (1995)
The Last Supper / A Funeral Without A Cry / Impalement Without Mercy / March Of The Dead / The Rapture Of Cremation / Engulfed In Eternal Frost / D.rwere I.n E.xcrements / In Remembrance Of Hate And Sorrow / Bloodbath In Paradise Part II / Krucifixion
BLUTSABBATH, Last Episode (1997)
Abschworung / Blackest Ecstasy / Purity Through / Behind The Black Moon / Blutsabbath / No Resurrection / The Requiem Of Hell / Untergang der Gekreusigten
NECRODAEMON TERRORSATHAN, Last Episode (2000)
Necrodaemon Terrorsathan / Vomit Upon

The Cross / Diabolical Possession / Lust Perishes In A Thirst For Blood / S.B.S.R. / Sadism Unbound / Tanzwut Totengesange / Cremation Of Holiness / Necrodaemon Terrorsathan Pt 2 / Outro-Anal Jesus
INFERNAL LIVE ORGASM, Last Episode (2001)

BELSHAZZAR (UK)
Line-Up: Arioch (vocals / guitar), Mars (drums / bass)

Scottish duo from Glasgow. BELSHAZZAR quite uniquely attempt to fuse the melodies of mid 80's classic Rock acts within the Black Metal format. A demo 'Sic Itur Ad Astra' was issued and plans are afoot for an album 'Resurrecting Metal'.

BELTANE (AUSTRALIA)
Line-Up: Bonnie Radibratovic (vocals), Karina Eames (vocals / guitar), Aaron Hewson (guitar), Paul Handley (bass / keyboards)

Albums:
THE FIRE OF BECOMING, Definitive Recordings DIFFD 1002 (2000)
The Fire Of Becoming / Mysterium / Until The New Moon / Angel Of May / Kinship / Dionysian Blood / Spell Of Harmony / The Enchanted Ocean / A Self Willed Commission / Impasse

BENIGHTED (Salisbury, NC, USA)
Line-Up: Zacathus (vocals), Demoniaque

BENIGHTED employed the talents of Adina Blaze of ACHERON and CERNUNNOS for live keyboard work. The 'Harbingers Of The Victorium Aeternus' album included a cover version of BATHORY's 'Satan My Master'.
Both BENIGHTED's Demoniaque and a previous band member Storm Ravensbane created the 2000 act WINDS OF ABBADON.

Albums:
HARBINGERS OF THE VICTORIUM AETURNUS, Arcadia Productions ARC001 (2000)
Arise From The Depths / Upon A Throne Of Blood / Darkened Hollow / Prelude To The Battle To Come / Under An Igneous Luming / Satan My Master
HOTVA, Arcadia Productions (2001)

BENIGHTED LEAMS (UK)

BENIGHTED LEAMS is the brainchild of Alex Kurtagic, owner of the Supernal Records mail order company and sleeve artist for bands such as DIMMU BORGIR and ANCIENT.

Albums:
CALIGINOUS ROMANTIC MYTH, Supernal AURA001CD (1996)
Tenebraious Arcadian Dream / The Fnead / Oeillades Into Paenumbral Mirth / Wood Nymph Of Summer Twilight / Caliginous Romantic Myth
ASTRAL TENEBRION, AURA002CD Supernal (1998)
Astral Tenebrion / Stellar Desideration / Aurora Of Despondance On Valles Marineris / Succeeding Departure From The Chryse Planitia / Hermetically Leering As Frigid Blores Obumber / Saturnine Fury Adumbrated The Aestival Castellations Of Iberia / The Ark Of Infinity / Sinister Demurral Estranged The Seductive Looming / Floundering Of The Aeons

BERGTHRON (GERMANY)

German Black Metal band BERGTHRON released a 1995 demo 'Duch den Nebel der Finsternis…'. The 1997 album is comprised one of solitary track a mammoth 333 minutes in duration.

Singles/EPs:
Uralte Gedanken, (1999)

Albums:
VERBORGEN IN DEN TIEFEN DER WÄLDER, Perverted Taste (1997)
Den treuen dienem der Nacht

BESTIAL SUMMONING (HOLLAND)

An infamous early Dutch Black Metal act issued the 'Sodomastic Rituals' demo in 1992. BESTIAL SUMMONING member Conscicide Dominus Arcula would following the break up of the band attempt suicide by slashing his wrists. After a period of psychiatric treatment he would found another Black Metal outfit BHOABHAN SIDHE.
BESTIAL SUMMONING vocalist Sephiroth (real name Maurice) would found OCCULT but would drop the pseudonym and corpsepaint in 1994.

54

Albums:
THE DARK WAR HAS BEGUN, No Fashion (1992)

BESTIAL WARLUST (AUSTRALIA)
Line-Up: Damon Bloodstorm (vocals), K.K. Warslut (guitar), Joe Skullfucker (guitar), Chris Corpse Molestor (bass), Markus Hellcunt (drums)

Notorious Australian Black Doom band. The unit was assembled by Damon Bloodstorm in 19990 titled CORPSE MOLESTATION evolving into BESTIAL WARLUST in 1992 following the demo 'Descension Of A Darker Deity'.
The 1994 debut album 'Vengeance War 'Til Death' had Bloodstorm joined by guitarists K.K. Warslut and Joe Skullfucker, bassist Chris Corpsemolester and drummer Markus Hellkunt. However, Warslut would make his exit to create the equally notorious DESTROYER 666.
The band's line up for their 'Blood And Honour' debut featured Bloodstorm, Hellcunt and Skullfucker alongside fresh recruits guitarists Battleslaughter and bass player Fiend Of The Deep.
BESTIAL WARLUST underwent a further line up change after the second album with bassist Inferno joining but the band would fold soon after.
Damon Bloodstorm created ABOMINATOR for the 1999 album 'Damnations Prophecy'. Markus Hellcunt joined ANATOMY.

Albums:
VENGEANCE WAR 'TIL DEATH, Modern Invasion MIM 7316-2 CD (1994)
Dweller Of The Bottomless Pit / Satanic / Heathens / Hammering Down The Law Of The New Gods / Holocaust Wolves Of The Apocalypse / Storming Vengeance / At The Graveyard Of God
BLOOD AND VALOUR, Modern Invasion MIM 7321-2CD (1995)
Blood And Valour / Death Rides Out / Descention, Hellsblood / Barbaric Horde / ... Til The End / Within The Storm / Legion Of Wrath / Orgy Of Souls (Hallowed Night) / I The Warrior

BESTIAL WRATH (GREECE)

Greek Black Metal group BESTIAL WRATH shared their 19893 7" single with LEGION OF DOOM.

Singles/EPs:
Passage Through.. The Circle, Molon Lave (1993) (Split single with LEGION OF DOOM)

BETHLEHEM (GERMANY)
Line-Up: Classen (vocals), Matton (guitar), Bartsch (vocals / bass), Rolf (drums)

Bartsch and Matton (both previously with the group DARK TEMPEST) formed BETHLEHEM in order to pursue a more Death Metal direction in late 1991than the way they had been travelling in their previous act. The pair both brought a unique set of experiences to bear on shaping BETHLEHEM's particular brand of melancholia as both had suffered from eerily alike suicides of family members

BESTIAL WARLUST

with Bartsch's girlfriend and aunt hanging themselves and Matton's father doing likewise. From their inception the authorities were intent on making life difficult for the band with gigs banned in Germany. Such was the persecution record label Adipocere even took the step of censoring references to the devil from BETHLEHEM lyric sheets.

After several line-up changes the group released the debut 'Dark Metal' album, although the second album ('Dictius Te Necare'; translation: 'Kill You') is far more notorious with sick German lyrics.

Classen (as 'Andras'), in spite of press reports claiming he was dead, would in fact found PARAGON BELIAL for the 'Hordes Of The Dark' album and later reunite with BETHLEHEM drummer Rolf to forge DARK CREATION.

PAVOR bass player Rainer Landfermann performs vocals on the second BETHLEHEM record although would be supplanted by Marco Kehran of DEINONYCHUS along with female vocals from Catharin Campen.

Singles/EPs:
Supplementary Exegis / Wintermute, Red Stream RSR 0109 (1996) ('Thy Pale Dominion' EP)

Albums:
DARK METAL, Adipocere CDAR022 (1994)
The Elbereth Commandment / Apocalyptic Dance / Second Coming / Vargtimmen / 3rd Nocturnal Prayer / Funeral Owlblood / Veiled Irreligious / Gepreisen Sei Der Untergang / Supplementary Exegis / Wintermute
DICTUS TE NECARE, Red Stream RSR 012 (1996)
Schatten aus der Alexander Welt / Die Anarchische Befreiung der Augenzeugenreligion / Aphel - Die Schwarze Schlange / Verheißung - Du Krone des Todeskultes / Verschleierte Irreligiosität / Tagebuch einer Totgeburt / Dorn meiner Allmacht
SARDONISCHER UNTERGANG IN ZEICHEN IRRELIOGIÖSEN DARBIETUNG, (199-)
Durch Beflechte Berührung Meiner Nemesis / Du Sollst Dich Töten / Gestern Starb ich schon Heute / Teufelverrückt Gottdreizehn / Tote Weiße Marder / Nexus / Luftstehs'Ibläh / Als ich Noch Caulerpa Taxifolia Erbrach / Tod ist Weicher Stuhlin Gar Fleischlos Gift

REFLEKTIONEN AUF'S STERBEN, (199-)
Wolfsstunde / Gestern Starb ich schon Heute / Angst Atmet Mord / Du Sollst Dich Töten / Vargtimmen / Reflektionen Auf's Sterben
PROFANE FETMILCH LENZT ELF KRANK, Prophecy Productions (2000)
Gar Albern Es Uns Totgebar / Von Bittersüssem Suizid

BETHZAIDA (NORWAY)
Line-Up: Lars Ruben Hirsch (vocals / flute), Brian III (guitar / keyboards), André Svee (guitar), Nils Arve Sandberg (bass), Terje Myhre Krabol (drums)

A very technical Black Metal act named after the supposed birthplace of the anti-Christ BETHZAIDA began life as a duo of drummer Terje Myhre Kråbøl and guitarist André Svee during October 1993.

The band had evolved early the following year with the addition of vocalist/flautist Lars Ruben Hirsch and bassist Olav Malmin and, with this line-up, BETHZAIDA cut the debut 'Dawn' demo. Although founded in Black Metal territory the group has always displayed a far keener grasp of melody than many of their counterparts and are eager to cite traditional Metal acts amongst their influences.

A second guitarist, Brian III (real name Brian Morsund) was brought into the fold before the close of 1994, just prior to the recording of second demo 'Nine World' and, in March 1995, Malmin was replaced by Nils Arve Sandberg.

The group released their debut album, 'Nine Worlds', through Seasons Of Mist later on in '95. Later added bassist Tom Wahl.

In 1996 Hirsch and Svee created the side project MIST ENTICER and were soon joined by Wahl in this endeavour. The BETHZAIDA split album 'War Vol. II' shared with ANATA included two new tracks, a rendition of a traditional folk tune and a version of ATANA's 'Under Azure Skies'.

Albums:
NINE WORLDS, Season Of Mist SOM 002 (1995)
Dawn (Part II) / Divinemant / ...And Then I Turned Towards Darkness / Frozen Wastes / Nine Worlds / The Outsider / The Tranquility Of My Last Breath / Burn, Fire For The Ancient Vampire / Forever Night / 1349

LXXVIII, Season Of Mist (1997)
The Blasphemer / Wolf's Desire / Black Winter / The Curtain Falls / No Regrets Before Death / Lengsel LXXVIII / Sumarian Rebirth / Brief Is The Flame / Et Natans Eventyr
A PRELUDE TO NINE WORLDS, Season Of Mist SOM 005 (1998)
All My Life / Decay / Dawn / Nine Worlds / Outsiders
WAR VOL. II, Season Of Mist (2000) (Split CD with ANATA)
Last Days Of Sodom / Expulsion / Fredmans Epistel Nr. 30: Drick Ur Ditt Glas / Under Azure Skies

BETRAYER (ISRAEL)
Line-Up: Yishai Swearts (vocals),

Albums:
MY TWISTED SYMPHONY, Raven Music (199-)
On The Wings Of Time / Rock Solid / Battles Within / Garden Of Memories / Dead End

BETWEEN THE FROST (SPAIN)

Albums:
INSTINCT OF SURLINESS Abstract Emotions (1998)
Immortalized Darkness / My Crystal Tower / Naked Between The Frost / Lost In The Immensity Of Time / Let Me Die / Forgotten In Ice / Morning Soul / Enjoying The Nothingness (Enjoying The Silence)

BEWITCHED (CHILE)
Line-Up: Doomicus (vocals), Ahran Evil (guitar), J.P. Stormlord (bass), Astralis Domina (keyboards), War Hammer (drums)

BEWITCHED date back to 1993. Founder members vocalist Doomicus and guitarist Ahran Evil were at first joined by guitarist Cuto, bassist Christian and drummer Snow.
BEWITCHED's second album 'Dragonflight' included a cover version of MERCYFUL FATE's 'Black Funeral'.

Albums:
DRAGONFLIGHT, Conquistador (2000)
Intro / Poetry Of The Forest / Funeral / Dragonflight / Wotan's Curse / Candles Of Doom / The Prophecy- Aquarian Revelation / The Threat Of Winter Community / Warfare / Snowfall / Dancing Upon Your Grave / Black Funeral / Souls Tears (Remix 666) /

Seven Sorrow (Hades Remix Including Trance Exorcism 666)

BEWITCHED (SWEDEN)
Line-Up: Vargher (vocals / guitar), Blackheim (guitar), Wrathyr (bass), Reaper (drums)

One of a myriad of Satanic Death Metal studio project acts put together by members of other bands on the side, BEWITCHED vocalist Vargher (real name Marcus Norman) is also a member of ANCIENT WISDOM, while guitarist Blackheim (real name Anders Nyström) is in both DIABOLICAL MASQUERADE and KATATONIA.
BEWITCHED debuted with the 1995 'Hellspell' demo. Their 1996 EP 'Encyclopedia Of Evil' is made up of covers of bands such as BLACK WIDOW's 'Sacrifice', MERCYFUL FATE's 'Come To The Sabbath', VENOM's 'Warhead', CELTIC FROST's 'Circle Of The Tyrants' and BATHORY's 'Hellcult'.

Singles/EPs:
Intro / Warhead / Sacrifice / Evil / Circle Of The Tyrants / Come To The Sabbath / Hellcult, Osmose OPCD 041/SPV 076-20642 (1996) ('Encyclopedia Of Evil' EP)

Albums:
DIABOLICAL DESECRATION, Osmose OPCD034 (1996)
Hard As Steel (Hot As Hell) / Hellcult / Born Of Flames / Deathspell / Bloodthirst / Burnin' Paradise / Holy Whore / Triumph Of Evil / Firehymn / Dressed In Blood / Blade Of The Ripper / The Witches Plague / Diabolical Desecration
PENTAGRAM PRAYER, Osmose Productions OPCD 057 (1997)
Blood On The Altar / Hallways To Hell / Demondawn / Night Of The Sinner / Satan's Claw / Hellblood / Beastchild / Cremation Of The Cross / The Night Stalker / Sacrifice To Satan / Hellcult Attack / Pentagram Prayer
AT THE GATES OF HELL, Osmose Productions (1999)
Sabbath Of Sin / Heave Is Falling / Black Mass / The Devils Daughters / At The Gates Of Hell / Let The Blood Run Red / Lucifer's Legacy / The Sinner And The Saint / Enemy Of God / Infernal Necromancy

BEYOND BELIEF (HOLLAND)
Line-Up: A.J. Van Drenth (vocals / guitar), Robbie Woning (guitar), Ronnie Van Der

Way (bass), Jacko Westendorp (drums)

Formed in 1986, BEYOND BELIEF feature two ex DEADHEAD members guitarist Robbie Woning and bassist Ronnie Van Der Way. Having released the 'Remind The Skull' demo in 1990, a further demo, 'Stranded', followed in 1992.
BEYOND BELIEF toured their native Holland with CREEPMINE, ANCIENT RITES and DEADHEAD.

Albums:
TOWARDS THE DIABOLICAL EXPERIMENT, Shark 029 RTD (1993)
Intro: Ave / Shapes Of Sorrow / Stranded / The Experiment / The Nameless / Silent Are The Holy / Fade Away / Untouched / Prophetic Countdown / Kissing In XTC / The Finishing Touch / Outro: Never
RAVE THE ABYSS, Shark 102 (1995)
Rave The Abyss / Cursed / Blood Beach / High On The Moon / The Burning Of Redlands / Crushed Divine / The Grand Enigma / Tyrants Of The Sun / Lost

BEYOND DAWN (NORWAY)
Line-Up: Tore Gjedrm (vocals / bass), Espen Ingierd (guitar), Petter Haavik (guitar), Einar Sjurso (drums), Dag Midbrod (Trombone)

BEYOND DAWN display a very original, depressive and bizarre mixture between Doom, Psychedelic and Avant Garde Rock including the novel use of a trombonist.
Original BEYOND DAWN guitarist Sindre Goksöyr left to found PILEDRIVER making way for Espen Ingierd.
After one demo tape BEYOND DAWN were able to release a four track record on Adipocere Records before later changing labels to Candlelight Records with whom they released 'Pity Love' in 1996.
Drummer Einar Sjurso guess on FLEURETY's 2000 album 'Department Of Apocalyptic Affairs'.

Singles/EPs:
Up Through The Linear Shades, Adipocere (1993) (7" single)

Albums:
LONGING FOR SCARLET DAYS, Adipocere CD AR019 (1994)
Cold / Moonwomb / Chaosphere / Clouds Swept Away The Colours
PITY LOVE, Candlelight CANDLE 012

(1996)
When Beauty Dies / The Penance / (Never A) Bygone Tendance / As The Evening Falters, The Dogs Howl / Embers Storm / Ripe As The Night / Daughter Sunday
REVELRY, Misanthropy AMAZON14CD (1998)
Love's (Only) True Defender / Tender / Resemblance / Stuck / Three Steps For The Chameleon (How To Seduce Modestly) / I Am A Drug / Breathe The Jackal / Life's Sweetest Reward / Chains / Phase To Phase
IN REVERIE, Eibon (1999)
Need / Rendezvous / Prey / Atmosphere / Confident As Hell / Naked / Phase-Juxtaposition / Chameleon
ELECTRIC SULKING MACHINE, Peaceville (2000)

BEYOND NORTH (GERMANY)

The multi-talented Michael Pelkowski wrote and recorded BEYOND NORTH's 1994 debut on his own. Pelkowksi is also the drummer of PAVOR.

Albums:
THE DARK IS MY FATHER, Imperator Grim 002 CD (1995)
Fullmonn Symphony / Blew Into The Horns Of The North / Beyond North / Inferno / The Dark Is My Father

BEYOND SERENITY (DENMARK)
Line-Up: Carsten Holm (vocals), Morten R. Jorgensen (guitar), Johnny Larsen (guitar), Anders Duus (bass), Thomas Maaetoft (drums)

Singles/EPs:
Cold / Childhood's Important / Time Turns The Key / Angel Of Revenge, Rox BSCD 9601 (1996) ('Bursting Into Leaf' EP)

THE BEZERKER (AUSTRALIA)
Line-Up: The Bezerker

The 'Reality' video was banned from British TV stations for it's violent content.

Albums:
THE BEZERKER, Earache (2000)

BHOABAN SIDHE (HOLLAND)

A Black Metal band in their early stages, and in particular their 1993 demo 'Cocoon Hides The Immortal', Dutchmen BHOABHAN SIDHE would evolve into an

58

Electronic act by 1994.
The band was in fact a duo of Aliborn and former BESTIAL SUMMONING member Conscicide Dominus Arcula.

Singles/EPs:
The New Order, Wimp (1995)

Albums:
CORPSE CRATER, Wild Rags (1996)

BI FROST (HOLLAND)
Line-Up: Guido 'Hammerheart' Heijnens (vocals), Jean Winants (guitar), Roger Hermans (guitar), Rob Wendler (bass), Sjoerd Rokx (drums)

Black Metal band BIFROST were borne out of the collapse of HORDES in 1993. Two demos, starting with 1994's 'Western Magick', and a live cassette led to a record deal with Nazgul's Eyrie Productions.
The band's debut 'Pagan Reality' soon sold out of its initial 1'500 pressing prompting recording of a second effort 'The Wildest Fire'.
However, BIFROST had split in October 1996 shortly after the album's release.
Vocalist Guido 'Hammerheart' Heijnens forged an alliance with guitarist Skuld to form CONQUERED MY FEARS and with this act undertook various support dates including to Japanese Metal band SABBAT, COUNTESS and ROTTING CHRIST among many others.
CONQUERED MY FEARS lost their original drummer and erstwhile BIFROST man Sjoerd Rokx filled the gap.
CONQUERED MY FEARS steadily began to introduce BIFROST material into their live set and eventually the decision was taken to resurrect the name.
The late 1997 version of BIFROST comprised of Heijnens, guitarists Skuld and Danny, bassist Kasper and Rokx on drums. A keyboard player was introduced for live shows.

Albums:
PAGAN REALITY, Nazgul's Eyrie Productions NEP004CD (1995)
Fimbulwinter: A Tale Of Hate / Bird Of Prey / My Ancestor, Now A Dark Woodspirit / Pagan Reality / Children Of The Black Hill / My Lady Of Winterfire / Battlefield Odinn (Father Of Victories) / Choosers Of The Slain / Lost Times, In Darkness Forgotten
THE WILDEST FIRE, Nazgul's Eyrie Productions NEP011CD (1996)

The Dark In The Past / Heathen Apotheosis / I Suffer In Silence / Blood In My Veins / Do I Decide Dreams / Beyond The Border Of Solitude / Midwinter Celebration / The Midgard Drama / Eburonic Pride / My Wicked Smile / The Wildest Fire / The Bright In The Future

BISHOP OF HEXEN (ISRAEL)
Line-Up: Balzamon (vocals), Lord Velkaarm (guitar), Dimort (keyboards), Prof. Van Helsing (drums)

Keyboard dominated Black Metal act BISHOP OF HEXEN debuted with a demo in 1996 entitled 'Ancient Hymns Of Legends And Lore'.

Albums:
ARCHIVES OF AN ENCHANTED PHILOSOPHY, Hammerheart (1997)
Crossing The Borders Between Light And Darkness / The Surreal Touch Between Steel And Flesh / Live My Spelled Emotions / Wading Through Sensuous Journeys / When A Witch Becomes A Pale Bride / Diaries Of Primeval Tragedies / To Being The Quest Towards The Noble Dark Cause / The Fascinating Installment Of Triumph

THE BLACK (ITALY)

Albums:
RELIQUORIUM, Minotauro (1989)
REFUGIUM PEGGATOTUM, Black Widowe (1994)

THE BLACK (SWEDEN)
Line-Up: Rietas (vocals / guitar / keyboards), Leviathan (bass), The Black (drums / keyboards)

A Satanic outfit formed in 1991, THE BLACK issued the 'Black Blood' demo in 1992, securing a deal with Necropolis Records.
Vocalist Rietas (real name Jon Nödtveit) is a member of DISSECTION. Drummer The Black (real name Make Pesonen) remained a member of ETERNAL DARKNESS.
Although THE BLACK released their debut album, 'The Priest Of Satan', in 1994, the earlier 'Black Blood' demo was pressed up on CD two years later and released using the same title.

Albums:
THE PRIEST OF SATAN, Necropolis NR003 (1994)

59

The Beast Of Fire / The Book Of Leviathan / Towards The Golden Dawn / The Sign Of The Evil Spirit / Lady Lilith / Black Blood / The Spirit Of Solitude / After My Prayers / The Goat Of Mendes / The Priest Of Satan / The Black Opal Eye / Whirlwinds Through The Land Of Ice
BLACK BLOOD, Necropolis NR012 (1996)
Book Of Leviathan / Lady Lilith / Towards The Golden Dawn / Black Blood / The Spirit Of Solitude / The Goat Of Mendes / The Black Opal Eye

BLACK CRUCIFIXION (FINLAND)
Line-Up: Timo Iivari (vocals), Juha Kullpi (guitar), E. Henrik Juujärvi (bass), Jari Pirinen (drums)

BLACK CRUCIFIXION, having issued 'The Promethean Gift' EP in 1993 eventually evolved into PROMETHEAN, releasing the 1997 album 'Gazing The Invisible'.

Singles/EPs:
Promethean Gift / Serpent Of Your Holy Garden / Journey Into Myself (Through A Ritual) / Flowing Downwards, Lethal Records LMCD 222 (1993) ('The Promethean Gift' EP)

BLACK FUNERAL (USA)

Solo outing from former SORATH member Michael Ford, also known as Baron Von Abaddon. BLACK FUNERAL opened proceedings with the 1994 demo 'Journeys Into Horizons' followed by a further tape 'Spells Of Darkness And Death' in 1996.
The inaugural album 'Vampyr- Throne Of The Beast' witnessed keyboard contributions from DEMONCY's Desolate Wings Of The Pagan Dawn.
Ford laid BLACK FUNERAL to rest to concentrate on other projects DARKNESS ENSHROUD, PAYCONAUT and the electronic act VALEFOR. With the latter band Ford goes under the title of Nachtotter although he has also been known as Talnagraph 108.

Albums:
VAMPYR- THRONE OF THE BEAST, Fullmoon (1996)
Ex Sanguini Draculae / The Floating Blue Witchlight / Valley Of The Shadow / Spectral Agony Of Pain And Lonliness / Vampyr- Throne Of The Heart / Spirit Of The Werewolf / Rising From A

Dishonored Grave / Of Dark And Crimson Spheres
EMPIRE OF BLOOD, Fullmoon (1997)
Vampire: The Wisdom Within, The Truth Without / Opferblut / The Land Of Phantoms / Bathory Incarnate: Goddess Of Death Arises / Der Werewolf / Leviathan: The Black Oceans Roar / Empire Of Blood / Nihilist / Lord Sathanas Returns / The Funeral Procession Descends / Journeys Into Horizons Lost
MOON OF CHARACITH, Fullmoon (1999)
Totentanz / Seduction And Devourment / Evocation In The Lunar Lodge / Rite Of Enveloping Shadows / Blood Rite- Manifestation Of Marchosias / Death Gnosis / Moon Thirst / The Vampire Born- Totentanz II / Banishing

THE BLACK LEAGUE (FINLAND)

Act founded by ex SENTENCED and IMPALED NAZARENE bassist / singer Taneli Jarva and drummer Sir Luttinen of IMPALED NAZARENE, LEGENDA and BEHERIT.
THE BLACK LEAGUE was completed by MYTHOS, IMPALED NAZARENE and LEGENDA bassist Florida and guitarists Alexi Ranta and Maike. The latter has credits with infamous Finnish Punk bands TERVEET KADET and FAFF BEY.
Ranta also busies himself with IGNIS FATUUS whilst Florida is a members of SHADOWS OVER SHADOWLAND.

Albums:
ICHOR, Spinefarm (2000)
Doomwatcher / One Colour: Black / Deep Waters / Goin' To Hell / Avalon / We Die Alone / The Everlasting Part II / Ozymandias / Blood Of The Gods / Bunker King / Winter Winds Sing / Ecce Homo! / Night On Earth

BLACK LODGE (NORWAY)
Line-Up: Vegar Hoel (vocals), Monica Pedersen (vocals), Kim G. Andersen (guitar), Preben Z. Moller D. (guitar), Halvor Larsen (bass), Frode Gundersen (drums)

A Doom Metal act with female vocals.

Albums:
COVET, Head Not Found HNF 010 (1995)
Dissonance / Mother Urge / Cube / Tower Inertia / Travesty / Mortal (1995)

BLACK MESSIAH (GERMANY)

Albums:
SCEPTRE OF BLACK KNOWLEDGE,
Last Episode 007385 2 LEP (199-)
Intro / Old Gods / Diabolic Rites / Queen
Of Darkness / Sceptre Of Black
Knowledge / Crusade Of The Blackened
/ Pagan Winter / Outro

BLACK PENTECOST (PA, USA)
Line-Up: Jerry Blase (vocals / guitar),
Ganwir (bass)

Frontman Jerry Blase, a well known
figure on the S&M scene, revealed that
the 'Funeral Winds In Paradise' album
was recorded whilst he was being
tortured by two females with beatings and
cigarette burns to achieve the desired
eerie howls. Apparently his favourite past
time is having his head jumped on by
barefoot women!
Blase also divides his time with other acts
such as EVIL GOD REVIVAL and his solo
project PRIME MINISTER ROFOCALE.

Albums:
FUNERAL WINDS IN PARADISE, Gothic
(1999)

BLACKRISE (DENMARK)

Albums:
MOONCULT, A Koffin Not Found (1997)

BLACK SHEPERD (BELGIUM)
Line-Up: Yvon Verhaegen (vocals), Igor
Plint (guitar), Michel Oluf (guitar), Patrick
Minnebier (bass), Alain Verhaegen
(drums)

A Belgian Thrash act with Black Metal
influences. Ex BLACK SHEPERD
guitarist Luc Vervelot created
CONSPIRACY OF SILENCE.

Albums:
IMMORTAL AGGRESSION, Punk Etc
(1988)
Immortal Aggression / State Of Decay /
Make Love War / Corpses / Preacher Of
Death / Trash / Another Day To Die / Kill
The Priest / Animal / Lord Of The
Darkness / I Am God / Evil Revenge

BLACKSTORM (AZ, USA)
Line-Up: Anthony Storm, J. Animal
Diamond, Michael Wright (guitar)

A symphonic outfit mixing Black Metal
with ambient overtones. Following
BLACKSTORM's debut album the band
dispensed with both corpsepaint and
guitarist Ryan Kibler. New recruit was
EXCESSIVE BLEEDING man Michael
Wright.
BLACKSTORM's 2000 album 'As Black
As Thy Candles Burn' was produced by
renowned erstwhile TESTAMENT,
CANCER, DEATH and AGENT STEEL
guitarist James Murphy.

Albums:
BLACK CIRCLE CRUSADER, Darque
(1999)
Eternal Fall / Black Circle Crusader /
Arrival Of The Winterhorde / Folklore /
Through Cold Mist / Knightgoria- The
Wizard Waltz / Knightgoria- The Wizard
Waltz II / Hammers Of Battle / The Birth
Of Darkness
AS BLACK AS THY CANDLES BURN,
Darque (2000)

BLACKWINDS (SWEDEN)

Line-Up: Lord Kraath (vocals / guitar), Zathanel (bass), Lord Alastor Mysteriis (drums)

A 1999 collaboration with strong SETHERIAL connections. Both vocalist / guitarist Lord Kraath and drummer Lord Alastor Mysteriis are SETHERIAL members whilst bassist Zathanel is a former SETHERIAL member.
ZATHANEL also has credits with MIDVINTER and SORHIN.

Singles/EPs:
The Watchers / The Black Wraiths Ascend / Share My Doom, Bloodstone Entertainment (1999) (7" single)

BLACK WITCHERY (FL, USA)

Line-Up: IMPURATH (vocals / bass), Tregenda (guitar), Vaz (drums)

BLACK WITCHERY evolved from the early 90's act IRREVERENT. By 1996 the band had retitled itself WITCHERY. A further title change occurred in 1999 as BLACK WITCHERY was adopted.
The 2000 album 'Hellstorm Of Evil Vengeance' was a shared affair with Canadian act CONQUEROR. As part of their contribution BLACK WITCHERY cut a cover of BLASPHEMY's 'Demoniac'.
BLACK WITCHERY have also contributed versions of SLAYER's 'Fight Till Death' to a Dwell Records tribute album and KREATOR's 'Tormentor' for a Fullmoon tribute affair.
Guitarist Tregenda (Steve Childers) participated in the BURNING INSIDE project in collusion with renowned ICED EARTH, DEMONS & WIZARDS, DEATH, CONTROL DENIED and INCANTATION drummer Richard Christy and fellow axeman Michael Estes from famed Black Metal merchants ACHERON.

Singles/EPs:
Summoning Of Infernal Legions, Dark Horizon DHR002 (1999) (7" single)

Albums:
HELLSTORM OF EVIL VENGEANCE, Dark Horizon DHR004 (2000) (Split album with CONQUEROR)

BLASPHEMY (CANADA)

Canadian Black Metal crew BLASPHEMY preceded their debut album with a 1989 demo 'Blood Upon

The Altar'.

Albums:
FALLEN ANGEL OF DOOM, Wild Rags (1990)
Winds Of The Black Gods / Fallen Angel Of Doom / Hording Of Evil Vengeance / Darkness Prevails / Desecration / Ritual / Weltering In Blood / Demoniac / Goddess Of Perversity / The Desolate One
GODS OF WAR, Osmose Productions (1993)
Elders Of The Apocalypse / Blood Upon The Altar / Blasphemous Attack / Gods Of War / Intro / Atomic Nuclear Desolation / Nocturnal Slayer / Emperor Of The Black Abyss / Intro / Blasphemy / Necrosadist / War Command / Empty Chalice

BLAZING ETERNITY (DENMARK)

Line-Up: Nattevogter P.T.M. (vocals), Morten Souren Lybecker (guitar), Hunger Darkenfeld (bass), Lars Korsholm (drums)

Copenhagen's BLAZING ETERNITY would bow in with the 1996 demo 'Soer Sorte Leder' and capitalized on by the 1998 session 'Der Hviler En Nat Under Sorte Virten Borge'. Previously the act had operated under the handle of ANCIENT SADNESS having issued a 1993 demo 'Tragedies'.
BLAZING ETERNITY's debut album of 2000 included guest sessions from SATURNUS members guitarist Kim Larsen and keyboard player Anders Nielsen.
Bass player Hunger Darkenfeld is an erstwhile VINTERMISKE member.

Albums:
TIMES AND UNKNOWN WATERS, Prophecy Productions (2000)
Concluding The Die Of Centuries / Fortable Horisorter / Of Times And Unknown Waters / Still Lost In The Autumn Of Eternity / (Sagnet Om) Manden Med Dew Sorte Hat / Dead Inside / Dark Summernights Of Eternal Twilight / End- Midnight

BLAZEMTH (SPAIN)

Line-Up: Volkarr, Lord Erlick, Eödar, Hissar Zui

A Spanish Black Metal act. Debuted with the 1994 demos 'Daemonium' and 'Unholycaust'.

FOR CENTURIES LEFT BEHIND,
Abstract Emotions AE001 (1995)
Marching Across The Path Of Glory / It's
Suffering Age / Kingdome Of Black
Emperor / Majesties Of War / To The
Valley Of Winds Master
FATHERLAND, Abstract Emotions
(1997)

BLESSED BE THE WOODS (ITALY)

Milan act BLESSED BE THE WOODS
was forged by erstwhile RAS ALGETHI
members. Musically the band offer Black
Metal with female vocals.
BLESSED BE THE WOODS also operate
the project band ALKAID.

Albums:
BLESSED BE THE WOODS, Alkaid
(1997)

BLODSRIT (SWEDEN)

BLODSRIT was forged as a duo of
Nazgúl and Kettil of PAGANIZER and
DEAD SUN in 1998 originally billed as
SKUGGRIKE. A demo 'The Arrival Of
Chaos' followed prior to a namechange to
BLODSRIT as the project became a solo
venture of Nazgúl.
A second session 'Dödens Sändebud' led
to a deal with the Asian label Psychic
Screams Entertainment and a split album
with Indonesian act RITUAL
ORCHESTRA.
MASSMURDER man Vampyr became
BLODSRIT's drummer in October of
1999.

Albums:
BLODSRIT, Psychic Screams
Enterainment (1999) (Split album with
RITUAL ORCHESTRA)
Shadowed Star Of Darkness / Goddess
Of Life Eternal / Blinded By Fire / Master
Of The Grey Domains / Torturing A
Feeble Priest / A Blaze In The Winternight

BLOOD AXIS (USA)
Line-Up: Michael Moynihan, Robert
Ferbrache, Annabel Lee

The debut 1994 BLOOD AXIS album
includes themes from J.S. Bach and
Prokofiev alongside texts by Nietzsche
and narrations of Charles Manson.
Driving force behind BLOOD AXIS
Michael Moynihan also has credits with
NON, SLAVE STATE and SLEEP

CHAMBER.
Albums;
IN GOSPEL OF INHUMANITY, Storm
STRM05 (1994)
The Gospel Of Inhumanity / The Voyage
(Canto I) / Eternal Soul / Between Birds
Of Prey / Herr, Nun Loss In Freude /
Reign I Forever / absinthe / Storm Of
Steel
BLOT: SACRIFICE IN SWEDEN: LIVE,
Cold Meat Industry CMI X (1998)
Sarabande Oratia / Herjafather / Secher /
Electricity / Land Of Ages / The March Of
Brian Boru / The Gospel Of Inhumanity /
eternal Soul / Between Birds Of Prey /
Reign I Forever / The Hangman And The
Papist / Storm Of Steel

BLOODBATH (SWEDEN)
Line-Up: Dan Swanö (vocals), Mikael
Akerfeldt (vocals), Blackheim (guitar),
Jonas Renske (bass)

A genuine Black Metal supergroup
project. The unholy union includes EDGE
OF SANITY's Dan Swanö, OPETH's
Mikael Akerfeldt, KATATONIA and
DIABOLICAL MASQUERADE's guitarist
Blackheim and KATATONIA / OCTOBER
TIDE bassist Jonas Renske.

Singles/EPs:
Breeding Death / Ominous Bloodvomit /
Furnace Funeral, Century Media (2000)
('Breeding Death' EP)

BLOOD COVEN (Kent, OH, USA)
Line-Up: Dann Saladin (vocals / guitar),
Dave Ingram (guitar), Jason Woolard
(bass), Brian Kerr (drums)

Ohio's BLOOD COVEN began life with ex
SIN EATER frontman Dann Saladin. By
1993 Saladin had split away from his
former act and the title BLOOD COVEN
was adopted for a new venture. The band
contributed a track 'Statuary' to the
'Midnight Offerings II' compilation album.
Guitarist Dave Ingram was drafted and a
1995 demo 'Dark Harmonies' followed.
BLOOD COVEN at this juncture also
comprised of bassist Chuck Smith and
drummer Andy Wiper. A further tape
emerged in 1997 'Serenades For The
Bleeding'.
Both Smith and Wiper bailed out of the
project. Undaunted BLOOD COVEN
enlisted former AD NAUSEUM drummer
Brian Kerr and set about gigging minus a
bassist. However, by 1996 ex HATE

THEORY four stringer Jason Woolard had been enrolled.

In their time BLOOD COVEN have guested for MERCYFUL FATE, OVERKILL and MORBID ANGEL amongst others.

Singles/EPs:
A Tribute To Warriors Lost, Blood Coven (1997) (7" single)

Albums:
ASHES OF AN AUTUMN BURNING, Bloodfiend (1998)
Ashes Of An Autumn Burning / The medium / The Burning Season / Firm Grip Of Darkness / To Reach Serenity / Kiss Of Akhkharu / The True Name Of God

THE BLOOD DIVINE (UK)
Line-Up: Darren White (vocals), Paul Ryan (guitar), Paul Allander (guitar), Benjamin Ryan (keyboards), Was Sarginson (drums)

Colchester's THE BLOOD DIVINE came together in late 1995 as a vehicle for ex ANATHEMA vocalist Darren White and features ex CRADLE OF FILTH guitarists Paul Allander and Paul Ryan along with keyboard player Benjamin Ryan. Drummer Was Sarginson also plies his trade with DECEMBER MOON.

In support of the 'Awaken' album dates opening for labelmates MY DYING BRIDE were undertaken in Europe prior to a batch of British headliners. Further forays into Europe saw BLOOD DIVINE appearing at many festivals, including the 'Rock In Madrid' show alongside BRUCE DICKINSON and NAPALM DEATH.

THE BLOOD DIVINE gave two cover tracks to Peaceville Records 1998 tenth anniversary compilation 'X' in JOY DIVISION's 'Love Will Tear Us Apart' and THE OSMONDS 'Crazy Horses'.

Sarginson enjoyed a brief spell as drummer for CRADLE OF FILTH. Allander quit to create a new act LILLITH with former ENTWINED keyboard player Mark Royce and ex CENOBITE vocalist / guitarist Mark Giltrow. The band adopted a new name of PRIMARY SLAVE but Allander was re-enlisted into the ranks of CRADLE OF FILTH in late 1999.

Benjamin Ryan founded CROWFOOT with form WITCHFINDER GENERAL, BAJJON and LIONSHEART bassist Zakk Bajjon. This band, with the addition of ex CRADLE OF FILTH guitarist Rishi Mehta and former INCARCERATED drummer

Mark Cooper became RAINMAKER 888.

Singles/EPs:
And With The Day's Dying Light, Peaceville (1996)

Albums:
AWAKEN, Peaceville CDVILE 62 (1996)
So Serene / Moonlight Adorns / Visions (Of A Post Apocalyptic World) Part One / Wilderness / These Deepest Feelings / Aureole / Oceans Rise / Artemis / In Crimson Dreams / Heart Of Ebony / Warm Summer Rain
MYSTICA, Peaceville (1997)
Mystica / As Rapture Fades / Visions In Blue / The Passion Reigns / Leaving Me Helpless / Visions Part II: Event Horizon / I Believe / Enhanced By Your Touch / Sensual Ecstasy / Fear Of a Lonely World / Prayer

BLOODHAMMER (FINLAND)

BLOODHAMMER would originally issue their 'Ancient Kings' album in 10" vinyl format. It was reissued on CD adding a further four tracks. The band also planned a split 12" release in alliance with INCRIMINATED.

Albums:
ANCIENT KINGS, Northern Heritage NH007 (2000)
Intro / Masters Of Alcohol / I'm Your Hell / Hellborn Fire / Destruction / Venom For God / Total End / Holocaust In Heaven / Outro / In Cold Blood / Satan Behind My Face / Suffering Is Eternal / Hellborn Fire

BLOOD OF CHRIST (CANADA)
Line-Up: Greg Idasz (vocals / bass), Jeff Longo (guitar), Jay Longo (drums)

Canadian Black Metal act BLOOD OF CHRIST announced their arrival with the 1994 demo 'Frozen Dreams'. A further effort 'Lonely Flowers Of Autumn' followed.

Albums:
A DREAM TO REMEMBER, Pulverizer (1997)
Moonlight Eclipse / Lonely Winter Morning / The Last Shrine / Dreams Of Winter Landscapes / As The Roses Wither / Nocturnal Desire / Act IX… The Ancient Battles / Winter Thee… A Forest Of Tragedy / Whispers From The Forest

BLOODSHED DIVINE (LA, USA)

One man project of multi instrumentalist Troy LeBlanc. BLOODSHED DIVINE's inaugural 1999 demo 'To The Ancient Dawn' would be reissued as 'Summoned To The Ancient Dawn' by Largactyl Records.

Albums:
SUMMONED TO THE ANCIENT DAWN, Largactyl (2000)

BLOODSTAINED DUSK (AL, USA)
Line-Up: Dageth (vocals / guitar / keyboards), Agares (guitar), Oroan (bass), Profana (drums)

Black Metal purveyors BLOODSTAINED DUSK were assembled in 1997. Their initial demo 'The Legions Reign Over Christondom' was later pressed up onto CD by Red Stream Records. Early members guitarist Sacrament and keyboard player Sekhem would quit prior to the debut album.

Singles/EPs:
The Legions Reign Over Christondom, Red Stream (1999)

Albums:
DIRGE OF DEATH'S SILENCE, Baphomet (2000)
Moon Behind The Storm / Bringer Of Everlasting Damnation / Renounce The Dawn / The Infernal Prairie / Vastland Of The Empire Lost / Sanguinas Path- The Blood I Follow / Funeral Of Lamentation

BLOOD STORM (PA, USA)

BLOOD STORM is the act of ABSU touring member Mezzadurus (real name Chris Gamble). The vocalist / bassist had previously fronted GOREAPHOBIA, an act that released a solitary EP on Relapse Records.
BLOOD STORM emerged with a brace of demos with 1995's 'Iron Flames Of Battle' and the following year's 'Death By The Storm Wizard'. Following the release of the debut album 'Atlantean Wardragon' on French label Osmose Productions both these earlier recordings would be reissued on CD in 1998. Drummer Telco Coraxo would session on the 1998 KRIEG album 'Rise Of The Imperial Hordes'.
BLOOD STORM put on an impressive old school black metal performance at the

1997 Milwaukee Metalfest.

Singles/EPs:
An Attack Of Sonic Torment (Live), Hellframe (1999) (7" single)

Albums:
THE ATLANTEAN WARDRAGON, Cacophonous (1997)
Spell Of The Burning Wind / All Of One Doom / Iron Flames Of Battles / The Atlantean Wardragon / Destroyer / Yuggothian Slayers / Steel Burning Thunder
DEATH BY THE STORMWIZARD, Nightfall (1998)
PESTILENCE FROM THE DRAGON STAR, Soul Sold (1999)

BLOODTHORN (NORWAY)
Line-up: Krell (vocals / guitar), Tom (guitar), Kai Nergaard (guitar), Knarr (drums)

BLOODTHORN is the result of a partnership between ex MANES guitarist Tom and former MORTUIS guitarist Krell. BLOODTHORN launched themselves with the 'Natteskyggen' demo. BLOODTHORN elaborated upon their trademark sound with the addition of female vocals but as the music got more adventurous internal frictions resulted. The band effectively imploded and surviving members took BLOODTHORN back in the direction of a stripped down Black Metal approach.
The 2000 split album with label mates AND OCEANS included covers of AND OCEANS and G.G.F.H. songs.
Both Krell and Knarr would aid a resurrected MANES in the late 90's. Guitarist Kai Nergaard issued a 2000 album 'Wasteland Serenades' from his side project band GRIFFIN.

Albums:
IN THE SHADOW OF YOUR BLACK WINGS, Seasons Of Mist SOM006 CD (1997)
The Embodied Core Of Darkness / Breeding The Evil Inside / March To War / Scarred Lands / Nightshadow / Clouds Of Sadness / ... With A Bloodstained Axe
ONWARDS TO BATTLE, Seasons Of Mist (1999)
As One In Darkness / ...Of Aeons To Come / Death To King / Dead Silence / The Day Of Reckoning / Sounds Of Death / Beneath The Iron Sceptre / The Brighter The Light, The Darker The

Shadow
WAR VOL. 1, Seasons Of Mist (2000)
(Split CD with AND OCEANS)
Spite / The End Offensive / Dead Men
Don't Rape / Kärsinyksien Vaa Leat
Kädet

BLO-TORCH (HOLLAND)
Line-Up: Michel (vocals), Hassan (guitar),
Marvin Vriesde (guitar), Sander (bass),
Pascal (drums)

Albums:
BLO-TORCH, Wicked World (1999)
Spanish Sun / Mount Ygman / King Of
Karnage / In Black Sky / Panzerstorm /
Quatrain / Seen To Be The Enemy /
March Of The Worm / Bloodstains

BLUT AUS NORD (FRANCE)

Previously known as VLAD, under which
title the band released two demos. BLUT
AUS NORD started as a one man project
by a musician called Vinsdal. After the
debut album, which saw bass contributed
by Ogat, bassist Ira Aeterna came into
the band and, together, they produced
the second album 'Memoria Ventusta I'.
Both musicians also worked on the
CHILDREN OF MAANI and THE EYE
projects.

Albums:
ULTIMA THULE, Impure Creations
(1996)
The Son Of Hoarfrost / The Plain Of Ida
/ From Hlidskjalf / My Prayer Beyond
Ginnungagap / Till I Perceive Bifrost / On
The Way To Vigrid / Rig Sthula / The
Last Journey Of Ringhorn
**MEMORIAVETUSTA - FATHERS OF
THE ICY AGE**, Impure Creations IRC 005
(1996)
Slaughterday (The Heathen Blood Of
Ours) / On The Path Of Wolf...Towards
Dwarfhill / Sons Of Whisdom, Master Of
Elements / The Forsaken Voices Of The
Gosthwood's Shadowy Realm / The
Territory Of The Witches / Guardians Of
The Dark Lake / Day Of Revenge (The
Impure Blood Of Theirs) / Fathers Of
The Icy Age

BONEWIRE (UK)

Initially known as INCARCERATED,
BONEWIRE's debut album was produced
by LIONSHEART bassist Zakk Bajjon.

Albums:
THROWN INTO MOTION, Cacophonous
NIHIL 3CD(1995)
Drowning Stain / Opium / Hollow /
Beneath The Sun / Shed This Skin / As
Far As The Eye / Forgive Me / Tides /
Awake

BOOK OF WISDOM (ITALY)

Albums:
JAEGERSKREUTZ, Nature And Art
(1995)
CATACOMBS, Nature And Art NACD 201
(1995)
Wir Vergehn' Wie Rauch In Starken
Wind / Parentatio / Soul Extinguished /
Estampie / Gia Ebbi Liberate / Crypt /
Acheron

BORGNAKER (SWEDEN)
Line-Up: Garm (vocals), Infernus (guitar),
Oystan G. Brun, Ivar Bjornson, Grim
(drums)

BORGNAKER is made up of members of
various Death Metal acts including Ivar
Bjornson of ENSLAVED, Grim of
IMMORTAL / GORGOROTH, Oystein G.
Brun of MOLESTED, Infernus of
GORGOROTH and ULVER's Chris.
BORGNAKER undertook a European
tour in September of 1997 alongside
HECATE THRONED, ROTTING CHRIST
and OLD MAN'S CHILD. All did not run
smoothly however as vocalist Garm
unexpectedly withdrew his services on
the eve of the tour. Borgnaker rapidly
supplanted Garm with erstwhile VED
BUENS ENDE and ARCTURUS man
Ilder at the same juncture bolstering their
live sound with a second guitarist Jens.
BORKNAGER put in a tour of America
during 1999 as part of a package bill
including EMPEROR, WITCHERY,
PECCATUM and DIVINE EMPIRE. This
was despite the band being an
understrength trio of Brun, bassist /
vocalist Simen Hastnaes (known as
I.C.S. Vortex) and guitarist Jens Ryland.
Grim had committed suicide shortly
before and bassist Kai K. Lee had quit.
BORKNAGER quickly recruited Lars
Solefald on keyboards and guest
drummer Nick Barker of CRADLE OF
FILTH and DIMMU BORGIR.
The 2000 album 'Quintessence',
produced by HYPOCRISY's Peter
Tägtgren, was recorded with fresh
drummer Asgeir Mickelson of Progressive
Rock act SPIRAL ARCHITECT and

ANESTHESIA. However, the band had to pull out of a projected tour with MAYHEM after Hastnaes, who had been a part time member of DIMMU BORGIR under his pseudonym of I.C.S. Vortex on bass guitar, decided to concentrate solely on that act.
Mickelson would join ENSLAVEMENT OF BEAUTY in late 2000.

Albums:
BORGNAKER, Malicious MR012 (1996)
Vintervredets Sjelesagn / Tanker Mot Tind (Kvelding) / Svartskogs Gilde / Ved Steingard / Krigsstev / Dauden / Grimskalle Trell / Nord Naagauk / Fandens Allheim / Tanker Mot Tind (Gryning)
THE OLDEN DOMAIN, Century Media 77175-2 (1997)
The Eye Of Oden / The Winterway / Om Hundrede Aar Er Alting Glemt / A Tale Of Pagan Tongue / To Mount And Rove / Grimland Domain / Ascension To Our Fathers / The Dawn Of The End
THE ARCHAIC COURSE, Century Media 7936-2 (1998)
Oceans Rise / Universal / Witching Hour / The Black Token / Nocturnal Vision / Ad Noctum / Winter Millenium / Fields Of Long Gone Presence
QUINTESSENCE, Century Media 77289-2 (2000)
The Rivalry Of Phantoms / The Presence Is Ominous / The Ruins Of Future / Colossus / Inner Landscape / Invincible / Icon Dreams / Genesis Torn / Embers / Revolt

BRANDPEST (DENMARK)
Vrykolatious (vocals), Diabolos (guitar), Hr. Alfast (bass), Sorgh (drums)

BRANDPEST are fronted by Vrykolatious, also singer for MALA FIDE. The band is in fact comprised of all the members of APOLLYON
The single was limited to 333 copies of which 111 were transparent vinyl.

Singles/.EPs:
Monstrum Marinum (Kraken) / Sagen Om Chresten Pedersen, Horror HOR002 (1998) ('I Fanderns Vold Og Magt' 7" single)

BRISEN (ITALY)
Line-Up: Elymas (vocals / bass), Unborn (guitar), Arymon (drums)

A Black Metal trio, BRISEN's 'Shade Of

Soul' album was made up of tracks from their 1993 'Holocaust Sky' demo with newer tracks. The band was previously known as DUNGEON.

Albums:
SHADE OF SOUL, Holocaust MS 006 (1995)
Hills Of Thunder / Thoughts On The Wind / Earth (Without God With Us) / Sea Of Darkness (Brisen Sleep) / Tree Of Agony / Nema / Only The Silence Around Me / Evil Power / Holocaust Sky / The Flame Of Hate / From A Mystic Land

BUNDESWEHRA (POLAND)

Polish Black Metal band BUNDESWEHRA had their 'Kings Return' demo pressed onto vinyl for a shared 12" single with Swiss act NERGAL.

Singles/EPs:
Kings Return, Warmaster (1993) (Split 12" single with NERGAL)

BURIAL MOUND (FINLAND)
Line-Up: T.S. Raven (vocals), Orth (guitar), Bone Collector (bass), Mordja (drums)

BURIAL MOUND was originally titled UTGARD issuing a brace of demos in 1995's 'Northern Glory' and 1997's 'Nightly Verses'. The band is led by the Sääksinieni brothers, more commonly known as T.S. Raven and Orth.

Singles/EPs:
Skinless Ones / Horror, Arte De Occulta Productions (1998) (7" single)

BURIED BENEATH (NY, USA)

BURIED BENEATH would issue a barrage of demos upfront of the debut album 'The Last Rays Of The Moon'. Their first session 'Creed Of The Unholy Spirit' emerged in 1992. 'Vivisect The Virgin Matu' followed topped by 1994's 'And This Too Shall Pass Away'.
The band would evolve into NIGHT CONQUERS DAY.

Albums:
THE LAST RAYS OF THE MOON, Dark Trinity (1997)
Reveal The Legacy / A Fate Worse Than Death / Remember Salem / Make Them Die Slowly / Wallowing In Misery /

Forgotten Not The Natural Splendour / Gothic Sorrow / Into A Depressive Shade Of Crimson / Spectrum Of Infinity / In Fields Of Green I Wander…

BURIED DREAMS (MEXICO)
Line-Up: Erich Olguín (vocals), Antonio De Yta (guitar), Ndua Valdespino (guitar), Ezequiel Mendoza (bass), Ivan Sartos (keyboards), Oscar Doniz (drums)

Albums:
BEYOND YOUR MIND, Oz Productions (1997)
The Sword And The Cross / Black Dragon / Reflexions Of The Light / The Battle / Beyond Your Mind / Limits Of Fantasy / Looking Through The Fire / Irony / Moxtla / Her Beauty
PERCEPTIONS, Oz Productions (2000)
Illlhamiqui / The Riddle / The Mind's Subconscious / At The End / Cosmic Prophecies / 360 / Perceptions / God's Of Fire / Buried Dreams

BURNING INSIDE (USA)
Line-Up: Jamie Prim (vocals / bass), Steve Childers (guitar), Michael Estes (guitar), Richard Christy (drums)

Studio Metal project centred on renowned ICED EARTH, DEMONS & WIZARDS, DEATH, CONTROL DENIED and INCANTATION drummer Richard Christy. Guitarist Steve Childers is a member of BLACK WITCHERY whilst his fellow axeman Michael Estes is from Black Metal merchants ACHERON.
The 2000 debut album 'The Eve Of The Entities' was released on the Polish label Still Dead Productions.

Albums:
THE EVE OF THE ENTITIES, Still Dead Productions (2000)
Words Of Wyndhym / The Eve Of The Entities / My Own / The Unknown / Masque / Engulfed In Flames / The Valley Of Unrest / Blood To All That Exist / Chapels Of Youth / Drained Of Essence / Everlasting Sleep

BURZUM (NORWAY)

The infamous Norwegian Black Metal band BURZUM formed in mid-1987 under the original title of URAK-HAI. In the early days the group was steeped in Tolkein lore with the names URAK-HAI, Grisnackh and BURZUM ('Darkness') all lifted from Orc titles and languages.

The band split in 1990 with band mentor Count Grisnackh (real name Varg Vikernes) formed SATANEL with IMMORTAL members Demonaz and Abbath. Grisnackh also dabbled in a Death Metal side project OLD FUNERAL. SATANEL disintegrated in 1991 with Grisnackh resurrecting URAK-HAI under the new name of BURZUM. Essentially a solo project BURZUM did feature EMPEROR guitarist Samoth on the 'Aske' mini album released in 1992.
Grisnackh was implicated in a number of church burnings along with other members of the Norwegian Black Metal scene. Count Grisnackh murdered MAYHEM vocalist Euronymous (real name Øystein Aarseth) on August 9th 1993. Before his arrest Grisnackh, when asked of Euryonymous's death, offered to "dance and piss on his grave"! Charged with first-degree murder Grisnackh was given a life sentence of 21 years. BURZUM's fourth album 'Hvis Lyset Tar Oss' ('If The Light Take Us') was completed just prior to the murder.
Grisnackh once more provoked headlines in early 1997 when a T-shirt he had designed whilst in jail for BURZUM caused outrage and was banned. Featuring the SS death's head logo on the chest and the slogan 'Support your local Einsatzkommando' Grisnackh proved his philosophies could still make an impression from the prison cell.
Grisnackh completed work on the 'Daudi Baldrs' (Death of Balder) album in 1997, the music, being a conceptual piece based around the Norse God Balder, son of Odin and Frigga, the deity of innocence and light, recorded on the keyboards he is allowed to keep in his cell.
Somewhat disturbingly the album cover featured Viking warriors, one in a cloak bearing the distinctive insignia of the Scandinavian SS division 'Wiking' and another cradling both a baby and sword.
Grisnackh's anti-hero status was partly revealed when his mother, Lena Bore, was jailed for helping to finance an attempt by the right wing organization Einsatzgrupe to spring her son from jail. The intended destination for BURZUM's leader was South Africa.
A BURZUM tribute album was released in 2000 on the Cymophane label featuring the likes of STARCHAMBER, EWIGKEIT, NOKTURNAL MORTEM and SCHIZOID. Vikernes' early OLD FUNERAL tapes would be released in 1999 by Hammerheart Records.

Singles/EPs:
Aske / Stemmen Fra Taarnet / Dominus
Sathanas / A Lost Forgotten Spirit, DSP
Anti Mosh 005 (1993)

Albums:
BURZUM, DSP Anti Mosh 002 (1993)
Feeble Screams From Forests Unknown
/ Ea, Lord Of The Deeps / Black Spell Of
Destruction / Channeling The Power Of
Souls Into A New God / War / The
Crying Orc / A Lost Forgotten Sad Spirit /
My Journey To The Stars / Dungeons Of
Darkness
HVIS LYSET TAR OSS, Misanthropy
AMAZON 001 (1994)
Det Som En Gang Var / Hvis Lyset Tar
Oss / Inn I Slottet Fra Droemmen /
Tomhet
DET SOM EN GANG VAR, Misanthropy
AMAZON 002 (1994)
Den Onde Kysten / Key To The Gate / En
Ring Til Aa Herske / Lost Wisdom / Han
Som Reiste / Naar Himmelen Klarner /
Snu Mikrokosmos Tegn / Svarte Troner
FILOSOFEM, Misanthropy AMAZON 009
(1996)
Dunkelheit (Darkness) / Jesus Tod /
Erblickte Die Töchter Des Fermaments /
Gebrechlichkeit (Decrepitude) /
Rundgang Um Die Tranzendentale
Saule Der Singularitat / Gebrechlichkeit
II (Decrepitude Part Two)
DAUDI BALDRS, Misanthropy AMAZON
013 (1997)
Daudi Baldrs / Hermodr A Helferd /
Balferd Baldrs / I Heimr Heijar / Illa
Tidandi / Moti Ragnarokum
HLIDSKJALF, Misanthropy AMAZON
021 (1999)
Tuistos Herz / Der Tod Wuotans /
Ansuegardaraitivo / Die Liebe Nerus /
Das Einsame Trauern Von Frijo / Die
Kraft des Mitgetuhls / Frijos Goldene
Tranen / Der Weinende Hadnar

CALVARY (ITALY)
Line-Up: Mauro Pirino (vocals), Chris Scarponi (guitar), Ignis Sechi (guitar), Wally Garay (bass), Alex Landis (drums)

An Italian Black Metal act. CALVARY first hit the scene with their 'And You Die!' demo followed by the 'In Solitude' session. Various members also operate the equally black TEARS OF CHRIST side project.

Albums:
ACROSS THE RIVER OF LIFE, Lollypop Dream 001 (1995)
Thy Fading Throne / From The Forest Of My Deepest Thoughts / Path To The Fiery Stars / Answer For Yourself / Across The River Of Life

CALVARY DEATH (BRAZIL)

Albums:
JESUS INTENSE WEEPING, Cogumelo CG017 (1999)
Sacred With Blessed / Penetrating In The Eternal Frost / Scum / The Fall Of Lucifer / I'm Spring / Reborn From Hell / Spiritual Suffocation / Predicting The Death / Batismode Fogo / Jesus Intense Weeping / Suffering / Immortal Sinbols / Cursed Be / Gritos Da Baca Do Inferno / Santuário Da Eterna Dor

CANDLE SERENADE (PORTUGAL)
Line-Up: Stregoyck (vocals / guitar), Belfegor (guitar), Nihasa (bass), Demogorgon (keyboards), Vrolok (drums)

Portuguese Black Metal band CANDLE SERENADE employ female vocals. The band debuted with the 1994 demo 'Tales From Walpurgis'.

Albums:
NOSFERATU'S PASSION, Guardians Of Metal (1995)
Overture / Balakian Rider / Chama Iberica / Celtic Lir's Son (Sab Grin's Legend) / Interlude For Gothic Kings / Spell Of Carpathian Winter / Transylvanic Mistress / Last Vampire Dance (Finale)

CARDINAL SIN (SWEDEN)
Line-Up: Dan Ola Persson (vocals), Magnus Andersson (guitar), John Zweetslot (guitar), Alex Losbäck (bass), Jocke Göthberg (drums)

CARDINAL SIN, whose musicians openly state to be rooted in 80's Metal, boast ex MARDUK members guitarist Magnus 'Devo' Andersson and drummer Jocke 'Grave' Göthberg. Guitarist John Zweetslot was previously with DISSECTION.
Following this line up's recording of the 'Spiteful Intent' EP the rhythm section was completed with the addition of bassist Alex Losbäck and a new vocalist was added in the form of Dan Ola Persson.
Göthberg created DARKIFIED. Zweetslot is now in DECAMERON while Andersson now fronts OVERFLASH.

Singles/EPs:
Spiteful Intent / Probe With A Quest / The Cardinal Sin / Language Of Sorrow, Wrong Again WAR 010 CD (1996) ('Spiteful Intents' EP)

CARDINAL SIN (UK)

Singles/EPs:
Spiteful Intents / Probe With A Quest / The Cardinal Sin / Language Of Sorrow, (1996) ('Spiteful Intent' EP)

Albums:
BLACK HORIZON, Cosh CSCD1 (1994)

CARNAL FORGE (SWEDEN)
Line-Up: Jonas Kjellgren (vocals), Johan Magnusson (guitar), Jari Kuusisto (guitar), Petri Kuusisto (bass), Stefan Westerberg (drums)

The founding line up of CARNAL FORGE comprised of DELLAMORTE man Jonas Kjellgren, drummer Stefan Westerberg of IN THY DREAMS and STEEL ATTACK personnel guitarist Jari Kuusisto and bassist Dennis Vestman. Following the debut album 'Who's Gonna Burn' Vestman departed to be replaced by another IN THY DREAMS man Petri Kuusisto.
Vocalist Jonas Kjellgren was guitarist with CENTINEX between 1999 and September 2000.

Albums:
WHO'S GONNA BURN, Wrong Again (1998)
Who's Gonna Burn / Sweet Bride / Twisted / Godzilla Is Coming Thru' / The Other Side / Part Animal- Part Machine / Born Too Late / Evilizer / Moggotman / Confuzzed

FIREDEMON, Century Media (2000)
Too Much Hell Ain't Enough For Me /
Covered With Fire (I'm Hell) / I Smell
Like Death (Son Of A Bastard) / Chained
/ Defacer / Pull The Trigger /
Uncontrollable / Firedemon / Cure Of
Blasphemy / Headfucker / The Torture
Will Never Stop / A Revel In Violence

CARPATHIAN FOREST (NORWAY)
Line-Up: R. Nattefrost (vocals / guitar),
Nordavind (guitar), Thchort (bass), A.
Kobro (drums)

CARPATHIAN FOREST comprise of
Nordavind and Nattefrost assisted by
EMPEROR bassist Tchort and IN THE
WOODS drummer A. Kobro. Nordavind
quit the band previous to the release of
the 2000 album 'Strange Old Brew'.
Nattefrost ('Vrangsinn') also operates
WORLD DESTROYER.

Singles/EPs:
In These Trees Are My Gallows, (1993)
(7" single)
He's Turning Blue / Ghoul, (199-) (7"
single)

Albums:
**THROUGH CHASM, CAVES AND
TITAN WOODS**, Avantgarde AVO11
(1995)
The Pale Mist Hovers Towards The
Mighty Shores / The Eclipse: The Raven
/ When Thousand Moon Have Circled /
Journey Through The Cold Moors Of
Svarttjern
BLOODLUST AND PERVERSION, NYX
(1997)
Through The Black Veil Of Burgo Pas /
Bloodlust And Perversion / Return Of
The Freezing Winds / The Woods Of
Wallachia / Wings Over The Mountain Of
Sighisoora / Journey Through The Cold
Moors Of Svarttjern / The Eclipse: The
Raven / The Last Sigh Of Nostalgia /
Carpathian Forest / Call From The
Grave / Return Of The Freezing Winds /
In The Circle Of Ravens / Warhead
BLACK   SHINING   LEATHER,
Avantgarde (1998)
Black Shining Leather / The Swordsmen
/ Death Triumphant / Sadomasochistic /
Lupus / Pierced Genitalia / In Silence I
Observe / Lunar Nights / Third Attempt /
The Northern Hemisphere / A Forest
STRANGE OLD BREW, Avantgarde
(2000)
Damnation Chant / Bloodcleansing /
March Of The Slave / Martur: Sacrificium

/ Thanatology / The Suicide Song / House
Of The Whipchord / Cloak Of Midnight /
Return Of The Freezing Winds / There
From Nekromantik / The Good Old
Enema Treatment / He's Turning Blue

CARPATHIAN FULLMOON
(NORWAY)
Line-Up: Henrik Petersson (vocals /
drums), Jorgan Hansen (guitar), Endre
Begby (guitar), Jon F. Bakker (keyboards)

Previously known as PENDULUM in
1991 with a line up of guitarist Henrik
Hansen, vocalist guitarist Geir, bassist
Lars and drummer Henrik Peterrsson.
In 1992 Geir departed leaving Peterrsson
to take over lead vocals. This line-up
recorded the demo 'Hecate' which
included a cover of BATHORY's 'Call
From The Grave'. Signed to American
label After World Records to release the
single 'Caedes Sacrilegae / Ketzerblut'.
At the close of the year a name change to
CARPATHIAN FULLMOON was decided.
The previous single was released in
Europe by Adipocere Records in 1993.
Added ex BALVAZ keyboard player Jon
Frederick and ex ABYSMAL second
guitarist Endre Begby.

Albums:
SERENADES IN BLOOD MINOR,
Avantgarde AV006 (1995)
Moonrise / Caedse Sacrilegae / De
Prestigiis Daemoneum 1563 / Luna
Garden / Sara Ellen / Mena Glade /
Serenade In Blood Minor / The Ancient
Of Days / Ggal Hannanh / Dawn

CARPE TENEBRUM
(AUSTRALIA / NORWAY)
Line-Up: Astennu (guitar), Nagash

Project album conceived by guitarist
Astennu of LORD KAOS and DIMMU
BORGIR and COVENANT man Nagash.
Astennu had relocated from Australia to
Norway following LORD KAOS' album
'Thorns Of Impurity'. He was eventually to
join DIMMU BORGIR for their 'Spiritual
Black Dimensions' album.
By 2000 Astennu was sacked from
DIMMU BORGIR and Nagash had left of
his own volition to concentrate on the
renamed KOVENANT renaming himself
Lex Icon.

Albums:
MAJESTIC NOTHINGNESS, Head Not
Found (1997)

Temptress Luna / Requiem Spell / Velvet Claws / Drain The Labyrinth / Perpetual Dancer / Sullen Becometh / Blood Dance **MIRRORED HATE PAINTING**, Hammerheart (1999) The Abyss Mystic Haze / Lured Like You Thought / The Painting / Mirrored In Scary Skies / And Fewer / Ludus / Void Dress / Dreaded Chaotic Reign

CARPHARNAUM

Albums:
REALITY ONLY FANTASIZED, Carphanaum (1997) Eternal Descent / Night Terror / Sinister Perceptions / Sightless / Drawn In Misery / Journey Beyond / Delusional Imprisonment / Soul Dissolved

CASKET (GERMANY)
Line-up: Jörg Weber (vocals / guitar), Karin Trapp (vocals), Jürgen Bischoff (guitar), Marc Fischer (bass), Tobias Demel (keyboards), Steffan Klein (drums)

CASKET were created in 1992 issuing their first demo recordings 'Voices From Beyond', the following year. A further cassette, '...But Death Comes Soon', followed in 1994 as CASKET added secondary female vocals from Karin Trapp and performed shows opening for PYOGENESIS and PANDEMONIUM.

Albums:
EMOTIONS... DREAMS OR REALITY, Serenades (1997) Way To Happiness / Emotions... / Black Mountain / Confessions / ... Dream Or Reality / Life-Elixir / Near Heaven **TOMORROW**, Serenades SR013 (1997) A Piece Of Love / Suicide / Questions Of Life / Secrets / Last Days / No More / Feel The Fire / Tomorrow/ Tears Of Sorrow

CASTRUM (CROATIA)
Line-Up: Morsus Sordahl (vocals), Insanus (guitar / keyboards), Dirgloch (guitar), Fra. Mortes Amaltha (bass)

Not to be confused with the contemporary Ukrainian Death Metal act of the same title. The original drummer for CASTRUM, Set, would decamp after the demo 'Nocturnal Eden Behind Serpents Eyes'. Both guitarists Insanus and Dirgloch are active members of GORTHAUR'S WRATH.
CASTRUM members united with musicians from ASHES YOU LEAVE to

forge NELDORETH in 2000.

Albums:
BLACK SILHOUETTES ENFOLDED IN SUNRISE, Folter (199-) Weeping Inside Plagued Mirrors- Burial Of Ashen Bride / A Symphony In Moonlight And Nightmare / Veiled With Threats One Age Before / Infernal Howling Through Pathless Silence / Black Silhouettes Enfolded In Sunrise / Tears Of Piano / On The Wings Of Dark Angel / Beyond The Mountains Of Frozen Spell / Obscurity Within Funeral Moon / For Those Wistful Moments In The Mist **IN THE HORIZONS OF THE DYING THEATRE**, Folter (2000)

CATAMENIA (FINLAND)
Line-Up: Mika Tönning (vocals), Riku Hopeakoski (guitar), Sampo Ukkola (guitar), Heidi Riihinen (keyboards), Timo Lehtinen (bass), Toni Tervo (drums)

A Finnish Black/Death Metal sextet from Oulu, CATAMENIA opened their account in early 1998 with the release of the debut album, 'Halls Of Frozen North', through Massacre.
Produced by Gerhard Magin, the band had been signed on the strength of their 'Winds' demo of 1995. Vocalist Mike Tönning guested as lead vocalist for fellow Finns DAWN OF RELIC on their debut 'One Night In Carcosa' album.

Albums:
HALLS OF FROZEN NORTH, Massacre MAS CD0153 (1998) Dreams Of Winterland / Into Infernal / Freezing Winds Of North / Enchanting Woods / Halls Of Frozen North / Forest Enthroned / Awake In Dark / Song Of The Nightbird / Icy Tears Of Eternity / Burning Aura / Child Of Sunset / Land Of The Autumn Winds / Pimea Yo / Outro **MORNING CRIMSON**, (1999) **ETERNAL WINTER'S PROPHECY**, Massacre MAS CD0258 (2000) Gates Of Anubis / Soror Mystica / Blackmansions / Kingdom Of Legions / Half Moons, Half Centuries / Forever Night / Dawn Of The Chosen World / Eternal Winter's Prophecy / In The Void / The Darkening Sun / In The Capricorns Cradle

CATHOLICON (Baton Rouge, LA, USA)
Line-Up: I.N.R.I. (vocals), Sovereign V (guitar), Patrick Conlan (bass), Blasphyre (keyboards), Rekcilyssup (drums)

Black Metal act CATHOLICON display strong Death Metal tendencies. The band bowed in with the 1994 demo 'Children Of The Lost Generation' followed up by the 'Redemption' tape of 1996.

The original line up included guitarist Vrykoulak (later to retitle himself Sovereign V) and keyboard player Troy Thomas. After the inaugural demo Thomas decamped. Vocalist I.N.R.I. added backing vocals to the 'Redemption' sessions before being asked to join full time. Bass in the studio was supplied by Gnosis (Jonathon Joubert) of DESPONDANCY. Erstwhile MISANTHROPY four stringer Patrick Conlan was later recruited.

CATHOLICON operated with second guitarist Forrest for a while. With his departure Gnosis stepped in yet again prior to founder member Troy Thomas returning to the fold.

Drummer Rekcilyssup also operates a side project PECKERNUT whilst Blasphyre bides his time with THE ABSITH TABLE.

Albums:

LOST CHRONICLES OF THE WAR IN HEAVEN, Underworld (1998)
Contract In Blood / Anti-Life / Heir To The Throne / Eve Bewitched / Ashes Of Eden / Virulent / Thorns Of The Crown / The Banks Of River Styx / Redemption / Altar Of Science / The General's Lament / Catholicon

CELTIC DANCE (PORTUGAL)

Line-Up: Conqueror (vocals), Natasha (vocals), Winter (guitar), Slain (bass), Bellicus Tebricosious (drums)

Portuguese Black Metal band CELTIC DANCE, founded upon the combining of forces from DARK PROPHECY, OCCULT BAPTISM and CHRIST TEARS in 1994, released a 1995 demo 'Goddess Of A Thousand Knights'. The band's line up at this juncture comprised of vocalist Conqueror, guitarist Laklaboath, bassist Tzaboath and drummer Andras. The latter would be supplanted in 1997 by Nygurien.

An album was recorded for the Shivadarshana label 'Ancient Battlecry' but was shelved only seeing the light of day in cassette form.

By 1999 Conqueror had resurrected the band name pulling in an all new group comprising guirtarist Winter, bassist Slain, drummer Bellicus Tebricoius and female vocalist Natasha.

Both Winter and Natasha had made their exit by 2000.

CELTIC FROST (SWITZERLAND)

Line-Up: Tom G. Warrior (vocals / guitar), Martin Eric Ain (bass), Reed St. Mark (drums)

A highly influential Zurich Thrash Metal act who pushed the musical boundaries of the genre to the limit, CELTIC FROST blended a fusion of extreme aggression with classical and jazz leanings to create a unique 'avant garde' eclectic style. The band rapidly built a strong fan base and, at their peak, looked set to rival the big name American Speed Metal outfits for world domination.

CELTIC FROST had a strange genesis as mentor and renowned 'death grunter' Warrior and bassist Martin Eric Ain were members of what was generally acknowledged to have been one of the worst bands ever- HELLHAMMER. Tom himself started out musically in GRAVE HILL who were heavily influenced by the NWoBHM bands such as DIAMOND HEAD and VENOM.

The original CELTIC FROST, so named after a combination of song titles on a CIRITH UNGOL album sleeve, line-up in May 1984 comprised of Warrior, Ain and drummer Isaac Darso. The latter lasted precisely one rehearsal before being usurped by SCHIZO's Stephen Priestly on a temporary basis as a session drummer for recording. At this stage CELTIC FROST were still working on NWoBHM favourites such as songs by ANGELWITCH and ARAGORN.

With HELLHAMMER's reputation preceding them (magazines reviews polarized at either the genius or dreadful end of the spectrum) CELTIC FROST retained their previous deal with Noise Records by submitting a master plan detailing the names of all future releases. The strategy called for an initial demo to be entitled 'A Thousand Deaths' but the label soon persuaded the band that this should form the basis of an opening commercially available product.

CELTIC FROST's first product, the mini-album, 'Morbid Tales' was recorded with Martin Eric Ain's former colleague in SCHIZO drummer Stephen Priestly. As soon as the sessions were completed though Priestly decamped. CELTIC FROST set about negotiations with American drummer Jeff Cardelli of Seattle act LIPSTICK. However, the band hired another American, ex CROWN drummer Reed St. Mark (real name Reid Cruickshank).

As with HELLHAMMER media views on 'Morbid Tales' ranged in their extremity from excellent to dire. The controversy stoked up by these opposing views would serve the band well. CELTIC FROST were still at this juncture wearing the stage make up later to be given the name 'corpse paint' by later generations of Black Metal bands. A further EP 'The Emperors Return' followed to equally polarized reviews and even condemnation from the band themselves. By now CELTIC FROST were being acknowledged as leaders in their field.

CELTIC FROST's inaugural live performances came with a run of shows opening for German bands BEAST and MASS in Germany and Austria. Planned shows in Italy with ASTAROTH were shelved.

Ain had been asked to leave during recording of the next album 'Into Megatherion' and CELTIC FROST pulled in Dominic Steiner of the Glam Rock act JUNK FOOD. The album, which saw the band utilizing timpanis, French horns and operatic vocals courtesy of Claudia-Maria Mokri, would be the first to be graced with lavish album sleeve artwork from the renowned artist H.R. Giger.

Friction between the band members resulted in Steiner's dismissal as soon as 'Into Mega Therion' had been completed. For CELTIC FROST's debut show outside of Europe at the November 1985 'World War Three' festival in Montreal alongside VOIVOD, POSSESSED, DESTRUCTION and NASTY SAVAGE with Martin Eric Ain back in the bass position.

Warrior also worked as producer for fellow Swiss Metal band CORONOR, a gesture they repaid by becoming CELTIC FROST's roadcrew!

1986 saw CELTIC FROST back on the live circuit touring Europe sharing billing with HELLOWEEN and GRAVE DIGGER. Later shows saw a headline at a Belgian festival, the band's debut in England in London with GRAVE DIGGER and HELLOWEEN supporting and also touring in America alongside RUNNING WILD and VOIVOD.

With CELTIC FROST's status rising sharply the 'Tragic Serenades' EP was issued to keep fans happy between albums. The EP consisted of remixed tracks from 'Into Megatherion' and new numbers.

'Into The Pandemonium' provided fans with another bizarre offering comprising tracks such as a cover of WALL OF VOODOO's 'Mexican Radio' and the Rap cut 'One In Their Pride'. Before the album had been recorded New York based guitarist Ritchi Desmond was briefly linked with a position in the band, but, having travelled to Switzerland to work with the group Desmond returned home citing "too many conflicting attitudes" as the reason why he failed to join CELTIC FROST. Warrior countered that Desmond brought uninvited family members along to the audition and looked nothing like his submitted photograph! Desmond was to front SABBAT for their 'Mourning Has Broken' album and subsequent disastrous tour.

During a break in recording the band played a series of European gigs with ANTHRAX, CRIMSON GLORY and even METALLICA.

For livework to promote 'Into The Pandemonium' CELTIC FROST added second guitarist Ron Marks and toured Britain in winter of 1987 with support from KREATOR then America on a bill with EXODUS and ANTHRAX. The tour succeeded in dumbfounding many of the band's established fans with such radical tracks as the aforementioned 'Mexican Radio' cover and the band was dogged throughout it's duration by legal wrangles with Noise Records. Disillusioned, Marks quit to be replaced by former JUNK FOOD guitarist Oliver Amberg.

Upon their return to Europe CELTIC FROST hit further problems when Martin Ain decided to abandon the music business entirely in favour of wedded bliss (!), so Warrior quickly drafted in Curt Victor Bryant.

CELTIC FROST was in a state of flux besieged by business and financial problems. Even an offer from director Ken Russell to lay down the soundtrack to the movie 'The Lair Of The White Worm' had to be declined because the group was in such disarray. However, the final blow to the classic line-up came when Reed St. Mark upped and left to join MINDFUNK and his position was filled by a returning Stephen Priestly. This was the line-up that was to record the disastrous 'Cold Lake' album produced by Tony Platt; a record that effectively killed the band's career in Europe.

With this effort CELTIC FROST appeared to ditch all of their former pretensions artistically and even adopted a new 'Glam' image, much to the horror of their most hardcore following. Tom dropped the 'Warrior' from his stagename and became plain old Thomas Gabriel Fischer, sporting an L.A. GUNS T-shirt on official press photos.

It was heavily rumoured that the band had, in a SPINAL TAP style move, adopted Tom's girlfriend as manager and that the new look was her masterplan for CELTIC FROST's step into the big league. CELTIC FROST themselves maintained that tracks like 'Teaze Me' were a parody of Glam Rock, but fans were outraged and the media universally attacked the album. The European tour fared badly with audiences deserting in droves. However, in America 'Cold Lake' was in actual fact making serious sales headway and a U.S. tour beginning in March 1989 was judged a success..

In late '89 the badly bruised CELTIC FROST announced a return to their former style and regrouped with Ron Marks. Martin Eric Ain was also persuaded to put down some guest bass tracks and contribute lyrics. The 'Vanity / Nemesis' Roli Mossiman produced album was cited by many as the band's best record to date, but the legacy of 'Cold Lake' still haunted the quartet to such a degree that sales suffered.

CELTIC FROST only managed minimal touring to back up the release of 'Vanity / Nemesis' including a British tour. By now Warrior was to be seen spotted playing a guitar emblazoned with his wife's name 'Michelle', the lady in question also having become a backing singer for the band.

New management hooked up a deal with major label BMG in America. However, the deal was shelved at the last minute leaving CELTIC FROST high and dry.

A further CELTIC FROST album did emerge titled 'Parched With Thirst Am I And Dying'. The record comprised of rare material and completely reworked older tracks. Promoted as a new album it sold extremely well.

Warrior took the band into an even more radical direction when he mooted the idea of working with ex THE TIME guitarist Jesse Johnson on a projected Funk-Metal project. Stephen Priestly meantime would perform drums for French act TREPONEM PAL's 1991 'Aggravation' album.

Following a 1992 four track demo, featuring the tracks 'Honour Thy Father', 'Seeds Of Rapture', 'Icons Alive' and Oh Father', the band searched in vain for a new deal. Initial tapes were laid down with Priestly on drums but sessions in Texas saw Reed St. Mark back behind the kit and Renée Hernz on bass. Nothing came of this latest venture and CELTIC FROST effectively split; Marks relocating to America to form STEPCHILD then SUBSONIC.

In 1992 Noise released a CELTIC FROST epitaph in the form of 'Parched With Thirst Am I And Dying'; a collection of rare and unreleased studio out-takes as the band bowed out.

In more recent years Martin Ain has produced the debut album from doom band SADNESS in 1995, whilst Tom Warrior was found fronting APOLLYON'S SON in 1996.

Singles/EPs:
The Usurper / Jewel Throne / Return To Eve, Noise N0041 (1986) ('Tragic Serenades' EP)
Dethroned Emperor / Circle Of The Tyrants / Morbid Tales / Suicidal Winds / Visual Aggression, Noise N0042 (1986) ('Emperor's Return' EP)
I Won't Dance / One In Their Pride / Tristesses De La Lune, Noise N094 (1986)
Wine In My Hand (Third From The Sun) / Heroes / Descent From Babylon, Noise NO (1990)

Albums:
MORBID TALES, Noise N 0017 60-1673 (1984)
Into The Crypt Of Rays / Visions Of Mortality / Procreation (Of The Wicked) / Return To Eve / Danse Macabre / Nocturnal Fear
TO MEGATHERION, Noise N0031 (1985)
Innocence And Wrath / The Usurper / Jewel Throne / Dawn Of Megiddo / Eternal Summer / Circle Of Tyrants / (Beyond The) North Winds / Fainted Eyes / Tears In A Prophet's Dream / Necromantical Screams
INTO THE PANDEMONIUM, Noise N0065 (1987)
Mexican Radio / Mesmerised / Inner Sanctum / Sorrows Of The Moon / Babylon Fell / Caress Into Oblivion / One In Their Pride / I Won't Dance / Rex Irae (Requiem-Opening) / Oriental Masquerade
COLD LAKE, Noise NUK 125 (1989)
Intro- Human / Seduce Me Tonight / Petty Obsession / (Once) They Were Eagles / Cherry Orchards / Juices Like Wine / Little Velvet / Blood On Kisses /

Downtown Hanoi / Dance Sleazy / Roses Without Thorns / Tease Me / Mexican Radio (New Version) **VANITY/NEMESIS**, Noise-EMI EMC 3576 (1990) The Heart Beneath / Wine In My Hand (Third From The Sun) / Wings Of Solitude / The Name Of My Bride / This Island Earth / The ReLstless Seas / Phallic Tantrum / A Kiss Or A Whisper / Vanity / Nemesis / Heroes **PARCHED WITH THIRST AM I AND DYING**, Noise N 191-2 (1992) Idols Of Chagrin / A Descent To Babylon / Return To The Eve / Juices Like Wine / The Inevitable Factor / The Heart Beneath / Cherry Orchards / Tristesses De La Lune / Wings Of Solitude / The Usurper / Journey Into Fear / Downtown Hanoi / Circle Of The Tyrants / In The Chapel In The Moonlight / I Won't Dance / The Name Of My Bride / Mexican Radio / Under Apollyon's Sun

CEMETARY OF SCREAM
(POLAND)

Albums:
MELANCHOLY, (1995)
Prologue / Melancholy / Dolor Ante Lucem / Gods Of Steel / Apocalyptic Visions Part II / Anxiety / Landscape Of Sadness / Lost Flowers / Violet Fields Of Extinction / Epilogue / The Shadow Of Notre Dame Cathedral
DEPRESSION, (1998)
Whisper- Touch / Breeze / Episode Man / Ironic / Walkin' On Air / Reveal The Rainbow / Cruel / Float To Escape

CENOTAPH (ITALY)

Trieste based Black group with Death Metal tendencies. CENOTAPH bowed in with a 1991 demo 'The Lurking Fear On Consecrated Ground' in 1991 followed up by the 'Demonolatreia Larve In Corpre Christi' tape.
Not to be confused with the plethora of other CENOTAPH's hailing from Mexico, America, Spain and Turkey.

Albums:
THIRTEEN THRENODIES, Planet K (1994)

CENOTAPH (MEXICO)
Line-Up: Edgardo (vocals), Pala (guitar), Julio Viterbo (guitar), Curro (bass), Oscar (drums)

An illustrious Mexican Death Metal act founded in 1989. Although traditionally Death Metal musically CENOTAPH employ strong Satanic themes. Ex member Daniel Corchado would go on to forge the highly rated and industrious act THE CHASM. He would be later joined by Julio Viterbo for THE CHASM 2000 album 'Procession To The Infraworld'.
Following a Milwaukee Metalfest performance CENOTAPH folded but recently have regrouped.

Singles/EPs:
Tenebrous Apparitions, Distorted Harmony (1990) (7" single)
The Eternal Disgrace, (1991) (7" single)

Albums:
THE GLOOMY REFLECTION OF OUR HIDDEN SCROLLS, Horus Corporation (1992)
The Gloomy Reflection Of Our Hidden Sorrows: i) requiem For A Soul Required, ii) Ashes In The Rain, iii)... A Red Sky, iv) Evoked Doom, v) Tenebras Apparitions, vi) The Spiritless One, vii) Infinite Meditation Of An Uncertain Existence In The Cosmic Solitude, viii) Repulsive Odor Of Decomposition
EPIC RITES (9 EPIC TALES OF DEATH RITES), Oz Productions CDOZ001 (1996)
Intro / Crying Frost / Lorn Ends / Navegate / Towards The Umbra / As The Darkness Borns / Angered Tongues / Epic Rites / Dethroned Empire / Thornes Of Fog
RIDING ON BLACK OCEANS, (1998)
The Solitudes / Severance / Grief To Obscuro / Macabre Locus Celesta / Among The Abrupt / Infinitum Valet / The Silence Of Our Black Oceans / Soul Profundis / Ectasia Tenebrae

CENOTAPH (USA)
Line-Up: Roger Scott (vocals / guitar), David Allen (bass), Darrell (drums)

Satanic Death Metal band CENOTAPH previously included ex DEUTSCH THREAT drummer Karl 'Killer' Schmitt. He would be replaced by Darrell of LOS REACTORS.

Albums:
BLOOD RITUAL, (1989)
APOSTASY, (1993)

CENTINEX (SWEDEN)
Line-Up: Mattias Lamppu (vocals),

Kenneth Wiklund (guitar), Andreas Evaldsson (guitar), Martin Schulman (bass), Joakim Gustafsson (drums)

Renowned Death Metal act that have increasingly bolstered their sound and imagery with Satanic lyrical references. CENTINEX opened their career in September 1990 issuing the debut demo cassette 'End Of Life' the following year. The band signed to Swedish label Underground for release of the album 'Subconscious Lobotomy' which saw a limited release of 1'000 copies. The CENTINEX line up at this juncture comprised of twin vocalists Erik and Mattias Lamppu, guitarist Andreas Evaldsson, bass player Martin Schulman and drummer Joakim Gustafsson.

A further three track demo session 'Under The Blackened Sky' followed. CENTINEX's next cassette release 'Transcend The Dark Chaos', released on the band's own novelly titled Evil Shit Productions, was repressed by Sphinx Records.

The second CENTINEX full length album 'Malleus Malefaction' was recorded for the German Wild Rags label and produced by Peter Tägtren of HYPOCRISY.

1996 saw the release of a shared 7" single in collusion with INVERTED and a fresh band line up retaining Lamppu, Schulman and Evaldsson but with new faces in UNCURBED guitarist Kenneth Wiklund and drummer Kalimaa. The band also featured on a split EP with Sweden's VOICES OF DEATH and German act BAPHOMET.

Early 1997 found CENTINEX on tour in Scandinavia as guests to CRADLE OF FILTH. However, a split in the ranks came the following year when both Lamppu and Evaldsson made their exit. It was to be July 1999 before CENTINEX enrolled UNCANNY and DELLAMORTE drummer Kennet Englund. For touring later in the year CENTINEX pulled in DELLAMORTE and CARNAL FORGE man Jonas Kjellgren on guitar and UNCURBED and DELLAMORTE vocalist Johan Jansson. The same year had CENTINEX contributing their version of 'Ripping Corpse' to a Full Moon Productions KREATOR tribute album.

2000 witnessed yet more ructions when Kjellgren and Englund decamped. Replacements were AZURE vocalist Robban Kanto and drummer Johan.

2001 had CENTINEX sharing vinyl with the infamous American act NUNSLAUGHTER with their take on SODOM's 'Enchanted Land' for the 'Hail Germania' EP on the Belgian Painkiller label.

Singles/EPs:
Sorrow Of Burning Wasteland / , (1996) (Split 7" single with INVERTED)
Shadowland / Eternal Lies, Oskorei Productions 004 (1998)
Apocalyptic Armageddon / Seeds Of Evil / Everlasting Bloodshed, Deadly Art DAP 095 (2000)
Enchanted Land / , Painkiller (2001) ('Hail Germania' Split 7" with NUNSLAUGHTER)

Albums:
SUBCONSCIOUS LOBOTOMY, Underground UGR05 (1992)
Blood On My Skin / Shadows Are Astray / Dreams Of Death / Orgy In Flesh / End Of Life / Bells Of Misery / Inhuman Dissections Of Souls / The Aspiration / Until Death Tear Us Apart
TRANSCEND THE DARK CHAOS, Sphinx SIXR 003 (1994)
MALLEUS MALEFACTION, Wild Rags WRR 043 (1995)
Upon The Ancient Ground / Dark Visions / Sorrow Of The Burning Wasteland / Transcend The Dark Chaos / Thorns Of Desolation / Eternal Lies / At The Everlasting Evil
REFLECTIONS, Diehard RRS 954 (1997)
Carnal Lust / Seven Prophecies / Before The Dawn / The Dimension Beyond / My Demon Within / In Pain / Undivined / Darkside / Into The Funeral Domain
REBORN THROUGH FLAMES, Repulse RPS 032CD (1998)
Embraced By Moonlight / Resurrected / Summon The Golden Twilight / The Beauty Of Malice / Under The Guillotine / Through Celestial Gates Molested / In The Arch Of Serenity
BLOODHUNT, Repulse RPS 042CD (1999)
Under The Pagan Glory / For Centuries Untold / Luciferian Moon / Bloodhunt / The Conquest Infernal / Like Darkened Storms / Mutilation
HELLBRIGADE, Repulse RPS 046CD (2001)
Towards Devastation / On With Eternity / The Eyes Of The Dead / Emperor Of Death / Last Redemption / Blood Conqueror / Neverending Hell / Nightbreeder / Hellbrigade

CENTURIES OF DECEPTION
(CA, USA)

CENTURIES OF DECEPTION previously went under the title of MYOCARDITIS adopting the new title in 1996. Band leader Atrox has also served time with ENCHANTED SORROW.

Albums:
HEIC NOETUNN PAX, Blood, Fire, Death (1997)

CENTURION (HOLLAND)

CENTURION were previously known as INQUISITOR.

Singles/EPs:
Of Purest Fire EP, (199-)

Albums:
CHOROZONIC CHAOS GODS, Full Moon Productions (1999)
Damned And Dead / The Law Of Burning / Hail Caligula!!! / Misanthropic Luciferian Onslaught / Let Jesus Bleed / Blood For Satan / Soul Theft / Cross Of Fury / In The Name Of Chaos

CEREMONY (HOLLAND)
Line-Up: Micha Verboom (vocals), Peter Verhoef (guitar), Johan Vd Sluijs (guitar), Ron Vd Polder (bass), Patrick Van Gelder (drums)

Singles/EPs:
Indemnicy, (1995)

Albums:
TYRANNY FROM ABOVE, Cyber Music Cyber CD6 (1993)
Inner Demon / Drowned In Terror / Solitary World / Ceremonial Resurrection / When Tears Are Falling / Humanity / Beyond The Boundaries / Of This World / Tribulation Foreseen

CERNUNNOS (GREECE)

One man Black Metal undertaking. Cernunnos also operates in WOLFNACHT and BAKXEIA NERAIDA.

CERNUNNOS WOODS (USA)

A one man ambient folkloric act of Bard Algol. CERNUNNOS WOODS bowed in with a well received stream of tapes including 'Tears Of A Weeping Willow',

'Lost Woods' and 'Immrama'.
Algol also contributes lyrics to mediaeval act THE SOIL BLEEDS BLACK.

Albums:
AWAKEN THE EMPIRE OF DARK WOODS, Cruel Moon International (2000)
Dark And Ancient Visions / The Lost Velvet Horn / Gad Goddeu / Echoes Of Knowledge In Ancient Stone / The Song Of Taliesin / Into Glory We Ride

CHAINED AND DESPERATE
(GREECE)
Line-Up: C.M. Ain (vocals), Panos Makris (guitar), George Pavlides (drums)

Created in 1990 as DESPERATION DEATH comprising of vocalist C.M. Ain (real name Nick Giagiakos), guitarist Panos Makris, keyboard player Manos and drummer Chris. By February of 1992 the band had become CHAINED AND DESPERATE debuting with a Pagan flavoured Doom demo tape in 1994 entitled 'Grieving For The Last Sun'.
After CHAINED AND DESPERATE's first gig in December 1994 both Manos and Chris broke ranks. Undeterred the band laid down recordings for Dark Side Records for a projected mini album produced by Magus Wampyr Daoloth of NECROMANTIA. However, the label went down and the band resorted to issuing the tracks as the demo 'Oracles For The Neither World'.
Further delays occurred when the group fell foul of negotiations with Neat Metal Records.

CHAKAL (BRAZIL)

Vocalist Korg is credited with penning the lyrics for SEPULTURA's 'To The Wall'. Vocalist Korg also sang with THE MIST, a band including ex SEPULTURA guitarist Jairo T. in it's ranks.

Albums:
THE MAN IS HIS OWN JACKAL, Coguemelo COG036-A (1991)

CHAOSTAR (GREECE)

Side project by SEPTIC FLESH guitarist Chris Antoniou. All his SEPTIC FLESH band mates contribute to the 2000 album.

Albums:
CHAOSTAR, Holy (2000)

Project Atom Traveller / An Electric Storm Of Thoughts / No Gravity / The Field Of Ante Cun / The Accident In Amarer / Time Was Running Out / The First Meeting / Finale

THE CHASM (OH, USA)

Line-Up: Daniel Corchada (vocals / guitar), Julio Viterbo (guitar), Alfonso Pol0 (bass), Antonio Leon (drums)

Mexican Death Black band THE CHASM, who opened their career with the demo 'Awaiting The Day Of Liberation', relocated to Ohio. The band's mentor and founder is former CENOTAPH man guitarist Daniel Corchada.
Corchada would loan himself out to the infamous INCANTATION in mid 1997. The group has undergone many changes in line up and by 1999 was down to a duo of Corchado and drummer Antonio Leon. Numbers were boosted with the recruitment of another erstwhile CENOTAPH member Julio Viterbo.
The 2000 album 'Processions To The Infraworld' saw the enlistment of bassist Roberto V. but he would soon bail out in favour of former ALLUSION four stringer Alfonso Polo.
THE CHASM has cut versions of KREATOR and DESTRUCTION songs for tribute albums.

Albums:
PROCREATION OF THE INNER TEMPLE, Bellphegot BELLCD 95011-2 (1994)
Conqueror Of The Mourningstar / A Dream Of An Astral Spectrum (To An Eternal Hate) / Confessions Of Strange Anxiety / Honoris Lux Infinitus (A Whipper To The Moon) / The Day Of Liberation / The Lonely Walker (My Pride And My Wrath) / The Cosmos Within / Stair To Aspirations
FOR THE LOST YEARS, Reborn CD001 (1995)
The Gravefields / Secret Winds Of Temptation / The Pastfinder / Deathcult For Eternity / Ascention Of Majestic Ruins / Our Time will Come… / Procreation Of The Inner Temple / An Arcanum Faded / Torn (By The Sunrise) / My Tideless Seas / Lost Yesterdays Impossible Tomorrows
DEATHCULT FOR ETERNITY: THE TRIUMPH, Oz Productions (1998)
Revenge Rises- Drowned In Mournful Blood / No Mercy (Our Time Is Near) / I'm The Hateful Raven / A Portal To

Nowhere / Channeling The Bleeding Over The dream's Remains / Possessed By Past Tragedies (Tragic Shadows) / Apocalypse / In Superior Torment… / The Triumph (Of My Loss)
PROCESSIONS TO THE INFRAWORLD, Dwell (2000)
Spectral Sons Of Mictlan / The Scars Of My Journey / At The Edge Of Nebulah Mortis / Fading… / Return Of The Banished / Cosmic Landscapes Of Sorrow / Architects Of Melancholic Apocalypses / Storm Of Revelations

CHILDREN OF BODOM (FINLAND)
Line-Up: Alex Laiho (vocals / guitar), Ale Kuoppala (guitar), Henkka 'Blacksmith' Seppäiä (bass), Janne Viljami Wirman (keyboards), Jaska Raatikainen (drums)

Espoo based Black Death metal act named after Finland's infamous Lake Bodom, the scene of a horrific series of murders. The band was previously titled INHEARTED. Founder member and vocalist Alex Laiho made his name as part of THY SERPENT maintaining CHILDREN OF BODOM, created in 1993 with drummer Jaska Raatikainen, as a going concern.
The band supported DIMMU BORGIR on their 1997 Finnish dates and would also feature on the high profile compilation album 'Metallilitto'. The praise received for this release scored the band a deal with Spinefarm Records. CHILDREN OF BODOM's debut album 'Something Wild' was an instant best seller and sales were strengthened when the band also scored a priority licensing deal with Germany's Nuclear Blastr Records.
Later the same year the industrious Laiho would team up with IMPALED NAZARENE and would also form part of Kimberley Goss' SINERGY line ups.
CHILDREN OF BODOM would quite spectacularly land a national number 1 single with 'Downfall' in early 1999.
Wirman, under the title of WARMAN, cut a solo album in 2000 titled 'Unknown Soldier'.
The B side to CHILDREN OF BODOM's 2000 single 'Hate Me' features a cover version of W.A.S.P.'s 'Hellion'. The ensuing album 'Follow The Reaper' found the Japanese version with an extra bonus track, a version of OZZY OSBOURNE's 'Shot In The Dark'.
CHILDREN OF BODOM supported PRIMAL FEAR for a German tour in February 2001.

CHILDREN OF BODUM
Photo : Martin Wickler

Singles/EPs:
Downfall / No Command, Spinefarm (1999) 1 FINLAND
Hate Me / Hellion, Spinefarm (2000)

Albums:
SOMETHING WILD, Nuclear Blast NB 308-2 (1998)
Deadnight Warrior / In The Shadows / Red Light In My Eyes (Part I) / Red Light In My Eyes (Part II) / Lake Bodom / The Nail / Touch Like Angel Of Death
HATEBREEDER, Nuclear Blast (1999)
Warheart / Silent Night, Bodom Night / Hatebreeder / Bed Of Razors / Towards Dead End / Black Widow / Wrath Within / Children Of Bodom / Down Fall
TOKYO WARHEARTS- LIVE, Nuclear Blast (1999)
Intro / Silent Night, Bodom Night / Lake Bodom / Bed Of Razors / War Of Razors / Deadnight Warrior / Hatebreeder / Touch The Angel Of Death / Downfall / Towards Dead End
FOLLOW THE REAPER, Nuclear Blast (2000)
Follow The Reaper / Bodom After Midnight / Children Of Decadence / Every Time I Die / Mask Of Sanity / Taste Of My Scythe / Hate Me / Northern Comfort / Kissing The Shadows / Hellion

CHILDREN OF MÄANI (FRANCE)

A side project of Vindesval of BLUT AUS NORD.

Albums:
THE VEIL OF OSIRIS, Velvet VMI 010 (1999)
Tradition: The Birth / In The Middle Of The Macrocosme "Those Who Are Called Vlad" / Tiphareth... And Beams Of Malchuth "After The Five Ones" / Tradition: My Birth "Where Is The Sky Of The First?"

CHIVA (SWITZERLAND)

Solo project from SADNESS guitarist Chiva.

Singles/EPs:
Fire And Ice / Noces Noir / Ifoss / Prelude Á La Nuit, Witchhunt (1997) ('Oracle Morte' EP)

CHOIR OF VENGEANCE (SWEDEN)

Singles/EPs:
Choir Of Vengeance EP, (1996)

CHOROZON (MA, USA)

Albums:
MAGOG AGAOG, Nocturnal Art (1998)
Dust / Love, Strength, Lies / Perdurabo-Magog Agog / Under The Leaves / Crimson Awakening / Demon / Void / 333 / Choronzon

CHRIST AGONY (POLAND)
Line-Up: Cezar (vocals / guitar), Mauser (vocals / bass), Gilan (drums)

CHRIST AGONY cut their debut demo 'Sacronocturn' in 1990. Further tapes 'Epitaph Of Christ' and 'Unholy Union'. Cezar also operates side act MOON issuing two albums to date.

Singles/EPs:
Inceremonical / Darkthurnal / Dies Irae / Ritualis Sceptrus, (1993) ('Unholy Union' EP)

Albums:
DAEMOONSETH, (1995)
DAEMOONSETH ACT II, Carnage CDAR024 (1995)
Introit Moon / Urtica Diaoica Cultha / Athyrium Typha Luciferi / Diaboli Necronasti / Sacronocturn / Abasatha Pagan (Prophetical p. III)
MOONLIGHT- ACTIII, Cacophonous NIHIL 14 (1996)
Asmoondei / Devilish Sad / Paganhorns / Mephistospell / Moonlight / Eternal Hate
DARKSIDE, Hammerheart (1997)
The Triangle / Hereditary / Dark Beauty / Kingdom Of Abyss / My Spirit Seal (Dream Version) / Dark Poem / Dark Goddess / Darkside / The Key / My Spirit Seal (Blood Version)
TRILOGY, (1998)
Spell Of Death / Hellspawn / Eternal Desires / Hail Darkness / Spying Star / Elysium / Downfall / Unvirtue Diabolical / Faithless / Necro 'No' Romanticism / Prophetical Part III
ELYSIUM, (1999)
Sadness Of Immortality / Fiery Torches / Demon's Lover / Immortal Dust / Eternal Stars / Elysium / Lords Of The Night / Cold Eyes / Bleeding Heart / Unvirginity Sin

CHRISTBAIT (AUSTRALIA)
Line-Up: Jason Vassallo (vocals), Craig Westwood (guitar), Jason Miszewski

(guitar), Nadia Markovic (bass), Jason Dutton (drums)

Melbourne Death Metal band founded in 1989 as REQUIEM. CHRISTBAIT issued a 1992 demo after which Lenny Markovic took over the drum position.

CHRIST DENIED (SPAIN)
Line-Up: Dave Rotten (vocals), David Nigger (guitar / bass / programming)

Studio duo of former INTOXICATION man David Nigger and AVULSED's Dave Rotten. The latter also operates in Grindcore band ANEAMIA. The 'Got What He Deserved' album includes a cover of ONSLAUGHT's 'Angel Of Death'.
CHRIST DENIED have also cut a version of PYREXIA's 'The Uncertain' for a split EP shared with ABORTED in 2000.

Singles/EPs:
The Horned God, Morbid (1995) (Double split 7" single with HAEMORRAGE)
The Uncertain, Soulreaper (2000) (Split single with ABORTED)

Albums:
... GOT WHAT HE DESERVED, Gulli GR005 (1996)
Banish The Vanished / A Monk's Wet Dream / Pay To Pray / Deserved No Less / Useless Sinless Life / No Salvation / Misery / Angels Of Death / Body Of Christ / Hierarchy Of Hypocrisy
CHRIST DENIED, Soulreaper (2000) (Split CD with ABORTED)

CHRISTIAN DEATH (USA)
Line-Up: Rozz Williams (vocals), Rikk Agnew (guitar), James McGearly (bass), George Belanger (drums)

Notorious Gothic Punk act centred upon vocalist Rozz William's (real name Roger Alan Painter) obsession with organized religion. CHRISTIAN DEATH courted controversy at every turn frequently utilizing swastikas and anti religious rhetoric. Confusion has masked the band's career as throughout most of their career CHRISTIAN DEATH has been operating under dual identities with two groups laying claim to the band name. The 'original' American band was led by Rozz Williams, the 'imposter' band based in Europe by Valor Kand.
The band's initial 1979 Los Angeles line up, originally known as THE UPSETTERS, included former ADOLESCENTS guitarist Rikk Agnew, bassist James McGearly and drummer George Belanger. It would be three years before CHRISTIAN DEATH debuted with an obscure EP, made up of tracks from a compilation shared with GRAVE 45 and THE SUPERHEROINES, followed by the full length 'Only Theatre Of Pain'.
CHRISTIAN DEATH's appreciation in France led to a deal with the L'Invitation Au Suicide label. The debut album was reissued and a follow up mini album 'Deathwish' released in 1984. Such was the apathy in America compared to the favour afforded by Europe that Williams relocated to Paris. The singer promptly built a new version of the band comprising Australian Valor Kand on guitar his wife and keyboard player Gitane Demone and drummer David Glass. All of these musicians were members of POMPEII 99, a band intended to back Williams on a CHRISTIAN DEATH European tour. A further French only release 'Catastrophe Ballet', recorded at Rockfield studios in Wales, ensued by which time the various members had gelled into CHRISTIAN DEATH mk 2.
After the 'Decomposition Of Violets' album Williams quit to concentrate on his other projects PREMATURE EJACULATION and HELTIR. The parting of the ways was initially amicable with the remaining band members intending to use the name SIN AND SACRIFICE. However, the band toured Europe minus Williams billed as CHRISTIAN DEATH and next album 'The Wind Kissed Pictures', only available as an Italian release, was credited to THE SIN AND SACRIFICE OF CHRISTIAN DEATH. By the time 'Atrocities' hit the market Kand was now simply billing the band CHRISTIAN DEATH.
Kand opted to persevere pulling in guitarist James Beam, flautist Sevan Kand (Valor & Gitane's son) and bassist Constance for 1987's 'The Scriptures'.
Meantime Williams founded the uncompromising SHADOW PROJECT with his wife Eva O and Jill Emery, both of THE SUPERHEROINES, and ex CHRISTY AND THE FLESHEATERS man Tom for the 'Dreams Of A Dying' album. Also involved in both SHADOW PROJECT and CHRISTIAN DEATH was bassist Dan Canzonieri, later to found Punk band ELECTRIC FRANKENSTEIN. Williams would also work on solo material with Gitane Demone resulting in the

'Dreamhome Heartache' album. Demone also worked with Dance act THE ALPHA PROJECT and German Goths PHALLUS DEI.

Further albums throughout the 80's found the Kand version of the band unable to break out from their existing fan base and into the mainstream. By 1988 Bean and Constance had quit. The almost commercial 12" single 'Church Of No Return' witnessed the recruitment of guitarist Barry Galvin and the session bass of Johann Schumann. The follow up album 'Sex, Drugs and Jesus Christ' came with deliberately provocative artwork featuring the messiah injecting heroin.

In 1989 the European CHRISTIAN DEATH was down to a duo of the Kand brothers. A double set of releases 'All The Love All The Hate' saw new members Nick The Bastard on guitar, Mark Buchanan on saxophone and drummer Ian Thompson. The same year Williams, Agnew and Eva) put in a comeback CHRISTIAN DEATH tour of Canada. An album, 'The Iron Mask', was recorded for Cleopatra Records but subsequently disowned by Williams who believed unfinished master tapes had been used. William's CHRISTIAN DEATH next recorded 'The Path Of Sorrows', seen by many as one of his finest works.

1993 had only Valor Kand remaining augmented for the European CHRISTIAN DEATH 'Sexy Death God' album by Matri on bass, Streamer on drums and Cullen and Marcel Trussell on violins and cellos. Williams, Agnew, Eva O and a returning Belanger laid a claim to the title of CHRISTIAN DEATH. This 'original' line up, also including Frank Agnew on guitar and bassist Casey Chaos, put out the 'Iconologica' live album through Triple X as a legal battle raged between the two parties.

Kand's CHRISTIAN DEATH signed to German Metal label Century Media for the 'Amen' album. Line up for this release being Kand, guitarist Flick, Matri on bass and Steve on drums. The following year a set of William's CHRISTIAN DEATH tracks was remixed by LAIBACH among others for the 'Death In Detroit' album.

Williams hung himself in April of 1988. He was 35. Kand's version of the band continues.

Chaos has since formed AMEN releasing a 1999 album.

Eva O issued a solo album 'Damnation' during 1999 on Massacre Records. Demone began a project with Paul Morden of THE BRICKBATS.

CHRISTIAN DEATH, now including ex CRADLE OF FILTH / BLOOD DIVINE drummer Was Sarginson toured Europe with Black Metal leaders CRADLE OF FILTH in late 2000. Various other members of CRADLE OF FILTH guested on the 2000 album 'Born Again Anti Christian'.

Singles/EPs:
Desperate Hell / Cavity / Spiritual Cramp / Romeo's Distress / Death Wish, Bemis Brain BB 127-128 (1982)
Believers Of The Unpure, Jungle JUNG 24T (1986)
Sick Of Love, Jungle JUNG 35T (1987)
Church Of No Return, Jungle JUNG 40T (1988)
What's The Verdict / This Is Not Blasphemy, Jungle JUNG 45T (1988)
I Hate You / We Fall Like Love, Jungle JUNG 055CD (1988)
Zero Sex, Jungle JUNG050T (1989)

Albums:
ONLY THEATRE OF PAIN, No Future FL 2 (1983)
Cavity- First Communion / Figurative Theatre / Burnt Offerings / Mysterious Iniquitatis / Dream For Mother / Deathwish / Romeo's Distress / Dogs / Stairs- Uncertain Journey / Spiritual Cramp / Resurrection- Sixth Communion / Prayer / Desperate Hell / Cavity
DEATHWISH, L'Invitation Au Suicide SD 4 (1984) (French release)
Deathwish / Romeo's Distress / Dogs / Desperate Hell / Spiritual Cramp / Cavity
CATASTROPHE BALLET, L'Invitation Au Suicide SD 5 (1984) (French release)
Awake At The Wall / Sleepwalk / The Drowning / The Blue Hour / Evening Falls / Andro Gynous Noise Hand Permeates / Electra Descending
THE DECOMPOSITION OF VIOLETS, R.I.O.R. A 138 (1985)
Awake The Wall / Sleepwalk / The Drowning / Theatre Of Pain / Cavity / The Blue Hour / Electra Descending / As Evening Falls / Face / Cervix Couch / This Glass House / Romeo's Distress
SCRIPTURES, Jungle FREUD 18 (1987)
Prelude / Song Of Songs / Vanity / Four Horsemen / 1983 / Omega Dawn / A Ringing In Their Ears / Golden Age / Alpha Sunset / Slit Blood / Raw War / reflections / Jezebel's Tribulation / Wraeththu
PAST AND PRESENT, Castle Showcase SHCD 163 (1987)

ANTHOLOGY OF BOOTLEGS, Nostradamus NOS 1006 CD (1988) Awake At The Wall / Sleepwalk / Theatre Of Pain / Cavity- First Communion / The Blue Hour / When I Was Bed / Birth / Coming Forth By Day / This Glass House / The Drowning / Cervix Couch / Figura Five Theatre / Untitled (Followed By Crowd Chaos)

ASHES, Normal NORMAL 15 (1988) Ashes (Part 1 & 2) / When I Was Bed / Lament (Over The Shadows) / Face / The Luxury Of Tears / Of The Wound

THE WIND KISSED PICTURES (PAST AND PRESENT), Supporti Fonografici SF 003 (1988) (Italian release) Believers Of The Unpure / Ouverture / The Wind Kisses Pictures / The Lake Of Fire / Blast Of Bough / Amaterasu / The Absoloute / Lacrima Christi / Lacrima Christ (Italian version)

ATROCITIES, Normal NORMAL CD 18 (1988) Bastinado Silhouettes / Foaming Dogs With Whips Sharp Teeth / Polished Buttons / Pelting Cadavernous Flesh / Belladonna For You Now Blue Eyes / Shuddering Following The Slice / Orgasmic Flush With Scalpel In Hand / O The Soothing / Is Such Heedless Deliverance / Worship Ye Nearing Quietus

SEX, DRUGS AND JESUS CHRIST, Jungle FREUD CD 25 (1988) This Is Heresy / Jesus Where's The Sugar / Wretched Mankind / Tragedy / The Third Antichrist / Erection / Ten Thousand Hundred Times / Incendiary Lover / Window Pain

THE HERETICS ALIVE, Jungle FREUDCD 29 (1989) This Is Heresy / Wretched Mankind / Sick Of Love / The Nascent Virion / Golden Age / Erection / Chimere De Si De La / Four Horsemen / Church Of No Return

THE IRON MASK, Cleopatra CLEO 57512 (1989) Spiritual Cramp / Sleepwalk / Skeleton Kiss / Figurative Theatre / Desperate Hell / Deathwish / Luxury Of Tears / Cervix Couch / Skeleton Kiss (Death mix) / Down In The Park (Live)

PART 1: ALL THE LOVE (ALL THE LOVE, ALL THE HATE), Jungle FREUDCD 33 (1989) Live Love Together / We Fall In Love / Love Don't Let Me Down / Suivre La Trace De Quelqu'un / Love Is Like A (B)Itchin' In My Heart / I'm Using You (For Love) / Deviate Love / Angel / Woman To Mother Earth

PART 2: ALL THE LOVE (ALL THE LOVE, ALL THE HATE), Jungle FREUDCD 34 (1989) Born In A Womb, Died In A Tomb / Baptized In Fire / I Hate You / Children Of The Valley / Kneel Down / Climate Of Violence: Part 1- The Relinquishment, Part 2- The Satanic Verses (Rushdie's Lament), Part 3- A Malice Of Prejudice / The Final Solution / Nazi Killer / Man To Father Fire

INSANUS, ULTIO, PRODITO, MISERICORDIAQUE, Jungle FREUD CD 48 (1991) Sevan Au Rex / Malus Amor / Tragicus Conatus / Infans Vexatio / Somnium / Venenum / Mors Voluntaria / Vita Voluntaria

JESUS POINTS THE BONE AT YOU, Jungle FREUD CD 39 (1992) Believers Of The Unpure / After The Rain / Sick Of Love / The Loving Face / Church Of No Return / Church Of No Return (Endured version) / What's The Verdict / This Is Heresy / Zero Sex / The Nascent Virion (New version) / We Fall In Love / I Hate You

LOVE AND HATE, Jungle FREUDBX 334 (1992)

LIVE IN HOLLYWOOD, Contemp CONTE 138 (1993)

TALES OF INNOCENCE: A CONTINUED ANTHOLOGY, Cleopatra CLEO 91092 (1993)

THE RAGE OF ANGELS, Cleopatra CLEO 81252 (1994) Trust (The Sacred And Unclean) / Lost Minds / Still Born-Still Life Part I / Sex / Her Only Sin / Bad Year / Torch Song / Still Born- Still Life Part II (The Unknown Men) / Procession / Panic In Detroit

THE DOLL'S THEATRE- LIVE, Cleopatra CLEO 62082 (1994) Birth-Death / Cavity / Spiritual Cramp / Desperate Hell / Deathwish / Skeleton Kiss / Dream For Mother / Burnt Offerings / Resurrection / Figurative Theatre / Romeo's Distress / Dogs

MANDYLION, Apollo APOL 001 (1994)

SEXY DEATH GOD, Bulletproof VEST 26 (1994) At The Threshold / Kingdom Of The Tainted Kiss / Heresy Act Two / Damn You / Into Dust / Eternal Love/ The Serpent's Tail / Kingdom Of The Solemn Kiss / Temples Of Desire / Deeply, Deeply / Drilling The Hole / Up On The Sea Of Blood / Eyelids Dancing / Invitation Au Suicide

AMEN, Century Media CD 77107-2 (1995) Prelude / Prologomemenon / The Nascent Virion / Damn You / Into Dust /

Sick Of Love / Drilling The Hole / The Serpent's Trail / Wretched Mankind / Kingdom Of The Tainted Kiss / Children Of The Volley
ICONOLOGIA: DREAMS, APPARITIONS AND NIGHTMARES, Triple X 51164-2 (1994)
Excommunicamus / Cavity- First Communion / Figurative Theatre / Cry Baby / Dream For Mother / Deathwish / Some Men- The Other / Mysterium Iniquitatis / Kill Your Sons / Stairs (Uncertain Journey) / Spiritual Camp / Resurrection- 6th Communion / Sleepwalk / Romeo's Distress / Dogs
THE PROPHECIES, Jungle FREUD CD 053 (1996)
DEATH IN DETROIT- REMIXES, Cleopatra CLEO 9591CD (1996)
PORNOGRAPHIC MESSIAH, Trinity TRI 006CD (1998)
BORN AGAIN ANTI CHRISTIAN, Candlelight CANDLE 045CD (2000)
Betrayal / Zodiac (He Is Still Out There…) / In Your Eyes / The Knife / Peek A Boo / Superstition And Fear / Dead Sorry / Malevolent Shrew / Blood Dance / Fucking In Slow Motion / The Darkest Aura / Kill Me / Peek A Boo (Cradle Of Filth version)

CHRONIC DECAY (SWEDEN)
Line-Up: Jocke Hammar (vocals / guitar), Roger (guitar), Gunnar Norgren (bass), Micke Karlsson (drums)

Singles/EPs:
Ecstasy In Pain / 1st Of September / Dark Before Dawn, Studiefrämjandet SFRS 613 (1990)
Silent Prayer / Vision Of A Madman, Studiefrämjandet SFRCS 9305 (1993) (Split EP with EXANTHEMA & RETURN TO HEAVEN)

CIRITH GORGOR (HOLLAND)
Line-Up: Nimroth (vocals), Asmoday (guitar), Astaroth Daemonum (guitar), Lord Mystic (bass), Levithmong (drums)

Teenage Tolkein inspired Black crew debuted as DARK SOCERESS in 1993 led by guitarists Astaroth Daemonum and Asmoday. Shortly after Levithmong was drafted on drums and Lord Mystic on bass. At this formative stage in their careers the band performed mainly cover versions from their heroes such as SLAYER, DARKTHRONE and MAYHEM. A change of lead singer to Nimroth in 1995 also provoked the name change to CIRITH GORGOR. However, it would be a full two years before the band's debut gig and their inaugural tape 'Mystic Legends'.

Following the debut album release Asmoday decamped in favour of new guitarist Marchosias for gigs opening for TESTAMENT, ASPHYX and SINISTER.

Albums:
ONWARDS TO THE SPECTRAL DEFILE, Osmose Productions (1999)
The Declaration Of The Neverending War / Winter Embraces Lands Beyond / Through Burning Wastelands / Sons Of The New Dawn / A Hymn To The Children Of Heimdal / Darkness Returns / Wandering Cirith Gorgor / Ephel Duth (A Warrior's Tale) / Shadow Over Isengard / Thorns Of Oblivion

CLANDESTINE BLAZE (FINLAND)

Anonymous solo venture of minimalist raw Black Metal. The initial 1998 demo, released in only 100 copies, included a thoughtful inclusion of burnt bible pages. Taking the conjcept one step further vinyl versions of the debut album 'Fire Burns In Our Hearts' on End All Life Records would include instructions on how to manufacture a fire bomb- complete with disclaimer.

Albums:
FIRE BURNS IN OUR HEARTS, Northern Heritage NH001 (2000)
NIGHT OF THE UNHOLY FLAMES, Northern Heritage NHBMC009CD (2001)
Intro / Chambers / Cross Of Black Steel / Night Of The Unholy Flames / Invisible Death / There's Nothing… / Aikakausi On Lyhyt / Future Lies In Hands Of The Strong

CON ANIMA (NORWAY)
Line-Up: Stian Culto (vocals), Embia (vocals), Amon (guitar / bass / keyboards / drums)

CONANIMA is the brainchild of Stian Danza Culto, once very briefly vocalist for MAYHEM. Previous to CON ANIMA the man had fronted Gothic Rock act SHADOW DANCERS.

Albums:
THE BOOK OF RIDDLES, Scarlet (1999)
Interludio I / Mindman / Interludio II / Eating Eyes / Interludio III / The Angel Of Melancholy / Interludio IV / Empyrean /

The House On The Hill / Interludio V / The Riddle / Interludio VI / The Book Of Eibon

CONQUEROR (CANADA)
Line-Up: Ryan Foster, J. Read

Brutal Black Metal band CONQUEROR preceded their 1997 debut album with a demo session entitled 'Anti Christ Supremacy'. The band was founded by former DOMINI INFERI man Ryan Foster. CONQUEROR's 'War, Cult, Supremacy' album includes a cover version of SLAUGHTER's 'The Curse'. The band also shared a split album with American band BLACK WITCHERY.

Albums:
WAR, CULT, SUPREMACY, Evil Omen (1997)
Infinite Majesty / Chaos Domination (Conquer The Enslaver) / Age Of Decimation / Kingdom Against Kingdom / Bloodhammer / Hammer Of Antichrist / The Curse / War Cult Supremacy / Domitor

CORPUS CHRISTI (PORTUGAL)
Line-Up: Nocturnus Horrendous (vocals / bass), Guardiäo (guitar), Ignis Nox (keyboards)

CORPUS CHRISTI is the product of two NOCTU members keyboard player Ignis Nox and multi instrumentalist Nocturnus Horrendus. Guitarist Guardiäu enrolled in 1999. A demo 'Anno Domini' arrived upfront of the debut album 'Saeculum Domoni'.

Albums:
SAECULUM DOMONI, So Die Music (2000)
Flamma Tenebrarum / Victoria Crueth / Jesus Cunt Lickers / Crown Denied / Throne Of The Proud / Holy Masturbation / Ave Domini / All Hail (Master Satan)

CORVUS CORAX (USA)
Line-Up: Mallus Stormcrow, Paul Martin (bass), Johan Cleereman

New York trio not to be confused with the German Mediaeval act of the same name. Johan Cleereman also operates THE RED KING whilst Mallus Stormcrow has involvement with ANIMA NOCTURNA.

Albums:
THE ATAVISTIC TRIAD, Dark

Symphonies (2000)
Sons Of The Earth / Terminum Est / Sojourn / Mystagogue

COUNT DE NOCTE (FINLAND)
Line-Up: T, Nieminen (vocals), J. Orpana (guitar), W. Sauren (guitar), J. Salonen (bass), J. Aronen (keyboards), J. Hohtari (drums)

COUNT DE NOCTE emerged with the demo 'Nos Omnes Unamanet' under their previous name of ENDOPARASITES.

Albums:
SORORES NOCTE GENITAE, (199-)
Pimeys / Ravenbeauty / Sorores Nocte Genitae / As Darkness Descends / Into The Night / Nos Omnes Una Manet

COUNTESS (HOLLAND)
Line-Up: Orlok (vocals / bass), Zagan (guitar), Warhead (drums)

Black Metal quartet COUNTESS were created in 1992 cutting their debut demo 'Permafrost' the following year. After many attempts at forming a stable line up the COUNTESS finally settled in 1995 on the trio of vocalist / bassist Orlok, guitarist Zagan and drummer Warhead. The band released an interim demo following their second album 'The Gospel Of The Horned One' titled 'The Wolves Awake'. COUNTESS toured with MORTUARY DRAPE in 1995, hitting the road again in 1997 sharing a billing with SABBAT and BARATHRUM.
The album 'The Shining Swords Of Hate' includes a cover version of BATHORY's 'Return To Darkness And Evil'.

Singles/EPs:
Hell's Rock n' Roll / Son Of The Dragon / Dokkum 754 / On The Wings Of Azazel (Live), Prowler Productions PRO9766601 CD (1997)

Albums:
THE GOSPEL OF THE HORNED ONE, Thurisaz 001 (1993)
Overture / Highland Victory / Doomed To Die / Full Moon Baptism / Crossing The Fires Of Darkness / Under The Sign Of The Celtic Cross / Kneel Before The Master's Throne / March Of The Clans
THE RETURN OF THE HORNED ONE, Nazgûl's Eyrie Productions NEP003CD (1994)
Into Iniquity / Aleivis / Fire And Blood / A Cry Of Hope Forever Gone / Ritual Of

The Seven Priests / Into Battle / The Wolf Cries Evil / Deisdaimonia / Since Man Has Wielded Swords / Blood In De Sneeuw
AD MAIOREM SATHANAE GLORIAM, Nazgûl's Eyrie Productions NEP009CD (1994)
Ad Maiorem Sathanae Gloriam / The Priest Must Die / The Wrath Of Satan's Whore / Thus Spoke The Master / Blood On My Lips / Sheltered Under The Claw / Ere A Bitter End / Ad Maiorem Satahanae Glorium (Reprise) / Born Too Late
THE BOOK OF THE HERETIC, Nazgûl's Eyrie Productions NEP014CD (1996)
I Believe / On The Wings Of Azazel / Forgotten / In Hate Of Christ / Give Me Your Soul / Creation / A Warlord's Swansong / Mediaeval Shadows / Chapel Of Doom / All The Master's Children / The Heretic's Torch / Be Gist Der Goden
THE SHINING SWORDS OF HATE, Barbarian Wrath (2000)
Children Of The North Star / Total War / Hate From Hell / Te Vuur En Te Zwaard / Totenkopf (Satan's Soldaten) / When The Raven Flys / return To Of Darkness And Evil

COVENANT (NORWAY)
Line up- Amund, Sarah Jezebel Diva (vocals), Nagash, Astennu (guitar), Sverd, Blackheart, Hellhammer (drums)

Somewhat of a black metal supergroup heralded with a 1994 demo 'From The Storms Of Shadows'. The 1998 album, produced by Xy of SAMAEL, boasts main protagonist Amund abetted by CRADLE OF FILTH / THERION female vocalist Sarah Jezebel Diva, DIMMU BORGIR members Nagash and guitarist Astennu, MAYHEM's drummer Hellhammer and Sverd of ARCTURUS.
By the 2000 album the band had altered dramatically with Sverd and Astennu departing. The band name now became a trio titled KOVENANT (in an effort to quell the confusion over so many act's titled COVENANT and in particular Swedish Industrial band COVENANT who made legal claim to the title). Whilst the band was changing it's name the band members duly followed. Nagash retitled himself Lex Icon, Hellhammer became Von Blomberg and Blackheart was now known as Psy Coma.
Psy Coma and Von Blomberg guested on Nagash's project TROLL album of 2000 'The Last Predators'.

Albums:
IN THE TIMES BEFORE THE LIGHT, Mordgrimm (1997)
Towards The Crown Of Nights / Dragonstorms / The Dark Conquest / From The Storm Of Shadows / Night Of The Blackwinds / The Chasm / Visions Of A Lost Kingdom / Through The Eyes Of The Raven / In Times Before The Light / Monarch Of The Mighty Darkness
NEXUS POLARIS, Nuclear Blast NB 301-2 (1998)
The Sulphar Feast / Bizarre Comic Industries / Planetarium / The Last Of Dragons / Bringer Of The Sixth Sun / Dragonheart / Planetary Black Elements / Chariots Of Thunder

THE COVENANT (UK)

Albums:
SPECTRES AT THE FEAST, Covenant COVCD002 (1994)

CRADLE OF FILTH (UK)
Line-Up: Dani (vocals), Stuart Anstis (guitar), Brian Hipp (guitar), Robin Eaglestone (bass), Damien Gregori (keyboards), Nicholas (drums)

Probably the foremost exponents of the British Black Metal scene. CRADLE OF FILTH have built their reputation on hard gigging and inventive albums all aided by an impressive merchandising campaign with a vast range of deliberately provocative, but still highly creative, T shirt slogans.
CRADLE OF FILTH was created in Suffolk during 1991 by former PDA and FEAST ON EXCREMENT vocalist Dani Filth (real name Dani Lloyd Davey), guitarist Paul Ryan, bassist Jon Richard and drummer Darren. This inaugural line up cut the opening demo 'Invoking The Unclean' in 1992, shortly after which second guitarist Robin Graves (real name Robin Mark Eaglestone- previously with MALICIOUS INTENT) was added. Further recordings were made titled 'Black Goddess Rises'.
A further demo 'Orgiastic Pleasures' ensued after which Jon Richard departed to create HECATE ENTHRONED, the band manouevering Graves to bass to plug the gap and drafting Paul Allender on second guitar and Benjamin Ryan on keyboards. It was to be the act's third demo, 'Total Fucking Darkness' issued in December of 1993, that really set the mould for future works and scored a deal

with Cacophonous Records.

Former SOLEMN drummer Was Sarginson joined but lasted a handful of gigs.

The debut album, 1994's 'The Principle Of Evil Made Flesh', found the band with yet another new face as Nicholas took over the drumstool. The ructions did not stop there though as Paul Ryan, Benjamin Ryan and Paul Allender all bailed out. This CRADLE OF FILTH triumvirate of refugees formed THE BLOOD DIVINE with ex ANATHEMA vocalist Darren White in late 1995.

Vowing to carry on Dani quickly filled the ranks with guitarists Stuart Anstis and Jared Demeter together with Darren Gregori on keyboards. (rumours abounded that 'Jared Demeter' was in actually Stuart Anstis).

The band's second album 'Vempire Or Dark Faerytales In Phallustein' was produced by ex WITCHFINDER GENERAL and LIONSHEART bassist Zakk Bajjon and, in a trend which continues to this day, found the band utilizing two female backing vocalists Sarah Jezebel Deva (Sarah Jane Ferridge) and Danielle Cneajna Cottington.

Rishi Mehta was also a guitarist for CRADLE OF FILTH during 1994 but would unite with Benjamin Ryan and Zakk Bajjon to create CROWFOOT then RAINMAKER 888.

Just as media interest peaked on the Black Metal scene CRADLE OF FILTH found themselves embroiled for most of 1995 involved in legal proceedings against their record company. With the release of the 'Vempire' album CRADLE OF FILTH quickly established themselves as the leading contenders in the Death Metal stakes and signed up to a bigger label Music For Nations replacing (?) Demeter with former SOLSTICE and SHIP OF FOOLS man Gian Pyres (real name John Piras) in the process.

The 1996 album 'Dusk And Her Dark Embrace', produced by Kit Woolven-better known for his mellower work, propelled the band into the mainstream garnering high sales globally. Sarah Jezebel Deva once again featured and would become a staple part of the band's recording and live line up.

In outside activities Graves created the side band DECEMBER MOON with former CRADLE OF FILTH drummer Was Sarginson for a 1996 album.

Added ex BRUTALITY guitarist Brian Hipp for live work in 1996. Shortly after the band's appearance at the 1997 Milwaukee Metalfest they announced their new keyboard player as being erstwhile ANATHEMA and SHIP OF FOOLS member Lez Smith.

Barker was to depart in early 1999 to another high profile Black Metal outfit DIMMU BORGIR and appearing as part of the highly successful LOCK UP collaboration with HYPOCRISY's Peter Tägtgren, NAPALM DEATH's Shane Embury and Jesse Pintado. The ex drummer would also figure on the notorious 'Mexican' Death Metal band BRUJERIA's 'Brujerizmo' album.

CRADLE OF FILTH meanwhile set to work on their next album title track, and accompanying first full length video directed by Alex Chandon of 'Pervirella' fame, with the temporary employment of THE BLOOD DIVINE and DECEMBER MOON sticksman Wes Sargison. An even more temporary drummer was Dave Hirschheimer of INFESTATION.

By the summer of the same year the band fractured once again with both Gian Pyres and Hirschheimer departing, the drum stool now being occupied by former AT THE GATES man Adrian Erlandsson. CRADLE undertook American festival dates with a stand in session guitarist.

Allender was brought back into the ranks in late 1999 from his post THE BLOOD DIVINE act PRIMARY SLAVE as the band line up splintered once more with Pyres returning to the fold. The turbulence was far from complete however with keyboard player Les Smith and guitarist Stuart Anstis both given their marching orders. Anstis would create APHELION.

With all this turbulence the 'From The Cradle To Enslave' EP emerged featuring new tracks plus covers of THE MISFITS 'Death Comes Ripping' and ANATHEMA's 'Sleepless'. Former keyboard player Damien Gregori rejoined the band for these sessions. Predictably his tenure was brief, the man's work only appearing on the American version of the EP.

CRADLE OF FILTH pulled in former MY DYING BRIDE keyboard player Mark De Sade (real name Mark Newby Robson) but after a handful of gigs his place was taken by another erstwhile MY DYING BRIDE man Martin Powell.

Limited edition's of 2000's 'Midian' included a cover of SABBAT's 'For Those Who Died' with guest vocal from SABBAT and SKYCLAD vocalist Martin Walkyier.CRADLE OF FILTH toured Europe in late 2000 with guests veterans

Gothics CHRISTIAN DEATH. There was a huge degree of fraternization between the two bands as members of CRADLE OF FILTH including ex drummer Was Sarginson appeared on CHRISTIAN DEATH's 2000 album 'Born Again Anti Christian'.

The CRADLE OF FILTH line up for Midian stood at Filth, Pyres, Allender, Graves, Powell and Erlandsson.

Singles/EPs:
From The Cradle To Enslave / Of Blood And Fucking / Death Comes Ripping / Sleepless, Music For Nations (1999)

Albums:
THE PRINCIPLE OF EVIL MADE FLESH, Cacophonous NIHL1CD (1994)
Darkness Our Bride (Jugular Wedding) / The Principle Of Evil Made Flesh / The Forest Whispers My Name / Iscariot / The Black Goddess Rises / One Final Graven Kiss / A Crescendo Of Passion Bleeding / To Eve The Art Of Witchcraft / Of Mist And Midnight Skies / In Secret Love We Drown / A Dream Of Wolves In The Snow / Summer Dying Fast
VEMPIRE, OR DARK PHAERY TALES IN PHALLUSTEIN, Cacophonous NIHIL6CD (1996)
Ebony Dressed For Summer / The Forest Whispers My Name / Queen Of Winter / Throned / Nocturnal Supremacy / She Mourns A Lengthening Shadow /

The Rape And Ruin Of Angels
DUSK AND HER DARK EMBRACE-LITANIES OF DAMNATION, DEATH AND THE DARKLY EROTIC, Music For Nations MFN 208 (1996)
Humans Inspired To Nightmare / A Gothic Romance (Red Roses For The Devil's Whore) / Haunted Shores / Dusk And Her Dark Embrace / Heaven Torn Asunder / Carmilla's Masque (Portrait Of The Dead Countess) / Beauty Slept In Sodom / The Graveyard By Moonlight / Funeral In Carpathia
CRUELTY AND THE BEAST, Music For Nations (1998) **48 UK**
Once Upon Atrocity / Thirteen Autumns And A Widow / Cruelty Brought The Orchids / Beneath The Howling Stars / Venus In Fear / Desire In Violent Overture / The Twisted Nails Of Faith / Bathory Aria / Benighted Like Usher / A Murder Of Ravens In Fugue / Eyes That Witnessed Madness / Portrait Of The Dead Countess / Lustmord And Wargasm (The Lick Of Carnivorous Winds)
MIDIAN, Music For Nations (2000) **11 FINLAND, 30 GERMANY, 63 UK**
At The Gates Of Midian / Cthuhlu Dawn / Saffron's Curse / Death Magick For Adepts / Lord Abortion / Amor E Morte / Creatures Kissed In Cold Mirrors / Her Ghost In The Fog / Satanic Mantra / Tearing The Veil From Grace / Tortured Soul Asylum / For Those Who Have Died

CRANIUM (SWEDEN)
Line-Up: Chainsaw Demon (vocals), Fredrik Söderberg (guitar), Grave Raper (guitar), Necro Nudist (drums)

CRANIUM's history dates back to 1985 founded by brothers bassist Phillip Von Segebaden and guitarist Gustaf. The act was rounded off with guitarist Fredrik Söderberg and drummer Fredrik Engqvist. The band changed titles to LEGION for the 1986 demo 'The Dawn' but soon folded.
Söderburg would found OBDURACY then the highly rated DAWN.
By 1996 the band reformed as CRANIUM once more to release the 'Speed Metal Satan' mini album comprised of early 80's tracks re-recorded. The band, now with Phillip Von Segebaden retitled 'Chainsaw Demon', employed the services of DAWN drummer Jocke Petterson before he decamped to THY PRIMORDIAL rebilling himself Morth.
For the 'Speed Metal Slaughter' album UTUMNO man Johan Hallberg was recruited although under the pseudonym of Necro Nudist.
Phillip Von Segebaden also has a side project band DEFENDER.

Albums:
SPEED METAL SATAN, Necropolis (1997)
Lucifer's Breath (The Storm To Come) / Storm Of Steel And Hate / Riders Of Damnation / Bestial Butcher / Raped By Demons
SPEED METAL SLAUGHTER, Necropolis (1998)
Slaughter On The Dance Floor / Lawnmower Lover / Dentist Of Death / S.R.T. (Satanic Rescue Team) / A Devil On The Drums- Sluts Of Satan / Graveyard Romance / Satanic Holiday
SPEED METAL SENTENCE, (1999)
Speed Metal Sentence / Nymphomaniac Nuns / Full Moon Fistbanger / Satanic Sect / Pestilential Penis / Samurai Satan / Taxi Terror / Cranium- Crushers Of Christ

CREMATORIUM (Whittier, CA, USA)

CREMATORIUM offered their homage to JUDAS PRIEST by including their version of 'Breaking The Law' to the 'Hell Bent For Metal' tribute album.

Albums
EPICEDIUMS OF THE DAMNED,
Crematorium (1997)

CREPUSCULUM CONSCIENTIAE
(ITALY)

Band forged by former NECROSIS members. CREPUSCULUM CONSCIENTIAE released a brace of demos in 1994's 'Brain Damage' and the following year's 'Rape Of The Mind'.

CREST OF DARKNESS (NORWAY)
Line-Up: Kristin Fjellseth (vocals), Akke (guitar), Ingar Almein (bass), Jan Petter Ringvold (keyboards), Frelløs (drums)

CREST OF DARKNESS was founded by former CONCEPTION bassist Ingar Almein. The band bowed in with the 'Quench My Thirst' EP as a trio featuring Almein on bass and guitar, keyboard player Lars Christian Narum and drummer Nils H. Maehlum. This line up was retained for the full length album 'Sinister Scenarios'.
1999's 'The Ogress' saw a shift to Listenable Records and a new look band with Almein pulling in PALE FOREST vocalist Kristin Fjellseth, his former CONCEPTION (and now KAMELOT) vocalist Roy Khan, keyboards from both Narum and Jan Petter Rinvold with drums from former CONCEPTION man Arne Heimdal.
The 2000 album 'Project Regeneration' sees contributions from Kristin Fjellseth on vocals, guitarist Akke, drummer Frekkøs with Ringvold retained on keyboards and arrangements from French Industrial act MELEK-THA.
CREST OF DARKNESS put in their inaugural live shows during November 2000.

Singles/EPs:
On A Sea Of Darkness / Quench My Thirst / This Is The Morning Magic / Absorption, Head Not Found (1996) ('Quench My Thirst' EP)

Albums:
SINISTER SCENARIO, Head Not Found (1997)
Under The Sign Of The Horned God / Sinister Scenario / The Acknowledgement / Recall The Earth / This World Is Mine / The Voice / Substitute Lover / Beautiful Monstrosity / Desire / Lunacy Souls
THE OGRESS, Listenable POSH015 (1999)

Eucharist / The Thousand Years / The Ogress / Reference / The Inheritance / Gift Of Grace / Euphoria / Sweet Scent Of Dark / Her Crown
PROJECT REGENERATION, Listenable POSH025 (2000)
Computerized / Luciferian Light / Project Regeneration / Sector 63 S / Hominis Nocturna / A Place With No Memories / Virus Control / Soulhunter / Living Dead / Electronic Art (Computerized Part 2)

CRIMSON MIDWINTER (FINLAND)
Line-Up: Jussi Kelenius (vocals), Jari (guitar), Jaako Like (guitar), Atte Makala (drums)

Some confusion over CRIMSON MIDWINTER's early line up as their first demo tape listed guitars credited to 'Kukko' and 'Jaska', in actual fact these being nicknames for longstanding members Jari and Jaako Like. However, the band's early rhythm section of bassist Mikko and drummer Teppo was soon dispensed with.

Albums:
RANDOM CHAOS, (199-)
Carnal Inferno / The Burden Of Immortality / Metalglory! / Random Chaos Logic / Flames Forseed / Bloodmetalfist / Loneliness, Bitterness: Utopia Falls / Like Pearls Before Swine

CRIMSON MOON
(Indianapolis, IN, USA)
Line-Up: Vampir Scorpio (vocals / bass), Nocturnal Overlord (guitar / drums), Pact Of Blood (keyboards)

Black Metal band CRIMSON MOON preceded their 'To Embrace The Vampyric Blood' album with a 1995 demo 'Into The Nocturnal Forest'. The album was in fact recorded in the bass player's front room!
All the members of CRIMSON MOON divide their time with other acts. Nocturnal Overlord operates in ARISE, ABYSMAL NOCTURNE and NEBIRU, frontman Vampir Scorpio is a member of SABNACK and AKRABUA whilst keyboard player Pact Of Blood figures in AKHKHARU.

Albums:
TO EMBRACE THE VAMPYRIC BLOOD, Abyss Productions (1997)
The Dirge Of The Apocalypse / Kingdom Of Shadows / Praise Be The Blood Of

The Serpent / Carpe Noctem / The Stormbringer / Sender Of Nocturnal Visions / To Offer Thy Crimson Sacrament / The Eye Of Draconis / Embraced

CRIMSON MOONLIGHT (Sweden)
Line-Up: Pilgrim (vocals), Petter (guitar), Samuel (guitar), David (bass), Alexander (keyboards), Gustav (drums).

CRIMSON MOONLIGHT are one of the few acts to pursue Black Metal music with the most ironic of twists-they are clearly stated Christians. The band's first demo 'Glorification Of The Master Of Light' saw VITAL DECISION singer Simon Rosén taking a guest lead vocal role.
Following the self financed EP 'Eternal Emperor' guitarist Jonathon would break away to concentrate full time on his other band SANCTIFICA. CRIMSON MOONLIGHT enlisted Samuel as replacement. Guitarist Petter is also involved with OBSECRATION.
The band bill themselves as Pilgrim-'Screams To Shatter The Walls Of Ignorance', Gustav-'Rhythms To Awaken The Dead And Feed The Fire Of Resolution', David-'Sounds To Tumble The Mountain Into The Ocean, Clear Vocal To Dry Your Eyes', Petter-'Melodies Haunting The Negative Forest, Cries To Pierce Your Heart', Samuel-'Tones Travelling The Rays Of Moonlight' and Alexander-'Dark Symphonic Art Of Sheer Beauty'.

Singles:
Where Darkness Cannot Reach/ Symphony Of Moonlight/ Eternal Emperor/ The Final Battle, (1999) (Eternal Emperor' EP)

CRONOS (UK)
Line-Up: Cronos (vocals / bass), Mike Hickey (guitar), James Clare (guitar), Chris Patterson (drums)

After nine years fronting one of the archetypal Black Metal outfits VENOM mainman Conrad Lant (a.k.a. Cronos) left the group in 1988 to form CRONOS, the result of the disappointing sales of 1987's 'Calm Before The Storm' album.
Conrad took both VENOM guitarists Mike H. (real name Mike Hickey) and Jimi C. along with him and soon added drummer Chris P. (at this point the band's musicians were known only by the initial letters of their surnames).

Scheduled tours of America and Japan were postponed in late 1989 when Cronos sustained a broken hand in a car accident. The band later toured the east coast of America, but after the release of the 'Dancing In The Fire' debut album live activity became limited.

CRONOS were due to tour Britain on a double bill with WARFARE on the so dubbed 'Dancing With The Firehammers' tour, but this was cancelled due to lack of interest! The band did, however, support MASSACRE at London's Marquee in 1992, by which time a second album, 'Rock n' Roll Disease' had appeared the previous year.

Lant guested on the 1994 album 'When War Begins… Truth Disappears' from German act WARPATH. Hickey emerged as temporary member of CATHEDRAL and then as live guitarist for CARCASS during 1994 touring to promote their 'Heartwork' album.

A third album was recorded during 1994, but Cronos decided - somewhat inevitably - to participate in the reformation of the original VENOM line-up in 1995 that headlined the Waldrock festival.

A new CRONOS album was released during 1995 to record the 'Venom' album with a brand new membership that contained Cronos, Hickey and ex CATHEDRAL drummer Mark Wharton. The album oddly featured re-works of classic VENOM songs.

As VENOM geared up for their reformation album 'Cast In Stone' and subsequent touring CRONOS was inevitably put on the back burner despite sessions for a planned fourth album titled 'Triumphirate' already being in the can.

Albums:
DANCING IN THE FIRE, Neat ODIO48 (1990)
Fantasia / Terrorize / Dancing In The Fire / Speedball / I'll Be Back / Vampire / Chinese Whispers / Old Enough To Bleed / Painkiller / My Girl / Hell To The Unknown
ROCK N' ROLL DISEASE, Neat D1051 (1991)
Messages Of War / Rock n' Roll Disease / Lost And Found / Midnight Eye / Sexploitation / Aphrodisiac / Sweet Savage Sex / Dirty Tricks Department / Bared To The Bone
VENOM, Neat Metal NM003 (1995)
In League With Satan / Superpower / Vempyr / Fire / 1000 Days In Sodom / Know Evil / Messages Of War / 7 Gates

Of Hell / Painkiller / Don't Burn The Witch (In Nomine Satanas) / Ye Of Little Faith / Satanachist / At War With Satan / Babylon

CROTALO (ITALY)
Line-Up: Gaetano Bucci (vocals / drums), Massimo Quinzio (guitar), Stefano Di Stasi (keyboards), Fabrizio Bolognani (bass)

Albums:
NEL CUORE DEL MONDO, WMMS 122 (1997)
Nel Cuore Del Mondo / In Viaggio Da Sempre / Oltre Il Buio Della Notte / Espressioni / Anime In Cammino / La Forza Della Disperazione / Geneazione X / Vivere Degliattimi / Davanti Ai Tuoi Occhi

CROWNFALL (NORWAY)
Line-Up: Geir Horn (vocals / guitar), Terje Andersen (guitar), Sverre Stokland (bass), Thomas Berglie (drums)

Although only having achieved demo releases CROWNFALL, previously known as ENDLESS upon their formation in late 1991, have made their mark on the Black Metal scene with the exploits of guitarist Terje Andersen.

Better known as Cyrus the six stringer has been employed as live guitarist for SATYRICON as well as boasting membership of OLD MAN'S CHILD, SENSA ANIMA and SUSPERIA.

CROWNFALL vocalist Geir Horn also has credits with OLD MAN'S CHILD under the pseudonym of Lupus.

CROWN OF AUTUMN (ITALY)
Line-Up: Diego Balconi (vocals), Emanuele Rastelli (bass / keyboards),

Albums:
THE TREASURES ARCANE, Elnor ELN 001 (1997)
Equinox / Towers Of Doleful Triumph / A Lyre In The Vesper's Calm / Nocturnal Gold Part 1: In Ageless Slumber / Nocturnal Gold Part 2: The Name Of Inquietude / The Nettle Path Of Grief / Thou Mayst In Mee Behold / The Treasures Arcane / And The Cold Came O'er The Feud / 'Neath Selenic Majesty / Forlorn Elven Realms

CRUACHAN (IRELAND)

Irish Folk Metallers. Signed up new

drummer Joe Farrell in late 1999.

Albums:
TUATHA NA GAEL, Nazgûl's Eyrie Productions NEP005 (1995)
I Am Tuan / The First Battle Of Moytura / Maeves March / Fall Of Gondolin / Cú Chulainn / Táin Bó Cuailgne / To Invoke The Horned Gods / Brian Boru / To Moytura We Return
THE MIDDLE KINGDOM, Hammerheart (2000)
A Celtic Mourning / Celtica (Voice Of The Morrigan) / The Fianna / A Druids Passing / Is Fuair An Chroi / Cattle Raid Of Cooley (Tain Bo Cuailigne) / The Middle Kingdom / Oro Se Do Bheatlia / Abhaile / Unstabled (Steeds Of Macha) / The Butterfly

CRUCIFIED WHORE (GERMANY)
Line-Up: Ferron Deduwath (vocals), Blackwinged Svarog (guitar), Nattvind (drums)

CRUCIFIED WHORE featured a track on the 'Only Death Is Real IV' compilation album. The band has issued the demo 'Beyond Nocturnal Senses' and 'Of Dark Ages'.

CRUCIFIER (PA, USA)

Black Metal band CRUCIFIER, centred on Cazz Grant of GRAND BELIAL'S KEY, have issued a whole array of demos starting with 'Humans Are Such Easy Prey' in 1991. Further sessions included 1993's 'By Disgrace Of God' and 1994's 'Powerless Against'.
Grant founded a new act BLUDGEON in 1997.

Singles/EPs:
Unparalleled Majesty, Pagan (1993) (7" single)
Split, Crucifer (1998) (Split 7" single with NUNSLAUGHTER)

CRUCIFORM

Albums:
ATAVISM (1993)
Prologue / Reduced To Dust / Necropolis / Proboscis / I, To The Heavens Shall lift My Eyes

CRY HAVOC (FINLAND)
Line-Up: Kaapro Ikonen (vocals), Jouni Lilja (guitar), Risto Lipponen (guitar), Kari Myöhänen (bass), Pauli Tolvahen (drums)

CRY HAVOC began their musical journey entitled PREPROPHECY issuing the Death Metal demos 'A Tomb Of Sanity' in 1993 and it's follow up 'Season Of Sorrows'. A name switch to RAVENSFALL saw the addition of ABSURDUS rhythm section bassist Taneli Nyholm and drummer Matti Roiha in 1996. However, when ABSURDUS were signed by the British Candlelight label Nyholm and Roiha disembarked back to their priority act. (Nyholm, billed as 'Daniel Stuka', would later join BABYLON WHORES).
A deal was struck with a Singapore based label and RAVENSFALL began preparation for recording of a debut album. Fate intervened when the label in question folded leaving the band high and dry. Noted label Spinefarm came to their rescue and the band, now billed as CRYHAVOC, cut their debut entitled 'Sweet Briars'.
Sales of the album were high (no doubt aided by the artistic sleeve photo cover imagery) and 'Pitch Black Blues' emerged in 1999.

Albums:
SWEET BRIARS, Nuclear Blast NB 326-2 (1998)
Bloodtie / Repent (Whore) / Come With Me / Wolfdance / Pagan Uprise / I Fade Away / Armageddon Y'Know / Misanthropy
PITCH BLACK BLUES, Spinefarm (1999)
Cryscythe / Metamorphosis / The Wind / Snowsong / Spree / The Serpent And Eve / Wild At Heart / Pitch Black Ink

CRYOGENIC (GERMANY)
Line-Up: Sven (vocals), Johanna (vocals), Harpokrates (guitar), Imperus (guitar), Jormundgander (bass), Theehomok (keyboards), Trismegistos (drums)

Berlin's CRYOGENIC had their debut album 'Celephais' produced by the noted figure of Harris Johns. The band, then in 1993 with early members singer Ruben and guitarist Niddhoggar, heralded their arrival with the demo 'Ignis Occultus In'.

Albums:
CELEPHAIS, Solistitium SOL034 (1999)
Celephais- Overture / wanderer / Die Rueckkehr / Fimbulwinter / Nactwache / Ignis Occultus In… / Processia Nocturna- Teil I / Processia Nocturna-

Teil I / Celephais / Celephais- Finale

CRYPTIC CARNAGE (GERMANY)

German Black Metallers CRYPTIC CARNAGE set the stage with the demos 'Return Of The Damned' and 'The Ancient'.

Albums:
... AND ANOTHER KINGDOM WAS BORN, Folter (1996)
Beyond The Burning Horizon / And A Star Of Glory Began To Shine / ... And Another Kingdom Was Born / With The Wind / Illusion / Mephistopholes / Lords Of Blackness / Nameless
ROZELOWE, Last Episode (1998)
Rozelowe / However Rich A Man May Be... / The Wizard / Beauty At Everytime / Primae Noctis / Franzikus / Lived To Die / Liebe, Hass, Neid Und Verderben / Disobedience / Timewarp

CRYPTICAL REALM (BELGIUM)

CRYPTICAL REALM opened proceedings with the 1996 demo 'Jus Caedis' followed up by a live cassette 'Celtic Rage'.
The 'La Tené' EP was limited to a mere 100 copies.
Although CRYPTICAL REALM is firmly centred upon multi instrumentalist Bart Uytterhaegen other contributing musicians included the soprano vocals of Wendy Supere, guest vocals from Sven of ANESTHESY and Hugo Tack on bass and keyboards.

Singles/EPs:
Death Wish / Fall Into Your Darkest Dream / Golgota (Live) / The Celtic Rage (Live), (1998) ('La Tené' EP)

Albums:
OPUS INFINITY, (1999)
Intro / Imman Curaig Maldruin Inso / The Excalibur Sonate: The Lady In The Lake / The Three Nights Of Samhain / Opus Infinity / The Excalibur Sonate II: The Uther Pendragon Pact

CRYPTIC WINTERMOON
(GERMANY)
Line-Up: Ronny Dörfler (vocals), Larsen Beattie (guitar), Michael Scharger (guitar), Jason (bass), Andrea Walter (keyboards), Goatlord (drums)

CRYPTIC WINTERMOON emerged in 1993 with a line up of guitarist Larsen Beattie, vocalist Bernd Seeberger, bass player Christian Reichel and drummer Marek Karakasevic. The following year saw the exit of both Seeburger and Karakasevic.
The frontman's position was taken by Ronny Dörfler but it was to be 1996 before Alexander Pohlmanni occupied the drumstool for the demo 'Voyage Dans Le Luna'. The same year saw Reichel departing in favour of Christian Ender and the addition of keyboard player Andrea Walter and guitarist Jochen Kressin.
Kressin was replaced by Michael Scharger in 1998. Goatlord took the drummer role in 2000.

Albums:
CRYPTIC WINTERMOON, (1997)
Shadowland / Angels Never Die / Visions Of Eternal Darkness / Doomsday
FRANCONIAN FROST, (1998) (Split album)
THE AGE OF CATACLYSM, Ars Metalli (1999)
The Cataclysm / The Abysssal Spectre / Born In Fire / Into Ashes / Fallen Kingdoms / When Daylight Dies / Blood Of The Dragon / Winter Of Apocalypse / Black Moon / Angels Never Die / Gods Of Fire And Ice / Necrobiosis / Dawn Of Ages

CRYPT OF KERBEROS (SWEDEN)
Line-Up: Christian Eriksson (vocals), Johan Löhnroth (guitar), Peter Petersson (guitar), Stefan Karlsson (bass), Jessica Stranbdell (keyboards), Mikael Sjöberg (drums)

Founded in 1990 under the original moniker of MACRODEX, releasing a demo cassette under that title, the group transformed itself into CRYPT OF KERBEROS. After the release of the 'Visions Beyond Darkness' single guitarist Johan Löhnroth and drummer Mikael Sjöberg split and Jonas Strandell and Mattias Bough were drafted in to fill the respective vacancies.
Although CRYPT OF KERBEROS issued a follow up single in 1992 and the 'World Of Myths' album in 1995, the group has now folded, guitarist Peter Petersson becoming a member of ARCANA.

Singles/EPs:
Visions Beyond Darkness / Darkest Rites, Sunabel SUNABEL 001 (1991)
Cyclone Of Insanity / The Ancient War, Adipocere AR004 (1992)

Albums:
WORLD OF MYTHS, Adipocere CDAR
913 (1995)
The Canticle / Cyclone Of Insanity /
Dream... / Stormbringer / The Ancient
War / Nocturnal Grasp / The Sleeping
God / World Of Myths

CULTUS SANGUINE (ITALY)

CULTUS SANGUINE is the side project
of MONUMENTUM's Roberto
Mammarella.
CULTUS SANGUINE's 2000 album 'War
Vol. III' was recorded in collaboration with
French Black Metal act SETH. The record
included a cover version of DEPECHE
MODE's 'Behind The Wheel'.

Singles/EPs:
The Evil Side, Adipocere (199-)

Albums:
CULTUS SANGUINE, Adipocere (1995)
Il Richiamo In Rosso / I Ride The Winds
Of Hate / My Journey Is Long But My
Time Is Endless / Into The Fields Of
Screaming Souls
SHADOWS BLOOD, Candlelight 021CD
(1998)
The Calling Illusion / Il Sangue /
Shadow's Blood / We Have No Mother /
The Graves Forget My Name / Lady Of
Lies / On These Nocturnal Wings / Le
Tombe / Silent Tunes Of Falling Blood /
Among Shadows
THE SUM OF ALL FEARS, Season Of
Mist (1999)
The Sum Of All Fears / Verrá Il Tempo Dei
Morti / Dominatress / Highest Depression /
The Fortune Unveiled / A Grace Upon
Mankind / In The Days Of Sombre /
Ultimat Madre / As A Funeral Inside
WAR VOL. III, Season Of Mist (2000)
(With SETH)
My Journey Is Long But My Time Is
Endless / We Have No Mother (Sir
Grave's Remix) / L'Hymne Au Vampire /
Behind The Wheel

CUTTHROAT (JAPAN)
Line-Up: Mirai (vocals), Shinichi (guitar),
Yasuyuki (bass), Youhei (drums)

CUTTHROAT was a 1999 project forged
by the alliance of two of Japan's most
esteemed extreme acs SIGH and
ABIGAIL. CUTTHROAT signed to Greek
label Iso666 for the subtly titled 'Rape,
Rape, Rape' album.

Albums:
RAPE, RAPE, RAPE, Iso666 (2000)

DAEMON
(NEW ZEALAND)

DAEMON, hailing from Nelson on New Zealand's south island, have endured turbulent times with persisting line up fractures leading up to the release of the 1997 'Neodeath' album.

The band's roots lay in the 1992 act BLOODWYCH which included vocalist Beezle and guitarist Xanataph. Later additions Jude Haenga on guitar, Jim Whyte on bass and drummer Peter Hockey saw the band evolve into the CARCASS inspired SLASH DEMENTIA. Kori Barrett took the drum stool as the group morphed yet again into DAEMON. However, Beezle would decamp in late 1993 to be replaced by Steve Doubrey of CATALYST. This line up redictably floundered and after a short spell with a female lead singer Xanataph added the vocal role to his duties. In a period of confusion Barrett made his exit. His replacement Amoniath was in turn ousted by the returning Barrett.

At this juncture DAEMON leader Xanataph forged a side outfit ANALYST with ex member Amoniath and bassist Nostohein from THE ADVERSARY. By 1997 ANALYST had retitled themselves DAEMON to record the 'Neodeath' album.

Later line ups of DAEMON would see Dead BC on drums and Lord Goatfuck on bass. The latter would bail out, his temporary replacement in 2000 being Thyiendalen on loan from BELTANE.

Albums:
NEODEATH, (1997)

DAEMONARCH (PORTUGAL)

DAEMONARCH is the side project of MOONSPELL's Fernando Ribeiro a.k.a. Langsuyar. Other MOONSPELL personnel are anonymously involved.

Albums:
HERMETICUM, (1998)
Lex Talonis / Of A Thousand Young / Corpus Hermeticum / Call From The Grave / Samyaja / Nine Angles / Incubus / The Seventh Daemonarch / Hymn To Lucifer

DAEMONIUM (FRANCE)

A supposed secret project by AKHENATON mentor Lord Vincent Akhenaton. All instruments are performed by the great one himself.

Akhenaton is also a member of AMAYMON and latterly fronts WINDS OF SIRIUS billed as Signeuer V. Sandragon.

Albums:
DARK OPERA OF THE ANCIENT WAR SPIRIT (OR SEARCH THE LIGHT), Adipocere CD AR020 (1994)
Act I- Necromancy / Act II- Chaos's Resurrection / Act III- By The Sword / Act IV- Close The Eve Of Seth / Act V- Black Like The Hate / Act VI- De Legions / Act VII- Of Desolation / Act VIII- De Arcanium Daemonium / Act Final (IX)- And You'll Raise Into The Light

DAIMONIA NYMPH (GREECE)

DAIMONIA NYMPH also operate as FIENDISH NYMPH.

Albums:
BAKXIKOE XOPOE TAN NY MORN, Solistitium SOL017 (1997)
The Calling Of Naiaaes / The Bacchic Dance Of The Nymphs / Calling The Twelve Gods / Calling Pan, Solistium SOL017 (1997)

DAKRIA (GERMANY)

Cologne based DAKRIA would fold after the 'Immortal Silent Heaven' album. Vocalist Oemer Hamzuoglu, also singer with Bonn's SYRE, would found ASEYEAM. Guitarist Martin Schaefer would join him in 1999.

Albums:
IMMORTAL SILENT HEAVEN, (1997)
Intro / The Battle To Call / Immortal Silent Heaven / Distance Longing Desire / The Endless Bereavement

DAMNATION (POLAND)
Line-Up: Les (vocals / guitar), Bart (guitar), Nergal (bass), Inferno (drums)

DAMNATION feature two members of BEHEMOTH: vocalist / guitarist Les and bassist Nergal. The band formed in 1991 releasing their first demo 'Everlasting Sickness' in 1993. A further tape, 'Forbidden Spaces', followed the next year which led to a deal with Polish label Pagan Records.

Following the debut album's release bassist Dagon was replaced by Nergal.

Vocalist Les was to create a side project titled HELL-BORN together with BEHEMOTH's Lord Ravenlock releasing an eponymous album.

Singles/EPs:
Coronation / Spell Master / Sworn To The Darkside / The Land Of Degradation, Last Episode 007300-2 LEP (1997) ('Coronation' EP)

Albums:
REBORN, Pagan Moon CD 002 (1995)
Pagan Prayer- The Antichrist / The Land Of Degradation / Leaving Into New Reality / From Broken Cross (Bleeding Jesus) / Time Of Prophets / Infestation-Maldoror Is Dead / Forbidden Spaces / The Rulling Truth / Behind The Walls Of Tears / Reborn (Outro)
REBEL SOULS, Last Epitaph Productions LEP010 (1996)
Prelude To Rebellion / Who Your God Is / Son Of Fire / Rebel Souls / Azarath- Watching In Darkness / From The Abyssland / Deliverance / Might Returns

DÄMONENDONNER (GERMANY)

Essentially a solo project of Arzachel. DÄMONENDONNER did benefit from the vocals of Isegrimm.

Albums:
DER FALL DES LICHTES, (1999)

DANSE MACABRE (HOLLAND)
Line-Up: Gunnar Theys, Jan Yrlund

DANSE MACABRE was originally one of the voluminous projects of NECROMANTIA mentor Magus Wampyr Daoloth with Gunther Theys of ANCIENT RITES and Sotiris of SEPTIC FLESH. Recordings cut for a projected single with the bankrupt Molon Lave label were shelved and Theys took the concept on to a full blown album.

Albums:
TOTENTANZ, Mascot M 7029-2 (1998)
Dust Of Centuries / Totentanz / Death In Midsummer / Gott Ist Tot (Where Science Prevailed) / Jester's Farewell (Solitude) / Decline Of Romanticism / Tristesse (Of Cardinals And Skeletons) / Ignorance Is Bliss (Di Talem Terris Avertite Pestem) / Overture To The Sun (Finsternis) / Megalomania / Psychopompos / A Dream Within A Dream

DARGAARD (AUSTRIA)

DARGAARD is just one of many creative outlets for Tharen, a veteran of such renowned names as ABIGOR, AMESTIGON and HEIDENREICH. His latest venture was forged in 1997 and fronted by vocalist Elizabeth Toriser. The lady in question having credits with ABIGOR, ANTICHRISIS and Tharen's other project DOMINION.

Albums:
ETERNITY RITES, Draenor Productions (1998)
Eternity Rite I / Demon Eyes / Fuer Isa Est Drakuna / Down To The Halls Of The Blind / Nightvision / Arcanum Mortis / Eternity Rite II / Temple Of The Moon / … Of Broken Stones / Seelenlos / Transfer Complete
IN NOMINE AETERNITATIS, Draenor Productions DPR009 (2000)
Dark Horizons / Underworld Domain / Pantheon In Flames / The Infinite / Temple Of The Morning Star / Caverna Obscura / Only The Blind Can See… / In Signo Mortis / The March Of Shadows / In Nomine Aeternitatis / The Seas Of Oblivion

DARKEST HOUR
(Washington DC, USA)
Line-Up: John Blakemore Henry (vocals),

Albums:
PROPHECY FULFILLED, (199-)
Choir Of The Prophecy Fulfilled / Reflections Of Ruin / Broken Wings / This Side Of Nightmare / This Curse / Coda XIII
THE MARK OF JUDAS, MIA (2000)
For The Soul Of The Savior / A Blessing In Tragedy / The Legacy / Part II / Eclipse / The Mark Of Judas / Escape Artist / Messiah Complex / How The Beautiful Decay

DARKEST OATH (GREECE)

DARKEST OATH involves the talents of NECROMANTIA's industrious Magus Vampyr Daoloth.

Singles/EPs:
Paradise Of The Infernal Torment, Molon Lave (1995)

DARK FUNERAL (SWEDEN)
Line-Up: Emperor Magus Caligula (vocals / bass), Blackmoon (guitar), Lord

Ahriman (guitar), Alzazmon (drums)

DARK FUNERAL date back to a band project assembled in 1993 by guitarists Blackmoon (real name David Parland and ex NECROPHOBIC) and Lord Ahriman (real name Micke Svanberg). The band line-up was completed by Themgoroth and Draugen and DARK FUNERAL issued the four track 'Dark Funeral' EP on Hellspawn Records in 1994. This record was also released in Poland on Carrion Records and retitled 'Open The Gates'.

Following the EP's release Draugen departed (eventually turning up as a member of SVARTSYN) and was succeeded by Equimanthorn as DARK FUNERAL began playing their first live shows.

Upon the eve of release of DARK FUNERAL's first full length album, 'The Secrets Of The Black Arts' (produced by HYPOCRISY's Peter Tägtgren), the band again underwent a roster change with the addition of vocalist/bassist Emperor Magus Caligula and drummer Alzazmon. The album, incidentally, includes a cover of VON's 'Satanic Blood'.

Guitarist Blackmoon also played guitar for NECROPHOBIC. He quit the band he quit in 1996 to concentrate on a solo project BLACKMOON his place being taken by Typhos, previously a member of Stockholm's FUNERAL MIST.

Touring in Europe saw the band supported by Italians NECROMASS. The band made every effort to lay on a terrifying spectacle with pigs heads on spikes gracing the stage flanked by inverted crosses. These dates, the first leg of what would become the 'Satanic War' tour, were so successful DARK FUNERAL toured Europe once more in February of 1997. For this batch of shows BAL SAGOTH and ANCIENT opened. The group's reach extended into their debut American shows later in the year with a short East coast tour.

1998 had DARK FUNERAL forming part of a European package bill sharing stages with CANNIBAL CORPSE and INFERNAL MAJESTY. The following year witnessed West coast American dates and a brief foray into Mexico upfront of European support slots to DIMMU BORGIR.

DARK FUNERAL would pay homage to their mentors by cutting cover versions of MAYHEM's 'Pagan Fears', KING DIAMOND's 'The Trial', SODOM's 'Remember The Dead' and SLAYER's Dead Skin Mask' for the 'Teach Children To Worship Satan' EP.

During 2000 Caligula and Dominion united with DARK FUNERAL session drummer Gaahfaust to found side project DOMINION CALIGULA releasing the 'A New Era Rises' album in 2000.

Not to be outdone Lord Ahriman created WOLFEN SOCIETY with ex ACHERON leader Vincent Crowley, Kyle Severn of INCANTATION and erstwhile VITAL REMAINS man Jeff Gruslins.

DARK FUNERAL added former DEFLESHED drummer Matte Modin to the ranks in late 2000.

Singles/EPs:
Open The Gates / Shadows Over Transylvania / My Dark Desire / In The Sign Of The Hordes, Hellspawn HELL001 (1994) ('Dark Funeral' EP)
The Trial / Dead Skin Mask / Remember The Fallen / Pagan Fears / An Apprentice To Satan, (2000) ('Teach Children To Worship Satan' EP)

Albums:
THE SECRETS OF THE BLACK ARTS, No Fashion NFR011 (1996)
The Dark Age Has Arrived / The Secrets Of The Black Arts / My Dark Desires / The Dawn No More Rises / When Angels Forever Die / The Fire Eternal / Satan's Mayhem / Shadows Over Transylvania / Bloodfrozen / Satanic Blood / Dark Are The Path To Eternity (A Summoning Nocturnal)
VOBISCUM SATANAS, No Fashion NFR027 (1998)
Ravenna Strigoi Mortii / Enriched By Evil / Thy Legions Come / Evil Prevail / Slava Satan / The Black Winged Horde / Vobiscum Satanas / Ineffable King Of Darkness

DARK HERESY (UK)

DARK HERESY debuted with the demo 'Diabolus in Musica' before the 'Abstract Principles…' album saw the light in 1995.

Albums:
ABSTRACT PRINCIPLES... TAKEN TO THEIR LOGICAL EXTREMES, Unisound (1995)
Engines Of Torture / The Last Temptation Of Pan / The Ceremony / Thy Blood / Ofermord / Hole / The Millstone / Tyler's Stand

DARKIFIED (SWEDEN)
Line-Up: Martin Gustavsson (vocals),

98

Martin Ahx (guitar), Robert Karlsson (bass), Jocke Göthberg (drums)

Ex MARDUK and CARDINAL SIN drummer Jocke 'Grave' Göthberg was a key figure in DARKIFIED, EDGE OF SANITY's Dan Swano also making his presence felt contributing keyboards on the 'A Dance On The Grave' album.
Bassist Robert Karlsson also sings lead vocal for Swano's act PAN-THY-MONIUM.

Singles/EPs:
Sleep Forever / The Forgotten City / The Whispers In The Darkness, Drowned Products DS003 (1992)

Albums:
A DANCE ON THE GRAVE, Repulse RPS005 (1995)
Intro / Howlings From The Darkness / A Summon For The Nameless Horrors / The Forgotten City / Outro For The Darkness / Sleep Forever… / The Forgotten City (1992) / The Whisperer In The Darkness

DARK MOON (Charlotte, SC, USA)
Line-Up: John Vesano (vocals / guitar), Chuck (guitar), Devon Penrod (bass), Scott Pletcher (drums)

South Carolina Black Metal band assembled by way of an en masse elopement from DEMONIC CHRIST. Guitarist Chuck features on DEMONIC CHRIST's debut album 'Punishment For Ignorance' whilst bassist Devon and drummer Scott were later members.

Singles/EPs:
Writhing Glory / Ceremonies Of Flesh Devine / Spirits In My Eyes, (199-) ('Dark Moon' EP)

Albums:
SEAS OF UNREST, Music For Nations (1999)
King Enthroned Upon Ashes / Vengeance For Withered Hearts / From The Moon's Mist We Rise / Wolf Cry / Writhing Glory / Ceremonies Of Flesh Devine / Spirit In My Eyes

DARKNESS ENSHROUD (NORWAY)

Essentially a solo project by ex SORATH man Baron Von Abaddon dating to 1993, DARKNESS ENSHROUD's first demo

'Winter Of Sorrow', was recorded with the aid of one Rahu. However, the debut album 'Ancient Kingdoms' was purely a solo effort.

Albums:
ANCIENT KINGDOMS, Moribund (1995)
I Will Deliver You To A Distant And Hostile Plane Of Gehenna / Bring Forth A Winterlike Frost / Evil Lords Await / Ancient Kingdoms / God Of Murder (Bring Forth Decay) / Twisting Funnels Of Violence That Swept The Summerlike Realm / Lust In A Dark Land Of Ice Beyond The Vision Of Mortal Knowledge / Winter Of Sorrow

DARK NOVA (GREECE)

Albums:
THE DARK RHAPSODIES, (1994)

DARK PHASE (TURKEY)

Albums:
WANING MOON, SETTING SUN, Istambul Muzik (1997)

DARK SANCTUARY (FRANCE)

An ambient melancholic Black soundscape project led by Arkdae (real name Fabien Pereira) with ethereal female vocals courtesy of Marquise Ermia. DARK SANCTUARY debuted with the 'Bruises' demo.
Arkdae is an industrious and much honoured musician featuring on the DEINONYCHUS album 'Mournument' and on the debut SETH album. Since 1997 he has also benn a member of OSCULAM INFAME and has a side project BEKHIRA.

Singles/EPs:
Funeral Cry, Ancestral Craft Productions (1998)

Albums:
ROYAUME MELANCOLIQUE, (1999)
L'Autre Monde / L'Ombre Triste / Night Rain / La Reve De La Nymphe / Miserere / Valley Of The Pain / The Final Battle / Maze / Anatheme
DE LUMIERE ET D'OBSURITÉ, Wounded Love (2000)
Preludia / De Lumiere Et D'Obscurite / Le Paradis Noir / Reve Mortuaire / Cet Enfer Au Paradis / La Chute De L'Ange / Interludia / Au Milieu Des Sepultures / Ordre Et Decadence / Les Entrailles De

Ce Purgatoire / Funerailles / Que Mon Dernier Soupir M'Emporte / Summoning Of The Muse

THE DARKSEND (SWEDEN)

Line-Up: Richfer (vocals), Bergman (guitar), Stefko (bass), Vires (drums)

Singles/EPs:
The Luciferian Whisper EP, X-Treme X-TR 001 (199-)

Albums:
UNSUNNED, Head Not Found (1996)
Bathing In Moonlight / In Shadows Dark Embrace / The Nocturnal Winter / When Frost Covered My Palace / A Brewing Storm / Raseri / As Shadows Call My Name / Unsunned
ANTICHRIST IN EXCELSIS, X-Treme X-TR 007 (2000)

DARK STORM (CZECH REPUBLIC)

Singles/EPs:
Black Hordes Of Saaz, View Beyond (1995) (Split single with MANIAC BUTCHER)

Albums:
FOUR LUCAN EMPERORS, Pussy God (1996)
Intro / Trial With All Gods / Vengeance / Vatican In Flames / Svatá Krev / The Shedding Of Holy Blood

DARKTHRONE (NORWAY)

Line-Up: Ted Skjellum (guitar / vocals), Ivan Engar (guitar), Dag Nilson (bass), Hank Amarillo (drums)

Self proclaimed 'True Norwegian Black Metal' band DARK THRONE have courted a great deal of controversy over a string of brutal Death Metal albums.
The band was convened in 1987 and issued a couple of demos, starting with 1988's 'Land Of Frost' and 'A New Dimension' before 1989's 'Thulcandra' then 'Cromlech' (which was recorded live). DARKTHRONE had yet to play an actual gig when they signed to Yorkshire based Peaceville Records and issued the Tomas Skogsberg produced 'Soulside Journey' in 1991.
Following the release of 'A Blaze In The Northern Sky' bassist Dag Nilsen quit.
Despite lining up a British tour in 1992, DARKTHRONE amazingly cancelled all dates, wishing to disassociate themselves from the Death Metal boom

and subsequently closed ranks, insisting on no press interviews and vowing never to play live again. One of their scarce performances from Esberg in Denmark would later be immortalized on the bootleg CD 'Roots Of Evilness'.
Adopting pseudonyms more suitable for their chosen creative path, Nocturno Culto (bass / vocals), Zephyrous (guitar) and Fenriz (drums) released 'Under A Funeral Moon' in early 1993, a record that appeared just prior to the spate of Satanic church burnings in Norway. Still refusing to commit themselves to any interviews DARKTHRONE remained silent on the whole affair. In 1994 Fenriz released the solo album 'Vinterskugge' under the project name ISENGARD.
Despite the arrival of a solo album from Fenriz under the ISENGARD handle, entitled 'Vinterskugge', DARKTHRONE remained active. A fourth album emerged entitled 'Transylvanian Hunger' in 1994 although it was preceded by a notorious and allegedly "fascist" press release, which saw many distributors refusing to handle the record. In a quite productive year for Fenriz, a further ISENGARD project album was released in late 1994 under the guise of NUCLEAR TEMPLE. The same year the industrious Fenriz created DØDHEIMSGARD. Although he left this project following the debut album the band continued.
In early 1995 Fenriz assembled VED BUENS ENDE ('AT THE END OF THE BOW") together with ULVER / ARCTURUS bassist Skoll, drummers Vicotnik of DØDHEIMSGARD and Carl-Michael ex SATYRICON and ULVER. He also turned up on VALHALL's 1997 second album, 'Heading for Mars', performing drum duties under the pseudonym of 'Lee Bress'.
Although a new DARKTHRONE album was released in 1997, 'Goatlord' is in fact a CD pressing of the band's early demos. The band were honoured by such contemporaries as IMMORTAL, SATYRICON and even EMPEROR on the Moonfog tribute album 'Darkthrone Holy Darkthrone'.
2000 found Fenriz involved in al all star project act EIBON. Issuing one track on the 'Moonfog 2000' compilation album EIBON consisted of Fenriz, PANTERA frontman Phil Anselmo, SATYRICON's Satyr Wongraven, NECROPHAGIA's Killjoy and MAYHEM's Maniac.

Albums:
SOULSIDE JOURNEY, Peaceville VILE

22 (1991)
Cromlech / Sunrise Over Locus Mortis /
Soulside Journey / Neptune Towers /
Sempiternal Past - Presence View
Sepulcharity / Grave With A View /
Iconoclasm Sweeps Cappadocia / Nor
The Silent (Whispers) / The Watchtower
A BLAZE IN THE NORTHERN SKY,
Peaceville VILE 28 (1992)
Kathaarian Life Code / In The Shadow
Of The Horns / Paragon Belial / Where
Cold Wind Blows / A Blaze In The
Northern Sky / The Pagan Winter
UNDER A FUNERAL MOON, Peaceville
VILE 35 (1993)
Natassja In Eternal Sleep / Summer Of
The Diabolical Holocaust / The Dance Of
Eternal Shadows / Unholy Black Metal /
To Walk The Infernal Fields / Under A
Funeral Moon / Inn I De Dype Skogers
Fabn / Crossing The Triangle Of Flames
TRANSYLVANIAN HUNGER, Peaceville
VILE 43 (1994)
Transylvanian Hunger / Over Fjell Og
Gjennom Torner / Skald Au Satans Sol /
Slottet I Det Fierne / Graven
Takeheimeus Saler / I En Hall Med Flesk
Og Mjod / As Flittermice As Satans Spys
/ En As I Dype Skogen
PANZERFAUST, Moonfog FOG005
(1995)
En Vind An Sorg / Triumphant Gloom /
The Hordes Of Nebulah / Hans Siste
Vinter / Beholding The Throne Of Might /
Quintessence / Snø Og Gransvog
(Utfero)
TOTAL DEATH, Moonfog FOG011
(1996)
Earth's Last Picture / Blackwinged /
Gather For Attack On The Pearly Gates /
Black Victory Of Death / Majestic
Desolate Eye / Blasphemer / Ravnajuv /
The Serpents Harvest
GOATLORD, Moonfog FOG021 (1997)
Rex / Pure Demonic Blessing / (The)
Grimness Of Which Shepherds Mourn /
Sadomasochistic Rites / As
Desertshadows / In His Lovely Kingdom
/ Black Daimon / Toward(s) The
Thornfields / (Birth Of Evil) Virgin Sin /
Green Cave Float
RAVISHING GRIMNESS, Moonfog
FOG023 (1999)
Lifeless / The Beast / The Claws Of
Time / Across The Vacuum / Ravishing
Grimness / To The Death
PREPARING FOR WAR, Peaceville
CDVILE 33 (2000)
Transylvanian Hunger / Snowfall /
Archipelago / I En Hall Med Flesk Og
Mjod / The Pagan Winter / Grave With A
View / Eon- Thulcandra (Live) / Soria

Moria (Live) / Natassja In Eternal Sleep /
Cromlech / In The Shadow Of The Horns
/ Neptune Towers (Live) / Under A
Funeral Moon / Skald Av Satans Sol /
Iconoclasm Sweeps Cappadocia

DARK TRANQUILLITY (SWEDEN)
Line-Up: Anders Friden (vocals), Fredrik
Johansson (guitar), Niklas Sundin
(guitar), Martin Henriksson (bass),
Anders Jivarp (drums)

DARK TRANQUILITY date back to 1989,
but started life under the rather bizarre
moniker of SCEPTIC BOILER!
Changing names to DARK
TRANQUILITY, the band issued two rare
7" singles. The first of these 1992 efforts,
the "Trial Of Life Decayed' EP, was limited
to a thousand copies while only a mere
five hundred pressings were made of the
'A Moonclad Reflection' EP. Both these
recordings were re-released in Poland
the following year on Carnage Records.
In the wake of the release of the
'Skydancer' debut album vocalist Anders
Friden left for IN FLAMES and was
replaced by Mikael Stanne for the second
album 'The Gallery'. In between these
albums DARK TRANQUILITY contributed
a version of 'My Friend Misery' to the
METALLICA tribute album "Metal Militia'
which was released on Black Sun
Records in 1994
Stanne contributed guest vocal on
DENIAL's debut EP 'Rape Of The
Century'. Perhaps a more significant
moment in the band's history was the
decision taken by Stanne and Sundin to
create a trad-Metal side project with
former CEREMONIAL OATH drummer
Jesper Strömbold and CRYSTAL AGE
guitarist Oscar Dronjac titled
HAMMERFALL.
With the original intention of creating a
non serious, kickabout band,
HAMMERFALL signed to Nuclear Blast
and quite amazingly shifted over 50'000
copies of their debut album 'Glory To The
Brave' in Germany alone. Unfortunately
for Stanne this was after he had dropped
out of the band to concentrate on DARK
TRANQUILITY.
In November 1997 DARK TRANQUILITY
headlined the Osmose touring
extravaganza known as the 'World
Domination' tour in headlining over
ENSLAVED, BEWITCHED,
SWORDMASTER, DEMONIAC and
DELLAMORTE.
The band toured Japan in 1999 with
Finnish act CHILDREN OF BODOM. The

band also performed to their biggest audience the same year as part of the Italian 'Gods Of Metal' festival headlined by IRON MAIDEN. DARK TRANQUILITY added bassist Michael Nicklasson and keyboard player Martin Brändström for 2000's 'The Haven'.

Singles/EPs:
Mid Vinter / Beyond Enlightenment / Void Of Tranquility, Guttaral (1992) ('Trial Of Life Decayed' EP. Limited edition of 1,000)
Unfurled By Dawn / Yesterworld, Exhumed Productions CORPSE001 (1992) ('A Moonclad Reflection' EP. Limited edition of 500)
Of Chaos And Eternal Night / With The Flaming Shades Of Fall / Away, Delight, Away / Alone, Spinefarm SPI23CD (1995) ('Of Chaos And Eternal Night' EP)
Zodijackyl Light / Razorfever / Shadowlit Facade / Archetype, Osmose OPMCD 049 (1995) ('Enter Suicidal Angels' EP)

Albums:
SKYDANCER, Spinefarm SPI 16CD (1993)
Nightfall By The Shore Of Time / Crimson Winds / A Bolt Of Blazing Gold / In Tears Bereaved / Skywards / Through Ebony Archways / Shadow Duet / My Faeryland Forgotten / Alone
THE GALLERY, Osmose Productions OPCD 033 (1995)
Punish My Heaven / Silence, And The Firmament Withdrew / Edenspring / The Dying Line / The Gallery / The One Brooding Warning / Midway Through Infinity / Lethe / The Emptiness From Which I Fed / Mine Is The Grandeur...And... / Of Melancholy Burning
SKYDANCER + CHAOS AND ETERNAL LIGHT, Spinefarm SP143CD (1996)
Nightfall By The Shore Of Time / Crimson Winds / A Bolt Of Blazing Gold / In Tears Bereaved / Skywards / Through Ebony Archways / Shadow Duet / My Faeryland Forgotten / Alone / Of Chaos And Eternal Night / With The Flaming Shades Of Fall / Away, Delight, Away / Alone '94
THE MIND'S I, Osmose Productions (1997)
Dreamlore Degenerate / Zodijackyl Light / Hedon / Scythe, Rage And Roses / Constant / Dissolution Factor Red / Insanity's Crescendo / Still Moving Sinews / Atom Heart 243.5 / Tidal Tantrum / Tongues / The Mind's Eye

PROJECTOR, Century Media (1999)
Freewill / Therin / Undo Control / Auctioned / To A Bitter Halt / The Sun Fired Blanks / Nether Noras / Day To End / Dobermann / On Your Time
HAVEN, Century Media 215668 (2000)
The Wonders At Your Feet / Not Built To Last / Indifferent Suns / Feasts Of Burden / Haven / The Same / Fabric / Ego Drama / Rundown / Emptier Still / At Loss For Words

DARKWOODS MY BETROTHED
(FINLAND)
Line-Up: Pasi (vocals / acoustic guitar), Jouni (guitar), Teemu Kautonen (bass), Tero (drums)

Purveyors of Black Metal, DARKWOODS MY BETROTHED have been strongly influenced by BATHORY and the Swedish outfit's 'Hammerheart' album in particular. The act arrived with a 1993 demo 'Reborn In Promethean Flame' although at the time the band was rather tastelessly titled VIRGINS CUNT. A further VIRGINS CUNT demo was released in 1994 'Dark Aureoles Gathering'. Later versions of the same demo would be sold under the new band name of DARKWOODS MY BETROTHED.
Bassist Teemu Kautonen later went to NATTVINDENS GRAT and WIZZARD. By 2000 WIZZARD had released three albums including the latest 'Songs Of Sin And Decadence'.
Drummer Tero also had a spell in WIZZARD during 1997.

Albums:
HEIRS OF THE NORTH STAR,
Hammerheart, Hammer 1 (1995)
My Eyes Are Frozen / One Son Of The Northstar / Uller / From The Snowy Hillsides They Came / In A Silent Night / Come Fimbulvetr / Yggdrasil's Children Fall
AUTUMN ROARS THUNDER,
Solistitium SOL 006 (1996)
Autumn Roars Thunder / Nightowl / When Ancient Spirits Battled / The Conspiracy Of The Pagan Cult / Hymn Of The Darkwoods / On The Top Of The Falconhill / King's Gray Shadow / I Burn At The Stake / Red Sky Over The Land Of Fells
WITCHHUNTS, Spinefarm (1999)
Without Ceremony And Bell Toll / Inside The Circle Of Stones / The Crow And The Warrior / Dying To Meet You / The

Preacher Came To Town / Burn,
Witches, Burn / The Witch Hunters

DARZAMAT (POLAND)
Line-Up: Kate (vocals), Flauros (vocals),
Simon (guitar), Daamr (guitar), Bomba
(drums)

DARZAMAT were founded by ex
MASTIPHAL member Flauros. The debut
'In The Flames Of Black Art' saw
DARZAMAT as a trio of vocalists Kate
and Flauros with Simon on guitar, bass
and drums. The band pulled in guitarist
Daamr and drummer Bomba for the 1998
follow up.

Albums:
IN THE FLAMES OF BLACK ART,
Faithless (1996)
In The Flames Of Black Art / Legend? /
Inevitable Eclipse / Seven Golden Fires /
Theatre Of Rapture / The Dream / The
Storm
IN THE OPIUM OF BLACK VEIL,
Faithless Productions (1998)
Beyond The World / In The Opium Of
Black Veil / For The Earth To The Stars /
Ancient Philosophy / Secret Garden
(Mystic Version)
SEVEN GOLDEN FIRES, Faithless
(2000)

DAWN (SWEDEN)
Line-Up: Henke Fors (vocals), Andreas
Fullmestad (guitar), Fredrik Söderberg
(guitar), Lars Tängmark (bass), Karsten
Larsson (drums)

OBDURACY guitarist Andreas
Fullmested and MORGUE guitarist
Fredrik Söderberg formed DAWN in late
1991 after they left their respective acts.
Previous to OBDURACY Söderberg had
been a member of the mid 80's acts
CRANIUM and LEGION.
Membership was completed with
additions from FUNERAL FEAST and
MESENTARY. Two demo cassettes
followed in 1992's 'Demo 1' and
'Apparition' in 1993, with the latter being
eventually released as a 7" EP the same
year on a shared EP with
PYPHOMGERTUM.
The DAWN debut album arrived in 1995
and it's title is translated as 'When The
Sun Sets Forever' and boasts lyrics in
medieval Swedish.
Outside the confines of DAWN vocalist
Henke Fors has found the time to perform
temporary vocal duties for fellow Swedes

IN FLAMES appearing on their debut
mini-album. The singer also found time to
create an extreme Black Metal band
called NIDEN DIV. 187 with A
CANOUROUS QUINTET guitarist Leo
Pignon and members of THY
PRIMORDIAL, releasing two albums for
Necropolis Records: 'Towards
Judgement' and 'Impergium'.
Extra curricular activity clearly being
contagious in Swedish Death Metal
circles, DAWN bassist Lars Tängmark
also has a side project with the Gothic act
THE WOUNDED MEADOW.
DAWN reappeared in 1996 with the mini
album 'Sorgh Pa Sverte Vingar Flogh' (or,
translated. 'Sorrow Flew On Black
Wings') and featured a cover version of
INFERNAL MAJESTY's 'Night Of The
Living Dead'.
Söderberg would resurrect his old group
CRANIUM as a side project during 1998
issuing three albums.
DAWN's drummer Jocke Petterson is
also known as Morth in THY
PRIMORDIAL and has sessioned with
both UNMOORED and CRANIUM.

Singles/EPs:
The Eternal Forest EP, Bellphegot
(1993) (Split EP with PYPHOMGERTUM)
Vya Kal / Sorrow Flew On Black Wings /
Soil Of Dead Earth / Night Of The Living
Dead, Necropolis NR 6664 (1996)
('Sorgh Pa Svarte Vingar Flogh' EP)

Albums:
NAER SOLEN GAR NIBER EVOGHER,,
Necropolis NR006 (1995)
Eyesland / The Ethereal Forest /
Diabolical Beauty / In The Depths Of My
Soul / Ginom Renande Lughier / As The
Tears Fall / Svarter Skiner Solen /
Everflaming
**SLAUGHTERSUN (CROWN OF THE
TRIARCHY)**, Necropolis NR021 (1998)
The Knell And The World / Falcula / To
Achieve The Ancestral Powers / Ride
The Wings Of Pestilence / The Aphelion
Deserts / Stalkers Blessing / Malediction
Murder

DAWNFALL (GERMANY)
Line-Up: Berischer (vocals / guitar), Birgit
(bass), C. Talbert (drums)

German Black Metal band DAWNFALL
opened proceedings with the 1993 demo
'Mysterical Darkness' demo.

103

Albums:
DOMINANCE OF DARKNESS, Nazgûl's
Eyrie Productions NEP001CD (1994)
Intro / Reach The Deep / Dominance Of
Darkness / Eye Of Haze / The Rise Of
The Fields Beyond / Ancient Sounds In
The Vault Of Wind / In My Rituals / Black
Silence / Eternal Lands / Into The
Darkened Season Of The Moon / With
Dark Winds

DAWN OF DREAMS (GERMANY)

Commonly confused with the Austrian
Gothic Doom band of the same name.

Albums:
DARKLIGHT AWAKENING, Last
Episode CD 5 7067 20 561 (2000)
Dark Black Conscious / Desires Origin /
Hell Beneath / Eclipse / To Watch The
Sunrise / Swallow This Fire / A Forgotten
Yearning / The Sirenes Dreaming / Dwell
In My Embrace

DAWN OF RELIC (FINLAND)
Line-Up: Rauli Roininen (guitar), Teemu
Luukinen (guitar), Pekka Mustonen
(bass), Pekka Malo (keyboards), Jukka
Zaan Juntunen (drums)

DAWN OF RELIC's 1994 demo 'Of The
Ambience', which featured vocalist Jarmo
Juntunen, resulted in their signing to
Earache Records subsidiary Wicked
World. The band's unique brand of Black
Metal is heavily infused with H.P.
Lovecraft references.
Session vocalists for the 'One Night In
Carcosa' album were CATAMENIA's Mika
Tönning and HORNA's Nazgul Von
Armageddon.

Albums:
ONE NIGHT IN CARCOSA, Wicked
World (1999)
Fimbulveir / When Aldebaran Is Visible /
The Last Dance Of Sarnath / Kadath
Opened: Part I- To Dream, Part II:
Through The Cavern Of Flame, Part III:
Nether Seas Boiling / Welkins Gar / Just
A River / Oceans
WRATHCAST, (2000)
Wrathcast / N.W.S. / Scions Of The
Blackened Soil / Awakenings / The Wall
Of Tartarean Well's / Dawn Of Relic / No
Sign Of The Dawn / Harvest Moon /
Instru-Mentally-III

DEAD BEGINNERS (FINLAND)
Line-Up: T. Sitomaniemi, E. Lahdenperä

DEAD BEGINNERS was previously titled
AUTUMN VERSES. The band in their
previous guise would record a further two
projected albums for release post the
'Tunes Of Disconsolation' debut.
However, the recordings were shelved
only to be combined for issue as the
'Sinners Rebellion' under the acts new
name of DEAD BEGINNERS.

Albums:
SINNER'S REBELLION, Spikefarm
(2000)
Calling Ruby / Treason Via Magdalene /
The Wounderable One / The Paragon
And The Beast Of Burden / Arradeus
2000 / Ex Cathedra / The Illfated /
Sinner's Rebellion / Dead Beginners

DEAD CHRIST (GREECE)

Singles/EPs:
Satanas Hunger, (1995)

DEAD SILENT SLUMBER
(SWEDEN)

Solo project from NAGLFAR's Jens
Ryden.

Albums:
ENTOMBED IN THE MIDNIGHT HOUR,
Hammerheart (1999)
In The Glare Of The Moon / Reborn By
The Seed Of Death / Smell The Incense
/ Entombed In The Midnight Hour / Blood
Collapse / Raining The Suicide Chalice /
Lick The Wound

DEATH POEMS (BRAZIL)
Line-up: Parosh (vocals), Undarkgoat
(guitar), Adonikan (bass), Baruch
(keyboards), Leviticum (drums).

It is unclear as to whether DEATH
POEMS are in fact one of the growing
movement of Christian Black Metal bands
or not. The band have proclaimed that
they are against "false Christianity".
Guitarist Undarkgoat (real name Evandro
Sudré) and bassist Shadrach were
previously with PEACEMAKER. This pair
would found ORDINANCE in 1998 pulling
in former IMMER GOTT members
Merenoth and keyboard player Baruch
(real name Leandro Simonato). With the
addition of drummer Leviticum (real name
Fabio Ribereiro this act evolved into
DEATH POEMS issuing the demo
'Devotional Tour'.
By October of 1999 Adonikan (real name

Samir Lima) had superseded Shadrach. Meremoth would depart too.
For touring to promote the debut album 'Pseudoprophatae' DEATH POEMS enlisted female vocalist Tabatha Martinez and new lead vocalist Parosh.

Albums:
PSEUDOPROPHETAE, (2000)
The First Sunrise/ Triumphant March/ Apocalyptic Visions/ Et Claris Det Mortis (Et Inferni)/ Øde Sted/ Pseudoprophetae/ The Satanic Majesty Oversight

DEATH SENTENCE
(CZECH REPUBLIC)

Albums:
THE WORLD DESPAIRES..., (1997)
Screams Of The Shadows / The Last / Faces From My Dreams / The Flames Of Hope In My Head / The World Despaires... / Death Is Only Life / Walpurgis Night / Dead World / Obituary Memories / Decameron

DEATH SS (ITALY)
Line-Up: Vampire (vocals), Death (guitar), Zombie (guitar), Mummy (bass), Werewolf (drums)

Italian Gothic horror Metal act DEATH SS date back to 1977 and have, over the years, become a cult institution, although the band has gone through various guises and titles; with the mainstay and lynch pin being founder Steve Sylvester. DEATH SS first made an impression with the 1981 demo tape 'Horned God Of The Witches'.
The first stable line-up of DEATH SS comprised vocalist Sylvester ('Vampire'), Paul Chain ('Death'), Claud Galley ('Zombie'), Danny Hughes ('Mummy') and Thomas Chaste ('Werewolf') and the group eventually debuted with a series of limited edition singles sold at gigs. Only 500 of each were pressed
In 1982 DEATH SS appeared on their first compilation album, 'Gathered', with the song 'Terror' and would then add the track 'Black And Violet' to the 1983 Italian Metal compilation album 'Heavy Metal Eruption'. However, DEATH SS split later the same year with Chain forming PAUL CHAIN VIOLET THEATRE. In the interim however Chain issued the 'Chains Of Death' single under the title of DEATH SS minus Sylvester!
Sylvester himself went solo and issued an EP of his own, 'The Free Man', using

the services of ex DEATH SS members. Having since reformed DEATH SS Sylvester now fronts the mothership act and his spin-off solo outfit SYLVESTER'S DEATH.
The 1997 album 'Do What Thou Wilt', recorded in England, sees DEATH SS with a line up of Sylvester, guitarists Emil Bandera and Felix Moon, bassist Andrew Karloff and drummer Ross Lukather.
As a footnote, former DEATH SS drummer Mimmio Palmiotta is now a member of DOMINE appearing on their 1997 album 'Champion Eternal'.
Steve Sylvester guested on the 2000 TENEBRE album 'Mark Ov The Beast'. Chain founded LOOSIN 'O' FREQUENCIES in 1999 for the 'Regeneration' album.
DEATH SS cut their versions of 'Come To The Sabbat' and 'Ancient Days' to the BLACK WIDOW tribute album 'King Of The Witches'.

Singles/EPs:
Zombie / Terror, (198-) (Band pressing. 500 copies)
Night Of The Witch / Black Mummy (Live), (198-) (Band pressing. 500 copies)
The Profonation / Spiritualist Séance, (198-) (Band pressing. 500 copies)
In The Darkness / The Mandrake Root, (198-)
Chains Of Death / Inquizitor / Schizophrenic, Metal Eye (1983)
Kings Of Evil / Gethsemane / Murder Angel, Metalmaster MET 127 (1989)
The Cursed Singles, Avantgarde (1995) (Limited edition. 666 copies.)
Hi Tech Jesus / Hi Tech Jesus (Digital Redemption mix) / The Devilish Meetings / Hi Tech Jesus (Virtual Messiah Ultra mix) / Jack The Ripper, Lucifer Rising (1999)

Albums:
THE STORY OF DEATH SS 1977-1984, Minotaur DEA 101 (1988)
Terror / Murder Angels / Horrible Eyes / Cursed Mania / Zombie / Violet Overture / Chains Of Death / Inquisitor / Schizophrenic / Black And Violet / The Bones And The Grave
IN DEATH OF STEVE SILVESTER, Metalmaster MET111 (1989)
Vampire / Death / Black Mummy / Zombie / Werewolf / Terror / The Hanged Ballad / Murder Angels / In Ancient Days / Come To The Sabbat (Live) / Zombie (Demo) / Black Mummy (Live 1980)
BLACK MASS, Metalmaster MET 120

(1990)
Kings Of Evil / Horrible Eyes / Cursed Mania / Buried Alive / Welcome To My Hell / Devil's Rage / In The Darkness / Black Mass

HEAVY DEMONS FEATURE, Rosemary's Babydisc 002 (1992)
Walpurgisnacht / Where Have You Gone? / Heavy Demons / Family Vault / Lilith / Peace Of Mind / Way To Power / Baphomet / Inquisitor / Templar's Revenge / All Souls' Day / Sorcerrous Valley

THE CURSED CONCERT- LIVE, Lucifer Rising (1992)
Ave Satani- Peace Of Mind / Horrible Eyes / Cursed Mama / Lilith / Vampire / Family Vault / Terror / Baphomet / Inquisitor / Templar's Revenge / Drum Solo / Where Have You Gone? / Heavy Demons / Kings Of Evil / Straight To Hell / Futilist's Lament / Heavy Demons ('92 remix) / Dog Man

FEAR OF EVIL, (199-)

THE CURSED SINGLES, Lucifer Rising (1996)
Zombie / Terror / The Night Of The Witch / Black Mummy / Profonation / Spiritualist Séance / In The Darkness / The Mandrake Root

HORROR MUSIC- THE BEST OF DEATH SS, Lucifer Rising (1996)
The Night Of The Witch / Profonation / Spiritualist Séance / Zombie / Terror / Vampire / Horrible Eyes / Cursed Mama

/ Kings Of Evil (Long mix version) / In The Darkness / Where Have You Gone? / Heavy Demons (Remix) / Blood And Violet ('95 version) / Chains Of Death ('95 version)

DO WHAT THOU WILT, Bossy Ogress 561 3016 20 BO (1997)
Liber I: The Awakening Of The Beast / Liber II: The Phoenix Mass / Liber III: Baron Samedi / Liber IV: Scarlet Woman / Liber V: The Serpent Rainbow / Liber VI: Crowley's Law / Liber VII: Guardian Angel / Liber VIII: The Shrine In The Gloom / Liber IX: The Way Of The Left Hand / Liber X: Liber Samekh

PANIC, Lucifer Rising (2000)
Paraphenalia / Let The Sabbath Begin! / Hi Tech Jesus / Lady Of Babylon / Equinox Of The Gods / Ishtar / The Cannibal Queen / Rabies Is A Killer!! / Tallow Doll / Hermaphrodite / Panic / Auto Sacramental

DEATHWITCH (SWEDEN)
Line-Up: Af Necrohell (guitar), Lady Death (bass), Terror (drums)

DEATHWITCH is a side project act of SACRAMENTUM drummer Niklas 'Terror' Rudolfsson. The mysterious Reaper adds vocals to the debut album. 1998's 'The Ultimate Death' was produced by former KING DIAMOND guitarist Andy LaRocque. DEATHWITCH's line up for this opus

DEATHWITCH

being Terror switching from drums to vocals, Doomentor on guitar, DISSECTION bassist Peter Palmdahl and new drummer Horror. Rudolfsson issued a side project album 'Enter The Realm Of Death' under the band name RUNEMAGICK in 1999.

Albums:
TRIUMPHANT DEVASTATION, Desecration DR001 (1996)
Intro - Black Dawn / Triumphant Devastation / Flag Of Black Death / Unholy Destruction / Soul Crusher / Bestial Mutilation / Storm Of Damnation / Infernal Gates Of Hell / Under The Black Wings / Deathwitch / Nocturnal Sacrifice / Sadistic Sodomizer
DAWN OF ARMAGGEDON, Necropolis DR02 (1997)
Intro- Dawn Of War / Ichora Shall Bleed / Angel Execution / Wrath Of Sathanas / Hellfuck Sodomy / Dawn Of Armageddon / Eternal Fornication / Blasphemous Desecration / Beast Of Holocaust / Diabolical Tormentor / Desecration Of The White Christ / Outro (Armageddon) / Infernal Gate (demo) / Triumphant Devastation (demo) / Beast Of Holocaust (demo) / Evil Blood (demo) / Wrath Of Sathanas (demo) / Nocturnal Sacrifice (demo)
THE ULTIMATE DEATH, Necropolis (1998)
Prelude To Grand Darkness / The Ultimate Death / Necromancers Rites / Violent Carnage / Dark Gift / Grave Symphony / Condemned To The Grave / Witches Morbid Lust / Prelude To Grand Conquest / Monumental Massacre / Revel In Sin / Monster Perversion / Death Machine / Pestilent Pandemonium / Demon Sabbath / Dawn Of Ymodus Millenium
MONUMENTAL MUTILATIONS, Necropolis NR035 (1999)
The Return Of Evil / Demonic Witch / Possessed Sadist / Fire Fuck / Jehova Shall Bleed / Total Cremation / Dark Beast / Sacrifice In Fire / The Rite Of Darkness / Terror Doom / Flag Of Black Death / Executioner 1999 / Necromancer

DECAMERON (SWEDEN)
Line-Up: Alex Losbäck (vocals / bass) / Johannes Losbäck (guitar), Johan Norrman (guitar), Tobias Kjellgren (drums)

Previously known as NECROFOBIC, the Swedes changed titles to DECAMERON

in 1991 and released their first demo in 1992 titled 'My Grave Is Calling'. Frontman Alex Losbäck also moonlighted with RUNEMAGICK in the early 90's. Drummer Tobias Kjellgren is ex SWORDMASTER. One of the band's original guitarists Johan Norrman quit to join DISSECTION in mid 1994 and also joined SACRAMENTUM.
DECAMERON soldiered on utilizing the temporary services of LORD BELIAL guitarist Dark. A permanent member was later found in Johnny Lehto. Drummer Tobias Kellgren departed following completion of the debut album, which was issued in 1996. Kjellgren would later joined DISSECTION in December 1995.

Albums:
MY SHADOW..., No Fashion NFR013CD (1996)
Mörker / Carpe Nocem / Our Time Has Come / Satanised / Le Roi Triste / The Scar Of Damnation / Sexual Immortality / Skabma / My Shadow... / Prophecy Of Life To Come / Mistress Of Sacrifice

DECAYED (PORTUGAL)
Line-Up: J.M. (vocals / bass), J.A. (guitar / keyboards), V.J. (guitar), J.B. (drums)

Black Metal merchants DECAYED released their 'Thus Revealed' demo in 1992 after which then then trio augmented their sound with the inclusion of second guitarist V.J. A single, 'The Seven Seals', followed before recording of the debut album 'Conjuration Of The Southern Circle' after which J.M. departed. DECAYED regrouped shifting J.A. to lead vocals and V.S. to bass guitar. The band's second album in 1995 'In Lustful Mayhem' included cover versions of VENOM and SODOM tracks. A theme that would weave through DECAYED's career.
1998 saw a split album shared with ALASTOR.
The 'Book Of Darkness' collection included previously laid down cover versions amongst which are CELTIC FROST, VENOM, BATHORY, SODOM, DEATH, AC/DC and even GEORGE THOROGOOD & THE DESTROYERS 'Bad To The Bone'.
The band issued two limited edition tapes in 2000 '9.9.99 Live' and 'Ataque Infernal', the latter including cover versions of songs from such cult artists as GROG, VIOLENT FORCE, KREATOR,

BATHORY and SODOM. The band also released the CD, limited to a mere 69 copies, entitled 'French Attack' to celebrate their first live shows in France. A further split affair, an alliance with CORPUS CHRISTII, was issued in 2001 on Hibernica Records.
Former DECAYED guitarist Tanngrisnir (V.S.) would join Portuguese favourites MOONSPELL.

Singles/EPs:
The Seven Seals / Valley Of Dreams, Dark (1993) (7" single)
From Blues To Black / One With The Gods (Rites Of Tenenir), Skyfall (1996) ('Satanic Rock n' Roll' free single with 'Ressurectionem Mortuorum' album)
Decadencia Christii, Hibernica EP01 (2001) (Split 7" single with CORPUS CHRISTII)

Albums:
CONJURATION OF THE SOUTHERN CIRCLE, Monastirium MST 001 (1993)
Immortal's Entreaty / Pagan Winds Return / Unholy Deity (Set) / Last Sleep / Nocturnal Prayers / Moon Of A Wulferian Shadow / Inquisitor's Delight / Circle Of The Castrian Mountains / Drums Of Valhalla / … Shall Ascend / Goddess Of The Ancient
IN LUSTFUL MAYHEM: THE SEVEN SEALS, Skyfall (1995)
RESSURECTIONEM MORTUORUM, Skyfall (1996)
Into Depths / Darkness Falls / A Realm Beyond / Thy Summoning / Archdemon / By The Candlelight / City Of The Horned One / Fuck Your God! / Countess Bathory / Abyssic Winds
SACRIFICE TO DARKNESS, (1998) (Split album with ALASTOR)
THE BOOK OF DARKNESS, Drakkar (1999)
Death Chimes In Armageddon / Sacrificial Rites / Tribulation / Rise At Dusk / Ethol Mishrak (Of Endless Night) / Flesh To Ashes / Halls Of Torment / Into The Crypt Of Rays / Call From The Grave / The Return Of Darkness And Evil / Bad To The Bone / Blasphemer / Touch Too Much / Infernal Death / In League With Satan / Witching Hour
FRENCH ATTACK, Decayed (2000)
Necromance / Behold The Wrath (Live) / Darkness Falls / Death Chimes Of Armageddon (Live) / Goddess Of The Ancients (Live)

DECEASED (GERMANY)

Line-Up: Lars (vocals / guitar), Martin (bass), Dirk (drums)

Singles/EPs:
Darkened Soul / As I Die / Eternal Devastation / The One Who Cared, Wilde Welt WWR 94-004-07 (1994) ('Blessed By Demons' EP)

DECEMBER (NORWAY)

Singles/EPs:
River Of Blood / Venus In Chains, Elfenblut (1997)

DECEMBER DAWN (GERMANY)
Line-Up: Jörg Schlichting (vocals), Ira Wohlgemuth (vocals), Olaf Pinnow (guitar), André Pasedeg (guitar), Martin Diers (bass), Markus Meyer (keyboards), Armin Wätjen (drums)

Albums:
OF GLOOM AND LIGHT, December Dawn (1997)
In The High Tower / Final Certainty / Tears In A Torrent / The Curse Of Knowledge / Wretched Thing / Darkened Lives / Life's Labour Lost / Via Dolorosa

DECEMBER MOON (UK)
Line-Up: Robin Graves (vocals / guitar), Was Sarginson (drums)

A Doom inspired Black Metal side project by CRADLE OF FILTH's Robin Graves and EXTREME NOISE TERROR and BLOOD DIVINE drummer Was Sarginson.
Sarginson was previously a member of SOLEMN and an early incarnation of CRADLE OF FILTH.
DECEMBER MOON's debut release was released through Finnish label Spinefarm in 1996.
Sarginson joined CRADLE OF FILTH in 1999 for a short spell.

Albums:
SOURCE OF ORGIN, Spinefarm SPI32 (1996)
Exaltation Of Power / You Can't Bless The Damned / Nocturnal Transcendency / Winter Sunset / Black Millenium / The Apparition Of Mother Earth / Twinned With Destiny / An Empty Gesture

DECEMBER'S FIRE (POLAND)

Reputedly a violent Orchestral Gothic Metal project founded in 1994.

BEHEMOTH's Nergal guests on the album which is essentially a solo outing by Piotr Weltrowski who performs all instruments.

Albums:
VAE VICTIS, Last Epitaph LEP 008 (1996)
Vae Victis / Patrz, Jak Ptona Dzikie Róze... / Pragne Twej Krwi / Aniot Samotnych

DECEMBER WOLVES
(Salem, MA, USA)
Line-Up: Devon (vocals), Joe (guitar), Tim (guitar), Brian (bass), Scott DeFusco (drums)

DECEMBER WOLVES debuted with the 1994 demo 'Wolftread'. The band issued their Celtic flavoured Black Thrash Metal debut album 'Til Ten Years' on the Korean label Hammerheart. Drummer Scott DeFusco, who also had a solo project TURAGHAN, would leave the band following the 'Completely Dehumanised' album.
DECEMBER WOLVES pulled in a fresh rhythm section in 2000 of bassist Dave Ebola and drummer Joe Kill.
Latterly members of DECEMBERS WOLVES have renounced any Black Metal connections.

Singles/EPs:
We Are Everywhere / Not With Tainted Blood, December Wolves (1997)

Albums:
'TIL TEN YEARS, Hammerheart (1996)
Ode To The Master Therion / The Night That I Died / Our Centuries Have Been Found / Lycanthropy: Yonder Through Ice Storms / Til Ten Years / When The Clouds Cry / Outro
COMPLETELY DEHUMANISED, Wicked World SICK03CD (1998)
Conditioned By The Thoughts That I Transmit To You / Completely Dehumanised / We Are Everywhere / Time Flies When You Wish You Were Dead / Friday The 13th / The Gard Division / My Bible / Not With Tainted Blood / To Kill Without Emotion

DECOLLATION (SWEDEN)
Line-Up: John Lesley (vocals / guitar), John Jeremiah (guitar), Charles Von Weissenberg (bass), Nick Sheilds (keyboards), Chris Steele (drums)

Despite their anglicised pseudonyms DECOLLATION are all Swedish natives. Bassist Charles Von Weissenberg (real name Tomas Johansson) is ex CEREMONIAL OATH whilst drummer Chris Steele (real name Kristian Wåhlin) is ex GROTESQUE and LIERS IN WAIT. Both Wåhlin and vocalist John Lesley (real name Johan Österberg) are now in DIABOLIQUE.

Singles/EPs:
Dawn Of Resurrection / Point Of No Return / The Godborn / Cursed Lands, Listenable POSH0004 (1992) ('Cursed Lands' EP)

DECORYAH (FINLAND)
Line-Up: Jukka Vuorinen (vocals / guitar), Jani Kakko (guitar / bass), Jonne Valtonen (keyboards), Mikko Laine (drums)

DECORYAH, although dating back to 1989, only released their debut demo 'Whispers From The Depth' in 1992. A second demo, entitled 'Cosmos Silence', was released at the close of the year. This tape provoked attention from Switzerland's Witchhunt Records prompting a 7" single release.

Singles/EPs:
Ebonies, Witchhunt (1993)

Albums:
WISDOM FLOATS, Witchhunt WIHU 9416 (1995)
Astral Mirage Of Paradise / Wisdom Floats / Monoliths / Beryllos / Reaching Melancholia / Circle Immortality / When The Echoes Start To Fade / Cosmos Silence / Intra-Mental Ecstasy / Ebonies / Infinity Awaits
FALL- DARK WATERS, Metal Blade 3984-14111-2 (1996)
Fall - Dark Waters / Submerged Seconds / Envisioned (Waters?) / Some Drops Behind The Essence / Endless Is The Stream / Gloria Absurdiah / Wintry Fluids (Portal) / She Came To Me In The Form Of Water / She Wept In The Woods

DEEPSKIN (PORTUGAL)

Solo project from MOONSPELL bassist Ares.

Albums:
JUDAS, Dreamcatcher (2000)

DEFACED CREATION (SWEDEN)
Line-Up: Thomas Dahlström (vocals), Jörgen Bylander (guitar), Zeb Nilsson (bass), Arrtu Malkku (drums)

Anti Christian tinged Death Metal act DEFACED CREATION bowed in with the 1994 demo 'Santeria'. The band had been forged by guitarist Jörgen Bylander, vocalist Thomas Dahlström and bassist Zeb Nilsson. A second guitarist Stefan Dahlberg broke ranks after the demo recording.
A further eponymous demo session arrived in 1995 followed by the EP 'Resurrection'. DEFACED CREATION teamed up with ACTERNUM for the split 'Fall' EP of 1997 which featured a new rhythm section of bass player Jock Wassberg and drummer Arrtu Malkku.
The band, with Johan Hjelm now on bass, also shared space in 1998 on the 'Infernal' EP with STANDING OUT.
DEFACED CREATION toured Europe as part of the 'Brutal Summer' package including DYING FETUS and DERANGED.
Bylander is also a member of Death Metal band CONDAMNED.

Singles/EPs:
Resurrection, Paranoya Syndrome (1996)
Fall, Paranoya Syndrome (1997) (Split EP with ACTERNUM)
Infernal, Rockaway (1998) (Split EP with STANDING OUT)

Albums:
SERENITY IN CHAOS, Vod VODCD005 (2000)
Baptized In Fire / Macabre Exposure Of Fleshly Devotion / Fire Temple / Kill The Light / Devastation / Return In Black / Cannibalistic Feast / Stillborn / The Victorious Underworld / Infernal / Enslave The Christians / Fall

DEFENDER (SWEDEN)

DEFENDER is the side project act of AFFLICTED bassist Philip Von Segebaden. The man is also a member of the notorious CRANIUM where he goes under the title Chainsaw Demon.

Albums:
THEY CAME OVER THE HIGH PASS, Necropolis NR043 (1999)
They Came Over The High Pass / The Siege Of Armengar / High Himalayan Valley / Summit Day / Dragon / City In The Clouds / Maze Of The Minotaur / Nomads Of The Stars

DEHUMANISED (New York, NY, USA)

Albums:
PROPHECIES FORETOLD, Pathos (1988)
Kingdom Of Cruelty / Fade Into Obscurity / Solitary Demise / Infinite Despair / Doomed To Die / Terminal Punishment / Condemned / Drawn By Blood

DEICIDE (FL, USA)
Line-Up: Glenn Benton (vocals / bass), Eric Hoffman (guitar), Brian Hoffman (guitar), Steve Asheim (drums)

DEICIDE, emerging from the cult troupe AMON in 1987, were the first American Black Metal band to push the novelty factor into the realms of the dangerous. Early shows had arch protagonist vocalist / bassist Glen Benton drenched in the blood of a pig bedecked in studded body armour sporting an upside down cross the frontman had burned into his own forehead.
Further controversy was whipped up after the second album 'Legion' when two New Jersey teenagers tortured and killed a dog leaving it's carcass hanging in a tree. When questioned by authorities the youngsters claimed inspiration from DEICIDE.
The band built up a loyal fanbase with surprising speed and Roadrunner Records were quick off the mark in re-issuing the AMON demos re-credited to DEICIDE and marketed as 'Amon: Feasting The Beast'.
The singer's more than vocal appreciation of a Satanic belief system, his willingness to engage in media sponsored set discussions on good and evil with church members (including the late former TWELFTH NIGHT vocalist and vicar GEOFF MANN) and his apparent witnessed shooting of squirrels in his house (!) put DEICIDE firmly in the Black Metal camp.
So vociferous was the media against DEICIDE that their notoriety spread into areas not normally troubled by Black Metal. Benton's comments regarding his supposed treatment of animals led to bomb threats which blighted a European tour. A more pointed message left with the media from the Animal Militia organisation informed Benton he would be killed if he

stepped on English soil. DEICIDE's British and European shows went according to plan until the Scandinavian leg when a bomb planted at the Fryshuset club in Stockholm, Sweden exploded. However, it was unclear as to the object of the assault as support band GOREFEST had also received death threats from another source.

Benton, whose first son he tactfully named Daemon, rather intriguingly voiced premonitions that he will die aged 33. Needless to say his 33rd Birthday passed without event.

Quite remarkably for a Black Metal band DEICIDE has maintained a rock solid line up since it's inception and continues to maintain a strong unyeilding fan base. Latest release 'Insinerate Hymn' is as uncompromising as ever.

Albums:
DEICIDE, Roadrunner RO 9381 (1990)
Lunatic Of God's Creation / Sacrificial Suicide / Oblivious To Evil / Dead By Dawn / Blasphericion / Deicide / Carnage In The Temple Of The Damned / Mephistopheles / Day Of Darkness / Crucifixion
LEGION, Roadrunner RC 91922 (1992)
Satan Spawns The Caco-Daemon / Dead But Dreaming / Repent To Die / Trifixion / Behead The Prophet (No Lord Shall Live) / Holy Deception / In Hell I Burn / Revocate The Agitator
AMON: FEASTING THE BEAST, Roadrunner RR 91112 (1993)
Lunatic Of God's Creation / Sacrificial Suicide / Crucifixation / Carnage In The Temple Of The Damned / Dead By Dawn / Blasphereion / Feasting The Beast / Day Of Darkness / Oblivious To Nothing
ONCE UPON THE CROSS, Roadrunner RR 8949-2 (1995)
Once Upon The Cross / Christ Denied / When Satan Rules His World / Kill The Christian / Trick Or Betrayed / They Are All Children Of The Underworld / Behind The Light They Shall Rise / To Be Dead / Confessional Rape
SERPENTS OF THE LIGHT, Roadrunner RR 8811-2 (1997)
Serpents Of The Light / Bastard Of Christ / Blame It On God / This Hell We're In / I Am No One / Slaves To The Cross / Creatures Of Habit / Believe The Lie / The Truth Above
WHEN SATAN LIVES, Roadrunner (1998)
When Satan Rules His World / Blame It On God / Bastard Of Christ / They Are

The Children Of The Underworld / Serpents Of The Light / Dead But Dreaming / Slave To The Cross / Believe The Lie / Trick Or Betrayed / Behind The Light Thou Shall Rise / Deicide / Father Baker's Dead By Dawn / Sacrificial Suicide
INSINERATE HYMN, Roadrunner RR 8570-2 (2000)
Bible Basher / Forever Hate You / Standing In The Flames / Remnant Of A Hopeless Path / The Gift That Keeps On Giving / Halls Of Warship / Suffer Again / Worst Enemy / Apocalyptic Fear / Refusal Of Penance

DE INFERNALI (SWEDEN)

Actually the solo project of DISSECTION's Jon Nodveidt, DE INFERNALI's album features EDGE OF SANITY's Dan Swäno singing lead vocal on the track 'Sign Of The Dark'.

Albums:
SYMPHONIA DE INFERNALI, Nuclear Blast (1997)
Into The Labyrinths Of Desolation / Ave Satan / Orcus Cursus / Sign Of The Dark / Revival / Paroxysmal Winds / Forever Gone / Atomic Age / Liberation / X

DEINONYCHUS (HOLLAND)

Previously known as MALEFIC OATH, changing names to DEINONYCHUS in 1993, this Dutch band, actually more of a solo project by Marco Kehren- previously known as Odin, released the 'After The Rain Falls An Empty Sky Remains' demo. The Mainman behind DEINONYCHUS, now titled Sephiroth, is a former member of BESTIAL SUMMONING and he also has a side band; OCCULT.

DEINONYCHUS made their live debut, complete with "Vampyric Theatre By The Brides Of Dracula" in August 1997 suitably at the Dracula Centenary celebrations.

Kehren would later become lead vocalist for German Black Metal band BETHLEHEM.

Albums:
THE SILENCE OF DECEMBER, Cacophonous NIHIL 5 CD (1995)
Intro-Black Sun / I, Ruler Of Paradise In Black / The Silence Of December / The Final Affliction Of Xafan / A Shining Blaze Over Darkland / Under The Autumn Tree / Here Lies My Kingdom /

My Travels Through The Midnight Sky / Red Is My Blood ...Cold Is My Heart / Outro-Bizarre Landscape
THE WEEPING OF A THOUSAND YEARS, Cacophonous NIHIL 13CD (1996)
The Romantic Sounds Of Death / A Gathering Of Memories / Upon The Highlands I Fought / A Last Lament / I Have Done As You Did / Lost Forever / The Awakened / The Gothic Statue
AFTER THE RAIN FALLS... AN EMPTY SKY REMAINS, Gutteral (1997)
Intro / A Throne On My Long Awaited Desires / A Ruler Of Paradise In Black / A Shining Blaze Over Darkland / Tears Will Flow
ARK OF THOUGHT, Supernal FERLY 001CD (1997)
Chrysanthemums In Bloom / Revelation / My Days Until / Oceans Of Soliloquy / Serpent Of Old / Leviathan / The Fragrant Thorns Of Roses / Birth And The Eleventh Moon

DELIVERANCE (UK)
Line-Up: Kris Krowe (bass / vocals), Sin (guitar), Master Daniels (drums)

Albums:
DEVIL'S MEAT, Metalworks VOV666 (1987)
Desire / Your Death / Rotten To The Core / Devil's Meat / R.I.P. / Killing For Jesus / Deliverance / Twenty One Steps To Hell
EVIL FRIENDSHIP, AVM (1989)
Dies Irae / Tongues Of Lies / Lord Of Vice / Bell, Book And Scandal / No Way Out / Alive Forever / The Drowning / Turn Me To Stone / Evil Friendship / Rabid / Trooper Of Death / Requiem
BOOK OF LIES, Metalworks (199-)
The Devil's Instrument Parts I-III / Nightmare / Sympathy / Book Of Lies / Runaway / The Evil / Tear Down The Walls / R.I.P.
THE ULTIMATE REVENGE, Griffin GN 5931-2 (1993)
The Devil's Instrument Parts I-III / Turn Me To Stone / Devil Friendship / Deliverance / Bell, Book And Scandal / Runaway / Troopers Of Death / Alive Forever / R.I.P. / 21 Steps To Hell / The Evil / Vision / Stealer Of Dreams / The Church Of Deliverance

DEMANTOR (GERMANY)

Albums:
YOUR ONLY SATISFACTION, Galdre (1997)

White Chappel / The Church / Death's Door / Your Only Satisfaction / shadows / Behind His Face / Buried Alive / Moments In The Laboratories / Dangerous Worship / Isolate / Army Of Corpses / Publish Lies / Scientology / Destroy (The Picture Of Jesus)

DEMENTOR (CZECH REPUBLIC)
Line-Up: Rene Blahusiah (vocals / guitar), Roman Calpas (guitar), Miro Kucej (bass), Milos Hornak (drums)

Founded as far back as 1988 the present day line up of Black Death Metal band DEMENTOR features none of the original line up. DEMENTOR bowed in as a trio of guitarist Roman Lukac and siblings Lubos Gazdfik on bass and brother Roman on drums. Some time later vocalist Rene Blahusiah was added to the ranks and it was to be this personality that would prove to be the staying power of the band.
DEMENTOR opened proceedings with the 1992 demo 'The Extinction Of Christianity' before striking a deal with Czech label Immortal Souls Productions for the cassette album 'The Church Dies'. Signing to Spanish label Qabalah Productions. At this stage Blahusiah had been joined by guitarist Roman Calpos, bassist Miro Kucej and drummer Milos Hornak.
DEMENTOR signed to the infamous French concern Osmose Productions for a 2001 album.

Albums:
THE CHURCH DIES, Immortal Souls Productions (1994) (Cassette album)
KILL THE THOUGHT OF CHRIST, Immortal Souls Productions (1997)
Devils Rebirth / The False Faith / Time For Death / Waiting For Death / Love / Requiem To The Cursed Lust / The Art Of Blasphemy / Taste Of Dead Meat / Gates Of Eternity / The Eyes Of The Beast
THE ART OF BLASPHEMY, Qabalah Productions (1999)
In The Name Of God / Kill The Thought Of Christ / The Law Of Karma / The Lost Humanity / Fate Of Emptiness / Rotting God / Suppuration Of My Soul / Mortal Melody / Prometheans
ENSLAVE THE WEAK, Osmose Productions (2001)

DEMIGOD (FINLAND)
Line-Up: Esa Linden (vocals), Mika Naapasalo (guitar), Jussi Kiiski (guitar),

Tero Laitinen (bass), Seppo Taatila (drums)

Black Thrash Metal act DEMIGOD first issued the demo 'Unholy Domain' prior to the 'Slumber Of Sullen Eyes' album. The act split after only one album. In 1993 Seppo Taatila joined ADRAMELCH. Esa Linden would also join ADRAMELCH in 1996.

Albums:
SLUMBER OF SULLEN EYES, Drowned DC008 (1993)
Apocryphal / As I Behold I Despise / Dead Soul / The Forlorn / Tears Of God / Slumber Of Sullen Eyes / Embrace The Darkness / Blood Of The Perished / Fear Obscures From Within / Transmigration Beyond Eternity / Toward The Shrouded Infinity / Perpetual Ascent / Darkened

DEMIMONDE (CZECH REPUBLIC)
Line-Up: Tanya (vocals), Kashtan (vocals / guitar), Klouzek (guitar), Ankaabrt (guitar), Pendaran (bass), D'Aven (keyboards), Ton (drums)

Prague based Black Metal act with strong Doom influences. Members of DEMIMONDE also divide their activities with the ambient Black act AFAGDDU and the album 'The Book Wanth, Rooting Out The Beast'.

Albums:
DEMIMONDE, (199-)
Sound Terror System / Where The Sun The Moon Doesn't Relieve / Shadow Symphony / Baroque Thunders / We Are Luring The Fire / Queens Pilgrimage / Empire Of Bal-Sagoth, The Chronicles

DEMOGORGON (GREECE)

DEMOGORGON is the side project of LEGION OF DOOM and WINTERGODS members. The act arrived with a 1995 demo 'Lycaon Pictus'.

Singles/EPs:
The Horned Moon / The Seal Of The Dragon, Melancholy Productions (1996) (7" single)

DEMONCY (GA, USA)
Line-Up: Synvorlath- Lord Of The Ancient Moon (vocals), Ixithra- Lord Of The Sylvan Shadows, Vorthrus- Lord Of The Frozen Planes, Elsiferian- Lord Of The Mystic Isles, Drathirul- Lord Of The

Mournful Mists, Vetharanyn- Empress Of The Withered Stars, Keagan- Lord Of The Archaic Stones

Black Metal act DEMONCY, previously titled DARKENED SKIES, has for many years been a one man project of Ixithra. DEMONCY first surfaced in 1991 with the demo tape 'Impure Blessings (Dark Angel Of The Four Wings)'. A second session 'Joined In Darkness' followed in 1992. The same year Uxithra joined PROFANATICA for one gig (billing himself 'Wicked Warlock Of Demonic Blasphemy') but returned to action with DEMONCY and a third demo effort in 1993 'Faustian Dawn'.
DEMONCY kept demoing with 1994's 'Hypocrisy Of The Accursed Heavens' and 1995's 'Ascension Of A Star Long Since Fallen'.
The 1995 Damnation Records album comprises the 1991 and 1994 demo recordings. DEMONCY were still demoing in 1996 issuing the 'Commencement Of The Dark Crusades' tape.
Ixithra lent his deft keyboard touches to the debut 1996 BLACK FUNERAL album. The industrious Ixithra also boasts membership of RAVEN'S BANE, MYSTERIAN, PROFANE GRACE and SUBKLINIK.

Singles/EPs:
Dawn Of Eternal Damnation, Shadows Of Black (1996) (7" single)

Albums:
FAUSTIAN DAWN, Damnation (1995)
Whispers Of Undesired Destinies / Winter Bliss / Satanic Psalms / Descending Clouds Of Immortality / Denial Of The Holy Paradise / The Enchanted Words Of Forgotten Love / Hidden Path To The Forest Beyond / The Chill Winds Of Time / Fullmoon Twilight / Departure Of The Dismal
JOINED IN DARKNESS, Baphomet (1999)
Hymn To Ancients / Impure Blessings (Dark Angel Of Four Wings) / Demoncy / Joined In Darkness / Winter Bliss / Hypocrisy Of The Accursed Heavens / Spawn Of The Ancient Summoning / Hidden Path To The Forest Beyond / Angel Of Dark Shadows (Goddess Of The Dark) / The Dawn Of Eternal Damnation / Embraced By Shadows
WITHIN THE SYLVAN REALMS OF FROST, So It Is Done (1999)

DEMON DAGGER (PORTUGAL)
Line-Up: Pedro Mendes (vocals), Vitor Carvalho (guitar), José Figueiredo (bass), Miguel Carvalho (drums)

DEMON DAGGER date back to 1995. The band was founded as a quartet of vocalist Pedro Mendes, guitarist Vitor Carvalho, bassist José Silva and drummer Miguel Carvalho.
Silva departed in 1997. A 1997 demo featured W.C. NOISE guitarist Rodolfo Carduso as guest.

Singles/EPs:
Soul Of Steel / A Stand Below, Recital (1999)

Albums:
AFTERSHOCK, Recital BOX002 (2000)
Etched Face / Sinking / Wrecking Wrench / A Stand Below / Broadmoor / Corundura Pursuit / Don't Look Back / Sinful Bles-sin / Sweet Turning Sour / Frenzy Wraith / Soul Of Steel

DEMONIAC (NEW ZEALAND)
Line-Up: Behemoth (vocals), Heimdall (guitar), Shred (guitar), Diccon (bass), Matej (drums)

New Zealand Black Metal band DEMONIAC issued the 1994 demo 'The Birth Of Diabolical Blood'. DEMONIAC relocated to England during 1997 to take part in the 'World Domination' tour of Europe headlined by DARK TRANQUILITY and ENSLAVED.
Frontman Behemoth would relinquish the bass role in 1998 to former ADORIOR man Chris Hastings as singer Adromelech exited. By 2000 the position was in the hands of erstwhile VOICE OF DESTRUCTION bassist Diccon. Drums were handed over to new Slovenian recruit Matej.

Singles/EPs:
Moonblood, United Blasphemy (199-)

Albums:
PREPARE FOR WAR, Evil Omen EOR 003 CD (1995)
Intro (Prologue Of War) / Prepare For War / The Birth Of Diabolic Blood / The Earth Calls Me / Missein Anthropos / Hammer Of Damnation / The Return Of The Darkness And Evil / Celtic Sword Of Iron / A Narain / Evocation / Chaoist / So Bar Gar / Dormant Entity / Final

(Epilogue Of War)
STORMBLADE, Evil Omen EOR 005 CD (1997)
Burn The Witch / Domination / Red Light / Into The Cavern Light / Hatred Is Purity / Fight The War / Red Headed Maniac / Nigger Slut / Stormblade

DEMONIC (NORWAY)
Line-Up: Witchdemon (vocals / bass / drums), Fiend (guitar / keyboards)

Black Metal outfit DEMONIC debuted with the 1994 demo 'Naer Mørket Faller'. This session plus extra material would surface on the Necropolis Records album 'Lead Us Into Darkness' the following year.
The band also shared a 12" single with Dutch act FUNERAL WINDS.

Singles/EPs:
Split, (1996) (12" single split with FUNERAL WINDS)

Albums:
LEAD US INTO DARKNESS, Necropolis NR6661 (1995)
Spell Of The Witchdemon / Unholy Gates Of Limbo / His Eyes Burn Hate / Nar Morket Faller
THE EMPIRE OF AGONY, Necropolis NR018 (1997)
The Everlasting Shadow / A Dark Journey Towards Desolation / His Eyes Burn Hate / Evoke The Demon Lord / Diabolic Blood War / Wandering Through A Cold Mist / Spell Of The Witch Demon / Lead Us Into Darkness / Torment Their Christian Souls With Infernal Powers

DEMONIC CHRIST (NC, USA)

North Carolina Black Metal band DEMONIC CHRIST, founded in 1992, is centred upon former MYTHIC member Dana Duffey Clayton.
Duffey's striking image is backed up with a dedication to uncompromising Black Metal and her presence as the undoubted leader of a band rather than a side musician stands DEMONIC CHRIST apart from the crowd.
MYTHIC had been a Doom Metal act with Duffey in collaboration with Terri Heggen and Mary Bielich (now a member of NOVEMBER'S DOOM) releasing the EP 'Mourning In The Winter Solstice' on Relapse Records.
DEMONIC CHRIST issued the 1993 demo 'Deceiving The Heavens' which

DANA DUFFEY of DEMONIC CHRIST
Photo : Danielle Duffey Baker

featured the late Aragon Amori of PROFANATICA and INCANTATION on bass guitar. The demo received worthy praise and found distribution in America through Wild Rags and Europe from Osmose Productions. The impact of the tape led in turn to a deal with the German Moribund label for the album 'Punishment For Ignorance'. Session musicians in use at this time included guitarist Jon Vesano, bassist Devon Penrod and drummer Scott Pletcher.

A heavy schedule of touring in America was punctuated with further cassette releases and the inclusion of tracks on the Dwell Records compilation 'Awakening: Females In Extreme Music'. Following the debut album Duffey split away from the rest of the band who all promptly founded DARK MOON. Duffey herself took time out to raise her new born baby girl.

DEMONIC CHRIST are still an active concern although now a solo outfit. Early material was collated by Dutch label Cryonics for the 1999 'Demonic Battle Metal' album. The record was issued in only 250 hand numbered copies.

Albums:
PUNISHMENT FOR IGNORANCE, Moribund DEAD11CD (1995)
Mendacious Messiah / We Have Risen / Concubine Of The Gods / Slaughter Of The Sheep / I Am Lord / Veins Of Frost / Outro- Eve's Descent
DEMONIC BATTLE METAL, Cryonics CRY03 (1999)
We Have Risen / Church Of Profane Masturbation / Deceiving The Heavens / Nocturnal Empire / Passing Of The Storms / Witches Fall / Blut Und Ehre

DEMONIC RESURRECTION (INDIA)
Line-Up: The Demonsteler (vocals / guitar), Nikita (vocals / keyboards), Asish (guitar), Count Varathura (bass), Yash (drums)

Albums:
THE DREAMSTEALER, (2000)
My Words Of Sadness / From The Ashes / Darkened Moon / My Misery / The Demonsteler / Crestfallen / The Sadness Still Remains / My World Of Sadness (Acoustic)

DEMONREALM (DENMARK)
Line-Up: Sharuen (vocals), Nocturnaz (guitar), Astraborgnasyl (bass)

DEMONREALM contributed the track 'Commence The Final War' to the four way split 'Awaiting The Glorious Damnation Of Mankind' EP sharing vinyl with F.R.O.S.T., GARWALL and AXIS OF ADVANCE.

DENETHOR (HOLLAND)
Line-Up: Dracul (vocals), Schmerzen (guitar), Profane (bass), Nocturnasz (drums)

Corpsepainted DENETHOR was the creation of former OBSCURITY members Schmerzen and vocalist Myst. 1995 saw the addition of female vocalist Gineke but her tenure was brief. Myst departed in September 1997 in favour of the fire breathing Dracul.
Although DENETHOR released a 1997 demo session the band had folded by 1998.

DENIAL OF GOD (DENMARK)
Line up: Ustumallagum (vocals) / Azter (guitar), Fargel (bass), Uksul (drums)

Satanic Metallers DENIAL OF GOD, featuring ex APOLLYON guitarist Azter, were created in 1991.
The group released two demos, 'Oscularium Infame' in 1992 and 'The Dawn Of Aemizaez' in 1993 before following up with the debut EP 'The Statues Are Walking'. The 1998 7" single 'The Curse Of The Witch' featured female bassist Isaz of cult act FEIKN.
Oddly, DENIAL OF GOD have been known to throw maggots into their audience!

Singles/EPs:
The Statues Are Walking EP, Maggot (1995) (7" single)
The Curse Of The Witch / Black Horror Metal, (1998) (7" single)

Albums:
THE GHOULS OF D.O.G., Dark Trinity Productions DTP002CD (1996)
The Ghouls Of D.O.G. / Robbing The Grave Of The Priest / Follow Those Who Died / The Crypt Has Eyes

DEPRAVED (GERMANY)

DEPRAVED include members of RIGER.

Albums:
DESTORTED THEORIES, CCP 100203-2 (199-)

116

DEPRAVITY (FINLAND)
Line-Up: Martti (vocals), Olli (guitar), Enska (guitar), Pete (bass), Matti (drums)

Albums:
SILENCE OF THE CENTURIES,
Adipocere CD AR017 (1993)
Silence Of The Centuries / Sleepy Ocean / Remasquerade / Phantasmagoria / Vacuum Of Thoughts

DEPRESION (AUSTRIA)
Line-Up: Daniel, Milan, Radim, Alex

Albums:
DEPRESION, Depresion (1997)
Intro / Time To Die / Life Of My Soul / Mendacious Faith / Bitches Of Your Mind / Depressions / Face Of Religion / Torture Of Defenceless / Yearning / Kladivo Na Carodejnice

DER TOD (ITALY)
Line-Up: Simone B. (vocals), Fausto B. (guitar / bass / keyboards / drums)

Albums:
DER TOD, Last Scream SCREAM 004 CD (1995)
(I'm Really) Bored / Black Sun (I'm Not Of This World) / I Scream / Everything / Tragic Feeling / Indecisions / Lifetime / The Meaning Of Life

DESASTER (GERMANY)
Line-Up: Okkulto (vocals), Infernal (guitar), Odin (bass), Tormentor (drums)

Koblenz based outfit specializing in Black Metal in its rawest form. DESASTER, who hark back to 1988, debuted with the demo 'The Fog Of Avalon' followed by a further demo session in 1994 'Lost In The Ages'. Early member Creator departed enabling guitarist Infernal ("Six silver strings of Hellish crossfire") to build a brand new band with vocalist Okkulto ("Blasphemic death threat"), bassist Odin ("Roaring four string battle axe") and drummer Tormentor ("Sadomized drum chaos").
DESASTER shared their inaugural single with UNGOD. The 1997 album 'Stormbringer' includes a cover of KREATOR's 'Tormentor'.
Tormentor himself would join up with the Japanese / German collective METALUCIFER alongside Jochen of METAL INQUISITOR.
The 1998 DESASTER album 'Hellfires

Dominion' includes guest sessions from Thorsten of LIVING DEATH, Wannes of ASPHYX and Lemmy of VIOLENT FORCE.
Drummer Riger would join ANTROPOFAGUS in early 2001 appearing on their 'A Waste Of Flesh' album.

Singles/EPs:
Hill Of A Thousand Souls, Merciless (1995) (Split single with UNGOD)

Albums:
A TOUCH OF MEDIEVEL DARKNESS,
Merciless MR CD003 (1996)
Skyline In Flames (Intro) / In A Winter Battle / A Touch Of Medieval Darkness / Fields Of Triumph / Devil's Sword / Into A Magical Night / Crypts Of Dracul / Visions On The Autumn Shades / Porter Of Hellgate / Home For The Brave (Outro)
STORMBRINGER, Merciless (1997)
Stormbringer / The Swords Will Never Sink / Sacrilege / Face Of Darkness / Tormentor / Emerging Castleland
HELLFIRE'S DOMINION, Merciless 008 (1998)
Intro / In The Ban Of Satan's Sorcery / Expect No Release / Tuetonic Steel / Metalized Blood / Thou Shalt Be King / Hellfire's Dominion / Past…Present…Future / Castleland / Across The Bloodfields

DESASTRIOUS (USA)

DESASTRIOUS, a one man project of Nocturnus Desastrious, debuted with the demo 'Necroanal Ceremonium'. The 'Loekr Inn Nefilhim' album sees keyboard contributions from Klawdia. Desastrious also runs the side project HELVINTR.

Albums:
LOEKR INN NIFLHEIM, (1998)
Dyrd Tyd / Al Svartur / Svartur Andstyggilegur Malmur / Magical Night Of Eternal Evil / At-Sokn / Norskripi Af Hinn O-Katr Skogland / Loekr Inn Niflheim / Managarmr / Far-Bjodr / Moonlight Harvest Of immortal Hate / Drekka Blod Dyrsins / In The Souls Of Night / Heimdall's Gjallarhorn / Hrafn

DESCEND (GREECE)

DESCEND were previously known as EPIDEMIC. A split album was issued with ALL THAT IS EVIL.

Albums:
DESCEND, (199-) (Split album with ALL THAT IS EVIL)
Unseen / Visions To Come / Toutatis Strikes / To Infinity We Shall Find
BEYOND THY REALM OF THROES, Black Lotus (1999)

DESEKRATION (GERMANY)
Line-Up: Christian Grünewald (vocals), Anne Weyl (vocals), Jörg Hoffmann (guitar), Michael Beutel (guitar), Marc Ziegenbein (bass), Markus Wegerer (drums)

Albums:
NAUDHIZ, Desekration (1998)

DESEKRATOR (NORWAY)
Line-Up: Panzerschwanz, Total Sleazer, Dr. Love, Prof. Powder, Capt. Killroy, Ali Gator, Bassnel Brekk

Black Metal with a rare showing of humour. In spite of the pseudonyms credited DESEKRATOR in reality boast Infernus and Tormentor of GORGOROTH and ex OLD FUNERAL man and 'Slayer' magazine editor Ali Gator (Tore Brathseth). ENSLAVED's Ivor Bjornson and Grutle Kjellson are also involved.

Singles/EPs:
Krucifixion Overdose, (199-) (Triple picture disc 7")

Albums:
METAL FOR DEMONS, Hammerheart (1999)
Metal For Demons / Aphice / Overdose / Texas Joe / Revenge Of The Hellhammer / Trommenaskinhelvete / Take Us To The Pub / Hot In The City / Execution / Bergen-Belsen Svinepelsen / Tormentor

DESIRE (PORTUGAL)
Line-Up: Tear (vocals), Mist (guitar), Eclipse (guitar), Dawn (keyboards), Flame (drums)

DESIRE was originally titled INCARNATED upon their foundation in 1992 by vocalist Tear and drummer Flame. Although a promo single 'Death Blessed By A God', was issued by September 1994 the band decided upon a name change to DESIRE.
The 'Infinity..' album included contributions from female vocalist Joana Pereira, bassist Jaime Souza and ex guitarist Luis Lamelas.

Second guitarist Eclipse was added following the debut album release. Although having been a going concern for some years DESIRE have played live on only a handful of occasions.

Albums:
INFINITY...A TIMELESS JOURNEY THROUGH AN EMOTIONAL DREAM, Skyfall SKY 85.003 (1996)
Chapter I: (Prologue) / Chapter II: (Leaving) This Land Of The Eternal Desires / Chapter III: A Ride In The Dream Crow / Chapter IV: The Purest Dreamer / Chapter V: In Delight With The Mermaid / Chapter VI: Forever Dreaming... (Shadow Dance) / Chapter VII: Epilogue

DESTINY (FRANCE)

Albums:
SUPREME DOMINATION'S ART, Psychic Scream (2001)

DESTROYER 666 (AUSTRALIA)
Line-Up: K.K. Warslut (vocals / guitar), Shrapnel (guitar), S. Beserk (bass), Jarro Deceiver (drums)

DESTROYER 666, founded by ex BESTIAL WARLUST and CORPSE MOLESTATION vocalist / guitarist Keith 'K.K.' Warslut, emerged with the 1995 demo 'Six Songs With The Devil'. The band, whose legend is 'Australian And Antichrist' have trod an uncompromising path of brutal Black Metal personified by their stage presence bedecked in vicious spikes and studs.
DESTROYER 666's debut line up for the first album 'Violence Is The Prince Of This World' included drummer Chris Volcano, former HOBB'S ANGEL OF DEATH and BESTIAL WARLUST bassist Bullet Eater (Phil Gresik) and DAMAGED guitarist Matt Sanders.
The follow up 'Unchain the Wolves saw Warslut retaining Bullet Eater but drafting in new faces Shrapnel on guitar and Howitzer (Coz of GOSPEL OF THE HORNS) on drums. Volcano went on to forge ABOMINATOR.
Howitzer would relinquish the drum stool to Jarro Deceiver in late 1997 the new recruit debuting on the 'Satanic Speed Metal' 7" single. Another casualty was Bullet Eater who, decamping to found LONG VOYAGE BACK, lost his place to S. Beserker.
Former SINISTER singer Evil Eric is

KEITH WARSLUT of DESTROYER 666

presently DESTROYER 666's drummer.

Satanic Speed Metal / The Sirens Call, Merciless (1998) (7" single)
King Of Kings / Lord Of The Wild, Ajna Productions (2000) (7" single)

Albums:
VIOLENCE IS THE PRINCE OF THIS WORLD, Modern Invasion (1996)
Hail To Destruction / An Endless Stream Of Bombers / … True Sons Of Satan / Burning The Veil Of Falsehood / Death Metal Winds (Howl Again) / Song For A Devil's Son / The Eternal Glory Of War
UNCHAIN THE WOLVES, Modern Invasion (1997)
Genesis To Genocide / Australian And Anti Christ / Satan's Hammer / Tyranny Of The Inevitable / Six Curses For A Spiritual Wasteland / Unchain The Wolves / Damnations Pride / Onward To Arktoga
PHOENIX RISING, Seasons Of Mist (2000)
Rise Of The Predator / The Last Revelation / Phoenix Rising / I Am The Wargod (Ode To The Battle Slain) / The Eternal Glory Of War / Lone Wolf Winter / Ride The Solar Winds / The Birth Of Tragedy

DETERIORATE (USA)

Previously a straight forward Death Metal band DETERIORATE would evolve into a more Black incarnation with later releases. The band folded in 1997. Erstwhile members of DETERIORATE would form ZAHGURIM.

Albums:
ROTTING IN HELL, JL America (1993)
Agonized Display / A Thousand Years Of Anguish / Cannibal Autopsy / Devoured / The Sufferance / Rotting In Hell / Asphyxiation Cremation / Shadows Of Death / Beyond The Grave / Decomposed Anatomy
THE SENECTUOUS ENTRANCE, Pulverizer (1996)
The Senectous Entrance / In The Presence Of Eurus / Xipe Totec / Stealing Strength For The Ivory Bear / Kiev 1237 / Religious Fatum / Ode To A Mortal / Darea Come… / Gather The Nebbish… / Evaporated Battle Ground

DETEST (DENMARK)

Line-Up: Peter Jørgensen (vocals), Ole Christiansen (guitar), Hardy Akira Madsen (guitar), Peter Frandsen (bass), Brian Andersen (drums)

Brøndby based DETEST supported DEATH and CARCASS in Denmark and appeared at the Roskilde Festival.

Albums:
DORVAL, Progress Red Labels PRL010 (1995)
The Assault On Dorval / The Process Of Doom (Preface Of Invasion) / A Black Sea Rose / Inhaled Through The Body / Unavoidable Encounter / Defiled / Dorval (Revenging Hour) / Bound / (Chapter VI) Legio / Deathbreed (The Description Of Legio) / Gathering Of Darkness (The Conclusion) / Shadows Of Dissolution / Obscurity Devised

DET HEDENSKE FOLK (NORWAY)

The single - a split 7" convened together with Australian act ABYSSIC HATE - is made up of demo recordings by Norwegian outfit DET HEDENSKE FOLK. The band feature former OLD FUNERAL, SATANEL, GORGOROTH and IMMORTAL man Abbath on drums.

Singles/EPs:
United By Heathen Blood, Bloodless Creations (1997) (Split 7" with ABYSSIC HATE)

DEVASTACION (ARGENTINA)

Line-Up: Walter Ortiz (vocals / guitar), Fabian Cejas (guitar), Gonzalo Giuliano (bass), Gustavo Quiroga (drums)

Albums:
… QUE LO PARIÓ!!, Icarus 004 (1999)
Intro / Raza Vengada / Pata, Sudor Y Sangre / Evolucion / Muerte Cumbia / Q'Lo Pario / Resistiendo Al Engano / La Patria Olvidada / Condicio Humana / Trotando De Zafar / El Enganero / La Rura Interior / El Informador Oficiel / Barbara Imposicion

DEVIL CHILDE (USA)

Line-Up: Lucifer (guitar), Matthew Hopkins (drums)

Anonymous Black Thrash outing. In reality guitarist 'Lucifer' is Jack Starr, previously a member of VIRGIN STEELE and presently with BURNING STARR whilst drummer 'Matthew Hopkins' is RAVEN and PENTAGRAM man Joe Hasselvander.

DEVIL CHILDE, (1984)
Devil Childe / Rain Of Terror / Son Of A
Witch / Repent Or Die / Thru The Shadow
/ Grave Robber / Beyond The Grave

DEVIL DOLL (SLOVENIA / ITALY)

An Extreme cult outfit based around the
personality of Mr. Doctor, DEVIL DOLL
were created in 1987 and in a very short
space of time built up an enormous
underground fanbase for their unique
eclectic amalgam of Speed Metal,
Classical music and Industrial Folk (!)
packaged into elaborate concept albums.
Bizarrely, the band's first release, 'The
Mark Of The Beast' is an unattainable
collector's item for only one copy, in a
hand painted sleeve, was pressed!
For the second album, 'The Girl Who
Was... Death', a concept album based
around the 60s TV series 'The Prisoner',
DEVIL DOLL actually performed live in
Ljubljana where cassettes were given out
free to the audience. The finalized album
once more leapt into the collectors
market when only 150 records survived
destruction from a limited pressing of
500.
The following year DEVIL DOLL worked
on a project titled 'The Black Holes Of
The Mind' and a Mr. Doctor side project
known as 'Mr. Doctor Sings Hans Eisler'.
Neither saw release, with the latter only
making the test pressing stage.
'The Black Holes Of The Mind' was
retitled 'Mr. Doctor' / 'Eliogabulus' and
recording was finished amidst the early
stages of the break up of Yugoslavia.
During 1991 DEVIL DOLL recorded a
further album, 'Sacriligium', as Ljubljana
was being attacked by Serbian soldiers.
Fate finally caught up with the band
though when fire destroyed both the
recording studio and the tapes for an
album to have been titled 'The Day Of
Wrath'.

Albums:
THE MARK OF THE BEAST, (1988)
THE GIRL WHO WAS... DEATH, Hurdy
Gurdy HG1 (1989)
ELIOGABALUS, Hurdy Gurdy HG6
(1990)
SACRILIGIUM, Hurdy Gurdy HG7 (1992)
SACRILIGE OF FATAL ARMS, Hurdy
Gurdy HG9 (1993)
DES IRAE, Hurdy Gurdy (1996)

DEVILS WHOREHOUSE (SWEDEN)

The 2000 mini album 'The Howling' is a
homage to the MISFITS and SAMHAIN
from MARDUK members Morgan and B.
War.

Albums:
THE HOWLING, Regain BLOOD 004
(2000)
The Howling / Blood Nymphoman /
Erotikill / We Live Again / Halloween /
Black Dream / All Hell Breaks Loose /
Moribound

DEVISER (GREECE)
Line-Up: Matt Hnaras (vocals / guitar),
George Triantafilakis (guitar), Nick
Cristogianis (bass / keyboards), Mike
Tsembertzis (drums)

Black Metal outfit DEVISER was founded
in 1989. The band's first demo 'Forbidden
Knowledge' ensued the following year as
did second effort 'Psychic Completion'. In
1993 a further tape surfaced entitled 'Into
His Unknown'.

Singles/EPs:
The Revelation Of Higher Mysteries,
Teutonic Existence (1995)

Albums:
UNSPEAKABLE CULTS, Mascot M
7024-2 (1997)
Stand & Deliver / Darkness Incarnate /
Threnody / When Nightmares Begin / The
Rape Of Holiness / Ritual Orgy
(Instrumental) / Dangers Of A Real And
Concrete Nature / The Fire Burning Bright
/ In The Horror Field / Afterkill (Outro)
TRANSMISSION TO CHAOS, II Moons
(1998)

DIABLERIE (FINLAND)
Line-Up: Henri Villberg (vocals), Kimmo
Tukainen (guitar), Eric Lundén (guitar),
Alessi Ahokas (bass), Juha Suorsa
(keyboards), Antti Ruokola (drums)

Created in late 1997 by former
CEREMONY OF ECLIPSE members
vocalist Henri Villberg and guitarist Kimmo
Tukainen. Original second guitarist Jukka
Gråsten would decamp after recording of
the 'Astro' demo necessitating bassist Erik
Lundén covering the guitar role and the
enrollment of Alessi Ahokas on bass.
Ahokas has credits with RAPTURE,
EXCELSIOR, PROPHET and
SNOWGARDEN. Lundén has a side band

entitled STILL LIFE. Villberg has sessioned as guest 'growling' vocalist for PROPHET.

Albums:
SERAPHYDE, Avantgarde (2001)
Dystphia Show / Nervine / Float / Astronomicon / Weltschmerzen / Until Death Do Us Apart / Nations Collide / Bitter Utopia / Death Wired To The Bleak / Seraphyde / Oppressions

DIABLOS RISING
(FINLAND / GREECE)
Line-Up: Mikka Luttinen, Magus Vampyr Daoloth

Industrial Black Death Metal project by Mikka Luttinen of IMPALED NAZARENE and Magus Vampyr Daoloth of NECROMANTIA, DIABLOS RISING's debut album features one Phillip Glass inspired track that is three minutes of complete silence!
Daoloth formed a further side project RAISM in 1996, issuing an album 'The Very Best Of Pain'.

Singles/EPs:
S.N.T.F., Kron-H (1995) (7" single)

Albums:
666, Osmose Productions OPCD023 (1995)
Genocide- I Am God / Vinnum Sabbati / Give Me Blood Or Give Me Death / Satanas Lead Us Through / Sorcery-Scientia Maxima / 666 / X-X-ST
BLOOD, VAMPIRISM AND SADISM, Kron-H 001 (1995)
Satanic Propaganda / Blood Lunar Cult / Blood Communion / Ilsa / Sadism Unbound / Mantle Of Suffering / Necrommanteion / Ashes To Ashes, Flesh To Dust

DIABOLI (FINLAND)

A one man project previously titled SILGIUM DIABOLI upon their formation in 1992 issuing the 'Descent Into Hell' demo. Became DIABOLI during 1995.

Albums:
MESMERISED BY DARKNESS, Unisound USR 026 (1996)
Into The Northern Darkness / Under The Leadership Of A New God / Mesmerized By Darkness / Thy Must Prepare To Fall / Fall Of The Human Race / Victory Celebration / Chaos / Supreme

TOWARDS DAMNATION, Full Moon Productions (1997)
Under A Bloodred Sky / To Burn The Kingdom Of God / Totaalituho / Twilight / Dream Unknown / Saatanan Viha / Under The Leadership Of A New God / Jumalan Tuhoaminen

DIABOLIC (Tampa, FL, USA)
Line-Up: Paul Ouellette (vocals), Briam Malone (guitar), Brian Hipp (guitar), Ed Webb (bass), Aantor Coates (drums)

Tampa blasphemous Black Death Metal band DIABOLIC feature former HORROR OF HORRORS, EULOGY and EXMORTIS drummer Aantor Coates. Bassist Ed Web is also a former EULOGY member.
DIABOLIC's June 1997 demo 'City Of The Dead' would be reissued as a mini album by Fadeless Records. The act's debut gig came with a high profile appearance sharing the stage with heavyweights VADER, MONSTROSITY and BROKEN HOPE. The band took to the road with gusto appearing in 1998 at the Milwaukee Metalfest and New York Demonfest, the New England Death And Hardcore festival and the Texan November To Dismember gig in 1999.
Touring in America saw DIABOLIC as part of the 'Death Metal Massacre' package alongside CANNIBAL CORPSE, GOD DETHRONED and HATE ETERNAL. The tour, although a great sucess, was marred by the band having all their equipment stolen after the first gig. Undaunted, DIABOLIC put in further touring supporting MORBID ANGEL the same year.
Ouellette would later be sacked for alleged "weakness" as bass player Ed Webb took over lead vocal duties. The band would also draft fomer BRUTALITY and CRADLE OF FILTH guitarist Brian Hipp. With this line up DIABOLIC cut a version of SLAYER's 'Killing Fields' for a tribute album. Later shows would see erstwhile ANGEL CORPSE guitarist Gene Palubicki filling in.

Albums:
CITY OF THE DEAD, Fadeless (1999)
Denounce God / City Of The Dead / Vortex / Encarta / Inborn
SUPREME EVIL, The Plague (2000)
Insacred / Sacrament Of Fiends / Ancient Hatred / Treacherous Scriptures / Grave Warnings / Rack Of Torment / View With Abhorrence / Dwelling Spirits /

Wicked Inclination / Supreme Evil
SUBTERRANIAL MAGNETUDE, (2000)

DIABOLICAL (PARAGUAY)

Albums:
SACRED REMAINS, (199-)
Monstrous Birth / (Nothing) Sacred
Remains / Enslaved By Darkness / The
Morning Madness / Innocencia Mortis /
Never Again / Final Retribution / I Hate…
/ Black Sepulcher / Totally Insane /
Abandoned
DOMINUS INFERNAL, Icarus (2000)
Revelation Of The Infernal Power / The
Laws Of Hell / Ready For The Ceremony
/ The Ancient God Serpent / Unholy
Darkness For The Occult Abyss /
Almighty Force Of Truth / Three Lords
From Hell / The Warriors / Recibe El
Nuebo Fuego

DIABOLICAL MASQUERADE (SWEDEN)

DIABOLICAL MASQUERADE is the solo
project of KATATONIA vocalist / guitarist
Blackheim. As well as DIABOLICAL
MASQUERADE Blackheim also fronts
BEWITCHED, a duo project with
ANCIENT WISDOM's Vargher.
EDGE OF SANITY's Dan Swano
produced the first effort.

Albums:
RAVENDUSK IN MY HEART, Adipocere
CDAR036 (1996)
The Castle Of Blackheim / Blackheim's
Quest To Bring Back The Stolen Autumn /
Beyond The Spiritual Moon / The Sphere
In Blackheim's Shrine / Under The
Banner Of The Sentinel / Blackheim's
Forest Kept The Season Forever / The
Dark Blue Sea Journeys Of The Sentinel
/ Blackheim's Hunt For Nocturnal Grace /
Ravendusk In My Heart
**MY PHANTOM LODGE (CLOAKED BY
THE MOONSHINE MIST)**, Adipocere CD
AR 039 (1998)
Astray Within The Coffinwood Mill / The
Puzzling Constellation Of A Deathrune /
Ravenclaw / The Walk Of The
Hunchbacked / Cloaked By The
Moonshine Mist / Across The Open Vault
And Away / Hater / The Blazing
Demondrome Of Murmers And Secrecy /
Upon The Salty Wall Of The Broody
Gargoyle
NIGHTWORK, (199-)
Rider On The Bonez / Dreadventurouz /
The Zkeleton Keyz To The Dead / This

Ghoultimate Omen / All Onboard The
Perdition Hearze! / The Eerie Obzidian
Cirkuz / Haunted By Horror
DEATH'S DESIGN, Avantgarde Music
(2000)

DIABOLICUM (NORWAY)
Line-Up: Blackblood (vocals), Sasrof
(guitar), Nathzion (guitar), Gorgorium
(bass), Mysteriis (drums)

DIABOLICUM evolved from the mid 90's
act IMPERIAL. Founded by guitarist
Sasrof and drummer Thorne IMPERIAL
issued an inaugural demo in 1994 entitled
'Mori Voluntaria' with session vocals
courtesy of Blackblood.
Throne decamped and new blood
drummer Amath and bassist Gorgorium
were enrolled for a 1996 session 'The
Imperial Darkness' with singer Thyrfing.
IMPERIAL's line up problems were
exacerbated when Amath quit. Session
drums were supplied by Lord Mysteriis of
SETHERIAL as Blackblood returned to
take over the lead vocal position
permanently for the third demo 'De
Fördömdos Legion'.
IMPERIAL was put on ice whilst various
members tried their hand at a new act
HELVETE with Lord Mysteriis and his
SETHERIAL colleague Kraath. By 1999
this outfit became DIABOLICUM with the
addition of guitarist Nathzion.

Albums:
THE GRANDEUR OF HELL, Napalm
NPR065 (2000)
The Grandeur Of Hell (Moloch) /
Chained On Demonwings / The Wind
Shall Slay / Serenade Of The Imperial
Darkness / Infernalord (The Prey Of
Black Souls) / The Man With Thousand
Shapes / Reaper Of The Orb / Perished
(The Manifestation Of Suicide) / Her
Divine Hatred (Tiamat) / Evocation
(Longing For Armageddon)

DIABOLIQUE (SWEDEN)
Line-Up: Kristian Wählin (vocals / guitar),
Johan Österberg (guitar), Bino Carlsson
(bass), Hans Nilsson (drums)

DIABOLIQUE is the brainchild of
GROTESQUE and LIERS IN WAIT
founder Kristian Wahlin. Guitarist Johan
Österberg is ex DECOLLATION.
Drummer Hans Nilsson is another LIERS
IN WAIT member and also has credits
with LUCIFERION and DIMENSION
ZERO.

The debut album was produced by KING DIAMOND's Andy La Rocque.
Wählin also goes under the pseudonym of Necrolord as cover artist for many Black Metal bands.

Albums:
WEDDING THE GROTESQUE, Black Sun (1997)
Dark Man / Shaven Angel Forms / Blood Of Summer / Sacrificial Highway / The Unchaste Bittersweet / Sorrow Piercing Art / The Smiling Black / Beggar Whipped In Wine / The Diabolique
THE DIABOLIQUE, Listenable POSH 011 (1998)
Stealing The Fire From Heaven / Blood Of Summer / Beggar Whipped In Wine / Sorrows Piercing Art / Deep Shame Of God
THE BLACK FLOWER, Black Sun (1999)
Catholic / Dark Rivers Of The Heart / Absinthe / And Deepest Sadness / Yesmine / Eternal Summer / Cannula / Morphine / A Golden Girl From Somewhere / Silver / Play In The Dark
BUTTERFLIES, Necropolis NR044CD (2000)
Rain / Losing You / Butterflies / Summer Of Her Heart / Stolen Moments / Beneath The Shade

DIES IRAE (POLAND)

Offshoot act from VADER men Mauser and Docent.

Albums:
IMMOLATED, Metal Blade 3984143562 (2000)
Zonak / Message Of Aiwas / Sirius / Immolated / The Nameless City / Bestride Shatak / Turning Point / Hidden Love / Lion Of Knowledge / Unheavenly Salvation / Fear Of God / Blasphemous Words

DIES ATER (GERMANY)
Line-Up: Nuntius Trisis (vocals / guitars), Torgrim (guitar), Obskur (bass), Ole Caust (keyboards), Imperus (drums)

Black Metal act DIES ATER was created in November 1994 with a line up of vocalist / guitarist Nuntius Tristis, guitarist Torgrim, bassist Obskur, keyboard player Ole Caust and drummer Imperus. The band's first demo in 1996 'Rabenflug' led to a deal with English label Mordgrimm for the debut John Harris produced album 'Reign Of Tempests'. DIES ATER toured as support to ABLAZE MY SORROW,

SIGH and DESASTER.
DIES ATER signed to German label Last Episode for the 2000 follow up 'Through Weird Woods'.

Albums:
REIGN OF TEMPESTS, Mordgrimm (1998)
…Das Erwachen Der Nacht / King Of Tempests / Konigsblut / Engelsnacht / Der Schwur / Der Fluch Der Seele / A Mourner's Dream / Rabenflug / Das Geleit
THROUGH WEIRD WOODS, Last Episode LEP 049 (2000)
…Wo Anmut Wacht / Scorned Heroine / Infested Night / Wintersturm / Der Schwur (Part II) / Das Tor- Des Dunkeln Schein / Through Weird Woods / Of Prophecies To Come…

DIE VERBANNTEN KINDER EVA'S (AUSTRIA)

Darkwave Ambient act DIE VERBANNTEN KINDER EVA'S ('The Banished Children Of Eve') founder member Silenius is also a member of ABIGOR and THE SUMMONING.

Albums:
DIE VERBANNTEN KINDER EVA'S (1995)
Einleitung / The Serpent's Voice / Darkened Skies / Quod Olim Erat / Beneath The Veil Of The Ocean / Requiem / May No Tears Stain This Holy Ground / The Messenger / Futile Belief / Reflexion Beyond Boundaries / Craving Dreams / Shadowvale / Withering Existence / Das Letzte Kapital
COME HEAVY SLEEP, Napalm (1997)
The Beginning / Come Heavy Sleep / Sad Silent Home / Misery / Dim Atmosphere / The Post / Unred Mystery / House Of Glass / Waters Of Wide Agony / The End
IN DARKNESS LET ME DWELL, Napalm (1999)
Intro / Brief Even As Bright / On A Faded Violet / Overcast / Cease Sorrows Now / In Darkness Let Me Dwell / Shall I Strive? / Sunrise From Dreams Of Thee / From Silent Night

DIMMAK (USA)
Line-Up: Shaune, Scott, Brandon, Dennis (bass)

DIMMAK consist of former RIPPING CORPSE members Shaune, Scott and Brandon together with ex TORTURE KRYPT bassist Dennis.

SHAGRATH of DIMMU BORGIR
Photo : Martin Wickler

Albums:
ENTER THE DRAGON, Dies Irae (1999)

DIMMU BORGIR (NORWAY)
Line-Up: Shagrath (vocals), Jens-Peter (guitar), Erkejetter Silenoz (guitar), Nagash (bass), Stian Aastad (keyboards), Tjodalv (drums)

Norwegian Black Metal exponents founded in 1993. DIMMU BORGIR have with a combination of tenacity on the touring front and the undoubted maturity of successive album releases quickly risen to the very top echelons of the Black Metal scene. The band now rank alongside CRADLE OF FILTH as the best selling Black Metal acts today. In spite of their status the band has weathered the storm of ever fluctuating line ups.

DIMMU BORGIR's vocalist Shagrath had previously been a member of FIMBULWINTER and RAGNAROK. Guitarist Erkjetter Silenoz was previously a member of NOCTURNAL BREED, going under the stage name of Ed Dominator. Drummer Åxellson Tjodalv was also an active member of OLD MAN'S CHILD and KOSMOS RØST. This initial trio soon completed the line up with the top hat wearing keyboard player Stian Aastad and bass player Brynjard Tristian.

The band signed to Nuclear Blast Records in 1996, although had to replace bassist Brynjard Tristan for the 'Devil's Path' EP with ex COVENANT man Nagash (Stian Thoresen). Said EP featured two cover versions of CELTIC FROST tracks.

The band toured Europe in 1997 alongside CRADLE OF FILTH, IN FLAMES and DISSECTION touring to promote the 'Enthrone Darkness Triumphant' album. With the support of Nuclear Blast DIMMU BORGIR were to find themselves thrust to the top of the Black Metal league as their album even broke into the national German charts.

Aarstad failed to turn up for a festival performance and the band pulled in AVERNUS, THERION and ANCIENT keyboard player Kimberly Goss for these shows and the American was announced as a permanent member shortly after. Aarstad would later emerge as a member of ENTHRAL releasing albums coincidentally enough on the Hot record label, owned by Shagrath.

Touring saw Tjoldav, at home with a new born child, temporarily replaced by Aggressor (Carl Michael Eide) of ULVER and INFERNO infamy. In true Black Metal tradition members of DIMMU BORGIR managed to get themselves into a few scrapes, which included Nagash being hospitalized after burning himself during a fire breathing routine and Silenoz punctured a car's tyre when a Volkswagen ran over his heavily spiked boots!

In more musical related matters, Shagrath was also to appear on his countrymen RAGNAROK's album 'Arising Realm' performing keyboards.

With the album still selling in Europe DIMMU BORGIR rounded off the year as guests to KREATOR on a batch of metal festival shows. This even included an impromptu acoustic performance at a Finnish rock club.

DIMMU BORGIR's next album 'Spiritual Black Dimensions' broke the band into the mainstream with accelerated sales worldwide. Joining the band on guitar was the Australian Astennu, a member of Nagash's side project CARPE TENEBRUM, and previous to that in his homeland LORD KAOS. Goss meantime had opted out to create her own Power Metal act SINERGY.

Various members of the group continued to be prolific however and both Astennu and Nagash, together with CRADLE OF FILTH, MAYHEM and ARCTURUS members forged yet another project act COVENANT.

The 1998 mini album includes a rather surprising cover of ACCEPT's 'Metal Heart'. DIMMU BORGIR also beefed up their sound with the addition of ex VIDDER keyboard player Mustis (real name Øyvind Mustafarta).

DIMMU BORGIR toured Britain with sell out shows. Support coming from DARK FUNERAL, DØDHEIMSGARD and EVENFALL.

In a surprise move the high profile Nick Barker from the British Black Metal band CRADLE OF FILTH, probably DIMMU BORGIR's only real competitors at the time in terms of sales, was poached to join the band.

Tjovald meantime rejoined his former colleagues in OLD MAN'S CHILD for their 'Revelation 666' album before creating a band project SUSPERIA with his OLD MAN'S CHILD colleagues guitarist Cyrus and bassist Memnock in 2000. Mustis would also session on the debut SUSPERIA album.

Although still very much Nagash's vehicle his main side act COVENANT adopted the new title of KOVENANT for their 2000 album 'Animatronic' and Nagash himself

DIMMU BORGIR
Photos : Martin Wickler

was renamed Lex Icon. Nagash left DIMMU BORGIR to concentrate on KOVENANT and the band drafted BORKNAGER / ex ARCTURUS bassist Simen Hestnaes as replacement.
DIMMU BORGIR dispensed with Astennu in mid 2000 replacing him swiftly with Archon. This alliance was brief in the extreme though as within weeks it was announced that OLD MAN'S CHILD driving force Galder had taken the position. DIMMU BORGIR's grip on Hestnaes tightened as he decamped permanently from BORKNAGER resulting in his former act having to cancel their European tour.
Barker also spread his talents to the highly successful LOCK UP collaboration with HYPOCRISY's Peter Tägtgren, NAPALM DEATH's Shane Embury and Jesse Pintado. He also figured anonymously with 'Mexican' Death Metal band BRUJERIA for their 'Brujerizmo' album.
Promoting their 2001 album 'Puritanical Euphoric Misanthropia' DIMMU BORGIR toured the European circuit heading a strong bill bolstered by IN FLAMES, SUSPERIA, NEVERMORE and LACUNA COIL.
KING DIAMOND guitarist Andy LaRocque would guest on the album performing on the Japanese bonus track 'Devil's Path'.

Singles/EPs:
Inn I Evighetens Morke, Necromantik Gallery Productions (1994)
Master Of Disharmony / Devil's Path / Nocturnal Fear / Nocturnal Fear (Celtically Possessed), Hot SHAGRAT 006 (1996) ('Devil's Path' EP)

Albums:
FOR ALL TID, No Colours NC003 (1995)
Det Nye Riket / Nader Korpenvinger / Over Bleknede Blaaer / Til Dommedag / Stien / Glittertind / For All Tid / Hunnerkongenssorgsvarte Ferd Over Steppene / Raabjoran Speiler Draugnejmenp Skodde / Den Gjente Sannhets Herpker
STORMBLAST, Cacophonous NIHIL 12CD (1996)
Alt Lys Er Svunnet Hen / Broderkapets Ring / Nar Sjelen Hentes Til Helvete / Sogens Kammer / Da Den Kristne Satte Live Til / Stormblast / Dodsferd / Antikrist / Vinder Fra En Ensom Grav / Guds Fortapelse / Apenbaring Av Dommedag
ENTHRONE DARKNESS

TRIUMPHANT, Nuclear Blast NB CD 247-2 (1997)
Mourning Palace / Spellbound (By The Devil) / In Death's Embrace / Relinquishment Of Spirit And Flesh / The Night Masquerade / Tormentor Of Christian Souls / Entrance / Master Of Disharmony / Prudence's Fall / A Succubus In Rapture / Raabjørn Speiler Draugheimens Skodde
GODLESS SAVAGE GARDEN, Nuclear Blast (1998)
Moonchild Domain / Hunnerkongen Sorgsvarte / Ferd Over Steppene / Chaos Without Prophecy / Raabjorn Speiler Draugheimens Skodde / Metal Heart / Stormblast (Live) / Master Of Disharmony (Live) / In Death's Embrace (Live)
SPIRITUAL BLACK DIMENSIONS, Nuclear Blast NB 110521 (1999)
Reptile / Behind The Curtains Of Night Phantasmagoria / Dreamside Dominions / United In Unhallowed Grace / The Promising Future Aeons / The Blazing Monoliths Of Defiance / The Insight And The Catharsis / Grotesquery Concealed (Within Measureless Magic) / Arcane Lifeforce Mysteria
PURITANICAL EUPHORIC MISANTHROPIA, Nuclear Blast NB527 (2001) **16 GERMANY**
Fear And Wonder / Blessings Upon The Throne Of Tyranny / Kings Of The Carnival Creation / Hybrid- Stigmata- The Apostasy / Architecture Of A Genocidal Nature / Puritania / Indoctrination / The Maelstrom Mephisto / Absolute Sole Right / Sympozium / Perfection Of Vanity / Burn In Hell

DISAFFECTED (PORTUGAL)

DISAFFECTED was created in January 1991 issuing two demos prior to gigging. A tape of a rehearsal landed the band a deal with Skyfall Records in 1995 although shortly after the release of 'Vast' DISAFFECTED lost both their vocalist and drummer Quim Aries, the latter going on to join SACRED SIN.
The debut album, which includes a cover of ACHERON's 'Thou Art Lord', was produced by Marsten Bailey, the Englishman responsible for the HEAVENWOOD album 'Diva'.

Albums:
VAST, Skyfall (1995)
Cold Tranquility / No Feelings Left / Unlimited Vision / The Praxis Of The Non

128

DISMAL EUPHONY
Photo : A. Dittman / Bitmap

Being / Dreaming I / Dream II (Another Form) / Allusion / Dead Like My Dreams / Vast- The Long Tomorrow / ... And Flesh Will Be My Bride / Thou Art Lord

DISHARMONY (GREECE)

Black Metal band DISHARMONY started life with the 1991 demo 'Day Of Doom' followed by a 1992 session 'Angels Lament'. DISHARMONY adopted the new title of THE RENAISSANCE DANCE in 1993. The band shed their Black Metal roots to become a Gothic flavoured Power Metal band.

Singles/EPs:
The Gate Of Deeper Sleep, Molon Lave (1993) (7" single)

DISMAL EUPHONY (NORWAY)
Line-Up: Keltziva (vocals), Kristoffer Austrheim (guitar / bass / drums), Elin (keyboards)

Hafrsfjord's DISMAL EUPHONY released the demo 'Spellbound' on CD prior to a name change to SORIA MORIA SLOTT. However, upon signing to Napalm Records the band reverted back to their previous title.
During early 1997 the band lost both their bass player and second guitarist. New recruits to DISMAL EUPHONY in 2000 were bassist Etland Casperson and keyboard player Axel Hemviksen.

Singles/EPs:
Dismal Euphony / A Winter's Tale /

Spellbound / The Mournful Silence, Napalm NPR 018 (1996) ('Dismal Euphony' EP)
Lady Ablaze / Abandon / Cabinet Bizarre / 150 MPH / Bortgag, Napalm NPR 072 (2000) ('Lady Ablaze' EP)

Albums:
SORIA MORIA SLOTT, Napalm NPR 021 (1997)
Prolog / Et Vintereventyr / Nattan Loftet Sitt Tunge Ansikt / Alvedans / Trolloundet / Ekko / Isgrav, Det Siste Hvilested / Epilog
AUTUMN LEAVES (THE REBEL LION OF TIDES), Napalm NPR 033 (1997)
An Autumn Leaf In The Circles Of Time / Simply Dead / A Thousand Rivers / Mistress Tears / Carven / Spire / In Remembrance Of A Shroud / Splendid Horror
ALL LITTLE DEVILS, Napalm (1999)
Days Of Sodom / Rage Of Fire / Victory / All Little Devils / Lunatic / Psycho Path / Shine For Me Misery / Scenario / Dead Words
PYTHON ZERO, Nuclear Blast (2001)
Critical Mass / Python Zero / Zentinel / Needle / Magma / Birth Reverse / Plasma Pool / Flyineye

DISSECTION (SWEDEN)
Line-Up: Jon Nodtveidt (vocals / guitar), John Zwetsloot (guitar), Peter Palmdahl (bass), Ole Öhman (drums)

Gothenburg Death Metallers DISSECTION date back to their formation in 1989 by ex OPTHALAMIA and THE

BLACK vocalist / guitarist Jon Nodveidt and bassist Peter Palmdahl.

The band's first offering was the demo 'The Grief Prophecy' in 1990 followed by a limited edition single on the French label Corpsegrinder Records. A further demo in 1992 led to an album deal with another French label, namely No Fashion.

Nodtveidt was already operating his side project THE BLACK at this stage going under the pseudonym of Rietas.

Following the release of 'The Somberlain' album in late 1993 guitarist John Zwetsloot was to leave and in came replacement Johan Norman, previously with DECAMERON and SACRAMENTUM. Meantime Nodtveidt extra curricular act THE BLACK released their debut record 'The Priest Of Satan'.

DISSECTION signed to Germany's Nuclear Blast label in early 1995 but not before releasing two tracks on a compilation album for Wrong Again Records namely a cover of TORMENTOR's 'Elizabeth Bathory' and an original 'Where Dead Angels Lie'. The Swedes have also contributed SLAYER's 'Anti-Christ' to the Black Sun Records compilation 'Slatanic Slaughter'.

The band toured Europe with label mates DISMEMBER in December 1995. For these shows DISSECTION debuted a new drummer, Tobias Kjellgren, ex of SWORDMASTER and DECAMERON. The departing Öhlman temporarily teamed up with SWORDMASTER then joined OPTHALAMIA.

Having started 1996 touring America on a bill alongside AT THE GATES and MORBID ANGEL DISSECTION's return shows in Europe were on a bill with SATYRICON and GORGOROTH.

During a down period in the band's activity frontman Jon Nodvelt created a dark ambient side project titled DE INFERNALI during 1997. Fans were kept interested with the Necropolis Records release 'The Past Is Alive' which collected together the early demos and singles as well as two tracks from SATANIZED, yet another side project outfit that included Nodtveidt, guitarist Johan Norman and drummer Kjellgren.

As 1998 dawned DISSECTION's future was thrown into doubt when Nodtveidt, in keeping with recent Black Metal musicians behaviour patterns, was arrested on suspicion of the murder of an Algerian homosexual. Nodtveidt would ultimately be imprisoned for the crime.

Palmdahl joined RUNEMAGICK for 'The Supreme Force Of Eternity' album. The bassist also appeared on the 1998 album from DEATHWITCH 'Ultimate Death'.

Singles/EPs:
Into Infinite Obscurity / Shadows Over

DISSECTION
Photo : Martin Wickler

A Lost Kingdom / Son Of The Mourning, Corpsegrinder CGR 003 (1990)
Where Dead Angels Lie (Demo Version) / Elisabeth Bathory / The Anti-Christ / Feathers Fell / Son Of the Mourning / Where Dead Angels Lie (Album Version), Nuclear Blast NB 1672 (1996) ('Where Dead Angels Lie' EP)

Albums:
THE SOMBERLAIN, No Fashion NFR 006 (1993)
Black Horizons / The Somberlaine / Crimson Towers / A Land Forlorn / Heaven's Damnation / Frozen / Into Infinite Obscurity / In The Cold Winds Of Nowhere / The Grief Prophecy / Shadows Over A Lost Kingdom / Mistress Of The Bleeding Sorrow / Feathers Fell
STORM OF THE LIGHT'S BANE, Nuclear Blast NB129 (1995)
At The Fathomless Depths / Soulreaper / Night's Blood / Where Dead Angels Lie / Feather's Fell / Unhallowed / Thorns Of Crimson Death / Retribution: Storm Of The Light's Bane / No Dreams Breed In Breathless Sleep
THE PAST IS A LIVE (THE EARLY MISCHIEF), Necropolis NR017 (1996)
Shadows Over A Lost Kingdom / Frozen / Feathers Fell / Son Of The Mourning / Mistress Of The Bleeding Sorrow / In The Cold Winds Of Nowhere / Into Infinite Obscurity / The Call Of The Mist / Severed Into Shreds / Satanized / Born In Fire

DIVINE SIN (SWEDEN)
Line-Up: Fredde Lundberg (vocals), Micke Andersson (guitar), Peter Halvarsson (guitar), Buddy Goude (bass), Martin Knutar (drums)

Albums:
WINTERLAND, Black Mark BMCD 83 (1995)
Gates Of Everbe / Children Of Conformity / Dead Again / Memories / All Alone / A Twilight Dream / Winterland / Years Of Sorrow / Endless Sleep / My Best Nightmare / In The Wake Of Perfection

DØDHEIMSGARD (NORWAY)
Line-Up: Aldrahn, Vicotnik, Fenriz

Founded in 1994 the uncompromising DØDHEIMSGARD were created as a trio of Aldrahn, Vicotnik and DARKTHRONE's drummer Fenriz on bass. After the debut album Fenriz departed making way for AURA NOIR's

Apollyon and Alver. Czral joined forces with the band later on drums.
In early 1995 Fenriz and Vicotnik assembled VED BUENS ENDE ('At The End Of The Bow") together with ULVER and ARCTURUS bassist Skoll, and Carl-Michael ex SATYRICON and ULVER. DØDHEIMSGARD enrolled bassist Jonas Alver.
The same year found Aldrahn involved with the ZYKLON B project for the 'Blood Must Be Shed' album working alongside Frost of SATYRICON and EMPEROR men Ihsahn and Samoth.
In 1997 Alver joined EMPEROR for their 'Anthems To The Welkin At Dusk' album. DØDHEIMSGARD men Apollyon and Czral resurrected classic Swedish Death Metallers CADAVER with Anders Oden in 2000. Czral also helped out with drums on demos for British band VOID.

Albums:
KRONET TIL KANGE, Malicious (1995)
Å Slakte Gud / En Krig Å Seire / Jesu Blod / Midnattsskogens Sorte Kjerne / Kuldeblest Over Evig Isode / Kronet Til Kange / Mournful Yet And Forever / Når Vi Har Dokket Grads Hjerte / Starcave, Depths And Chained / When Heavens End
MONUMENTAL POSSESSION, Malicious MR010 (1996)
Intro / Utopia Running Scarlet / Marbled Wievs In The Corridor / An Alien Dreamworld Cyclone / Monumental Possession / Seremonial Unshapped Spell / Angel Death / Lost In Faces / Pages
SATANIC ART, Moonfog FOG017 (1998)
Oneiroscope / Traces Of Reality / Symptom / The Paramount Empire / Wrapped In Plastic
666 INTERNATIONAL, Moonfog FOG018 (1999)
ShivaInterfere / Ion Storm / Carpet Bombing / Regno Potiri / The Final Conquest / Sonar Bliss / Magic / Completion

DOG FACED GODS (SWEDEN)
Line-Up: Johnny Wranning (vocals), Conny Jonsson (guitar), Peter Tuthill (bass), Richard Evensand (drums)

DOG FACED GODS were named after the TESTAMENT song. Vocalist Johnny Wranning and guitarist Conny Jonsson also have credits with EBONY TEARS. Wranning is also an ex MISCREANT member. Before too long all the membership of EBONY TEARS were involved with DOG FACED GODS operating both bands in tandem. Pelle Saether of ZELLO produced and added guest vocals to the 1998 album. Keyboards came courtesy of ZELLO's Mats Olsson.

Albums:
RANDOM CHAOS THEORY IN ACTION, GNW GNW04 (1998)
Blindfolded / The Man Inside / God All Over / Face My Rage / Fractured Image / Dirge / Prozac 3105 / Purge / All Worlds Collide / Swallowtail / The Chaos
DOLORIAN (FINLAND)
Line-Up: Antti Haapapuro (vocals / guitar), A. Kukkohori (bass / drums), J. Ontero (keyboards)

A multi faceted act DOLORIAN, based in Oulu and previously entitled TEMPLES BEYOND, employ elements of Black and Death Metal slowed down to labouring Doom crawl. The band themselves describe their music as leaving the listener "spiritually cramped".

Albums:
WHEN ALL LAUGHTER HAS GONE, Avantgarde (1999)
Desolated Colours / My Weary Eyes / A Part Of Darkness / When All Laughter Has Gone / Collapsed / Fields / With Scorn I Perish

DOMINANCE (ITALY)

Albums:
ANTHEMS OF ANCIENT SPLENDOUR, Scarlet SC004-2 (1999)
Intro- Forgotten Age Awakening / Between The Sands / Fallen Winter / Immemorial Iced Lake / Anthem Of Ancient Splendour / Celestial Tormentors / Engraved / Outro- Fallen Asleep Again

DOMINION CALIGULA (SWEDEN)

Side project of DARK FUNERAL personnel Dominion, Emperor Magus Caligula and drummer Gaahfaust. The 2000 album 'A New Era Rises' was produced by Tommy Tägtgren.

Albums:
A NEW ERA RISES, No Fashion (2000)
A New Era Rises / Dominion / Praise Thy Victorious / In Love With The Gods / Let Them Hate Me / Drink The Royal seed (Fellatio Me Scrotum) / Let Me

Become / Cold Black

DOMINION 3 (AUSTRIA)
Line-Up: Elizabeth Toriser (vocals), Tharen (instruments)

DOMINION 3 is another offshoot of Tharen's talents. The man also has credits with ABIGOR, AMESTIGON, DARGAARD and HEIDENREICH. Vocals are handled by Elizabeth Toriser of ABIGOR, ANTICHRISIS and DARGAARD. Session guitars come courtesy of AMESTIGON's Jørg Lanz.

Albums:
THE HAND AND THE SWORD, Draenor Productions DPR 010 (2000)

DOMINIUM (VA, USA)
Line-Up: Dominus (vocals / guitar), Mortalis Kabal (bass), Malignus (drums)

DOMINIUM debuted with the demo tape 'Curses Of Wisdom'. Bassist Ancalagon was replaced by Arkon in early 200. However, realising that the high profile Norwegian act DIMMU BORGIR also employed an Arkon the four stringer became Mortalis Kabal. The band's problems in their rhythm department continued when Kabal bailed out in November of 2000. William Carter of FROM WITHIN would deputise.
DOMINIUM have in their time supported visiting artists such as MAYHEM and KOVENANT.

Singles/EPs:
Into The Black War / With Blade, Kingdom Conceived / Decieve The Shadows Of Untold Times / With Blade, Kingdom Conceived (Demo), Dominium (2000) ('The Black War Comes' EP)

DORNENREICH (GERMANY)
Line-Up: Eviga (vocals / guitar / bass), Dunkelkind (guitar), Moritz Neuner (drums)

DORNENREICH offer Black Metal with the novel use of a cello courtesy of Stefan Nielerwieser. The band debuted with the demo 'Mein Flügelschang'. Drummer Moritz Neuner is a much in demand veteran of ABIGOR, DARKWELL, EVENFALL and KOROVA.

Albums:
NICHT UM ZU STERBEN, CCP 100186-2 (1997)
Hasses Freigang / In Die Nacht /

Verlorenes Gefunden, Gefundenes Empfunden / Schlaflos Traumend / Im Flatternden Schleier Der Verganglichkeit / Und Wie Ein Kind In Deiner… / Durch Die Schluchten Der Kalte / Hotesfest **BITTER IST'S DEM TOD ZU DIENEN**, CCP 100198-2 (1998) Nachtlich Liebend / Wunderküssen / Reime Faucht Dem Märchensarg / Federstrich In Grabesnähe / Leben Lechzend Herzgeflüster / Woran Erkennt Michdeine Sehnsucht Morgen? **HER VON WELKEN NÄCHTEN**, (2000)

DOXODEMON (SINGAPORE)

Line-Up: Paat (vocals), Pearce Arai (guitar), Sham (guitar), Joehanis (bass), Azli (drums) Black Grindcore act founded as LIBATION during 1992 by NECRONANISM vocalist / bassist Paat, guitarist Ash and drummer Zul. This group would switch names to ITNOS for the less than tactfully titled EP 'Christ Mary Bitch' released on the Dutch Superior Creation label in 1994.
ITNOS folded with Zul (as Dajjal) joined ABBATOIR and IMPIETY. Paat reassembled a new band with erstwhile MIXES guitarist Jumaat and former MARTYRDOM drummer Azli for the promotional cassette 'Hymnenic Promonancy'. By 1997 the band had filled out with second guitarist Sham, previously an OSSUARY member.
December 1998 witnessed further changes with the enlistment of ex HARVESTER guitarist Pearce Arai and former OSSUARY and MARTYRDOM bassist Joehanis. With this line up the group adopted the new title of DOXODEMON.

Albums:
EVANESCE, Darkartz (1999)

DRACONIS (Los Angeles, CA, USA)

Albums:
OVERLORDS OF THE GREYING DAWN, Dark Realm (1999)
Overlords Of The Greying Dawn / Black Horde Of Blasphemy / When Darkness Lasts Forever / Descending The Shadowed Passage To Nocturnal Realms / Medieval Spirits From The Seven Gates / The Oracle Of Eternal Doom / Alongside Subconscious Souls Of eternity / Unseen Reflections Of Interdimensional Transfixions / Beneath The Dismal Aura Of Stormfog / Cryptic Chasms Shroud The Everdark **THE HIGHEST OF ALL DARK POWERS**, Greying Dawn (1999)

DRAINED (MA, USA)

Line-Up: Bob Mendell (vocals), Neal Delongchamp (guitar), Mike Cardoso (bass), Roger Chouinard (drums)

Albums:
SUSPENSION OF DISBELIEF, Martyr Music Group (1999)

DREAM INTO DUST
(New York, NY, USA)

A one man Electro Folk Metal project of Derek Rush.

Albums:
THE WORLD WE HAVE LOST, Elfenblut (1999)
Maelstrom / Cross The Abyss / Mercury Falling / Nothing But Blood / Enemy At The Gates / Farewell To Eden / Eternal Inquisition / The World We Have Lost / Not Above But Apart

DREAMS OF DAMNATION (USA)

Line-Up: Charlie Silva (vocals / bass), Jimmy Durkin (guitar), Al Mendez (drums) DREAMS OF DAMNATION are led by former DARK ANGEL guitarist Jimmy Durkin and the gargantuan figure of Brazilian Charlie Silva.

Albums:
LET THE VIOLENCE BEGIN, Necropolis NR064 CD (2000)
Blood To Free A Soul / Unholy Invocation / Cremation Day / Demonic Celebration / Hammer Of Sickness / Release Me

DROTTNAR (NORWAY)

Line-Up: Sven-Erik Lind (vocals), Karl Fredrik Lind (guitar), Bjarne Peder Lind (bass), Glenn-David Lind (drums)

Although just as vicious and chaotic as many pure Black Metal bands DROTTNAR are in fact ardent Christians. The band employs strong use of mythical imagery from the books of revelation to achieve their aim.
DROTTNAR (translating as 'Master'), made up of the four Lind siblings, was originally convened as the Doom Metal band VITALITY. Bengt Olsson would intrude into the family harmony when he supplanted Bjarne Peder Lind.

Albums:
SPIRITUAL BATTLE, Plankton (2000)
A White Realm / Natter På Harmageddon / Spiritual Battle / Away

From The Destruction / Doom Of
Antichrist / Missing Souls / Frykt Ikke

DUNKELGRAFEN (GERMANY)
Line-Up: Dunkelgrafen, Lord Asgaqlun ,
Gabriel, Ishariot

DUNKELGRAFEN toured Germany as
support to EMINENZ. Guitarist Lord
Asgaqlun departed the ranks in 2000.

Albums:
SCHATTEN DER EWIGKEIT, Last
Episode (1998)
Intro / Der Hoffnung Sät der Haß /
Schatten der Ewigkeit / Dämonen der
Seele / Reich Hades / Dunkelheit /
Bastard Jesus Christus / Herr des
Schweigens / Der Scher / Outro
BAPHOMETS AEON, Last Episode
(1999)
Einleitung / Im Schatten Des Todes / Die
Saat des Bösen / Mysterium einer Macht
/ Baphomet / Nehter der Bergiede /
Rückkehr der Kaisen / Tempel der
Offenbarung / Im Zeichen des Chaos /
Ausklang des Mysterious

EBLIS (SWEDEN)

**...AND OUR TIME
ANNOUNCES BLACK,**
(1998)
Fall Of The Usher / ...And
Our Time Announces Black / Ceremony
(Dance Macabre) / Travel Through
Eternity / Rise Of The Pass Away / Last
Dream In Darkness

EBONY LAKE (UK)

Albums:
**ON THE EVE OF THE GRIMLY
INVENTIVE**, Cacophonous NIHIL31CD
(1999)

EBONY TEARS (SWEDEN)
Line-Up: Johnny Wranning (vocals),
Conny Jonson (guitar), Thomas Thun
(bass), Iman Zolgharnian (drums)

EBONY TEARS vocalist Johnny
Wranning also operates with
MISCREANT and DOG FACED GODS.
Guitarist Conny Jonson is also a DOG
FACED GODS man. Eventually the
membership of DOG FACED GODS
mirrored EBONY TEARS with the
recruitment of ex BULLDOZER bassist
Peter Tuthill and drummer Richard
Evensand with the two bands functioning
in tandem.

Albums:
TORTURA INSOMNIA, Black Sun (1998)
Moonlight / Freak Jesus / Nectars Of
Eden / With Tears In My Eyes /
Involuntary Existence / Opacity /
Spoonbender / Evergrey / Skunk Hour
A HANDFUL OF NOTHING, Black Sun
(1999)
Inferno / Harvester Of Pain / A Handful
Of Nothing / Scenario / When
Depression Speaks / Erised / Cosmical
Transformation / The End

ECLIPSE (POLAND)

Albums:
**DORSA CHARMS VENOMOUS
COLOURS**, Blackened BLACK021CD
(1999)

EDGE OF SANITY (SWEDEN)
Line-Up: Dan Swanö (vocals), Dread
(guitar), Sami Nerberg (guitar), Anders
Lundberg (bass), Benny Larsson (drums)

Influential Metallers noted the
involvement of mentor Dan Swano (a big
name on the Swedish music scene
renowned for his production and
involvement in other acts as diverse as
UNICORN, PAN-THY-MONIUM,
GODSEND, WOUNDED KNEE and
NIGHTINGALE among others) EDGE OF
SANITY came together in 1989. Guitarist
Sami Nerberg was previously with Punk
act F.Z.Ö. while Swano and bassist
Anders Lundberg had been in another
Punk band by the name of ULANBATOR.
EDGE OF SANITY debuted with the
demo tape 'Kur-Nu-Gi-A' and the band
has managed to sustain a stable line-up.
The act signed to the Black Mark label in
1990 recording their debut 'Nothing But
Death Remains' at the legendary
Montezuma Studios, home previously to
THERION, HEXENHAUS, BATHORY,
CANDLEMASS and CREMATORY
among others.
Their 1995 EP 'Until Eternity Ends'
contains a version of THE POLICE's hit
'Invisible Sun'. Don't be fooled by the one
credited track on 1996's 'Crimson' album-
the song is over 40 minutes in duration.
Despite a prolific recording schedule
various members of EDGE OF INSANITY
have found the time to work on other
projects. Guitarist Dread (real name
Andreas Axelsson) contributes to LUCKY
SEVEN and sang lead vocal on
Deathsters MARDUK's first album.
Drummer Benny Larsson also records
with OPHTHALAMIA under the
pseudonym 'Winter', whilst Swano sang
lead vocals for Danish Metallers
MACERATION on their 'A Serenade Of
Agony' album using the nom de plume of
Day Disyraah.
However, somewhat surprisingly the
1997 album 'Cryptic' found Swanö no
longer involved and his position was
taken by PAN-THY-MONIUM /
DARKIFIED vocalist Robban Karlsson.
Swanö created the project band
BLOODBATH with OPETH's Mikael
Akerfeldt and KATATONIA men
Blackheim and Jonas Renske in 2000.

Singles/EPs:
Until Eternity Ends / Eternal Eclipse /
Bleed / Invisible Sun, Black Mark BMCD
58 (1994)
Sacrificed, Black Mark BMCD 37-P
(1994) (Radio Promotion release)

Albums:
NOTHING BUT DEATH REMAINS,

135

Black Mark BMCD 10 (1991)
Tales... / Human Aberration / Maze Of
Existence / The Dead / Decepted By The
Cross / Angel Of Distress / Impulsive
Necroplasma / Immortal Souls
UNORTHODOX, Black Mark BMCD 18
(1992)
Unorthodox / Enigma / Incipience To The
Butchery / In The Veins / Darker Than
Black / Human Aberration / Everlasting /
After Afterlife / Beyond The Unknown /
Nocturnal / Curfew For The Damned /
Cold Sun / Day Of Maturity / Requiscon
By Page / Dead But Dreaming / When
All Is Said
THE SPECTRAL SORROWS, Black
Mark BMCD37 (1994)
The Spectral Sorrows / Darkday / Livin'
Hell / Lost / The Masque / Blood Of My
Enemies / Jesus Cries / Across The
Fields Of Forever / On The Other Side /
Sacrificed / Waiting To Die / Feedin' The
Charlatan / A Serenade For The Dead
PURGATORY AFTERGLOW, Black
Mark BMCD 61(1994)
Twilight / Of Farksome Origin / Blood
Colored / Silent / Black Tears / Elegy /
Velvet Dreams / Enter Chaos / The
Sinner And The Sadness / Song Of
Sirens
CRIMSON, Black Mark BMCD 68 (1996)
Crimson
INFERNAL, Black Mark BMCD 108
(1996)
Hell Is Where The Heart Is / Helter
Skelter / 15: 36 / The Bleakness Of It All /
Damned (By The Damned) / Forever
Together Forever / Losing Myself / Hollow
/ Inferno / Burn The Sun / The Last Song
CRYPTIC, Black Mark BMCD 125 (1997)
Hell Written/ Uncontrol Me/ No Destiny/
Demon I/ Not Of This World/ Dead I Walk/
Born, Breed, Bleeding/ Bleed You Dry
EVOLUTION, Black Mark (2000)

EIBON (NORWAY/ USA)

A dramatic project band including some
true heavyweights of the Metal scene.
EIBON include in its ranks PANTERA
frontman Phil Anselmo, Fenriz of
DARKTHRONE, Killjoy of
NECROPHAGIA, Satyr Wongraven of
SATYRICON and MAYHEM's Maniac.
EIBON debuted deliberately low key with
a solitary track on the 'Moonfog 2000'
compilation album.

EINHERJER (NORWAY)

Line-Up: Rune 'Nidhogg' Bjelland
(vocals), Frode 'Grimmar' Glesues

(guitar), Audun Wold (guitar), Stein Sund
(bass), Gerhard 'Vivar' Storesund
(drums)

Undisputed Viking Metal named after the
mythical Nordic warriors who rise to fight
in Valhalla after being killed on the
battlefield.
EINHERJER, then a quartet of vocalist
Nidhogg, guitarist Grimmar, bassist
Thonar and drummer Vivar, debuted in
1994 with the 'Aurora Borealis' tape.
EINHERJER pulled in second guitarist
Audun Wold and bassist Stein Sund
('Eldern' of HELLSTORM) for the
'Dragons Of The North' album. The 1998
'Far Far North' EP includes two
recordings dating back from 1994.
Sund joined forces with ENSLAVED
drummer / vocalist Harald to found the
side project THUNDRA issuing the 2000
album 'Blood Of Your Soul'.

Singles/EPs:
Leve Vikingaanden, Necromantik
Gallery Productions (1995) (7" single)
De Sorte Sioers Land / Aurora Borealis /
Witchking / Einherjer, Necropolis NR
6662 (1994) ('Aurora Borealis' EP)
Far Far North / Naar Hammeren Haves /
Naar Aftensolen Rinner, Century Media
(1998)

Albums:
DRAGONS OF THE NORTH, Napalm
NPR023 (1996)
Dragons Of The North / Dreamstorm /
Forever Empire / Conquerer / Fimbul
Winter / Storms Of The Elder / Slaget
Ved Harfsfjord / Ballad Of The Sword
ODIN OWNS YE ALL, Century Media
(1998)
Leve Vikingeaanden / Out Of
Ginnungagap / Clash Of The Eldar /
Odin Owns Ye All / Remember Tokk /
Home / The Pathfinder And The
Prophetess / Inferno / A New Earth
NORWEGIAN NATIVE ART, Native
North (2000)
Wyrd Of The Dead / Doomfaring /
Hugins Eyes / Burning Yggdrasil /
Crimson Rain / Howl Ravens Come /
Draconian Umpire / Regicide

EISREGEN (GERMANY)
Line-Up: M. Roth, Yantit M., M. Lenz,
D.F., R. Matthes

Singles/EPs:
Des Heilands Haut (Album version) /
Zeit Zuspielen (Version extreem) /

Herzblut 2000 / Fleischfestival (Neuinspielung) / Scharlachrotes Kleid (Version Schopfheim), Last Episode MCD 5 7053 20 561 (1999) ('Fleischfestival' EP)

<u>Albums:</u>
ZERFALL, Last Episode CD 007356-2 (1998)
…Und Über Allem Weht Der Wind So Kalt (Post I) / Legende Des Liedes (Post II) / In Der Grube (Post III) / Auferstehung (Post IV) / Ich Bin Viele / Eispalast / Ode An Den Niedergang / Herzblut / End Zeit
KREBS KOLONIE, Last Episode CD 007395-2 (1998)
Veroabend Der Schlact / Nachtgeburt / Scharlachrotes Kleid / Krebskolonie / Fur Eüch, Die Ihr Lebt / Das Kleine Leben / Blass-Blau-Lippen / Abglanz Vom Licht / Futter Für Die Schweine / Thueringen
LEICHENLAGER, Last Episode CD 5 7054 20 561(2000)
Des Heilands Haut / Leichenlager / Feindhild Mensch / Und Sie Blutete Far Einen Sommer Lang / Das Ier (Sado Mix) / Salz Der Erder / Die Seele Der Toteburt / Nur Dein Fleisch / Bei Den Grabern / Schwarze Rese / Zeir Zu Spielen

ELBERETH (SPAIN)
Line-Up: Lola Marquinez (vocals), Asier Gonzalez (guitar), Fernando Averalo (guitar), Alvaro Castro (bass), David Diaz (drums)

Melodic Gothic Doom Metal band with not only female vocals to assert their individuality but violins, flutes and even bagpipes!

<u>Singles/EPs:</u>
Reminiscences From The Past, Drowned Productions (1992)

<u>Albums:</u>
... AND OTHER REASONS, Witchhunt WIHU 9520 (1995)
From The Sea Cliff / The Idyllic Place Of Innocence / The End Of The 2nd Act / April Rain / Four Roses In My Heart / The Beautyful Short Story / Crystal World / ...And Other Reflections / So Much Affliction / Fallen Leaves / Forgotten Forever / Nostalgic Harmonies Brings The Wind / Autumn Concert

ELEGION (AUSTRALIA)

<u>Albums:</u>
ODYSSEY INTO DARKNESS,
Candlelight CANDLE 020MCD (1998)

ELEND (AUSTRIA / FRANCE)
Line-Up: Eve Gabrielle Siskind (vocals), Renaud Tschirner (vocals / keyboards / violin) / Alexandre Iskandar (vocals / violin / keyboards)

ELEND, one of France's brightest and most innovative hopes on the current Metal scene were founded by former orchestra players Renaud Tschirner and Alexandre Iskander in 1992 adding vocalist Eve Gabrielle Siskand to complete the debut album.
ELEND's first album is a conceptual piece exploring John Milton's epic poem 'Paradise Lost'. The theme of Lucifer and the coming of pandemonium was continued for the second album. Sales were so strong for 'Les Ténebre Du Dehors', now with the additional female vocals of Nathalie Barbary, that the closing chapter of the saga promised on album number three was delayed due to significant interest being shown by the major labels. As it was the band stuck by the French label Holy Records for 1997's 'Weeping Nights'.
ELEND have a non album 12 minute track 'Birds Of Dawn' released on the 1996 compilation album 'The Holy Bible'.

<u>Albums:</u>
LECONS DE TENEBRAES, Holy HOLY08CD (1994)
Lecon De Tenebres / Chanting / Into Bottomless Perdition / Deploration / Infernal Beauty / Lucifer / Eclipse / The Reign Of Chaos And The Old Night / The Emperor
LES TÉNÉBRE DU DEHORS, Holy HOLY 17 CD (1996)
Nocturne / Ethereal Journeys / The Luciferian Revolution / Eden (The Angel In The Garden) / The Silence Of Light / Antienne / Dancing Under The Closed Eyes Of Paradise / Les Ténébres Du Dehors
WEEPING NIGHTS, Holy HOLY 17 CD (1997)
Weeping Night / O Solitude / The Embrace / Nocturne / Ethereal Journeys / The Luciferion Revolution / Eden / Dancing Under The Closed Eyes Of Paradise / Les Ténébres Du Dehors
UMBERSUN, Music For Nations CDMFN 239 (1998)
Du Tréfonds Des Ténébres / Melpomere / Moon Of Amber / Apocalypse / Umbra / The Umbersun / In The Embrace Of

Heaven / The Wake Of The Angel / Au Tréfonds Des Ténébres

ELYSIAN FIELDS (GREECE)
Line-Up: Bill (vocals / guitar), Michalis Katsikas (guitar / bass)

Death Metal band previously known as DESULPHARIZE for their inaugural demo 'Nihilistic Era'. The title ELYSIAN FIELDS was adopted in 1994.
Guitarist Michalis Katsikas also operates HAVORUM.

Albums:
ADELAIN, Unisound (1995)
I Of Forever / As One / Unsentiment- I Was Dying Once Again / Of Purity And Black / Foredoomed Elegy / Father Forgive Them (For They Don't Know) / Elysian Fields / Deicide- The Auspice
WE... THE ENLIGHTENED, Wicked World WICK02CD (1998)
Their Blood Be On Us / I Am The Unknown Sky / Until The Night Cries Rise In Your Heart / ... And The Everdawn Faded Away / Shall They Come Forth Unto Us / Arcana Caelestia / The End Shall Be Tragically Fulfilled / The Last Star Of Heaven Falls / Wither, Oh Divine, wither

ELYSIUM (POLAND)
Line-Up: Maciej Miskiewicz (vocals),

Albums:
DREAMLANDS, Black Mark (2000)

EMBER (IL, USA)

Singles/EPs:
Into Death / These Darkened Wings / Divinity, (1998) ('Chapter II: The Gate' EP)

Albums:
CONCESSION, Ember (1999)

EMBRACED (SWEDEN)
Line-Up: Kalle Johansen (vocals), Michael Hakansson (vocals / bass), Davor Jepic (guitar), Peter Mardklint (guitar), Julius Chmielewski (keyboards), Daniel Lindberg (drums)

EMBRACED members bassist Michael Hakansson and keyboard player Sven Karlsson joined EVERGREY in late 2000. Hakansson also has credits with MORTUM.

Albums:
AMOROUS ANATHEMA, Regain (1998)
A Dying Flame / The End... And Here We All Die / Nightfall / Princess Of Twilight / Into The Unknown / Memento Of Emotions / The Beautiful Flow Of An Autumn Passion / Dirge Of The Masquerade
WITHIN, Regain RR0008 (2000)
Solitude Of My Own / Within Me / The Fallen / Putrefaction / Era Of Changes / Nightmare Drama / Sacred Tears / Blessed Are Those / Outro

EMINEZ
Photo : Martin Wickler

EMINENZ (GERMANY)
Line-Up: Leviathan (vocals), Darkman (guitar), Karsten Breitung (guitar), Butcher (bass), Henry Kuhnert (drums)

EMINENZ were a union of ex Death Metal musicians, the previous influences plainly audible on the two albums. Guitarist Karsten Breitung also operates BELMEZ.

Albums:
EXORIAL, Lethal LRC9666 (1994)
Introduction Black Thoughts / Jesus Wept Nevermore / Demons From The Black Abyss / Angel Rip Angel / The Unholy (Preachers Of Darkness) / Blasphemy / Ghost / Demons Awake / Only Flesh / Dark Millennium / Exorial / Outro
THE HERETIC, Lethal LRC24 (1996)

Demons Cross The Fiery Path /
Bloodred Nights / Day Of Battle, Night
Of Thunder / Lucifers Return / Thousand
Blasphemies / The Gate / Necronomicon
Exmortis / The Heretic / Lucifers Return
ANTI GENESIS, (199-)
Nocturnal Horizon / God's Downfall /
Praise The Death / Army Of Immortals /
Apocalypse / Triumph Of The
Nightforces / Grey Souls / Conspiracy Of
The Witches / Anti Genesis
THE BLACKEST DIMENSION, Last
Episode LEP 045 (2000)

EMPEROR (NORWAY)
Line-Up: Ihsahn (vocals / guitar), Samoth
(guitar), Tyr (bass), Trym (drums)

Overtly Satanic act based in Telemark
that gained a fair degree of attention on
the back of the MAYHEM / BURZUM feud
in 1993. However a few short years later
EMPEROR's star has eclipsed many
other Black Metal acts and the band can
truly be regarded as amongst the handful
of leading bands in their chosen field.
EMPEROR tour globally and their record
sales are into the hundreds of thousands.
EMPEROR started young with the debut
single featuring a fourteen year old
vocalist / guitarist Ihsahn (real name
Vegard Sverre Tveitan) and fifteen year
old Samoth (real name Tomas
Thormodsaeter Haugen). The band's
early line up also included bassist Mortiis
(Haavard Ellefsen) who appears on the
band's 1992 demo, the 7" single 'As The
Shadows Rise' and EMPEROR's split
1993 album with ENSLAVED.
Prior to EMPEROR Samoth and Ihsahn
had operated in the bands DARK
DEVICE, XERASIA and EMBRYONIC.
This latter act released the demo 'The
Lord Of Lost Souls'.
EMBRYONIC evolved into the Death
Metal outfit THOU SHALT SUFFER
comprising of Ihsahn on lead vocals and
guitar, Samoth on guitar, bassist Ildjarn
and drummer Thorbjørn. A demo session
'Into The Woods Of Belial' was
undertaken and a 7" EP released on the
Mexican label Distorted Harmony entitled
'Open The Mysteries Of Your Creation'.
This latter release saw a switch in the
band membership with Thorbjørn taking
over the bass role and Ronny taking on
drums.
In mid 1991 Samoth had got a further
project up and running titled EMPEROR.
The band's debut line up had the guitarist
joined by vocalist / guitarist Ygg, Samot
(Samoth) on drums and bassist Mortiis

for the inaugural 'Wrath Of The Tyrant'
demo. After this tape 'Orcutus' magazine
founder and THORNS member Faust
(real name Bård Eithun) then of STIGMA
DIABOLICUM took the drummers role
and Samoth switched to guitar.
Faust had in the late 80's played in a
proto Black Metal band made up of Frost
(later of SATYRICON), Messiah (pre
MAYHEM and IMPOSTER), Nemo
(another future IMPOSTER member) and
bassist Jonas Alver (later to join the
EMPEROR family tree).
EMPEROR's CD debut came with a split
album shared with Viking Metallers
ENSLAVED. Samoth also established his
own label Nocturnal Arts to issue the 'As
The Shadows Rise' EP.
Scheduled to support DEICIDE in London
prior to the headliners cancelling at the
last minute EMPEROR went on to play
their own hastily arranged show which
highlighted their many weaknesses as an
inexperienced live act. EMPEROR
proved that scary facepaint was not
enough. Strangely enough their support
band for the London show was Christian
Thrash band MOURN who brandished a
large golden cross onstage much to
EMPEROR's displeasure. Following this
shaky start further touring with CRADLE
OF FILTH in 1995 EMPEROR opted to
dispense with the corpsepaint and from
this juncture would quickly establish
themselves as one of the premier acts of
the genre.
1994 also found both Ihsahn and Samoth
involved with the ZYKLON B project for
the 'Blood Must Be Shed' album working
alongside Frost of SATYRICON and
DØDHEIMSGARD man Aldrahn.
However, shortly after completing the
ZYKLON B sessions Faust, Samoth and
Tchort were imprisoned in for church
burning, which delayed the recording of
the debut album. These charges related
to the arson of the Holmenkollen chapel
and others in which it is alleged members
of EMPEROR participated with Count
Grisnackh of BURZUM and MAYHEM's
Euronymous. Faust was also implicated
in the murder of a homosexual in August
1992 and is currently serving a life
sentence. He is due for parole in 2003.
The band achieved further notoriety in
France when a youth obsessed by the
Black Metal genre actually went as far as
to desecrate a child's grave, stealing the
corpse and fashioning himself curtains
from the cadaver's skin. When
questioned by Police he claimed
inspiration from EMPEROR.

In the face of EMPEROR's enforced lay off Samoth was far from idle contributing as a guest musician to albums by GORGOROTH and ARCTURUS. Samoth would also undertake some live gigs with SATYRICON and put down bass and guitar on their release 'The Shadowthrone'. Samoth also performed on BURZUM's 'Aske' mini album, the cover art for which featured a photograph of the burning church at Skjold.

Ishahn meantime breathed new life into THOU SHALT SUFFER pursuing this as an electronic project.

Mortiis departed to concentrate on his Black Electronic solo project MORTIIS. Ildjarn of THOU SHALT SUFFER was employed on bass. The incarcerated Faust's position for recording was taken by MAYHEM's Hellhammer, with keyboards supplied by Sverd of ARCTURUS. Hellhammer quit in late 1994 and Mefisto had a brief tenure on the kit but despite these uncertainties as to their future stability EMPEROR remained at the forefront of the Scandinavian Satanic Metal scene.

In 1996 EMPEROR cut a cover version of a HELLHAMMER track 'Massacre' for a tribute album 'In Memory Of Celtic Frost' recorded with ENSLAVED and GEHENNAH man Dirge Rep (Per Husebø) on drums.

With Samoth finding his freedom after serving his sentence EMPEROR settled their line up for recording with Ihsahn and Samoth joined by bassist Tchort and erstwhile ENSLAVED drummer Trym Torsen.

1997's 'Anthems To The Welkin Dusk' album found Tchort supplanted by DØDHEIMSGARD man Jonas Alver. Tchort would leave the fold for SATYRICON but would later be jailed for six months convicted of desecration and knife assault.

Drums were supplied by Trym for the 'Reverence' outing and keyboards from April of 1998 were in the hands of Charmand Grimloch of TARTAROS. 1998's 'Wrath Of The Tyrants' CD comprises all the Mortiis era EMPEROR material including the band's 1992 demo and four tracks cut for the split 'Hordanes Land' CD. The band also appeared with their version of 'Gypsy' for a MERCYFUL FATE tribute album on Listenable Records and also with a version of BATHORY's 'A Time To Die' on a further tribute effort.

The 1998 Moonfog release 'Thorns Vs. Emperor' included EMPEROR covering 'Aerie Descent' and 'I Am' from Faust and Snorre's act THORNS.

EMPERORS line up problems were far from over though and in June of 1998 Alver quit. European touring on the festival circuit in April of 1999 found EMPEROR enlisting MORPHEUS WEB bassist Tyr.

Grimloch released 'The Red Jewel' album by his project act TARTAROS in 1999.

In 2000 Ihsahn's side project PECCATUM (in conjunction with his brother Lord PZ and girlfriend Ihriel) released the 'Oh, My Regrets' single. Meanwhile Samoth and Trym created ZYKLON with MYRKSKOG's guitarist Destructhor.

Portuguese Black Metal band, signed to Samoth's Nocturnal Arts label, covered an EMPEROR track on their second album 'Spectral Transition- Dimension Sirius'. The song featured Samoth on bass and even Faust on spoken word and drums.

EMPEROR recently announced they intend to continue only as a studio project leaving the 'Emperial Live Ceremony' album as their epitaph.

Singles/EPs:
As The Shadows Rise, Nocturnal Art (1994)
The Loss And Curse Of Reverence / In Longing Spirit / Opus A Satana, Candlelight CANDLE018 (1997)

Albums:
HORDANES LAND, Candlelight 002CD (1993) (Split CD with ENSLAVED)
I Am The Black Wizard / Wrath Of The Tyrant / Night Of The Graveless Souls / Cosmic Keys To My Creations And Times
IN THE NIGHTSIDE ECLIPSE, Candlelight 008CD (1995)
Into The Infinity Of Thoughts / The Burning Shadows Of Silence / Cosmic Keys To My Creations And Times / Beyond The Great Vast Forest / Towards The Pantheon / The Majesty Of The Night Sky / I Am The Black Wizard / Inno A Satana
ANTHEMS TO THE WELKIN AT DUSK, Candlelight CANDLE023CD (1997)
Al Svartr (The Oath) / Ye Entrancemperium / Thus Spake The Nightspirit / Ensorcelled By Khaos / The Loss And Curse Of Reverence / The Acclamation Of Bonds / With Strength I Burn / The Wanderer
THORNS VS. EMPEROR, Moonfog (1998) (Split CD with THORNS)

Exördium / I Am / Aerie Descent / Thus
March / The Night Spirit
WRATH OF THE TYRANT, Century
Media 7879 (1998)
I Am The Black Wizards / Wrath Of The
Tyrant / Night Of The Graveless Souls /
Cosmic Keys To My Creations And Times
/ Introduction / Ancient Queen / My
Empire's Doom / Forgotten Centuries /
Night Of The Graveless Souls / Moon
Over Kara-Shehr / Witches Sabbath /
Lord Of The Storms / Wrath Of The Tyrant
IX EQUILIBRIUM, Candlelight (1999)
Curse You All Men! / Decrystallising
Reason / Elegy Of Icaros / Source Of
Icon E / Sworn / Nonu Aequilibrium /
Warriors Of Modern Death / Of
Blindness And Subsequent Seers
EMPERIAL LIVE CEREMONY,
Candlelight CANDLE 048CD (2000)
Curse You All Men / Thus Spake The
Nightspirit / I Am The Black Wizards / An
Elegy Of Icaros / With Strength I Burn /
Sworn / Night Of The Graveless Souls /
Inno A Satana / Ye Entrancemperuim

EMPYRIUM (GERMANY)
Line-Up: Markus (vocals / guitar / bass /
drums), Andreas (keyboards)

A Black Metal band utilizing synthesizers
EMPYRIYUM began as a fully fledged
band project in 1992 before various band
members drifted away to leave the group
as a duo of vocalist / guitarist Markus and
keyboard player Andreas.
With this line-up EMPYRIUM released
their first tape 'Der wie ein Blitz vom
Himmel Fiel' in December 1994 and
subsequently gained a deal with
Prophecy Productions.
The second album was aided by the flute
and cello of Nadine.

Albums:
A WINTER SUNSET, Prophecy
Productions PRO001 (1996)
Moonromanticism / Under Dreamskies /
The Franconian Woods In Winter's
Silence / The Yearning / Autumn Grey
Views / Ordain'd To Thee / A Gentle
Grieving Farewell Kiss
**SONGS OF MOORS AND MISTY
FIELDS**, Prophecy PRO 007 (1997)
When Shadows Grow Longer / The Blue
Mists Of Night / Mourners / Ode To
Melancholy / Lover's Grief / The
Ensemble Of Silence
**WHERE AT NIGHT THE
WOODGROUSE PLAYS**, Prophecy
Productions (2000)

Where At Night The Woodgrouse Plays /
Dying Brokenhearted / The Shepherd
And The Maiden Ghost / The Sad Song
Of The Wind / Wehmut / A Pastoral
Theme / Abendrot / Many Moons Ago /
When Shadows Grow Longer '99

ENCHANTED (NORWAY)

Singles/EPs:
With Eyes I Am Cursed / Daylight Wing
Collides, Edged Circles EDGE003 (1998)

ENDLESS (GERMANY)
Line-Up: Tom Küchler (vocals), Eric
Hofmann (guitar / keyboards), André
Hager (bass), Jan Erdtel (keyboards),
Sven Drechsler (drums)

Albums:
BEYOND THE ABYSS, Spirit (199-)
Calamity / Church In Chaos / Plastic
Flowers / Brocken Der Zerfalls / Wake
Again In Heaven (Sometimes) / Death
Kiss / Walking Flame / Elaine / Love Is
The Real Drug
FIRE, Spirit 27361 61932 (1996)
Beyond The Abyss / Expiratory Death /
Twilight Of Delusion / Cascade /
Between The Devil And The Deep Sea /
Angel Shield / Desire To Rule / Victim Of
Fire / Son Of Time / Confidential Eyes /
Endzeitgedanken / No Reason (Destroy
Mix) / Virgin Eyes

ENDLESS TEARS (FRANCE)
Line-Up: Vince (vocals / guitar), Philippe
(guitar), Francois (bass), Roulo (drums)

After the release of two demos this four
piece band from Talant recorded their
first, self-financed CD.
'Emotion' finds this Bi-lingual outfit (lyrics
are in French and English) offering
technical, melancholic Thrash Metal.

Albums:
EMOTION, ENT001 (1994)
Emotion / Sacrifice-Le Poete / Lies /
Retour / Sister Love / L'Acte / Wait / Le
Dernier Survivant

ENDURA (UK)
Line-Up: Stephen Pennick, Christopher
Walton

The duo of ENDURA were previously
titled ABRAXAS.

Albums:
DREAMS OF DARK WATERS, Nature

141

And Art NACD 202 (1995)
Dreams Of Dark Waters / Intra-Uterine Sabbat / Colours / R'lych Awakens / Stelluris / Black Eidolon / Dance Of Quliefi / The Frozen Moon / Varuna / Twilyte Language
BLACK EDEN, Red Stream RSR 0114 (1996)
Satanas Ex Machina / The Left Hand Of The Dead / The Devils Stars Burn Cold / When God Was A Snake / The Sun No Longer Sets Me Free / A Golden Heresy
LIBER LEVIATHAN, Aesthetic Death (1996)
Gods Of The Sea / Fish Eyed Daemon / Cyclopean Silo / Engine Of Typhoon / Nan Ma Dol / Abysmal Deeps / Island Of The Dead / Dagon Is My Weapon / Earthoscope / Cthulhu Fhtagn

ENGORGE (NJ, USA)

New Jersey's ENGORGE comprise erstwhile DISCIPLES OF MOCKERY and NEBULA 666 members, After an initial demo 'Enchanted By The Battles Of Azazel' ENGORGE issued an extremely rare album. The 'Within The Realms Of Blasphemous Fornication' CD was pressed in only 100 copies.
A further demo 'Grave Desecration' was issued in 2000. Kyle of ENGORGE was previously a stand in drummer for Death Metal act MORTICIAN.
Not to be confused with the Dutch Death Metal act of the same name that released the 'Awaiting To Subside' album.

Albums:
WITHIN THE REALMS OF BLASPHEMOUS FORNICATION, Engorge (1999)

ENID (GERMANY)

A one man mediaeval Metal act of Martin Wiese. ENID's second album sees contributions from drummer Moritz Neuneer of DORNENREICH and EVENFALL wit female vocals by Maria Dorn of AGONY and STARDUST.

Albums:
NACHTGEDANKEN, CCP 100198-2 (199-)
ABSCIEDSREIGEN, CCP 100206-2 (2000)
Erinnerungen / Weg Der Weisung / Reverie Of Youth In Spheres Of Dreams / Meer Der Vergessenen Reiter / Bondage's Coronation / Herbststurm /

Whispering Of Good Bye
ENOCHIAN (CZECH REPUBLIC)

Albums:
NIGHT MONUMENTAL EVIL, Leviathan (1996)
En Tragisk Symfoni / Vikingsverd (Lindisfarn- Frostormenes Brann) / Fucked Holy Truth / Mysterious Empire Of The moon / Monumental Demonium / Black Consil Of Satan / Ancient War Rites Of Evil And Hate / Impalergrave Of The Winterstorm / Hedningenes Hymne I Landet I Nord / Den Skandinavske Is Saegen / Nordisk Folklor / Snowland

ENOCHIAN CRESCENT (FINLAND)
Line-Up: Wrath (vocals), Michael (guitar), Eappa (guitar), Harald (bass), Generis (drums)

A highly rated if troubled act Finns ENOCHIAN CRESCENT have had their career blighted by line up problems. The band began in 1995 with a line up of singer Wrath, guitarist Anshelm, bassist Harald and drummer Generis. This version of the band cut the opening 1996 demo 'Anno Bastardi' after which Anshelm decamped.
The band signed a deal with domestic label Woodcut Records for the debut 'Telecvovim' album, ENOCHIAN CRESCENT now featuring the guitar talents of Michael and Eappa.
However, Michael would quit the ranks prior to the follow up 'Omega Telecvovim'. Drums were now in the hands of AND OCEANS and BLACK DAWN man Grief. (There is some conjecture that Generis and Grief are one in the same person). Latterly bassist Harald has departed.

Singles/EPs:
Pestilence And Honey / Vabzir Camliax / Thirteen Candles / Mortiferum Of Ptormaire Malaise / A. Mathilde, Avantgarde Music (1998) ('Babylon Patralx De Telecvovim' EP)

Albums:
TELOCVOVIM, Woodcut (1997)
Kun Ihmisliha Itki / Closed Gates Of Tomorrow (The Cold Forest) / Crescentian Under Autumn Trees / Arma I P 'Lad' Sa Madriaax / Wolf Among Sheep / A Dream Of Basaltic Submarine Towers Of Titanic Proportions And Nightmare Angles / Afar (The Age Of Dust) / When Tears Run Dry / Bonedancer / Black Flame Of Satan

142

Burning
OMEGA TELOCVOVIM, Avantgarde
AV045 (2000)
Oceans On The Dry Land / Abaiuonin /
Transversary / 'Tis The Sound Of
Tempest That Drowns Us Out / Ye
Crystall Sphears / Igne Natura
Rewovatur Integra / Väkisinkastettu / De
Siatris Od Teloch / Grey Skin

ENSHROUD (MALTA)
Line-Up: Conrad Borg (vocals), Josef
Bajada (guitar), Carlo Aquilina (guitar),
Sean Pollacco (bass), Gordan Zammit
(keyboards), Kenneth Pace (drums)

Black Death Metallers ENSHROUD came
onto the scene in 1997. With keyboard
player Charlotte Schembri the band
submitted the track 'Miseries' to the
'Tomorrows Millionaires' compilation
album on Toppling Colossus Records.
ENSHROUD lost the services of
Schembri but added vocalist Conrad Borg
and keyboard player Gordan Zammit
during 1999.

ENSLAVED (NORWAY)
Line-Up: Grutle Kjellson (vocals / bass),
Ivar Bjornson (guitar / keyboards), Trym
Torson (drums)

Probably one of the foremost exponents
of 'Viking Metal'. Previous to ENSLAVED
vocalist Grutle Kjellson and guitarist Ivar
Bjornson operated under the title of
PHOBIA.
ENSLAVED debuted in 1992 with their
'Yggdrasill' demo, although the group's
first real available product was a split CD
with countrymates EMPEROR.
ENSLAVED were to later issued a split
album with SATYRICON in 1996 titled
'Yggdrasill'. ENSLAVED also cut their
version of CELTIC FROST's 'Procreation
Of The Wicked' to a tribute album 'In
Memory Of Celtic Frost'.
The band undertook a mammoth
European tour during 1997 to promote
the 'Eld' album alongside ABSU and
INFERNO.
Drummer Trym Torson departed for
EMPEROR giving Harald Helgesson a
brief tenure behind the kit. A permanent
replacement was found with Dirge Rep
(in actuality Per Husebø of GEHENNA)
as ENSLAVED also welcomed second
guitarist Richard Kronheim. The resulting
1998 album 'Blodhemn' was produced by
HYPOCRISY's Peter Tägtgren.
Both Kjellson and Bjornson were involved
in the spoof Viking Metal act
DESEKRATOR in the late 90's in
collusion with GORGOROTH and OLD
FUNERAL members.
Helgesson meantime forged a union with
EINHERJER's bassist Stein Sund to
found THUNDRA issuing the 'Blood From
Your Soul' album in 2000. ENSLAVED
toured Europe in December 2000 as part

ENSLAVED
Photos : Martin Wickler

ENSLAVED

143

of an almighty Death Metal package that included MORBID ANGEL, THE CROWN, BEHEMOTH, HYPNOS and DYING FETUS.
Bjornson is also a member of BORKNAGAR.

Albums:
HORDANES LAND, Candlelight CD001 (1993) (Split CD with. EMPEROR)
Slagst I Skogen Bortenfor / Epilog / Slagen / Allfoor Ooinn / Balfer / Andi Fara / Prologr
VIKING LIGRVELDIS, Deathlike Silence ANTI-MOSH 008 (1994)
Lifani Lif Undir Hamri / Vetranótt / Midgards Eldar / Heimdallr / Novegr (Instrumental)
FROST, Osmose Production OPCD025 (1994)
Frost / Loke / Fenris / Svarte Vidder / Yggdrasil / Jotunblod / Gyfaginning / Wotan / Isöders Dronning
YGGDRASIL, Moonfog FOG009 (1996) (Split CD with SATYRICON)
Heimalle / All For Odinn / Hal Vale / Niunda Heim
ELD, Osmose Productions OPCD 053 (1997)
793 (Slaget Om Lindisfarne) / Hordalendingen / Alfablot / Kvasirs Blod / For Lenge Siden / Glemt / Eld
BLODHEMN, Osmose Productions OPCD 063 (1998)
Audhumla / I Lenker Til Ragnarok / Urtical Gods / Ansuz Astral / Nidingaslakt / Eit Auga Til Mimir / Blodhemn / Brisinghamen / Suttungs Mjod / Perkolator
MARDRAUM- BEYOND THE WITHIN, Osmose Productions OPCD 100 (2000)
Større Enn Tid-Tyngre Enn Natt / Daudningekvida / Entrance-Escape / Ormgard / Aeges Draum / Mardraum / Det Endelege Riket / Ormgard II- Kvalt I Kysk Høgsorg / Krigarem Eg Ikkse Kjerde / Sterneheimen / Frøyas Smykke

ENSLAVEMENT OF BEAUTY
(NORWAY)
Line-Up: Ole Alexander Myrholt (vocals), Tony Eugene Tunheim (guitar), Hans Age Holmen (bass), Asgeir Mickelson (drums)

ENSLAVEMENT OF BEAUTY started out in 1995 as a duo of vocalist Ole Alexander Myrholt and guitarist Tony Eugene Tunheim. Following the debut 'Traces O' Red' album the group added bassist Hans Age Holmen and SPIRAL ARCHITECT and BORKNAGER

drummer Asgeir Mickelson.

Albums:
TRACES O' RED, Head Not Found HNF061CD (1999)
In Thro' The Cave Of Impressions / Traces O' Red- The Fall And Rise Of Vitality / Be Thou My Lethe And Bleeding Quietus / Dreams / Something Unique / The Poem Of Dark Subconscious Desire / Eerily Seductive / My Irreverent Pilgrimage / And I Still I Wither / I Dedicate My Beauty To The Stars

ENTHRAL (NORWAY)
Line-Up: Kjetil Hektoen (vocals / drums), Gunnhild Bratset (guitar), Espen Simonsen (bass), Stian Aarstad (keyboards), Martin Rafoss (bass)

ENTHRAL was convened by drummer and vocalist Kjetil Hektoen, formerly of THE FLESH, and guitarist Gunnhild Bratset. An early bass player Gunnleik Fjellseth soon decamped and by March of 1996 Thomas Kjørnes was filling in for ENTHRAL's debut demo.
In an attempt to stabilize the line up guitarist Magnus Krogsveen and keyboard player Martin Løchsen were enlisted but both made their exit swiftly. Fortunately Martin Rafoss and erstwhile guitarist of THE FLESH Espen Simonsen plugged the gap in time for recording of the debut album 'Prophecies Of The Dying'. Keyboards were later in the hands of former BORKNAGER and DIMMU BORGIR man Stian Aarstad.
Simonsen bailed out in November 1998 upfront of recording for a third album.

Albums:
PROPHECIES OF THE DYING, Hot HR009 (1997)
Salig Er Den Som Lir / Prophecies Of The Dying- Kundalini (Serpent Power) / Prophecies Of The Dying- Part II / A Divine Tragedy / Enchanted By The Serpents Spell / Thy Passionate Despair
THE MIRROR'S OPPOSITE END, Hot HR011 (1998)
When The Sky Touched The Earth / In Passion Swept / Weltschmerz / The Sins Of Man / Salvation Mother / Monochrome / The 9th Sphere / Call Of The Horned Piper- The Sabbat Song / The Leaper Play

ENTHRONED (BELGIUM)
Line-Up: Lord Sabathan (vocals / bass), Nornagest (guitar), Nebiros (guitar),

Namroth Blackthorn (drums)

Renowned Belgian band ENTHRONED found infamy with the suicide of their drummer Cernunnos. The sticksman had been a founder member of the group in late 1993 when he united with Lord Sabathan of BLASPHERION and erstwhile SLANESH guitarist Tsebaoth. ENTHRONED released a demo 'Blackwinds' and a split EP with ANCIENT RITES prior to signing with Osmose Productions' subsidiary label Evil Omen.

Added ex INFECTED and HERESIA guitarist Nornagest following completion of the debut album 'Prophecies Of Pagan Fire' and ENTHRONED would tour with the likes of BLOOD, ANCIENT RITES, ENSLAVED and MARDUK. However, Tsebaoth would quit in favour of Nebiros. Cernunnos, suffering from severe depression, would hang himself in April 1997. ENTHRONED recorded a tribute to their late drummer in 1998, the album including material written by Cernunnos whilst in his pre ENTHRONED act MORBID DEATH and a cover of SODOM's 'The Conqueror'. Drums were now in the hands of Namroth Blackthorn. Touring in Europe found the band as guests to DARK FUNERAL prior to a second bout with HECATE ENTHRONED and USURPER.

The band's fourth album 'The Apocalypse Manifesto' was co-produced by Peter Tägtgren. ENTHRONED supported MARDUK on their epic European tour in late 1999.

The debut album was reissued in 1999 by Blackened Records with extra demo tracks, live tracks and the out take 'Post Mortem Penetration'.

Former ENTHRONED guitarist Dimitrus created a new act FLATULATION in 1999 debuting with an intriguingly titled demo 'Autopsy D'une Intoxication Chilli Con Carne'.

Singles/EPs:
Split, Afterdark (1995) (Split 7" single with ANCIENT RITES)

Albums:
PROPHECIES OF PAGAN FIRE, Evil Omen (1996)
Intro / Deny The Holy Book Of Lies / Under The Holocaust / Scared By Darkwinds / Tales From A Blackened Horde / At Dawn Of A Funeral Winter / Rites Of The Northern Fullmoon / Skeldenland / At The Sound Of The Millenium Black Bells / As The Wolves Howl Again
TOWARDS THE SKULLTHRONE OF SATAN, Blackend BLACK008CD (1997)
Satan's Realm (Intro) / The Ultimate Horde Fights / Ha Shaitan / Evil Church / The Antichrist Summons The Black Flame / The Forest Of Nathrath / Dusk Of Forgotten Darkness / Throne To Purgatory / When Horny Flames Begin To Rise / Hertogenwald / Final Armageddon (Epiligue)
REGIE SATHANAS (A TRIBUTE TO CERNUNNOS), Blackend BLACK 011 CD (1998)
Prelude To Satan's Avengers / By Dark Glorious Thoughts / Walpurgis Night / Satan Never Sleeps / The Conqueror / Deny The Holy Book Of Lies / Outro
THE APOCALYPSE MANIFESTO, Blackend (1999)
Whisperings Of Terror- The Apocalypse Manifesto / Death Faceless Chaos / Retribution Of The Holy Trinity / Postmortem Penetrations / Genocide (Concerto No. 35 For Razors) / Völkermord der Antigott / Alastor Rex Perpetuus Dölöris / The Scourge Of God / Anal Lust

ENTIRETY (ITALY)

Varese based Black Metal band ENTIRETY first emerged with the 1995 demo 'Deserts'.

Albums:
IN CAELO OMNIA ACCIDERUNT, Northern Darkness (1997)

ENTWINED (UK)
Line-Up: Stephen John Tovey (vocals), Lee James (guitar), Simon (bass), James Southgate (drums)

ENTWINED feature erstwhile ESTRANGED members vocalist Stephen John Tovey, bassist Simon and drummer James Southgate. Guitarist Lee James has credits with MORTAL TIDE and METAL STORM. As ENTWINED the band bowed in with the demos 'XIII' and 'Hot Cherished Mask'.

ENTWINED supported MORBID ANGEL on their 1998 European tour but would fold shortly after.

Albums:
DANCING UNDER GLASS, Earache (1998)
The Sound Of Her Wings / Shed

Nightward Beauty / Under A Killing Moon / The Forgotten / A Moments Sadness / The Sacrifice Of Spring / Red Winter / Heaven Rise / XIII

EPIC (USA)

<u>Albums:</u>
OF TEARS AND BLOOD, (1997)
Chronicles Of The Dragon Knights Part One: Of Tears And Blood… i) The Ages Of War, ii) The Howling Of The Dark Sword, iii) The Garden Of Sin, iv) Of Tears And Blood, v) The New Dawn, vi) Where The Night Never Ends, vii) The Walking Shadow

EPOCH OF UNLIGHT (USA)
Line-Up: Jason Smith (vocals / bass), Randy Robertson (vocals / guitar), Pierce Totty (bass), Tino Losicco (drums)

Black Metal previously known as ENRAPTURED upon their inception in 1990. By 1993 the band had switched titled to REQUIEM to issue the 'As The Storm Slowly Fades' demo'. The band finally became EPOCH OF UNLIGHT during 1994.
Their fresh guise was heralded by the demo 'Beyond The Pale'.

<u>Singles/EPs:</u>
Of Feral Eyes / Winters Seed / Den Ubrum / Immortal Crucify, Exhumed (1996) ('Within The Night' EP)

<u>Albums:</u>
BLACK AND CRIMSON GLORY, Y.F.L.H.D. (1997)
Intro I / (From Northern Aeries To) The Infinite Cycle Of The Unborn Land / Intro II / Silver Mistress / Intro III / Conflagration Of Hate
WHAT WILL BE HAS BEEN, The End (1997)
Ad Infinitum / Undone Within / Silver Mistress / Burning As One / What Will Be Has Been / Crimson Might (And Glory) / (From Northern Aeries To) The Infinite Cycle Of The Unborn Land / The Day The Light Hath Died / Conflagration Of Hate / Immortal Crucify

EQUINOX (USA)

Black Metal act EQUINOX issued the demos 'Anthem To The Moon' and 'Equinox' prior to the release of their inaugural 7" single.

<u>Singles/EPs:</u>
Upon The Throne Of Eternity, (1995) (7" single)

<u>Albums:</u>
RETURN TO MYSTERY, Unisound (1996)
Rites Of Red Giving / Return To Mystery / Until The Dawn's Mist / The Mourning River / Valley Of The Kings / Dreams Of The Winter Solstice / Winds Of Autumn / Infernal Atavism (Descend To Tetragrammaton) / Path To Eternal Ruin

EROS NECROPSIQUE (FRANCE)
Line-Up: Oliver (vocals / keyboards), Cof (bass)

<u>Albums:</u>
CHARNELLE TRANSCENDANCE, Adipocere (1995)
Introduction / L'Appel De Dionysos / Le Mélodieux Écoulment Du Temps / Réminiscence / Avortement Suicidaire / Pardon / A L'Ami Décédé / Communion / Delirium De L'Étré Send
PATHOS, Adipocere CD AR 043 (1998)
Le Depart / Mathilde / Ultime Reverence / La Scission Dechirante D'Une Illusiore Fusion / Le Deuil Du Merveilleux / Noyade / Selene / Aujourd Hui, Deux Mains / Le Douloureaux Souffle De L'Authenticite

ESOTERIC (UK)
Line-Up: Greg Chandler (vocals), Steve Peters (guitar) (guitar), Gordan Bickwell (guitar), Bryan Beck (bass), Keith York (drums)

A Birmingham based ultrasludge Black Doom band founded in 1992. ESOTERIC debuted in 1994 with an 82 minute long demo tape! The debut album 'Epistemological Despondency' was recorded with drummer Darren although he quit shortly after recording. ESOTERIC employed the services of a drum machine for the highly praised follow up 'The Pernicious Enigma'.
The 'Metamorphogenesis' EP includes Tom Kvalskoll of Norwegian act PARADIGMA on guest vocals.
ESOTERIC are a rare sight on the live scene only having completed a handful of gigs.

<u>Singles/EPs:</u>
Dissident / The Secret Of The Secret / Psychotropic Transgression, Eibon (1999) ('Metamorphogenesis' EP)

Albums:
EPISTEMOLOGICAL DESPONDENCY,
Aesthetic Death (1995)
Bereft / Only Hate (Baresark) / The
Name Of Despair / Lamented
Despondency / Edadification (Of Thorns)
/ Awaiting My Death
THE PERNICIOUS ENIGMA, Aesthetic
Death (1997)
Creation Through Destruction / Dominion
Of Slaves / Allegiance / Nox: BC
9701040 / Sinstrous / At War With The
Race / A Worthless Dream / Stygeon
Narcosis / Passing Through Matter

ESTATIC FEAR (AUSTRIA)
Line-Up: Beowulf (vocals / bass), Stauff
(guitar), Calix Miseriae (guitar /
keyboards), Astaroth Magus (drums)

This Doom / Death / Black / Gothic Metal
band was formed in 1993 and has
featured a stable line-up since 1994.
On the debut album, which features
strong medieval themes, the band was
assisted by female vocalist Marion and
the flute playing of Petra Hölzl.
Drummer Astaroth Magus ('Milan Dejak')
also operates in ASTAROTH, THIRD
MOON and SEPTIC CEMETARY.

Albums:
SOMNIUM OBMUTUM, CCP 100151-2
(1996)
Des Nachtens Suss' Gedone / Somnium
Obmutum / As Autumn Calls / Ode To
Solitude
A SOMBRE DANCE, CCP 100197-2
(199-)
Intro (Unisomo Lute Instrumental) /
Chapter I / Chapter II / Chapter III /
Chapter IV / Chapter V / Chapter VI /
Chapter VII / Chapter VIII / Chapter IX

ETERNAL AUTUMN (SWEDEN)
Line-Up: John Carlsson (vocals / guitar),
Thomas Ahlgren (guitar), Thomas
Ahlgren (bass), Ola Sundström (drums)

Albums:
THE STORM, Black Diamond BDP005
(1999)
The Storm / Autumn Fire / In My Recent
Shape / As The Last Leaf Fell /
Moonscape / Autumn Opus, No 1 /
Floating... / In A Land Dawn Never
Reached

ETERNAL CONSPIRACY
(HOLLAND)

Singles/EPs:
Serenades Of Dark Angels / Reborn In
Moonlight / Existence / Words Of Despair,
(199-) ('Serenades Of Dark Angels' EP)

ETERNAL DARKNESS (SWEDEN)
Line-Up: Janne (vocals), Jompa (guitar),
Tony (guitar), Tero Viljanen (bass), Make
Pesonen (drums)

Singles/EPs:
Doomed / Psycopath, Distorted Harmony
DH006 (1992)

ETERNAL DIRGE (GERMANY)
Line-Up: Timo (vocals / guitar), Pethe
(guitar), Boelmi (bass), Ralf (drums)

This band, from Marl, Westfalia, was
formed in the mid 80s and released
several demos before 'We Are The Dead'
led to a record deal.
Both of ETERNAL DIRGE's albums
highlight the group's brand of Death /
Thrash Metal with keyboard leanings on a
grand scale. Indeed, during the recording
of the 'Chaos Magick' album permanent
keyboardist Sascha R. joined the group.

Albums:
MORBUS ASCENDIT, HASS Production
(1994)
Out The Eons / The Crawling Chaos /
Exploring The Depths / Blind Idiot God /
The Decadence Within / We Are The
Dead / Sinustis Maxillaris / Evolved
Mutations
KHAOS MAGICK, Moribund MR024
(1996)
I, Unameable / The Threshold Of
Sensation / Anthem To The Seeds (Of
Pure Demise) / Feaster From The Stars /
Rending The Veils / Kallisti / Like Roses
In A Garden Of Weed / In Praise Of
Biocide / Hymn To Pan / My Sweet Satan

ETERNAL TEARS OF SORROW
(FINLAND)
Line-Up: Altti Veteläinen (vocals), Antti
Talala (guitar), Jarmo Puolakanaho
(guitar), Olli Pekka- Torro (guitar /
keyboards), Pasi Hiltula (keyboards),
Petri Sankala (drums)

Death Metal act with Black overtones
although the band themselves are
reluctant to label their brand of music
'black'. The group rose from the ashes of

147

an early 90's act ANDROMEDA which comprised of Altti Verläinen on bass, Jarmo Puolakanaho on guitar, vocalist Mikko Komulainen, guitarist Olli Pekka Törrö and drummer Petri Sankala. ANDROMEDA folded after their rehearsal rooms burnt down but did manage a 1993 demo 'Beyond The Fantasy'.

By the following year Verläinen, Törrö and Puolakanaho founded ETERNAL TEARS OF SORROW bowing in with the tape 'The Seven Goddesses Of Frost'. The group was far from happy with the end result citing the facts that it had been recorded at school on a four track! Fortunately a follow up session 'Bard's Burial' secured a deal with the Swedish X-treme Records label. However, although the 'Sinner's Serenade' opus was laid down in 1996 it was to be September 1997 before its release.

The band switched to the Finnish Spinefarm concern for sophomore outing 'Vild Mánnu'. In 1999 Törrö decamped and new members Antti Talala on guitar, bassist / keyboard player Pasi Hiltula and erstwhile ANDROMEDA colleague drummer Petri Sankula were welcomed into the fold.

The 'Chaotic Beauty' album, which includes a cover of EDGE OF SANITY's 'Black Tears', was produced by Mikko Karmila featured backing vocals from SINERGY's Kimberley Goss.

Touring to promote the album resulted in the exit of Talala with Antti Kokko taking his position.

Albums:
SINNERS SERENADE, X-Treme XTR003 (1997)
Another One Falls Asleep / The Law Of The Flames / Dirge / Into The Deepest Waters / Sinners Serenade / My God, The Evil wind / March / Bard's Burial / The Son Of The Forest / Empty Eyes
VILD MÁNNU, Spinefarm SPI68CD (1999)
Northern Doom / Burning Flames Embrace / Goashem / Scars Of Wisdom / Nightwinds Lullaby / Raven (In Your Eyes) / Vild Mánnu / Coronach / Nodde Rahgan / Seita
CHAOTIC BEAUTY, Spinefarm (2000)
Shattered Soul / Blood Of Faith Stains My Hands / Autumn's Grief / The Seventh Eclipse / Bride Of The Crimson Sea / Black Tears / Tar Of Chaos / Bhéan Sidhe / Nocturnal Strains / Flight Of Icarus / Coronach / Nightwinds Lullaby / Burning Flames Embrace

ETERNE (UK)
Line-Up: David Dando (vocals / guitar / bass / programming), Martyn Lear (keyboards / programming)

ETERNE offer Avant Garde Doom.

Albums:
STILL DREAMING, Candlelight 009CD (1995)
Flesh Made World / Divine / The Crawling Chaos / Scarlet Field / Marionette / The Endless / Forever / A Certain Kind Of Bitterness / Epilogue / Thanatos / Still Dreaming / In Retrospect
DEAD AUTHOR, Candlelight 016CD (1997)
Bleed / Pandora / Jyhad / Naked / Complicity / Heal / Delirium / Lexicon / Numb / Dead Author

ETHERIAL (GREECE)
Line-Up: Anton (vocals / keyboards), Chris (guitar / bass), Vangelis (drums)

A deliberately primitive Metal act. An ETHEREAL member, Alessandro Monopolii, would later join Doom act MORNINGRISE.

Albums:
OM SANTHI, Unisound (1995)
DOMINION, Uniforce (1996)

EVEMASTER (FINLAND)

EVEMASTER emerged with the 1996 demo session 'In Thine Majesty'. Although essentially a duo of vocalist J. Taskula and guitarist Tomi Mykkänen EVEMASTER undertook touring in Poland. Session musicians for these gigs included guitarist Tommi Vaittinen, bassist Matti Gran, keyboard player Erkka Huikuri and drummer Migus Neuvonen.

In typical Scandinavian fashion Gran, Neuvonen, Vaittinen, Mykkänen and Kuikuri also operate the sixties flavoured Rock band SHAMOS.

Albums:
LACRIMAE MULDI, K.T.O.K. (1998)
Pandemonium / Whispers / Embraced / Archways / Lacrimae Muldi / Epistelium (The Storm Rises) / Equinox Nocturne

EVENFALL (GERMANY)
Line-Up: Ansgar Zoschg (vocals), Ivan D'Alia (guitar), Roland Wurzer (bass), Max Boy (keyboards), Moritz Neuner (drums)

EVENFALL used to go under the handle of RESURRECTUS, a band that issued an EP in 1997.

Albums:
STILL IN THE GREY DYING, Century Media CD 77266-2 (1998)
Forbidden Tales / Black Bloody Roses / Garden Of Sadness / Still In The Grey Dying / Fallen From Grace / Frozen Mystery / Evenfall / Sales Of Charon / Dark Is The Season / In Between Days

EVENSONG (HUNGARY)
Line-Up: Gabor Olah (guitar), Gergely Cseh (bass), Agnes Toth (vocals / keyboards), Gabor Vegh (drums)

Albums:
PATH OF THE ANGELS, Displeased (1999)

EVENVAST (ITALY)
Line-Up: Antonietta Scilipoti (vocals), Luca Martello (guitar), Diego Maniscalco (bass), Roberto Risso (drums)

EVEN VAST include the former CHAOS AND TECHNOCRACY duo of vocalist Antonietta Scilipoti and guitarist Luca Martello.

Albums:
HEAR ME OUT, Black Lotus BLRCD 009 (1999)

EVERDARK (NY, USA)
Line-Up: Storm (vocals), Tom Death (guitar), Chris (guitar), John Berzerker (bass), Jay (drums)

Black Metal band EVERDARK issued the 1994 demo 'Graveyard Rites' upfront of their debut album.

Albums:
ARMAGEDDON'S BIRTH, Full Moon Productions (1996)
NOT OF GOD, II Moons TM 1203 2 (1997)
Heaven's Damnation / Winter Eve / Gravesite Rites / Tombstone / Infernal / Scarlet Treason (Her Thorns Bleed Me) / Like Wolves Among Sheep / Within My Chilling Grasp / In Darkness, I Dwell

THE EVERDAWN (SWEDEN)
Line-Up: Pierre Törnkvist (vocals / guitar / bass), Patrick Törnkvist (guitar), Niklas Svensson (bass), Oskar Karlsson (drums)

THE EVERDAWN were created by erstwhile GATES OF ISHTAR members drummer Oskar Karlsson and bassist Niclas Svensson together with former SCHEITAN guitarist Pierre Törnkvist. In fact, all three - previous to the formation of GATES OF ISHTAR in 1994 - had been members of DECORTITION.
Svensson and Törnkvist also have credits in THE MOANING.

Singles/EPs:
The Everdawn / Nightborn / The Silent Winter Sky / Opera Of The Damned, Black Diamond IRS (1996) ('Opera Of The Damned' EP)

Albums:
POEMS – BURN THE PAST, Invasion (1997)
Territory Loss / When The Sunset Forever Fades / Needlework / Where Pain Never Dies / Autumn, Sombre Autumn / Burn / Poems / Opera Of The Damned

EVEREVE (GERMANY)
Line-Up: Tom Sedotschenko (vocals), Thorsten Weißenberger (guitar), Stephan Kiefer (guitar), Stefan Müller (bass), Michael Zeissl (keyboards), Marc Werner (drums)

Singles/EPs:
Intro / Darkmere / Salvation / Stormbirds / Autumn Child, Promo-Split-CD (1995) (Promotion Split CD with PARRACIDE)

Albums:
SEASONS, Nuclear Blast NB222-2 (1996)
Prologue: The Bride Wears Black / A New Winter / The Phoenix, Spring / The Dancer, Under A Summer Sky / Twilight / Autumn Leaves / Untergehen Und Auferstehen / To Learn Silent Oblivion / A Winternight Depression / Epilogue
REGRETS, Nuclear Blast (1999)
Misery's Dawn / Fall Into Oblivion / Holyman / Redemption / House Of The Rising Sun / The Eclipse Of The Seventh Sun / Passion And Demise / Dies Irae (Grave New World) / Where No Shadows Fall / House Of The Rising Sun (Club edition)

EVERTICUM (DENMARK)
Line-Up: Rolf Ljungberg (vocals), Jan Lauridtsen (guitar), Rasmus Andersen (bass), Lars Roed (drums)

Danes EVERTICUM released a brace of

demos prior to the 1999; 'In Infinitium' EP namely 'Human Nature' and its follow up 'In Eternal Sleep'.

Singles.EPs:
The Other Side / Shamefull Memories / Philosophies Put To rest / Born In Flames, (1999) ('In Infinitium' EP)

EVIL DIVINE (PA, USA)
Line-Up: J. Demonic (vocals), R. Moll (guitar), B. Becht (guitar), Matt Moore (bass), J. Zignacht (keybpoards), Patrick Battagla (drums)

A notorious force on the American Black Metal scene. EVIL DIVINE announced their inception with the 1996 demo 'Wolf Slay' and a line up of frontman J. Demonic, guitarist J. Kennish and drummer M. Myers. Demonic has credits with MASKIM XUL, BAPTISED IN BLOOD and TORQ III.
For a track included on the compilation album 'Eat The Evidence Vol. II' the band pulled INSATANITY vocalist Jay Lipitz on backing vocals.
EVIL DIVINE then underwent what was to be the first of many turbulent line up changes as Demonic drafted guitarist V. Geryson (also known as B. Becht), second guitarist Peter and keyboard player C. Zignacht (sometimes Zigmont). Myers would break ranks to join forces with the already departed Kennish in another band as EVIL DIVINE drafted the mysterious Shadow (C. Rehill) on drums for their inaugural gig on Halloween 1997. Further shuffles saw the adoption of guitarist R. Moll (billed as 'C.L.O.P.S.'), bassist Fester and drummer Clev for a round of gigs. Shadow made his way onto Industrial band LOST SIGNAL. However, predictably the group fractured again with Zignacht and Pete bailing out. Keyboard player Sekkmet Syatha was enrolled for the debut album 'Feathers Have Fallen', recording of which took a mere three days.
Syatha bade his farewell in September of 1998 as Zignacht promptly rejoined. Stability was still elusive though as Fester, Clev and Geryson departed en masse.
Tracks for a projected 7" single 'Graveland Mist' were cut with new faces Chris on drums and guitarist S. Diabolica. Former member J. Kennish would also deputize on bass during this period in order to keep up the band's live presence.

EVIL DIVINE then struck a monumental setback when Chris was jailed. The drummer receiving a 78 year sentence. Demonic was also given a term of a year in a psychiatric hospital. With the band in disinitigration Kennish reunited with Myers in Hardcore act PNEUMA.
With Demonic hospitalised Moll, Becht and Zignacht created INNOCENCE FALLEN in alliance with SOLACE IN THE SHADOWS members bassist Matt Moore and drummer Patrick Battagla. When Demonic was granted his freedom he was asked to join this new act which promptly renamed itself EVIL DIVINE for the second album 'Dawn Before The Dawn'.
The latests EVIL DIVINE line up is listed as J. Demonic ('88mm Flak Vokills'), R. Moll ('Lead Chainsaw Assault'), B. Becht ('Rhythmic Razor Suicide'), M. Moore ("Basstard Sword'), J. Zigmont ('Symphonic Torment') and P. Battagla ('Thermonuclear Global War').
J. Demonic, in keeping with Black Metal tradition, also leads a double life as bass player 'Lord Sedit' for VUKODLAK. He is also a member of Industrial band SYNTHETIK FORMS as well as performing drums in ARYAN TORMENTOR and INFERNAL HATRED.

Albums:
FEATHERS HAVE FALLEN, Evil Divine (1998)
Evil Divine Intro / Achtung / Bitch Of The Devil / Apocalyptic Prophecy / The Journey / Last Class Soul / And The Angels Fell / Blood / Revenge / Broken Love / Crying Cain
DAWN BEFORE THE DAWN, Evil Divine (2001)
Forged In Fire / Drawn By Moonlight / All Creation / Polarity / Self Inflicting / Shadow Out Of Time

EVIL GATE (SWITZERLAND)
Line-Up: Lord Dead (vocals / bass), Evelyne (vocals / keyboards), Hammer (guitar), Lord Kraken (guitar), Jofheim (drums)

EVIL GATE stayed the course little over a year. Founded in 1997 the band performed their final gig in March 1998.

Albums:
INTO THE DARKNESS, Blackmoon Circle (1997)
Intro / Shadow Moon / Infernal Winter / Summon The Evil Spirit / Into The

Darkness / Evil Gate

EVIL INCARNATE (USA)
Line-Up: Mike Eisenhauer (vocals / bass), Rob Rigney (guitar), Dave Gally (guitar), Andy Vehnekamp (drums)

Previously known as APOLLYON and forged by erstwhile NUM SKULL members frontman Mike Eisenhauer and guitarist Tom Brandauer in 1994. A series of demos started with 'Beyond Blasphemy and 'Deliverance From Salvation'. Brandauer departed and was replaced by former MORBID CORPSES and FEAR SPAWNED RELIGION man Dave Gally The third effort 'Christ Destroyed' was issued before Deathgasm Records compiled these early recordings for the 'Blood Of The Saints' album. These recording were also issued on cassette by the Czech label Ramu Records.
EVIL INCARNATE have also offered tribute to VENOM, SLAYER and BLACK SABBATH by appearing on various tribute albums.
EVIL INCARNATE drummer Andy Vehnekamp is better known as a member of JUNGLE ROT.
Brandauer returned following the exit of Gally.
A second album entitled 'Blackest Hymns Of God's Disgrace' was recorded in 2000.

Albums:
BLOOD OF THE SAINTS, Deathgasm (2000)
First Born Of The Wicked / Last Suffer Of Nazarene / Blood Of The Saints / Heaven Lay Burned / His Only Bastard Son / Twist Of The Serpents Head / Raised From The Deep / The Sacrificial Lamb / Dead Corpse Of Jesus Christ / Sculpture Of Impurity

EVILUTION (New Haven, CT, USA)

Albums:
SHRINE OF DESECRATION, Pure Death (1998)
Act Of Attrition / The Rebirth Of Azazel / Cowering Messiah / Nailed To The Cross / Baptimisal Rite To Deity / Shrine Of Desecration / In Constant Obscure / Extracted From The Womb

EVILWAR (BRAZIL)
Line-Up: Sabatan (vocals), Azarack (guitar), Typhon Seth (bass), Ichthys Niger (drums)

EVILWAR, founded in mid 1999, include former MURDER RAPE personnel vocalist Sabatan, guitarist Azarack and drummer Ichthys Niger. Both Azarack and Niger also have credits with INSANE DEVOTION.

Albums:
UNHOLY MARCH, (2000)

EVOKE (UK)

EVOKE, a Mansfield based Black Metal band, debuted with a 1994 demo tape before eventually issuing two singles during 1997, the second of which is a split 7" green vinyl affair shared with Germany's KADATH.

Singles/EPs:
Behold The Twilight / Await The Inevitable, Megagrind (1997)
As I Bleed / Among Mere Mortals, Paranoia Syndrome (1997) (Split 7" with KADATH)

Albums:
DREAMING INTO REALITY, (1997)
Intro / The Sign Of Solitude / Through Blood Stared Eyes / Body Rites / Among Mere Mortals / No Repeat / Rouge / Die Before My Eyes / When Beauty Dies / Equanimity Lost / Manipulate The Ridicule / As I Bleed / While You Decay I Live
THE FURY WRITTEN, System Shock (2000)

EVOKEN (NJ, USA)
Line-Up: John Paradiso (vocals / guitar), Nick Orlando (guitar), Steve Moran (bass), Dario Derna (keyboards), Vince Verkay (drums)

Black Metal band EVOKEN have undergone a series of transformations since their inception. The band was initially formed in April 1992 by PUTRIFACT guitarist Nick Orlando together with bassist / vocalist Rob although under the name of FUNEROUS. A switch to ASMODEUS came in 1993 with an accompanying demo but by 1996 the name EVOKEN was finally settled on. The 1999 line up comprises of Orlando, former GRIM LEGION vocalist / guitarist John Paradisdo, ex INNER CONFLICT bassist Steve Moran, BODY OF CHRIST man Vince Verkay on drums and ex INFESTER keyboard player Dario Derna. Derna also operates with

ABAZAGORATH. Orlando also performs in a side act FUNEBRERUM with ABAZAGORATH members.

Albums:
SHADES OF NIGHT DESCENDING, Adipocere CD AR 031 (1996)
Intro / Engraven Image / Shades Of Night Descending / Towers Of Frozen Dusk / Into The Autumn Shade
QUIETUS, Avantgarde (2000)
In Pestilence Burning / Withering Indignation / Tending The Dire Hatred / Where Ghosts Fall Silent / Quietus / Embrace The Emptiness / Atremertus Journey

EVOL (ITALY)
Line-Up: Prince Of Agony (vocals / keyboards), Princess Of Disease (vocals), Lord Of Sorrow (guitar / bass/ drums)

EVOL, named after the black principle of existence and founded in 1993 by vocalist and keyboard player Prince Of Agony, were to add a fourth member in 1996, namely drummer Count De Saba. Prior to their 1995 debut album EVOL issued the demo 'Dark Dreamquest'.

Singles/EPs:
The Tale Of The Witchlord / Ancient Abbey (Thunder remix) / Das Gemiedene Schloß / Phenomena / Prologue (Waiting For His Country) (Demo), Adipocere (199-) ('Ancient Abbey' EP)

Albums:
THE SAGA OF THE HORNED KING, Apidocere CDAR026 (1995)
The Present Age / The Chant Of The Witch / From The Unknown Domain... / Through Foggy Plains And Mystic Woods He Rides... / Prologue / The Eve / The Return Of The Horned King / The Feast / Sorrow Of The Witch / The Sag Of The Horned King
DREAMQUEST, Adipocere CDAR 037 (1996)
Dreamquest / Sad Doom Of A Dark Soul / Sona-Nyi / Flying With The Night Gaunts / Celephais / The Ancient King Of Ice / Sarkomand / Darkmere / Ulthar / Dark Stairs Of R'Lyeh / Cathuria / The Black Crystal Of Astar / ...Verso La Citta Del Tramonto
PORTRAITS, Adipocere (199-)
Overture / Portraits / Ancient Abbey / Inquisition Begins / Once Upon A Time / Il Principle Di Anghista / March For Evol

/ Il Castello Evitato / Il Chierico Grigio / Grigia Signora / Tower Of The Necromancer / Epilogue (Fading Black)

EWIGKEIT (UK)

One man Black Metal project of J. Fogarty. EWIGKEIT translates as 'Eternity'. EWIGKEIT contributed to the 2000 BURZUM tribute album on Cymophane Records.

Albums:
BATTLE FURIES, Eldethorn ELD001 (1998)
Jewel Of My Empire / Wonder Of The Cosmos / Christendom Falls / Dragons Burning / Kingdom In The Clouds (My Astral Journey) / Time Reborn / Gods Of Ages Awakened / 'O Elbereth' / Keshara Rise / As Shadows Dance
STARSCAPE, Eldethorn (1999)
Point Of Origin / Unveiling The Mysteries / The Legend Of Keshara / The Return Of Planet X / Deviant / Lightspeed Evolution / Starscape / Capsule / Birth Of Hours / Space Symphony / Dragon Burning

EXHUMATION (GREECE)
Line-Up: John Nokteridis (vocals), Marios Iliopoulos (guitar), Panagiotis Giatzoglu (guitar), Thomas Bairachtaris (keyboards), Pantelis Athanasiadis (drums)

The 1998 album 'Dance Across The Past' has guest appearances from Kimberley Goss of DIMMU BORGIR and SINERGY and Jesper Strombald of IN FLAMES. EXHUMATION folded in 2000 with guitarist Mario creating NIGHTRAGE.

Albums:
SEAS OF ETERNAL SILENCE, Diehard (1997)
Intro / Seas Of Eternal Silence / Dreamy Recollection / Beyond The Eyes Of Universe / Forgotten Days / Passing Suns / Ceaseless Sorrow / Guilty Of Innocence / Monuments
DANCE ACROSS THE PAST, Holy (1998)
Images Of Our Extinction / Whithered Sky / Dance Across The Past / The Slender Light / Moonless Night / Regrettable Remains / Sin / My Depression / Territory
TRAUMATICON, (199-)
Awakening / Nightrage / Befalling / Traumaticon / Blemished / Disguised Failure / Voracious Sleep / Secrecy / Nemesis / Wounded Eyes

EXHUMATOR (BELARUS)
Line-Up: Alexander Bourei (vocals / guitar), Pavel Bolokhov (bass), Jouri Golovach (drums)

Extreme Metal act EXHUMATOR was forged in Minsk, capitol of Belarus, in 1989. The band started out as a quartet of vocalist Slava Korsakov, guitarist Vova Lisishin, bassist Igor Silnichenko and drummer Anton Arkhipov. This line up cut the debut album 'Welcome And Die' and the follow up EP 'Arising Of Suspicions'.
Vadim Akimov was added on lead vocals in 1992 to appear on the sophomore album 'Resurrected'. The bass position then switched to accommodate Pavel Bolokhov.
The 1994 demo 'Sacrificial Bleeding' would be the last recording made by Akimov who died the following year. Undaunted EXHUMATOR relocated to Western Europe in order to further their career. Settling in Brussels EXHUMATOR were by now a trio of Bourei, Bolokhov and drummer Jouri Golovach.

Singles/EPs:
Arising Of Suspicions EP, (1993)

Albums:
WELCOME AND DIE, (1990)
RESURRECTED, (1993)

EXHUMATOR (BULGARIA)

Solo venture from the strangely titled 'The Piff' who records alone in his basement. Not to be confused with the Belarus Black Metal band or the German Thrash Metal band. Both albums, heavily inspired by BATHORY, are available only on cassette.

Albums:
FITS OF MADNESS, WU 100.011 (1997)
CHAINS OF DARKNESS, WU 100.037 (1998)

EXORCISM (PA, USA)

EXORCISM, a one man venture, trade in Black Death Metal. A demo 'Suspended Above The Flesh' was issued in 1997 preceding a string of self financed releases.

Albums:
AFTERLIFE, (1998)
VANISH INTO THE DEPTHS, (1999)
A JOURNEY INTO THE NIGHT CHASM,

Nascent Frost Productions (2000)

EXORCIST (USA)
Line up- Damien Rath (vocals), Marc Dorian (guitar), Jamie Locke (bass), Geoff Fontaine (drums)

Although on the surface a Thrash Black Metal act EXORCIST are rumoured to be none other than trad metallers VIRGIN STEELE going under pseudonyms.

Albums:
NIGHTMARE THEATRE, Roadrunner RR 9700 (1986)
Black Mass / The Invocation / Burnt Offerings / The Hex / Possessed / Call For The Exorcist / Death By Bewitchment / The Trial / Execution Of The Witches / Consuming Flames Of Redemption / Megawatt Mayhem / Riding To Hell / Queen Of The Dead / Lucifer's Lament / The Banishment

EXPIRATION (SPAIN)
Line-Up: Carlos (vocals), Felix 'Lombriz' (guitar), Ed Brain (guitar), Angel (bass), Sergio 'Larva' (drums)

After the band's 'Deviated' EP EXPIRATION vocalist Carlos left and was replaced by Guanche Artemi'.
In their time EXPIRATION have played with the likes of AVULSED, DERANGED and GOLGOTHA.

Singles/EPs:
Deviated / Don't Bury Me / The Hidden Voices / Maze Of Sadness / Number Four, Expiration EXP-001 (1996)

EXPULSER (BRAZIL)
Line-Up: Alessandro Profano (vocals), Weber Daeahmon (guitar), Alessandro Lima (bass), Marcon N. Rodrigus (drums)

EXPULSER set the scene with the 1989 demos 'Fornications' and 'Bloody Cross Of J. Christ'. EXPULSER would fracture following the release of the 1992 'The Unholy One' album. With only guitarist Weber Daeahmon surviving he built a new band comprising of vocalist / bassist José L. Borgleux, guitarist Luciano Andrade and drummer Kiko Tiotlola.

Albums:
FORNICATIONS, Maggott (1990) (Split album with BRUTAL DISTORTION)
Vomiting In Paradise / The Offensor / No Resurrection

THE UNHOLY ONE, Cogumelo (1992)
Praise To The Almighty God / Cirrhosis
(Let's Get Drunk) / Bleeding At Cross /
Fornications (At The Church) / The
Unholy One / Screams Of Delights /
Christ's Saga / The Evil Orgasm / Gore
Pussy Of Virgin (The Rape) / The Slut

EXTERMINATOR (BELGIUM)

Albums:
MIRROR IMAGES, Exterminator (2000)

EXTOL (NORWAY)
Line-Up: Christer Espevoll (guitar), Emil
Nicolaisen (guitar), Eystein Holm (bass),
David Husvik (drums)

EXTOMORE (HUNGARY)

Albums:
KALYIJAG, Rise Up 5 4507 20 561
(2000)

EXTREME DEFORMITY
(HUNGARY)

Black Metal act from Hungary.

Albums:
INTERNAL, LMS (199-)

THE EYE (FRANCE)

Albums:
SUPREMACY, Velvet Music International
(1997)
The Eternal Oath Of Life / The Land /
The Call Of A thousand Souls / My
Supremacy / Aidyl / The Purest
Domination In Wisdom (The Eternal
Eye) / Your Weakness (Bastard Son Of
Fear) / The Eye

EYEFEAR (AUSTRALIA)
Line-Up: Jim Georgopoulos (vocals),
Anthony Porchia (guitar), Con
Papazoglou (guitar)

Albums:
DAWN.. A NEW BEGINNING, Fotia
(1999)

EZURATE (IL, USA)

Until 1994 EZURATE was known as
AMAMYON.

Albums:
INFERNAL DOMINATION, Ezurate
(2000)

FAERGHAIL (FINLAND)
Line-Up: Jussi Ranta (vocals), Kai Lehtinen (guitar), Tuomas Murtojärvi (guitar), Petri Moisio (bass), Tomi Kangassalo (drums)

Albums:
HORIZON'S FALL, Shiver SHR027 (1999)
In Portraits Of Shadowed Life / Frostmaiden's Veil / As I Wither Away / Witches Dance / Reveries Night / My Beloved / When Stormclouds Gather… / Hämärän Kutsu
WHERE ANGELS DWELL NO MORE, Shiver SHR036 (2001)
Suicidal Rites / Silver Moon Child / Faerghail (Where Angels Dwell No More) / Summer Sadness / Horizon's Fall / Behold A Sinful Shade / Strife For Blood / Dying Memories… / In The Arms Of A Nightmare / Masked For Death

FALKENBACH (ICELAND)

FALKENBACH's Viking Metal is the one man project of Vratyas Vakyas. The man would add guest vocals to the 2001 AD INFERA album.

Singles/EPs:
Laeknishendr / Gadralag, (1995) (Promotion release)

Albums:
...EN THEIR MEDH RIKI FARA..., No Colours NC 008 CD (1997)
Galdralag / Heathenpride / Laeknishender / Ultima Thule / Asum Ok Alfum Naer… / Winternight / Into The Ardent Awaited Land…
MAGNI BLANDINN OK MEGINTIRI, Napalm NPR 037 (1998)
… When Gjallarhorn Will Sound / … Where Blood Will Soon Be Shed / Towards The Hall Of Bronzen Shields / The Heathenish Foray / Walhall / Baldurs Tod

FALLEN EMPIRE (Ward, AR, USA)
Line-Up: Lord Hellspawn (vocals / guitar), Nazareth (guitar), Tora (bass), Valkyr (keyboards), Dragonphir (drums)

Arkansas based FALLEN EMPIRE debuted with the demo 'From The Ashes'. The band contributed their version of 'The Exorcist' to a MERCYFUL FATE tribute album.

Albums:
SHADOWS, Fallen Empire (1999)

FALL OF THE LEAFE (FINLAND)
Line-Up: Tuomas Tuominen (vocals), T. Hatakka (guitar), Juha Kouhi (bass), Petri Hannuniemi (keyboards), Marko Hyytiä (drums)

A highly rated Finnish atmospheric Black inclined outfit. FALL OF THE LEAFE's first release, the demo 'Storm Of The Autumnfall', included early members vocalist Jani Lindstrom and guitarist Kaj Gustafson.
Following the recording of the 'Evanescent, Everfading' album singer Jani Lindstrom parted ways with the group being replaced by Tuomas Tuominen. Gustafson would later bail out being supplanted by M. Rostedt. T. Hatakka displaced him in turn.
Longstanding bassist Juha Kouhi exited in 2000 with his place being filled by P. Santola then P. Burka. However, Kouhi was to return to the fold the following year. For their third album the band signed with the Argentinian Icarus concern.
Members of FALL OF THE LEAFE also operate in UNHOLA. Tuominen also fronts Gothic Rock artists SARANTH.

Albums:
STORM OF THE AUTUMNFALL, Northern Sound (1996)
Into The Autumnsphere / Storm Of The Autumnfall / The Garden Of The Shoreless Sea / Starfire / Upon The Verdant Vales Of North
EVANESCENT EVERFADING, Defiled DLF 4724-2 (1998)
The Celestial Keeper / … And My Heavens Fall / The Garden By The Shoreless Sea / Wings Of My Desire Untamed / My Weeping Goddess / Starfire / With Each Fall Of The Leafe / Within The Everfrozen Winternight / Evanescent, Everfading
AUGUST WERNICKE, Icarus ICARUS07 (2000)
Into The Autumnsphere / Deference, Diminuend / Platinum / A Feather To The juniper / Machina Mimesis (In The Corner Café) / Lectured By The Demons Of Dreams / Wonder Clouds Rain / Effloresce Black And White / In Morning Mood And Utopia Revelation / Bleak Picture, August

FANGORN (GERMANY)

One man Black Metal project.

Albums:
NON RHAPSODIAN, G.U.C. 001 (1997)
Deprivation / Uisge Beatha / Sorrow Is
Knowledge / Hydra (The Head Of The
Gorgon Is Mine) / Keep On Rotting /
Palastalied / Suffer The Scornful, Die /
Part Of The Gate / (And I Leave) /
Fangorn / Wenn wir Toten Erwachen /
Der Metalmann

FATAL EMBRACE (SWEDEN)
Line-Up: Tommy Gronberg (vocals /
bass), Andreas Johansson (guitar),
Manne Engstrom (guitar), Henrik Serholt
(drums)

Gothenburg's FATAL EMBRACE came
together in 1994. A demo secured an
immediate deal with Candlelight Records.

Albums:
SHADOWSOULS GARDEN, Candlelight
CANDLE018 (1997)
Our Rotten Thirst / Path Of Virtues- That
Tepid Torment / Well Of Starclouds /
Shadowsouls Garden / Blood's Icon /
Drowned In The Grossway Water /
Under Dark Red Sunburst / As Heaven
Stood Seasonless And Dead

FEIKN (DENMARK)
Line-Up: Isaz (vocals / guitar), Inanna
(bass), Charon (drums)

Female fronted cult act FEIKN arrived
with the demo 'Visse Ting Som Haerder',
later pressed onto 7" vinyl. The band's
debut single 'Helhessen' was limited to
333 copies.
FEIKN vocalist Isaz also performed bass
with DENIAL OF GOD.

Singles/EPs:
Helhessen / Aamarden, Horror HOR001
(1998)
Visse Ting Som Haerder, Horror
HOR007 (2000)

FERMENTING INNARDS
(GERMANY)
Line-Up: Mario Weinhold (vocals), Rico
Spiller (guitar / bass), Andreas Hilbert
(guitar / bass / keyboards), Marek
Kassubeck (drums)

Originally a Death Metal outfit, this East
German group rapidly turned into more of
a Black Metal touting outfit.

Singles/EPs:
In Hate / Innocent Or Incident / Drowned
/ Eternal Sadness, Invasion IR 006 (199-
) ('Drowned' EP)

Albums:
MYST, Invasion IR 016 (1995)
Blood And Thunder / Myst / Those
Burning Thorns / Hatefid /
Transfiguration Of The Withered Beauty
/ Eternal Sadness / Mourning / The
Rising In Northern Storm / Svantfeldet
Hat / Battles On Ice

FESTER (NORWAY)
Line-Up: Rolf Tommy Simonsen (vocals /
guitar), Tiger Mathisen (vocals / guitar),
Jörgen Skjolden (bass), Jan Skjolden
(drums)

This Norwegian outfit combine Doom /
Death Metal with a brand of Black Metal
that, on the 'Silence' album, incorporates
mainly whispered vocals!

Albums:
WINTER OF SIN, No Fashion NFR 002
(1994)
Winter Of Sin / Senses Are The True
You / The Ancient Gods Wore Black /
Entering... / Victory!!! / Liberation / As
The Swords Clinch The Air / A Dogfight
Leaves A Trace / The Commitments That
Shattered
SILENCE, Lethal LRC 756 (1995)
Dream / Silent Is The Raven /
Frustrations / The Maze / The
Conformists / Voices From The Woods /
Elisabeta In My World Of Thoughts /
Growing Thirst / Nar Noen Dor

FIENDISH NYMPH (GREECE)
Line-Up: Domenica Manteli (vocals),
Pandelis Giasafakis, Spyridon Giasafakis

FIENDISH NYMPH have also issued a
Hellenic folkloric album entitled 'O
Bakxikos Choros Ton Nymphon' under
the alternate title of DAEMONIA NYMPH.
The band would fold with members
founding ARKANEX.

Albums:
THE SYBIL OF ELIKONA, Solistitium
(2000)

FILLI NIGRANTIUM INFERNALIUM
(PORTUGAL)

Portuguese Black Metal band FILLI NIGRANTIUM INFERNIUM began life as BACHTERION adopting the new title in 1992.
As BACHTERION the group issued the demo 'The Miracle Of Death'. A year later now retitled a second demo 'Os Metodos Do Pentagrama' was released.

Albums:
A ERE DO ABUTRE, Monasterium (1995)

FIMBULWINTER (NORWAY)

FIMBULWINTER is a side project of ULVER's Skoll and Shagrath of DIMMU BORGIR.

Albums:
SERVANTS OF SORCERY, Hot HR001 (1996)
Intro / When The Fire Leaps For The Ash Mountain / Servants Of Sorcery / Black Metal Storm / Fimbulwinter Sacrifice / Morbid Tales / Roaring Hellfire

FINNTROLL (FINLAND)
Line-Up: Katia (vocals), Somnium (guitar), Skrymer (guitar), Tundra (bass), Trollhorn (keyboards), B. Dominator (drums)

A quite unique proposition in Black Metal circles in that FINNTROLL base their lyrics upon the Trollish myths of Scandinavia and back it all up with Polka inspired Metal.
The band was forged by Katia and THY SERPENT and BARATHRUM guitarist Somnium who cut the demo 'Rivfader'. Later recruits were RAPTURE and ex BARATHRUM drummer B. Dominator. MOONSORROW's Trollhorn on keyboards, bassist Tundra and live guitarist Ørmy.
After the 'Midnattens Widunder' album Skrymer supplanted Ørmy.

Albums:
MIDNATTENS WIDUNDER, Spikefarm (2000)
Intro / Svartberg / Rivfader / Vätteanda / Bastuvisan / Blodnatt / Midnattens Widunder / Seger Sång / Svampfest
JAKTERS TID, Spikefarm (2001)

FIURACH (ITALY)
Line-Up: Vanth (vocals), Deathmaster (guitar), Avenir (guitar), Avadon (bass), Adonai (keyboards), Wrathlord (drums)

FIURACH is the coming together of erstwhile AGARTHI members. When AGARTHI dissolved band members created various acts including DEATHRAID, DEMON'S GATE and DOOMSWORD.
During the late 90's vocalist Vanth and keyboard player Adonai combined forces with DEMON'S GATE guitarist Avenir and Deathmaster of DOOMSWORD to forge FIURACH. Drums were handled by Wrathlord, a one time member of Norwegian act ANCIENT.

Albums:
CHAOSPAWNER, Scarlet SC007 (1999)
Prologue / Descent Of The Apocalypse Lords Part I / Descent Of The Apocalypse Lords Part II / The Rebirth / Enter The Triangle / … With Doom / Impaler's Skullchalice / The Hunt / The Divine Sword Conquest / Om Mani Padme Um / Chaospawner Part I / Chaospawner Part II

FLAMES (GREECE)
Line-Up: Nigel Foxxe (vocals), Chris Lee (guitar), Andy Kirk (bass), Gus Collin (drums)

FLAMES significantly changed line-up for the 'Summon The Dead' album bringing in vocalist Alex Oznek, guitarist Athan Schitsos and drummer George Adrian. Mainman Nigel Foxxe later formed THANATOS and NIGEL FOXXE'S INC releasing an album.
Foxxe would later figure in FORTRESS UNDER SIEGE.

Albums:
MADE IN HELL, (1985)
MERCILESS SLAUGHTER, Famous Music (1986)
Murder / Legend / Beloved Dead / Moorgile / Werewolf On The Hunt / Cocksuckin' Slave / Evil / Infidel
LIVE IN THE SLAUGHTERHOUSE, Famous Music (1987)
SUMMON THE DEAD, Famous Music FM0053 (1988)
Eastern Front / Summon The Dead / Kill For Mummy / Alcohol And Beer / Legend II (The Demon's Mind) / Legions Of Death / Avenger / Slaughterhouse / Ballad Of A Skinbeating Maniac

LAST PROPHECY, Famous Music (1989)
Revenge / Deathra / Agnostic Front /
Destiny Of Hate / Red Terror / Silo / Acid
Rain / Drinking All Night
NOMEN ILLI MORS, Molon Lave (1991)
IN AGONY WE RISE, (1992)

FLAUROS (FINLAND)
Line-Up: Wraith (vocals / guitar),
Nightswan (guitar), Thoth Sinkkonen
(bass), A. Kartzu (drums)

Albums:
MOMENTS OF TOTAL HOLOCAUST,
Twelfth Planet (2000)
Monuments Of Weakness / Paradise
Filled With Orgies / For The Twentieth
Time The Leaves Fall To The Ground /
Why Do I Bleed / Total Holocaust

THE FLESH (NORWAY)
Line-Up: Einar Fredriksen (vocals / bass),
Espen Simonsen (guitar), Morten Vaeng
(guitar), Anders Eek (drums)

THE FLESH are a very brutal Death
Metal band formed in 1993 in Drammen,
near Oslo. The quartet features two ex
members of FUNERAL (bassist Einar
Fredriksen and drummer Anders Eek)
and was originally conceived as a side
project from the duo's mothership.
Prior to debuting with the 'Storming The
Heaven's Gate' EP THE FLESH had
received some rave reviews for their
'Icecold Macabre Lust' demo.

Singles/EPs:
The Weeping Of Wrists / Inadvertent
Battery / Last Day Of Your Life / Inhuman
Misbehaviour, Arctic Serenades SERE
004 (1995) ('Storming The Heaven's
Gate' EP)

FLESHCRAWL (GERMANY)
Line-Up: Alex Pretzer (vocals), Stefan
Hanus (guitar), Mike Hanus (guitar),
Markus Amann (bass), Bastian Herzog
(drums)

FLESHCRAWL's first demo tape in 1991
was titled 'Festering Flesh'. This was
quickly followed by the self financed mini
album 'Lost In A Grave'.
1993's 'Impurity' release was produced
by EDGE OF SANITY's Dan Swano.
Prior to recording the third album,
'Bloodsoul', bassist Amann quit leaving
Mike Hanus to take up four string duty.
Although the group pursued a Doomier
direction in the early part of their career

they have since progressed into a pure
Death Metal outfit with increasingly
Satanic lyrical tendencies. The 'Bloodred
Massacre' album includes a version of
SLAYER's 'Necrophiliac'.
2000 found FLESHCRAWL on tour in
Europe as part of the 'No Mercy' festival
package alongside Poland's VADER,
America's VITAL REMAINS and
Brazilians REBAELLIUN.
FLESHCRAWL's 'As Blood Rains From
The Sky...' album sees covers of
EXCITER's 'Swords Of Darkness' and
CARNAGE's 'The Day Man Lost'.

Singles/EPs:
Lost In A Grave EP, Morbid (1991)

Albums:
DESCEND INTO THE ABSURD, Black
Mark BMCD 27 (1992)
Between Shadows They Crawl /
Phrenetic Tendencies / Perpetual Dawn /
Purulent Bowel Erosion / Lost In A Grave
/ Never To Die Again / Festering Flesh /
Infected Subconscious / Evoke The
Excess
IMPURITY, Black Mark BMCD 48 (1993)
From The Dead To The Living /
Withering Life / Reincarnation /
Subordinated / Disfigured / After
Obliteration / Stiffen Souls / Center Of
Hate / Inevitable End / Incineration
BLOODSOUL, Black Mark BMCD 88
(1996)
Bloodsoul / In The Dead Of Night /
Embalmed Beauty Sleep / Contribution
Suicide / The Age Of Chaos / Recycling
The Corpses / Nocturnal Funeral / Tomb
Of Memories
BLOODRED MASSACRE, (199-)
Hellspawn / Dark Dimension / Bloodred
Massacre / Awaiting The End / The
Messenger / Through The Veil Of Dawn /
Necrophiliac / Beyond Belief / Slaughter
At Dawn
**AS BLOOD RAINS FROM THE SKY ...
WE WALK THE PATH OF ENDLESS
FIRE,** Metal Blade (2000)
March Of The Dead / Path Of The
Endless Fire / Under The Banner Of
Death / As Blood Rain From The Sky /
Embraced By Evil / The Dark Side Of My
Soul / Swords Of Darkness / Impure
Massacre Of Bloody Souls / Creation Of
Wrath / Graves Of The Tortures / Feed
The Demon's Heart / The Day Man Lost

FLEURETY (NORWAY)
Line-Up: Alexander Nordgaren (vocals /
guitar), Svein Egil Hatlevik (vocals /

keyboards / drums)

Duo from Ttre Enebakk formed in 1991 FLEURETY debuted with a 1993 demo titled 'Black Snow' and are particularly noted for their distinctive high pitched screaming vocal technique.

During 1997 guitarist Alexander Nordgaren became live guitarist for MAYHEM's world tour.

FLEURETY's 2000 album 'Department of Apocalyptic Affairs' boasts an impressive guest list of Black Metal elite. On drums is Einar Sjurso of BEYOND DAWN and Carl Michael Eide of AURA NOIR and VED BUENS ENDE. Keyboards are contributed by Sverd of ARCTURUS. Even MAYHEM's Maniac puts in a showing.

Nordgaren also operates I LEFT THE PLANET.

Singles/EPs:
A Darker Shade Of Evil / ...And The Choirs Behind Him / My Resurrection In Eternal Hate, Aesthetic Death ADEP001 (1994)
Facets / I Saw Claws / Vortex / Outro, Supernal (1999) ('Last Minute Lies' EP)

Albums:
MIN TID SKAL KOMME, Misanthropy-Aesthetic Death AD002 (1995)
Fragmenter Av En Fortid / En Skikkelse I Horisonten / Hvileløs / Englers Piler Har Ingen Brodd / Fragmenter Av En Fremtid
DEPARTMENT OF APOCALYPTIC AFFAIRS, Supernal (2000)
Exterminators / Face In A Fever / Shotgun Blast / Fingerprint / Facets 2.0 / Last Minute Lies / Barb Wire Smile / Snap Art Version

FLOWING TEARS (GERMANY)

Line-Up: Manfred Bersin (vocals), Benjamin Buss (guitar / keyboards), Frederic Lesny (bass), Christian Zimmer (drums)

Previously known as FLOWING TEARS AND WITHERED BEAUTY issuing the 1996 album 'Swansongs'.

Albums:
JADE, Century Media (2000)

FLOWING TEARS AND WITHERED BEAUTY (GERMANY)

Line-Up: Manfred Bersin (vocals), Benjamin Buss (guitar / keyboards), Frederic Lesny (bass), Christian Zimmer (drums)

Experimental 'Dark Wave' Rock act FLOWING TEARS AND WITHERED FLOWERS were assembled in 1994 issuing their first recordings in February the following year in the form of the 'Bijou' demo.

Several line up shuffles ensued prior to a follow up tape 'Flowers In The Rain' preceding the 1996 debut album 'Swansongs'.

By 2000 the band were simply known as FLOWING TEARS releasing the 'Jade' album.

Albums:
SWANSONGS, Seven Art Music SA CD 001 (1996)
Flowers In The Rain / Waterbride / Fallen Leaves / Arion / Crystal Dance / Flowing Tears & Withered Flowers / ...Along A Dreamin' Ocean... / ...And I Drown...
JOY PARADE, Seven Art (1998)

FOG (IN, USA)

FOG heralded their arrival with the demo 'Thy Darkest Empire' in 1999. The band has also issued a shared single with Finns HORNA.

Singles/EPs:
Split, Dark Horizon (2000) (Split 7" single with HORNA)

FORBIDDEN SITE (FRANCE)

Albums:
STURM UND DRANG, Solistitium SOL 011 (1997)
Ars Gallica / Serenade Macabre / Der Sieg Der Finsternis / Aurelia / Dark Embrace / Evanescence / Ars Vampirica / Renaissance Noire / Pleurs Nocternals
ASTRALGEIST, Solistitium SOL033 (1999)
Ex Cathedra- Dies Irae / Venus Erotica / Plue Ne M'Est Rien / The Fall Of Usher / La Chouanne / Ex Cathdrea- Engels Lied / Alltagstod / Marrianne / Invocation A La Momie / "I Have Led Astray Some Stars" (Astralgeist) / "A Stone Like Still Flushes My Heart" (Astralgeist) / Ex Cathedra-Apotheose / Durch Leiden Freude

FOREFATHER (UK)

FOREFATHER is an "angolo Saxon heathen Metal" outfit forged by brothers Athelstan and Wolfstan. Session drums are from Tiowulf.

DEEP INTO TIME, Angelisc (1999)
Intro / Natural Chaos / Deep Into Time / Immortal Wisdom / Visions Of Elders / Dusk To Dawn / Ancient Voice / The Ornamented Sword / The Wilde Dance
LEGENDS UNFOLD, Millennium Metal Music MMM002 (2000)
The Fyrdman Cometh / Winds Of Eternal Freedom / Visions Of Elders / These Lands / The Path Of Yesterdays / These Lands II / Ancient voice
THE FIGHTING MAN, Angelisc (2000)
The Fighting Man / Together They Stood / For These Shores / The Call To Arms / Out Of Darkness / The Paths Of Yesterdays / The Last Battle / When Our England Died

FOREST OF IMPALED (USA)

Line-Up: Vassyl (vocals / bass), Adrian Adams (guitar), Mark Trela (guitar), Zielu (keyboards), Losiu (drums)

FOREST OF IMPALED include Polish emigrees and former NOCTURNAL SERENITY guitarist Mark Trela. The band, founded in 1992, opened with the demo 'The Dark Wilderness'. Frontman Vassyl is in reality Dan Prawica, keyboard player Zielu is Mike Zielinski whilst drummer Losiu is Andy Rusin.
Another FOREST OF IMPALED drummer Duane Timlin would also figure in the Black Death Metal act SARCOPHAGUS led by JUDAS ISCARIOT mentor Akhenaten. Under the pseudonym of Cryptic Winter the man was also part of Akhenaten's other project WELTMACHT.

Albums:
MORTIIS DEI, Vox Mortis (1995)
Beckoning Midnight Dreams / Orgy Of Unearthly Delights / Mortiis Dei / Mystic Sight Of The Infernal Horde / Dark Shadows Of The Astral World
DEMONVOID, Red Stream (1999)
For Ours Is The Kingdom (Desecrate The Heaven) / Beyond The Black Mountain Realm / The Impaler / I Metamorphosis (Birth Of The Seventh) / II Diabolis (The Seventh Dominion) / Wings Of Apocalypse / Demonvoid / The Gateway Of The Gods / Mortiis Dei

FOREST OF SOULS (FRANCE)

Line-Up: Jerome Deres (vocals / guitar), Denis Barjettas (bass / keyboards), George Noguerira (keyboards), Wilfrid Rodel (drums)

FOREST OF SOULS mix a heady brew of Doom Metal and Gothic overtones. For the 1998 album the band added guitarist Fred Mariotti.

Albums:
WAR AND POETRY, Adipocere ADS CD 001 (1995)
War And Poetry – Act I: The Ritual / The Anthem Of Eternity / War And Poetry – Act II: The Curse / Into The Infinity Sorrow Of My Mind / The Time Of Broken Gates
CONTES ET LEGENDES D'EFEANDAYL, Adipocere CD AR 041 (1998)
The Discreet Korrigan's Presence / Esmahilv / Deliverance / Dream's Challenger / … When They Watch Out / Watcher's Line / Song For The Autumn Lady / A Strange Family / Two Disturbing Souls / The Time Of Broken Gates – Part II / La Venue Du Grand Brouillard / Le Marin Des Mers De L'Ouest

THE FORGOTTEN (NY, USA)

THE FORGOTTEN embarked upon their Black Metal career with demos 'To Wake The Forest Black' in 1997 and 1998's 'The Grave'. The band drafted former DISLLUSIONED bassist Maureen Murphy in late 1998.

Albums:
CASKETS FULL OF NOISE, (1998)
L'ALDILA, Paragon (2001)

FORGOTTEN SILENCE (CZECH REPUBLIC)

Line-Up: Hanka Nogolova (vocals), Alexander Novacek (vocals / bass), Pavel Urbanek (guitar), Jan Friedman (keyboards), Miloslav Nahodil (drums)

Founded by a union of erstwhile REMEMBRANCE and SAX members. FORGOTTEN SILENCE debuted with a cassette album 'The Nameless Forever… The Last Remembrance'.
Following the 1995 'Thots' album various collaboration EP's ensued with artists such as AGONY, NOTRE DAME and DISSOLVING OF PRODIGY.
FORGOTTEN SILENCE contributed their version of 'Utok' to a planned tribute to MASTER'S HAMMER. Latterly the band has been credited as having a line up of vocalist Hanka, bassist Krusty, guitarist Medvid and drummer Chrobis.

Split, (1996) (Split EP with DISSOLVING OF PRODIGY)
Split, (1997) (Split EP with AGONY)
Split, (1999) (Split EP with NOTRE DAME)

Albums:
THOTS, Metal Age MA 0008-2-331 Obscene OBP 011 (1995)
Clara Writes… / Rosa – The Beauty / Tres Marias Part I / Tres Marias Part II / Clara – The Clairvoyant / A Night At 'Christabel Colon' / Blanca – The Endless Desire / The Awakening / Alba – The Little Girl / The Evenings / The Old Memories 'The House Of The Spirits' / … And You Read
SENYAAN, Red Black Productions (1997)
KA BA ACH, (1999)
Red Paiom- The Yellow Blue Snake / Rostau- The Sandwaves / Al Qáhir- In The Marble Halls (Of Fame) IV / Saqqára- The Sitting Statue / FL2C- The Morning In Cairo / Vaset- The Breath Of Tasechetaat / Memnon- The Ancient Moaning / Ipet Insuit- The Sunflames / Dendara- In The Deepest Depth, In The Darkest Dark… / Idfú- Under The Hor's Wings / Syere- The Water Lines / As Suwars- One Step To Another World

FORGOTTEN SUNRISE (ESTONIA)
Line-Up: Anders Meltz (vocals), Margus Gustavson (guitar), Jan Talts (bass), Tarvo Valkm (drums)

A band from Tallinn formed in 1993, after the debut demo ('Behind The Abysmal Sky') appeared FORGOTTEN SUNRISE signed to the Finnish label Rising Realm. The band's debut CD highlighted their melodic Death Metal laced with plentiful Doom influences to nice effect; the group utilizing violin, flute, keyboards and female backing vocals in the mix.

Albums:
FOREVER SLEEPING GRAVESTONES, Rising Realm REALM 003 (1994)
Unknown Land Of Silence / Ode To The Depressive Timedance / Enjoyment Of Sunrise / In Your Eyes

FORGOTTEN WOODS (NORWAY)
Line-Up: Thomas (vocals), Olaf (guitar / drums), Rune (bass)

Norwegian Black Metal act FORGOTTEN WOODS arrived with two 1993 demo sessions 'Sjel Av Natten' and 'Through

The Woods'. The first demo would later be commercially released as a single by Last Epitaph Records.
Released two albums on the No Colour label in the mid 90s although by 1997 they had retitled themselves JOYLESS and released the 'Unlimited Hate' album on the same label.

Singles/EPs:
Sjel Av Natten / En Natt Med Storm Og Ravners Skrik / Hvor Vinteren Rar, Last Epitaph CCD 102 (1996)

Albums:
AS THE WOLVES GATHER, No Colour NC002 (1995)
Eclipsed / As The Wolves Gather / In My Darkest Visions / Winter / Grip Of Frost / Dimension Of The Black Dark / Svartedauden / Through Dark And Forgotten Valleys
THE CURSE OF MANKIND, No Colour NC 006 (1996)
Overmotets Pris / My Scars Hold Your Dreams / The Starlit Waters -I, The Mountain / With Swans I'll Share My Thirst / Den Ansiksløse / The Velvet Room

FORLORN (NORWAY)
Line-Up: Alvarin (vocals / guitar / keyboards), C. Worhn (bass), Blod (drums)

FORLORN was the result of a trad Metal experiment by GEHENNA and 122 STAB WOUNDS members Sanrabb, Alvarin and C. Worhn. Alvarin also has early credits with AURVINDIR.
FORLORN drummer Blod (real name Jan Egil Fosse) also has credits with GEHENNA, ANTAIOS and INFEST. Bass player C. Worhn would also join GEHENNA.
Other stand in members for FORLORN included bassist Laeturnus and drummer S. Winter from A WINTER WITHIN.
Not to be confused with the Swedish Doom Metal FORLORN.

Albums:
FORLORN, Head Not Found (1997)
A Battle So Bright / Aerefull Ferd / Drommefanger / Heroes / Ragnarok
THE CRYSTAL PALACE, Head Not Found (1998)
Lik Av Falne Menn / Aerfull Ferd / Boerer Av Nordstjeinen / The Magellenic Clouds / The Crystal Palace / Ragnarok / Gate Of Mystic / Lunar Eclipse

AD CAELESTIS RES, Napalm NPR077 (2000)

THE FORSAKEN (SWEDEN)
Line-Up: Anders Sjöholm (vocals), Stefan Holm (guitar), Patrick Persson (guitar), Michael Hakansson (bass), Nicke Grabowski (drums)

THE FORSAKEN, previously titled SEPTIC BREED, offer Death Metal with Satanic overtones. Vocalist Anders Sjöholm also fronts MASSGRAV and OMINOUS whilst bass player Michael Hakansson plays with EVERGREY and EMBRACED.

Albums:
MANIFEST OF HATE, Century Media (2001)
Seers Hatred / Deamon Breed / Betrayal Within Individuals / Collection Of Thoughts / Soulshade / Intro- Manifest Of Hate / Dehumanised Perspective / Truth Of God / Incinerate / Inseminated By The Beast

FORSTH (SWITZERLAND)
Line-Up: Gonahr (vocals / bass), Ragnath (guitar), Thonger (keyboards), Aragorn (drums)

Undoubted Black Metallers with all the right accessories (corpsepaint, studded wristbands and unwieldy swords etc), FORSTH were previously known as GORGON, under which title the band released the 1996 album 'Winterfrost' on M.O.S. Records.

Albums:
HELVETIC WAR, Last Episode LEP017CD (1997)
Intro / True Helvetic War / Forgotten Woods / The End Of A Damned Dominion / Blutaar / Snowdance / Frozen Land / Mitternachtsnebel / Misanthropic Perfection

FROM DEPTHS (ITALY)

Singles/EPs:
The Burning Ice, Anonymous (1995) (12" single)

FROM THE DEPTHS (USA)

Black Metal band FROM THE DEPTHS issued a demo entitled 'Bereavement' after the release of their 1996 album.

Albums:
FROM THE DEPTHS, Dismal (1996)
Into The Mystery And Beyond / The Magic Of October Moons / The War Of The Captive Spirits / Fuck That Witch / Curse Of The Scarecrow / Bring Forth The Detractor / Apparitions Of Myself / Dawn Of The Crimson Harvest / And They Shall Rise Again / It Lurks / Autumn Colored Day / The Wraths Of The Others Begins / From The Depths / Outro: The Echoes Of Distant Dreams
ELYSIUM, Nightfall (1999)
Seperation / Sunshine / Regret / Elysium / Dark Angel / Thy Bright Night / Forever / Epidemic / Iron Maiden

FROSTMOON (NORWAY)
Line-Up: Massacra, Vinterfrost

FROSTMOON was originally a duo of multi instrumentalist Massacra and vocalist Tundra. Following the first demo 'Nordgesriket' Tundra exited leaving Massacra to release a further four tapes as a solo venture. Vocalist Vinterfrost was enrolled for a split EP in 1998 shared with ORK.
Tundra, also known as Arctander, performed drums for TAAKE and has his own solo project suitably titled TUNDRA.

Singles/EPs:
Ancient Vordöhus, Oskorei Productions (1998) (Split 7" single with ORK)

Albums:
TORDENKRIG, Sound Riot (2000)
Skogsrost / Vikingmakt / Iskaldt Raseri / Norgesriket Hylles / Hersker Au Morket / For Alltid / A Funeral Memorial / Behind The Snowcovered Mountains / Attack Of The Northern Frostwinds / Black Bestial Funeral
BLACK BESTIAL FUNERAL, Sound Riot (1999)

FROSTMOON ECLIPSE (ITALY)

Although essentially a solo project of guitarist Claudio Alcara FROSTMOON ECLIPSE have included vocalist and drummer Gionata Potenti within the ranks. FROSTMOON ECLIPSE has issued the demos 'Cold Silvery Eyes' in 1996 and its 1997 follow up 'To Exalt My Triumph'.
Potenti is also drummer with HANDFUL OF HATE.

Singles/EPs:
Where Possessed Souls Stand On Dark Walls EP, (1999)
Supreme Triumph In Black EP, Black Tears Productions (2000)

FROZEN SHADOWS (CANADA)
Line-Up: Amyrkhaal (vocals / keyboards), Alvater (guitar), Namtar (bass / drums)

French-Canadians FROZEN SHADOWS was created in 1995 by erstwhile members of TENEBRAE. The initial line up include guitarist Valaach and drummer Forrkas.
Valaach was superseded by Alvater and with Forrkas quitting after the 1996 demo 'Empires De Glace' bassist Namtar took on drum responsibilities.
FROZEN SHADOWS debut album 'Dans Les Bras Les Immortals' was a self financed affair. German label Millennium Metal Music reissued the inaugural demo on CD format in 2000.

Albums:
DANS LES BRAS LES IMMORTALS, Sepulchral (1999)
Dans Les Bras Les Immortals / Beyond The Pallid Vales / Au Sevil De Ténébres / Under Horrid Skies / Forsaken Whispers / Of Pure And Insufferable Torment / Lunes Funébres
EMPIRES DE GLACE, Millennium Metal Music (2000)
Au Sevil De Ténébres / Adrift In The Sepulchral Snow / Return To supremacy / Forests Of Perdition / Coldest Infinity

FROZEN SOULS (GERMANY)

German Black Metal band released a demo entitled 'Flesh In Armour'.

Singles/EPs:
The Second Gate Of Fsab Wolfenstein, (199-) (7" single)

FULGOR (GERMANY)

Black Metal band FULGOR issued the demos 'To Be One With The Stars' and 'Our 10 Urphar Visions' prior to the 'Eyequinox' single.

Singles/EPs:
Eyequinox, Merciless (1995) (7" single)

FUNERAL EVE (NJ, USA)

FUNERAL EVE arrived with the provocative demo 'Fuck Norway' in 1999. Follow ups the same year were delivered swiftly with further sessions 'Hymns For Hell' and 'Angelfuck'. 2000 found a fourth demo issued 'War And Fucking Armageddon'.

Singles/EPs:
Necrowolf EP, (2000)

Albums:
THROUGH THE GATES OF DAMNATION, (2000)

FUNERAL FROST (SWEDEN)

Swedish Black Metal crew FUNERAL FROST arrived in 1994 with the 'Midnight Speeches'.

Albums:
QUEEN OF FROST, Wolfnacht Domain (1996)

FUNERAL MIST (SWEDEN)
Line-Up: Arioch (vocals / guitar / bass), Necromorbus (drums)

Stockholm's FUNERAL MIST issued the demos 'Darkness' and 'Havoc' prior to the 'Devilry' debut album but would lose all their founder members along the way.
The band in it's original form comprised of vocalist and guitarist Typhos, guitarist Vintras and drummer Velion. Bass player Arioch was added later supplanting a previous incumbent who apparently is unworthy of even naming. FUNERAL MIST's debut gig came in 1995 and the first demo 'Darkness' the year after.
The strife began when Velion was fired and Necromorbus took the role. However, in 1996 FUNERAL MIST lost Typhos to the high profile DARK FUNERAL and subsequently Vintras was sacked due to "impressive laziness". Vintras would later join up with THYRFING but would be ejected from that band too.
FUNERAL MIST was now down to a duo of Arioch and Necromorbus. Songs destined for Arioch's side project WINDS were utilized for the sophomore 'Havoc' demo.
The mini album 'Devilry' was issued in CD and vinyl format. The latter having an exclusive track 'Hellspell 2' but limited to 300 copies.
Arioch is also a member of TRIUMPHATOR featuring on the 'Wings Of Antichrist' album.

163

Albums:
DEVILRY, Shadow 003 (1998)
The Devil's Emissary / Bringer Of Terror / Nightside Phantom / Funeral Mist / The God Supreme / Hellspell 2

FUNERAL MOON (MEXICO)
Line-Up: Impure Ehiyeh (vocals / guitar), Demogorgon (vocals / drums)

Mexican Black Metal band were created as LETO in 1993. As FUNERAL MOON released the 1994 demo 'In The Shadows' and its 1995 follow up 'Silent Night Of full Moon Shine' prior to signing to Gutteral Records for their debut album.

Singles/EPs:
Grim... Evil, Defuntes (1997) (12" single)

Albums:
BENEATH THE CURSED LIGHT OF A SA, Gutteral (1996)

FUNERAL NATION (USA)
Line-Up: Mike Pahl (vocals / bass), Chaz (guitar), Dave Chiarella (drums)

FUNERAL NATION drummer Dave Chiarella also shared employment with DISINTER. Chiarella joined USURPER in 1997 retitling himself Dave Hellstorm.

Albums:
REIGN OF DEATH, Turbo (1991)
Your Time Has Come / State Of Insanity / Reign Of Death / Midnight Hour / Sign Of Baphomet

FUNERAL ORATION (ITALY)
Line-Up: The Old Nick (vocals), Luca (guitar / keyboards), Fabban (bass), Rodolfo (drums)

A Death Metal band formed in 1989 not to be confused with the Dutch Hardcore band of the same name. FUNERAL ORATION has only one surviving member from the original line-up, guitarist Luca being that man.
Having released two demos 'Domine A Morte' and 'XXX A.S. 1995 E.V.' and a 7" EP FUNERAL ORATION toured Italy extensively before line-up changes forced the group to adopt a slightly bizarre Black Metal direction in 1993.
Having issued a new, two track demo and the 'Christic Depravations' live video Avantgarde Records stepped in to offer the Italian outfit a deal, with debut album 'Sursum Luna' arriving in 1996.

Albums:
SURSUM LUNA, Avantgarde AV 017 (1996)
Beltane's Night / Pregnant Whore / Intermezzo I / Me A Morte Libera Domine / Intermezzo II / The Age Of Apotheosis / Intermezzo III / Sursum Luna (Lunesta Trilogia) / Intermezzo IV / Stigmata / Intermezzo V / Pagan Joy / Finale

FUNERAL URN (GREECE)

Black Metal band FUNERAL URN would share a split single with NERGAL.

Singles/EPs:
Split, (1995) (Split 7" single with NERGAL)

FUNERAL WINDS (HOLLAND)
Line-Up: Golgotha (vocals), Hellchrist Xul (guitar), Esteban (drums)

Black Metal band FUNERAL WINDS first offered the demo 'La Majeste Infernale'. In 1995 the group shared a split album 'Screaming For Grace' with Japanese band ABIGAIL.
In a period of flux for FUNERAL WINDS Golgotha forged the equally nasty LIAR OF GOLGOTHA. Drummer Esteban would also join this project. Upon FUNERAL WINDS reformation Hellchrist Xul rejoined but Esteban would be replaced.
A FUNERAL WINDS 12" bootleg single emerged in 1996 sharing tracks with DEMONIC.

Singles/EPs:
Resurrection, Pagan (1993) (7" single)
Funeral Winds, Black Arts (1995) (7" single)

Albums:
SCREAMING FOR GRACE, Warmaster (1995) (Split album with ABIGAIL)
GODSLAYER XUL, Lethal (1995)

FUNERIS NOCTURNUM (FINLAND)
Line-Up: Torment (vocals), Impresoovenairmort-Nérgal (guitar), Sinéquamnon (guitar), Horgath (bass), Ruho (keyboards), Draco (drums)

FUNERIS NOCTURNUM was the result of an alliance between vocalist Torment and guitarist Grimort during 1998. The band made their entrance with the 'Slay And Burn' demo as various line up changes, including the brief recruitment of ALGHAZANTH man Veilroth, rocked the band. A stable line up was established for recording of the 'Pure Satanic Blasphemy' album but shortly after founder member Grimort bowed out. His replacement was Sinéquamnon of MACHINE MEN.

Both keyboard player Ruho and drummer Draco also play in Random while other FUNERIS NOCTURNUM members also have non Black outside projects including Torment in Death Metal act ENTER MY SILENCE and bassist Horgath in GOLD DUST.

Albums:
PURE SATANIC BLASPHEMY, Woodcut CUT011 (2000)
Burying The Last Breath Of Christianity / Damnation Of Inri / Withering Life / Slay And Burn / Pure Satanic Blasphemy / Kuolontoire / Seitsemäs Portti / Three Steps Closer To The Truth / The August Hammer Of Satan

FURTHEST SHORE (FINLAND)
Line-Up: E. Nattasett (vocals), Hexenmeister (guitar), R. Puukko (guitar), Thomas (keyboards), Thypsy (drums)

FURTHEST SHORE is one in a long line of guitarist Hexenmeister's projects. He is better known as Teemu Kautonen of WIZZARD, DARKWOODS MY BETROTHED and NATTVINDENS GRÄT.

Albums:
CHRONICLES OF HETHENESSE-BOOK 1: THE SHADOW DESCENDS, Skaldic Art (1999)

FUTURE ALIENS (GERMANY)

A Solo project from Judas Cadaver

Albums:
CRAZY, WILD AND SEXY, Outcast (1993)
Party Of A Lie / Stupid's Gonna Fuckin' Mad / Wonderworld / Warning Heart / Rational Type / Die Or Be Vicious / Nothing To Lose / Teenage Damage / Gun To Loose / Wasted Politics / Undercover Maniac / Like Those Battles Will / Ben K. Na Na Na / Work Out, Search Out / One Day Livin' / Speed Boy / Magical Night

FUTURE TENSE (HOLLAND)
Line-Up: Cock Von Drumen (vocals), Rob Weber (guitar), Tjerk Kiesel (bass), Ruud Beunder (drums)
Singles/EPs:
Go To Hell / Condemned To The Gallow / La Guilltine / Swords Of Vengeance / Evil Attack, Universe (1984) ('Condemned To The Gallow' EP)

GAAHLSKAGG
(NORWAY)
Line-Up: Gaahl (vocals)

Albums:
EROTIC FUNERAL, No Colours (2000)
Lek No Lit(t) M.O.K. / Skullfuck / N-13 / Whipper / Moralens Hammer / Great Joy / I Am Sin / Come To My Kingdom / Mankind- Development / P.T.K. / Erotic Funeral / In Memory Of... / Helveteslokk- Kom Brenne

GALLOWS OF GOLGOTHA
(AUSTRALIA)
Line-Up: Ben (vocals / guitar), Dane (vocals / bass), Mick (drums)

New South Wales trio GALLOWS OF GOLGOTHA, previously known simply as GALLOWS for their 1995 tape 'Demolition, feature erstwhile TORN drummer Mick.

Singles/EPs:
Vale Of Descending Insanity / Thoughts Forbidden / Australian Apocalypse / Galgathian Dream, (1999) ('Human Desires Of Tortured Minds' EP)

GANDALF (FINLAND)
Line-Up: Jari Hurskainen (vocals), Timo Nyberg (guitar), Sami Vauhkonen (guitar), Kirka Sainio (bass), Nalle Osterman (drums)

Albums:
DEADLY FAIRY TALES, Wicked World WICK04CD (1998)
End Of Time / Marionette / The Cradle / Dark Memories / Fade Away / The Price Of My Deeds / Forlorn / Eternal Fire / Stronger Than Hell / Never Again

GATES OF ISHTAR (SWEDEN)
Line-Up: Mikael Sandorf (vocals), Tomas Jutenfäldt (guitar), Andreas Johansson (guitar), Niklas Svensson (bass), Oskar Karlsson (drums)

Very young Lulea based GATES OF ISHTAR were created at the end of 1994. Drummer Oskar Karlsson and bassist Niclas Svenssson were previously with DECORTITION.
The band released a modestly titled demo tape the following year titled 'Best Demo Of '95' which landed them a deal with Finnish label Spinefarm Records.
The debut album, although typical Death

Metal, did also include a cover version of the W.A.S.P. hit 'I Wanna Be Somebody' and GATES OF ISHTAR were to subsequently tour with the likes of AT THE GATES, DARK TRANQUILITY and LUCIFERION.
However, both Karlsson and Svensson departed and formed THE EVERDAWN together with ex DECORTITION and SCHEITAN man Pierre Törnkvist and wound up releasing the 1997 album 'Poems- Burn The Past'.
GATES OF ISHTAR's own 1997 album, 'The Dawn Of Flames', was the last album recorded at the legendary Unisound studios.
Apparently former NECROMICON member Baron De Samedi was briefly a GATES OF ISHTAR member prior to forging BATTLELUST.

Albums:
A BLOOD RED PATH, Spinefarm SPI 31 CD (1996)
Inania / Where The Winds Of Darkness Blow / The Silence / Tears / The Dreaming Glade / When Day Light's Gone / Into Seasons Of Frost / A Bloodred Path / I Wanna Be Somebody
THE DAWN OF FLAMES, Invasion (1997)
Perpetual Dawn / Trail Of Tears / Forever Scarred / Dream Field / Dawn Of Flames / eternal Sin / No Time / The Embrace Of Winter / Where The Winds Of Darkness Blows / A Bloodred Path / The Dreaming Glade / The Silence
AT DUSK AND FOREVER, Invasion (1998)
Wounds / The Nightfall / At Dusk And Forever / Battles To Come / The Burning Sky / Never Alone Again / Always / Red Hot / Forever Beach

GEHENNA (NORWAY)
Line-Up: Sanrabb (vocals / guitar), Dolgar (guitar), Noctifer (bass), Sarcana (keyboards), Dirge Rep (drums)

Black Metal band GEHENNA debuted with the 1993 demo 'Black Seared Heart'. The band's initial line up comprised of Sanrabb and Dolgar, both on vocals and guitar, with drummer Sir Vereda. The latter soon departed in favour of Dirge Rep (real name Per Husebø) and bass was taken over by Svartalv. With this line up GEHENNAH undertook their first live performance in February 1994. Keyboard player Sarcana offered his services after this gig.

GEHENNA
Photo : Martin Wickler

GEHENNA
Photo : Martin Wickler

Svartalv was replaced by Noctifer following the second album 'Seen Through The Veils Of Darkness'.

In 1996 drummer Dirge Rep took the drum stool for EMPEROR for their contribution of HELLHAMMER's 'Massacre' to a CELTIC FROST tribute album.

Vocalist Sanrabb and other GEHENNA members Alvarin and Whorn conducted a trad Metal experimental band known as FORLORN during 1997 releasing a self titled mini album on Head Not Found Records.

The 1998 album sees the debut in GEHENNA of 122 STABWOUNDS and FORLORN drummer Blod (real name Jan Egil Fosse) and PENITENT and VINDSVAL keyboard player Damien (Asbjørn Beyer Log). Dirge Rep having joined ENSLAVED.

Blod sessioned on the 1999 TSJUDER album 'Kill For Satan'.

Singles/EPs:
Ancestor Of A Darkly Sky, Necromantik Gallery Production (1994) (7" single)
Deadlights / In Mothers Tomb / Master Satan, Moonfog (1998) (7" single)

Albums:
FIRST SPELL, Head Not Found HNF003 (1995)
The Shivering Voice Of The Ghost /

Unearthly Loose Palace / Angelwings And Ravenclaws / The Conquering Of Hirsir / Morning Star
SEEN THROUGH THE VEILS OF DARKNESS, Cacophonous NIHIL CD 9 (1996)
Lord Of Flies / Shairak Kinnummh / Vintereket / A Witch Is Born / Through The Veils Of Darkness / The Mystical Play Of Shadows / The Eyes Of The Sun / A Myth... / Dark Poems Author
MALICE-THE THIRD SPELL, Cacophonous NIHIL 16CD (1996)
She Who Loves The Flames / Made To Suffer / Touched And Left For Dead / Bleeding The Blue Flame / Manifestation / Ad Arma Ad Arma / The Pentagram / Malice / The Word Became Flesh / Before The Seventh Moon
BLACK SEARED HEART, Holycaust (1996)
Intro / Two Demons Eight Spirits / Black Seared Heart / Angelwings And Ravenclaws / The Chariots That Carried Her To The... / Outro Part I / Outro Part II / A Witch Is Born / Night Of The Serpents Judgement / Midwinter Forest
ADMIRON BLACK, Moonfog FOG 016 (1999)
The Killing Kind / Deadlights / Admiron Black / Seal Of Mans Destruction / Devils Work / Slowly Being Poisoned / Eater Of The Dead
MURDER, Moonfog FOG 025 (2000)
Murder / Worthy Exit / Devout Dementia

/ The Crucified One / Perfect Hate / To The Grave / Trail Of Blood / Master Satan / The Death

GEHENNAH (SWEDEN)
Line-Up: Mr. Violence (vocals), Rob Stringburner (guitar), Ripper Olsson (bass), Hellcop (drums)

GEHENNAH made their presence known via two now infamous demos 1993's subtly titled 'Kill' and the following year's 'Brilliant Loud Overlords Of Destruction'. A deal with Primitive Art Records was struck for the 'Hardrocker' album after which GEHENNAH launched the 'No Fucking Christmas' EP, in a limited run of 500 golden vinyl copies.
GEHENNAH's next effort 'King Of The Sidewalk' saw the band signing up to French Black Metal experts Osmose Productions. Although disowned by the band as rushed and underproduced the album made sufficient impact to score a European 1996 tour billed alongside IMPALED NAZARENE and ANGELCORPSE.
With GEHENNAH gaining ground Primitive Art Records reissued both 'Hardrocker' and 'No Fucking Christmas' in vinyl format although only 100 copies of each surfaced.
A split EP with RISE AND SHINE was also recorded.
Ronnie 'Ripper' Olson also shares his duties with VOMITORY whilst Michael 'Helltop' Birgersson operates with DAWN OF DECAY.
Members of GEHENNAH contributed to the SATANARCHY band project of 2000 with personnel from RISE AND SHINE and FURBOWL.

Singles/EPs:
Satanclaws / Merry Shitmas, Primitive Art PAR005 (1995) ('No Fucking Christmas' EP)

Albums:
HARD ROCKER, Primitive Art PAR004 (1995)
Hardrocker / Skeletons In Leather / Say Hello To Mr. Fist / Brilliant Loud Overlords Of Destruction / Winter Of War / Beerzerk / I Am The Wolf / Blood Metal / Crucifucked / Bombraid Over Paradise / The House / Gehennah / Piss Off, I'm Drinking / Psycho Slut
KING OF THE SIDEWALK, Osmose OPCD 046 (1996)
Rock n' Roll Patrol / Hellstorm / Bitch

With A Bulletbelt / King Of The Sidewalk / (You're The) Devil In Disguise / Bang Your Heads For Satan / Chickenrace / Tough Guys Don't Look Good / Saturdaynight Blasphemer / Bulldozer / Demolition Team
DECIBEL REBEL, Osmose OPCD 065 (1998)
Beat That Poser Down / Six Pack Queen / Hangover / Decibel Rebel / Hellhole Bar / Get Out Of My Way / Under The Table Again / Street Metal Gangfighters / Rocking Through The Kill / 666, Drunks And Rock n' Roll / I Fucked Your Mom / We Love Alcohol

GENOCIDE (PORTUGAL)

Albums:
GENOCIDE, Musica Alternativa MA041 (1995)
Obscure Brain / Black Plague / Brutal Evolution / World Lying / Die By Allergy / Human Thoughts / Silent Song / Mind Despair / Twisted Corpses

GENOCIDIO (BRAZIL)

GENECIDIO covered HELLHAMMER's 'Aggressor' as a secret uncredited track.

Albums:
ONE OF THEM, (1998)
DEPRESSION, (1999)
HOCTAE DROM, (1999)
POSTHUMOUS, (2000)
Pilgrim / Condemnation / Lilit And Nahemah / The Sphere Of Lilit / The Sphere Of Nahemah / Black Depth / Luciferic Man / Goodbye Kisses / Cloister / Ways / Black Planet / Illusions

GHOST (POLAND)
Line-Up: Krzysztof Berlik (vocals), Dariusz Engler (guitar), Roman Pegza (guitar), Mieczyslaw Klimek (bass), Krzysztof Jankowsky (drums)

Albums:
THE LOST OF MERCY, Loud Out CD 0011 (1994)
Anthem Of Vengeance / Morbid Game / Flag Of Shadowmaster / Alien / Bestial Rites / Cross Of Stone / Extreme Reality / The Day After / Kings Of Darkness / Fight For Your World

GHOSTORM (LITHUANIA)
Line-Up: Marius (vocals), Omenas (guitar), Tarailia (guitar), Andius (bass), Smarve (drums)

GHOSTORM, a technical Death Metal band, debuted with a 1993 demo 'The End Of All Songs' and would follow it up with the Black Mark released 'Frozen In Fire' two years later.
The album was recorded at Unisound studios in Sweden and produced by EDGE OF SANITY's Dan Swano.

Albums:
FROZEN IN FIRE, Black Mark BMCD 65 (1995)
Fraud Of Dark / There / Solitude / Frost / Dreamland / Come Back / The Sea / At Boundary / Unnormal

GLOOMY GRIM (FINLAND)
Line-Up: Whisper (vocals), Mörgoth (guitar), Lord (guitar), Ceasar (bass)

An act with a rich heritage. Guitarist Lord also operates under his alter ego of Agathon Frosteus as drummer for SOULGRIND, THY SERPENT, NOMICON and BARATHRUM. Bassist Ceasar T. MacLaunone is also a member of WALHALLA, SOUGRIND and NOMICON.
GLOOMY GRIM were borne out of the short lived HELLSTORM and bowed in with the demo 'Fuck The World, Kill The Jehovah' follwed by 'Friendship Is Friendship, War Is War' in 1998.
The debut album 'Blood, Monsters, Darkness' includes a cover version of OZZY OSBOURNE's 'Over The Mountain'.
Female vocalist Whisper has also aided SOULGRIND and NOMICON.

Albums:
BLOOD, MONSTERS, DARKNESS, (1998)
War / Asylum / Children Of The Underworld / Crucifixion / Pope Of The Black Arts / Blood / Ocean Of Candles / Ashes / The Summoning / Over The Mountain

GOAT (DENMARK)

Albums:
SACRED PILGRIM (ALLE HADER GOAT), Die Hard RRS 950(1996)
Brotherfucker / Goat / Alle Hader Goat / Goat's Revenge / Leave Goat Alone / Kill The Church / Spraeng Tarmen / Fucking Frenzy / Rip Apart / In Die Svartze Lock Ein - Dein Svin / Killing Is Goat's Game (Part I) / Killing Is Goat's Game (Part II0 / I'm Goat (We're Goat) / Daughter In

The Slaughter

GOATLORD (Las Vegas, NV, USA)

One of the earliest American Black Metal bands. GOATLORD debuted with the less than tactfully titled 'Sodomize The Goat' demo in 1988.

Albums:
REFLECTIONS OF THE SOLSTICE, Turbo (1991)
GOATLORD, JL America (1992)
Voodoo Mass / Blood Monk / Distorted Birth / The Fog / Underground Church / Chicken Dance / Acid Orgy / Possessed Soldiers Of War / Sacrifice

GOAT OF MENDES (GERMANY)
Line-Up: Marcochias (vocals / guitar), Surtur (spoken vocals), Achchazzu (guitar), Aratron (bass), Thyphaon

Black Pagan Metal outfit GOAT OF MENDES have been mostly inspired by the multitude of similar groups that emerged in the 80s.

Albums:
HYMN TO ONE ABLAZE, Perverted Taste PT 014 (1996)
Awakening / Reflections Of A Black Seared Heart / Night Of Beltane / A Pagan Lament / Crom - Cruach (Maggot Of Time) / A Crimson Flood On Frozen Snow / Hymn To One Ablaze / Belated Divine Abortion / Succubus, My Betrothed / Transcendence / Christendomes Fall / Requiem
TO WALK UPON THE WICCAN WAY, Perverted Taste (1997)
Invoking The Watchtowers / Beneath The Eye Of Hecate / I Soar The Moonless Skies / Boudicca's Triumph / Amidst The Frozen Forest / Witchfires / Pale Prince Of The Ruins / The Spirit Of Heathendom / Carnilex / Ordo Templi Orientis / Closing The Circle

GOATPENIS (BRAZIL)

Black Metal band GOATPENIS arrived with a 1992 demo 'Htaed No Tabbas' (designed to be read backwards) followed by 1994's 'Blessed By War' and a further 1995 session 'Jesus Coward'.
GOATPENIS are not noted for their subtlety.

Albums:
INHUMANIZATION, Evil Horde (1996)

GODBLOOD (CYPRUS)
Line-Up: Deceased (vocals), Adorian (guitar / bass), Panos (drums)

GODBLOOD, founded as far back as 1991, issued a split EP with MACABRE OMEN following the debut demo 'Flowers' in 1994.

Singles/EPs:
Godblood, Demonian (1998) (Split with MACABRE OMEN)

Albums:
THOSE FUNERAL TIMES, Throne Productions TAV003 (1999)
The Windfall / Midnight Reign's Circle / Like The Wolf's Skin / Tormented / In Slow Motion / Spring Delight / Funeral / The Cursed And The Ruined / Spring Delight

GODBOMB (GERMANY)
Line-Up: Peter König (vocals / bass), R.V.F. (vocals / guitar), Jan Hoffmann (drums)

Previously known as GOMORRHA. GODBOMB's album was self financed. Original drummer Thomas Henning was replaced by Jan Hoffmann.

Albums:
...STILL GOMORRHA, Godbomb BEST NR. 666 (1995)
Lost In You / Sweet Stench Degradation / D.K. / Penis Envy / ... Still Gomorrah / Refugee / No Reason (For Her Pleasure) / Micro Mortal Mental / A Hole In Head / Don't Move / Conquista 1492 / Show Me Your Butt

GODDEFIED (SWEDEN)
Line-Up: Janne Arvidsson (vocals / guitar), Jonas Aneheim (guitar), Rickard Eriksson (bass), Mattias Petersson (drums)

Albums:
ABYSMAL GRIEF, Wild Rags WRR041 (1994)

GODDESS OF DESIRE (HOLLAND)
Line-Up: Grev Drake (vocals / guitar), Count August (vocals / bass), Emperor Mark (drums), Lilith (Female Effects), Delilah (Female Effects)

Formed in 1995,by the end of the year GODDESS OF DESIRE had appeared on an RTL 4 Dutch TV special ('Ooggetuige')

and followed up the TV exposure with three support slots to GWAR the following year.
GODDESS OF DESIRE's stageshow has become notorious for the employment of two 'nasty nuns' Lilith and Delilah.
Latter day band recruits include drummer Master Blaster, second guitarist Lord Arydon and 'nun' Medusa.

Albums:
LET US WIN THIS WAR, Shivadarshana SR 1014 (1997)
Intro (Midnight Overture) / Mistress Of Inferno / War Of The Crusade / Glory In Metal / Goddess Of Desire / The Battleground / Metal To The Metals / Wall Of Terror / (The Perversity Of) Satan's Ugliest / Doomsday Warrior
LET US WIN THIS WAR II, Shivadarshana SR 1014 (1997) (Vinyl release)
Mistress Of Inferno / War Of The Crusade / Worship Me / Glory In Metal / The Battleground / Blasphemic Beasts Convoked / Wall Of Terror / Diabolic Demolition / Doomsday Warrior / (The Perversy Of) Satan's Ugliest
SYMBOL OF TRIUMPH, Metal Blade 3984 14248-2 (1999)
Blasphemic Beasts Convoked / Infernal Bestialities / Brother To Brother / Ride / Diabolic Demolition / Ruina Regnorum / Live For Metal / Worship Me / Metal Forever / Wimps And Bastards

GOD DETHRONED (HOLLAND)
Line-Up: Henri Sattler (vocals), Jens (guitar), Beef (bass), Roel Sander (drums)

Having been sensationally snapped up by American label Metal Blade Dutch outfit GOD DETHRONED then had to stand back in amazement when, quite surreally, Metal Blade announced that GOD DETHRONED's debut album, 'The Christhunt', was "boring"!
The debut album of 1992 was in fact such a hurdle for the band to overcome that GOD DETHRONED actually split up after it's release. Salkes were not exactly startling as the record company neglected to include the band's name on the cover artwork!
During the interim front man Henrik Sattler joined Thrash act MINISTRY OF TERROR and following a European support tour to IMPALED NAZARENE refounded GOD DETHRONED.
It wasn't until 1997 that the group were

170

able to follow the debut record up with 'The Grand Grimoire' album the musicians were novelly portrayed as dark age heroes, their faces juxtaposed onto medieval paintings of knights with accompanying legends testifying as to the manner of their death.

In support of the new record GOD DETHRONED opened for label mates SIX FEET UNDER on their lengthy 1997 European tour.

Hammerheart Records released GOD DETHRONED's original demo 'The Ancient Ones' on CD in 2000. The band geared up for fresh product by supplanting drummer Roel Sander with American Tony Laureano, a veteran of ACHERON, ANGELCORPSE and MALEVOLENT CREATION. Sander created INHUME.

Albums:

THE CHRIST HUNT, Shark CD034 (1992)
Necrosapiens / Hordes Of Lucifer / Christ Carnage / Infernal Sights Of A Bloody Dawn (Morbid Rites) / Necromagnon / The Christhunt / Cadavers / Unholdin' Of The Hewe / God Dethroned
THE GRAND GRIMOIRE, Metal Blade 3984-14148-2 (1997)
The Art Of Immolation / The Grand Grimoire / The Luciferion Episode / Under A Silver Moon / The Somberness Of Winter / Sickening Harp Rasps / Into A Dark Millenium / Coliseum Serenades / Fire
BLOODY BLASPHEMY, Metal Blade 39841427-2 (1999)
Serpent King / Nocturnal / The Execution Protocol / Boiling Blood / A View Of Ages / Soul Capture 1562 / Under The Golden Wings Of Death / Firebreath / Bloody Blasphemy
THE ANCIENT ONES, Hammerheart (2000)
RAVENOUS, Metal Blade (2001)
Swallow The Spikes / The Poison Apple / Villa Vampiria / Cursed By Darkness / The Mysteries That Make You Bleed / The Iconoclast Deathride / The Crowd For The Morbid / Ravenous / Autumn Equinox / Winter Campaign 2002 / Evil dead

GOD FORSAKEN (FINLAND)
Line-Up: Mika (vocals), Hannu Kujanen (guitar), Sami Ketola (bass), Teemu Hautaniemi (drums)
Previously known as PUTRID, Finnish quartet GOD FORSAKEN suffered an almost immediate setback just after the debut 1992 release, 'Dismal Gleams Of Desolation', when vocalist Mika fell victim to hearing problems in late 1993.

The band was able to record a further demo with guitarist Hannu Kujanen handling most of the vocal duties prior to Mika's return. However, shortly after recording the demo drummer Juha Pohto quit to be temporarily replaced by MYTHOS member Teemu Hautaniemi. A European tour with ANATHEMA and PYOGENESIS followed with Hautaniemi until a new drummer, Jani Viskari, could be found. This liaison was short-lived however and in late 1994 original drummer Pohto rejoined.

More line-up struggles hit the band in early 1995 after the recording of 'The Tide Has Turned' with both bassist and drummer being sacked. Quick stand-ins were found in former colleague Hautaniemi and bassist Sami Ketola.

Albums:

DISMAL GLEAMS OF DESOLATION, Adipocere AR 008 CD (1992)
Loveless / Dismal Glease Of Desolation / Waiting For The Unknown / The End Of Eternity / Who Lives Will See / In My Darkness / Exhaling Timeless Tedium / There Were Seven Suns Shine
THE TIDE HAS TURNED, Adipocere AR 025 CD (1995)
November / Forsaking The World / Until Death Joins Us Again / Jupiter / Astral Voyager 69 / The Tide Has Turned / Nowhere To Be Found / Giving It All away / It's All The Same in The End / She Dies / Goodbye

GODFUCK (ITALY)

The obviously Black Metal band GODFUCK is the product of NECROMASS member Charles Blasphemy. The eponymous mini album, an ambitious effort blending Black Metal with Electronic passages, was issued in 3" CD format.

Albums:
GODFUCK, Northern Darkness (1993)

GODGORY (SWEDEN)
Line-Up: Matte Andersson (vocals), Stefan Olsson (guitar), Mikael Dahlqvist (guitar), Fredric Danielsson (bass), Thomas Heder (keyboards), Erik Andersson (drums)

Swedish outfit GODGORY are amongst a

number of rising new groups to have been produced by EDGE OF SANITY's Dan Swano, the man having worked on the GODGORY debut 'Sea Of Dreams'. Vocalist Matte Andersson also fronts a side project band GRAVE FLOWERS releasing the 2000 album 'Solace Me'. Various other members of GODGORY are also musicians that form part of Progressive Metal act WORD OF SILENCE.

Albums:
SEA OF DREAMS, Invasion IR 021 (1995)
Intro / Sick To The Gore / Walking Among The Dead / Inside My Head / Sea Of Dreams / Surrounded By Dreams / Corporal Infection / Key To Eternity / In Silence Forever / Deathwish / Religious Fantasy
SHADOW'S DANCE, Invasion IR 025 (1996)
Abandon / Tear It Down / Rotten In Peace / Leavetaking / God's Punishment / Make You Pay / In The Ocean Sky / Shadow's Dance
RESURRECTION, Nuclear Blast (1999)
Resurrection / Crimson Snow / Adultery / My Dead Dreams / Death In Black / Collector Of Tears / Waiting For Lunacy To Find Me / Princess Of The Snow

GODKILLER (MONACO)

Extreme Satanic Death Metallers GODKILLER hail, quite bizarrely from the millionaire's playground known as the principality of Monaco!
Formed in 1994 the band released their debut demo 'Ad Majorem Satanae Gloriam' the same year. It was a tape GODKILLER swiftly capitalized on in February of the following year by offering a further tape entitled 'The Warlord'. The group has since released two albums.
GODKILLER concentrate on medieval paganistic themes and are so fundamentalist in their beliefs that mainman Duke Satanael even denounces Anton La Vey's Church of Satan as being 'weak'!!
Recent GODKILLER outings have veered towards the electronic. 'Deliverance' even quotes passages from the Bible.

Albums:
THE REBIRTH OF THE MIDDLE AGES, Wounded Love (1996)
Hymn For The Black Knights / From The Castle In The Fog / Path To The Unholy

Frozen Empire / Blood On My Swordblade / The Neverending Reign Of The Black Knights
IN GOD WE TRUST, Wounded Love (1997)
THE END OF THE WORLD, Wounded Love 737323 (1998)
The End Of The World / The Inner Pain / Down Under Ground / Following The Funeral Path / Day Of Suffering / Nothing Left But Silence / Still Alive / Waste Of Time / De Profundis
DELIVERANCE, Wounded Love WLR021 (2000)
Nothing Is Sacred / Wailing / At Dusk / When All Hope Is Gone / Dust To Dust / Far My Days Are Vanity / Wisdom / I Am A Stranger In The Earth / Deliverance

GOD MACABRE (SWEDEN)
Line-Up: Per Boder (vocals), Ola Sjöberg (guitar), Jonas Ståhlhammar (guitar), Thomas Johansson (bass), Niclas Nilsson (drums)

Albums:
THE WINTERLONG..., MBR MANGLED 6 (1995)
Into Nowhere / Lost / Teardrops / Ashes Of Mourning Life / Spawn Of Flesh / Lamentation / In Grief

GODSEND (NORWAY)
Line-Up: Gunder Audun Dragsten

A one man project pioneered by erstwhile SUFFOCATION and ATROX guitarist Gunder Audun Dragsten, GODSEND issued a three song demo in 1992 featuring drummer / vocalist Dan Swano of EDGE OF SANITY for the tracks 'Starfall', 'Slaydream' and 'Silence Of Time'. 'Slaydream' later appeared on the compilation album 'Against All Gods'.
For the debut album, 'As The Shadows Fall', Dragsten drafted in Swano once more plus another EDGE OF SANITY member, drummer Benny Larsson.

Albums:
AS THE SHADOWS FALL, Holy HOLY03 (1994)
Slaydream / As The Shadows Fall / With The Wind Comes The Rain / Autumn Leaves / Spiritual Loneliness / Beyond The Mist Of Memories / My Lost Love / Walking The Roads Of The Unbeheld / Silence Of Time
IN THE ELECTRIC MIST, Holy HOLY15CD (1995)
Down Upon You / Nobody Home / Life

Must Go On / In The Bitter Waters / Clarion Call / Voyage In Oblivion / the Sun Will Shine Again / Lost / Under Silver Linings / Tranquility / Thoughts And Shadows

GODS TOWER (BELARUS)
Line-Up: Lesley Knife (vocals), Alexander Urakoff (guitar),

Albums:
THE EERIE, Metal Agen (1993)
Reign Of Silence / When Life Ends / Inis Afalon / Till Death Do Us Part / The Eerie / Beyond Praying
THE TURNS, Metal Agen (1993)
The Turns / I Am The Raven / Seven Rains Of Fire / Twilight Sun / An Eye For An Eye / Rising Arrows / Blood / Mysterious
EBONY BIRDS, Sturmfluegel (1999)
Seven Rains Of Fire / An Eye For An Eye / Rising Arrows / Till Death Do Us Part / The Eerie / Beyond Praying / Twilight Sun / Blood / Mysterious

GOETIA (POLAND)

Albums:
WOLFTHORN, (2000)

GOLDEN DAWN (AUSTRIA)

On the surface it would seem odd that Austrian Black Metal act GOLDEN DAWN shared their first demo with Ambient band APEIRON. However, it was soon revealed that both brands were the product of just one man Dreamlord. A further GOLDEN DAWN demo 'Way Of The Sorcerer' followed in 1995.
The debut album 'The Art Of Dreaming', produced by former PUNGENT STENCH man Martin Schirenc, saw Pazuzu of the SUMMONING on guest vocals.
Dreamlord also has another act VANITAS that has issued the 'Worlds End' tape.

Albums:
THE ART OF DREAMING, Dark Matter (1997)
Ideosynchricity / The Art Of Dreaming / Nothing But The Wind / My Confession To War / Subspecie Aeternitatis / The Majesty Of The Kingdom After / The Sorcery Of The Nagual Side / Per Aspera Ad Astra / Beyond The Mortal Shell
A SOLEMN DAY, (199-)
As If All Light Had Passed Away / Soulwinter / Presence Of The Dark / A Solemn Day / Rising Sun- Sublimity Part

II / Forever Free / One And Everything / Wandering Between The Worlds

GOLGOTHA (SPAIN)
Line-Up: Amon Lopez (vocals), Vicente J. Paya (guitar), Ivan Ramos (guitar), Toni Soler (bass), Jose Nunez (keyboards), Ruben Alarcon (drums)

More of a project than an actual band, Spain's GOLGOTHA was the brainchild of UNBOUNDED TERROR's Vicente J. Paya, who felt he needed a vehicle for songs that he'd written that didn't fit the concept of his main outfit.
The debut GOLGOTHA release, the 'Caves Of Mind' mini album, received glowing reviews in Europe and this gave Paya the incentive to put something a little bit more permanent together, adding DEHUMANIZED members Ivan Ramos and Ruben Alarcon amongst others.
GOLGOTHA are believed to be one of the few Spanish acts to truly have what it takes to break on an international scale.

Albums:
CAVES OF MIND, Repulse (1994)
MELANCHOLY, Repulse (1995)
Lonely / Lake Of Memories / Nothing / Raceflections / Lost / Immaterial Deceptions / Stillness / Virtualis Demens / Caves Of Mind

GORBALROG (GERMANY)

A venture from duo Zargonath and Mortynoth.

Albums:
UNTERGANG, Millenium Metal Music SOL030 (2000)
Blutige Schwingen / Wildergeist / Stille / Ars Mortis / Sternengriff / Untergang / … Und Es Beginnt / Aeonen Verwesender Anmut

GORGON (FRANCE)
Line-Up: Chris (vocals / guitar / keyboards), Brice (guitar), Joel (bass), Seb (drums)

French Death Metallers GORGON were founded around the 1992 demo tape 'Call From Unknown Depths' which led directly to a deal with the Italian label Wounded Love Records for the 'Immortal Horde' EP.
In 1995 GORGON released their first, full length album with a dose of brutal Death Metal. The band also contributed songs

to a number of compilation albums and played shows with SAMAEL, MERCYLESS and SADIST. Indeed, guitarist Khaos was to join Swiss outfit SAMAEL during 1996!

Singles/EPs:
Immortal Horde-EP, Wounded Love (1993)

Albums:
THE LADY RIDES A BLACK HORSE, Dungeon 001 (1995)
Among Fogs Of Oblivion (Intro) / Tower Of Gargoyles / The Lady Rides A Black Horse / Call From Unknown Depths / As A stone / The Union / At The Memory Of The Past / Elizabeth / Swallowed Thoughts / Immortal Horde / The Day Required
REIGN OF OBSCENITY, Gorgon (1997)

GORGON (SWITZERLAND)
Line-Up: Ragnath (vocals / guitar), Gonahr (bass), Aragorn (drums)

Black Metal act GORGON changed titles to FORSTH after the 'Winterfrost' album and issued a 1997 album entitled 'Helvetic War' on Last Episode Records.

Albums:
WINTERFROST, MOS (1996)
Intro / Waldpfad / In The Gleam Of The Burning Timberabstract / Snowly Mountains / Mit den Gedanken im Nordischen Altertum / Winterfrost / Horde Of Avengers / Wolfshowl In The Moonshinelight / Battles Of The Dusk

GORGOROTH (NORWAY)
Line-Up: Infernus (guitar), Storm (bass), Erik 'Grim' (drums)

GORGOROTH, named after the Tolkein mythical landscapes that breed evil and led by guitarist Infernus, emerged in 1992 as a trio including vocalist Hat and drummer Goatpervertor.
The band debuted in 1994 with a demo featuring the two tracks 'Sexual Bloodgargling' and '(Under) The Pagan Megalith'. The debut 'Pentagram' album featured EMPEROR's Samoth on bass. However, due to the group's original bassist Kjetter being imprisoned for his involvement in the burning of the 800 year old church Skjold Stavkirke. Further contributions also came from SATYRICON drummer Frost. Samoth himself was imprisoned for church

burning and was duly replaced by Storm. The 1996 'Antichrist True Norwegian Black Metal' album featured second vocalist Pest of OBTAINED ENSLAVEMENT. For touring in Europe alongside SATYRICON and DISSECTION the band's line up evolved further to comprise Infernus, ex IMMORTAL drummer Erik (as 'Grim') with AETURNUS frontman Ares on bass.
It was all change again as further line up ructions hit GORGOROTH after the 1997 'Under The Sign Of Hell' opus. Infernus now joined by guitarist Tormentor, MALIGNENT ETERNAL and OBTAINED ENSLAVEMENT bassist T. Reaper, TRELLDOM vocalist Graahl with AETURNUS and THY GRIEF drummer Vrolok. GORGOROTH switched to the aggressive Nuclear Blast label in Germany for the high profile 'Destroyer' album.
Grim and Infernus also operate as members of BORKNAGER. Infernus featured on the DESEKRATOR 'Metal For Demons' album of 1999. In October of the same year erstwhile drummer Grim would commit suicide.
GORGOROTH's 2000 album 'Incipit Satan' saw the drum stool now occupied by Sjt Ericksen.

Singles/EPs:
Revelation Of Doom (Live) / Ritual (Live), Malicious (1996) (7" single)

Albums:
PENTAGRAM, Embassy TE01 (1994)
Begravelsenatt / Crushing The Sceptre (Regaining A Lost Domain) / Ritual / Drommer Om Dod / Katharinas Bortgang / Huldelokk / (Under) The Pagan Megalith / Maaneskyggens Slave
ANTICHRIST TRUE NORWEGIAN BLACK METAL, Malicious MR008 (1996)
En Stam Lukt Av Kristenblod / Bergtrollets Hevn / Gorgoroth / Possessed / Heavens Fall / Sorg
UNDER THE SIGN OF HELL, Malicious (1997)
Revelation Of Doom / Krig / Funeral Procession / Profeterus Penbaring Postludium / Deleggebe Og Undergang / Blood Stains The Circle / The Rite Of Infernal Invocation / The Devil Is Calling
DESTROYER, Nuclear Blast NB 321-2 (1998)
Destroyer / Open The Gates / The Devil, The Sinner And His Journey / Om Kristen Og Jödisk Tru / Pa Slagmark

Langt Mot Nord / Blodoffer / The Virginborn / Slottet I Det Fjerne
INCIPIT SATAN, Nuclear Blast NB 423-2 (2000)
Incipit Satan / A World To Win / Litani Til Satan / Unchain My Heart!!! / An Excerpt Of X / Ein Eim Av Blod Og Helveetesild / Will To Power / When Love Rages Wild In My Heart

GOSPEL OF THE HORNS
(AUSTRALIA)

The vocalist of GOSPEL OF THE HORNS would later fold the band to create a fresh act titled GOTH.

Singles/EPs:
Desolation Descending / Gospel Of The Horns / Eve Of The Conqueror / Time To Strike, Damnation D15 (2000) ('Eve Of The Conqueror' EP)

Albums:
THE SATANIST'S DREAM, Polyphemus (1995)
Cold Endless Seasons Of Darkness / The Satanist's Dream / Rites Of Demonic Possession / Calling For The Gods / Land Of Ancient Forests

GOTHICA (ITALY)
Line-Up: Alessandra Santovito (vocals), Roberto Del Vecchio (vocals), Carmine Giagiacomo (guitar), Laura Vinciguerra (violin), Daniele Prosperi (oboe), Luigi Pagano (percussion), Marco Bacceli (drums)

GOTHICA emerged with a self titled 1995 demo. Adding violinist Laura Vinciguerra the band contributed the track 'Nothingness' to the 1996 Italian compilation album 'Screams From Italy'. GOTHICA's first album was released on the Cruel Moon label, a sub division of Sweden's Cold Meat Industry concern.

Albums:
NIGHT THOUGHT, Cruel Moon (2000)
Stagione Oscura / Nothingness / Medusa / Spirits Of The Dead / Proserpina / Spirit Dance / The Land Under The Waves / Penelope / The Pure Nymph / The Grave / Lost In Reverie / Sepulchres

GRABESMOND (AUSTRIA)
Line-Up: Lucia M. Faroutan (vocals), Peter

175

Another in the long line of Austrian project acts. GRABESMOND comprised initially of Peter from ABIGOR and Protector of THE SUMMONING in an effort to experiment with atmospheric sounds. The duo cut the demo 'in Schwindenden Licht' prior to disbanding to concentrate fully on their main acts.

However, Peter resurrected GRABESMOND in collusion with Lucia M. Faroutan for the debut 'Mordenheim' album.

Albums:
MORDENHEIM, Draenor Productions DPR 004 (1997)
Evocation / Min Grau / Hoffest / Mordenheim / Mitternachtsball / Gravlik Staämma / Tränenmeer / Dimman Kommer Rullande / Traumwelt / Fortuna / Carnival Of Fear / Midnattssol / Endzeit
XENOGLOSSIE, Draenor Productions (1999)
Screams Of The Past / Multisum Lacrimis / Night's Dominion / Isis-Norega / Min Svart Ängel / D'Helle Phat Wirt Im Entrant / Spectacle Of Death / Blodström / Von Wolfe / Obscene Obsession / At The Edge Of The World / Totgeboren / Balder's Sturz / Totentanz

GRAND BELIAL'S KEY (USA)

GRAND BELIAL'S KEY, fronted by vocalist / drummer Lord Vlad Luciferion, opened proceedings with the 1992 demo 'Goat Of A Thousand Years' followed by a second 1994 session 'Triumph Of The Hordes'.

would join esteemed Norwegian Black Metal act ANCIENT rebilling himself Lord Kaiaphas. Meantime the band pulled in CRUCIFIER man The Black Lourde Of Crucifixion (Cazz Grant) as replacement for the 'Mocking The Philanthropist' album.
Other erstwhile band members created ARGHOSOLENT.

Singles/EPs:
A Witness To The Regicide, Sistrum (1996) (7" single)
The Tricifixion Of Swine, Spikekult (1999) (7" single)

Albums:
MOCKING THE PHILANTHROPIST, Wood Nymph (1998)
Foul Parody Of The Lord's Supper / Shemhamforash / Reflections Of The Coffin Lid / The Slums Of Jerusalem /

Castrate The Redeemer / Sumerian Fairytale / At The Blessed Grotto / Savouring The Virgin's Pessary / In Rapture Of The Fenrir Moon / Demonarchy / The Centaur / Conspicuous Imagery Adorns The Nunnery / The Seventh Enochian Key / The Holocaust Trumpeter

GRAVE FLOWERS (SWEDEN)

GRAVE FLOWERS is the Doom side project of GODGORY front man Matte Andersson. Prior to the 'Solace Me' album GRAVE FLOWERS had tested the waters with the 1997 demo "Gamonbozia'.

Albums:
SOLACE ME, Last Episode CD 5 2030 20 561 (2000)
Insomnia / Mentally Exposed / No More Winters / Wistful Whispering / Voluntary Silence / Dayexchange / Different Moods

GRAVELAND (POLAND)

Polish extreme Black Metal act GRAVELAND arrived with the 1992 demo sessions 'Necromanteion' and 'Drunemeton'. The following further demos were released titled 'Epilogue', 'In The Glare Of Burning Churches' and 'Celtic Winter'. Many of these demos were subsequently pressed onto vinyl.
Darken of GRAVELAND is also a member of INFERNUM and has issued the albums 'Forgotten Songs' and 'Heralds Of Flight' with his solo venture LORD WIND. He also contributes to the debut VELES album 'Night On The Bare Mountain'.

Singles/EPs:
Hordes Of Empire / The Gates To The Kingdom Of Darkness / The Return Of Funeral Winds, No Colours (1994) ("The Celtic Winter' EP)
Intro- Day Of Fury / Sons Of Fire And Steel- Servants Of War / Sacrifice For Honour / Outro- To Die In Glory, (1998) ('Immortal Pride' EP)

Albums:
CARPATHIAN WOLVES, Eternal Devils (1994)
Carpathian Wolves / Barbarism Returns / In The Northern Carpathians / Impaler Of Wallachia / Witches Holocaust / At The Pagan Samhain Night / Unpunished Herd / Into The War

THOUSAND SWORDS, Lethal (1995)
Intro / Blood Of Christians On My Sword /
Thousand Swords / The Dark Battlefield /
The Time Of Revenge / Born For War /
Black Metal War / To Die In Fight / Outro
THE CELTIC WINTER, (199-)
Intro / Call Of The Black Forest / Hordes
Of Empire / The Night Of Fullmoon /
Prolog / The Gates To The Kingdom Of
Darkness / The Return Of Funeral Winds
**IN THE GLARE OF BURNING
CHURCHES**, No Colours (1996)
In The Glare Of Burning Churches / The
Night Of Fullmoon / The Dark Dusk
Abyss / Through The Occult Veil / For
Pagan And Heretics Blood / Instrumental
/ Hordes Of Empire / Outro- The Gates
To The Kingdom Of Darkness
FOLLOWING THE VOICE OF BLOOD,
No Colours NC012 (1997)
Intro / White Hands power / Thursaz /
Following The Voice Of Blood / Forge Of
Souls / Raise The Swords / And The
Horn Was Sounding Far Away / Fed By
The Beasts / Outro
EPILOGUE, (199-)
Intro / The Eyes Of Balor / Shadow Of
Doom / The Forest Nementon Part II /
children Of The Moon / Outro / In The
Glare Of Burning Churches / The Night
Of Fullmoon / The Dark Dusk Abyss /
Through The Occult Veil / For Pagan
And Heretics Blood

GRAVEWORM (ITALY)
Line-Up: Stefan Flori (vocals), Stefan
Unterpertinger (guitar), Harald Klenk
(guitar), Didi Schraffl (bass), Sabine Mair
(keyboards), Martin Innerbichler (drums)

The sophomore GRAVEWORM release
contains a version of HELLOWEEN's
'How Many Tears' and a guest vocal
appearance by CRADLE OF FILTH
backing vocalist Sarah Jezebel Diva.

Albums:
WHEN DAYLIGHT'S GONE, Serenades
SR010 (1997)
Awake / Lost Yourself / Far Away / Eternal
Winds / Dark Silence / Tears From My
Eyes / When The Sky Turns Black /
Another Season / Aeons Of Desolation
UNDER THE CRESCENT MOON, Last
Episode (1998)
Awaiting The Shining / Awake... Thy
Angels Of Sorrow / By The Grace Of
God / How Many Tears
**AS THE ANGELS REACH THE
BEAUTY**, Serenades (1999)
A Dreaming Beauty / Portrait Of A

Deadly Nightmare / Ceremonial
Requiem / Nocturnal Hyns / Behind The
Curtains Of Darkness / Pandemonium /
Prophecies In Blood / Into The Dust Of
Eden / Graveyard Of Angels
SCOURGE OF MALICE, Last Episode
(2001)

GRAVEWURM (NM, USA)
Line-Up: Tyrant (vocals), Funeral Grendel
(guitar), Massacre (bass), Desecrator
(drums)

New Mexico's GRAVEWURM released
the demos 'Possessed By Darkness',
'Massacre In Blood' and 'Nocturnal
Spells' during the mid 90's. A fourth effort
'Command Of Satan's Blade' emerged in
1998.
The GRAVEWURM album 'Ancient
Storms Of War', although issued in 1999,
was recorded some four years earlier.

Albums:
ANCIENT STORMS OF WAR, Barbarian
Wrath (1999)
At The Gates Of Armageddon / Riders
Of The Cursed One / On Icy Plains I Die
/ Nocturnal Spells / Dwellers Of
Darkness / Descend Into The
Underworld / Slaughtered On The Altar /
Beneath The Moonfog / Cranial
Splendour / Ancient Storms Of War / The
Dark Horde / Cadaveric Dementia / A
Once Forgotten Kingdom / The Gorging /
Rise From The Crypts / Possessed By
darkness / Black Candles
COMMAND AT SATAN'S BLADE, (1999)
At The Gates Of Armageddon / When
Death Is Near / Summon The Dead /
Diabolic Storm / Funeral Tyrant / Visions
Of Centuries Past / Necrowitch / Minions
Of The Sinister / Massacre In Heaven
(Demo) / Invert The Cross (demo) /
Wizards Of War (Demo)

GRAVHEIM (NORWAY)
Line-Up: H.M. Cron (vocals), Hegal
(guitar), Abaddon (bass)

GRAVHEIM are fronted by H.M. Cron
(real name Ronny Muggerud) and
guitarist Heval (real name Torstein
Aaring). Hevel also has credits with
MOLOCH and SANZIA.

GREEN CARNATION (NORWAY)

GREEN CARNATION are a project band
assembled by ex EMPEROR and
SATYRICON member Tchort, guitarist

177

Christer C.H. Botteri and bassist X. Botteri of IN THE WOODS as well as personnel from DRAWN, CARPATHIAN FOREST along with TRISTANIA's Vibeke. GREEN CARNATION is in fact the band Tchort decamped from to join EMPEROR in 1990. With this reversal the other band members evolved the act into IN THE WOODS.

Guest vocals on the 2000 album come courtesy of Synne Soprana.

Tchort would go on to create BLOOD RED THRONE with Death of SATYRICON and vocalists Ronni Thorsen and Vidar Helseth.

Albums:
JOURNEY TO THE END OF THE NIGHT, Prophecy Productions (2000)
Falling Into Darkness / In The Realm Of The Midnight Sun / My Dark Reflections Of Life And Death / Under Eternal Stars / Journey To The End Of Night (Part I) / Echoes Of Despair (Part II) / End Of Journey (Part III) / Shattered (Part IV)

GRIEF OF EMERALD (SWEDEN)
Line-Up: Johnny Lehto (vocals / guitar), Anders Tång (bass), Robert Bengtsson (keyboards), Jonas Blum (drums)

GRIEF OF EMERALD was founded by former DECAMORON and ODERU man Johnny Lehto with bassist Anders Tång of NECROFEAST and MASTEMO. The band later added NIDEN DIV 187 drummer Fredrik.

An album provisionally titled 'Signs From A Stormy Past' was recorded for Scottish label Deviation but was shelved. Some tracks from these sessions were used for the 'Nightspawn' mini album.

Fredrik made an exit being replaced by Jonas Blum of RUNEMAGICK and DEATHWITCH for the 'Malformed Seed' album.

Albums:
NIGHTSPAWN, Listenable POSH013 (1998)
The Beginning / Winds Of Vengeance / Warsworn / Famine / Revival / Nightspawn / Day Of Doom / Trinitia Damnation / The Second Dynasty
MALFORMED SEED, Listenable (2000)
Like The Plague We Shall Spread / Wingless / Threshold To Fire / Nightstalker Pentagram Warrior / Holy Book- Holy Shit / Beaten Beyond Recognition / Malformed Seed / Life Has Lost

GRIFFIN (NORWAY)
Line-Up: Tommy Sebastian (vocals), Kai Nergaard (guitar), Marcus (guitar), Johnny Wangberg (bass), Marius Karlsen (drums)

Initially a project of BLOODTHORN guitarist Kai Nergaard and ATROX and BETHZAIDA man Tommy Sebastian GRIFFIN would evolve from a kickabout rehearsal hobby to a fully fledged band. Second guitarist Marcus was added in December 2000. GRIFFIN cut tracks for a limited edition EP in early 2001 comprising of live tracks and cover renditions of TURBONEGRO's 'Bad Mongo' and IRON MAIDEN's 'Wrathchild'.

Albums:
WASTELAND SERENADES, Season Of Mist (2000)
Mechanized Reality / The Usurper / Spite Keeps Me Silent / Obsession / New Business Capitalized / Hunger Strike / Always Closing / Punishment Macabre / Exit 2000 / Wasteland Serenade / Dream Of Dreamers (Bliss 2)

GRIMOIRE (ISRAEL)

Israeli Black Metal act GRIMOIRE first surfaced in 1995 with their demo 'In The Darkwoods Sovereignty'.

Albums:
A REQUIEM FOR THE LIGHT, Euphonious PHONI003 (1996)
A Requiem For The Night / At Dark / Above The Silvery Fog / The Immortal Warrior Spirit / Nevuath Ha'Tom / In The Darkwoods Sovereignty / Our Agony / Vampires / … And On With Darkness

GRIMTHORN FOREST (AUSTRIA)

Solo outing from VOBISCUM, CLANDESTINE and SERAPH member Count Grimthorn. The multi instrumentalist Grimthorn had operated as a drummer with his previous acts going under the stage name of Dunkelfürst.

Albums:
GRIMTHORN FOREST, DMS Productions (2000)

GROMS (NORWAY)
Line-Up: Øyvind Haugland (vocals / guitar), Hans Dalen (guitar), Haakon

Johannesson (bass), Petter Gordon
Jensen (drums)

Kristiansand based Doom Metal outfit
GROMS date back to 1992. The group
toured Poland in 1993 and issued the
'Ascension' album two years later.

Albums:
ASCENSION, Arctic Serenades SERE
002 (1995)
Ascension / From Dust To Dust / True
Wisdom / The Riddle / Truth
Misunderstood / Noone / The End Of
The Age / The Voice Of Righteousness /
The Just Shall Live By Faith

HADES (ALMIGHTY)
(NORWAY)
Line-Up: Janto Garmanslund (vocals / bass), Jorn Inge Tunsberg (guitar), Stig (guitar), Remi (drums)

Previously known as HADES (NORWAY) due to confusion with the American HADES. In their previous incarnation HADES (NORWAY) released the 'Alone Walkying' EP in 1993 and full length albums 'Again Shall Be...' in 1995 and 1997's 'Dawn Of The Dying Sun'.

Albums:
MILLENNIUM NOCTURNE, Hammerheart (1999)
Millennium Overture / Dream Traveller / Carnival Blaspheme / Nemesis / To Reach Divine Fulfillment / Candles Of Chaos / A Ballad Of Death And Obsession / Nighttime Endurance / Warcry

HADES (NORWAY) (NORWAY)
Line-up: Janto Garmanslund (vocals / bass), Jorn Inge Tunsberg (guitar), Stig (guitar), Remi (drums)

HADES (NORWAY), founded in 1992 by erstwhile IMMORTAL bassist Janto Garmanslund, adopted the addition of their home country to their name after their 1993 demo 'Alone Walkyng' appeared following protests from the American HADES. Drummer Remi is ex DARK.
Guitarist Jorn Inge Tunsberg had pre HADES (NORWAY) been involved with both OLD FUNERAL and SATANAEL, two almost mythical acts that included both Varg Vikernes of BURZUM notoriety and IMMORTAL's Abbath.
HADES (NORWAY)'s debut album, issued in 1995, found the group offering familiar Norwegian Black Metal based around Viking and pagan themes.
With the release of the 1997 album 'Dawn Of The Dying Sun' the record company took the opportunity to reacquaint the public with the 1995 debut, releasing both albums together as a double vinyl album set limited to 1'000 copies.
HADES (NORWAY) became HADES (ALMIGHTY) for 1999's 'Millenium Nocturne' album.

Singles/EPs:
Unholy Congregation / Hecate (Queen Of Hades) / Alone Walkyng, Wounded Love WLR008 (1993) ('Alone Walkyng' EP)

Albums:
AGAIN SHALL BE..., Full Moon (1995)
Pagan Triumph / Hecate (Queen Of Hades) / The Ecstasy Of An Astral Journey / An Oath Sworn In Bjorguin / ...Again Shall Be / The Spirit Of An Ancient Past / Unholy Congregation / Glorious Again The Northland Shall Become / Be-Witched / In The Moonless Sky
DAWN OF THE DYING SUN, Full Moon (1997)
Dawn Of The Dying Sun / The Awakening Of Kings / Apocalyptic Prophecies (The Sign Of Hades) / Alone Walkying / Crusade Of The Underworld Hordes / The Tale Of A Nocturnal Empress / The Red Sun Mocks My Sadness / Pagan Prayer

HADEZ (PERU)
Line-Up: Ron King (vocals), Jhon Agressor (guitar), Walter Crucifer (guitar), Frank Silent (bass), O.A.D.M. (drums)

Peruvian Black Death Metal outfit HADEZ, founded in 1989, debuted with the 'Extreme Badness On The World' demo.

Albums:
AQUELAREE, Brutal (1996)
IF YOU DIE A THOUSAND TIMES, Conquistador (199-)

HAGALAZ' RUNEDANCE
(NORWAY)

HAGALAZ' RUNEDANCE is the project of AGHAST's Nebel, real name Andrea Meyer-Haugen.

Singles/EPs:
When The Trees Were Silenced, Elfenblut (1997)
On Wings Of Rapture, Well Of Urd (2000)

Albums:
THE WINDS THAT SANG OF MIDGARD'S FATE, (1998)
When The trees Were Silenced / Behold The Passionate Ways Of Nature / The Home That I Will Never See / The Oath He Swore On Wintersday / Seidr / Das Fest Der Wintersonne (Ein Wihnachtsliel) / A Tale Of Fate (Folksgang Awaits) / When The Falcon Flies / serenade Of

The Last Wolf / Mother Of Times
VOLVEN, Well Of Urd (2000)
The Dawning / Seeker Divine / Volven /
Alva / Solstice Past / On Wings Of
Rapture / Wakle Skaldi / Dreaming Wild
White Horses / Your World In My Eyes /
On Wings Of Rapture (Vision Of Skuld)

HAIMAD (SWEDEN)
Line-Up: Agilma (vocals / bass), Azradan
(guitar), Ammith (guitar), Fenalk
(keyboards), Keuron (drums)

Sundsvall Black Metallers HAIMAD
bowed in with the 1996 demo 'A Dream
Vision Vanished'. A second session 'The
Horned Moon' was pressed onto CD by
Occult Records.

Albums:
THE HORNED MOON, Occult (1997)

HA LELA (LITHUANIA)
Line-Up: Vaidas (vocals), Laura (vocals),
Vilma (vocals / kankles), Lauras (guitar /
keyboards), Ramûnas (guitar / bass /
keyboards), Donatas (pipe / dambrelis /
lumzdelis), Aurius (drums)

HA LELA are named after an ancient
legendary Lithuanian war cry. Their first
demo 'Rauda' in 1994 was a poorly
produced affair but the quality material
garnered the band exposure in the
worldwide Black Metal press.
A further tape in 1996 'Pabudimas'
('Awakening') led to a deal with Eldethorn
Records, an offshoot of Neat Metal
Records.
Guitarist Ramūnas also plays with
ZPOANVTENZ and POCCOLUS.

Albums:
PABUDIMAS, Eldethorn ELD003 (1998)
Pabudimas / Sidabrinés Saulés Simbolis
/ Audros Sirdis Ir Kraujas / Isjojo Bernelis
/ Prakeiktas Troskimas / Sokis... Septyni
Ratai / Reikejo Zengti Tris Zingsnius

HANDFUL OF HATE (ITALY)
Line-Up: Nicola B. (vocals / guitar), Marco
M. (guitar), Enrico S. (bass), Gionata
Potenti (drums)

Italian Black Metal band based in Lucca.
HANDFUL OF HATE arrived in 1995 with
the demo session 'Goetia Summa'. The
band, centred upon vocalist / guitarist
Nicola B., had been founded some two
years earlier unfortunately suffering the
tragedy of having bassist Urgo die in

1994.
HANDFUL OF HATE has had numerous
line ups with their rhythm section of J.M.
and bassist Andrea B. decamping in early
1998. A short term replacement was ex
DEATH SS man Felix Moon.
Latterly the band has drafted
NECROMASS guitarist Marco M,
MIDGARD bass player Enrico S and
drummer Gionata Potenti of
FROSTMOON ECLIPSE.

Albums:
GLYPHOTIC SUPREMACY, Northern
Darkness (1997)
Reborn From Ashes- Phoenix Mass /
Erection- Delightful Rape Of The Stellar
Virginity / Urd Va Rundan / Prophecy Of
A New Assiah's Supremacy / A Red
Moon Ariseth Upon The Silent Sky /
Nuit- Lustful Receptacle Of Erected
Power / Undicias Ah-Qliphah / astral
Offspring Of Abhorrence / Beyond The
Everwhelming Circles / La Notre Di Pan
HIERARCHY, Northern Darkness (1999)
The XI Wings Of Death / Disparity /
Fleshcrawling Blasphemy / Stifled Into
Extremism / The Slaughter Of The Slave
Gods / Scars Of Damnation / Masters
Pleasure / The Bleeding Lips Of Grace /
Submission (The Fine Art Of Sodomy) /
The Rise Of Abomination

HATE ETERNAL (USA)
Line-Up: Erik Rutan (vocals / guitar), Alex
Webster (bass), Tim Yeung (drums)

HATE ETERNAL, alongside ALAS, is one
of the two bands led by MORBID ANGEL
and ex RIPPING CORPSE guitarist Erik
Rutan and CANNIBAL CORPSE bassist
Alex Webster
For recording of the 'Conquering The
Throne' album HATE ETERNAL pulled in
ex INTERCINE bassist Jared Anderson
and SUFFOCATION's guitarist Doug
Cerrito.
Rutan still assists MORBID ANGEL as
live guitarist and is a noted producer,
having handled Brazilian act KRISIUN's
2000 album.
HATE ETERNAL toured as support to
CANNIBAL CORPSE and DETHRONED.
The band's latest line up including former
MALEVOLENT CREATION drummer
Derek Roddy.
Rutan also operates a Symphonic female
fronted Metal project titled ALAS.

Albums:
CONQUERING THE THRONE, (1999)

Praise Of The Almighty / Dogma Condemned / Catacombs / Nailed To Obscurity / By His Own Decree / The Creed Of Chaotic Divinity / Dethroned / Sacrilege Of Hate / Spiritual Holocaust / Darkness By Oath / Saturated By Dejection

THE HAUNTED (SWEDEN)

Line-Up: Marco Aro (vocals), Jensen (guitar), Anders Bjorler (guitar), Jonas Bjorler (bass), Per Moller Jensen (drums)

A Death / Thrash act with strong Black Metal links. THE HAUNTED was founded by former SÉANCE guitarist Jensen during the summer of 1996 bringing in erstwhile INFESTATION, AT THE GATES and TERROR guitarist Anders Bjorler together with drummer Adrian Erlandsson. THE HAUNTED also drafted former DISSECTION and CARDINAL SIN man John Zweetsloot on bass. Zweetsloot's tenure would be brief and another ex AT THE GATES man Jonas Bjorler would take his place.

The band attempted to lure in a lead vocalist and discussions were held with Toxine of SATANIC SLAUGHTER and WITCHERY, and Rogga of MERCILESS. Ultimately it would be Peter Dolving of MARY BEATS JANE that landed the job. During 1997 Erlandsson created the side project HYPERHUG. Within time he would decamp from THE HAUNTED to concentrate on this act full time. THE HAUNTED attempted to fill the drum position with DISSECTION and OPTHALAMIA man Ole Öhman. Fate intervened when HYPERHUG's singer damaged his hearing curtailing the group. Erlandsson rejoined his former colleagues.

A deal was soon struck with Earache Records and THE HAUNTED undertook touring in Europe with NAPALM DEATH. Shortly after Dolving quit to found ZEN MONKEY. His replacement was FACEDOWN's Marco Aro. With this new line up the band toured the European festival circuit in 1999.

THE HAUNTED was offered the support slot to TESTAMENT's American dates the same year but in mid rehearsal for these shows Erlandsson quit to join premier British Black Metal band CRADLE OF FILTH. The tour went ahead with Per Moller Jensen of KONKHRA and INVOCATOR fame.

Albums:
THE HAUNTED, Earache (1999)
Hate Song / Chasm / In Vein / Undead / Choke Hold / Three Times / Bullet Hole / Now You Know / Shattered / Soul Fracture / Blood Rust / Forensick
THE HAUNTED MADE ME DO IT, Earache (2000)
Dark Intentions / Bury Your Dead / Trespass / Leech / Hollow Ground / Revelation / The World Burns / Human Debris / Silencer / Under The Surface / Victim Iced

HAVAYOTH (SWEDEN)

Line-Up: Andreas Hedlund (vocals), Morgan Hansson (bass)

HAVAYOTH, a project of Markus E. Norman of BEWITCHED and ANCIENT WISDOM with NAGLFAR guitarist Morgan Hansson on bass.

Albums:
HIS CREATION REVERSED, Hammerheart (2000)
Transcendence / Mirrors / The Watcher / Burn / Starfall / Teleon / Wound / Dreaming / Fallen

HAVOHEJ (USA)

Extreme Black Metal band founded by Paul Ledney of PROFANITICA. Ledney also has credits with INCANTATION and REVENANT.
Erstwhile PROFANATICA and INCANTATION man Brett Makowski performed session guitars on the 'Dethrone The Son Of God' album.

Singles/EPs:
Unholy Darkness And Impurity / Behold The Prince Of Peace / March Of The Seven Priests Of Mockery, Damnation Of God (1993) ('Unholy Darkness And Impurity' EP. 7" single)
Black Perversion / Unholy Godown / Mary Goddess Of Shit, (1994) (12" single)
The Black Mist / Enlightened One, Axtion (1994) (7" single)

Albums:
DETHRONE THE SON OF GOD, Candlelight (1993)
Spilling Holy Blood / Final Hour Of Christ / Weeping In Heaven / I Arose / Heavenly Father / Once Removed Saviour / Raping Of Angels / The King Of Jews / Behold The Prince Of Peace / Holy Blood, Holy

Grail / Fucking Of Sacred Assholes / Nazarene Decomposing

HECATE ENTHRONED (UK)
Line-Up: Jon (vocals), Marc (guitar), Nigel (guitar), Paul (bass), Michael (keyboards), Craig (drums)

An industrious British Black Metal style outfit that debuted with the demo 'An Ode For A Haunted Wood'. Vocalist Jon was previously bass player with CRADLE OF FILTH.
The 1999 album saw fresh faces as ex EWOC vocalist Dean Seddon supplanted Jon, keyboard player Michael made way for Daz and drummer Rob returned to the fold.

<u>Albums:</u>
UPON PROMETHEAN SHORES (UNSCRIPTURED WATERS), Blackened BLACK002CD (1996)
Promethea- Thy Darkest Mask Of Surreality / The Crimson Thorns (My Immortal Dreams) / A Graven Winter / To Feed Upon Thy Dreams / An Ode For A Haunted Wood / Through Spellbinding Branches (Deepest Witchcraft)
THE SLAUGHTER OF INNOCENCE, A REQUIEM FOR THE MIGHTY, Blackend (1997)
Goetia / Beneath A December Twilight / The Spell Of The Winter Forest / A Flame In The Halls Of Blasphemy / A Monument For External Martyrdom / The Slaughter Of Innocence / At The Haunted Gallows Of Dawn / Christfire / Within The Ruins Of Eden / The Danse Macabre / The Beckoning
DARK REQUIEMS AND UNSILENT MASSACRE, Blackened BLACK012CD (1998)
In Nomine Satanas / The Pagan Swords Of Legend / Centuries Of Wolven Hunger / Forever In Ember Drowning / Upon The Kingdom Throne / For Thee In Sinful Obscurity / Dark Requiems And Unsilent Massacre / Thy Sorrow Bequethed / The Scarlet Forsaken / Ancient Graceless Dawn
KINGS OF CHAOS, Blackened (1999)
Miasma / Perjuror / Deceiving The Deceiver / Malignant Entity / Blessing In Disguise / I Am Born / Exalted In Depravity / Conquest Complete / The Downfall / Repent / Witch queen Ascending

HEFEYSTOS (POLAND)
Line-Up: Nantur Aldaron (vocals / bass), Alicja Szumska (vocals), Zeffar (guitar), Heiglot (guitar), Piotr Weltrowski (keyboards), Piastun Aothar (drums)

Formed at the end of 1994, by the summer of the following year Polish outfit HEFEYSTOS had recorded their 'Vilce Sjen' EP, although this was never actually released officially! Still, a full album followed in 1996.

<u>Singles/EPs:</u>
Vilce Sjen EP, (1994) (Never officially released)

<u>Albums:</u>
HEFEYSTOS, Atratus Last Epitaph (1996)
Urok Samotnosci / Magiczny Strumién / Czarna Lza / Starych Legend Czar / Glos Z Ogrodow Niwy / Gdzie Milczy Kazdy Cién
PSYCHO CAFÉ, Wounded Love WLR 016 737224 (1998)
Love Is The Law / Our Lady Of The Whores / Credo / 3 Is The Key / Away / U Gonna Bleed For Me / Everyone Is A Star / Rats / Adoration Of The Earth / Thursday Evening / The Kingdom Is Mine / Psycho Cafe

HEIDENREICH (AUSTRIA)

Chaos Metal assemblage of ABIGOR and AMESTIGON members.

<u>Albums:</u>
A DEATH GATE CYCLE, Napalm (1998)
A Death Gate Cycle / The Prophet's Sacrifice / Frozen Tears / Todeswunsch / The Goat Shrine / Memories Of A Descending Moon
TRANCE OF AN UNHOLY MAN, Napalm (1999)
An Incarnations Dream / Cosmic Reflections / The Shadoweaver / The Slumbering terror / grim And Bitter Heart / Trance Of An Unholy Man / Das Astrale Element / Heart Of Midnight- Genocide

HELHEIM (NORWAY)
Line-Up: Vanargandr (vocals / bass), Hrimgrimmir (guitar), Hrymr (drums / keyboards)

Formed in 1992 by Vanargandr and Hrimgrimnir, skinsman Hrymr completed the trio in 1993 whilst a fourth member, Nidhogg, was briefly a member of the group for the recording of the first HELHEIM demo before leaving after it

was completed.
The band next recorded a fifty minute long demo entitled 'Nidr Ok Nord Liggt Helvegr'. This tape gained the group a deal with the German based Solistitium label. The 'Jormundgand' album was produced at the legendary Grieghallen Studios.

Stylistically, HELHEIM deal in aggressive Black Metal, although they are not lacking in melody in places. Not to be confused with the other Norwegian HELHEIM that issued the 1996 'Fenris' album.

Albums:
JORMUNDGAND, Solistitium SOL003 (1996)
Jormundgand / Vigrids Vard / Nidr Ok Nordr Liggr Helvegr / Gravlagt I Eljudne / Svart Wisdom / Jotnevandring / Nattravnens Takt / Galder
AV NORRØN AETT, Solistitium SOL009 (1997)
En Forgangen Tid / Vinterdoden / Fra Ginnunga- Gap Til Evig Tid / Mork, Eng Vinter / Apenbaringers Natt / De Eteriske Andevesenes Skumringsdans / Av Norrøn Aett
BLOD & ILD, Ars Metalli (2000)
Blod And Ild / Evig / Helten (Pt II) / Jernskogen / Asgardsreien / Kjenn Din Fiende / Odins Moy / Terrorvelder / Yme

HELHEIM (NORWAY)

One of two Norwegian HELHEIM's.

Albums:
FENRIS, Necropolis (1996)
Synders Makt / Saga Morket / Amok / Fimbulwinter

HELL (UK)
Line-Up: Dave G. Halliday (vocals), Kev Bower (guitar), Tony Speakman (bass), Tim Bowler (drums)

A Nottingham based theatrical Black Metal band way before their time, HELL were local heroes and their influence could later be seen plainly in SABBAT.
The band, including ex RACE AGAINST TIME vocalist Dave G. Halliday and former PARALEX trio of Kev Bower, Tony Speakman and Tim Bowler, toured extensively, supporting the likes of THIN LIZZY, JAGUAR, MORE, URIAH HEEP and MAMA'S BOYS. Their self financed single, recorded at Ebony Records studios, sold well but was slated in 'Kerrang!' magazine who simply failed to

comprehend the band's direction. A further cassette single followed in 1984 featuring 'In The Depths Of Despair', 'Land Of The Living Dead' and 'Plague And Fire'. The band also drafted in an additional guitarist in Sean Kellen.
HELL also demoed 'Devil's Deadly Weapon' before signing to Belgian label Mausoleum, but two weeks prior to recording a proposed album the label collapsed. Disillusioned, HELL split and, sadly, Halliday later committed suicide.
Bassist Tony Speakman was to join SYZ releasing the 1986 single 'Rock n' Roll Children', while drummer Tim Bowler formed LIFE AFTER.

Singles/EPs:
Save Us From Those Who Would Save Us / Death Squad, Deadly Weapon (1983)

HELL BORN (POLAND)
Line-Up: Lord Ravenlock (vocals / drums), Les (guitar / bass)

Polish Black Metal duo HELL BORN is the secondary pursuit of DAMNATION's Les and BEHEMOTH's Lord Ravenlock. Describing themselves as "Hell on earth!" HELL BORN included a cover version of DESTRUCTION's 'Antichrist' on their 1996 mini album.

Albums:
HELL BORN, Pagan Moon CD 006 (1996)
Inverted / Hellraiser / Those Are Dead But Shall Rise / Merciless Onslaught / Antichrist

HELLHAMMER (SWITZERLAND)
Line-Up: Satanic Slaughter (vocals / guitar), Savage Damage (bass), Bloodhunter (drums)

Formerly known as HAMMERHEAD, this bizarre and primitive extreme Metal outfit was founded in 1982.
Previous to HAMMERHEAD frontman Thomas Gabriel Fischer and bassist Steve had been involved with various fledgling acts emulating their NWoBHM heroes VENOM.
During the August of 1982 Fischer, transferring from bass to guitar, was now fronting a trio of Priestly and drummer Jörg Neubart. Inspired apparently by Newcastle NWoBHM band RAVEN and their Gallagher brothers team Fischer and Priestly adopted the joint stage surnames

of 'Warrior'. Neubart became 'Bruce Day'. Their debut demo, 'Triumph Of Death', was widely regarded as one of the worst examples of a Heavy Metal band ever! 'Metal Forces' magazine editor Bernard Doe in particular cited it as the most appalling thing he had ever heard. History however would dictate that HELLHAMMER would later be recognized as one of the root catalysts of the Black Metal genre.

Although in later years band members have admitted their knowledge of music was basic to say the least when the HELLHAMMER recordings were made nevertheless the band were in possession of an artistic vision which would undoubtedly shape the Metal scene over many years.

In 1983 HELLHAMMER enrolled bass player Martin Eric Ain and drummer Stephen Priestly from SCHIZO. However, invited to submit a fresh demo to Berlin's Noise Records HELLHAMMER very nearly split as Ain felt he did not have the necessary talent to go through with the session!

Still, positive or negative press encouraged Noise to sign the band and the Berlin based label released the 'Apocalyptic Raids' EP which had no details as to what RPM the record should be played at; sounding just as strange at 33RPM as it did at 45!

Metal Blade Records released the EP in America with an extra two tracks.

HELLHAMMER mainman 'Satanic Slaughter' later swopped identities to become Tom G. Warrior and started the avant garde Metal legends CELTIC FROST in May of 1984 retaining the deal with Noise. CELTIC FROST issued a stream of critically praised outings before fizzling out.

Still an influence in some circles over ten years later, Sweden's ABYSS covered the HELLHAMMER track 'Massacra' on their 1995 album 'The Other Side'.

Warrior forged a new project in the late 90's billed as APOLLYON SUN.

Singles/EPs:
The Third Of The Storms (Evoked Damnation) / Massacra / Triumph Of Death / Horus / Agressor, Noise N008 50-1668 (1984) ('Apocolyptic Raids' EP)

HELLKULT (FINLAND)

HELLKULT include personnel from AZAGHAL. Members of HELLKULT

would found WYRD for the album 'Unchained Heathen Wrath'.

Albums:
OF PURE HEATHEN BLOOD, Dragonthrone DCD004 (2000)

HELLSPELL (SWEDEN)
Line-Up: Chrille Andersson (vocals / drums), Daniel Andersson (vocals / guitar / bass)

Guitarist Daniel Andersson and bass player Chrille Andersson are both fulltime members of NON SERVIUM.
In their main act Daniel Andersson goes under the title of 'Janos' whilst Chrille operates under the pseudonym 'Tyr'.

Albums:
DEVIL'S MIGHT, Invasion (2000)
To Summon The Devil / When The Seals Have Been Broken / Sent To Destroy / In Blasphemy / Warlust / Reconstruction Of The Lost World / Sacrilegious Immolation / Den Evjga Striden / Demon Load / Devil's Might

HELLSTORM (NORWAY)
Line-Up: Amok (vocals / guitar), Koma (bass), Kjekle (guitar), Penis (guitar), Vargon (drums)

HELLSTORM was forged as a trio of frontman Amok, bassist Elden and drummer Vorgon. After an initial demo session Elden departed to join EINHERJER and was duly replaced by Koma.

Signing to Head Not Found Records recording for the debut album was apparently delayed by the death of drummer Vorgon. According to press releases the vacancy left was confusingly filled by the similarly titled Vargon.

HELLSTORM's line up has fluctuated ever since with members Knattemar and Ihizag having brief stints. Latterly HELLSTORM has included second guitarist Kjektle and (allegedly) a third guitarist for live work entitled 'Penis'!

Singles/EPs:
Murder, Oskorie Productions (1996)

Albums:
FUCKING BLEED, Head Not Found HNF059CD (1999)

HELLWITCH (FL, USA)
Line-Up: Pat Raneiri (vocals / guitar),

Tommy Mouser (bass), Joe Schnessel (drums)

HELLWITCH, formed in 1984, released a 1987 demo titled 'Mordrivial Dissemination'.

Albums:
SYZYGIAL MISCREANCY, Wild Rags WRE 902 (1990)
The Ascent / Nosferatu / Viral Ehogence / Sentient Transmography / Mordirivial Dissemination / Pyrophoric Seizure / Purveyor Of Fear
TERRASYMMETRY, Lethal LMCD 1111 (1993)
Terrasymmetry / Satan's Wrath / Dawn Of Apostasy

HELREID (ITALY)
Line-Up: Franco Violo (vocals), Yorick (guitar), Alessandro Arcuri (bass), Daniele Soravia (keyboards), Luca Roggi (drums)

Albums:
MÉMORIES, Underground Symphony US CD 021 (1997)
Exordium / Mark The Wizard / Tale Of The Crypt / Endless Wars / Interludium / Suite De F. / The Departing Muse / Congedum

HEMLOCK (Brooklyn, NY, USA)

Black Metal act that include former ANTHRAX, NUCLEAR ASSAULT and BRUTAL TRUTH bassist Dan Lilker. Besides HEMLOCK Lilker still operates in STORMTROOPERS OF DEATH.
HEMLOCK issued a split EP in 1997 shared with BLACK ARMY JACKET.

Singles/EPs:
Split, Sound Views (1997) (Split EP with BLACK ARMY JACKET)

Albums:
CRUSH THE RACE OF GOD, Head Not Found (1997)
FUNERAL MASK, Head Not Found (1997)
Frozen Tears / Way Of The Wolf / Hemlock / Black Dawn / October Sunrise / Necrofuck / Loyal To Evil / Reign Of Death / Funeral Mask
LUST FOR FIRE, Full Moon Productions (1998)

HERESIARH (LATVIA)
Line-Up: Rasa (vocals), Morguelder Dragonseye (vocals / keyboards), Hater,

Mourn Majesty, Burial Jester, Kalutun (drums)

HERESIAH is a union of noted Latvian outfits ALFHEIM and DARK REIGN. The band was forged when DARK REIGN members Burial Jester, Mourn Majesty and drummer Kaludun joined forces with ALFHEIM refugees Hater and Morguelder Dragonseye. The whole project is fronted by the female soprano vocals of Rasa of NEGLECTED FIELDS. Drummer Kalutun also performs as a member of SKYFORGER and BLIZZARD.

Albums:
MYTHICAL BEASTS AND MEDIEVAL WARFARE, Demolition DEMCD 103 (2000)
All Hail The Wyverns / Horns Of War / Dragons Domain / The Crownless King / The Cruel Bard / Saga Of The Shield Maid- Part I: The Old Forest (Of Lament), Part II: Of Her Triumph / Higher Than Hills / Trollstorm / Elfwine / Wolfghosts (In Winter)

THE HERETIC (SPAIN)

Albums:
THE BOOK OF FATE, Iberian Moon (1998)
Overture: Dream Master's Fall / Daemons Ride The Wind / Era / Karmic Wheel (Or The Never Ending Pass Of Time)
FALLEN FROM HEAVEN, Iberian Moon (2000)
The I / False Idol / Earth Of Untruth / Human Nature / Nocturnal Guest / No Answer / Nightflight / Frontal Collision / Global Suicide Century
THE APOCRIPHAL SCRIPTS, (2001)

HERMH (POLAND)
Line-Up: Bart (vocals), Kris (guitar), Tom (guitar), Marcel (bass), Mark (keyboards), Mark (drums)

Self styled Depressive Metal act HERMH convened with their 1994 demo 'Oremus Peccatum (Refaim)'. A second tape arrived in 1995 dubbed 'Crying Crown Of Trees' selling over 2'000 copies. The enterprising Italian label Entropy Productions cobbled together both demos to make up the 'Echo' CD.
HERMH signed to German label Last Episode for their official debut 'Taran'. Although the band were far from happy

with the finished sound of the album nevertheless HERMH went on the road to promote it supporting the likes of VADER, BEHEMOTH and LAKE OF TEARS.
In late 1996 HERMH signed to domestic label Pagan Moon records for their 'Angeldemon' outing.
The band changed titles to UNKNOWN DIMENSIONS in 2000.

Albums:
ECHO, Entropy Productions (1995)
TARAN, Last Episode (1995)
ANGELDEMON, Pagan Moon, CD 009 (1997)
Intro- Wonderlust / The Silent Touch Of Bloody Rain / Dreamdeath Lover / Winged Emptiness / Years Of Dying / Wolfish Flower / Vampire The Angeldemon / Streak From Kozmoz / Immortalize- Outro

HETSHEADS (SWEDEN)
Line-Up: Anders Strokirk (vocals / guitar), Stabel (guitar), Fredda (bass), Freimann (drums)

HETSHEADS are now known as BLACKSHINE. Vocalist Anders Strokirk also plays with NECROPHOBIC.

Albums:
WE HAIL THE POSSESSED, Repulse (1995)
Dissolution By Catatonia / Remonstrating The Preserver / Paganization / Brutal Exhordation / Cast In Silver / Phlebotomize (Fade Away In Silence) / When The Time Has Come / For His Sake

HIMINBJØRG (FRANCE)
Line-Up: Elvan, Zahaah (guitar / bass)

HIMINBJØRG, although French, offer Viking Metal. The band is founded upon Zahaah of CELESTIAL RITES and Elvan of NEHËMAH.

Singles/EPs:
Fiery September Fire EP, (1999)

Albums:
WHERE RAVENS FLY, (1999)
Lightening Of Blood / Conqueror / In The Haze Of The Summer Solstices Fire / Journey Through The Nine Worlds / Nidhöggr / When Ravens Fly
IN THE RAVEN'S SHADOW, Red Stream (2000)
Guided By The Stars / Thiazi's Oyne /

The Inverted Dimension / In The Raven's Shadow / In The Forest Of The Demons From Within / Rising / Dreamwalker / The Voice Of Blood / Valaskjastf

HIN ONDA (FINLAND)
Line-Up: Narqath (vocals / guitar / keyboards), Wind (keyboards), Vortex (drums)

HIN ONDA began life as SVARTALFHEIM, an act that issued the demo 'Well Of The Highest Knowledge'. Previous to this band central members Narqath and Wind had operated the 1996 band CALM after which Narqath joined AZAGHAL.
Reuniting as SVARTALFHEIM in 1998 Narqath and Wind were joined by AZAGHAL drummer Kalma. As HIN ONDA the outfit debuted with the 'Fiery September Fire' EP for Aftermath Records.
There are many offshoots to HIN ONDA as Narqath busies himself with WYRD, OATH OF CIRION with members of DRUADAN FOREST and VALAR. This latter project has issued the demos 'Towards The Great Unknown', 'The Arrival Of The Dragonlord', 'Where Dragons Forever War' and 'Hidden Paths'.
As a solo artist WIND has released a string of Black Ambient workouts such as 'Veil Of Death', 'One More For Melancholy' and 'Woodland Spirits'.

Singles/EPs:
24th September 1155 / Troll And Tom / Lores Of The Forgotten Ones / Paganheart, Aftermath (1999) ('Fiery September Fire' EP)

Albums:
SONGS OF BATTLE, Aftermath (2000)
Songs Of Battle / House Of Hel / The Rune Singers Path / Soulswan / Twelve Valiant Men / Burning The Lake Alive / Fimbulwinter / Through Sinister Landscapes / Language Of The Woods / 24th September 1155 / Paganheart / House Of Hel (Alternative version) / The Rune Singers Path (Alternative version) / Soulswan (Alternative version)

HIRILORN (FRANCE)
Line-Up: Shaxul (vocals / bass), Sinn (guitar), Hastarl (guitar), Yohann (drums)

HIRILORN, named after a mythical tree, came together in 1994 when two guitarists Sinn and Hastarl united with frontman Shaxul. The line up fluctuated as HIRILORN dispensed with apparent "unworthy" members until the band was solidified with the addition of drummer Yohann in 1996.

HIRLORN included tracks on the Velvet Music International compilation 'Encyclopedia Pestilentia' which in turn scored the band a split demo with MERRIMACK issued by Draffar Productions. The response was enthusiastc and Drakkar signed HIRILORN for a full length album 'Legends Of Evil And Eternal Death'.

In 2000 HIRILORN's demo 'A Hymn To The Ancient Souls' was coupled with tracks from Mexican act NASUV for a shared CD on Sempiternal Productions. HIRILORN have split up.

Singles/EPs:
Depopulated (Prelude To The Apocalypse), Sempiternal (2000) (7" single)

Albums:
LEGENDS OF EVIL AND ETERNAL DEATH, Drakkar DKCD05 (1998)
A HYMN TO THE ANCIENT SOULS, Sempiternal Productions (2000)
Return Of The Druids / Haxan / Haunted Castle Of Rising Solitude / Where Lightning Strikes Eternally / Astral Entities

HOBB'S ANGEL OF DEATH
(AUSTRALIA)
Line-Up: Peter Hobbs (vocals/ guitar), Mark Wooley (guitar), Phillip Gresik (bass), Darren McMaster-Smith (drums)

HOBB'S ANGEL OF DEATH was one of the few Australian acts to employ Satanic overtones with 80's Thrash Metal. Peter Hobbs had started his musical career in 1984 with TYRUS, creating ANGEL OF DEATH in 1986. The following year saw the release of two demos 'Angel Of Death' and 'Virgin Metal Invasion From Down Under'. These sessions were recorded with the assistance of Melbourne act NOTHING SACRED guitarist Mark Wooley, Karl Lean and Sham.

These tapes came to the attention of German label Steamhammer and the 1988 eponymous album was produced by Harris Johns in Berlin. HOBB'S ANGEL OF DEATH had now solidified around Hobb's, NOTHING SACRED guitarist Mark Wooley, former MASS

CONFUSION bassist Phil Gresik and ex NEW RELIGION drummer Darren McMaster-Smith. Back home HOBB'S ANGEL OF DEATH put in their debut live show opening for MORTAL SIN.

By 1989 the band had splintered with Hobbs and Wooley enlisting bassist Dave Frew and drummer Bruno Canziani. Following touring the band was then put on ice resulting in Wooley and Frew founding HATRED.

Bassist Phil Gresik would later join the notorious Black Metal band BESTIAL WARLUST and later the equally infamous DESTROYER 666. Latterly he has found LONG VOYAGE BACK.

Albums:
HOBB'S ANGEL OF DEATH, Steamhammer (1988)
Jack The Ripper / Crucifixion / Brotherhood / Journey / House Of Death / Satan's Crusade / Lucifer's Domain / Marie Antoinette / Bubonic Plague / Cold Steel
INHERITANCE, Shock (1995)

HOLLENTHON (AUSTRIA)

HOLLENTHON was founded by former PUNGENT STENCH vocalist Martin Shirenc initially titled VUZEM. As VUZEM the outfit included two tracks anonymously to the Austrian extreme music compilation entitled 'Norici Obscura Pars'. A name switch to HOLLENTON occurred for legal reasons. The man also busied himself with KREUZWEG OST in alliance with SUMMONING's Silenius for the 2000 album 'Iron Avantgarde'.

Albums:
DOMUS MUNDI, Napalm (1999)
Enrapture- Hinc Illae Lacrimae / Hornage- Magni Nominis Umbra / Vestige- Non Omnis Moriar / Lure- Pallida Mors / Interlude- Ultima Ratio Regum / Reprisal- Malis Avibus / Premonition- Lex Talonis / Eclipse- Vita Nova

HOMICIDE (GERMANY)
Line-Up: Matarru (vocals), Shocker (guitar), Mentor (guitar), M. (bass), Zarathrusta (drums)

HOMICIDE include DARK BEFORE DAWN guitarist Mentor in the ranks. The band's first drummer Doomhammer was succeeded by Zarathrusta.

188

SLAUGHTERS LEGACY, Undercover (2000)
Intro / Black Crusade / Slaughters Legacy / When Steel Gets Red / Raped By The Cross / Tiefen Der Ewigkiet / Triumph Of Death

HORDES (HOLLAND)
Line-Up: Guido Heijnens (vocals),

Black Metal band HORDES issued a 1993 demo 'Songs To Hall Up High' prior to their solitary single release. Vocalist Guido Heijnens ('Hammerheart') went on to BIFROST and CONQUERED MY FEARS. Other HORDES personnel created COUNTESS.

Singles/EPs:
Longing For The Kingdom Of Steel, Thurisaz (1993) (7" single)

HORNA (FINLAND)
Line-Up: Nazgul Von Armageddon (vocals), Shatraug (guitar), Thanatos (bass), Gorthaur (drums)

HORNA is a literal translation of 'Hell'. The band evolved from the 1993 band SHADOWED led by guitarists Shatraug and Moredhel. In 1994, with the addition of drummer Gorthaur the act became HORNA. During this formative stages various members drifted in and out of the ranks including bassist Nazgul Von Armageddon.
HORNA's first product was the 1995 demo 'Varjoissa'. Nazgul was re-recruited although this time as a lead vocalist. A further tape 'Hiidentorni' followed in 1997 which was pressed onto CD by Solistitium Records.
1998 saw the departure of guitarists Moredhel and Skratt. European dates saw HORNA employing stand in musicians prior to the band being put on ice whilst members undertook their military service.
Late 1998 saw the recruitment of Thanatos and the return of Moredhel. During 2000 HORNA issued a split 7" single with American act FOG.
Von Armageddon would guest as session vocalist for fellow Finns DAWN OF RELIC on their debut 'One Night In Carcosa' album.

Singles/EPs:
Yhdeksän Yö / Haudankmylmyyden Maille, Sota (1999) (7" single)

Albums:
HIIDENTORNI, Solistitium SOL015 (1997)
Avaus / Hun Lyömme Jumalan Kodin Liekkeihin / Hiidentorni Huokuu Usvansa / Ikuisesti Kalpeina Kuoleman Muistolle / Tappakaa Kristus / Sanoista… Pimeyteen / Hänen Synkkä Myrskynsä / Hornanväki / Sinulle Mätänevä Jehova
KOHTI UHDEKSAN NOUSUA, Solistitium SOL 018 (1998)
Örkkivuorilta / Imperial Devestation / Sword Of Darkness / White Aura Buried In Ashes / Sormus Ja Silmä / Outro
HAUDANKMYLMYYDEN MAILLE, Solistium SOL031 (1999)
Procogi / Yudeksän Yö / … Jeesuksen Veresiä / Ylle Kuihtuneen Ajan Ajattusten / Kun Jumalan Sydän On Murskattu / (Kaiken) Kristityn Kuolema / Viimeinen Sielu Jumalan Valosta / Haudankmylmyyden Maille / Hymni Toumiopäivänä / Peikkomaille / Epilogi
PERIMÄ VIHASSA JA VERIKOSTOSSA, Oskorei Productions (1999)
A Ring To Rule / Pimeys Yllä Pyhän Maan / Haudanusva / Verikammari / Ghash Inras

HOUSE OF USHER (SWEDEN)
Line-Up: Jani Ruhala (vocals), Mattias Kenhed (guitar), Martin Larsson (guitar), Stefan Källarsson (bass), Jani Myllärinen (drums)

Singles/EPs:
Revengeance / Rather Black, Obscure Plasma 911002 (1991)

HROSSHARSGRANI (GERMANY)
Line-Up:

HROSSHARSGRANI started initially as a 1998 dark ambient outlet for Hugin of HEIMATLEID and SCHLAGANFALL but would fast develop into a vicious Black Metal act. A series of tapes including debut 'Der Pfad Zum Tor der Toten' led to further cassette releases 'Lieder aus Mittelerde' and 'Der Ring den Macht'.
The inaugural album '… Of Battles, Ravens And Fire' utilized erstwhile SCHLAGANFALL and DOGMA guitarist Roland with female backing vocals courtesy of Eva.

Albums:
… OF BATTLES, RAVENS AND FIRE, CCP CCP100213-2 (2000)

Legend / Preparing For Battle / The Prayer / March Of The Einherjer / Ragnarok / The Ravenflight / Gjallarhorn

THE HUMBLE POET (NORWAY)
Line-Up: Per Flaa (vocals / bass), Gunnar Berg (vocals / guitar / keyboards), Aage Skar (guitar), Paal Iversen (drums)

Albums:
FIG LEAF, Head Not Found HNF 027 (1997)
New Ship / The Humble Poet / Shadowlands / And She Flies / On The Seventh Day / Hi There / Anyway / The Critic / Thanks

HYPNOS (CZECH REPUBLIC)
Line-Up: Bruno (vocals / bass), R.A.D. (guitar), Skull (drums)

Trio HYPNOS are in fact KRABATHOR men vocalist Bruno and drummer Skull. The 2000 album 'In Blood We Trust' sees Mike of IMPALED NAZARENE involved. An accompanying EP saw HYPNOS covering BULLDOZER's 'The Cave' HYPNOS toured Europe in December 2000 as part of an almighty Death Metal package that included ENSLAVED, MORBID ANGEL, BEHEMOTH, THE CROWN and DYING FETUS.

Singles/EPs:
Infernational / Breeding The Scum / The Cave / In Blood We Trust, Morbid (2000) ('Hypnos' EP)

Albums:
IN BLOOD WE TRUST, Morbid (2000)
Incantation / Burn The Angels Down / Fatal Shrine Of Sky / Infernational / Lovesong / Open The Gates Of Hell / Sacrilegious / Across The Battlefields / Breeding The Scum / In Blood We Trust / After The Carnage (Outro)
XXX, (2001)
Intro / The End Of God / X / Nath And Her Gun / XX / Phantasma Plasma / Mother / XXX / Neverland / XXXX? / Riddle / Mother (Father Edit) / The End Of God (Resurrection mix)

HYPNOSIS (FRANCE)

Albums:
SHADOWORLD, Black Lotus (1999)

HYPNOTIC SCENERY
(CZECH REPUBLIC)
Line-Up: Robert (vocals), Martin (guitar), Mike (bass), Catherini (keyboards), Angel (drums)

HYPNOTIC SCENERY recorded their first demo, quite bizarrely, in Latin before offering the more straight forward 'Crystal Curtain' in Czech.
In 1995 the quintet self-financed the recording and release of their debut album 'Vacuum'. It's not known whether they subsequently cleaned up the market back home with it....

Albums:
VACUUM, Hypnotic Scenery (1995)
Orgasme Flamme / Tenebrosa Alta / Detur / Scintilla Vitae / Flumen Maeroris / Voluptutis Incognitae / Quare? / Vacuum
DEEPER AND DEEPER, Sheer SR CD008 (1997)
Moonlighting / Sic Itur Ad Astra / Beautiful Nymph / Nothing Is A Chance / Deeper And Deeper / Deus Mortuus / Blind Journey / Wretched Man / My Trust / Mystery And Enigma / Hypogeum

HYPOCRISY (SWEDEN)
Line-up: Masse Broberg (vocals), Peter Tägtren (guitar), Jonas Österberg (guitar), Mikael Hedlund (bass), Lars Szöke (drums)

HYPOCRISY was formed by guitarist Peter Tägtren in October 1991 and were initially known as SEDITIOUS. Both Tägtren and drummer Lars Szöke had previously been members of CONQUEST, an act dating back as far as 1984. Tägtren had returned from America where he had been a member of MALEVOLENT CREATION and MELTDOWN. HYPOCRISY's line-up was augmented by ex EPITAPH guitarist Jonas Österberg and erstwhile VOTARY vocalist Masse Broberg.
As HYPOCRISY the band soon secured a deal with Germany's Nuclear Blast Records issuing the debut 'Penetralia' album in 1992.
For the second album HYPOCRISY were down to a quartet, with Peter Tägtren handling guitars. Tour dates included shows with DEICIDE and CANNIBAL CORPSE. However, on tour vocalist Masse Broberg suffered a breakdown, necessitating Tagtren taking over lead vocals. Following the dates HYPOCRISY decided to carry on as a trio releasing the 'Inferior Devotees' mini album which included the SLAYER cover 'Black Magic'. This track also appeared on the

SLAYER tribute compilation album 'Slatanic Slaughter Volume One'.

In 1995 HYPOCRISY toured such far flung places as Mexico and Portugal promoting their' Fourth Dimension' album.

During 1996, the year in which the band released the 'Maximum Abduction' mini album (which included a cover of KISS' 'Strange Ways') Tägtren fulfilled duties as stand in guitarist for MARDUK on their European tour as well as working on a solo project PAIN.

Tägtren, Hedlund and Szöke also pursued a side project act THE ABYSS having so far released two albums; "The Other Side' and 'Summon The Beast'.

As the seventh album, 1997's 'The Final Chapter' saw the light of day, Tägtren announced that this would signal HYPOCRISY's final fling, citing that he wished to concentrate on PAIN. However, this announcement combined with the resulting good reviews granted to 'The Final Chapter' persuaded Tägtren to change his mind. By now HYPOCRISY had shifted its lyrical content away from the evil from below to the evil from above with increasing alien themes and album imagery.

HYPOCRISY issued their first live album 'Destroys Wacken' followed by another critically acclaimed studio album simply titled 'Hypocrisy'. The man also involved himself in the commercially successful LOCK UP project with NAPALM DEATH bassist Shane Embury and guitarist Jesse Pintado with DIMMU BORGIR drummer Nick Barker. Although the LOCK UP album sold spectacularly well in Germany Tägtgren backed out of the project before live work ensued.

2000 found Tägtren busier than ever with a further PAIN album 'Rebirth' as well as a fresh HYPOCRISY effort 'Into The Abyss'.

Singles/EPs:
Pleasure Of Molestation / Exclamation Of A Necrofag / Necromonicon / Attachment To The Ancestor, Relapse RR 6040 (1993)
Roswell 47 / Carved Up / Request Denied / Strange Ways, Nuclear Blast NB 145 (1996) ('Maximum Abduction' EP)

Albums:
PENETRALIA, Nuclear Blast NB067-2 27361 60552 (1992)
Impotent God / Suffering Souls / Nightmare / Jesus Fall / God Is A ... / Left

To Rot / Burn By The Cross / To Escape Is To Die / Take The Throne / Penetralia
OSCULUM OSCENUM, Nuclear Blast NB 080-2 (1993)
Pleasure Of Molestation / Exclamation Of A Necrofag / Osculum Obscenum / Necromonicon / Black Metal / Inferior Devotees / Infant Sacrifices / Attachment To The Ancestor / Althotas
INFERIOR DEVOTEES, Nuclear Blast NA RED6104-2 (1994)
Inferior Devotees / Symbol Of Baphomet / Mental Emotions / God Is A Lie / Black Magic
THE FOURTH DIMENSION, Nuclear Blast NB112-2 / 2736168940 (1995)
Apocalypse / Mind Corruption / Reincarnation / Reborn / Black Forest / Never To Return / Path To Babylon / Slaughtered / Orgy In Blood / The North Wind / T.E.M.P.T. / The Fourth Dimension / The Arrival Of The Demons / The Abyss
ABDUCTED, Nuclear Blast NB133-2/27361 61332 (1996)
The Gathering / Roswell / Killing Art / The Arrival Of The Demons (Part Two) / Buried / Abducted / Paradox / Point Of No Return / When The Candle Fades / Carved Up / Reflections / Slippin' Away / Drained
THE FINAL CHAPTER, Nuclear Blast NB 283-2 (1997)
Inseminated Adoption / A Coming Race / Dominion / Inquire Within / Last Vanguard / Request Denied / Through The Window Of Time / Shamateur / Adjusting The Sun / Lies / Evil Invaders / The Final Chapter
HYPOCRISY DESTROYS WACKEN, Nuclear Blast NB 110493 (1999)
Roswell / Inseminated Adoption / A Coming Race / Apocalypse / Osculum Obscenum / Buried / Let It Rot / The Fourth Dimension / Pleasure Of Molestation / Killing Art / The Final Chapter / Time Warp / Til The End / Fuck U / Beginning Of The End
HYPOCRISY, Nuclear Blast (1999)
Fractured Millenium / Apocalyptic Hybrid / Fusion Programmed Minds / Elastic Inverted Vision / Reversal Reflection / Until The End / Paranormal Mysteries / Time Warp / Disconnect Magnetic Corridors
INTO THE ABYSS, Nuclear Blast NB 529-2 (2000) **64 GERMANY**
Legions Descend / Blinded / Resurrected / Unleash The Beast / Digital Prophecy / Fire In The Sky / Total Eclipse / Unfold The Sorrow / Sodomized / Deathrow (No Regrets)

HYPOCRITE (SWEDEN)

Line-Up: Johan Haller (vocals / bass), Nicke Åberg (guitar), Henrik Hedborg (guitar), Peter Nagy (drums)

Stockholm Death Metallers HYPOCRITE started out life in 1989 under the name of DARK TERROR.
HYPOCRITE's single is a split effort with ELECTROCUTION on the Italian Molten Metal label. Drummer Peter Nagy also plays for MÖRK GRYNING and ETERNAL OATH.

Singles/EPs:
Heaven's Tears, Molten Metal MOLTEN010 (1994) (Split single with ELECTROCUTION)

Albums:
EDGE OF EXISTENCE, Offworld OW005 (1996)
Vita Dolorosa / Deep Within This Flower Of Sin / Edge Of Existence / The Scream... / Voices From The Dark Side / Heaven's Tears / A Black Wound / When I'm Gone / Sanctuary Of The Sleeping God / Welcome To Abaddon / Forsaken by Christ / Beyond The Edge

IBEX THRONE
(Salt Lake City, UT, USA)
Line-Up: Azelcraz Marconis Witchborn (vocals), Lord Dying (guitar), Judas Drexor Arawn (guitar), Desecrator (bass), Mictlan (drums)

Based in the Mormon heartland of Salt Lake City IBEX THRONE has had a troubled history leading up to their 'D.E.A.D.' EP.
The band was founded in 1997 by erstwhile members of DEMENTED TORMENT and guitarist Lord Dying of LORD BEHERIT. The band debuted with the demo 'Transcend The Darkness' but tragically the following year vocalist Anihilist (Weston Madsen) committed suicide by shooting himself in the head.
IBEX THRONE also planned a split album 'Nihilistic Death War', featuring a version of SLAYER's 'At Dawn They Sleep', in collusion with CRAFT of Sweden.
IBEX THRONE performed at the legendary 'Sacrifice Of The Nazarene Child' Black Metal festival in Texas in 2000.
Lord Dying, guitarist Judas Drexor Arawn and drummer Mictlan also operate the side project YAOTL MICTLAN.

Singles/EPs:
Destructing The Saints / Enslavement Of The Weak / Armageddon Arrives / Death, Blasphemic Hymns (1999) ('D.E.A.D.' EP)

Albums:
TRANSCEND THE DARKNESS-D.E.A.D., Black Art Productions (2000)
Transend The Darkness / Onward To Conquer / Threshold Of The Ibex Horde / Abysmal Hate / The Blood Oath / Waging Our Dark War / Destructing The Saints / Enslavement Of The Weak / Armageddon Arrives / Death
IBEX THRONE, (2000)
Requiem Of The Sombreness Empire / Black Sand Through My Veins / Vomitorium Cruetes / Ibex Throne / Destructing The Saints / Enslavement Of The Weak / Armageddon Arrives / Death / Abysmal Hate / Transcend The Darkness / The Blood Bath

ICE AGES (AUSTRIA)

ICE AGES is another in the long line of SUMMONING offshoots. Main men

Protector and Silenius are the protagonists.

Albums:
STRIKE THE GROUND, Napalm (1997)
A Dream As Red As Darkness- Part I / A Dream As Red As Darkness- Part II / Strike The Ground / Time Of Dawn / Endless Circle / Shrunk To Nothing / Almost Invisible / Trapped And Scared / Dead But Wide Awake / Darkened World / Transparent Dreams / Eternal Sleep
THIS KILLING EMPTINESS, Draenor Productions DPR 012 (2000)
Far Gone Light / Lifeless Sentiments / The Fiend / I Come For You / This Killing Emptiness / Heartbeat / The Last Time / Shades Of Former Light / The Denial / Last In Daze

ILDJARN (NORWAY)

Black Metal band ILDJARN sometimes benefit from the assistance of EMPEROR's Samoth on their recordings. The band dates to 1992 with demos such as 'Ildjarn' and 'Minnesjoerd' preceding their first release the 'Norse' EP. As the band progressed, sometimes simply billed as ILDJARN NIDHOGG, experimentation came to the fore. Later albums are exercises in minimalist electronica alongside brutal and raw Metal.

Singles/EPs:
Mørklagt Sti / Svarte Hjerter / Nattens Ledestjerne / Natt Og Taake, Nocturnal Art (1995) ('Norse' EP)
I Anmarsj Gjennon Grangunn / Ved Tjernets Bredd / Vintermrk / Skogens Hatefulle Skapning, Napalm (1996) ('Svartfråd' EP)
Strength And Anger / Black Anger (Hate Meditation I) / Interchange / Midnight Strength, Black Anger (Hate Meditation II), Norse League (1997) ('Strength Of Anger' EP)

Albums:
DET FRYSENDE NORDARIKET, Norse League (1995)
Morklagt Sti / Svarte Hjerter / Nattens Ledestjerne / Natt Og Tåke / Innferd / Kronet / Sola Skjules / Ild / Fjerde Dag / Et Glimt / Stov Og Aske / Øde / Utsyn, Del: I-V / Demring / Minnesjord, Del: I-VI / Myrk Var / Dalens Ånd Avslutning
ILDJARN, Norse League (1995)
Skogslottet / Kulde / Tåkeheim / Snoen Dekker / Skogsvinet / Svarte Grangunn /

Krigere / Atter En Gang / Nordiske Morke / Blikkets Storket / Himmel Hvelv / Der Set Skjulte Lever / Huset I Skogen / Dralmehen / Svartetjell / Morkeheim / Himmelsen Svarter / Som En Ensom Borg / Vinden Riter / Morket Skynger Seg / Sygog Nummet / Innover Idalsakk / I Molst Over Åsen / Til Dekket Og Kalv / Det Morkner
FOREST POETRY, Napalm (1996)
Whispering Breeze / Blackened Might / Clashing Of Swords / No Gleaming Light / Blazing Eye / Sinking Deep / Chill Of The Night- Returning Part I / The Blade Flares In Red Light / Deepening In Grey / Midnight Interval / descending / Away From The Dawn / Before My Eyes Forever / Reflecting Mountains / Brother Of The Frest / Dead Years / Dark December / Cold And Waste / Visions Of The Earth- Returning Part II / Risen Seeds Of Time / Winter Embrace / No Place Nowhere
LANDSCAPES, Norse League (1996)

IMMOLATION (New York, NY, USA)
Line-Up: Ross Dolan (vocals / bass), Thomas Wilkinson (guitar), Robert Vigna (guitar), Craig Smilowski (drums)

Anti Christian Metal band IMMOLATION was created in February of 1988 by frontman Russ Dolan, drummer Neal and two erstwhile RIGOR MORTIS members guitarists Robert Vigna and Thomas Wilkinson. Two demos ensued prior to the 'Dawn Of Possession' album and the recruitment of drummer Craig Smilowski. IMMOLATION would later add former FALLEN CHRIST and DISASSOCIATE drummer Alex Hernandez for the 'Hereinafter' album. Touring saw shows in Europe with CANNIBAL CORPSE.
IMMOLATION toured America in 2000 sharing billing with SIX FEET UNDER. John McEntee deputized for Vigna on later tours.

Albums:
DAWN OF POSSESSION, Roadrunner (1991)
Intro Everlasting Fire / Despondent Souls / Dawn Of Possession / Those Left Behind / Internal Decadence / No Forgiveness (Without Bloodshed) / Burial Ground / After My Prayers / Fall In Disease / Immolation
STEPPING ON ANGELS... BEFORE DAWN, Repulse (1995)
Relentless Torment / Holocaust / Rigor Mortis / Warriors Of Doom / Immolation / Dawn Of Possession / Internal Decadence / Burial Ground / Despondent Souls / Infectious Blood / Despondent Souls (1990) / Burial Ground (Live) / Infectious Blood (Live) / Immolation (Live) / Despondent Souls (Live) / Dawn Of Possession (Live)
HEREINAFTER, Metal Blade 3984-14102-2 (1997)
Nailed To Gold / Burn With Jesus / Here In After / I Feel Nothing / Away From God / Towards Earth / Under The Supreme / Christ's Cage
FAILURES FOR GODS, Metal Blade (1999)
Once Ordained / No Jesus, No Beast / Failures For Gods / Unsaved / God Made Filth / Stench Of High Heaven / Your Angel Died / The Devil I Know
CLOSE TO A WORLD BELOW, Metal Blade (2000)
Higher Coward / Father, You're Not A Father / Furthest From The Truth / Fall From A High Place / Unpardonable Son / Lost Passion / Put My Hand In The Fire / Close To A World Below

IMMORTAL (NORWAY)
Line-Up: Abbath (vocals / guitar), Iscariah (bass), Horgh (drums)

IMMORTAL first emerged as a quartet in 1990. During the late 80's the band members vocalist Abbath Doom Occulta and guitarist Demonaz Doom Occulta (real name Harald Naevdal) were both in SATANEL, an outfit that also featured BURZUM's notorious Count Grisnackh. This triumvirate also operated the Death Metal unit OLD FUNERAL alongside Tyr and Alligator. SATAENAL and OLD FUNERAL ran parallel courses until Abbath and Demonaz broke away to forge AMPUTATION with drummer Armagedda and guitarist Jorn Inge Tunsberg. The latter exited in the Autumn of 1990 to create HADES (NORWAY) and AMPUTATION duly evolved into IMMORTAL.
IMMORTAL's first recording was the limited edition of 1000 'Immortal' single released by Listenable Records.
IMMORTAL then signed to noted black metal exponents Osmose Productions releasing their first full length album 'Diabolical Fullmoon Mysticism' in 1992. Shortly after Armagedda was fired and a temporary drummer Kolgrim was installed staying the course for just one gig in Bergen during December of 1992. Unfortunately for IMMORTAL this concert was the subject of a television broadcast

ABBATH of IMMORTAL
Photo : Martin Wickler

which showed the band in a less than flattering light.

By their next album, the faster paced 'Pure Holocaust', the band was down to a duo with Abbath handling drum duties despite sleeve credits acknowledging Erik as the drummer. Erik did in fact join IMMORTAL following the release of 'Pure Holocaust'.

IMMORTAL toured Europe to back up its release on a bill with BLASPHEMY quaintly titled the "Fuck Christ" tour. The dates were a success and a second batch of dates, known as 'Sons of northern darkness" were added with support act MARDUK. Erik (retitled 'Grim') lost his position upon the tour's completion later turning up as a member of GORGOROTH for their 1996 'Antichrist' album.

(Sadly Grim would commit suicide in October 1999).

IMMORTAL's drum position was now taken by one of the true Black Metal personalities as MAYHEM's Hellhammer stood in for European touring supporting MORBID ANGEL.

A permanent skinsman was found in the form of Horgh for 'Blizzard Beasts'. Although IMMORTAL were by now without among the elite of the Black Metal world with ever increasing album sales, even breaking into the national charts in some territories, the band was rocked by the forced exit of founder Demonaz. It was learned that the guitarist was suffering from a form of arthritis that made performing extremely painful. IMMORTAL soldiered on with Demonaz still offering lyrical contributions. The public face of the band evolved to accommodate the changes with Abbath taking guitar duties and Ares of AETURNUS performing bass guitar.

Outside of IMMORTAL Demonaz busied himself on the side project PERFECT VISIONS.

The 2000 album 'Damned In Black' provided evidence that recent turbulations had not altered IMMORTAL's onward pursuit as the record sold over 40'000 copies on pre sale and made an impression on the national German charts.

With Iscariah on bass guitar IMMORTAL undertook touring of America alongside ANGEL CORPSE and KRISIUN prior to headline Mexican shows.

IMMORTAL have recently left longstanding label Osmose Productions signing to the giant Nuclear Blast concern. Late 2000 had Horgh deputizing as live drummer for PAIN.

Abbath also has outside concerns as drummer for DET HEDENSKE FOLK.

<u>Singles/EPs:</u>
Immortal, Listenable (1990) (Split 7" single with ARMEGEDDA)
Unholy Forces Of Evil / Cold Winds Of Funeral Dust, Listenable (1991) (7" single)

<u>Albums:</u>
DIABOLICAL FULLMOON MYSTICISM, Osmose SPV CD084-08662 (1992)
The Call Of The Wintermoon / Unholy Forces Of Evil / Cryptic Winterstorms / Cold Winds Of Funeral Dust / Blacker Than Darkness / A Perfect Vision Of The Rising Northland
PURE HOLOCAUST, Osmose OPCD019 (1994)
Unsilent Storms In The North Abyss / A Sign For The Norse Hordes To Ride / The Sun No Longer Rises / Frozen By Icewinds / Storming Through Red Clouds And Holocaust Winds / Eternal Years On The Path To The Cemetery Gates / As The Eternity Opens / Pure Holocaust
BATTLES IN THE NORTH, Osmose SPV 84-20332 (1995)
Battles In The North / Grim And Frostbitten Kingdoms / Descent Into Eminent Silence / Throned By Blackstorms / Moonrise Fields Of Sorrow / Cursed Realms Of The Winter Demons / At The Stormy Gates Of Mist / Through The Halls Of Eternity / Circling Above In Time Before Time / Blashyrkh (Mighty Ravendark)
BLIZZARD BEASTS, Osmose (1997)
Intro / Blizzard Beasts / Nebular Ravens Winter / Suns That Sank Below / Battlefields / Mountains Of Might / Noctambulant / Winter Of The Ages / Frostdemonstorm
AT THE HEART OF WINTER, Osmose (1999)
Withstand The Fall Of Time / Solarfall / Tragedies Blow Out Horizon / Where Dark And Light Don't Differ / At The Heart Of Winter / Years Of Silent Sorrow
DAMNED IN BLACK, Osmose OPCDL 095 (2000)
Triumph / Wrath From Above / Against The Tide (In The Arctic World) / My Dimension / The Darkness That Embraces Me / In Our Mystic Visions Blest / Damned In Black

IMMORTAL DOMINION
(Fort Collins. CO, USA)

Singles/EPs:
Birth EP, Immortal Dominion (1996)

Albums:
ENDURE, Immortal Dominion (1999)

IMMORTALIS (GERMANY)

IMMORTALIS' debut album was produced by ex HOLY MOSES guitarist Andy Classen and featured a cover of VENOM's 'Countess Bathory'.

Albums:
INDICIUM DE MORTUIS, Morbid 08457062 (1991)
Burning Existence / Subordinate Gods / Bleeding Inheritance / Quo Vadis (Everlasting Life) / Indicium De Mortuis / My Requiem / Voices Of Forgotten Souls / Blasphemous Process / Countess Bathory

IMPALED NORTHERN MOONFOREST (USA)

A rare imposter in the Black Metal legions. IMPALED NORTHERN MOONFOREST are in fact those wacky ANAL CUNT guys.

Singles/EPs:
Flames Of Hell, MTS (1999)

IMPALED NAZARENE (FINLAND)
Line-Up: Sir Mikka Luttinen (vocals / drums), Dr J-Ace (guitar), The Fuck You Man (bass), Mr. ML GD 6th (keyboards)

IMPALED NAZERENE date back to 1990 and have created a unique niche market for themselves in the Death Metal scene. The band lean more towards Punk and have landed themselves in hot water with the Finnish authorities by branding Russians as "Red scum". Bassist 'The fuck you man' is in fact SENTENCED's Taneli Jarva.
The band's inaugural line up comprised of mika Luttinen on vocals, guitarists Ari Holappa and Mika Pääkkö, bass player Anti Pihkala and drummer Kimmo Luttinen. Both Luttinen brothers were previously members of MUTILATION.
IMPALED NAZARENE's presence was first felt in 1991 when the debut demo emerged titled 'Shemhamforash'. The tape was laid down on a primitive two

track and saw the departure of Pihkala in favour of Harri Holonen. In April of 1991 IMPALED NAZARENE put in their first live gig as support to BEHERIT. Further shows ensued as openers to SENTENCED.
The second session'Taog Eht Fo Htao Eht' quickly followed capitalised on by a festival appearance at the 'Days Of Darkness' event alongside AMORPHIS.
A 7" single 'Goat Perversion' was released by the Italian Nosferatu concern after which both Holappa and Halonen decamped. Undettered IMPALED NAZARENE gigged for a while as a power trio. New recruit Taneli Jarva is drafted for a second single for French label Osmose Productions pairing 'Sadogoat' with a JOHNNY CASH cover 'Ghost Riders'! However, Pääkkö broke ranks and Jarno Anttila deputises on guitar. This roll would soon turn into a full time tenure.
The debut full length album 'Tol Cormpt Norz Norz Norz' saw initial limited edition copies including an extra thirteen tracks comprising the earlier demos. IMPALED NAZARENE's third single 'Satanic Masowhore' was backed on the flip side with a cover version of EXTREME NOISE TERROR's 'Conned Thru Life'. Sales were strong enough to break the Finnish national top forty album charts.
Toured Europe with ANCIENT RITES in early 1994 upfront of recrding third album 'Suomi Finland Perkele'. The record's perceived right wing lyrics draw controversy and instructions are issued by French authorities to withdraw the album from the stores. Fortunately sales were not unduly harmed as misinformation led to the band's previous album being removed from racks. Embroiled in the resulting press frenzy IMPALED NAZARENE set out on tour around Europe with American's ABSU and Australia's SADISTIK EXEKUTION. However, by the following year founder member Sir Luttinen had decamped to concentrate on his solo project LEGENDA. A planned mini album, provisionally titled 'Hamnasnas', was shelved due to in fighting in the band. After Luttinen's departure he also operated in parallel BEHERIT and would session for CATAMENIA. Reima Kellokoski took the IMPALED NAZARENE drum stool for October tour dates in Europe with MINISTRY OF TERROR and KRABATHOR. The group also put in their first British show headlining a Halloween event at London's

Astoria.
In early 1996 added ex BELIAL bassist Lehto Saari, who replaced 'The Fuck You Man' Jarva immediately after recording of the 'Latex Cult' and 'Motorpenis' outings. Both Jarva and the wayward Luttinen would later found THE BLACK LEAGUE. The 'Motorpenis' mini album features covers of tracks from Finnish Punk acts FAFFBEY and TERVEET KADET as well as GANG GREEN's 'Alkohol'. April of 1996 had the band out on their lengthiest trek around Europe to date as part of the 'No Mercy' touring festival. IMPALED NAZARENE sharing the stage with CANNIBAL CORPSE, IMMOLATION, ROTTING CHRIST, KRABATHOR and GRAVE.
Recovering after these dates the band laid down an exclusive track 'I Am The Killer Of Trolls' for the compilation album 'World Domination II'. 1996 was rounded off by a further bout of European touring with ANGEL CORPSE and GEHENNAH. The band found themselves back in trouble in 1997 when the Hare Krishna movement objected to the use of artwork on the 'Ugra Karma' album.
During the summer of 1998 the group put in further prominent international shows playing the Milwaukee Metalfest, gigs in Canada and a series of dates in Mexico. In September of 1998 the band drafted THY SERPENT, CHILDREN OF BODOM and SINERGY guitarist Alex Laiho. However, Laiho's commitments kept him

out of the line up for another round of European shows this time with DRILLER KILLER and RITUAL CARNAGE. Laiho did perform with the band in February of 1999 on their second visit to America and Mexico but cut short his commitment returning to Finland. Nevertheless, IMPALED NAZARENE undertook their first Japanese shows as a quartet. The band would not let up the live work and by April were back in Europe as part of the 'No Mercy III' festivals in alliance with PECCATUM, LIMBONIC ART, THE CROWN, EMPEROR and MORBID ANGEL. Still as a four piece the band also put in shows in far flung Australia and New Zealand.
IMPALED NAZARENE's 2000 release saw a split effort with DRILLER KILLER. The band's status is such that several bootleg singles and albums exist most notably 'Live In The Name Of Satan'.

Singles/EPs:
Noisrevrep Taog / In The Name Of Satan / Noisrevrep Eht Retfa / Damnation, Nosferatu (1991) ('Goat Perversion' 7" single)
Sado Goat / Ghost Riders, Osmose Productions (1992) (7" single)
Satanic Masowhore / Conned Thru Life, Osmose Productions OPEP003 (1993) (7" single)
Motorpenis, Osmose Productions SPV 076 20622-2 CD (1996)

Albums:
TOL CORMPT NORZ NORZ NORZ,
Osmose Productions OPCD010 (1993)
Apolokia / I Al Purg Vompo / My Blessing
(The Beginning Of The End) / Apolokia
II: Aikolopa 666 / In The Name Of Satan
/ Impure Orgies / Goat Perversion / The
Forest (The Darkness) / Mortification
Blood Red Razor Blade / The God
(Symmetry Of Penis) / Condemned To
Hell / The Dog (Art Of Vagina) / The
Crucified / Apolokia III: Agony / Body-
Mind-Soul / Hoath: Darbs Lucifero /
Apolokia Finale XXVII AS / Damnation
(Raping The Angels)
UGRA KARMA, Osmose Productions
OPCD018 (1994)
Goatzied / The Horny And The Horned /
Sadhu Satana / Chaosgoat Law / Hate /
Gott Ist Tot (Antichrist War Mix) /
Coraxo / Soul Rape / Kali-Yuga /
Cyberchrist / False Jehova / Sadistic 666
- Under A Golden Shower
SUOMI FINLAND PERKELE, Osmose
Productions OPCD026 (1995)
Intro / Vituursen Multi Huipennus / Blood
Is Thicker Than Water / Steel Vagina /
Total War- Winter War / Quasb- The
Burning / Kuolema Kaikille (Paitsi Meille)
/ Let's Fucking Die / Genocide /
Ghettoblaster / The Oath Of The Goat
LATEX CULT, Osmose Productions
OPCD038 (1996)
66 6 S Foreplay / 1999: Karmakeddon
Warriors / Violence I Crave / Bashing In
Heads / Motorpenis / Zum Kotzen / Alien
Militant / Goat War / Punishment Is
Absolute / When All Golden Turned To
Shit / Masterbator / The Burning Of
Provinciestraat / I Eat Pussy For
Breakfast / Delirium Tremens
RAPTURE, Osmose Productions
OPCD069 (1998)
Penis Et Circes / 6th Degree Mindfuck /
Iron Fist With An Iron Will / Angels
Rectums Do Bleed / We're Satan's
Generation / Goatvomit And Gasmasks /
Fallout Theory In Practice / Burst
Command 'Til War / Healers Of The Red
Plague / The Pillory / The Return Of The
Nuclear Gods / Vitutation / J.C.S. /
Nuclear Metal Retaliation / Inbred /
Phallus Maleficarum
NIHIL, Osmose Productions (2000)
Cogito Ergo Sum / Human Proof / Wrath
Of The Goat / Angel Rectums Still Bleed-
The Sequel / Porteclipse Era / Nothing's
Sacred / Zero Tolerance / Assault The
Weak / How The Laughter Died / Nihil
**IMPALED NAZARENE VS DRILLER
KILLER**, Solardisk (2000)
DECADE OF DECADENCE, Osmose

Productions OPCD 108 (2000)
Intro / Condemned To Hell / The Crucified
/ Disgust Suite Op. I / Morbid Fate /
Disgust Suite Op. II / Worms In Rectum /
Conned Thru Life / Crucifixation /
Nuctermeron Of Necromanteion /
Condemned To Hell / Impurity Of Doom /
The Crucified / Infernus / Morbid Fate /
Ave Satanas / In The Name Of Satan /
Fall To Fornication / Damnation (Raping
The Angels) / Noisrevrep Taag / In The
Name Of Satan / Noisrevrep Taag /
Damnation (Raping The Angels) / The
Black Vomit / Ghost Riders / Sadogoat / I
Am The Killer Of Trolls / Kill Yourself /
Burst Command Til War / Nuclear Metal
Retaliation / Instrumental I / Instrumental
II / Instrumental III

IMPENDING DOOM (GERMANY)

German Black Metal band IMPENDING
DOOM shared a split album with UNGOD
in 1997.

Albums:
CAEDES SACRILEGAE, Perverted
Taste (1997)
Caedes Sacrilegae / Aeon Of Dreams /
Be My Blood Of The Night / Dracul's
Passion By The Light Of The Bloodmoon
/ My Goddess / Autumn Silence /
Funeral Pile / Revelation Of Baphomet /
Downfall Of God / Impending Doom
SPLIT, Merciless (1997) (Split album with
UNGOD)
SIGNUM OF HATE, (199-)
The Age Of Antichrist / Armageddon
Tales / Demon- (Mon)Archy / Land Of
Burning Coffins / Hellhammer / Sumerian
Awakening / The Rebirth / Domination
Of Suffering Souls / Forward To
Golgotha / Stigma (Signum Of Hate) /
Metal To The Metals

IMPERATOR (POLAND)
Line-Up: Bariel (vocals / guitar), Mefisto
(bass), Carol (drums)

One of the true veterans of the Polish
extreme Metal scene. IMPERATOR was
founded in the mid 80's as a duo of
vocalist / guitarist Bariel and drummer
Adrian. Even in these formative days
IMPERATOR's raison de etre was
uncompromising Metal.
Mefisto was added on bass guitar during
September 1985 in order to fulfill the
band's debut live shows. The first demo
tape 'Endless Sacrifice' surfaced in 1986
followed by a live cassette titled

'Deathlive'. For IMPERATOR's third demo, 1987's 'Eternal Might', Moloch took over drum duties. The band's burgeoning status kindled the interest of Euronymous of Deathlike Silence Records but as negotiations between the two parties dragged on IMPERATOR opted to sign to local label Nameless Records. Unfortunately due to Nameless being a Polish company distribution worldwide was severely restricted.
Pagan Records re-issued the debut in 1997 with bonus tracks.

Albums:
THE TIME BEFORE TIME, Nameless (1991)
Eternal Might / Abhorrence / Necromonicon / Persecutor / Defunct Dimension / External Extinction / Ancient Race
THE TIME BEFORE TIME, Pagan Moon CD 007 (1997)
Eternal Might / Abhorrence / Necromonicon / Persecutor / Defunct Dimension / External Extinction / Ancient Race / Love Is The Law (Love Under Will) / The Rest Is Silence

IMPERIAL (FRANCE)
Line-Up: Skrow (vocals / bass), Qujou (guitar), Richard (drums)

Marseille extreme Black act IMPERIAL go further than most in their attempts to shock with sickening lyrics. The band's albums are noted for their utter rawness.

Albums:
AUX CRÉPUSCULES, Osmose Productions (1998)
Le Narcissique / Aux Crépuscules / Montre Ton Regard / Orage Find / Un Adieu / La Femme Brülée / Vermin / Les Cavaliers De L'Oubli / La Lune Rouge / Impérial / Thrasheurs 13
THRASHEURS 13, Osmose Productions (1998)
Thrasheurs 13 / Censuré / Gouvener / Rebellion / Les Tableaux Rouges
MALMORT, Osmose Productions (2000)
Malmort / Gouverner / Paolla / Les Filles Mortes Ne Disent Jamais 'Non' / Le Metal / Caranaval / Domination / La Chiennasse / Confessé / L'Historie De Bobby Qui S'Est Abyé, Qui Revient, Et Que Sa Copine Trove Qu'Il Pue L'Egout / Paraboles

IMPERIUM (NORWAY)

IMPERIUM drummer Frode Clausen has credits with DISMAL EUPHONY.

Albums:
TOO SHORT A SEASON, (199-)
Silenced / To Things That Were / Too Short A Season / Slip Of Tongue / Play Of Compassion / Chemical Dreams / Left Meaningless / Messiah Mask / Awakening

IMPIETY (SINGAPORE)
Line-Up: Shyalthan (vocals / bass), Xxxul (guitar), Demonomancer (bass), Fauzzt (drums)

Singapore Black Metal act IMPIETY, founded in 1990, hailed their coming with a 1992 demo 'Ceremonial Necrochrist Redesecration'. The band at this stage comprised of frontman Shyalthan, guitarist Xxxul and drummer Iblyss. The group, minus Xxxul and with new guitarist Leprophiliac Rex, was signed up to the Shivadarshana label for a 7" single 'Salve The Goat'. This release sold well and was also licensed to the American Fudgeworthy label where it was pressed onto marble vinyl.
Following the single IMPIETY bolstered their sound with guitarist Abyydos as Rex took on bass duties. This incarnation of IMPIETY cut the debut album 'Asateerul Awaleen'. Response was strong again and a projected mini album 'Funeralight' was recorded. However, IMPIETY's record label collapsed and the EP surfaced only on tape format.
After this episide Iblyss was forced out and Abyydos was forced to depart to fulfill his national service obligations. IMPIETY was brought back up to strength with the addition of guitarist Fryaun and ex LIBATION drummer Dajjal.
Dajjal would later join Deathsters ABBATOIR whilst coincidently erstwhile ABBATOIR and ABHORER man Dagoth joined IMPIETY. Session bass at this juncture was being handled by ABATTORY's Kravnos for the 1999 album 'Skullfucking Armageddon'. Meantime Samhain Records in America issued 'Dragon Oath Diabolus' from the 'Funeralight' sessions on a split 7" single with the infamous PROFANATICA.
The turn of the millenium beckoned further line up changes when Fryraun was allegedly imprisoned for two years for posseession of heroin curtailing a planned Asian and European tour.

Regrouping founder member Xxxul rejoined alongside bassist Demonomancer and European shows ensued. Upon returning to Singapore Dagoth left the fold and was replaced by Fauzzt of HAIL for a second round of European dates. The French Drakkar label re-released 'Skullfucking Armageddon' with extra tracks from earlier EPs.
Recently IMPIETY signed to the established Black Metal haven Osmose Productions.

Singles/EPs:
Salve The Goat / Iblis Exelsi, Shivadarshana (1994) (7" single)
Sodomythical Frostgoats / Serpentspells / Sorcerique Baphostorms / Dragonoath Diabolus, Ultra Hingax Productions (1997) ('Funeral Light' EP. Cassette release)

Albums:
ASATEERUL AWALEEN, Shivadarshana (1996)
Intromancy: Dzuul Ar'Shil Jaheem / Anal Madonna / Divine Hutamahan Frostfuck / Hymnvocation Of Nazarethian Nunwhores / Magick- Consecration Goatsodomy / Ceremonial Necrochrist Redesecration / Bismishyaithan / Blasphemyth... The Seventh Goatspawn
SKULLFUCKING ARMAGEDDON, Iron Pegasus (1999)
Lords Of The Apokalypse / Nocturnized / Sodomythical Frostgoats / Ironflames Of Hate / Diabolical Witches Aggression / Skullfucked- The Speed Metal Hell / Sorcerique Baphostorms / Torment In Fire

IMPRESSIONS OF WINTER
(GERMANY)
Line-Up: Laikha, Joe, Tobias Franz, Andres Waldura

Albums:
CANTICA LUNAE- SONGS OF THE MOON, Spirit SON 228-2 (1996)
Canticum Lunae / Hi Versus / Flores Gelidi / From Dreamworld To Sunrise / Impressions Of Winter / Ignis Ardet In Pluvia / Triviality / Captivas (Instrumental) / My Father's Return / Elegy Of A Swan / Foreboding
DECEPTIVE SPRINGS AND FADING LANDSCAPES, Spirit 085-35082 SPV (1998)
Promising Wake / Langueo (Silence Of Wine) / Shadowed Grove / Bandar /

Transcendence / Festival Of Fools / Omnis Mundi Creatura / Ghosts Of The Forest / Auctoritas Libri / Urechinaria / Landscape Of The Meadow Lost / The Recovering Of Spring

IMPURITY (BRAZIL)

Albums:
INTO THE RITUAL CHAMBER, Cogumelo COG081 (1997)
SATANIC METAL KINGDOM, Cogumelo (2000)

INADE (GERMANY)

INADE describe their sound as "crushing Ambient". The band, a duo of Rene Lehman and Knut Enderlein, lace their releases with esoteric and occult themes. The 1996 'Aldebaran' release constructed around the ideas of the German Vril society.
INADE debuted with the 1992 'Schwerttu' cassette followed by the 'Burning Flesh' 1993 session. Signing to the British Cold Spring label INADE issued the 'Axxiarm' 7" single then the 'Aldebaran' release. A switch to the American Malignant concern saw the release of a 10" vinyl EP 'The Flood Of White Light'.
The band also performs as EX ORDER.

Singles/EPs:
Breaking The Walls / Above The Plains / Movement And Construction, Cold Spring (1996) ('Axxiarm Plains' 7" single)
Grinding Inside / Impulse / With The Flood To Light, Malignant (1997) (10" single)
Signals From 68 Dimensions / The Conquest Of Being Separated / The Cursing Of Enabling Foundations / The End Of Beginning, Cold Spring (1996) ('Aldebaran' EP)
V.I.T.R.I.O.L., Loki Foundation LOK120 (1997) (7" single)
Crackling Void I. / Quartered Conclusion II., MDP (1999) ('The Quartered Void' 7" single)

Albums:
BURNING FLESH, Loki Foundation LOK124CD (1997)
Overture Bells / Shattered Bones / The Coming Of The Black Legions / Final Prayer / Outcry / Storm Of Fire / Burning Flesh / Through The Gates Of Death / Genius Loci Part I / Genius Loci Part II / Genius Loci Part III / Genius Loci IV / Tat Twarm Asi

COLLIDING DIMENSION TOUR '99, (1999)
Signals From 68 Dimensions Part I / Signals From 68 Dimensions Part II / Inner Sphere Resonance / IRX Pulsar / With The Flood To Light / Vitriol Part I / Vitriol Part II
THE CRACKLING OF THE ANONYMOUS, Loki Foundation (2001)

IN AETURNUM (SWEDEN)
Line-Up: David Larsson (vocals / guitars), Paul Johansson (guitar)

Originally titled BEHEMOTH releasing demos prior to a name change to IN AETURNUM and the 1997 mini album 'And Darkness Came'.
IN AETURNUM toured Europe in 1999 alongside IMMORTAL.
Frontman David Larsson is also a member of WAR and INFERNAL.

Albums:
AND DARKNESS CAME, (1997)
FOREVER BLASPHEMY, Necropolis (1999)
Majesty Of Fire / Spawned To Crush / Reaper In Black / The Pale Black Death / Forever Blasphemy / Of Unhallowed Blood / When The Vultures Left
THE PESTILENT PLAGUE, Necropolis NR052 CD (2000)

INANNA UNVEILED (GERMANY)

Albums:
INANNA UNVEILED, Solistitium SOL023 (1997)
Trifixion: Kether, Chokmah, Binah / In Absence Of Inanna / Shadowkeep / I, The Allfather / No Peace Amongst The Stars / My Lady Unchanging / This Spell Was Wrought By Hatred / Write My Name In Dusk

IN BATTLE (SWEDEN)
Line-Up: Wiklund (drums / vocals), Fröléti (guitar / bass)

IN BATTLE was a "War Metal" amalgamation in 1996 of ODHINN members guitarist Fröléti, Ostlund and drummer Wiklund with SETHERIAL's Lord Moloch and Lord Alastor Mysteriis.
IN BATTLE's line up for the 1998 album was down to a duo of Wiklund and Fröléti.

Albums:
IN BATTLE, Napalm (1997)
Ruler Of The Northern Sphere / I Ofred Vi Drar Fram / The Nocturnal Moan / Enchant Me / År Av Köld / Doom Of The Unbeloved / Odhinn / A Sign Of Northern Triumph And Glory / De Hängdas Furste / Lokes Ätt / Helhorde / In Battle
THE RAGE OF THE NORTHMEN,

IN AETURNUM

Napalm (1998)
From The Flesh And Bones Of Our
Enemies / The Rage Of The Northmen /
The Sceptre Of Hate / The Conqueror /
The Destroyer Of Souls / Muspelheim
The Dominion Of The Flame / Storms Of
War / Armies Of The Northern Realms /
Endless War

INCANTATION (New Jersey, USA)
Line-Up: Craig Pillard (vocals / guitar),
John McEntee (guitar), Ronnie Deo
(bass), Jim Roe (drums)

A highly influential act that straddle the
borderline between Black and Death
Metal. INCANTATION are cited by many
of todays acts as being a direct
inspiration.
INCANTATION came together with a line
up of erstwhile BLOOD THIRTY DEATH
members guitarist Brett Makowski and
bassist Aragon Amori. Ex REVENANT
man John McEntree and Paul Ledney,
previously with G.G. Allin's
CONNECTICUT COCKSUCKERS.
A major fall out occurred with McEntree
being left alone as Makowski, Amori and
Ledney decamped en masse to found the
notorious Black Metal act PROFANATICA
releasing a string of highly controversial
EPs.
Following INCANTATION's debut album
'Onward To Golgotha' frontman Craig
Pillard broke away from the group. Before
long bassist Ronnie Reo and drummer
Jim Roe joined him to found WOMB, an
act that evolved into DISCIPLES OF
MOCKERY.
Competition between DISCIPLES OF
MOCKERY and INCANTATION was so
fierce that at the 1994 Deathstock festival
in New York Pillard's band played a full
set of INCANTATION numbers just before
INCANTATION themselves took the
stage!
Confusion reigned in Death Metal circles
when INCANTION's 1994 album 'Mortal
Throne Of Nazarene' was re-released
under the new title of 'Upon The Throne
Of Apocalypse' with a reversed track
order and a sticker proclaiming 'Pagan
Disciples Of Mockery'!! (Later Pillard's
mob became WOMB again but reverted
to DISCIPLES OF MOCKERY for the
1999 three track promotion CD).
Amidst all this INCANTATION relocated
entirely to Ohio with only founder member
John McEntee creating a completely
revised line up. INCANTATION performed
a short tour of Mexico in 1995 sharing a
bill with IMMOLATION and ACID BATH.

An American tour with Swedes GRAVE
was nearly curtailed when
INCANTATION's bassist decided not to
go along for the ride. Stoically the band
carried on without bass as a trio of
McEntee, guitarist Dwayne Morris and
drummer Kyle Severn. However,
INCANTION finally settled on bassist Rob
Yench.
The band later pulled in frontman Daniel
Corchado but for shows in Argentina
during 1996 DEATHRUNE's Mike Saez
took the position on a temporary basis.
The 1997 album, produced by Bill
Korecky, features a cover of DEATH's
'Scream Bloody Gore'.
By 2000 INCANTION's roster had shifted
once more. Corchado opted out to
concentrate on his other act THE CHASM
and in came the aforementioned Mike
Saez. The album was recorded with
session drummer Dave Culross of
MALEVOLENT CREATION and the band
pulled in DEATH, CONTROL DENIED
and ICED EARTH man Richard Christy
for tour work.
Kyle Severn meantime involved himself
with the high profile WOLFEN SOCIETY
project featuring ACHERON's Vincent
Crowley, VITAL REMAINS singer Jeff
Gruslin and DARK FUNERAL guitarist
Lord Ahriman.

Singles/EPs:
Entrantment Of Evil, Seraphic Decay
(1990)

Albums:
ONWARD TO GOLGOTHA, Relapse
(1992)
Golgotha / Devoured Death /
Blasphemous Creation / Rotting Spiritual
Embodiment / Unholy Massacre /
Entrantment Of Evil / Christening The
Afterbirth / Immortal Cessation /
Profanation / Deliverance Of Horrific
Prophecies / Eternal Torture
MORTAL THRONE OF NAZARENE,
Relapse (1994)
Demonic Incarnate / Emaciated Holy
Figure / Iconclasm Of Catholicism /
Essence Ablaze / Nocturnal Dominium /
The Ibex Moon / Blissful Bloodshower /
Abolishment Of Immaculate Serenity
**THE FORESAKEN MOURNING OF
ANGELIC ANGUISH**, Relapse RR 6974
(1997)
Shadows From The Ancient Empire /
Lusting Congregation Of Perpetual
Damnation (Extreme Eden) / Triumph In
Blasphemy (Interlude) / Forsaken

Mourning Of Angelic Anguish / Scream Bloody Gore / Twisted Sacrilegious Journey Into The Darkest Neurotic Delirium / Outro / The Ibex Moon / Blasphemous Cremation / Essence Ablaze / Blissful Bloodshower
DIABOLICAL CONQUEST, Relapse (1998)
Impending Diabolic Conquest / Desecration (Of The Heavenly Gracefullness) / Disciples Of Blasphemous Reprisal / Unheavenly Skies / United In Repugnance / Shadows From The Ancient Empire / Ethereal Misery / Masters Of Infernal Damnation / Horde Of Bestial Flames
THE INFERNAL STORM, Relapse (2000)
Anoint The Chosen / Extinguishing Salvation / Impetuous Rage / Sempiternal Pandemonium / Lustful Demise / Heaven Departed / Apocalyptic Destroyer Of Angels / Nocturnal Kingdom Of Demonic Enlightenment

INCHIUVATU (ITALY)

Sicilian Black Metal act.

Albums:
ADDISIU, Elegy (1997)
Veni / Inchiuvatu / Cu Sancu A L'Occhi / Ave Matri / Addisiu / Castiu Di Diu / Lu Jocu Dili Spiddi / Nenia / Unia / Cristu Crastu / Quiete Morete / Lu Jaddinu Di Lu Piacirim / Luciferu Re

IN DARKNESS (PORTUGAL)

Portuguese Black Metal band IN DARKNESS issued the 1995 demo 'Remembrance From The Ancients' prior to their 1997 debut album.

Albums:
TOO COLD INSIDE, Eclipse (1997)
Intro / Forever Broken Dream / My Tears / Long Autumn / As The moon / This Emptiness / The Cold Inside / In Passion / Whispers In The Dark

IN DEUM MALEDICUS (ITALY)

Rome based Black Metal project IN DEUM MALEDICUS is the work of two NOVEMBRE members.

Albums:
ACIES, Cysboiled (1995)

INDUNGEON (SWEDEN)

Line-Up: Mournlord (vocals / drums), Asmodeus (guitar), Cethulhv (guitar), L.V. Manngarmr (bass)

INDUNGEON is a project established in 1996 by Stefan Wienerhall and Karl Beckmann of MITHOTYN and THY PRIMORDIAL vocalist Michael Andersson and bassist J. Albrektsson. The act's debut demo was impressive enough to be repressed onto CD by American label Full Moon Productions. 'Machinegunnery Of Doom' includes a cover of BATHORY's 'Fire In Fire'.
Both Beckmann and Wienerhall would later create the Power Metal band FALCONER.

Albums:
MACHINEGUNNERY OF DOOM, Full Moon Productions (1997)
THE MISANTHROPACALYPSE, (1999)
Genocide / Powers Unbound / Misanthropalypse / Sentenced To The Flames / Mutilated / Propaganda Of War / Final Conflict / Battletank No. II

INFERIA (FINLAND)

Line-Up: Reijo Kortesniemi (vocals), Jani Huttunen (guitar), Jani Nikkilä (guitar), Petri Malinen (bass), Tero Järvinen (drums)

Singles/EPs:
Under The Skin Of The Split Body / The Art Of Self Mutilation / Lunatics Anal Fanatics / Spawned At The Dawn / They Bleed And Bleed, Invasion IR007 (1995) ('Spawned At The Dawn' EP) (1995)

INFERNAL BEAUTY (BELGIUM)

Line-Up: Thomas (vocals), Kristof (guitar / keyboards), Bart (guitar), Pieter (bass), Sara (keyboards), Joachim (drums)

INFERNAL BEAUTY formed in 1994, albeit under a different name. Originally founding members Maarten (vocals) and Kristof (guitar) pursued an avant garde direction, although once bassist Pieter and drummer Joachim joined the fold the Death Metal sound became more progressive.
After a few months rehearsing as a quartet Maarten opted to leave due, it seems, his voice not being up to the extreme style INFERNAL BEAUTY wished to offer. He was replaced by Thomas and, after completing gigs opening for SADIST, EXTERMINATOR

and AVATAR in August 1995, the group completed their first demo ('Drakensquar') which was voted 'Demo Of The Month' in the Dutch Rock mag 'Aardschock'.
The success of the demo led to a deal with Hammerheart Records and the first album would contain a remixed version of the 'Drakensquar' ('Ruler Of Darkness') demo.
Novelly, the band's lyrics are in 'Drakensliny', a language peculiar to the band and invented by Joachim.

Albums:
DARKENSQUAR, Hammerheart (1997)
Revüro Eud Vis Squarderik / Alcatara (As The Forest Calls) / Io Lindipnig / Atheria / Tis Emprio / Sinitiöm Eud Sanctimo / Victro Eud Vis Squaderik

INFERNAL GATES (SWEDEN)

Albums:
FROM THE MIST OF DARK WATERS, X Treme XTR 002 (1998)
Greet The Storm / In Times Of Sculptured Shadows / The Gathering Of Tears / Ember Of Illusions / A Void Unsealed / Under My Wings / Remembrance Of Things To Come / The Son Of Ancient Gloom

INFERNAL MAJESTY (CANADA)
Line-Up: Chris Bailey (vocals), Steve Terror (guitar), Kenny Hallman (guitar), Psychopath (bass), Rick Nemes (drums)

Following Thrash Metal band INFERNAL MAJESTY's debut 1987 album 'None Shall Defy' the band released the 'Nigresent Dissolution' and 'Creation Of Chaos' demos.
Dutch label Displeased re-issued the debut album with bonus tracks culled from the demo sessions. The 1999 'Chaos In Copenhagen' album added extra tracks of INFERNAL MAJESTY cover versions by CHRIST DENIED and DAWN.

Albums:
NONE SHALL DEFY, Roadrunner (1987)
UNHOLIER THAN THOU, Hypnotic HYP 1062 (1998)
Unholier Than Thou / The Hunted / Gone The Way Of All Flesh / Black Infernal World / Roman Song / Where Is Your God? / death Toll / Art Of war
NONE SHALL DEFY, Displeased (1997)
Overlord / R.I.P. / Night Of The Living

Dead / S.O.S. / None Shall Defy / Skeletons In The Closet / Anthology Of Death / Path Of The Psycho / Into The Unknown / Hell On Earth
CHAOS IN COPENHAGEN, Hypnotic (1999)
Birth Of Power / Unholier Than Thou / Where Is Your God? / R.I.P. / Night Of The Living Dead / S.O.S. / Night Of The Living Dead (DAWN) / Overlord (CHRIST DENIED)

INFERNI (HOLLAND)

Side project of FUNERAL WINDS members.

Albums:
INFERNI, Black Arts (1995)

INFERNÖ (NORWAY)
Line-Up: Aggressor, Necrodevil, Bestial Tormentor

A self proclaimed 'True' Metal band that includes in its rankings Carl Michael Eide ('Aggressor') of AURA NOIR, VED BUENS ENDE and also an ex SATYRICON and ULVER member.
INFERNÖ debuted with a 1995 demo session 'Massacre In Hell'.
For INFERNÖ's 1996 album 'Utter Hell' the frightening personality named as "Hazardous Pussy Desecrator" was found to be contributing "Session Guts"!
Following the debut record INFERNÖ delivered tracks to the Primitive Arts EP 'Headbangers Against Disco'.
The vinyl version of 1998's 'Downtown Hades' included two live tracks recorded on the band's 'Euro Holocaust' tour with ABSU and ENSLAVED.

Albums:
UTTER HELL, Osmose Productions OPCD 044 (1996)
Intro From Hell / Satanic Overkill / Tormentor / Ripping Hell / Storming Metal / Infernal Invasion / Sodom (Burning The Flag) / Necroslut / Torment Her / Massacre In Hell / Infernö
DOWNTOWN HADES, Osmose Productions OPCD 060 (1998)
Straight From Hell / Utter Hell / Rot In Hell / Roadkill / In Bed With Satan / Bulldozer / Alcoholocaust / Thrash Till Death / Metal Attack / Violator

INFERNUM (POLAND)

INFERNUM is a side project of members

of GRAVELAND. The act first issued the 1995 demo 'Damned Majesty'.

Albums:
TAUR-NUR-FINN, Astral Wings (1995)
Intro / In The Black Clouds Of War / The Ancient Order / Gammadion / Weltmacht Oder Niedergang / Meine Ehre Heisst Treue / Cathari Sects / Outro

INFESTATION (UK)
Line-Up: David Samuel (vocals), Giusseppe Cutispoto (guitar), Jeremy Gray (guitar), Declan Malone (drums)

Promising British Black Death Metal crew INFESTATION emerged in 1996. The band was dealt a blow in 1998 when drummer Dave Hirschmeiner joined the premier league act CRADLE OF FILTH. His replacement for the 'Mass Immolation' debut album was Declan Malone.

Singles/EPs:
Curse Of Creation EP, Infestation (1998)

Albums:
MASS IMMOLATION, Lunasound LUNA001CD (2000)
Necrospawn / Book Of Lies / Legions Of Death / Desecrate / The Hunt / Evil, Evil / Carrion / Black Pope / Butcher Knife / Curse Of Creation / Infest / Demons Of Darkness / Prophet Of Doom / Self Impaled

INFEST DEAD (SWEDEN)

A Death Metal project from EDGE OF SANITY's Dan Swanö based upon the temple of Lucifer and the burning of believers in Jesus Christ.

Singles/EPs:
The Rising / I'll Be Black / In The Spell Of Satan / Save Me From The Hands Of Christ / Fucked By Satan / Burn Me (Without The Grace Of God), Invasion IR 020 (1996) ('Killing Christ' EP)

Albums:
HELLFUCK, Invasion IR 026 (1997)
Rebirth (Intro) / The Desecration Of Christ / Infest The Dead / The New Empire / Mercenary, Merciless / Born Nailed / Susej Ilik Ot Tolp Eht / Blaspheme The Abyss / Polterchrist / Sacrifice The Saviour / Hellfuck / Darkness Complete / Haunting The Fly / Heaven Denied / Salvation Incomplete /

Bewitch The Virgin / Angeldemon / World Inverted / Son Of The Darkside / Hellborn / Satanic / Amen (Outro)
JESUSATAN, (1999)
Resurrection / Christiansanity / Born To Burn / Jesusatan / Undead Screaming Sins / The Burning Of The Son / Sinister / Evil / Antichristian Song / Black Knight

INKUBUS SUKKUBUS (UK)
Line-Up: Candia Riley (vocals), Tony McKormack (guitar), Bob (bass)

Gloucestershire Gothic esoteric Folk Metallers with an enviable reputation for high quality albums infused with Wiccan and Paganist themes. The band was founded in 1989 as a trio of vocalist Candia Riley, guitarist Tony McKormack and Adam Henderson. Originally titled after a local ancient monument BELAS KNAP the band soon evolved into INCUBUS SUCCUBUS releasing the 7" single 'Beltaine'. Despite the high profile nature of this release the band splintered with Riley and McKormack continuing as CHILDREN OF THE MOON.
By late 1991 the duo had resurrected INCUBUS SUCCUBUS with the addition of drummer Bob. Early material from the CHILDREN OF THE MOON sessions was issued as the debut INCUBUS SUCCUBUS album 'Beltaine'. The band toured Britain heavily promoting this and further releases such as 1993's 'Belladonna And Aconite' including dates with artists as diverse as NOSFERATU, ZODIAC MINDWARP, THE DAMNED and CLAWFINGER. The 1994 album 'Wytches', released on the Pagan Media label, saw a distinct shift in musical style. The album would quickly become a much sought after rarity.
Promoting the 'Heartbeat Of The Earth' album the band toured as guests to DANZIG and the GENITORTURERS before dates at major festivals in Germany. By 1995 the group changed both their name, subtly to 'INKUBUS SUKKUBUS', and their format to manouevre Bob to bass to accommodate the inclusion of a drum machine.
1996 had INKUBUS SUKKUBUS further enhancing their status with showings on British TV and further European touring. The band also cut a version of 'Spellbound' for a SIOUXSIE AND THE BANSHEES tribute album.
Latterly INKUBUSS SUKKUBUS have put in their inaugural American shows and are regulars at established Gothic

festivals and the Whitby Dracula events. INKUBUS SUKKUBUS toured Britain with CRADLE OF FILTH in 1999.

Albums:
BELLADONNA AND ACONITE, Resurrection ABCD 7 (1993)
Beltaine / Midnight Queen / Trinity / Belladonna And Aconite / Soul Inside / Song Of The Siren / Vampyres / Eternity / Incubus / All The Devil's Men / I Am The One / Old Hornie / Vlad / Samhain
WYTCHES, Pagan Media PMR CD7 (1994)
Wytches / Queen Of The May / Pagan Born / Gypsy Lament / Leveller / Call Out My Name / Conquistadors / Burning Times / Song To Pan / Enchantment / Catherine / Church Of Madness / The Rape Of Maude Bowen / Dark Mother / Devils
HEARTBEAT OF THE EARTH, Resurrection ABCD 5 (1995)
Heartbeat Of The Earth / Young Lovers / Underworld / Prince Of Shadows / Craft Of The Wise / Corn King / Witch Hunt / Fire Of Love / Love Spell / Song For Our Age / Intercourse With The Vampire / Sabrina / Catherine / Take My Hunger
BELTAINE, Resurrection ABCD 11 (1996)
Beltaine / Wytches I / Pagan Born / Song To Pan / Goblin Jig / Midnight Queen / Trinity / I Am The One / Vampyre Kiss / Wytches II / Burning Times / The Leveller / Church Of Madness / Wytches (Chant)
VAMPRYE EROTICA, Resurrection ABCD 17 (1997)
Heart Of Lilith / Woman To Hare / Hail The Holly King / Wake Of The Christian Knights / Paint It Black / All Along The Crooked Way / The Witch Of Berkeley / Danse Vampyr / Vampyre Erotica / Wild Hunt / Sweet Morpheus / Hell-Fire / Whore Of Babylon
AWAY WITH THE FAERIES, Resurrection ABCD 21 (1998)
Wytches Chant '98 / Away With The Faeries / Come To Me (Song Of The Water Nymph) / Turnera / Starchild / Io Pan / Woman To Hare / Paint It Black / Craft Of The Wise / Heartbeat Of The Earth / Witch Hunt / Queen Of The May / Take My Hunger / Vampyre Erotica / Belladonna And Aconite
WILD, Resurrection (1999)
Rune / Wounded / Kiss Of Hades / Struwwlpeter / Bright Star / Lord Of The Flame / Aradia / Storm / Smile Of Torment / Reptile / Nymphomania / Lammas Song / Wild / Delilah

INNER SHRINE (ITALY)
Line-Up: Luca Liotti (vocals/ guitar), Cecilia Boninsegni (vocals), Anna Vignozzi (vocals), Leonardo Moretti (bass), Claudio Tovagli (drums)

Gothic Metal from Florence featuring the operatic singing of Cecilia Boninsegni and the "mystic voices" of Anna Vignozzi.

Albums:
NOCTURNAL RHYMES ENTANGLED IN SILENCE, Dragonheart (1997)
Fatum (Intro) / Dream On / The Last Breath / Bleeding Tears By Candlelight (The Illusion Of Hope Act I) / Awaiting The Solar Awakening (The Illusion Of Hope Act II) / Soliloqium In Darkness (The Illusion Of Hope Act III) / Enveloped By A Conquest's Shadow / Subsidence / Breaking The Mortal Shell Of Love
FALLEN BEAUTY, Dragonheart (2000)
Sanguis Vitae / In The Garden Of Sadness / Angelic Visions / Free In Emptiness / Enlightened By Splendour / Symphony Of The Absolute Bulwark / Passage To Eternity / The Inner Research Of The Shrine

INQUISICIÓN (CHILE)
Line-Up: Pedro Galán (vocals), Manalo Schafler (guitar), Christian Maturana (bass), Carlos Hernández (drums)

Santiago's INQUISICIÓN was founded in 1993 by TORTURER guitarist Manalo Schafler together with drummer Carlos Hernández initially billed as SANTA INQUISICIÓN. The act was fronted by Erstwhile PANZER vocalist Freddy Alexis.
By 1995 the band title had been shortened to simply INQUISICIÓN and augmented their sound with bassist Christian Maturans, previously with PSYKIS.
The 1998 album 'In Nomine' is a collection of earlier demos released on CD format. In March 1999 Alexis made way for new singer Pedro Galán.

Albums:
STEEL VENGEANCE, Dreamland Music (1997)
Innocent Sinner / Sed Diabolus / Pagan Rites / Steel Vengeance / Fate Was Sealed / Message In Black / Torturer / The Ancient Light / Into The Labyrinth
IN NOMINI, Toxic (1998)
Innocent Sinner / Sed Diabolus / Pagan Rites / Fate Was Sealed / The Ancient

Light / Torture / Into The Labyrinth / Mayday's Eve / Bats In The Bellfry / Holy Fire / The Dream Quest Of The Unknown Avalon
BLACK LEATHER FROM HELL, (1998) Dragonslayer / Black Leather From Hell / Army Of Darkness / Midnight Avenger / The Axis Of The Mist / Witchcraft / Extermination / Devil Mistress / Mensage Oculto

INQUISITION (WA, USA)

INQUISITION shared a demo with Brazilians PROFANE CREATION in 1996.

Singles/EPs:
Inquisition EP, (1990)

Albums:
INCENSE OF REST, Defiled (1994) Chant Of The Unholy Victory-Whispering In The Tears Of Blood / Incense Of Rest / Encounter In The Deep Shadows / Visions Of The Pagan Lord / Meditation Before The Kill
INTO THE INFERNAL REGIONS OF THE ANCIENT CULT, (1998) Unholy Magic Attack / Those Of The Night / The Initiation / Empire Of Luciferian Race / Summoned By Ancient Wizards Under A Black Moon / Journey Ti Infernukeorreka / Into The Infernal Regions Of The Ancient Cult / Mighty Wargod Of The Templars (Hail Baphomet) / Solitary Death In The Nocturnal Woodlands / Hail The Cult

INQUISITOR (HOLLAND)
Line-Up: Alex (vocals), Erik (guitar), Hans (bass), Wim (drums)

Formed in 1992 from the merging of Dutch outfits MENTICIDE and DESULTORY. INQUISITOR soon became known for a style of hectic Thrash Metal with strong Death Metal influences.
Having debuted with the 'Blasphemous Accusations' demo after several line-up changes a second demo ('Your Pain Will Be Exquisite') led to a deal with Shiver Records.
The debut album caused problems however as the cover artwork was deemed obscene and was forced to be censored.
INQUISITOR became CENTURION in the late 90's debuting with the 'Of Purest Fire' EP.

Albums:
WALPURGIS - SABBATH OF LUST, Shiver (1996) Damnation For The Holy / Consuming Christ / Condemned Saints / Trial Of Denial / Chaos In Eden / Jehova's Downfall / Crypt Of Confession / Unholy Seeds / Cry Of The Christians / Fallen Missionary / Inquisitor

IN RUINS (USA)
Line-Up: J. Michael (vocals / guitar), Jason (bass), Sean James (drums)

Philadelphia Death Black act previously known as BLACK THORNS.

Albums:
FOUR SEASONS OF GREY, Metal Blade (1998) The Haunted Moon / Four Seasons Of Grey / Nocturne / Vampire, Garden Of Thorns / Forest Of The Impaled / Black Thorns / Beyond The Black Lake / The Gathering Storm

INSANE DEVOTION (BRAZIL)
Line-Up: Moloch (vocals), Mauricio Laube (guitar), Rodrigo (bass), Fernando Nahtaival (keyboards), Flavio (drums)

Founded as DAEMON in 1995 by keyboard player Fernando Nahtaival and drummer Rafael Reis. By 1996 the band had enrolled frontman Douglas Evanstorm of REVERANCE. Later ex NECROTERIO guitarist Adriano was drafted for the split CD 'Whores Of Babylon'.
1998 witnessed major changes as guitarist Mauricio Laube from Death Metal band SCORNER, singer Moloch of CAIFAZ and bassist Rodrigo of AKERONT and NOCTURNAL WHISPERS and FORNICATION drummer Flavio all enrolled. With this new look INSANE DEVOTION cut another split CD 'In Inferioribus Terrae' this time in alliance with SCORNER.
The 1999 incarnation of the band predictably shifted again with members including rhythm section bassist Azarack and drummer Icthys Niger of MURDER RAPE and EVILWAR and ex NECROTERIO guitarist Adrian Leatherface.
Nahtaival would session on the debut REVERANCE AETURNUM album in 2000.

Albums:

WHORES OF BABYLON, (1997)
IN INFERIORIBUS TERRAE, (1999)
(split album with SCORNER)
The Born Of The New King / Whores Of
Beelzebub / Marching In TheWrath Of
The Deads / Slaying For Satan

INSATANITY (USA)

Line-Up: Mark Rochar (vocals), Jan Lipitz
(guitar), Dan Roberts (guitar), Lou Suppa
(bass), Matt Mazzenga (drums)

Philadelphia extreme Black Metal band
INSATANITY released a plethora of
demos prior to signing to Greek label
Unisound for their debut 1996 album.
INSATANITY bowed in with an
eponymous demo in 1993 following it the
same year with 'Ad Maiorem Satanae
Glorium' and 'Unholiness Rising' in 1995.

Albums:

DIVINE DECOMPOSITION, Unisound
(1996)
Begooten, Not Made / Shemhamforash /
Diabolical Indignation / Transfiguration /
Divine Decomposition / Under The
Baphomet / Rex Judaeorum / Angels Of
The Apocalypse / The Blood Is The Tie
SPLIT, Mortal Coil (1997) (Split album
with IMMORTAL SUFFERING)
Holocaust / At One With Infinity /
Vengeance From Beyond The Grave /
Mortification / The Great Abstinence /
Unjaded / Dawn Of The Dead / Entangled
Upon Lies / 12 / God's Little Children / I
Murder / Corpse (Grave Robber)

IN THE WOODS (NORWAY)

Line-Up: Jan Ovl Svithjod (vocals),
Oddvar A.M. (guitar), Christer C.H. Botteri
(guitar), X. Botteri (bass), Anders Kobro
(drums)

IN THE WOODS formed in 1992 and the
group's first commercially available
demo, 'Isle Of Men', released the
following year gained a deal with British
label Misanthropy Records. The band
also re-released the band's demo in CD
format. The band's debut single was a
version of the 60's JEFFERSON
AIRPLANE druggie classic 'White
Rabbit'.
The Autumn of 1996 saw IN THE
WOODS on the road in Europe with
support from KATATONIA and VOICE OF
DESTRUCTION.
Vocalist Jan Ovl 'Overlord' Svithjod and
guitarist Christer guested on the 1999

DRAWN album 'A New World'.
Drummer Anders Kobro from IN THE
WOODS also moonlights with
CARPATHIAN FOREST and features as
part of SCARIOT for their 2000 album
'Deathforlorn'.
IN THE WOODS twins guitarist Christer
C.H. Botteri and bassist X. Botteri also
feature on the GREEN CARNATION
album 'Journey To The End Of Night'.

Singles/EPs:
White Rabbit / Mourning The Death Of
Aase, Misanthropy (1996)

Albums:
HEART OF THE AGES, Misanthropy
AMAZON 004 (1995)
Yearning The Seeds Of A New Dimension
/ (HE) Art Of The Ages / ...In The Woods /
Mourning The Death Of Aase / Wotan's
Return / Pigeon / The Divinity Of Wisdom
A RETURN TO THE ISLE OF MEN,
Hammerheart HHR 007 (1996)
The Wings Of My Dreamland / Tell De
Dode / In The Woods… / Creations Of
An Ancient Shape / Wotan's Return /
Heart Of The Ages / … And All This…
(Child Of Universal Tongue)
OMNIO, Misanthropy AMAZON 011
(1997)
299 796 kms / I Am Your Flesh / Kairos!
/ Weeping Willow / Omnio? (Pre- Bardo-
Post)
STRANGE IN STEREO, (199-)
Closing In / Cell / Vanish In The Absence
Of Virtue / Basement Corridors / Ion /
Generally More Worried Than Married /
Path Of The Righteous / Dead Man's
Creek / Titan Transcendence / Shelter /
By The Banks Of Pandemonium
**THREE TIMES SEVEN ON A
PILGRIMAGE**, Prophecy Productions
(2000)
Seed Of Sound / Karnakosmic / Epitaph
/ Empty Room / Let There Be More Light
/ Child Of Universal Tongue / Soundtrack
For Cycoz (1st Edition) / White Rabbit /
Mourning The Death Of Aase / If It's In
You

IN THOUSAND LAKES (SPAIN)

Albums:
LIFELESS WATERS, Arise ARISE 012
(1998)

IN THY DREAMS (SWEDEN)

Line-Up: Jonas Nyrén (vocals), Kakan
Stuvemark (guitar), Jari Kuusisto (guitar),
Fredrik Eriksson (bass), Stefan

Westerberg (drums)

Albums:
STREAM OF DISPRAISED SOULS,
Wrong Again WAR014 (1997)
Fateless / Glistening Truth / Fleeing
Illusion / Dreams Within / Stream Of
Dispraised Souls

INTO THE SUNLESS MERIDIAN
(NY, USA)

INTO THE SUNLESS MERIDIAN is a
side project of Mikael from NIGHT
CONQUERS DAY. A demo 'Sex Magick'
was issued prior to the debut album.

Albums:
INTO THE SUNLESS MERIDIAN, Near
Dark (1997)

INTROITUS (CZECH REPUBLIC)
Line-Up: Svantevid, Defluens

Albums:
SKIES OF THE UNHOLY DEPARTED,
C.C.P. CCP 100 187-2 (1997)
Towards The Enchanting Dark / Crimson
Night / Resurgent / Astral Crown (As The
Crowds Gather) / Pale Bride Of The
Black Wind / Damnation's Throne / I'm
The Spirit That Caressed Eternity / On
The Wings Of Holy Mist

INVERTED (SWEDEN)
Line-Up: Henric Heed (vocals), Mats
Blomberg (guitar), Larsken Svensson
(guitar), Joel Andersson (bass), Kristian
Hasselhuhn (drums)

Black Metal group INVERTED marked
their arrival with the 1991 demo 'Tales Of
Estaban'. INVERTED have shared space
on split singles with RESUCITATOR and
CENTINEX.

Singles/EPs:
Revocation Of The Beast / Beyond The
Holy Ground / Lost (With Christ) / Into
The Sign Of Chaos, Wild Rags WRR046
(1995) ('Revocation Of The Beast' EP)
Empire Of Darkness / Crawling
Underbellies, Regress BTT004 (1995)
Split, Wild Rags (1994) (Split single with
RESUCITATOR)
Split, Voice Of Death (1996) (Split single
with CENTINEX)

Albums:
THE SHADOWLAND, Shiver (1995)
THERE CAN ONLY BE ONE..., (199-)

Revenge / Fallen Saints / Longing For
Darker Times / As The Last Angel Falls /
Inverted / Metal Victory / Forever Death /
Wrath Of Sin

INVOCATION (GREECE)

Hellenic Black Metal band INVOCATION
issued a split 7" single shared with fellow
Greeks MEDIEVAL DEMON.

Singles/EPs:
Split, Dark Side (1995) (Split single with
MEDIEVAL DEMON)

ISEGRIM (HOLLAND)

ISEGRIM was founded in 1996 by the
duo of Ränz and Goldiloxxx. The band
was brought up to strength with the
addition of Krisz, Aaarghnita and Arydon
for the suitably titled 'Most Evil' demo of
November 1997.
ISEGRIM's live shows were reliant on
CELTIC FROST and KREATOR cover
versions but original material was issued
in the form of the 'Bird Of Prey' mini
album.
ISEGRIM adopted the new title of
IZEGRIM to avoid confusion with the
German project of the same name.
Arydon also operates with GODDESS OF
DESIRE.

Albums:
BIRD OF PREY, Damnation (1999)

ISEGRIM (GERMANY)

ISEGRIM is a solo project of one
Blackwar. Not to be confused with the
Dutch ISEGRIM that released the 'Bird Of
Prey' mini album and adopted a new title
of IZEGRIM in 1999.

Singles/EPs:
Diabolical Witchcraft / Rape Jesus
Christ / Seven Legions / Hear The
Screams Of Hell, Last Episode 007391-2
(1999) ('Isegrim' EP)

Albums:
DOMINUS INFERUS USHANAS,
Massacre MAS CD0253 (2000)
Domine Ushanas / Witch Of The
Northernlights / Lucifers Black Wings /
Blasphemous Hymns / ...The Eyes Of
Jesus Christ / Angel With Fire And
Sword / A Fistfuck Of Black Metal / Into
The War Of Satan

ISENGARD (NORWAY)

A solo project by DARKTHRONE drummer Fenriz (a.k.a. Gylve Nagell). ISENGARD bowed in with a 1989 demo 'Spectres Over Gorgoroth' and the follow up 1991 session 'Horizons'. ISENGARD's debut album 'Vinterskugge' ('Winter Shadow') was issued in 1994 on the Peaceville Records subsidiary Deaf records. A second album by Fenriz was released in late 1994 under the name of NEPTUNE TOWERS.

Albums:
VINTERSKUGGE, Deaf 16CD (1994)
Chapter One-Vandereren:
Vinterskugge- Gjennom Skogen Til Blaafjellene- Ut i Vannets Dyp Hvor Morket Hviler- Dommerdagssalme- In The Halls And Chambers Of Stardust The Crystallic Heavens Open- Fanden Lokker Til Stupet (Nytrad)- Naglfar / Chapter Two (Spectres Over Gorgoroth): Thy Gruesome Death- Deathcult- Rise From Below- Dark Lord Of Gorgoroth-Trollwandering (outro) / Chapter Three (Horizons): The Fog- Storm Of Evil-Bergtrollets Gravferd- Our Lord Will Come
HØSTMORKE, Moonfog (1995)
Neslepaks / Landet Og Havet / I Ei Gran Borti Nordre Åsen / Over De Syngende Ode Moer / Thornspawn Chalice / Total Death

ISHTAR (SWEDEN)

Albums:
KRIG, Hammerheart (1999)
The Abyss / The Shadow Warrior / Mörkrets Furste / Skuggtronen / De Svarta Följeslagarna / Damnation / Dimal Paradise / Vinterfrost

ISIDORE (TX, USA)

Black Thrash act ISIDORE is one of a triumvirate of solo projects from Endymion. Other operations include the ambient ENDYMION and the pre ISIDORE act HYLAS.

Albums:
SHADOW SEASON, Aphelion (1999) (Split album with HYLAS)

ISVIND (NORWAY)
Line-Up: Arak Draconiiz (vocals / guitar / bass), Goblin (drums)

Formed in Oslo during 1993, Black Metal band ISVIND ('Icewind') released the demos 'The Call Of The Icewind' and 'Nivelheimen' before the arrival in 1996 of a limited edition, 1'000 pressing 7" EP. Having shared rehearsal facilities with MAYHEM and ARCTURUS the influence of both bands would appear to have been considerable in shaping the ISVIND sound.
Mainman Arak Draconiiz also has credits with TSJUDER.

Singles/EPs:
Isvind / Herskerinnen / Et Slag Mot De Veike…, Solistitium SOL002 (1996) (7" single)

Albums:
DARK WATERS STIR, Solistitium SOL 007 (1996)
Intro / Ulv! Ulv! / En Gjennomratnet / Stille Sjel / Lysningen I Skogen / Dark Waters Stir / As Rane Came Down / Backend-Poltergeist

IZAKARON (RUSSIA)
Line-Up: Morkh (vocals), Azarlokh (guitar), Vesgoth (guitar / keyboards), Warslav (bass), Rhaven (drums)

IZAKARON emerged in 1997 with the demo cassette 'Thine Elder Forests Unfold'.

Albums:
CHAOCHRIST, Eternal Art (2000)
Hunting On Troyan Path / Aphrodite Of Hatred / Woods Of Thy Might / Thou Art Incarnated Souls / The Origin / Jam Of The Serpent / The Profound / Cold Kingdom / Benighted At The Ninth Gate

JOURNEY THROUGH THE DARK (ITALY)

Line-Up: Carlo Carbone (vocals), Gianluca Vecchio (guitar), Andrea Rizzuro (bass), Giuliano Pagliaro (keyboards), Francesco Caliri (drums)

Italian Black Metal band JOURNEY THROUGH THE DARK issued a 1995 demo 'Screams Of Sirens'.

Albums:
AMONG SECRETS, Nosferatu (1997)

JOYLESS (NORWAY)

Line-up: Thomas (vocals), Olaf (guitar / drums), Rune (bass)

JOYLESS are, in fact, a retitled FORGOTTEN WOODS. Under their previous guise the band released two albums; 'As The Wolves Gather' in 1995 and the follow up 'The Curse Of Mankind'.
JOYLESS issued a split 7" single shared with APOKRYPHUS limited to just 200 copies. The full length album 'Unlimited Hate' includes a cover version of MOTÖRHEAD's 'Religion'.

Singles/EPs:
Split, No Colours (1997) (Split single with APOKRYPHUS)

Albums:
UNLIMITED HATE, No Colours NC013 (1997)
Inherent Emptiness / Your Crystal Fragments / Bla Melankoli / (Don't Need) Religion / Overmotets Pris / Jomfrulysts / Dimension Of The Blackest Dark

JUDAS ISCARIOT (De Kalb, IL, USA)

Black metal solo vehicle for the industrious Akhenaten. The band is noted for its adherance to the purest of nihilistic Black Metal, its anti- commercialist approach and an exalted status on the underground scene. Many releases are issued in strictly limited edition formats. Initial recordings, billed as HEIDEGGER in 1992, were apparantly titled after the theorist Martin Heidegger.
JUDAS ISCARIOT bowed in with the 1993 demo 'Judas Iscariot'. It was to be two years before the follow up 'The Cold Earth Slept Below'. Further sessions ensued with 1996's 'The Dying Light',

'Distant In Solitary Night' and 'An Ancient Starry Sky'.
Two tracks from the 'Distant In Solitary Light' album were also issued in 7" single format entitled 'Arise My Lord' on Akhenaten's own Breath Of Night label.
Akhenaten would relocate to Germany for later releases and would also become bass player for the infamous Czech Black Metal act MANIAC BUTCHER.
JUDAS ISCARIOT have performed live as a trio with Akhenaton on vocals and guitar with Lord Imperial of KRIEG on bass and Proscripter McGovern of ABSU infamy on drums at the Texan 'Sacrifice The Nazarene Child' festival during 1999.
A later line up for a headlining performance at the 'Under The Black Sun' festival in Germany found Lord Imperial staying the course with MANIAC BUTCHER's Butcher on drums and secondary guitars courtesy of NARGAROTH's Kanwulf. This show was captured on the vinyl album 'Under The Black Sun- Live'. Limited to a mere 500 copies the album, which included alongside the live cuts an 11minute studio track 'Portions Of Eternity Too Great For The Eyes Of Man', would much to Akhenaten's chagrin command high prices on internet auction houses as demand far outstripped supply.
The bands 1993 demo was combined recordings from KRIEG, ETERNAL MAJESTY and MACABRE OMEN for release on the French Spikekult label.
Akhenaten was announced as forging part of the KRIEG live line up as bass player for the 2000 'Sacrifice The Nazarene Child' event but in the event it would be LUST's S. Diabolus who filled the role.
Akhenaten also operates WELTMACHT (with Lord Imperial) and the Black Death Metal act SARCOPHAGUS.

Singles/EPs:
The Wind Stands Silent / The Black Clouds Roll Under The Parapet Of The Sky, Breath Of Night BON002EP (1996) ('Arise My Lord' 7" single)
To The Coming Age Of Intolerance, Paniac (2001) (Split 7" single with KRIEG)

Albums:
THE COLD EARTH SLEPT BELOW..., Moribund DEAD14CD (1997)
Damned Below Judas / Wrath / Babylon / The Cold Earth Slept Below / Midnight Frost / Ye Blessed Creatures / Reign /

Fidelity / Nietszche
DISTANT IN SOLITARY LIGHT, Moribund (1996)
The Wind Stands Silent / Where The Winter Beats Incessant / The Black Clouds Roll Under The Parapet Of The Sky / The Clear Moon And The Glory Of Darkness / To The Black Tower Of Victory / In The Bliss Of The Eternal Valleys Of Hate
THY DYING LIGHT, Moribund (1997)
But Eternal Beheld His Vast Forests / His Eternal Life, Like A Dream Was Obliterated / Helpless It Lay, Like A Worm In His Frozen Track / Behold, Our Race Of Unstoppable Genius / From His Woven Darkness Above / Writhing Upon The Wind Of Mystic Philosophy And Dreams / They Saw His Pale Visage Emerge From The Darkness / Thy Dying Light, And Desolate Darkness / Arise, My Lord Of Infernal Wisdom
OF GREAT ETERNITY, Elegy (1997)
The Heavens Drip With Human Gore / I Filled With Woes The Passing Wind / Then Mourns The Wanderer / For The Last Judgement Draweth Nigh / Calls To Heaven For Human Blood / Our Sons Shall Rule The Empire Of The Sea
HEAVEN IN FLAMES, Red Stream RSR 0136 (2000)
An Eternal Kingdom Of Fire / Gaze Upon Heaven In Flames / Eternal Bliss… Eternal Death / Before A Circle Of Darkness / From Hateful Visions / Spill The Blood Of The Lambe / An Ancient Starry Sky
DETHRONED, CONQUERED AND FORGOTTEN, Red Stream (2000)
Descent To The Abyss / Benevolent Whore, Dethroned For Eternity / Journey Through Visions Of War / March Upon A Mighty Throne / Spill The Blood Of The Lamb (Special Blitzkrieg version)
UNDER THE BLACK SUN- LIVE, Paniac (2000)
Babylon In Ruin / Black Clouds Roll Under The Parapet Of The Sky / The Heavens Drop With Human Gore / Spill The Blood Of The Lamb / Karmageddon / Black Eternal Winds / Portions Of Eternity Too Great For The Eyes Of Men

JULIE LAUGHS NO MORE
(SWEDEN)
Line-Up: Danne (vocals), Blomman (vocals / guitar), Thomas (guitar), Babbaen (bass), Ronnie B. (drums)

Albums:
WHEN ONLY DARKNESS REMAINS,

JUDAS ISCARIOT

213

Voices Of Wonder (1999)
Only Darkness Remains / Morbid Dreams
/ Domains Of Darkness / The Cold
Awakening / The Ashes Of The Midnight
Sun / Silent Waters / Everything Dies

JUVENES (POLAND)

Albums:
RIDDLE OF STEEL, No Colours (2000)
Prolog / Chariots Of Gods / Ubi Sent /
Riddle Of Steel / Epilog

KAMPFAR (NORWAY)
Line-Up: Dolk (vocals / drums), Thomas (guitar / bass)

Self styled 'Black Pagan' outfit KAMPFAR were borne out of a previous band MOCK. With the dissolvement of MOCK guitarist Dolk created KAMPFAR, releasing a demo in late 1994.
The two tracks on the demo were remastered and a new recording added to create the EP, which was released by French label Seasons of Mist in 1997.

Singles/EPs:
Kamfar/ Kynig/ Kjenkorsten, Seasons Of Mist SOM003 (1997)
Norse / Troll / Taerreng, (199-) ('Norse' EP)

Albums:
MELLOM SKOGLEDDE AASER, Malicious MR 011 (1997)
Intro / Valdog / Valgalderkvad / Kledd I Bryne Og Smykket Blodorm / Hymne / Bukkeferd / Naglfar- Ragnarok
FRA UNDERVERDENEN, (199-)
I Ondskapens / Troll, Død Og Trolldom / Norse / Svart Og Vondt / Mork Pest / Fra Underverdenen

KAT (POLAND)
Line-Up: Roman Kostrzewski (vocals), Poitr Luczyk (guitar), Wojciech Mrowiec (guitar), Tomasz Jagus (bass), Irseneusz Loth (drums)

KAT were amongst the first Polish Metal bands to make a breakthrough into Western European Rock circles in the mid 80s. KAT's debut Polish release '666' was reissued for the Western market in the toned down form of 'Metal And Hell'.
Following the 1989 album 'Oddech Wymarlich Swiatów' ("The Breath Of Dead Worlds') KAT underwent line up changes. Losing guitarist Wojciech Mrowiec and bass player Tomasz Jagus the band would regroup with bassist K, Oset and guitar player J, Regulsji.
The 1992 'Bastard' album found KAT operating more furiously than ever before but the act calmed down considerably for the 1994 'Ballady' effort. Later work has seen KAT back on track.
The 1997 mini album 'Badz Wariatem, Zagraj Z Latem' (Get Crazy, Play With Kat') the band reworked earlier material alongside new tracks and Techno remixes.

KAT vocalist Roman Kostrzewski has also issued a double album inspired by Anton La Vey's 'Satanic Bible'.

Singles/EPs:
Ostatni Tabor / Noce Szatana, MMPR (1985) (7" single)

Albums:
666, Silverton (1986)
METAL AND HELL, Ambush (1986)
Metal And Hell / Killer / Time To Revenge / Devil's House Part I / (You Got Me) Vampire / Devil's Child / Black Hosts / Oracle / Devil's House Part II / 666
38 MINUTES OF LIVE, Silverton (1988)
ODDECH WYMARLYCH SWIATÓW, Metal Mind (1994)
BASTARD, Silverton (1992)
BALLADY, Silverton (1994)
RÓZE MILOSCI NAJCHETNIEJ PRZYJMUJA SIE NA GROBACH, Silverton (1995)
BADZ WARIATEM, ZAGRAJ Z KATEM, Silverton (1997)
SZYDERCZE ZWIERCIADO, Silverton (1997)

KATAKLYSM (CANADA)
Line-Up: Aquarius Sylvian Mars Venus (vocals), Jean Francois Dagenais (guitar), Maurizio Lacono (bass), Max Duhamal (drums)

Canadian Death Black act KATAKLYSM opened proceedings with the demo tape 'The Death Gate Cycle Of Reincarnation'. Line up initially was vocalist Aquarius Sylvian Mars Venus (Sylvian Houde), guitarist Stephan Core, bassist Maurizio Lacono and drummer Ariel Saide. The band signed to the German label Nuclear Blast for a debut 1993 album 'The Mystical Gate Of Reincarnation'.
Promoting the sophomore 'Sorcery' effort KATAKLYSM put in their inaugural European shows, including dates with DEICIDE, and became the first Canadian band to tour Mexico.
KATAKLYSM's drummer Max Duhamel was forced to leave the band in late 1995 following cartilage damage to his right knee. His replacement was American Nick Miller.
The band then switched to the Canadian Hypnotic label for the experimental 'Victim Of The Fallen World' album. However, this record saw limited distribution. By 1998 Duhamel had made his return as the band welcomed in new bassist Stephane Barbe.
Resigning with their former label Nuclear

Blast KATAKLYSM cut the 2000 'The Prophecy' outing. Guests included Rob of NECROMONICON and Mike DeSaho of CRYPTOPSY.

Singles/EPs:
Vision The Chaos (Kataklysm Part I) / Shrine Of Life (Chapter III- Reborn Through Death version II), Boundless (1994) (7" single)

Albums:
THE MYSTICAL GATE OF REINCARNATION, Nuclear Blast NB093 (1993)
The Mystical Gate Of Reincarnation: Trilogy. I) Frozen In Time (Chapter One- Will Of Suicide), II) Mystical Plane Of Evil (Chapter Two- Enigma Of The Unknown), III) Shrine Of Life (Chapter Three- Reborn Through Death / The Orb Of Uncreation
SORCERY, Nuclear Blast NB108 (1995)
Sorcery / The Rebirth Of Creation: Trilogy I) Mould In A Breed (Chapter One- Bestial Propagation), II) Whirlwind Of Withered Blossoms (Chapter Two- Forgotten Ancestors), III) Feeling The Neverworld (Chapter Three- An Infinite Transmigration) / Elder God / The Resurrected Portal Of Heaven: Trilogy I) Garden Of Dreams (Chapter One- Supernatural Appearance), II) Once...Upon Possession (Chapter Two- Legacy Of Both Lores), III) Dead Zygote (Chapter Three- Dethroned Son) / World Of Treason
THE TEMPLE OF KNOWLEDGE, Nuclear Blast NB 157-2 (1996)
The Transflamed Memories (Trinity) I) The Unholy Signature (Segment One- Utterly Significant), II) Beckoning The Xul (Segment II- In The Midst Of The Azonei's Dominion), III) Point Of Evanescence (Segment III- Of Sheer Perseverance) / Through The Core Of The Damned (Trinity IV) Fathers From The Suns (Act 1- The Occurred Barrier), V) Enhanced By The Lore (Act 2- Scholarship Ordained), VI) In Parallel Horizons (Act 3- Spontaneous Aura Projection) / Era of Aquarius (Trinity VII) The Awakener (Epoch 1- Summon The Legends), VIII) Maelstrom 2010 (Epoch 2- Omens About The Great Infernos), IX) Exode Of Evils (Epoch 3- Ladder Of Thousand Parsecs) / L'Odysee
VICTIM OF THE FALLEN WORLD, Hypnotic (1998)
As My World Burns / Imminent Downfall / Feared Resistance / Caged In / Portraits Of Anger / Extreme To The Core /

Courage Through Hope / A View From Inside / (God) Head / Embracing Europa / Remember / World Of Treason II
NORTHERN HYPERBLAST LIVE, Hypnotic (1999)
Maelstrom 2010 / Exode Of Evils / Enchant By The Lore / Sorcery / Elder God / Fathers From The Sun / Point Of Evanescence / Beckoning Of The Xul / The Awakener / Once... Upon Possession / The Unholy Signature / The Orb Of Uncreation / In Parallel Horizons / Vision The Chaos / Shrine Of Life
THE PROPHECY (STIGMATA OF THE IMMACULATE), Nuclear Blast NB 470-2 (2000)
1999: 6661: 2000 / Manifestation / Stormland / Breeding The Everlasting / Laments Of Fear And Despair / Astral Empire / Gateway To Extinction / Machiavellion / Renaissance

KATATONIA (SWEDEN)
Line-Up: Sombreius Blackheim (vocals / guitar), Israphael Wing (bass), Lord Seth (drums)

KATATONIA started life as a duo of guitar Sombreius Blackheim (real name Anders Nyström) and vocalist/drummer Lord Seth (real name Jonas Renske) in 1987. The group issued the 1992 demo 'JHVA Elohin Meth' which was later released in CD form by Dutch label Vic Records.
In late 1992 KATATONIA added bassist Israphael Wing (real name Guillaume Le Hucke) signing to No Fashion Records.
In addition to the material listed below the band have also contributed two tracks ('Black Erotica' and 'Love Of The Swan') to the Wrong Again Records compilation album 'W.A.R.' in 1995. Further recordings of interest included a split 7" EP with PRIMORDIAL the following year.
Blackheim also has a side project band titled BEWITCHED releasing the 'Diabolical desecration' album on Osmose Records in 1996. Seth is working on his OCTOBER TIDE project.
KATATONIA performed a short British tour in late 1996 with support acts IN THE WOODS and VOICE OF DESTRUCTION.
Blackheim and Seth also pursue another Death Metal project titled DIABOLICAL MASQUERADE. In 2000 the pair forged Black Metal project act BLOODBATH with EDGE OF SANITY's industrious Dan Swanö and OPETH's Mikael Akerfeldt.

Singles/EPs:
Midvinter Gates (Prologue) / Without God / Palace Of Frost / The Northern Silence / Crimson Tears (Epilogue), Vic VIC 1 (1994) ('Jhva Elohim Meth...The Revival' EP)
Funeral Wedding / Shades Of Emerald Fields / For Funerals To Come... / Epistal, Avantgarde AV 009 (1995) ('For Funerals To Come' EP)
Scarlet Heavens EP, Misanthropy (1996) (Split EP with PRIMORDIAL)
Nowhere / At Last / Inside The Fall, Avantgarde (1997) ('Sounds Of Decay' EP)
Saw You Drown / Scarlet Heavens, Avantgarde (1997)

Albums:
DANCE OF THE DECEMBER SOULS, No Fashion 005 (1995)
Seven Dreaming Souls / Gateways Of Bereavement / In Silence Enshrined / Without God / Elohim Meth / Velvet Thorns (Of Drynwhyl) / Tomb Of Insomnia / Dancing December
BRAVE MURDER DAY, Avantgarde AV022 (1996)
Brave / Murder / Day / Rainroom / 12 / Endtime
DISCOURAGE ONES, Avantgarde AV 029 (1998)
I Break / Stalemate / Deadhouse / Relention / Cold Ways / Gone / Last Resort / Nerve / Saw You Drown / Instrumental / Distrust
TONIGHT'S DECISION, (199-)
For My Demons / I Am Nothing / In Death, A Song / Had To (Leave) / This Punishment / Right Into The Bliss / No Good Can Come Of This / Strained / A Darkness Coming / Nightmares By The Sea / Black Session
SINGLES COLLECTION, (199-)
Midvinter Gates (Prologue) / Without God / Palace Of Frost / The Northern Silence / Crimson Tears (Epilogue) / Funeral Wedding / Shades Of Emerald Fields / For Funerals To Come... / Epistal / Nowhere / At Last / Inside The Fall

KATAXU (POLAND)

Black Metal band KATAXU's debut album was a split affair with THUNDERBOLT.

Albums:
ROOTS THUNDER, Cymphane AR001CD (2000)

KAVIAR KAVALIER
(CZECH REPUBLIC)

Albums:
+KLINIK+, Tentamen- Metal Age (1997)
Die Fetische Nacht / Du Ekelps / Spezial Gumiklinik / Der Nachtlichter Wasser Marsch / Zase To Zacalo / Ritual / Blue Velvet / Geile Frau / Einladung Zur Kaviar Party / 11th Street / Van Holst / Kaviar / Viva / Prejdi Jordan

KAWIR (GREECE)
Line-Up: Archenoros (vocals), Mentor (guitar / bass). E.S. Erichthonius (keyboards / drums)

A Greek Black Metal band with one single to their credit, a split affair with the Japanese group SIGH. Former members of KAWIR would go on to found CARPATHIAN LORDS and Death Metal act SICKNESS. Drummer Costas sessioned on the DEVISER album 'Unspeakable Cults'.

Singles/EPs:
Eumenidis, Cacophonous (1994) (Split single with SIGH)
To Kavirs EP, Dark Side (1996)

Albums:
PROS KAWEIROUS, Dark Side (1996)

KEEP OF KALESSIN (NORWAY)
Line-Up: Ghásh (vocals), Obsidian C. (guitar), Warach (bass), Vyl (drums)

Trondheim act previously known as ILDSKJAER. A 1996 demo 'Skygger Av Sorg' secured a label deal with the Avantgarde Music concern. Cernunnos of MANES sessions for the band as guitarist.
Bassist Warach (real name Øyvind Westrum) also runs a solo project BLOODSWORN.

Albums:
THROUGH TIMES OF WAR, Avantgarde Music (1997)
Through Times Of War / Den Sister Krieg / As A Shadow Cast / I Choose To Suffer / Skygger Av Sorg / Obliterator / Nectarous Red
AGNEN- A JOURNEY THROUGH THE DARK, Avantgarde (1999)
Dragonlord / As Mist Lay Silent Beneath / I Deny / Pain Humanized / Orb Of Man / Dryland / Towards I Roam / Agnen

217

KHAZAD DHUM (GERMANY)

Albums:
BLACKEST, Mindart Productions (1996)

KHISANTH (MS, USA)
Line-Up: Daemon (vocals), Dale (guitar), Chris (bass), Kevin (drums)

Mississippi band KHISINTH arrived with the demos 'Realm Of The Serpent' and 'Majestic Rites Of Chaos'.

Albums:
FORSEEN STORMS OF THE APOCALYPSE, Baphomet (2001)

KILLENGOD (AUSTRALIA)
Line-Up: Errol Nyp (vocals), Daniel Maynard (guitar), Corey Pagan (guitar), Drexler Roberts (bass), Jonathon Dao (drums)

Albums:
TRANSCENDUAL CONSCIOUSNESS, Warhead WHCD13 (199-)
Ever Death Flow / Funeral Fuck / Soul Mutilation / Believe In Divination / Experimental Evidence / Transcendual Consciousness / Luceferic Leviathan / Nordic Messiah
INTO THE ANCIENT MOON, (1998)
Ode To An Ancient Moon / Dominated Spirit / Temporary Skin / Thirteenth Universe / Masquerade Of The Masters / Lorde Of Whores / My Intention / Inhaling The Corpse / Everlasting Egypt / Black Miracle / Blasphemous Priest

KING DIAMOND (DENMARK)
Line-Up: King Diamond (vocals), Pete Blakk (guitar), Andy LaRocque (guitar), Hal Patino (bass), Mickey Dee (drums)

In April 1985 cult Satanic Metal band MERCYFUL FATE finally split and enigmatic vocalist King Diamond regrouped with MERCYFUL FATE guitarist Michael Denner and bassist Timi G. Hansen (formerly known as Timi Grabber) with a new band centred around his own stage personality KING DIAMOND. The other original band members were ex NADIR and GEISHA drummer Mickey Dee (real name Delaoglou) and guitarist Floyd Konstandin, the latter being superseded by former TRAFALGER guitarist Andy LaRocque.
King opted to concentrate his efforts mainly on America, where MERCYFUL

FATE had built a strong and loyal following. The debut album, 'Fatal Portrait' echoed heavily his former band but with more emphasis on overblown horror theatrics. The lyrical shift was a wise one as King had fallen into the trap of getting involved in a conversation with 'Kerrang!' magazine journalist Dave Dickson on the subject of Aleister Crowley and Magick. According to the interview that saw print, he had few answers. Allegedly an ardent follower of Crowley's philosophies and supposed Satanic practices (he was quick to claim responsibility for the 'demon' that electrocuted GIRLSCHOOL's Kim McAullife), King fell victim to someone who had recently taken a few widely available quotes inviting King to comment. King's credibility never really recovered in the eyes of the European media.
The second album, 'Abigail', was the first in a series of concept affairs that KING DIAMOND were to turn into highly elaborate stageshows. Following recording of 'Abigail' Michael Denner left due to feeling the pressure of being constantly on the road and was swiftly replaced with ex MADISON guitarist Michael 'Moon' Myllynen.
'Abigail' was toured around America with Chicago Christian Doom Metal band TROUBLE then undertook 15 shows in Germany opening for MOTÖRHEAD as well as headline shows. The hard graft of touring paid off and in America 'Abigail' reached number 123 in the Billboard charts selling over 150'000 copies.
Prior to recording next album 'Them', KING DIAMOND relocated to Los Angeles in order to have a realistic crack at the American market. The band also replaced Myllynen and Timi Hansen with ex GEISHA guitarist Pete Blakk and bassist Hal Patino.
'Them' (another conceptual affair) bolstered the continuing success of KING DIAMOND in America by charting in the Billboard top 100, but touring plans were initially shelved to allow the band to contribute soundtrack music to the horror movie 'Boggs'. Following the recording of 'Them' drummer Mickey Dee quit later to work with DON DOKKEN and WWIII before landing a permanent stay in MOTÖRHEAD. He was replaced with San Franciscan Chris Whitemyer, previously drum tech for WHITESNAKE's Tommy Aldridge, although the next record, 'Conspiracy' (which continued the plot of 'Them') beckoned in another

drummer in Swedish native Snowy Shaw. Shaw (real name Tommy Helgesson) would later record with MEMENTO MORI and WHIPPED CREAM in addition to joining King in a reformation of MERCYFUL FATE.

More line-up changes befell the group shortly after recording1990's 'The Eye' when longtime guitarist Pete Blakk quit to form his own band TOTEM.

Around the turn of the decade King chose to reform MERCYFUL FATE, although also carried on his solo career and was to add a new complement of band members for the KING DIAMOND comeback affair entitled 'The Spider's Lullaby' in 1995. The new band included recently added bassist Mike Webb and guitarist Charlie D'Angelo. The album proved a solid success, gaining chart places in Sweden, Denmark and Finland and was the first for new label Massacre, King having ended his long term association with Roadrunner Records with the 'Live In Europe '87 - Abigail' album back in 1991. A further record appeared in 1996 entitled 'The Graveyard' before, in late 1997, Roadrunner Records re-issued the KING DIAMOND back catalogue in re-mastered form, with some albums featuring additional bonus tracks. Both 'The Eye' and 'Live In Europe '87' were also re-mastered but do not have any additional material added. Meantime drummer Darrin Anthony was forced out of the band due to injuries suffered in a car accident.

1998's 'Voodoo' album, another horror conceptual effort, saw King and LaRocque (who, in the interim, had produced the debut album by Sweden's MIDVINTER during 1997) joined by second guitarist Herb Simonson, bassist Chrise Estes and drummer John Luke Herbert. The band added EIDOLON guitarist Glen Drover for tour work.

Shaw, D'Angelo and La Rocque ventured into outside activity by founding ILLWILL releasing a 1998 album.

Former bassist Hal Patino returned to the ranks in 2000 ousting David Harbour. Herbert would also decamp in October of 2000 making way for former SURGEON man Matt Thompson.

LaRocque would guest on the 2001 DIMMU BORGIR album 'Puritanical Euphoric Misanthropia' performing on the Japanese bonus track 'Devil's Path'.

Singles/EPs:
No Presents For Christmas / Charon,

Roadrunner RR12485 (1987)
The Family Ghost / Shrine, Roadrunner (1987)
Halloween / Them / No Presents / Shrine / Lake / Phone Call, Roadrunner RR 2455 1 (1988)
Welcome Home, Roadrunner (1988) (USA promotion)

Albums:
FATAL PORTRAIT, Roadrunner RR9721 (1986) **33 SWEDEN**
The Candle / The Jonah / The Portrait / Dressed In White / Charon / Lurking In The Dark / Halloween / Voices From The Past / Haunted
ABIGAIL, Roadrunner RR 9622 (1987) **39 SWEDEN, 123 USA**
Funeral / Arrival / A Mansion In The Darkness / Family Ghost / The 7th Day Of July 1777 / Possession / Abigail / Black Horsemen
THEM, Roadrunner RR 9550 (1988) **38 SWEDEN**
Out From The Asylum / Welcome Home / The Invisible Guests / Tea / Mother's Getting Weaker / Bye, Bye, Missy / A Broken Spell / The Accusation Chair / Them / Twilight Symphony / Coming Home
CONSPIRACY, Roadrunner RR 9461 2 (1989) **41 SWEDEN**
At The Graves / Sleepless Nights / Lies / A Visit From The Dead / The Wedding Dream / Amon Belongs To Them / Something Weird / Victimized / Let It Be Done / Cremation
THE EYE, Roadrunner RR 9346 (1990)
Eye Of The Witch / The Trial (Chambre Ardente) / Burn / Two Little Girls / Into The Convent / Father Picard / Behind These Walls / The Meetings / Insanity / 1642 Imprisonment / The Curse
LIVE IN EUROPE '87 -ABIGAIL (LIVE), Roadrunner RR 9287 (1991)
Funeral / Arrival / Come To The Sabbath / The Family Ghost / The 7th Day Of July 1777 / Portrait / The Possession / Abigail / The Candle / No Presents For Christmas
A DANGEROUS MEETING, Roadrunner RR 9117-2 (1992) (Best of compilation CD with MERCYFUL FATE)
The Candle / Charon / Halloween / No Presents For Christmas / Arrival / Abigail / Welcome Home / Sleepless Nights / Eye Of The Witch
THE SPIDER'S LULLABY, Massacre MASSCD 062 (1995)
From The Other Side / Killer / The Poltergeist / Dreams / Moonlight / Six

Feet Under / The Spider's Lullabye / Eastmann's Cure / Room 17 / To The Morgue

THE GRAVEYARD, Massacre MASS CD 103 (1996)
The Graveyard / Black Hill Sanatorium / Waiting / Heads On The Wall / Whispers / I'm Not A Stranger / Digging Graves / Meet Me At Midnight / Sleep Tight Little Baby / Daddy / Trick Or Treat / Up From The Grave / I Am / Lucy Forever

FATAL PORTRAIT, Roadrunner RR 8789-2 (1997) (Re-mastered, re-issue featuring bonus tracks)
The Cradle / The Jonah / The Portrait / Dressed In White / Charon / Lurking In The Dark / Halloween / Voices From The Past / Haunted / No Presents For Christmas / The Lake

ABIGAIL, Roadrunner RR 8788-2 (1997) (Re-mastered, re-issue featuring bonus tracks)
Funeral / Arrival / A Mansion In Darkness / The Family Ghost / The 7th Day Of July 1777 / Omens / The Possession / Abigail / Black Horsemen / Shrine / A Mansion In Darkness (Rough Mix) / The Family Ghost (Rough Mix) / The Possession (Rough Mix)

THEM, Roadrunner RR 8785-2 (1997) (Re-mastered re-issue featuring bonus tracks)
Out From The Asylum / Welcome Home / The Invisible Guests / Tea / Mother's Getting Weaker / Bye, Bye Missy / A Broken Spell / The Accusation Chair / "Them" / Twilight Symphony / Coming Home / Phone Call / The Invisible Guests (Rehearsal) / Bye, Bye Missy (Rehearsal)

CONSPIRACY, Roadrunner RR 8787-2 (1997) (Re-mastered re-issue featuring bonus tracks)
At The Graves / Sleepless Nights / Lies / A Visit From The Dead / The Wedding Dream / "Amon" Belongs To "Them" / Something Weird / Victimized / Let It Be Done / Cremation / At The Graves (Alternate Mix) / Cremation (Live Show Mix)

VOODOO, Massacre MAS CD0155 (1998)
Louisiana Darkness / 'L.O.A.' House / Life After Death / Voodoo / A Secret / Salem / One Down, Two To Go/ Sending Of Dead / Sarah's Night / The Exorcist / Unclean Spirits / Cross Of Baron Samedi / If Only They Knew / Aftermath

HOUSE OF GOD, Massacre (2000)
Upon The Cross / The Trees Have Eyes / Follow The Wolf / House Of God / Black Devil / The Pact / Goodbye / Just A Shadow / Help!!! / Passenger To Hell /

Catacombs / This Place Is Terrible / Peace Of Mind

KING DIAMOND AND BLACK ROSE: 20 YEARS AGO- A NIGHT OF REHEARSAL, Metal Blade (2001)
Locked Up In The Snow / Holy Mountain Lights / Crazy Tonight / Virgin / Kill For Fun / The End / Road Life / Soul Overture / Doctor Cranium / Disgrace / I Need Blood / Radar Love

KOHORT (POLAND)

Black Metal band KOHORT debuted in 1996 with the 'Meggido Eve' demo.

Albums:
CHRISTIAN MASQUERADE, Eternal Devils (1996)

KOROVA (AUSTRIA)

Line-Up: Christof Niederwiesr (vocals / guitar / keyboards), Georg Razeburger (guitar), Michael Kröll (bass), Moritz Neuner (drums)

Albums:
A KISS IN THE CHARNEL FIELD, Napalm NPR009 (1995)
Intro: Der Weltenbrand / Das Kreuz und der Meltzenapfel / After The Fruits Of Ephemeral Pulchritide / Lachrydeus Mittelgard (Slahan Fontagr Inn Awebi) / Entlebt in tristem Morgenblut / Latin Dreams In Turpentine / Intro: Im Teich erlischt ein Bächlein / Awakening From Perpetual Contemplation (Yellow Mahogony Tomb I) / Nordsciltim In The Filth Where All Cull Perambulates Pain / Salomeh, des Teufels Braut / A Kiss In The Charnel Fields

DEAD LIKE AN ANGEL, (1998)
Europa In Flammen / Strangulation Alpha / Our Reality Dissolves / Trip To The Bleeding Planets / Dead Like An Angel / Echoworld Caravans / Der Schlafmann Kommt / Tantra-Nova-Hyper Cannibalism

KOROZY (BULGARIA)

Line-Up: Possessor (vocals / guitar), Vampira (bass), Inscriptor (keyboards), Trolon (drums)

Albums:
LONG ROAD TO THE LAND OF BLACK, (1999)
Road To The Land Of Black / Dying Memories / Welcome To The Black Palace / Birth Of The Witch / The Blessing Of The Kehajota Witch / Soul Belongs To Evil / The Anger Of Servent

KORP (NORWAY)

KORP drummer Peter Andersson also operates with INCARNATED.

Albums:
DEMON REBORN, Vod VODCD006 (2000)
Into Everlasting Dreams / Night Of Temptation / Raven's Might / Demon Reborn / To Be Embraced By Darkness / In Thousand Years / The Infinite / I Månskenets Dystra Ijus / Until Eternity Calls

KOVENANT (NORWAY)

Line-Up: Lex Icon (vocals / bass), Psy Coma (guitar), Hellhammer (drums)

Previously known as THE COVENANT. Lex Icon, previously known as Nagash, is ex DIMMU BORGIR. Drummer Von Blomberg, better known as Hellhammer, has his priority act is MAYHEM whilst guitarist Psy Coma is in fact Blackheart. Previous members guitarist Astennu (DIMMU BORGIR / CARPE TENEBRAUM) and keyboard player Sverd were dispensed with upfront of the name change.

The band used the opportunity of changing titles to revamp their image, sound and names too from the earlier 'Nexus Polaris' album. These moves paid off as the band won two prestigious Spellmanprizen awards in Norway in the best band category.

The 1999 'Animatronic' album sees a cover of BABYLON ZOO's 'Spaceman' and heavy usage of female opera vocals.

KOVENANT, with second guitarist Angel, toured America for the first time as part of a package deal with MOONSPELL and AMORPHIS.

KOVENANT men Hellhammer and Psy Core appear on the 2000 TROLL album 'The Last Predators', a project assembled by Nagash.

The band has made huge strides to distance themselves from the Black Metal scene recently.

Albums:
ANIMATRONIC, Nuclear Blast (1999)
Mirror's Paradise / New World Order / Mannequin / Sindrom / Jihad / The Human Abstract / Prophecies Of Fire / In The Name Of The Future / Spaceman / The Birth Of Tragedy

KREUZWEG OST (AUSTRIA)

KREUZWEG OST is a union of SUMMONING's Silenius and HOLLENTHON / ex PUNGENT STENCH vocalist Martin Shirenc.

Albums:
IRON AVANTGARDE, Napalm DPR011 (2000)
Re-Kapitulation / Ein Bild Freudiger Lebens Bejaung / Eduard Rüttelmeier / Oh No Lo So, Magnifico / Stählerne Schwingen / Caki Voli / Kohlenklau / Der Feuersturm Von Dresden / Du, Gefangene! / Donautaufe / Na Wostoke Nechewo Nowogo

KREWEL (CZECH REPUBLIC)

Albums:
KREWEL, View Beyond (1994)

KRIEG (Bellerica, MA, USA)

Founded in 1995 until 1997 KRIEG went under the title of IMPERIAL. Bassist Lord Imperial has also formed part of the live line up for JUDAS ISCARIOT and has involvement with numerous projects including BLACK VIRGINITY, PROFONATION, DEVOTEE and VELTMACHT.

Session drums on the 1998 album 'Rise Of The Imperial Hordes' came courtesy of Telco Coraxo of BLOODSTORM. Other contributors were erstwhile ABOMINUS man Lord Soth and Ted of AUTUMN TEARS.

KRIEG would eventually become a solo endeavour of Lord Imperial once former member Lord Soth departed to DEVOTEE. A 1998 demo session 'A Crumbling Shrine' would be distributed as a multi band promotion release sharing space with JUDAS ISCARIOT and French band ANTAEUS. Soth would make a return to the group which also pulled in guitarist Azag.

Although a whole string of projected KRIEG releases was earmarked for 2000 on various labels the only release was a shared album in collusion with JUDAS ISCARIOT, ETERNAL MAJESTY and MACABRE OMEN on Spikekult Records. A further split affair was planned with Canadians ALLFATHER and Hungarian act NEBORA.

A live line up for KRIEG was announced for shows in 2000 comprising of Lord Imperial, S. Diabolis of LUST on bass and

THORNSPAWN's guitarist Lord Necron and drummer Blackthorn.

Singles/EPs:
To The Coming Age Of Intolerance, Paniac (2001) (Split 7" single with JUDAS ISCARIOT)

Albums:
RISE OF THE IMPERIAL HORDES, Blood Fire Death (1998)
The Arrival / Alarum / The Great Black Death / As Humanity Fades / My Weeping Soul- Part II / Coronation / End Of Time / Calamity From The Skies / Reunion Of The Ancients / Path Of Soth / The Ascension

KRISIUN (BRAZIL)
Line-up: Alex Carmago (vocals / bass), Moyses Kolesne (guitar / keyboards), Max Kolesne (drums)

Sao Paulo Death Metal merchants KRISIUN first offered their 1991 demo 'Evil Age'. A further tape 'Curse Of The Evil One' backed it up the following year leading to the band's first official product the 'Unmerciful Order' EP. Other releases included shared EP's with Germans HARMONY DIES and VIOLENT HATE. Signing to Germany's G.U.N. Records KRISIUN debuted proper with 1996's 'Black Force Domain'.
Switching to Century Media Records KRISIUN's 2000 album 'Conquerors Of Armageddon' was produced by MORBID ANGEL's Eric Rutan.

Albums:
UNMERCIFUL ORDER, (1993)
They Call Me Death / Unmerciful Order / Crosses Towards Hell / Agonize The Ending / Summons Of Irreligious / Meaning Of Terror / Infected Core / Insurrected Path (Depth Classic) / Rises From The Black
BLACK FORCE DOMAIN, G.U.N. GUN147 (1997)
Black Force Domain / Messiah Of The Double Cross / Hunter Of Souls / Blind Possession / Evil Mastermind / Infamous Glory / Respected To Perish Below / Meanest Evil / Obsession By Evil Force / Sacrifice Of The Unborn
APOCALYPTIC REVELATION, G.U.N. (1998)
Creations Scourge / Kings Of Killing / Apocalyptic Victory / Aborticide (In The Crypts Of Holiness) / March Of The Black Hordes / Vengeances Revelation /

Rites Of Defamation / Meaning Of Terror / Rises From Black
CONQUERORS OF ARMEGEDDON, Century Media (2000)
Intro- Ravager / Abyssal Gates / Soul Devourer / Messiah's Abomination / Cursed Scrolls / Conquerors Of Armageddon / Hatred Inherit / Iron Stakes / Endless Madness Descends

KULT OV AZAZEL (FL, USA)
Line-Up: Xul, Xaphan, Von (drums)

KULT OF AZAZEL, fronted by erstwhile DEVOURED BY DARKNESS man Xul, was borne out of AZAZEL, an act that issued the 'Enter Erebus' demo. Became KULT OF AZAZEL in February 2000.

Albums:
TRIUMPH OF FIRE, Arctic Music (2000)
La Messe Noir / Triumph Of Fire / Destruction Of The Throne Of God / My Misanthropy / To The Cold Beyond / In The Plagued Realm / Legions Unleashed / Altar Of Satan / Aether Cries / Embrace The Burning / Crown Of Fire
ORDER OF THE FLY, Blood, Fire, Death (2000)
Garden Of Shadows / Undeserving Fate / Transformation / Aether Cries / Crown Of Fire / Forever Heaven Gone / Garden Of Shadows (Live)
KULT OV AZAZEL, Genocide (2000) (Split album with KRIEG)
Intro / In The Plagued Realm / Symbionic 666 / Destruction Of The Throne Of God / Forever Heaven Gone

KVIKKSØLVGUTTENE (NORWAY)

Solo work from Necrobutcher of MAYHEM. Session musicians are vocalist Zathan and the strangely titled drummer Det Skal Du Drite I.

Singles/ EPs:
Skullcrusher / Grave Violater / Violent Death, Head Not Found (1997) ('Gamlem' EP)

Albums:
KRIEG, Head Not Found (1997)
In Den Arsch Gefickt / Torture / Krieg / More Murder / Anger / Ghoul / Sluts / Violent Death / Fisted Sisters / Naglekamp

KVIST (NORWAY)
Line-Up: Tom (vocals / bass), Hallvard Vergrimm (guitar / keyboards), Endre

(drums)

Black Metal act KVIST, founded in 1993,
trod the traditional path of a high selling
demo to attain their deal with French label
Avantgarde.

Albums:
FOR KUNSTEN MAA VI EVIG VIKKE,
Avantgarde AV014 (1996)
Ars Manifestia / Forbannet Veaere Jeg
Gar Pa / Stupet / Svartedal / Min Lekam
Er Meg Blott En Byrde / Vettenetter

LAMB OF GOD
(Richmond, VA, USA)
Line-Up: Randy (vocals), Mark (guitar), Will (guitar), John (bass), Chris Adler (drums)

LAMB OF GOD were previously known as BURN THE PRIEST.

Albums:
NEW AMERICAN GOSPEL, Prosthetic 3984143452 (2000)
Black Label / A Warning / In The Absence Of The Sacred / Letter To The Unborn / The Black Dahlia / Terror And Hubris In The House Of Frank Pollard / The Subtle Arts Of Murder And Persuasion / Pariah / Confessional / O.D.H.G.A.B.F.E.

LANGSUIR (MALAYSIA)
Line-Up: Batara Guru (guitar), Aznaniac (guitar), Azlan (bass)

Malaysian Black Metal crew LANGSUIR debuted with the demo 'Occultus Mysticum' in 1993.

Singles/EPs:
My Oath For Thee / Bastardized Regaman Sihir- Pontianik / The Seven Headed Dragon Of Peldangi / Tangisan Embun Pagi, Oriental Eruptions (1997) ('Eastern Cruelty' EP)

LEGENDA (FINLAND)
Line-Up: Sir Luttinen (vocals / guitar / keyboards), Niko Karppinen (bass)

A keyboard based outfit created by Sir Luttinen, previously a member of arch Black Metal protagonists IMPALED NAZARENE. The project was originally entitled GANDHARVA LEGENDA.

Albums:
AUTUMNAL, Holy HOLY25CD (1997)
All Flesh Is Grass / Bloodred Sunset / Legend / By The Moonlight / Wolves, Honey, Wolves / Kings / Luciette / Autumnal / At Nightfalls / Jacalian Cry / Black Sky / All Love Is Gone / Winter Night
ECLIPSE, Holy HOLY36CD (1999)
The Night Has Drawn Night / Where The Devils Dance / Rev. 66 / Shades And Shadows / Dead Red Roses / Cohorts Of Demons / Sister Shadow Sister (Blooddance mix) / The Fall Of Crow / Springrealm / The Heart Of The North / Eclipse

LEGION OF DOOM (GREECE)
Line-Up: Daimon (vocals / bass), Demogorgon (guitar), Aithir (drums)

Black Metal outfit LEGION OF DOOM shared their debut single with BESTIAL WRATH. The band recorded a demo titled 'Desecration' the following year as a duo of frontman Mortuary on vocals and bass and guitarist Demogorgon. The band embroiled themselves in notoriety from the off with debut album 'Kingdom Of Endless Darkness' being refused by many distributors due to its inclusion of a swastika on the inner sleeve artwork.
In 1996 LEGION OF DOOM utilized the temporary services of NAER MATARON drummer Aithir. The second album, produced by Magus Wampyr Daoloth of NECROMANTIA, saw Mortuary's place being taken by Daimon. Once again the presence of a stylized swastika created controversy.
Guitarist Demogorgon would issue a solo 7" single 'The Horned Moon' simply billed as DEMOGORGON. He would also form part of the duo WINTERGODS together with L.W. Darkoan of national socialist band DER STURMER.
Demogorgon also has a Gothic Rock project SHADOWS OF MAJESTY.

Singles/EPs:
Passage Through... The Circle, Molon Lave (1993) (split single with BESTIAL WRATH)

Albums:
KINGDOM OF ENDLESS DARKNESS, Soundphaze SIR 9510 (1995)
Holocaust Of David's Race / Kingdom Of Endless Darkness (Ades) / Hymn To The Fiendish Veleth / Aris...God Of Brutal War / The Black Queen / The Desecration / Meseonas
THOSE OF THE BLOOD, Hypervorea (1997)
Narjniians Eternal Winter / Sunrise Of The Golden Dawn / For Those Of The Blood / Erinuev- Daimone V Fterwtoi / Messenger / Kure / To Mustiko Tou Kocouliou

LEGION 666 (CANADA)
Line-Up: Asofoetida (vocals)

Albums:
KISS THE GOAT, Panzerlarm (2000)

LEMEGETHON (GREECE)

Black Metal band LEMEGOTHON first came to attention with a 1991 demo 'Dethronement Of The Light'.

Singles/EPs:
Demonic Hellhounds, Wounded Love (1995)

LENGSEL (NORWAY)

Line-Up: Tor Magne S. Glidje (vocals / bass), John Robert Mjåland (bass), Ole Halvardsveen (drums)

LENGSEL (which translates as 'Yearning') are fronted by Tor Magne S. Glidje who is also employed as bassist for EXTOL.

Albums:
SOLACE, Black Sun BS20 (2000)
Solace / Revival / Opaque / Hours / Coat Of Arms / Stille Dualisme / The World Monotone / Avmakt

LIAR OF GOLGOTHA (HOLLAND)

LIAR OF GOLGOTHA is a side project from Golgotha of FUNERAL WINDS.

Singles/EPs:
The Seventh Winter, Maggot (1995)
The Blood Of The Past / The Awakening Of The Vampire Lord / Forthcoming Bloodstorm, Cyronics (1996) ('Vendetta' EP)

Albums:
DANCING THROUGH THE PALACES OF UNHOLY BEAUTY, Shivadarshana (1996)
Into The Abysmal Night / Ancient Nature Rebels / The Strong Warlord / My Dreams Of Red / Dancing Through The Palaces Of Unholy Beauty / The Frozen Lakes Of Xastur / The Long Forgotten Wastelands / The Seventh Winter / In The Midst Of The Pagan Winterwar / Icons Of Seduction / Earning A Place On The Thrones / My Wisdom Of Truth / Dawn Of The Age Of Victory
DWELL WITHIN THE MYSTERIOUS DARK, Mascot M 7031-2 (1998)
The Dwelling / Merciless Rage / Towards The Time Centre / The Soul Above The Others / Creator / The Defloration Of Virgin Mary / My Spirit In The Web Of Purity / Into The Labyrinth Of Lamentation / The Long Forgotten Wastelands / The Mysterious Dark
ANCIENT WARS, Mascot (1999)

Ghost Of An Ancient Siberian Wolfcult / Night Of The Falling Stars / Mission Of Domination / Remembering The Ancient Wars / Forbidden Ancient Continent / In Praise Of Cthulhu / Atmospheres Of Elder Times / Goddess Rising / The Fall

LIERS IN WAIT (SWEDEN)

Line-Up: Christoffer Jonsson (vocals), Kristian Wahlin (guitar), Matthias Gustafson (bass), Hans Nilsson (drums)

Featuring the guitar talents of ex GROTESQUE man Kristian Wahlin. LIERS IN WAIT utilized the services of THERION vocalist Christoffer Jonsson to record the album. Drummer Hans Nilsson later joined LUCIFERON.
Both Wahlin and Nilsson founded DIABOLIQUE for a 1998 album.

Albums:
SPIRITUALLY UNCONTROLLED ART, Dolores DOL007 (1991)
Overlord / Bleeding Shrines Of Stone / Maleficent Dreamvoid / Liers In Wait / Gateways

LILITU (USA)

Line-Up: Derek Bonner (vocals / guitar), Jason Piona (guitar), Chris Todd (bass), Adina Blaze (keyboards), Evan Jones (drums)

LILITU was forged in 1995 with a line up of frontman Derek Bonner, fellow vocalist Evangelina, bassist Scott Harvey and bass player Holly Strong. In this incarnation the band cut two demos 1996's 'Our Vessels Of The Sea' and the following year's 'Servants Of Twilight'.
Despite the progress made with these releases the band would fold. However, Bonner resurrected LILITU in collusion with former ACHERON keyboard player Adina Blaze and session stand ins bassist Jonathon Potter and drummer Brian Mullis. By 1999 Bonner and Blaze had gelled a stable line up alongside guitarist Jason Piona, bassist Jason Barlous and drummer Evan Jones. The latter would be out of the picture by December of 1999 replaced by Dexter Young.
The summer of 2000 saw Blaze making an exit shortly after LILITU had recorded a version of WASP's 'Sleeping In The Fire' for a Dwell Records tribute album. Before the close of the year Chris Todd had taken the bass position and LILITU were also employing the temporary

services of ICEPICK drummer Cory Lang.

Albums:
THE EARTH GODS, Emerald Factory (2000)
Introduction- The Seventh Aeon / Firmament / To Burn Before The Sun / Dead Yesterday / Rise And Fall / The Earth We Stand To Inherit / The Earth Gods

LIMBONIC ART (NORWAY)
Line-Up: Daemon, Morpheus

A Black Metal project centred around former INFINITE DECAY man Daemon (real name Vidar Jensen). LIMBONIC ART started life as a quartet, but soon reduced to just Daemon and Morpheus. The duo were promoted heavily by Samoth of EMPEROR, leading to many press misjudgments that LIMBONIC ART were merely an EMPEROR offshoot.
Vinyl versions of the 1998 album 'In Abhorrence Dementia' were limited to a mere 500 signed copies.
In late 2000 Daemon featured as a guest on Samoth's side project ZYKLON's 2000 album 'World Ov Worms'.

Albums:
MOON IN THE SCORPIO, Nocturnal Art Productions ECLIPSE005 (1997)
Beneath The Buried Surface / Moon In The Scorpio / Through The Gleams Of Death / In Mourning Mystique / Beyond The Candles Burning / The Dark Rises Of The Heart / Darkzone Martyrdom
IN ABHORRENCE DEMENTIA, Nocturnal Art Productions ECLIPSE 008 (1997)
In Abhorrence Dementia / A Demonvoid Virtue / A Venomous Kiss Of Profane Grace / When Mind And Flesh Depart / Deathtrip To A Mirage Asylum / Under Burden's Of Life's Holocaust / Behind The Mask Obscure / Oceania / Misanthropic Spectrum
EPITOME OF ILLUSIONS, Nocturnal Art (1998)
Symphony In Moonlight And Nightmares / Path Of Ice / Sources To Agonies / Solace Of The Shadows / The Black Heart's Nirvana / Phantasmagorical Dreams / Arctic Odyssey
AD NOCTUM- DYNASTY OF DEATH, Nocturnal Art (1999)
The Dark Paranormal Calling / As The Bell Of Immolation Calls / Pits Of The Cold Beyond / Dynasty Of Death / The Supreme Sacrifice / In Embers Of Infernal

Greed / The Yawning Abyss Of Madness

LONG VOYAGE BACK
(AUSTRALIA)

LONG VOYAGE BACK was founded by the veteran HOBB'S ANGEL OF DEATH and DESTROYER 666 bass player Phil Gresik. In his previous act DESTROYER 666 the man had gone under the nom de guerre of Bullet Eater.
The second album saw drums courtesy of Sham with female vocals from Mel Watson and Sam Lohs

Albums:
LONG VOYAGE BACK, Destruktïve Kommandöh DSTK7664-2CD (1998)
Long Voyage Back / Poison Blood / Towards The Sun / The Search / Reflection / Nomadic Paths
LONG VOYAGE BACK II, Modern Invasion MIM7328-2CD (1999)
Naked And Wounded / Ghosts Of The Past / Phyrhic Battle / Heavy Stone / Behind The Eyes / The Struggle / The Pitiless Reality

LONG WINTER STARE
(Cranston, RI, USA)
Line-Up: Chris Listing (vocals / guitar), Madrigal (guitar), Scarab (keyboards), Greg Bull (drums)

An experimental Black symphonic act Rhode Island's LONG WINTER STARE was created as MANTHING in 1996. Evolving into LONG WINTER STARE the band for a time employed second guitarist Dwarn.
The bands second album, which included a twisted version of the KANSAS classic 'Carry On My Wayward Son', saw backing vocals courtesy of KRIEG's Lord Imperial.
Added female singer Dierdra Faith in 2000.

Albums:
COLD TALE ETERNAL, Pantheon (1998)
Enter / Timeless And Somber / Sigh / Eternal Slumber / Anastasia / Paranoid / Clawing Out
BEFORE THE DAWN, SO GO THE SHADOWS, Dragon Flight (1999)
Blood Of Nazarene / He Is Insane / War Epic / Carry On My Wayward Son / Into The Darkness / Hounds / Remain Life Eternal / Into The Sun
THE TEARS OF ODIN'S FALLEN, Dark

Symphonies (2000)
In The Hall Of Odin / Blood Of Steel /
Blood Of My Fathers / Neolyth / The
Last Call / In Arms / The Unknown God

LORD (FRANCE)
Line-Up: Lord Charon (vocals/bass),
Aragorn (guitar), Countess Hoggsogoth
(keyboards), Tipthereth (drums)

A Corpsepainted Black Metal act from
Hazebouck plying lethargic Doom riffs,
LORD evolved as a duo of Lord Charon
and keyboard player Countess
Hoggsogoth during 1994, adding guitarist
Kleudde and drummer Morgon before the
year was out.
Previous to LORD founder Lord Charon
had been a member of Thrash band
MEGATHRASH prior to founding Black
Metal outfit THESPIAN FLOW. The man's
next move was to become bass player for
Deathsters SEPULCHARAL. A meeting
with Countess Hoggsogoth led in turn to
the formation of FUNERAL PYRE, later
titled LORD.
The following year LORD issued a demo
cassette, 'Shadows Of Massacre', after
which the band once more trimmed down
to the founding duo.
Prior to recording the debut album
guitarist Aragorn and drummer Tipthereth
brought the ranks up to strength,
although both Kleudde and Morgon
contributed to the album sessions.
By 2000 LORD's roster comprised of Lord
Charon, Countess Hoggsogoth, guitarists
The Nazgûl and Samigina and drummer
Armageddon.

Albums:
**BEHIND THE CURTAIN OF
DARKNESS**, Eldethorn ELD002 (1998)
Intro / Live To Fight, Fight To Die / Into
Hell's Well / Midnight In The Graveyard /
When Funeral Pyres Ablaze The Black
Moon Sky / Under The Spell Of The
Diabolical Sorcerer / Shadows Of
Massacre / Calling From The Deepest
Darkness / Gates To The Blazing
Kingdom

LORD BELIAL (SWEDEN)
Line-Up: Dark (vocals), Vassago (guitar),
Bloodlord (bass), Lilith (flute), Sin (drums)

LORD BELIAL vocalist Thomas 'Dark' is
ex SATANISED. Guitarist Pepa 'Vassago'
and drummer Mikael 'Sin' are both ex
SADIST.
Prior to the 1995 debut album LORD

BELIAL had already made their presence
felt with the demos 'The Art Of Dying' in
1993 and 'Into The Frozen Shadows' in
1994.
Guitarist VASSAGO issued solo product
in 1997 in the form of a split 12" single
shared with ANTICHRIST.

Albums:
**KISS THE GOAT: SIC TRANSIT
GLORIA MUNDI**, No Fashion NFR010
(1995)
Hymn Of The Ancient Misanthropic Spirit
Of The Forest / Satan Divine / Grace Of
God / The Ancient Slumber / Into The
Frozen Shadows / The Art Of Dying /
Oscuum Obcenum / Mysterius Kingdom
/ In The Light Of The Fullmoon / Lilith-
Demonic Queen Of The Black Light
ENTER THE MOONLIGHT GATE, No
Fashion (1997)
Enter The Moonlight Gate / Unholy Spell
Of Lilith / Path With Endless Horizons /
Lamia / Black Winter Bloodbath / Forlorn
In Silence / Belial- Northern Prince Of
Evil / Realm Of A Thousand Burning
Souls (Part I)

LORDES OF ALL DESIRES (USA)
Line-Up: Le'Rue Delashay (vocals /
guitar), Caine (guitar), Gates (bass),
Armand (keyboards), Asmodechi (drums)

LORDES OF ALL DESIRES was founded
by the union of THEATRE OF THE
MACABRE and BLOODMOON members
in 1996. Following the debut album
Le'Rue Delashay reconvened his
previous act THEATRE OF THE
MACABRE for the 2000 album 'A
Paradise In Flesh And Blood'.

Albums:
CROWNED IN BLASPHEMY, (1998)
Crowned In Blasphemy / The Scars Of
Withered Beauty / Sins Of Thy Flesh /
This Most Precious Beast / The Feasting

LORD KAOS (AUSTRALIA)
Line-Up: Lord Of Night Summoning
(vocals), Frank (guitar), Darael (guitar),
Incubus (bass), Shaun (keyboards), Nigyl
(drums)

Black Metal act created in early 1994.
Debuted, with the aid of a drum machine,
in 1995 with the 'Path To My Funeral
Light' demo. As the band membership
ebbed and flowed LORD KAOS took to
using drum machines and programmed
keyboards onstage.

The first album 'Thorns Of Impurity' was recorded in 1995 as a trio for Warhead Records although did not see a release until late 1996 due to Norway's Head Not Found label bidding for the band. Although the album finally saw a release guitarist Astennu quit to relocate to Norway to create CARPE TENBRUM with Nagash of DIMMU BORGIR. Astennu eventually joined DIMMU BORGIR for their 'Spiritual Black Dimensions' album.

Undeterred LORD KAOS pulled in ex NEUROPATH guitarist Korps and various members of Newcastle's EMPERY OF THORNS. Live gigs followed including supports to CRADLE OF FILTH.

Vocalist Lord Of Night Summoning (Jamie) also operates CRUCIBLE OF AGONY.

Albums:
THORNS OF IMPURITY, Warhead (1996)
Crystal Lakes / Hall Of Sorrow / Golden Winds On Red Streams Of Ocean Lightning / Freezing Ornate Throne / Dark Tower Of Illumination / Under The Darkest Shade / Red Sky Of Angels Dying / In The Icy Realm / Fountains Of Impure Essence / Thorns Of Impurity

LORD WIND (POLAND)

A solo Pagan Folklore endeavour of GRAVELAND and INFERNUM's Rob Darken.

Albums:
FORGOTTEN SONGS, Full Moon Productions (1998)
Windstory Of Old Ghost / War Song / Song Like Wind / Going To War / Signal For Fight / Prolog- Sword For Sun / Father's Sword / Only Your Spirit Will Return / Pagan Holocaust / Funeral Song / Arianrod Heil!
HERALDS OF FLIGHT, No Colours (2000)
Gift Of Gods / Fighting Till Death / Hail To The Gods Of Victory / Mystery / Heralds Of Reborn Honour / Today Love, Tomorrow Death / Without Mercy And Forgiveness / Gates Of Valhalla / Dark Forges Of Hades

LOST DREAMS (AUSTRIA)
Line-Up: Maggo Wenzel (vocals), Andreas Maierhofer (guitar), Herbert Sopracolle (guitar), Auer Tom (bass), Phillip Hörtnagl (keyboards), Marco Eller (drums)

Austrian Death Black act LOST DREAMS have had a confused history streching back to the mid 90's Originally guitarist Andreas Maierhofer handled lead vocals until Böhm Martin took over in 1996. However, by mid 1997 Martin had been supplanted by Maggo wenzel and in addition LOST DREAMS pulled in female singer Tanja Falschunger. The keyboard position also changed as Haideggar Alexander made way for Babette Kach. 1999 had a switch on the drum stool with Stephan Zangerle having a brief term before Marco Eller landed the job. 2000 saw bassist Boris Hoerhager losing out to Auer Tom.

Albums:
REFLECTIONS OF DARKNESS, Lost Dreams (1999)
Reflections Of Darkness / Obsessed / Always Beside You / Burning Eyes / The Funeral Of God / Believe In Evil (Live)

LOTHLORIEN (SWEDEN)
Line-Up: Tobias Birgersson (guitar), Linus Wikstrom (guitar), Tobias Johansson (bass), Daniel Hannedahl (drums)

Albums:
THE PRIMAL EVENT, Black Mark (1999)
I Wear Mankind / Forever And Ever Alone / Moments / Sorrowsoul / The Other Side / Inside My Mind / Supernatural / Among Those Who Wept

LUCIFER (SWEDEN)
Line-Up: Johnny Fagerström (vocals / drums), Lars Thorsen (guitar), Mikael Andersson (guitar), Mikael Fasth (bass)

BELSEBUB vocalist Johnny Fagerström formed LUCIFER as a side act. When LUCIFER split Fagerström and bassist Mikael Fasth formed VALIUM.

Singles/EPs:
No Return / Endless Journey, Bellphegot BELL 93002 (1993)

LUCIFERION (SWEDEN)
Line-Up: Wojtek Lisiski (vocals / guitar), Mikael Nicklasson (guitar), Peter Wiener (drums)

LUCIFERION's guitarist Micke Nicklasson and drummer Peter Andersson are both ex SARCAZM, whilst vocalist Wojtek Lisicki previously sang

with HIGHLANDER. Nicklasson also sings lead vocal for LIERS IN WAIT. Following the recording of the group's debut 'Demonication (The Manifest)' drummer Peter Wiener quit to be superseded by ex LIERS IN WAIT drummer Hasse Nilsson. The album featured a version of SODOM's 'Blasphemer'.
LUCIFERION also covered METALLICA's 'Fight Fire With Fire' for the Black Sun Records tribute album 'Metal Militia'. Nilsson would join his erstwhile colleague guitarist Kristian Wahlin founding DIABOLIQUE.

Albums:
DEMONICATION (THE MANIFEST), Listenable POSH007 (1994)
Intro / On The Wings Of The Emperor / Graced By Fire / Rebel Souls / Satan's Gift / The Manifest / Risus De Lucifer (Suffering Of Christ) / Tears Of The Damned / Blasphemer / The Voyager.

LUCIFER'S HAMMER
(Mason, MI, USA)
Line-Up: Todd Cushman (vocals), Mike Seabrook (guitar), Andy Smith (bass), John Caldwell (drums)

LUCIFER'S HAMMER can trace their history as far back as 1988. The band opened up with the 1989 demo 'Tales Of The Midnight Hour' and a string of other tapes followed. The 1995 effort 'Hymns To The Moon' preceded the album 'The Mists Of Time'.

Albums:
THE MISTS OF TIME, (1997)

LUGUBRUM (BELGIUM)

Schizophrenic Electronic Black Metal act LUGUBRUM debuted with a 1993 demo 'Black Prophecies'. Initially the group, who classify themselves as "Boersk blek metle", consisted of Barditus and Zwelg. However, the departure of Zwelg to FINSTERNIS in 1993 heralded the arrival of Midgaard for the debut 'Winterstones' album.
Second effort 'Gedachte & Geheugen' was divided into two halves being all out War Metal and Symphonic ambience. This was followed by a split album 'De Zuivering' shared with SUDARIUM.
Zwelg would rejoin LUGUBRUM as bassist and his FINSTERNIS colleague drummer Svein would also enroll for LUGUBRUM's first ever gig in October of 1998.
The 'Bruyne Troon' album of 2001 cites the band members as being 'Pimping Midgaaars' on vocals, guitar and banjo (!), 'Juan Solo' on drums and most disturbingly 'Bobby Fatt' on bass and anus!!!

Albums:
WINTERSTONES, Skramasax SKR001 (1995)
Embracing The Moonlit Snowclouds / Sode Gilimida Sin / Aardmannen / Ogenboom / Dance Of The Winterking / Foltas / Fliegenpilz / Winds Enter My Mouth / Black Hag
GEDACHTE & GEHEUGEN, Skramasax SKR002 (1997)
Waar Et Vuur En De Kraaien Zingen / Stahlhelm I / Stahlhelm II / Als De Godenzwijgen / Zomermoord / Dampen Unten Ondiep Graf / Lugubrum / Trollenkloof / De Vlan Der Krijg / Het Dromen Der Berken / De Geheimenhelmen / Mijn Koninkrijk Van Groen
DE ZUIVERING, Skramasax SKR003 (1998)
Intro- Plaaggeesten / Buegman Met Het Boze Oog / Pankraker De Smeltkroes Het Madenmaal / Lluagor De Zuiverende / Outro- Zwavelzwijnen
DE TOTEM, Bezerker BRZRK004 (1999)
Intro- Beer / Hoornkluiten / Udder Of Death / De Totem / Ratteknaegher / Beard Of Disease / Midgets Of Evil / Inner Magma / Reet Reel / Voos / Outro- Oui Maitre
BRUYNE TROON, Skramasax SKR004 (2001)
Invade (Stinker Of Stink) / Gekloofd / Low Dog / Bruyne Troon / Druipstaarted / Kleigerukt / The Great Dressler / Het Spook Van De Gordmijn / Sponge / Staertgebroet / Kannibaal / Pump Room Brawl / Old Grey Hair / Schaambaard / Holebeard Blues / Expunge

LUNAR AURORA (GERMANY)
Line-Up: Whyrhd (vocals / bass), Aran (guitar), Sindar (keyboards), B.C. (drums)

A German Black Metal band founded in 1994, by the following October the group's first demo, 'A Wandering Winterdream Beneath The Cold Moon' (limited to 100 copies), appeared and, the following year ('96), second demo 'Auf Dunklen Schwingen' was released. An album finally arrived in 1996 after which the band drafted keyboard player Sindar.

During September of 1999 drummer Nathaneil made his departure. A split single was recorded in collusion with fellow German Black Metal band SECRETS OF THE MOON. Drummer B.C. made his exit in early 2000 to be replaced by Narg. However, in an about turn B.C returned usurping Narg.

Singles/EPs:
Auf Einer Wanderung / , Darkwind (2000) (split single with SECRETS OF THE MOON)

Albums:
WELTENGÄNGER, Voices (1996)
Grabgesänge / Rebirth Of An Ancient Empire / Flammende Male / Into The Secrets Of The Moon / Schwarze Rose / Conqueror Of The Ember Moon
SEELENFEUER, (1998)
Seelenfeuer / Mein Schattenbruder / Arger Aus Nichts / Schwarzer Seelenspiegel / Der Geist Des Grausamen
STARGATES OF BLOODSTAINED CELESTIAL SPHERES, Kettenhund (2000)
Kampfork / Schwarzer Engel / Die Quelle Im Wald / Blut Baum / Moorleiche / Drachenfeuer / Gebirgsmystizmus / Verwesung / Weltengaerger / Child Of The Apocalypse / Der Leidensweg / Sternenblut / Something Has Died Forever
ARS MORIENDI, Ars Metali (2001)

LUNGORTHIN (GERMANY)

Line-Up: Verjigorm (vocals / guitar), Arioch (bass), Gaefa (keyboards), Sulphar Fire (drums)

Yet another Black Metal band with A Tolkein inspired title. LUNGORTHIN came together in 1995 dispensing a brace of demos in 1997 entitled 'The Magister' and 'Glemt' prior to original guitarist Makabroth taking his leave. LUNGORTHIN then issued a self financed album 'As Night Gets Colder' after which they adopted guitarist Lord Chaos. However, he in turn exited for reasons of, according to the band, "humanity failure"!

LUNGORTHIN plugged the gap with keyboard player Gaefa in May 2000.

Albums:
AS NIGHT GETS COLDER, Lungorthin

(1998)
Intro / Ragnarok / The Path Of Omniscience / Outer Planes / The Assassin / Lands Of Darkness / Ancient Sun / … As Nights Get Colder / Infernal Dreams
PROPHECY OF ETERNAL WINTER, Folter (1999)
Schattentanz / Demiplane Of Dread / Captured In Grisly Death / Nightshades Upon Darksoul Domain / Prophecy Of Eternal Winter / Nethermancer / Der Turm

LUTHER BELTZ (UK)

Line-Up: Luther Beltz (vocals), Ronnie Reynolds (guitar), Rick Gilliat (guitar), Dave Hewitt (bass), Tez Brown (drums)

Chesterfield's LUTHER BELTZ, fronted by former WITCHFYNDE vocalist Luther Beltz, have operated under various names such as THE LUTHER BELTZ BAND, LUTHER BELTZ WITCHFYNDE and just WITCHFYNDE. However, in 2000 the tag LUTHER BELTZ was settled on under pressure from the remaining three ex WITCHFYNDE members refounding the band and taking the name. Joining Beltz are STORMWATCH members bassist Dave Hewitt (also an ex member of NWoBHMers WARRIOR) and guitarist Ronnie Reynolds. Second guitar is supplied by former FRONTIER member Rick Gilliat. However SAXON guitarist Graham Oliver has also made live appearances with the band.

Billed as WITCHFYNDE the band recorded 'Sign Of A Madman' for a German DEMON tribute album. A three track demo emerged in mid 2000.

Rebilled as WYTCHFYNDE the band appeared at the legendary Wacken Festival in Germany.

LUX OCCULTA (POLAND)

Line-Up: Jaro (vocals), Slav (vocals), G'Ames (guitar), Peter (guitar), Jack (bass), U. Reck (keyboards), Kriss (drums)

LUX OCCULTA first made an impression upon the Metal scene with their November 1995 demo 'The Forgotten Arts'. The band at this point included drummer Aemil.

Following the debut album 'Forever Alone, Immortal' the band pulled in new drummer Kriss, a flautist and female backing singers for the 1997 follow up 'Dionysos'.

Not to be confused with the Italian

Progressive Rock act of the same title.

<u>Albums:</u>
FOREVER ALONE, IMMORTAL, Pagan
Moon CD 005 (1996)
The Kingdom Is Mine: I Saw The
Beginning / Homodeus: Throne Of Fire /
Sweetest Stench Of The Dead: The
Battlefield / The Third Eye: Illuminatio /
Apokathsasis: Out Of Chaos / Bitter
Taste Of Victory
DIONYSOS, Pagan Moon CD 012 (1997)
The Birth Of The Race / Blessed Be The
Rain / Chalice Of Lunar Blood /
Nocturnal Dithyramb / Ecstasy And
Terror / Upwards To Conquer Heaven
**MAJOR ARCANA (THE WOUNDS THAT
TURN FLESH INTO LIGHT)**, Pagan
(1999)
Love (Garden Of Aphrodite) / Heart Of
The Devil / When Horned Souls Awake /
Burn / Creation / Love / war / Passing
Away / The Path
MY GUARDIAN ANGER, Pagan (1999)
The Heresiarch / Kiss My Sword /
Triangle / The Opening Of The Eleventh
Sephirah / Nude Sophia / Cube / Library
On Fire / Mane-Tehel-Fares

LYCANTHROPY (USA)
Line-Up: Asmodeus (vocals / bass),
Baalberith (guitar), Lamia (keyboards),
Arcanum (drums)

Black Metal band LYCANTHROPY first
emerged with the 'Sanctity Of The Black'
demo. A further session 'Amduscias'
followed the same year before signing to
the German Path To Enlightenment
concern.
Apparently all the members of
LYCANTHROPY are related with
keyboard player Lamia being the wife of
Arcanum.

<u>Albums:</u>
THE VEILS OF SORROW, Path To
Enlightenment (1996)
Of Dark Emotion / The Battle At The End
Of Time / In Umbra Cenare / Invocation
To Luna

MACABRE END
(SWEDEN)
Line-Up: Per Boder (vocals), Jonas Stålhammer (guitar), Ola Sjöberg (guitar), Thomas Johansson (bass), Niklas Nilsson (drums)

MACABRE END later changed their name to GOD MACABRE releasing an album in 1994. Guitarist Jonas Stålhammer also doubles as vocalist for UTUMNO.

Singles/EPs:
Consumed By Darkness / Ceased To Be / Spawn Of Flies, Corpse Grinder CGR001 (1991)

MACTÄTUS (NORWAY)
Line-Up: Hate Rodvitnesson (vocals), Gaut (guitar), Ty (guitar), Mefistofoles (bass), Mjolne (drums)

Vocalist Hate Rodvitnesson and guitarists Gaut and Ty first combined their talents in 1989 to found the band BLASPHEMY. With the addition of drummer Mjolne in 1993 this outfit evolved into MACTÄTUS issuing the demo tape 'In Sorrow'. A second cassette titled 'Sorgvinter' scored the band a deal with the French label Embassy Productions and a debut album 'Blot'. For this outing MACTÄTUS were joined by bassist Herr Bukkefot but his departure followed shortly after recording. As Embassy Productions was swallowed up in bankruptcy MACTÄTUS switched allegiances to the established Napalm label for second album 'Provenance Of Cruelty'. This record promoted the band into a whole new league and benefited from co-production of EMPEROR's Samoth and lyrical contributions courtesy of Nocturno Culto of DARKTHRONE. Female vocals were lent by Kathrine Abrahamsen.
'Provenance Of Cruelty' was recorded with SVARTHARID members bassist Istar and keyboard player Forn. Whilst the former would exit after the album sessions Forn stayed on as a permanent member. For the band's third album 'The Complex Bewitchment MACTÄTUS enrolled bassist Stian, better known as Mefistofeles.
Singer Per Erik Flatin, a man with apparent MACTÄTUS connections, would join ALSVARTR for a short spell in mid 1999.

Singles/EPs:
King Of The Dark Side / A Dark Journey, Mactätus (1998) (Promotion CD)

Albums:
BLOT, Embassy Productions (1997)
Black Poetry / Sorgvinter / Knustkrisiendom / Et Kaldt Rike / I Trollriket / Vandring / Når Et Kristent Liver Fortapt / Hat Og Kulde
PROVINENCE OF CRUELTY, Napalm (1999)
Draped In Shadows Of Satan's Pride / King Of The Dark Side / Sleepless Souls / The Emperor's Trial / En Trone Vevd Av Tid / Sonn Av Torden / Dark Journey / Provenience Of Cruelty
THE COMPLEX BEWITCHMENT, Napalm NPR 080 (2000)
Ornament Of Pettiness / Another Dimension / The Passage (To The Kingdom Of No Return) / Speak The Word Of The Winds / With Excellence / Iron Handed / Complexity In Vain / Dance Of Might

MAJESTIC MIDNIGHT (SPAIN)

Black Metal act MAJESTIC MIDNIGHT debuted with a 1995 demo 'A Blackened Rain Of Tears'. A debut album was recorded for Evil Omen Records but the two parties fell out and it is unclear as to whether the record was released.
Former members would unite with refugees from MYSTHICAL to found SYMAWRATH.

Albums:
A TRIP TO DARK..., Evil Omen (1997)

MALEFACTOR (BRAZIL)
Line-Up: Vladimir Mendes Senna (vocals), Danilo Coimbra (guitar), Wallace Guerra (guitar), Roberto Souza (bass), Luciano Gonzag Veiga Dias (keyboards), Alexandre Deminco Lemos (drums)

Guitarist Jafet Amoedo decamped in mid 2000 to be replaced by erstwhile MYSTIFIER and GRIDLOCK man Martin Mendonca.

Albums:
CELEBRATE THY WAR, Megahard (1999)
THE DARKEST THRONE, Demise (2001)

MALEVOLENCE (PORTUGAL)

Line-Up: Carlos Cariano (vocals / guitar), Frederico Saraiva (guitar), Aires Pereira (bass), Paulo Pereira (keyboards), Gustavo Costa (drums)

A Portuguese Black Death Metal band that has supported both SINISTER and CRADLE OF FILTH. MALEVOLENCE debuted with the demo 'Pleasure Of Molestation'.
1999's 'Martyralized' was recorded in Sweden with an all new line up centred upon surviving founder member vocalist Carlos Cariano.

Albums:
DOMINIUM, Danger (199-)
Desespero / Dominium Of Hate / The Burning Picture / Under Inhuman Torch / Enchanted Mask / Swallowed In Black / My Eyes (Throne Of Tears) / Sweet Bloody Vision / erotica / Ceremonial Gallery
MARTYRALIZED, Maquiavel Music Entertainment (1999)
The Brotherhood Of Christ / Diabolical Eve (Chronicles Of Master Lusitania) / Hunters Of The Red Moon / Les Salls Obscures De Rode Noire XVIII / Thy Extremist Operetta / Insubordination / A Shining Onslaught Of Tyranny / Oceans Of Fire / Martyralized

MALIFICARIUM (COLUMBIA)

Black Metal outfit MALIFICARIUM debuted with a 1996 demo 'The Dust Of The Real Path'.

Albums:
UNHOLY FALLDOWN OF CHRISTIANDOM, (1996)

MALIGNANT ETERNAL (NORWAY)

Line-Up: T. Reaper (vocals / guitar), Arrelsdal (guitar), Tom Stein (bass), Roy Ole Førland (keyboards), Brynjulv Guddal (drums)

An industrial style Black Metal band founded in 1991 with founding members T. Reaper (real name Torgrim Øyre) and drummer Brynjulv Guddal. Also involved was bassist Kenneth Horsvold for the inaugural demo 'In The Realms Of Flames'.
The 1998 EP '20th Century Boy' comprises earlier material re-recorded along with a version of IRON MAIDEN's 'Number Of The Beast'.

T. Reaper would join the ranks of OBTAINED ENSLAVEMENT for their 1998 'Soulblight' album and also figured in GORGOROTH.

Singles/EPs:
Glory / North / Zyklon / Number Of The Beast, (1998) ('20th Century Beast' EP)

Albums:
TÅRNET, Hot (1996)
Into Twilight / Vanished Winds / Warriors Dawn / Tarnet / Dark Clouds / North
FAR BENEATH THE SUN, Napalm (1997)
The Reaper / Far Beneath The Sun / My Empire / Prelude To Inferno / A Stonecold Heart / Daemon Song / Carpathian Stardust / Glory
ALARM, Napalm (1999)
Millenium Psycho / Deathcon 6 / Omniania / Neonhead / Exit Eden / Stained Sculpture / Beastwork / Palace Of Pleasure / Enigma II

MALKUTH (BRAZIL)

Line-Up: Priest Vampyr Ashtaroth (vocals / guitar), Daniela Nightfall (vocals), Holocausto (bass), Cyber Necro Daemon (keyboards), Lord Nightfall (drums)

Black Metal act MALKUTH have issued the demos 'Orgies In The Temple Of Christ (Bastard Son)' in 1995 and 'Glory And Victory' in 1996.
The band, founded in 1993, has endured numerous line up problems since their inception. MALKUTH debuted live in 1995 with a line up of Fazoth, twin guitarists Lord Nightfall and Priest Vampyr Ashtaroth, bassist Kleudde and drummer Invoker Diabolic Flame. The rhythm section would soon bail out in favour of Flammellian Azoth on bass as Maniac For War took over the drumstool. With this line up MALKUTH cut the demo 'Glory And Victory', the title track also appearing on the Canadian compilation album 'Under The Pagan Moon'.
Further ructions hit Malkuth with the absence of Azazel, Maniac For War and Azoth. New recruits were Foehnmephys on bass and drummer Samir. Before too long Holocausto had ousted Foehnmephys. Regrouping MALKUTH transferred guitarist Lord Nightfall over to drums and Priest Vampyr Ashtaroth took over the lead vocal role.
MALKUTH supported Greek pioneers ROTTING CHRIST on their Brazilian tour.

233

Singles/EPs:
Under Delight Of The Black Candle,
Demise (1997) (7" single)

Albums:
THE DANCE OF SATAN'S BITCH,
Demise (1998)
EXTREME BIZARRE SEDUCTION,
Demise (2000)

MÅNEGARM (SWEDEN)
Line-Up: L. Grawsio (vocals / drums),
Hemgren (vocals), Almgust (guitar), Ande
(guitar), P. Wilhelmsson (bass),

MåANEGARM debuted with the demo 'Ur
Nattvidar'.

Albums:
NORDSTJÄRNARS TIDSÅLDER, (199-)
Nordstjärnars Sken / Fädernos Kall-
Under Höjdn Nordbarén / Drakeld / Den
Dödes Drömmar / Nordanblod / En
Fallen Härskare / Ymer / Vindar Från
Glömda Tider / Blod, Jord Och
Stärnegans / Det Sargade Landet /
Tiden Som Komma Skall
HAVETS VARGAR, Displeased (2000)
Havets Vargar / Trädatanke (Fader Tids
Död) / Gryningstimma / En Del Av Allt
Som Bliuit Glömt / Fädernes Jord /
Vargtörne / Vanvett / Spjutsång / Ett
Gammult Bergtroll / Fylgians Dans Den
Sista Striden / Vinternattskväde

MANES (NORWAY)
Line-Up: Sargatanas (vocals), Cernunnos
(guitar)

Black Metal band MANES, a pairing of
vocalist Sargatanas and guitarist
Cernunnus, first emerged with the 1993
EP 'Maanens Natt' followed by 1994's
'Ned I Stillhetten' and finally the 1995
effort 'Til Kongens Grav De Døde
Vandrer'. The band was then forced out
of the spotlight for many years when main
member Cernunnos dealt with a serious
medical complaint coltitis ulcerosa.
During the interim former members
guitarist Tom founded BLOODTHORN
whilst guitarist Skei forged
SUFFOCATION- the act that evolved into
ATROX.
The band returned when Dutch label
Hammerheart offered to repress the
demos onto CD upfront of a new studio
album. During 1999 the duo forged a
band made up of ATROX guitarist Eivind,
BLOODTHORN bassist Krell, erstwhile
BLOODTHORN and ATROX member

Knarr on drums and Pilson of THE 3RD
AND THE MORTAL on keyboards.
Cernunnus sessions for KEEP OF
KALESSIN as live guitarist.

Singles/EPs:
De Morke Makters Dyp / Maaners Natt /
Under Den Blodraude Maanen / En
Hymne, (1993) ('Maanens Natt' EP)
Menn På Helveg Hastar / Månens Natt /
Dansen Gjennom Skuggeheimen / Uten
Liv Ligge Landet Øde / Ned I Stillheten,
(1994) ('Ned I Stillheten' EP)

Albums:
UNDER EIN BLODRAUT MAANE,
Hammerheart (1999)
Min Trone Star Til Evig Tid / Maanes
Natt / Uten Liv Ligger Landet Ode / De
Morke Maktens Dyp / Under Ein
Blodroud Maane / Til Kongens Grau De
Dode Vandrer

MANIAC BUTCHER
(CZECH REPUBLIC)
Line-Up: Barbarud Hrom (vocals), Vlad
Blasphemer (guitar), Ramus (guitar),
Akhenaten (bass), Butcher (drums)

One of the Czech Republic's foremost
Black Metal acts. As their name implies
MANIAC BUTCHER deal in raw and
unadulterated Metal with no concessions
keyboards or female vocals. Indeed, the
band state quite firmly 'We use the
mouths of girls for totally different
activities'!
Although the band first emerged with the
1993 demo 'Immortal Death' MANIAC
BUTCHER can trace their history as far
back as 1988. The debuting line up
comprised of vocalist Barbarud Hrom,
guitarist Vlad Blasphemer, bassist
Thomas and drummer Michael.
The 1994 session 'The Incapable Carrion'
saw Thomas being superseded by Jorg
on bass. MANIAC BUTCHER had their
1996 'Black Hordes Of Saaz' single
shared with DARK STORM. Following the
band's debut full length album Jorg
decamped.
Second album 'Lucan- Antikrist' saw the
inclusion of second guitarist Lord
Unclean. Line up troubles afflicted the
band further when Michael left the fold
followed by Lord Unclean. By this stage
MANIAC BUTCHER was down to the
pairing of Vlad Blasphemer and Barbarud
Hrom for the 'Cerna Krev' outing.
1999 had session players Ramus on
guitar and Butcher on drums filling the

vacant positions for a split album shared with INFERNO and SEZARBIL. A full length effort 'Invaze' was also released the same year. Meantime the 'Cerna Krev' album was re-released on the Brazilian Mega Therion label with extra tracks and retitled 'Sangue Negro'.

MANIAC BUTCHER achieved quite a coup in 2000 when the esteemed Akhenaten of noted American Black Metal project JUDAS ISCARIOT was inducted into the band on bass.

Both Blasphemer and Hrom also operate the side band NHAAVAH issuing the album 'Kings Of Czech Black Metal' and split a EP with KATHARSIS.

Singles/EPs:
Black Hordes Of Saaz, View Beyond (1996) (Split single with DARK STORM)

Albums:
BARBARIANS, Pussy God PGR 666 (1996)
Barbarians / Catheclasm / Sbaty Oter- Holy Father / Peklo- Hell / Second Creation / The End Of Messiah
LUCAN-ANTIKRIST, Pussy God PGR011 (1996)
Zrada- Treacherous / Pulnocni Rise- Midnight Empire / Lucane- Lucans / Zatechy Hrad- Castle Of Saaz / Posledni Bitva- The Lost Battle / Sordny Den- The Judgement Day
KRVESTREB, Pussy God PGR015 (1997)
CERNA KREV, Pussy God PG020 (1998)
PROTI VSEM, Pussy God PGR024 (1999) (Split CD with INFERNO and SEZARBIL)
INVAZE, Pussy God PGR027 (1999)
SANGUE NEGRO, Mega Therion (2000)
EPITAPH: THE LAST ONSLAUGHT OF MANIAC BUTCHER, Pussy God PGR031 (2000)

MANTAS (UK)
Line-Up: Pete Harrison (vocals), Mantas (guitar), Alistair Barnes (guitar), Mark Savage (drums)

VENOM guitarist Mantas' more melodic leanings are evident on this solo effort, released in the period prior to his re-involvement with the band. Mantas (real name Jeff Dunn) recruited guitarist Alistair Braacken for the project, with drums supplied by Mark Savage (ex WAR MACHINE).
Mantas rejoined VENOM, requisitioning

Barnes for the new line-up. Savage became lead vocalist for XLR8R.

Singles/EPs:
Deceiver / I'm On Fire / The Green Manalishi, Neat 60-12 (1989)

Albums:
WINDS OF CHANGE, Neat 1042 (1988)
Let It Rock / Deceiver / Hurricane / King Of The Ring / Western Days / Winds Of Change / Desperado /Nowhere To Run / Sayonara

MARDUK (SWEDEN)
Line-Up: Joakim Grave (vocals), Morgan Håkansson (guitar), Roger B. War (bass), Fredrik Andersson (drums)

An extreme Scandinavian Death Metal band initially called GOD switching names to that of the Sumerian illegitimate God MARDUK in 1990. Founder member guitarist Morgan Håkansson was previously a member of ABHOR and Punk Rock act MOSES.

The first demo featured ex LUCKY SEVEN vocalist Andreas Axelsson. Other musicians included guitarist Joakim Göthberg and bassist Rickard Kalm. MARDUK's less than tactfully titled 'Fuck Me Jesus' EP - actually their first demo pressed onto vinyl - was graced with a sleeve depicting a naked woman inserting a cross between her legs from behind and was subsequently banned across Europe.

By the time the group's debut album arrived in 1992 MARDUK's line-up had shifted to Håkansson, Axelsson, Göthberg, guitarist Magnus Andersson and Bogge Svensson of Viking Metallers ALLEGIANCE on bass.

Prior to the ensuing 'Those Of The Unlight' album, Göthberg assumed the lead vocal role as Axelsson had left to join EDGE OF SANITY. Andersson also left to concentrate on his various project bands; such as ALLEGIANCE, OVERFLASH and CARDINAL SIN. Göthberg joined Andersson as the drummer in CARDINAL SIN before founding DARKIFIED.

With third album 'Opus Nocturne' emerging in 1994, the group would tour Europe the same year supporting IMMORTAL on their 'Sons Of Northern Darkness" tour. MARDUK's roster at this juncture comprising of Håkansson, ex CHAINED bassist Roger 'B. War' Svensson, vocalist Joakim Av Gravf and A CANOUROUS QUINTET drummer

MARDUK

Fredrik Andersson.

In 1996 the 'Heaven Shall Burn...When We Are Gathered' album was issued and MARDUK also released the 'Glorification' EP, which featured the band's cover versions of tracks by PILEDRIVER, VENOM, DESTRUCTION and BATHORY.

At this point in time MARDUK's line-up consisted of Håkansson (also an active member of ABRUPTUM by now), vocalist Legion, guitarist Kim Osara, 'B. War' and Andersson.

For their 1996 European tour MARDUK drafted in their producer and HYPOCRISY and ABYSS guitarist Peter Tägtgren as a stand in member, although plans were laid to convene ex NECROPHOBIC and DARK FUNERAL member David 'Blackmoon' Parland into the fold.

Various members of MARDUK collaborated with Swedish Punk act WOLFPACK to create MOMENT MANIACS. The recordings resulted in the 1999 'Two Fuckin' Pieces' album.

2000 saw the issue of an MCD 'Obedience' featuring MARDUK's rendition of CELTIC FROST's 'Into The Crypt Of Rays'. MARDUK members also contributed to the 2000 album 'The Howling' by DEVILS WHOREHOUSE.

Singles/EPs:
Here's No Fucking Silence EP,

Slaughter (1992)
Fuck Me Jesus / Departure From The Mortals / The Black / Within The Abyss / Shut Up And Suffer, Osmose Productions OPCD 015 (1993) ('Fuck Me Jesus' EP)
Glorification Of The Black God (Remixed Version) / Total Desaster / Sex With Satan / Sodomise The Dead / The Return Of The Darkness And Evil, Osmose Productions OPMCD 043 (1996) ('Glorification' EP)
Obedience / Funeral Bitch / Into The Crypt Of Rays, Regain (2000) ('Obedience' EP)

Albums:
DARK ENDLESS, No Fashion Necropolis CDS17 (1992)
Still Fucking Dead (Here's No Peace) / The Sun Turns Black as Night / Within The Abyss / The Funeral Seemed To Be Endless / Departure From The Mortals / The Black... / Dark Endless / Holy Inquisition
THOSE OF THE UNLIGHT, Osmose Productions OPCD015 (1993)
Darkness Breeds Immortality / Those Of The Unlight / Wolves / On Darkened Wings / Burn My Coffin / A Sculpture Of The Night / Echoes From The Past / Stone Stands On It's Silent Vigil
OPUS NOCTURNE, Osmose Productions OPCD028 (1994)
Intro / The Appearance Of Spirits Of Darkness / Sulphar Souls / From

Subterranean Throne Profound / Autumnal Reaper / Materialized In Stone / Untrodden Paths (Wolves Part II) / Opus Nocturne / Deme Quaden Thyrane / The Sun Has Failed

HEAVEN SHALL BURN... WHEN WE ARE GATHERED, Osmose Productions OPCD 040 (1997)
Summon The Darkness / Beyond The Grace Of God / Infernal Eternal / Glorification Of The Black God / Darkness It Shall Be / The Black Tormentor Of Satan / Dracul Va Domni Din Nov In Transylvania / Legion

LIVE IN GERMANIA, Osmose Productions (1997)
Beyond The Grace Of God / Sulphar Souls / The Black / Darkness It Shall Be / Materialized In Stone / Infernal Eternal / On Darkened Wings / Wolves / Untrodden Paths (Wolves Part II) / Dracul Va Domni / Legion / Total Desaster

NIGHTWING, Osmose Productions (1998)
Preludium / Bloodtide (XXX) / Of Hell's Fire / Slay The Nazarene / Nightwing / Dreams Of Blood And Iron / Dracole Wayda / Kaziklu Bey- The Lord Impaler / Deme Quaden Thyrane / Anno Domini 1476

PANZER DIVISION MARDUK, Osmose Productions (1999)
Panzer Division Marduk / Baptism By Fire / Christraping Black Metal / Scorched Earth / Beast Of Prey / Blooddawn / 502 / Fistfucking God's Planet

INFERNAL ETERNAL, Blooddawn BLOOD 007 (2000)
Panzer Division Marduk / Burn My Coffin / Baptism By Fire / The Sun Turns Black As Night / Of Hells Fire / 502 / Materialized In Stone / Beast Of Pray / Those Of The Unlight / Sulphar Souls / Dreams Of Blood And Iron / Fistfucking God's Planet / On Darkened Wings (Live) / Into The Crypt Of Rays (Live) / Still Fucking Dead (Live) / Slay The Nazarene (Live) / Departure From The Mortals (Live) / Legion (Live) / Video

MÄRTYRER (GERMANY)
Line-Up: Kutty (vocals), Danny B. (guitar), Schratze (bass), Sascha (drums)

Albums:
RAGNARÖK, Metal Enterprises ME 570 CD (1995)
Ragnarök / Walhalla / Thor / Neptun & 3 Löwen / Bis Aufs Blut / Brautschau / Männer Müssen Manchmal / Wir Leben Das Leben / 0190-2728 / Zu Vati Ins Bett

/ Eine Ode An Das Leben / Verlier Nie Den Mut

MARTYRIUM (GERMANY)

Black Metal band MARTYRIUM issued a slew of demos prior to their debut 1995 album. Tapes included 1992's 'Invocation Of The Mist' and 1993's 'Through The Aeon' and 'Arcanum De Via Occulta'.
Ex members of MARTYRIUM founded SECRETS OF THE MOON.

Albums:
L.V.X. OCCULTUM, Merciless (1995)
Atum's Speech / A Living Ba / Enuma Elish / Lucifer Rising / Forgotten Spheres / Glory Of The Raging Storm / Scarlet Woman / Into Midnight Silence / Winds Of Apocalypse

MASKIM (ITALY)

Singles/EPs:
7 / Dusk / Lilith / Black Massacre, Zasko LAB ZL1 MK1 92 (1993) ('Maskim' EP)

MASKIM (IA, USA)
Line-Up: Septimus (vocals / guitar), Blakk (guitar), Anarchrist (bass), Zenn Von (drums)

MASKIM include ex MORTUARY OATH members. Following an eponymous 1996 demo MASKIM issued the 1998 'Impaled' tape. July of 1998 saw bass player Sinistra making way for Anarchrist.

Albums:
BATTLESTORM, Genocide (1999)
Arrival / Smoke On The Horizon / Black Serpent / Battlestorm / Desecrated Ground / Retribution
CONQUEST, Genocide (2000)
Cleansed By Fire / Age Of Chaos / Conquest / Blood Of The Enemy / Demise / Death Denied / Black Wings / Sacrifice / Eternal Darkness

MASOCHIST (USA)

Black Metal band MASOCHIST would provide the launch platform for members of WINDS OF THE BLACK MOUNTAIN and SUMMON.
The band issued a slew of less than subtly titled demos starting with 1992's 'Feast Of The Goat' followed by 1993's 'Fuck Your God' (later pressed as a single on the infamous Norwegian label Poserslaughter), 'Frost Of The Diabolical

Forest' and 'Sucking The Tongue Of The Ancient One' in 1994.

Singles/EPs:
Fuck Your God, Poserslaughter (1994) (7" single)

MASSHU (MN, USA)

Albums:
PANDEMONIUM, (2000)

MASTERS HAMMER
(CZECH REPUBLIC)
Line-Up: Frantisek Storm, Vlastimil Voral

A Black Metal act dating back to the early 80's. MASTERS HAMMER first came to attention with their 'Finished' demo of 1988, 'The Mass' demo in 1989, followed up by 'The Fall Of Idol' tape.
MASTERS HAMMER's first album, 'Ritual', was released solely in Czechoslovakia in 1991 selling over 25,000 copies.

Singles/EPs:
Cards Do Not Lie / Satrapold, Poserslaughter (1991) ('Klavierstück' single)

Albums:
RITUAL, Monitor (1991)
Intro / Bad Modley / Razdy Y Nae / Ritual / Genieve / Cerna Svatozar / Becny Navrat / Jama Petel / Japalili Jsme Onen Evet / Byfoupeni / Stolf / Zapalili Jsme / Vykoupeni
THE JILEMNICE OCCULTIST, Osmose Productions OPCD011 (1994)
Overture / Among The Hills A Winding Way... / I Don't Want Sirs To Pester / A Dark Forest Spreads All Around... / That Magnificent Deer Has Vanished... / My Captain... / By The Misery Of Fate I'm Haunted... / Oh, My Precious Sir... / Everything That Just On My Whim.. / Glory, Herr Hauptmann... / Sucharda's Home
RITUAL, Osmose Productions OPCD031 (1995)
Intro / Bad Modley / Razdy Y Nae / Ritual / Genieve / Cerna Svatozar / Becny Navrat / Jama Petel / Japalili Jsme Onen Evet / Byfoupeni / Stolf
SLÁGRY, Osmose Productions KRON-H 03 (1996)
Savlovy Tanec / Ach Saynku, Synku / Pujdem Spolu Do Betléma / Indiánská Písen Hruzy / Carl Czery Op 849 / Rock n' Roll Music / Vzpomínám Na Zlaté

Casy / Nabucco / Alava Modernistova

MASTIPHAL (POLAND)
Line-Up: Flauros (vocals), Cymeris (guitar), Abigor (bass), Sammach (keyboards), Sacruiel (drums)

Polish Black Metal act MASTIPHAL first emerged with a 1993 demo entitled 'Nocturnz Landscape'. The following year's effort 'Sowing Profane Seed' would eventually be issued commercially in 1997 on Faithless Records.
The band's original keyboard player Destructor would make way for Sammach in time for the album 'For A Glory Of All Evil Spirits, Rise For Victory'.
Following this release MASTIPHAL splintered with vocalist Flauros forging DARZAMAT.

Singles/EPs:
Aim / Confirmation / In The Shadow Of Nastrnd / Summoned Howling, Faithless (1997) ('Sowing Profane Seed' EP)

Albums:
FOR A GLORY OF ALL EVIL SPIRITS, RISE FOR VICTORY, Nocturne (1996)
Battle / For A Glory Of All Evil Spirits, Rise For Victory / Flames Of Fire Full Of Hatred / Winds Of Stakes / Tesknota Czasów Minionych / Calling From The Past / Aim / Legion / Nad Jeziorami Mys 'Linies' Miertelnej

MAYHEM (NORWAY)
Line-Up: Euronymous (guitar), Necro Butcher (bass), Maniac (vocals)

Instigators of the monumental Norwegian Black Metal scene. MAYHEM have inspired a myriad of imitators and their own personal heritage is woven with tragedy and controversy befitting the undisputed leaders of the genre. MAYHEM leader Euronymous was instrumental in establishing the notorious Norwegian Black Metal scene, running his own label Deathlike Silence and record shop Helvete (Hell). Not content with the blatant Satanic overtures, acts such as MAYHEM, DARKTHRONE and BURZUM have been blighted by supposedly propagating national socialist ideas.
MAYHEM came together in 1984 when the 16 year old Destructor (real name Oystein Aarseth) forged a union with bassist Necro Butcher and drummer Mannheim. Even though MAYHEM in

their formative stages were covering songs by the likes of CELTIC FROST, BATHORY and VENOM at live gigs Aarseth, now titled Euronymous was already experimenting with the ghoulish white make up later to be termed 'corpsepaint' and a staple of the Black Metal legions for many years to come.

Having released a demo in 1986 - subtly entitled 'Pure Fucking Armageddon' – MAYHEM, comprising of vocalist Messiah, Euronymous, Necro Butcher and Mannheim, were proud to announce that this tape featured "the worst possible sound quality" and few could disagree.

Following the tape Messiah's place was taken by Maniac (real name Sven Erik Kristiansen). Further demos were titled 'Voice Of A Tortured Skull'.

Their debut 1987 album was more of the same, although MAYHEM underwent an evolution. Maniac and Mannheim quit the band and in 1988 the band saw the acquisition of drummer Hellhammer (real name Jan Axel Blomberg) and ex MORBID vocalist Dead (real name Per Yngve Ohlin). MAYHEM's music evolved into paths ever bleaker and starker than before fuelled by Dead's lyrics.

The band were by now beginning to create waves internationally. Their extreme measures often found pig's heads scattered about the stage and Dead finally hospitalized himself after his penchant for cutting himself on stage led to severe blood loss at one gig.

Severe delays meant it was to be six years before a follow up to 'Deathcrush' appeared. During this time MAYHEM conducted only a smattering of live gigs, one of which was recorded for 'Live In Leipzig', the only recorded product to feature Dead.

Dead committed suicide under suspicious circumstances with Hellhammer accusing Euronymous of provocation at the very least. Apparently Dead was jocular on the day of his suicide, an act he carried out by slashing his wrists and blowing half his head off with a shotgun ironically with ammunition given to him as a present by Count Grisnackh of BURZUM.

It was Euronymous who found the body and before calling the authorities decided to take some photographs of it as a memento! Hellhammer himself made a necklace from pieces of Dead's skull as a gory keepsake.

Necro Butcher bailed out of MAYHEM seemingly at odds with Euronymous's attempts to position himself as a Black Metal figurehead. MAYHEM recruited ex THY ABHORRENT vocalist / bassist Occultus (real name Stian Johansen) and THORNS guitarist Blackthorn (real name Snorre Ruch) in an attempt to push forward. Occultus also happened to be editor of the 'Sepulchral Noize' fanzine and an employee of Euronymous working in the 'Helvete' shop.

Occultus lasted a matter of weeks exiting to found PERDITION HEARSE and later Goth Rock act SHADOW DANCERS.

Lacking a vocalist and bassist MAYHEM pulled in a guest for the 1993 album 'De Mysteriis Dom Sathanas' and were thus supplied by Atilla of Hungary's TORMENTOR. Bass was supplied by Varg Vikernes (alias Count Grisnackh of BURZUM).

MAYHEM and BURZUM began to vie for the title of Black Metal leaders and a bitter war of words erupted between Euronymous and Grisnackh. This culminated in Euronymous being stabbed to death by Grisnackh in 1994 amidst a wave of publicity on the Norwegian Black Metal scene, which also saw Grisnackh and Blackthorn jailed for arson attacks on local churches.

'De Mysteriis Dom Sathanas' was finally issued in September of 1993. As Grisnackh received a jail sentence of 21 years (not preventing his BURZUM career though) the myth of Euronymous began to grow.

Hellhammer actually teamed up with MYSTICUM during this period but was to reconcentrate his efforts on MAYHEM once more. MYSTICUM promptly replaced him with a drum computer!

Hellhammer vowed to continue with MAYHEM redrafting Maniac, Necro Butcher with Blasphemer of AURA NOIR. Hellhammer was involving himself in the side project ARCTURUS with ULVER vocalist Chris and Samoth of EMPEROR. However, he did briefly join EMPEROR in order to appear on their debut album. Seemingly unable to keep out of a recording studio, Hellhammer also appeared on the debut album by the COVENANT, yet another project act put together by DIMMU BORGIR, CRADLE OF FILTH and ARCTURUS members.

MAYHEM's 1997 single release is culled from the two studio tracks, originally laid down for the Swedish label CBR in 1991. Towards the end of 1995 a new semi-official MAYHEM album emerged entitled 'Dawn Of The Blackhearts'. The album grimly featured a photograph depicting the aftermath of Dead's suicide taken by his erstwhile band mates upon discovery of the body. The album itself was made up of early tracks including live cuts dating back to 1986 including two CELTIC FROST and two VENOM tracks.

A further release 'A Tribute To The Black Emperors' paired MAYHEM's demo songs together with tracks from Dead's band MORBID.

MAYHEM surprised many when they actually took to the world's stage in late 1997 for a whirlwind of live performances that easily re-established the veracity of their claim to lead the Black Metal clans. The touring line-up found Hellhammer alongside Maniac, Blasphemer (real name Rune Eriksen), Necrobutcher and stand-in guitarist Alexander on loan from FLEURETY.

Maniac appeared alongside PANTERA's Phil Anselmo, SATYRICON's Saytr Wongraven, NECROPHAGIA's Killjoy and DARKTHRONE's Fenriz for the EIBON side project that issued one track on the 'Moonfog 2000' compilation.

Hellhammer was still a prime mover in KOVENANT for their second album (the band previously known as COVENANT) adopting a fresh pseudonym. The drummer also guested on the TROLL 2000 album 'The Last Predators', a project of KOVENANT and ex DIMMU BORGIR man Nagash.

Maniac guests on FLEURETY's 2000 album 'Department Of Apocalyptic Affairs'. Meantime Trym teamed up with OLD MAN'S CHILD for a European tour during late 2000.

MAYHEM's 'Grand Declaration Of War' featured SPIRAL ARCHITECT singer Oyvind on backing vocals.

In keeping with their status MAYHEM's career has been well documented with a whole slew of bootlegs such as 'The True Black' album (sharing space with ZEMIAL and THOU SHALT SUFFER), 'Out From The Dark' (rehearsal recordings featuring Dead) and 'In Memorium'.

In keeping with Black Metal tradition Necrobutcher operates an obligatory side project titled KVIKKSØLVGUTTENE.

Singles/EPs:
Carnage / Freezing Moon, Black Metal (1997)
Ancient Skin / Necrolust, Misanthropy (1997) (Limited edition of 100 given away free at gigs)

Albums:
DEATHCRUSH, Posercorpse Music Frank 001 (1987)

Silvester Anfang / Deathcrush / Chainsaw Gutsfuck / Witching Hour / Necrolust / (Weird) Manheim / Pure Fucking Armageddon
DE MYSTERIIS DOM SATHANAS, Deathlike Silence ANTI-MOSH 006 (1994)
Funeral Fog / Freezing Moon / Cursed In Eternity / Pagan Fears / Like Eternal / From The Dark Past / Burned By Time And Lust / De Mysteriis Dom Sathanas
A TRIBUTE TO THE BLACK EMPERORS, Land Of The Rising Sun (1994) (Split album with MORBID)
Necrolust / Carnage / The Freezing Moon / Funeral Fog
LIVE IN LEIPZIG, Avantgarde Music (1994)
Deathcrush / Necrolust / Funeral Fog / The Freezing Moon / Carnage / Buried By Time And Dust / Pagan Fears / Chainsaw Gutsfuck / Pure Fucking Armageddon
DAWN OF THE BLACKHEARTS, Warmaster (1995)
Deathcrush / Necrolust / Funeral Fog / Freezing Moon / Carnage / Buried By Time And Lust / Chainsaw Gutsfuck / Pure Fucking Armageddon / Dance Macabre / Black Metal / Procreation Of The Wicked / Welcome To Hell
A TRIBUTE TO THE BLACK EMPERORS, Land Of The Rising Sun (1995) (Split album with MORBID)
The Freezing Moon / Deathcrush / Necrolust / Funeral Fog
WOLF'S LAIR ABYSS, Misanthropy AMAZON 012 (1997)
I Am The Labyrinth / Fall Of The Seraphs / Ancient Skin / Symbols Of The Bloodsword
MEDIOLANUM CAPTA EST, Avantgarde (1999)
Silvester Anfang / Deathcrush / Fall Of Seraphs / Carnage / Necrolust / Ancient Skin / Freezing Moon / Symbols Of Bloodswords / For The Dark Past / Chainsaw Gutsfuck / I Am Thy Labyrinth / Pure Fucking Armageddon
GRAND DECLARATION OF WAR, (2000)
Grand Declaration Of War / In The Lies Where Upon You Lay / A Time To Die / View From Nihil / II Principle / A Bloodsword And A Colder Sun / Crystallized Pain In Deconstruction / Completion In Science And Agony

MAYHEMIC TRUTH (GERMANY)
Line-Up: Belial, Leviathan (guitar), Lilith (bass)

Black Metal band MAYHEMIC TRUTH,

founded in 1992, first came to attention with the 1993 'Son Of Dawn' demo. Erstwhile member Balor would go on to create BLIZZARD.

Singles/EPs:
Cy Thraw, Folter (1995)

Albums:
IN MEMORIUM, Iron Pegasus (1999)
Intro / Lady Morgaine / When Thousand Candles Cry / Morrigan / Carrion Of War / Fire And Ice / Conspiracy Of The Golden Angels / Bluot Era Hathu / Cythraw / Hymn Of The Crow

MAZE OF CAKO TORMENTS
(LATVIA)

One man Black Metal project of Sit Kaimuc.

Albums:
DABALIBULA, (1995)
DEMONICAL SONGS OF YELLOW WATER, (1997)

MAZE OF TORMENT (SWEDEN)
Line-Up: Pehr Larsson (vocals / bass), Peter Karlsson (guitar), Kjell Enblom (drums)

Originally titled TORMENT upon the band's formation in 1994 by former HARMONY members drummer Kjell Enblom and guitarist Peter Karlsson. The duo were soon joined by VINTERLAND guitarist Pehr Larsson.
The trio, still operating under the name HARMONY, recorded a demo which came to the attention of Deviation Records based in Scotland. The band then switched titles to TORMENT for a three track demo. Upon signing to Corrosion Records the band title became MAZE OF TORMENT for the 1996 album 'The Force' produced by EDGE OF SANITY's Dan Swäno.
MAZE OF TORMENT added bass player Thomas Nyqvist shortly after the album's release.
MAZE OF TORMENT's 2000 album 'Death Strikes' was produced by Tomas Skogsberg.

Albums:
THE FORCE, Corrosion CR 6-503-2 (1996)
Shapeless In The Dark / Dream Of Blood / Souls Been Left To Die / The Force / Brave The Blizzard / Battle Of The Dead

/ The Last Candle / Land Unknown
FASTER DISASTER, Iron Fist Productions (1999)
The Reality / Five Inch / Dead Soul / Horror Visions / Ancient Treasure / Faster Disaster / The Devil's Kill / Hide The Light / Bite The Dust
DEATH STRIKES, Necropolis NR056CD (2000)
Death Strikes / Sodomizing Death Spell / Intense Slaughter / This Is Death / Aggressive Bloodhunt / The Infernal Force / The Sadist / Angels From Hell / The Evil Beneath The Flames

MEDIEVAL DEMON (GREECE)

Black Metal band MEDIEVAL DEMON issued the demo 'Night Of The Infernal Lords' before having a track from that session included on a 1995 shared 7" single with INVOCATION.
Members of MEDIEVAL DEMON, Bloodfrozen and Angel Of Decay (actually brothers Alexander and Kostas Karras), also bide their time with BLOODCULT.

Singles/EPs:
Split, Dark Side (1995) (Split single with INVOCATION)

Albums:
DEMONLATRIA, Unisound (1998)
Under The Twilight / Dark Widow / Field Of Tears / Queen Of Sorrow / Spirits Of The Dead / Doomsday / Lewdness In The Dark / Demonlatria / Warrior's Anthem / The Rise Of The Moon / Beyond The Clouds / No Flesh Shall Be Sharped / Melancholy

MEFISTO (SWEDEN)

Although released in 2000 the album 'The Truth' comprises of the 'Meglomania' and 'The Puzzle' demos laid down in 1986.

Albums:
THE TRUTH, Wrong Again (2000)
Missing In Action / Frost Of Inferno / Betrayal Of Truth / Act Dead / Hunting High, Die / The Puzzle Of Liberty / Underground Circus

MELECHESH (ISRAEL)
Line-Up: Melechesh Ashmedi, Proscriptor, Moloch, Alhazred

Black Metal group MELECHESH came to the fore with their 1995 demo 'As Jerusalem Burns'. Live bass player

Butchered also has a side project ARALLU.

Singles/EPs:
The Siege Of Lachish, Devilish Music Propaganda (1996)

Albums:
AS JERUSALEM BURNS... AL' INTISAR, Breath Of Night (1997)
Intro / Sultan Of Mischief / Assyrian Spirit / Planetary Rites / Hymn To Gilbil / The Sorcerers Of Melechesh / Dance Of The Black Genii / Baphomets Lust / Devil Night / As Jerusalem Burns... Al' Intisar

DJINN, Osmose Productions (2001)

MELEK TAUS (SWEDEN)

Black Metal band MELEK TAUS debuted with a 1995 demo 'We Unite'. MELEK TAUS drummer Kristeian would later join MIDVINTER.

Albums:
EXPULSION FROM THE REALMS OF LIGHT (ENCIRCLED BY FIRE), Near Dark (1997)
We Unite / Encircled By Fire / Where The Forest Never Ends / A Dedication To Northern Nature

MENHIR (GERMANY)
Line-Up: Heiko (vocals / guitar), Ralf (bass), Manuela (keyboards), Fix (vocals / drums)

Albums:
DIE EWIGEN STEINE, (1997)
Menhir / Winter / Die Auserwahlten / Warriors Of The North / Schwerzheit / Barditus / Tag Der Bergelung / Pagenlord

MEPHISTOPHOLES (GERMANY)
Line-Up: Nordischer Kunstler (vocals / keyboards), Xenien (guitar), Ferun (guitar), Jury Kowalkczyk (guitar), Hanno Weihe (guitar), Frurr (bass), Selphratus (drums)

Black Metal band MEPHISTOPHELES were previously titled ODIN.

Albums:
LANDSCAPE SYMPHONIES, Adipocere CD AR040 (1997)
A Landscape Symphony (Introduction) / Cosmos... / Dark Clouds Rise Above The Kingdom / Destiny Calls / The Overture Of The Night / My Throne Of Wisdom / Infinite Dreams / I Will Not Forget (Outro)

SONGS OF THE DESOLATE ONES, Last Episode (1999)

MERCYFUL FATE (DENMARK)
Line-Up: King Diamond (vocals), Hank Shermann (guitar), Michael Denner (guitar) Timi Grabber (bass), Kim Ruzz (drums)

MERCYFUL FATE were born out of the ashes of Danish Punk Heavy Rock outfit THE BRATS, a group formed in the late 70s by guitarists Hank Shermann and Michael Denner alongside vocalist Yenz (later to turn up fronting GEISHA and Y) and drummer Monroe.
THE BRATS recorded one track for a 1979 Punk/Metal crossover compilation album called 'Pair Punk' and released one full album on CBS Records '1980 Brats' which made quite an impact in Europe selling particularly well in France. It even led to the track 'Zombie People' picking up British airplay courtesy of Capital Radio's Alan Freeman.
'1980 Brats' was basically a Metal album with Punk overtones as THE BRATS although the album also included a quirky Russian Folk song sung in Russian by Denner!
However, the group disbanded and Hank Shermann soon linked up again with Michael Denner (who had formed DANGERZONE) and BLACK ROSE frontman KING DIAMOND (real name Kim Peterson) and DANGERZONE bassist Timi Grabber along with drummer Kim Ruzz and recorded a four track demo. The tape featured the tracks 'Some Day', 'Death Kiss', 'Love Criminals' and 'Combat Zone' once more under THE BRATS name.
Ex footballer King Diamond had already made a name for himself in Europe with the BLACK ROSE stageshow, which thrived on blood n" gore theatrics. This was a trait that was to spill over heavily into his new band.
Diamond immediately stamped his distinctive seal on the proceedings with his uniquely high range vocals. Shortly after the demo, the band switched monickers to MERCYFUL FATE and 'Love Criminals' began to pick up heavy airplay on Dutch radio thanks to the healthy state of the underground tape trading scene at the time.
MERCYFUL FATE demoed twice more and on the strength of the second tape were invited to England by Darryl Johnstone at Ebony Records to add a track ('Black Funeral') to the 'Metallic

Storm' compilation. MERCYFUL FATE also recorded 'Walkin' Back To Hell' during the Ebony session but this was never released.

With interest in Holland almost outpacing the rest of Europe, MERCYFUL FATE signed to Dutch record company Rave On in September 1982 and released the four track mini-album 'Corpse Without A Soul'. Its impact on the underground metal scene was huge and Ron Quintana's San Francisco magazine 'Metal Mania' voted it EP of the year

Whilst in England on a short tour in March 1983 (including a memorable show at the Clarendon Hotel in London's Hammersmith district) the band recorded a cult session for BBC Radio One's 'Friday Rock Show' featuring the tracks 'Evil', 'Satans Fall' and 'Curse Of The Pharoahs'.

As momentum gathered MERCYFUL FATE soon split with Rave On and signed to Roadrunner in Europe and Music For Nations for Britain in early 1983. They recorded their debut full length album 'Melissa', so titled in honour of a notorious Danish medieval witch whose skull Diamond claimed to own, A single 'Black Masses'/'Black Funeral' was also issued.

As a live act MERCYFUL FATE were an extremely heavy proposition, with the twin guitarwork of Shermann and Denner added to the distinctive, wailing histrionics of King Diamond's style and his penchant for microphone stands made of human thigh bones and pseudo satanic overtones. It's fair to say that the band certainly made an impression!

MERCYFUL FATE promoted the 'Melissa' album heavily, opening for the likes of URIAH HEEP, GILLAN and GIRLSCHOOL. Regrettably with the latter KING DIAMOND claimed responsibility for invoking the 'evil presence' which electrocuted GIRLSCHOOL vocalist Kim McAullife at a show in Copenhagen.

The band also courted controversy when they pulled out of a British tour supporting MANOWAR after just one date at St Albans City Hall. MERCYFUL FATE claimed that as they had contributed financially to the costs of the tour they were being treated unfairly by the headliners as regards set up times and soundchecking. MANOWAR refuted the allegations and MERCYFUL FATE were promptly ditched in favour of Birmingham support band CRAZY ANGEL.

In May 1984 MERCYFUL FATE recorded their second album, 'Don't Break The Oath', with producer Henrik Lund and embarked on their first American dates as headliners and as openers for MOTÖRHEAD. The album was another success, scoring many European chart positions.

The Danes were hit with the departure of Hank Shermann in 1985. The guitarist opted to form the much more commercial FATE. This group achieved critical acclaim but little else before Shermann reunited with Michael Denner to forge ZOSER MEZ in a more traditional Metal mould at the start of the new decade.

With Shermann out of the group it wouldn't be long before King opted to break the band up in order to pursue a different course with KING DIAMOND. Taking Denner and Timi Grabber (now using the moniker Timi G. Hansen) with him King would tend to eschew the satanic overtones of MERCYFUL FATE in order to pursue more conceptual, horror themes.

Having achieved a great deal of success with KING DIAMOND it would be after hearing some of the material the re-united duo of Shermann and Denner in ZOSER MEZ that King felt the time was right to reform MERCYFUL FATE with Shermann, Denner, and Hansen. Original drummer Kim Ruzz could not be torn away from his day job as a postman, so Morten Neilson laid down the drums for the comeback album. MERCYFUL FATE's reunion show was at the legendary Dynamo festival in Eindhoven, Holland during June 1993.

The 'In The Shadows' album from the reborn MERCYFUL FATE had the added interest of featuring guest drummer Lars Ulrich of METALLICA on a revamped version of the 1982 demo track 'Return Of The Vampire'.

The subsequent 'The Bellwitch' release turned out to be mini album comprising of three live numbers and two new songs ('The Bellwitch' and 'Is That You Melissa?', although the ensuing 'Time' release would witness the group on full throttle once more and touring America in early 1995 supported by SOLITUDE AETUNUS.

Having added drummer Bjorn T. Holm to the line-up in early 1996 the 'Into The Unknown' album featured new bassist Sharlee D'Angelo.

In late 1997 Roadrunner Records re-issued the early titles in re-mastered form and featuring the odd bonus track to boot, whilst Shermann and Holm have also busied themselves working on a band project under the name of GUTRIX and have so far released the album 'Mushroom Songs'. D'Angelo and Wead also created side project HEMISFEAR. Shermann released a side project album 'Sick In The Head' under the title VIRUS 7 in 2000.

Singles/EPs:
A Corpse Without A Soul / Nuns Have No Fun / Doomed By The Living Dead / Devil Eyes, Rave On RMLP002 (1982)
Black Masses / Black Funeral, Music For Nations MFNKUT 106 (1983)

Albums:
MELISSA, Music For Nations MFN 28 (1983)
Evil / Curse Of The Pharoahs / Into The Coven / At The Sound Of The Demon Bell / Black Funeral / Satan's Fall / Melissa
DON'T BREAK THE OATH, Roadrunner RR 9835(1984) 33 SWEDEN
The Oath / Gypsy / Desecration Of Souls / Nightmare / Come To The Sabbath / To One Far Away / Dangerous Meeting / Welcome, Prince Of Hell / Night Of The Unborn
THE BEGINNING, Roadrunner RR 9603 (1987)
Doomed By The Living Dead / A Corpse Without A Soul / Nuns Have No Fun / Devil Eyes / Curse Of The Pharoahs / Evil / Satan's Fall / Black Masses
RETURN OF THE VAMPIRE, Roadrunner RR 9184 (1992)
Burning The Cross / Curse Of The Pharoahs / Return Of The Vampire / On A Night Of Full Moon / A Corpse Without A Soul / Death Kiss / Leave My Soul Alone / MDA / You Asked For It
IN THE SHADOWS, Metal Blade ZORRO 61 (1993)
Egypt / The Bell Witch / The Old Oak / Shadows / A Gruesome Time / Thirteen Invitations / Room Of Golden Air / Legend Of The Headless Rider / Is That You Melissa? / Return Of The Vampire
THE BELL WITCH, Metal Blade ZORRO 78 (1994)
The Bell Witch / Is That You, Melissa? / Curse Of The Pharoahs / Egypt / Come To The Sabbath / Black Funeral
TIME, Metal Blade ZORRO 80 (1994)
Nightmare Be Thy Name / Angel Of Light / Witches Dance / The Mad Arab / My Demon / Time / The Preacher / Lady In Black / Mirror / The Afterlife / Castillo Des Mortes
INTO THE UNKNOWN, Metal Blade 3984-17026-2 (1996)

Lucifer / The Uninvited Guest / Ghost Of Change / Listen To The Bell / Fifteen Men (And A Bottle Of Rum) / Into The Unknown / Under The Spell / Deadtime / Holy Water / Kutulu (The Mad Arab- Part Two)
DEAD AGAIN, Metal Blade 3984 14159-2 (1998)
Torture (1629) / The Night / Since Forever / The Lady Who Cries / Banshee / Mandrake / Sucking Your Blood / Dead Again / Fear / Crossroads

THE MERLONS (GERMANY)
Line-Up: Antje (vocals), P.G. (guitar), Fritz (guitar), Alex (bass), Frank (drums)

Formed by guitarist P.G. and from the German town of Erlangen, THE MERLONS originally went under the title of THE MERLONS OF NEHEMIAH and released their first two albums under this title before adopting the easier THE MERLONS.
The group, who have a strong interest in medieval history, quite bizarrely invented their own language for lyric writing and aren't afraid to experiment with a whole host of instrumentation in order to give an authentic medieval touch.
1995's 'Romanoir' album came with a free CD ROM tarot computer game.

Singles/EPs:
Red Moon / Salamander / Anna's Days / Aergus, Musical Tragedies MT-337 (1996) ('Salamander' EP)

Albums:
CANTONEY, Musical Tragedies MT-236 (1992)
Au Sela Se La Jole / La Marche Funebre Sur Si / Testaroche / The Maiden And The Dragon / The Ork / The Whistle Of Love / Soldier
ELUOAMI, Musical Tragedies MT-285 (1994)
J.O.B. / A Long Time Ago / Execution / Rana / Winter / Eluoami Circle I: Praeludium, II: Eluoami, III: Coda / Damnation / Wasser / Achalamenjah / Devil Dance / Birth
ROMANOIR, Musical Tragedies MT 292 (1995)
Romanoir / Ork / Fieve / Execution / Utopia / I.O.B. / Devil Dance / Soldier III / Au Dela De La Joie

MESSE NOIR (Meriden, CT, USA)
Line-Up: Joe Gianetti (vocals), Matthew (guitar), Mike Morrill (drums)

Connecticut's MESSE NOIR debuted with the 1996 demo 'The Throne Of Ninninhagel'.

Albums:
MANDAL- GATE OF THE CALLING, (1998)
Excommunicated / The Ancients / Heralds Of Pestilence / Call Of Tiamat / Passage To Tchort / Impaled Existence / Messe Noir / Sacrifixion

MESSIAH (SWITZERLAND)
Line-Up: Andy Kaina (vocals), R.B. Brogi (guitar), Patrick Hersche (bass),

Founded in 1984 by guitarist R. B. Brogi, MESSIAH built up impressive sales of their first two albums. 'Extreme Cold Weather' sold in excess of 12'000 units alone, prompting a deal with Noise Records.
MESSIAH's line-up changed in 1993 with the departure of vocalist Andy Kaina and bassist Patrick Hersche. The bass position was filled by Oliver Koll and a new vocalist was found in ex THERION man Christofer Johnsson.

Singles/EPs:
Birth Of A Second Individual / Psychomorphia / Right For Unright / M.A.N.I.A.C., Noise N0244-3 (1994) ('Psychomorphia' EP)
The Ballad Of Jesus, Noise NO244-3 (1994)

Albums:
HYMN TO ABRAMELIN, Chainsaw Murder (1986)
Hymn To Abramelin / Messiah / Anarchus / Space Invaders / Thrashing Madness / Future Aggressor / Empire Of The Damned / Total Maniac / The Dentist
EXTREME COLD WEATHER, Chainsaw Murder 004 (1988)
Extreme Cold Weather / Enjoy Yourself / Johannes Paul Der Letzte (Dedicated In Hate To Pope John Paul II) / Mother Theresa (Dedicated In Love To Mother Theresa) / Hyper Bores / Radezky March: We Hate To Be In The Army Now / Nero / Hymn To Abramelin (Live) / Messiah (Live) / Space Invaders (Live) / Thrashing Madness (Live) / Golden Dawn (Live) / The Last Inferno (Live) / Resurrection (Live) / Ole Perversus (Live)
CHOIR OF HORRORS, Noise NO183-2 (1991)
Choir Of Horrors / Akasha Chronicle / Weeping Willows / Lycantropus Erectus

/ Münchhausen Syndrom / Cautio Criminalis / Northern Commans / Weena
ROTTEN PERISH, Noise CD084 04552 (1992)
Prelude: Act Of Fate / For Those Who Will Fail / Living With A Confidence / Raped Bodies / Lines Of Thought Of A Convicted Man / Conviction / Condemned Cell / Dreams Of Eschaton / Anorexia Nervosa / Deformed Creatures / Alzheimer's Disease / Ascension Of A Divine Ordinance
UNDERGROUND, Noise NO244-2 (1994)
Battle In The Ancient North / Revelation Of Fire / Underground / Epitaph / The Way Of The Strong / Living In A Lie / Screams Of Frustration / The Ballad Of Jesus / Dark Lust / One Thousand Pallid Deaths / The End

MIASTHENIA (BRAZIL)
Line-Up: Vlad D. Hades (vocals / guitar), M. Thormianak (guitar), Susan Hecate (keyboards), Mist (bass), A. Mictlan (drums)

MIASTHENIA's commercial debut was as part of a split album shared with fellow Brazilians SONGE D'ENFER. The band had issued the previous demos 'Paro O Encarte De Sabbat' in 1995 and 'Faun' in 1996.

Albums:
VISIONS OF NOCTURNAL TRAGEDIES, Evil Horde EH002 (1998) (Split album with SONGE D'ENFER)
Et Videt Quod esset Bonum (Sublime Blasphemy) / My Lady Princess Of Hell (Conjuration To Gorgon) / My Visions In The Forest / Hynn A Pa / Faun / Tragica Musica Nocture
XVI, Somber Music (2000)

MIDVINTER (SWEDEN)
Line-Up: Kheeroth (vocals), Damien (guitar / bass), Zathanel (drums)

The debut album by Death Metallers MIDVINTER was produced by KING DIAMOND guitarist Andy La Rocque. The band, founded by a union of erstwhile FOGBOUND and APOLLGON members, first tested the waters with the 'Midvinternatt' demo. MIDVINTER's initial line up comprised of vocalist Björn, guitarist Damien and drummer Krille.
Following the demo an alliance was struck with BEWITCHED and NAGLFAR personnel Adde and Stolle although this

version of MIDVINTER did not gel and the band folded. Unfortunately Björn, according to band sources, was subsequently admitted to a mental hospital. MIDVINTER was resurrected in 1996 with new members ex SETHERIAL vocalist Kheeroth and ex SETHERIAL and member of SORHIN Zathanel on drums. Guest musicians on the album included DISSECTION's Jon Nodtveidt and former AT THE GATES and OXIPLEGATZ guitarist Alf Svensson.

Zathanel would later renew his SETHERIAL links founding BLACKWINDS for a 1999 EP in collaboration with his former band colleagues vocalist / guitarist Lord Kraath and drummer Lord Alastor Mysteriis.

Albums:
AT THE SIGHT OF THE APOCALYPSE DRAGON, Black Diamond (1997)
Dod Fodd / All Things To End Are Made / Moonbound / Hope Rides On Devils Wings / Dreamslave / Noctiluca In Aeturnum- Of Nights Primeval / Ett Liv Fornekat / De Vises Hymn

MINAS TIRITH (NORWAY)
Line-Up: Frode (vocals), Stian (guitar), Gottskalk (bass)

Avant garde act founded in 1989 with Black persuasions combined with elements of Jazz, Doom and Death Metal. MINAS TIRITH bassist Gottskalk also has connections with TULUS and OLD MAN'S CHILD.

Singles/EPs:
Mythology, AR (1993)

Albums:
THE ART OF BECOMING, Art 196 (1996)
The Living Dead / The Colour Of Nothing / Sympathy From The Devil / The Art Of Becoming / In The Night I Walk / X = 666 / In Union We Die / A Child Is Born In Babylon / Holy Brother
DEMONS ARE FOREVER, Facefront (1999)

MIND COLLAPSE

Albums:
VAMPIRES DAWN, Vod VODCD007 (2000)

MINISTRY OF TERROR (HOLLAND)

Line-Up: Hans Mertens (vocals), Remco Hulst (guitar), Henri Satler (guitar), Elzo Nijboer (bass), Tjerk De Boer (drums)

MINISTRY OF TERROR, comprising of ex GOD DETHRONED members, first made an impression with their 1993 demo 'As Chaos Reigns'.

Albums:
FALL OF LIFE, Foundations 2000 (1995)
Move On To Hate / Agony / Darkened / Lost / Human Nature / Fall Of Life / As Chaos Reigns / Hollow / Tears Of Humiliation / Relentless

MISANTHROPE (FRANCE)
Line-Up: S.A.S. De L'Argeliere (vocals / guitar), Charles Henri Moreac (guitar), Jean-Jacques Moreac (bass), Oliver Gaubert (drums)

Self styled "Emotional Climate" band. Initially formed as a trio in 1988 by S.A.S. De L'Argeliere (real name Phillipe Courtois) MISANTHROPE soon made their presence felt with two demo tapes; 'Inductive Theories' in December 1989 and 'Crisis Of Soul' in June of 1990. The next step was the limited edition split album 'Hater Of Mankind'. This release was soon to sell out of all 2000 copies. Live work included dates in Europe with ASPHYX, THE ACCUSSED and MUTILATED amongst others. By June of 1992 a further release, 'Deus Puerilis', had appeared.

MISANTHROPE formed part of a touring package dubbed the "Macabre Dance Tour" alongside SADNESS and CELESTIAL SEASON during May 1994. The band's third record (credited by the band as their "true debut") secured the band valuable press internationally.

Having released the '1666..Theatre Bizarre' album in 1995 the group returned two years later. The 1997 album 'Visionnaire' greatly benefited from a production job courtesy of Fredrik Nordström. Recorded in Sweden, it is no surprise that HAMMERFALL / IN FLAMES drummer Jesper Strömblad and his IN FLAMES colleague Anders Friden make guest appearances.

MISANTHROPE embarked on an ambitious three album series entitled 'Recueil D'Ecueils: Les Épares... Et Autres Oeuvres Interdites' beginning with the rarities album 'Libertine Humiliation' in 1998, the 'Live Bootleg' record of 1999 taken from their European dates alongside SEPTIC FLESH and NATRON and finally February 2000's 'Oeuvres Interdites'.

Albums:
HATER OF MANKIND, (1991)
Mind Building / Paradoxical Burial / Unsubdued Redemption / Blaspheme The Earth / Hater Of Mankind
DEUS PUERILIS, (1992)
Deus Puerilis / In Silence / Totem Of Doubt / Velvet Solemn Quest
VARIATIONS ON INDUCTIVE THEORIES, Holy HOLY02 (1994)
Solstice Of Poetries / Aquarium / Childhood Memories / La Demiurge / My Black Soul / Aeternitas / The Grey Orchard / Atlas / Monolith In Ruins / And Also The Lotus / Mourning Humanity
MIRACLES: TOTEM TABOO, Holy HOLY06 (1994)
Standing At The Galaxy / L'Erotique Courtoise / Miracles / Aesthetic Fluttering / Maudit Sois-Tu Soleil / La Demiurge (Remix) / Deus Puerilis / In Silence / Totem Of Doubt / Velvet Solemn Quest
1666... THEATRE BIZARRE, Holy HOLY16CD (1995)
Gargantuan Decline / Courtisane Syphilitique / 1666...Theatre Bizarre / L'Autre Hiver / Pirouetting Through The Gloom / Aphrodite Marine / Medieval Embroidery / Mylene / Trumpets Of Hypochondria / Schattengesang / La Derniere Pierre
VISIONNAIRE, Holy HOLY27CD (1997)
Futile Future / Batisseur De Cathédrales / Hypochondrium Forces / Le Silence Des Grottes / 2666... / La Dandy / Hands Of The Puppeters / La Rencontre Revée / Irrévérencieux / O-Visionaire
LIBERTINE HUMILIATION, Holy (1998)
Misanthrope Necromancer / Matador De L'Etreme / At 666 Days... / L'Ecouans / Total Eclipse Chaos / Sous L'Eclat Blanc Du Nouveau Milenaire / Crisis Of Soul / Combattant Sans Sepulture / Antiquary To Mediocrity / Humiliations Libertines
LIVE BOOTLEG, Holy (1999)
Futile Future / Total Eclipse Chaos / L'Écume Des Chouans / 1666... Theatre Bizarre / Encore / Misanthrope Necromancer / Batisseur De Cathédrales / Humiliations Libertines / Le Roman Noir
OEUVRES INTERDITES, Holy (2000)
Le Lanceur D'Ames / L'Envol / Courtisane Syphilitique 2000 / Impermanence Et Illumination / Les Litanies De Satan / La Druidesse Du Gévaudan / L'Écume Des Solos / L'Erotique Courtoise (Live) / At 666 Days / Forever Shattered Failure v/ Movements For Hypochondriac Basses

And Libertine Tempus / Le Roman Noir 1995 / Ouverture D'Avant Scére
IMMORTAL MISANTHROPE, (2000)
Eden Massacre / Emperors Of Nothingness / Maimed Liberty / Diabolical Lamentations / Khopirroh / Androgyne Night / The Soul Thrower / Exiled Existance / Verdun 1917 / Millionaire Passion

MISERCORDIA (FRANCE)
Line-Up: Ludovic (vocals), Alexandra (vocals)

Albums:
PAINFUL DREAMS, Black Lotus BLRCD 019 (2000)

MISERY (AUSTRALIA)
Line-Up: Damon Robinson (vocals / bass), L. Kannanhinij (guitar), Scott Edgar (guitar), Anthony Dwyer (drums)

A Queensland Death Metal group with strong similarities to MORBID ANGEL. The band date back as far as 1988 issuing two demos 'Sorting Of The Insects' in 1992 and 'Astern Diabolous' in 1993.

Singles/EPs:
Seeds Of Doubt / Torn / Venganza Del / Innocent Torture, Valve (1994) ('Insidious' EP)
Dark Inspiration, Subcide Productions (1995) (7" single)

Albums:
A NECESSARY EVIL, Velvet Urge (1993)
Lifeless / Inverted Prophet / Born Dead / H.I.V. / Septic Octopus / I Endure / Sound Cancer / Body Farm / Sorting Of The Insects / Misery
REVEL IN BLASPHEMY, Warhead WHCD 18-2 (1997)
Godspeak / Act Of War / Plague Of Humanity / Dark Inspirations / Infinite Hate / Morbid Dreams / All That Is Evil / A Song Before Dying / Remembrance / Altered States / Revel In Blasphemy
CURSES, Venomous (2000)
Sweet Oblivion / Intent To Kill / Immortal / Swine / Blood For Blood / There Is No God / Consumate The Virgin / Two Faced / Zealot / Shitmouth / Eyes Wide Shut / The Chosen Fool

MISFORTUNE (SWEDEN)
Line-Up: Daniel Saidi (vocals), Peter Rudhberg (guitar), Martin Unoson

(guitar), Henrik Viklund (bass)

MISFORTUNE guitarists Peter Rudhberg and Martin Unoson both perform in MURDER MARKET featuring on the 'Undusted' album. Vocalist Daniel Saidi has side projects EBLIS and SAIDI.

Singles/EPs:
The Prophecy / Midnightenlightened / Pain Unbearable, Blackened (1999)

Albums:
FORSAKEN, Blackend (2000)
Forsaken / Scenary Of Despair / Rape Of Bewildered Dreams / In Matus / Burn! / Through Chaos Fulfilled / A Real Of The Unblessed / Apostates Of Hate

MISTELTEIN (SWEDEN)
Line-Up: Seron (vocals), Nagrinn (guitar), Baalzephon (guitar), Karagat (bass), Hel (keyboards), Nirag (drums)

Nalbow based MISTELTEIN are a classic corpse painted Black Metal act that include drummer Nirag of EMBRACED. The group, which include female keyboard player Hel, first emerged with the demo 'Spawn Of The Phantom Moon Wars'.
In 2001 guitarist Baalzephon bailed out with Nishrach plugging the gap.

Albums:
RAPE IN RAPTURE, No Fashion NFR041 (2000)
Darkness Scars My Soul / Twilights Sigh / Autumns Misty Might / Nevercoming / The Fire In My Eyes / Inquisition Of The Bleeding God / Hymn Of A Timeless Being / Dusk Rising / Silver Tears

MISTIGO VARGGOTH DARKESTRA (UKRAINE)

Solo endeavour from NOKTURNAL MORTUM's Kniazz Varggoth.

Albums:
THE KEY TO THE GATES OF APOCALYPSE, The End TE011 (1999)
The Key To The Gates Of Apocalypses

MITHOTYN (SWEDEN)
Line-Up: Rickard Martinsson (vocals / bass), Stefan Weinerhall (guitar), Karl Beckmann (guitar / keyboard), Karsten Larsson (drums)

Black Viking Metal act MITHOTYN emerged in February 1993 with the demo 'Behold The Shields Of Gold'. Previously the act had been borne out of guitarist Stefan Weinerhall and vocalist Schutz's 1992 band CEREBUS. Two further demos 'Meadows In Silence' in 1994 and 'Nidhogg' in 1995 would ensue before the band signed to Invasion Records. During these formative years the band gained and lost female keyboard player Helene whilst Schutz was superseded by vocalist Rickard Martinsson by the time of 'Nidhogg'.
Beckmann and Wienerhall were also involved in the INDUNGEON project album 'Machinegunnery Of Doom' in 1996 alongside Michael Andersson and J. Albrektsson of THY PRIMORDIAL. Beckmann would also guest on THY PRIMORDIAL's 'Signs Of Leviathan' EP. Members of MITHOTYN created ATRYXION for the 2000 'The Fall Of Ordexion' album. Weinerhall and Larsson forged the straight ahead Metal band FALCONER with vocalist Matias Bladh securing a deal with Metal Blade Records.

Albums:
IN THE SIGN OF THE RAVENS, Black Diamond (1997)
Upon Raving Waves / In The Sign Of The Ravens / Shadows Of The Past / Lost In The Mist / Embraced By Frost / In The Forest Of Moonlight / Tills Dagen Gyr / Stories Carved In Stone / Freezing Storms Of Snow / Where My Spirit Forever Shall Be / Let Thy Axe Swing
KING OF THE DISTANT FOREST, Invasion (1997)
King Of The Distant Forest / Hail Me / From The Frozen Palace / On Misty Pathways / The Legacy / Trollvosa / Under The Banner / We March / The Vengeance / Masters Of Wilderness / In A Time Of Tales
GATHERED AROUND THE OAKEN TABLE, Invasion (1999)
Lord Of Ironhand / Watchmen Of The Wild / In The Clash Of Arms / Hearts Of Stone / The Well Of Mimir / Chariot Of Power / Nocturnal Rivers / The Guardian/ Imprisoned / Guided By History / The Old Rover

MITT WINTER (NORWAY)

Solo Dark Ambient undertaking from one Grev Morsktorn.

Albums:
VINTERDRØM, CCP CCP100207-2 (2000)

THE MOANING (SWEDEN)
Line-Up: Mikael Grankvist (guitar), Patrick Tornkvist (guitar), Niklas Svensson (bass), Andreas Nilzon (drums)

Guitarist Mikael Grankvist is also a SATARIEL member. Fellow six stringer Patrick Tornkvist is with THE EVERDAWN. Bassist Niklas Svensson operates with THE EVERDAWN and GATES OF ISHTAR.

Albums:
BLOOD FROM STONE, No Fashion (1997)
Blood From Stone / Still Born / Of Darkness I Breed / Dying Internal Embers / A Dark Decade's Rising / Dreams In Black / Mirror Of The Soul / Dark Reflections

MOANING WIND (SWEDEN)
Line-Up: Johan Carlsson (vocals / bass), Tomas Bergstrand (guitar), Magnus Eronen (guitar), Martin Bjöörn (bass)

Karlstad Death Metal act. MOANING WIND had their track 'All My Gates Are Closed' included on a Belgian compilation issued by Shiver Records.

Albums:
VISIONS IN FIRE, Corrosion CR 6-505-2 (1996)
Hunted / Longing Away / Lost Forever / The Epoch That Died / Dark Side… Black Sun / A Fallen Arrow / Torn By The Wind / Awakened Spirit / Silence / Visions In Fire

MOCK (NORWAY)

Black Metal act MOCK debuted with a 1993 demo 'Cold Winter'. These tapes were used for a split album shared with TUMULUS in 1995 on the Dutch label Hammerheart Records.
Upon MOCK's dissolution bandleader Dolk founded KAMPFAR, releasing an EP on French label Seasons Of Mist and an album, 'Mellom Skoggledde Aaser', on Malicious Records.

Singles/EPs:
Vinterlandet / Call Thy Eternal Winter / Thy Sorrow Of Asgard, (1996) ('Vinterlandet' EP)

Albums:
COLD WINTER, Hammerheart (1995) (Split album with TUMULUS)
The Waves Of Agaar / Bonded By Thy Blood / Ner Af Vikingum Black / Northern Sins

MOLESTED (NORWAY)
Line-Up: Oystein G. Brun (vocals / guitar), Trond Furnes (guitar), Kenneth Lian (bass), Erien Erichsen (drums)

MOLESTED frontman Oystein G. Brun also operates in the higher profile Black Metal act BORGNAKER.

Singles/EPs:
The Usurpers Winterblood / Fogflames / Wolves Of Graven Hate / Pyre At The Tarn / Following The Growls, Effigy EFFIP 004 MCD (1995) ('Stormvold' EP)

Albums:
BLOD-DRAUM, Effigy EFFI 001 (1995)
A Strife Won At Wraith / Along The Misty Morass / Unborn Woods In Doom / Following The Growls / Blod-Draum / The Hate From Miasma Storms / Carved By Raven Claws / A Glade Of Ingrown Blood / Forlorn As A Mist Of Grief

MOMENT MANIACS (SWEDEN)

Jam session between members of one of Sweden's leading Black Metal acts MARDUK and Punk compatriots WOLFPACK.

Albums:
TWO FUCKIN' PIECES, Distortion (1999)
Forward / Flesh Power Dominion / When I Make You Bleed / No Win Situation / My Loss / Cold Deadly Steel / Haunted / Family Business / Do You Think I Care? / Time For War

MONASTYR (POLAND)
Line-Up: Master (vocals / guitar), Hodor (bass), Faja (drums)

Albums:
NEVER DREAMING, Morbid Noizz MN 003 (1994)
Intro / Leave The Dreams / Hung Upon The Crucifix / Suicide Sacrifice / Shepherd Of Dead Sheeps / Sin Your Soul / Never Dreaming / Eternal Flaw / Aggressor

MONUMENTUM (ITALY)

Line-Up: Andrea Zanetti (vocals), Francesca Nicoli (vocals), Roberto Mammarella (guitar / bass / keyboards), Mox Christadoro (drums)

MONUMENTUM came together in mid 1987 with a line-up of vocalist Mark, guitarist Roberto Mammarella, bassist Anthony and drummer Mox Christadoro. They released a 1989 demo, entitled 'Musaeum Hermeticum', and two tracks from this tape – 'Nostalgia Of The Infinite' and 'Nephtali' - were released on a split EP in 1991 shared with ROTTING CHRIST.

MONUMENTUM effectively split following the demo release, but increased recording offers saw the band sign to Norway's DSP label. Unfortunately, before a release could be made, DSP's mentor Euronymous was murdered.

Finally seeing the light of day on Misanthropy Records, the debut album 'In Absenti Christi' utilizes the talents of two vocalists in ICONOCLAST's Andrea Zanetti and ATARAXIA's Francesca Nicoli.

Drummer Mox Christadoro has since worked with numerous Italian bands including CRASH BOX, LAS CRUS and CARNIVAL OF FOOLS.

Roberto Mammarella also operates a Gothic Doom side project CULTUS SANGUINE.

Singles/EPs:
Nostalgia Of The Infinite / Nephtali, Obscure Plasma (1991) (Split single with ROTTING CHRIST)

Albums:
IN ABSENTIA CHRISTI, Misanthropy (1995)
Battesimo: Nero Opaco / A Thousand Breathing Crosses / Consuming Jerusalem / Fade To Grey / On Perspective Of Spiritual Catharsis / SeluhS AggeloS / From These Wounds / Terra Mater Orfanorumj / Nephtali / La Noia

MOON (POLAND)

Line-Up: Cezar (vocals / guitar), Doc (drums)

MOON is in fact the project band of CHRIST AGONY frontman Cezar and VADER drummer Docent.

Albums:
DAEMON'S HEART, (1999)
SATAN'S WEPT, (2000)

MOONBLOOD (GERMANY)

German Black Metal band MOONBLOOD were originally titled DEMONIAC issuing two demos under that name. Following the 1994 DEMONIAC demo 'Nosferatu' the band switched titles to MOONBLOOD for 'The Winter Falls Over The Land' demo.

A split 7" single with NEMA was their next move.

Singles/EPs:
Split, United Blasphemy (1997) (Split single with NEMA)
Blut & Krieg EP, (1997) (12" single)

MOONSPELL (PORTUGAL)

Line-Up: Langsuyar (vocals), Tanngrisnir (guitar), Mantus (guitar), Tetragrammaton (bass), Neophytus (keyboards), Nisroth (drums)

MOONSPELL are the band that put Portugal on the Metal map. Having been founded in the early 80s as MORBID GOD and gaining a deal with French label Adipocere via their 'Anno Satanae' demo MOONSPELL have quickly made inroads into the European Rock market.

Having made themselves almost instantly the frontrunners in the Portuguese Metal scene MOONSPELL were quick to accept an offer from major German independent label Century Media. The resulting 1995 album, 'Wolfheart', produced by GRIP INC. guitarist Waldemar Sorychta, garnered much favourable press.

MOONSPELL toured Europe as support act to TIAMAT and MORBID ANGEL in 1995 before returning to studio work in order to cook up the second album 'Irreligious'.

Promoting 'Irreligious', MOONSPELL conducted two European tours as their stature grew rapidly from a guest slot with SAMAEL to a much higher profile jaunt with TYPE O NEGATIVE.

1997 would witness the 'Second Skin Live' album before the group hit back in 1998 with the brand new studio effort 'Sin-Pecado'. The album displayed a far more adventurous style than previous efforts and the band's move away from Metal forced bassist Ares to depart. MOONSPELL persevered putting in

MOONSPELL
Photo : Martin Wickler

shows during 1997 supporting heavyweights such as KISS and MANOWAR. Ares meantime created DEEPSKIN for the 'Judas' album.
MOONSPELL toured Germany in early 2000 supported by veterans KREATOR newcomers and KATATONIA.

Singles/EPs:
Goat On Fire, Molon Lave (1994) (7" single)
Wolves From The Fog, Molon Lave (1994) (7" single)
Opium (Radio Edit) / Raven Claws / Ruin And Misery / Opium (Album Version), Century Media 77140-2 (1996)
Second Skin/ An Erotic Alchemy (Remix) / Sacred / Second Skin (Video Edit), Century Media 77189-3 (1997) ('Second Skin' EP CD1)

Albums:
UNDER THE MOONSPELL, Adipocere AR 021 (1994)
Allah Akbar! La Allah Ella Allah! / Tenebrarum Oratorium / Opus Diabolicum / Chorai Lusitania!
WOLFHEART, Century Media CD77097-2 (1995)
Introduction / Wolfshade (A Werewolf Masquerade) / Love Crimes /... Of Dream And Drama (Midnight Ride) / Lua D'Inverno / Trebraruna / Vampiria / En Erotic Alchemy / Alma Mater

IRRELIGIOUS, Century Media 77123-2 (1996)
Perverse...Almost Religious / Opium / Awake / For A Taste Of Eternity / Ruin And Misery / A Poisoned Gift / Subversion / Raven Claws / Mephisto / Herr Spiegelmann / Full Moon Madness
2ECOND SKIN, Century Media 77189-2 (1997)
2econd Skin/ Erotik Alchemy (Per Version)/ Sacred/ 2econd Skin (Video Edit)/ Opium (Live)/ Awake (Live) / Herr Spiegelmann (Live) / Of Dream And Drama (Midnight Ride) (Live) / Ruin And Misery (Live) / Mephisto (Live) / Alma Mater (Live)
SIN- PECADO, Century Media CD 77190-2 (1998)
Slow Down! / Handmade God / Second Skin / Abysmo / Flesh / Magdalene / VC (Gloria Domini) / Eurotic A / Mute / Dekadance / Let The Children Cum To Me... / The Hanged Man / 13!
THE BUTTERFLY EFFECT, Century Media (1999)
Soulsick / Butterfly FX / Can't Bee / Lustmord / Selfabuse / I Am The Eternal Spectator / Soulitary Vice / Disappear Here / Adapables / Angelizer / Tired

MOONTHRONE (WV, USA)
Line-Up: Andrew D'Cagna (vocals / guitar), Keith Loeffler (bass)

252

The MOONTHRONE duo of Andrew D'Cagna and Keith Loeffler previously went under the assumed names of Avernus and Darkhero respectively. MOONTHRONE's initial demos 'Among The Black Of Night' and 'Dust Thou Art, And To Dust Thou Has Returned' scored a deal with Abyss Productions. These demos would later be reissued on CD format by Frozen music.

D'Cagna would found ANGELRUST in October of 1999 in alliance with Frank Gordon of Death Metal band MASTICATED ENTRAILS.

Albums:
EMPTINESS, Abyss Productions (1998)
The Dawning / By Blizzard Of Norse Snow / Leviticus / Emptiness / Godless Eve / Gates Of Seeping Crimson / Planetary Serpents On Magnetic Winds / She Faded With The Shadows / Arkanum
ZODIAC, Frozen (1999)
Venution Trance: The Genesis / Shadowed Abduction: The Tragedy / Contempt: The Brooding / The Burning Spell: The Ascendance / Stellar Voyager: The Adventure / Purgatory Within: The Oracle / Clash At Saturn's Gates: The Confrontation / Dusk: The Triumph / Portrait Of Retribution: The Betrayal / Aquarius: The Transcendence / The Cosmic Path: The Revelation
AMONG THE BLACK OF NIGHT, Frozen Music FM08 (1999)
Shimmering Emerald Towers / Moonthrone / Destiny (Beyond The Black Horizon) / She Faded With The Shadows / This Sunset Eternal / Shadow Funeral / Raven Of Twilight / The Last Dawn Turned Black
DUST THOU ART, AND TO DUST THOU HAS RETURNED, Frozen Music FM09 (1999)
Moonlit Conquest / Twilight Of Misery / Gotterdammerung / … Of Golden Dust / Under A Canopy Of Stars / Spectral Vortex / Diabolique (Revelation In Red) / Storming The Gates Of The Cosmos
FLESHHOLD, Frozen Music FM12 (2000)
THE FOREST'S EDGE, Frozen Music FM14 (2000)

MORANNON (SWEDEN)
Line-Up: Henrik Lindenmo (vocals / bass), Vortex (guitar), Tobbe (bass), Goatlord (drums)

The Gavle based deliberately primitive Black Metal act MORANNON, created in 1993, issued a split demo in 1997 shared with MARTYRIUM. The band include HELLPIKE members vocalist / bassist Henrik Lindenmo and drummer Goatlord. Guitarist Vortex is in fact Daniel Bryntse of FORLORN, WINDWALKER and WITHERED BEAUTY. Lindenmo is also a member of FORLORN.

All the members of MORANNON also busy themselves with Punk band KALLT STAÄL.

MORBID (NORWAY)

An almost legendary Black Metal act. Frontman Dead would later come to prominence with MAYHEM and become an infamous 'Black Metal Martyr' after his apparent suicide.

MORBID first attracted attention with the 1987 demo 'December Moon' followed by the following years 'Last Supper'.

Quite horrifically Dead's corpse was photographed in all its gory detail for use on the MAYHEM bootleg 'Dawn Of The Black Hearts' album sleeve.

The 1994 album 'A Tribute To The Black Emperors' was a split affair shared with MAYHEM. The band's demo 'December Moon' was pressed onto vinyl for a 12" single in 1995.

Singles/EPs:
December Moon, Reaper (1995) (12" single)

Albums:
A TRIBUTE TO THE BLACK EMPERORS, Land Of The Rising Sun (1994) (Split album with MAYHEM)
My Dark Subconscious / Winds Of Funeral / From The Dark / Disgusting Semla

MORBID ANGEL (Tampa, FL, USA)
Line-Up: David Vincent (vocals / bass), Trey Azagthoth (guitar), Erik Rutan (guitar), Pete Sandoval (drums)

Florida Black Death metal act MORBID ANGEL, founded in 1984, broke down the barriers between extreme music and commercial success but seemingly blew their chances of entering the big league with a series of remarks attributed to main man Trey Azagthoth (real name George Emmanuel III) being allegedly fascist in nature. The world's rock media erupted in an outcry against these supposed nazi leanings. Nevertheless, despite the controversy and the band's denials,

MORBID ANGEL had racked up combined sales of over 1,000,000 albums sold by 1998.

At one time MORBID ANGEL featured a rhythm section of bassist Sterling Von Scarborough and drummer Mike Browning, both previously with INCUBUS. Coincidentally INCUBUS was also to donate guitarist Gino Marino to MORBID ANGEL in 1992. Browning eventually ended up after his MORBID ANGEL stint in NOCTURNUS (and much later AFTER DEATH) whilst Von Scarborough was to resurrect INCUBUS after his post MORBID ANGEL act USURPER.

What was to be the band's debut album 'Abominations of desolation', recorded in 1986, was shelved due to the band's ever fluctuating line up. MORBID ANGEL's commercial debut the 'Thy kingdom come' single featured drummer Wayne Hartshill.

Scarborough was supplanted by ex TERRORIZER man David Vincent. The bassist had been an acquaintance of the band for some time having produced the 'Abominations Of Desolation' sessions. With this more solid unit MORBID ANGEL's sales began to accelerate as did their worldwide recognition.

In 1991, just upfront of a lengthy American tour, MORBID ANGEL's planned debut album 'Abominations Of Desolation' finally saw a release through Earache Records. The album had been bootlegged relentlessly upon the band's ascendancy into the upper echelons of the thrash ranks.

Guitarist Richard Brunelle drifted away in mid 1992. MORBID ANGEL filled his shoes briefly with former INCUBUS man Gino Marino but before long Brunelle was back.

1993 saw MORBID ANGEL of such a stature that their 'Covenant' album was produced by Flemming Rasmussen and signed to the massive Warner Bros. corporation in America. With tour support now guaranteed the band criss crossed America opening for BLACK SABBATH and MOTÖRHEAD.

Brunelle departed for good in 1994 and the band closed the gap with ex RIPPING CORPSE guitarist Eric Rutan.

MORBID ANGEL undertook an enormous touring schedule throughout 1995 and into 1996. Dates began in their home state of Florida for an American tour before extensively covering Europe until February 1996 saw the band back in America prior top a return trip to Europe.

These shows yielded the live album 'Entangled In Chaos'.

The band seemingly suffered a double hammer blow in 1997 not only with the departure of Vincent, so often the band's mouthpiece, but also the collapse of their deal with Earache Records. However, Azagthoth picked up the pieces and renegotiated a revised deal with their former label and pulled in ex MERCILESS ONSLAUGHT / CEREMONY / INTERSINE man Steve Tucker to plug the gap left by Vincent.

In 1998 Vincent found himself playing bass in the S&M inspired GENITORTURERS, but then he is the husband of frontwoman Geni after all!

Although Rutan appeared as main songwriter and contributor to the 'Formulas Fatal To The Flesh' album MORBID ANGEL pulled in guitarist Richard Burnelle for live work as Rutan decamped to concentrate on his other two acts ALAS and HATE ETERNAL. However, rehearsals for the tour to promote the record did not go well and with Burnelle being dispensed with Rutan got the call for assistance. Following the 'Formulas Fatal To The Flesh' tour Rutan decamped yet again and produced the 'Conquerors Of Armageddon' album for Brazilian Black Metallers KRISIUN in 2000.

Rutan returned to the fold later in 2000 for the 'Gateways To Annihilation' album, a record that kicks off with an intro of a genuine swamp frog chorus!

MORBID ANGEL toured Europe in December 2000 headlining an almighty Death Metal package that included ENSLAVED, THE CROWN, BEHEMOTH, HYPNOS and DYING FETUS.

Singles/EPs:
Thy Kingdom Come / Abominations Of Desolation / Blasphemy Of The Holy Ghost, Morbid Angel (1988)
God Of Emptiness / Sworn To The Black / Sworn To The Black (Laibach remix) / God Of Emptiness (Laibach remix), Earache MOSH 112T (1994)

Albums:
ALTARS OF MADNESS, Earache MOSH 11 (1989)
Visions From The Darkside / Chapel Of Ghouls / Maze Of Torment / Damnation / Bleed For The Devil
BLESSED ARE THE SICK, Earache MOSH 31 (1991)

Intro / Fall From Grace / Brainstorm / Rebel Lands / Doomsday Celebration / Day Of Suffering / Blessed Are The Sick / Leading The Rats / Thy Kingdom Come / Unholy Blasphemies / Abominations / Desolate Ways / The Ancient Ones / In Remembrance
ABOMINATIONS, Earache MOSH 048 (1991)
The Invocation / Chapel Of Ghouls / Unholy Blasphemies / Angel Of Disease / Azaghoth / The Gate / Lord Of Fevers And Plagues / Hell Spawn / Abominations / Demon Seed / Welcome To Hell
COVENANT, Earache MOSH 081 (1993)
Rapture / Pain Divine / World Of Shit / Vengeance Is Mine / Lion's Den / Blood On My Hands / Angel Of Disease / Sworn To Black / Nar Mattaru / God Of Emptiness
ENTANGLED IN CHAOS-LIVE, Earache MOSH167 (1996)
Immortal Rites / Blasphemy Of The Holy Ghost / Sworn To The Black / Lord Of All Fevers And Plagues / Blessed Are The Sick / Day Of Suffering / Chapel Of Ghouls / Maze Of Torment / Rapture / Blood On My Hands / Dominate
FORMULAS FATAL TO THE FLESH, Earache MOSH180 (1998)
Heaving Earth / Prayer Of Hatred / Bil Ur-Sag / Nothing Is Not / Chambers Of Dis / Disturbance In The Great Slumber / Umulamahri / Hellspawn: The Rebirth / Covenant Of Death / Hymn To A Gas Giant / Invocation Of The Continual One / Ascent Through The Spheres / Hymnos Rituales De Guerra / Trooper
GATEWAYS TO ANNIHILATION, Earache (2000)
Kawazu / Summoning Redemption / Ageless / Still I Am / He Who Sleeps / To The Victor The Spoils / At One With Nothing / Opening Of The Gates / Secured Limitations / Awakening / I / God Of The Forsaken

MORDOR (SWITZERLAND)

Singles/EPs:
Dark Throne Of Blasphemous Evil / The Great Kat Is God / Lamentations For Corinne / Black Roses For The Dawn Of Chaos, (1995) ('Odes' EP)

Albums:
CSEJTHE (1995)
Bloody Countess / First Birth Of The Cruel Nymph / Last Demonic Invocation / Self Immolation For My Sweet Goddess / Of The Dark Dawn / The Moment Of The

Worship Of Total Evilution / In Search Of The Pure Negation / Agony: The Ascent Of The Mountain

MORGUL (NORWAY)
Line-Up: Jack D. Ripper (vocals / guitar / bass), Agarwaen Hiril

A solo work of multi instrumentalist Jack D. Ripper. MORGUL's early demo sessions 'Vargvinter' and 'In Gowns Flowing Wide' were recorded with drummer Hex.
The 1998 album 'Parody Of The Mass' was produced by Mikael Hedlund of HYPOCRISY.

Albums:
LOST IN SHADOWS GREY, Napalm NPR028CD (1997)
Enthroned / The Dark Infinity / Hunger Of The Immortals / My Bride… / River Of Princess
PARADY OF THE MASS, (1998)
Black Hearts Domain / Healing The Blind / Torn / Ballad Of Revolt / Adoration Of The Profane / Author Of Pain / The End
THE HORROR GRANDEAU, Century Media (1999)
The Horror Grandeur / Ragged Little Dolls / The Murdering Mind / A Third Face / Elegantly Decayed / Cassandra's Nightmare / The Ghost

MÖRK GRYNING (NORWAY)
Line-up: Goth Gorgon (vocals / guitar / bass), Draakh Kimera (guitar / keyboards / drums)

Swedes MÖRK GRYNING, which, in English, means 'Dark Dawn', were produced by EDGE OF SANITY's Dan Swanö.

Albums:
TUSEN ÅR HAR GÅTT..., No Fashion NFR012 (1996)
Dagon / Journey / Tusen År Har Gått / Omringen / Armageddon Has Come To Pass / Unleash The Beast / The Final Battle / Morkrets Gryning / Min Sista Färd (En Visa Om Döden)
RETURN FIRE, No Fashion NFR022 (1997)
World Of The Dragon / Supreme Hatred / The Doom Of Planet Yuconon / The Surrounding / Dreams, Sweet Dream / No Longer In Wait / Manhunter / Return Fire / Dawn Of The Magic Aeon / Master Of Fire / Necrophiliac

MORNINGRISE (GREECE)
Line-Up: Diego Balbo (vocals), Luigi Alberio (vocals), Roberto Fazari (guitar), Alessandro Monopoli (guitar), Maurizio Galazzi (bass), Micheler Ercolano (drums)

A Black Doom act that included former AGARTHI drummer Michele Ercolano. The band was founded by guitarists Roberto Fazari and Gabriele Castelnuous, bassist Maurizio Gallazzi and singer Diego Balbo. MORNINGRISE later pulled in Ercolano on drums and second vocalist Luigi Alberio whose clean vocals supplented Balbo's growls and grunts.
In 2000 Castelnuous departed to be replaced by former ACRON man Mirko Placido. However, within months he in turn had been ousted by ETHEREAL guitarist Alessandro Monopoli.

Albums:
DRAGONS OF THE SUN, (1998)

MORNINGSTAR (FINLAND)
Line-Up: Ari Honkonen (vocals / guitar / bass), Mikko Paavilainen (bass), Pasi Pasanen (drums)

Black Metal group from Finland. The act was previously titled TESTATOR upon their formation in 1989. A further name change to THOR'S HAMMER eventually led to MORNINGSTAR and the 1992 demo 'Obscure Aurora Above Us'.
A 1993 demo 'Inside The Circle Of The Pentagram' eventually led to a deal with German label Wild Rags.
Frontman Ari Honkonen also has allegiances with two other acts namely the Doom band MINOTAURI and the Nordic ancestral Metal grup IRONBIRD.

Singles/EPs:
Before The Dawn, Morbid 660733 (1996)

Albums:
AS THE WOLVES HOWL, Wild Rags (1995)
RIVENDELL, Wild Rags (1995)
Warriors Of Pagan Gods / (War) Legend / Pagan Dance / The Eyes Of Lamia / Kavlevala / My Purgatory / Déjà vu / Ancient Crypt / Iron Bird / The Morningstars (Saw My Death)
HERETIC METAL, Moonlight MOON 004 (1996)

Burning The Crucifix / War & Victory / Crushing Their Legions / Eternal Darkness / A Great Revolt / During A Fullmoon / Bloody Hammer / Twilight Of The Paradise / (Black) Power Of Shaman / The Phobia / Pierce His Eyes
HELL, (1999)
Speed Demon / Heavy Metal Heretics / Booze And Hate / Visitor From Death / The King / Maniaxe / Metalstorm / After The Battle / Chainsaw Philosophy / My Restless Soul / The Spirit (Of The Bottle) / Under The Stars
WEIGHT OF THE HAMMER, R.I.P. (2000)
Sylvester Night 1596 / Northern Summer / Electric Battlecry / Metal / Hakkapeliitta / Pirates Of The Northern Sea / The Last Dragon / Traitors Over The Edge / The Alchemist / Manala / The Death Of Klaus Fleming / The Sign Of Turisas

MORPHEUS (SWEDEN)
Line-Up: David Brink (vocals), Stefan Ekström (guitar), Sebastian Ramstedt (guitar), Johan De Daux (bass), Markus Rüden (drums)

MORPHEUS were formed by ex CARBONISED members drummer Markus Rüden and guitarist Stephan Ekström, together with ex members of EXHUMED. The single features guitarist Janne Rudberg, who left prior to the album to form EXCRUCIATE.

Singles/EPs:
In The Arms Of Morpheus, Opinionate OP003 (1991)

Albums:
SON OF HYPNOS, Step One STEP005 (1995)
Depths Of Silence / Through The Halls Of Darkness / God Against All / The Third Reich 3797 A.C. / Of Memories Made (The God Of Dreams) / Memento Mori / Among Others / Inflame The Mass / Wonderland / Dreams

MORTEM (NORWAY)
Line-Up: Marius Vold (vocals), Steiner Johnsen (guitar / bass), Hellhammer (drums)

MORTEM were complemented by the drumming of Hellhammer, was on loan from MAYHEM for this recording. Vocalist Marius Vold later came to attention in an early incarnation of ARCTURUS, then with THORNS and rebilled as Athera for the high profile 2001 act SUSPERIA.

Singles/EPs:
Slow Death / Agonised To Suicide, Putrefaction (1990)

MORTEM (PERU)

Peruvian Black Metal act MORTEM first came to attention with the 'Superstition' and 'Vomit Of The Earth' demos. MORTEM's 1998 album 'The Devil Speaks In Tongues' includes a cover of the SACRIFICE track 'Turn In Your Grave'.

Albums:
DEMON TALES, Merciless MR CD004 (1997)
Daemonium Vobiscum / End Of The Christian Era / A Demon's Tale / Satan II / Ungay Man (Mother Of Disease) / Vomit Of The Earth / Unearth The Buried Evil / Demonolatry / Blackened Arts / Tormented By The End
THE DEVIL SPEAKS IN TONGUES, Merciless (1998)
Fiat Obscuritas / Demons Haunt Loudun / Uma, Head Of The Witch / Summoned To Hell / Mutilation Rites / Devil Speaks In Tongues / Posthumous Magic / Turn In Your Grave / Zombie Plague / Sucubus / Lycanthropes (Howling Death) / Moon Of Cannibalism
DECOMPOSED BY POSSESSION, Merciless MR CD0014 (2000)

MORTIIS (NORWAY)

A solo project from the ex bassist Haavard Ellefsen of premier Black Metal act EMPEROR, MORTIIS specialize in ambient electronic Doom music. Mortiis also conducted another electronic band, VOND, in order to give vent to more "negative" music!
The album 'Crypt Of The Wizard' was also issued as separate set of five 12' singles. Early MORTIIS releases were issued in limited edition coloured vinyls only serving to increase the mystique surrounding the man. Signing to British label Earache Records for 'The Stargate' album, featuring CRADLE OF FILTH vocalist Sarah Jezebel Deva, brought the enigmatic figure to a wider audience.
MORTIIS employed a seven man band for a chaotic tour of America during 1999 which saw the act banned from many venues.
Mortiis, who always appears in public with fake elf ears and crooked nose, has also written a book titled 'Secrets Of My Kingdom' for future publication. Mortiis also operates FATA MORGANA and the vampyristic CINTECELE DIAVOLUI.

Singles/EPs:
Blood And Thunder, (199-) (7" single)
Ferden Og Kullet, Dark Dungeon Music (1996) (12" single)
En Sirkel Av Kosmisk Kaos, Dark Dungeon Music (1996) (12" single)
Vandreren's Sang, Dark Dungeon Music (1996) (12' single)
Stjernetödt, Dark Dungeon Music (1996) (12' single)
I Mörkret Drömmende, Dark Dungeon Music (1996) (12' single)

Albums:
FØDT TIL Å HERSKE, Malicious MA003CD (1995)
Født Til Å Herske Part I / Født Til Å Herske Part II
ANDEN SOM GJORDE OPPROE (THE REBELLIOUS SPIRIT), Cold Meat Industries CMI 31 (1995)
Det Var En Gang Et Menneske / Over Odermark / Opp Under Fjellet Toner En Sang / Tiden Er En Stenlagt Grar / Fra Fjelltronen / En Mork Horisont / Visioner Av En Eldgammel Frertid
KEISERN AV EN DIMENSION UKJENT (EMPEROR OF A DIMENSION UNKNOWN), Cold Meat Industry (1996)
Reisene Til Grotter Of Ødemarker / Keiser Av En Dimension Ukject
CRYPT OF THE WIZARD, Dark Dungeon Music (1996)
Ferden Og Kullet / Da Vibygde Tårnet / Under Tårnet's Skygge / En Sirkel Av Kosmisk Kaos / Vandreren's Sang / Den Bortdrevne Regnbuen / Trollmannen's Krypt / Stjernefødt / I Mørket Drømmende / Fanget I Krystal
THE STARGATE, Earache (1996)
Child Of Curiosity And The Old Man Of Knowledge / I Am The World / World Essence / Across The World Of Wonders / (Passing By) And Old And Raped Village / Towards The Gates Of The Stars / Spirit Of Conquest- The Warfare /Army Of Conquest- The Warfare (Ever Onwards)

MORTUARY DRAPE (ITALY)
Line-Up: Wildness Perversion (vocals), Old Necromancer (bass), Maniac Of Sacrifice (guitar), Diabolic Obsession (bass), Nequam (drums)
Italian Black Metal merchants MORTUARY DRAPE are known for the almost unique employment of two bass

players. The band debuted with the 1986 'Doom Return' demo. A further effort 'Necromancy' followed three years later.

Vocalist Wildness Perversion and bassist Old Necromancer (also known as 'Without Name') have always been the pivotal members of MORTUARY DRAPE with a constant everflowing cast of side members.

By 2000 the band included guitarists Andrea Taddei and Ricardo Messere, bassist Daniele Caniotti and drummer Luca Castasegna. However, on the album 'Tolling 13 Knell' group personnel were listed as drummer L.O.R.R. Will Revealed, bassist Left Hand Preacher and guitarists Roaming Soul and Demon Shadow.

Singles/EPs:
Mother / Crepusculor Whisper / Moon / Zombie / Vengeance From Beyond, Decapitated (1992) ('Into The Drape' EP)

Albums:
ALL THE WITCHES DANCE, Unisound (1995)
My Soul / Primordial / Astral Bewitchment / Funeral Chant / Larve / Tregenda (Dance In Shroud) / 13th Way / Intro (Chain) / Medium Mortem / Occult Abyss
MOURN PATH, Shivadarshana (1996)
SECRET SUDARIA, Nazgûl's Eyrie Productions NEP013CD (1997)
Obsessed By Necromancy / Wandering Spirits / Abbot / Necromancer / Evil Death / Madness / Secret Sudaria / Cycle Of Horror / Necromaniac / Presences / Malediction
TOLLING 13 KNELL, Avantgarde (2000)
Dreadful Discovery / Liar Jubelium / Vertical / Not Still Born / The Umber Plane / Laylah / Winged Priestess / The Last Supper / Birth's End / Defuncts / Lantern

MORTUM (SWEDEN)
Line-Up: Tinna Carlsdoller (vocals), Chrille Andersson (vocals / guitar), Michael Hakansson (vocals / bass), Rille Svensson (guitar), Bartek Nalezinski (drums)

Michael Hakansson is a member of EMBRACED. Chrille Andersson has credits with NON SERVIAM and HELLSPELL. Bassist Michael Hakansson also performs with EVERGREY.

A large contingent of MORTUM's membership (Andersson, guitarist Rille Svensson and drummer Bartek Nalezinski) would found the

straightforward Metal band SUPREME MAJESTY in 1999.

Albums:
THE DRUID CEREMONY, (1998)
Until Eternity / Punisher / Lady Lust / Night Spawned / The Druid Ceremony / Mother Of War / The Haunting / A Cursed Mankind / The Search For You / Outro

MOURNING (HOLLAND)
Line-Up: Marc (vocals / bass), Rene (guitar), Pim (guitar), Andre Van Der Ree (drums)

Death Metal act MOURNING, from Gouda, date to 1989. The band initially recorded a proposed split album with ETERNAL SOLSTICE in 1990, but this was not released as planned. However, three tracks were culled from these sessions for a demo.

With guitarist Pim having quit at the close of 1991, the original split album was finally released in 1992 and original drummer Misha Hak quit just before MOURNING signed a deal with Foundation 2000 Records. Hak later contributed drums to ETERNAL SOLSTICE's debut full length album 'The Wish Is Father To The Thought'.

By coincidence ETERNAL SOLSTICE added Hak's replacement in MOURNING, Andre Van Der Ree, to their line-up in 1994.

Albums:
MOURNING, Midian Creations (1992) (Split CD with ETERNAL SOLSTICE)
GREETINGS FROM HELL, Foundations 2000 FDN 2006 (1993)
Intro - Arma Satani / Sweet Dreams / Demon's Dance / Territorial / Denial Of Your Destiny / Only War And Hell / What? / Deranged Or Dead /

MUNDANUS IMPERIUM (NORWAY)
Line-Up: Jorn Lande (vocals), Peter Thuve (guitar), Bert E. Holm (keyboards), Lars Wiik (bass / drums)

Originally a Black Metal act MUNDANUS IMPERIUM, previously titled NATTEFALL, have evolved into a straight forward Power Metal band along classical 80s lines.

For the Nuclear Blast album MUNDANUS IMPERIUM were fronted by VAGABOND and THE SNAKES man Jorn Lande, a man of quite incredible vocal stature and recognized as one of Scandinavia's finest

258

talents. The 1999 album also features a version of RAINBOW's 'Stargazer'.
Lande also worked on a side project A.R.K. in 1999 with ex CONCEPTION men Tore Ostby and Ingar Amlien together with TNT and YNGWIE MALMSTEEN drummer John Macaluso. During 2000 Lande issued his debut solo album and also performed guest lead vocals for MILLENIUM. He joined YNGWIE MALMSTEEN's band in November.

Singles/EPs:
Ode To The Nightsky / Frozen Stars / Ridernde Pa Nattens Vinger, Velvet Music International (1997) ('Ode To The Nightsky' EP)

Albums:
THE SPECTRAL SPHERES CORONATION, Nuclear Blast NB 27361 63222 (1999)
Distant Conglomeration / The Life Of What You Seen / Beyond The Eternity / Starwars / Predominate / Stargazer / The Unborn Breaths In Silence / If The Universe Transformed

MURDER RAPE (BRAZIL)
Line-Up: Sabatan (vocals), Ipsissimus (guitar), Agathodemon (bass), Ichthys Niger (drums)

An extreme Brazilian Black Metal crew that include DAEMON drummer Ichthys Niger. MURDER RAPE debuted with the 1993 demo 'In Liaison With Satan'. The second album '...And Evil Returns' saw the inclusion of INSANE DEVOTION bassist Azarack.
In the summer of 1999 Azarack, vocalist Sabatan and drummer Ichtys Niger founded a new band EVILWAR for the 'Unholy March' album.

Albums:
CELEBRATION OF SUPREME EVIL, Cogumelo COG1010 (1994)
Intro / Embassy Of Satan / The Beginning Of Pain / Cries From The Abyss / Great Worshippers / Trace Of Omnipotence / Morbid Desires / Goat Rules / Outro
... AND EVIL RETURNS, Evil Horde EH001 (1996)
Pail Air Of Melancholy / For The Glory Of Evil Warriors / Echoes For The New Millenium / Descendents From Dark Side / Wonders Of Shadows / Celebration Of Supreme Evil

MUTANT (SWEDEN)
Line-Up: Peter Lake (guitar), Henrik Ohlsson (drums)

Black Metal formed by members of THEORY IN PRACTICE.

Albums:
EDEN BURNT TO ASHES, Mutant (1998)
Demon World / Beyond Bet Durrabia / Eden Burnt To ashes / Dark Spheres / Abduct To Mutate
THE AEONIC MAJESTY, Listenable (2000)
The Majestic Twelve / Demonworlds / Premonitions Erupt / Beyond Bet Durrabia / The Aeonic Majesty / Immemorial Lunacy / Dark Spheres / Eden Burnt To Ashes / Abduct To Mutate

MUTILATION (FRANCE)

French Black Metal band MUTILATION first issued the 1993 demo 'Satanist Stryken'.

Singles/EPs:
Hail Satanas We Are The Black Legions, (1994) (7" single)

Albums:
VAMPIRES OF BLACK IMPERIAL BLOOD, Draakar (1996)

MY INFINITE KINGDOM (POLAND)
Line-Up: Unholy Sirkis (vocals / guitar), Curche Sabasthor (bass), Thorn Chors (keyboards), Prince Mar Hellfrost (drums)

Albums:
ECSTASIES OVER DREAMING LADY, No Colours NC004 (1995)
In Scarlet Empires / Fairylands Of My Windmill / Shading The Dark / ... And Waves Flow Endlessly / A Trail In Evil Domain / dreams Of War / Painland / The Circle Of Naked Rocks

MYRIADS (NORWAY)
Line-Up: Mona Undheom Skottene (vocals), Alexander Twiss (guitar), J.P. (guitar), Morloc (keyboards), Rudi Junger (drums)

MYRIADS was founded by former OVERFLOATER guitarist Alexander Twiss. Both Twiss and vocalist Mona Undheom Skottene would join the ranks of TWIN OBSCENITY during 1997 but returned to concentrate on MYRIADS by the following year. MAJESTICS and AURVANDIR bassist Telal was involved during this period.

Bass player Knud Kleppe was employed for studio recording and MYRIADS utilize Christian Repper for live work.

Keyboard player Morloc (real name Mikael Stokdal) also operates with A WINTER WITHIN and MAJESTIC.

Singles/EPs:
In Spheres Without Time / Seductive Hate / The Day Of Wrath / Dreams Of Reality, (1998)

Albums:
IN SPHERES WITHOUT TIME, Napalm NPR 074 (2000)
Fragments Of The Hereafter / The Day Of Wrath / Spheres Without Time / Seductive Hate / Dream Of Reality

MYRING (FINLAND)
Line-Up: Skred Frostknight (vocals), Leka Frostknight (vocals / bass), Sargonnas (guitar), Demonica (keyboards)

MYRING was borne out of an acrimonious split in the ranks of TUONELA during 1997. The band originally included ex TUONELA drummer Mortarr but his services were soon dispensed with.

Albums:
ENGAGE THE ENEMY, Myring (1999)
Fall / Frostknives / Engage The Enemy / Jurret Mullasia / Pohjolan

MYRMIDION (TX, USA)
Line-Up: Buer (vocals / drums), Shade (guitar / bass)

The diabolical MYRMIDION pairing of Buer and Shade were originally joined by second guitarist Nunrape although the gentleman in question would depart after the EP.

Singles/EPs:
Utburd / Mystical Moon Eye / Seal Of Stolas / Blasphemous Torture / Somber Destiny, (199-) ('Divine Blasphemy' EP)

MYRKSKOG (SWEDEN)
Line-Up: Master V (vocals / bass), Savant M (guitar), Destructhor (guitar), Anders Eek (drums)
A highly individual approach to the genre makes MYRSKOG a unique proposition. The band, founded in the early 90's,

include former SUFFERING members and has had a fluid line up leading to the 1995 demo 'Apocalyptic Psychotasia'.

MYRKSKOG's Destructhor (real name Thor Anders Myhren) also features on the 2000 ZYKLON album, the side project of EMPEROR's Samoth and Trym. Drummer Anders Eek has credits with ODIUM, FUNERAL and THE FLESH. Drums on the 'Deathmachine' album were handled by Sechtdaemon.

Drummer Bjørn Thomas has also featured in the ranks of MYRKSKOG. Session keyboards were handled by Custer (real name Per Arvid).

Frontman Master V also operates a live keyboard player for LIMBONIC ART.

Singles/EPs:
A Poignant Scenario Of Death / Death Beauty Lust Ecstasy / A Macabre Death Fare To The Devil, (199-) ('Apocalptic Psychotasia- The Murder Tapes' EP)

Albums:
DEATH MACHINE, Candlelight (2000)
Discipline Misanthropy / The Hate Syndicate / A Poignant Scenario Of Horror / Sinthetic Lifeworm / Syndrome 9 / Morphinemangle Torture / Deathfare To The Devil / Death Machine / Pilar Deconstruction (Syndrome 9 Remix)

MYSTERIIS (BRAZIL)
Line-Up: Agares (vocals), Mantus (guitar), Trojan (guitar), Agramon (bass), Blitzgork (keyboards), Malphas (drums)

Rio De Janeiro old style Black Metal band MYSTERIIS emerged with the 1999 demo cassette 'Dreaming With The Darkness Cold'. Line up at this stage comprised of vocalist Agares, guitarist Mantus, bassist St. Damned and drummer Malphas. After the demo release St. Damned made way for former SONGE D'ENFER and NECROMANCER bassist Agramon.

A deal was struck with Brazilian extreme metal label Demise for the debut album 'About The Christian Despair' after which new members female vocalist Michelle Mania, second guitarist Trojan and keyboard player Blitzgork were enrolled. MYSTERIIS contributed their version of 'Nightmare' to a 2000 SARCÓFAGO tribute album.

In December 2000 both Blitzgork and Malphas made their exit.

Fucking In The Name Of God EP,
Demise (2000)

Albums:
ABOUT THE CHRISTIAN DESPAIR,
Demise (1999)
Ave Mysteriis (Baphomet Signs) / Song
For Anu / Feeling The Ancient Hordes Of
The Abyss / Blasphemy Calls / The
Valley Of The Triumphant / Nocturnal
Celebrations / Diabolical Cosmos
Dimensions / Sobre O Desespero Cristâo

MYSTERIUM (GERMANY)
Line-Up: Peter Domma (vocals / guitar),
Sabine Tiefensee (voices), Norman Al
Rubai (guitar), Timo Wolfahrt (guitar),
Andreas Landvoigt (keyboards), André
Holstein (drums)

Albums:
**THE GLOWERING FACADES OF
NIGHT**, Sturmesflügel FLUG003 (2000)
Primordium Mysteriorum / Where
Morning Still Stays Far Away / Ceremony
Of The Nightfall / The Red Eyed Wrath /
Ode To The Dark One / ere Lore Sank
Passing Far / Cynthia's Child / Winter
Enshrined

MYSTHICAL (SPAIN)

Erstwhile members of MYSTHICAL would
unite with former personnel of MAJESTIC
MIDNIGHT to found SYMAWRATH.

Singles/EPs:
Dusk Of The Myth, (1995)

MYSTIC CHASM (HOLLAND)

Singles/EPs:
Lost Empire, (1995)

Albums:
SHADOWS OF THE UNKNOWN, (1995)

MYSTIC CIRCLE (GERMANY)
Line-Up: Graf Van Beelzebub (vocals /
bass), Mephisto (guitar / keyboards),
Agamidion (guitar), Aaarrgon (drums)

Black Metallers MYSTIC CIRCLE were
founded in 1993 as a duo of vocalist /
bassist Graf Von Beelzebub and
drummer Aaarrgon. Adding guitarist
Mephisto, the band recorded debut demo
'Dark Passion' the following year.
Rhythm guitarist Agamidion bolstered the
band's sound as they switched from

Death Metal to Black Metal proving this
point with a further tape in 1995 titled 'Von
Kreigern Und Helden'. 1996 saw a further
demo in the form of 'Die Götter Der
Urväter'. The EP followed before a debut
album arrived later the same year.
The 2000 release 'Kriegsgotter II'
features demos and cover versions of
CELTIC FROST, ACHERON and
BATHORY numbers.

Singles/EPs:
Kriegsgötter, (1996)

Albums:
**MORGENRÖTE- DIE SCHREI NACH
FINSTERNIS MORGEN RÖTE**, Last
Epitaph LEP 007 CD (1996)
Mitternacht / Morgana's Curse /
Graveyard Dreams / Bloodlust (When
The Wolf Awake) / Throne Of The Night /
Octobermoon / Medina (Satan's Whore)
/ Kiss From A Vampire / Ravens Dusk /
Morgenröte
DRACHENBLUT, Last Episode (1998)
Ancient Words / Ancient Words /
Notrum- The Sword Of Might / The
Dragonslayer / King Of The
Nibelungenlord / Isenstein / Shadows
Over Worms / Hagen Von Tronje / Blood
From The Xanters King / Rheingold
INFERNAL SATANIC VERSES, Last
Episode (1999)
Intro- The Demons Call / Undestructable
Power Of Darkness / Hordes Of The
Underworld / The Devilstone / Thorns Of
Lies / One With The Anti Christ / Black
Legions / Fallen Christian Empire
KRIEGSGOTTER II, Last Episode CD
5.7061.20.561 (2000)
One Rode To Asa Bay / Die Gotter Der
Urvater / Azazel's Soulfly / Acheron
(Medley) / Circle Of The Tyrants

MYSTICUM (NORWAY)
Line-Up: Mean Malmberg, Prime Evil,
Cerastes (guitar)

MYSTICUM began life as the Industrial
Black Metal trio SABAZIOS releasing two
demos -'Wintermass' and 'Medusa's
Tears' - during 1992, both involving the
use of brutal drum computers.
The SABAZIOS tapes led to an
agreement with then MAYHEM member
Euronymous and his record label DSP.
Just prior to recording of the scheduled
album the name change to MYSTICUM
ensued.
The band's plans were thrown into
disarray with the murder of Euronymous

by BURZUM leader Count Grisnackh. However, former MAYHEM drummer Hellhammer was later to put in a stint with MYSTICUM. This liaison was brief though and MYSTICUM reverted back to a drum computer.

MYSTICUM issued a 1994 shared 7" single with ULVER.

The album was released by Fullmoon Records in 1995.

MYSTICUM
Photo : Martin Wickler

Singles/EPs:
Split, Necromantik Gallery Production (1994) (Split single with ULVER)

Albums:
IN THE STREAMS OF INFERNO, Fullmoon (1995)
Industries Of Inferno / The Rest / Let The Kingdom Come / Wintermass / Where The Raven Flies / Crypt Of Fear / In Your Grave / In The Last Ruins We Search For A New Planet

MYSTIFIER (BRAZIL)
Line-Up: Sathanael (vocals), Paulo Lisbon (guitar), Beelzebuth (bass), Louis Bear (drums)

Black Metal band MYSTIFIER debuted with a 1989 demo 'Tormenting The Holy Trail'. The act's debut line up comprised of vocalist Mengninousouan, guitarist Behemoth, bass player Beelzebubth and drummer Lucifuge Rofocale. A 7" single ensued before further demos 'Aleister Crowley' in 1991 and a further tape two years later.

MYSTIFIER scored a deal with renowned French label Osmose productions for their 'Wicca' album. After this release a line up shuffle saw the exit of Mengninousouan and the recruitment of ex HATRED singer Asmodeus and former CALVARY guitarist Astaroth. Following the 1993 album 'Goetia' both Astaroth and Behemoth departed. MYSTIFIER plugged the gap with Paulo Lisbon.

Longstanding member drummer Lucifuge Rofocale bailed out in August of 1998 prior to a Brazilian tour supporting ROTTING CHRIST. A temporary stand in was recruited for the dates as was second guitarist Thony D'Assys of CARNIFIED. Louis Bear, previously with DREARYLANDS, would then manouevre into the drum position.

1999 had the band industrious on the tribute album front and MYSTIFIER versions of POSSESSED's 'Fallen Angel', KREATOR's 'Storm Of The Beast', SEPULTURA's 'Morbid Visions' and SLAYER's 'Tormentor' all surfaced on various releases.

Latterly Asmodeus was forced out to enable Sathanael to front the band.

MYSTIFIER's original 1989 demo was made available on CD in 2000 by Russian label Eldritch Productions. Bonus tracks included cover versions of POISON's 'Leather And Metal' and SARCOFAGAS's 'Satanic Lust'.

2000 found MYSTFIER continuing the tradition of contributing tracks to tribute albums with the band donating METALLICA's 'Phantom Lord', MORBID ANGEL's 'The Invocation- Chapel Of Ghouls' and WASP's 'The Torture Never Stops'.

Former MYSTIFIER and GRIDLOCK guitarist Martin Mendonca would join fellow Black Metal band MALEFACTOR in 1999.

Singles/EPs:
The Evil Ascension Returns, Maniac (1990)
T.E.A.R., (1997)

Albums:
WICCA, Osmose Productions (1992)
The Witch Voisin Receives Our Gloat- Osculum Obscenum / Tormentum Aeternu / Cursed Excruciation / Defloration (The Antichrist Lives) /

262

(Invocatione) The Almighty Satanas / The Dark Kingdom (T.F.A.R.) / An Elizabethan Devil Worshipper's Prayerbook / Hyoseyannus Niger / Mystifier (Satan's Messengers) Our Gloat
GOETIA, Osmose Productions (1993)
Aleister Crowley And Ordo Templi Orientis / An Elizabethan Devil Worshipper's Handbook / The Sign Of The Unholy Cross / Caerimonia Sanguilentu (Goetia) / Beelzebub / The Realm Of Antichrists / The True Story About Doctor Faust's Pact With Mephistopheles / Cursed Excruciation- The Sinous Serpent Of Genesis (Leviathan) / The Baphometic Goat Of Knight Templar In The twelfth Century
THE WORLD IS SO GOOD THAT WHO MADE IT DOESN'T LIVE HERE, Osmose Productions (1996)
Give The Devil His Due / A Chant To The Goddess Of Love- Venus / The Death Of An Immortal (According To The Astral Light) / Idolatry / The Barbarian Dwelling With The Wise / Moonick (Why Does It Never Rain On The Moon?)
DEMYSTIFYING THE MYSTIFIED ONES (FOR A DECADE IN THE EARTHLY PARADISE), (1999)
The Evil One Invades The Earthy Paradise / The Supreme Power Of The Human Empire / False Superstitions Made By Tellers Of Legends / A Plague Spreads In The Earthly Paradise / Belzeebubth / Demystifier / Will Jews Praise The Antichist As Messiah? / The So Called God Abandons The Earthly Paradise
THE FOURTH EVIL CALLING FROM THE ABYSS- TORMENTING THE HOLY TRINITY, Eldritch (2000)

MYTHOLOGICAL COLD TOWERS
(BRAZIL)
Line-Up: Samej (vocals), Flagellum (guitar), Nechron (guitar), Leonard (bass), Akenaton (keyboards), Hamon (drums)

Albums:
SPHERE OF NEBADDON (THE DAWN OF A DYING TYFFERETH), (199-)
In The Forgotten Melancholic Waves Of Eternal Sea / Celestial Dimensions Into Silence / The Vastness Of A Desolated Glory / Slaves In The Imaginary Abysal Line / Erotic Voluptuousness Of A Lost Feeling Of Life / Golden Bells From The Eternal Frost / Mythological Cold Towers / … Of Inexistancy / A Portal Of My Dark Soul

REMOT MERIDIANI HYMNI- TOWARDS THE MAGNIFICENT REALM OF THE SUN, (20000

MYTHOS (FINLAND)
Line-Up: Tony Pekkala (vocals / guitar), Jukka Vappu (guitar), Mikko Laurila (bass), Teemu Hautanieemi (drums)

Formed in 1992 by erstwhile BELIAL guitarist Jukka Valppu, MYTHOS released a brace of demos starting with 'Moulded In Clay' whilst undergoing intense line-up changes. The group finally settling on the combination listed above before signing to French label Evil Omen. Having had tracks on the compilation album 'Vociferous And Machiavellian Hate', quite bizarrely MYTHOS would split following the release of their one and only album, 'Pain Amplifier', in 1994.

Albums:
PAIN AMPLIFIER, Evil Omen EORCD002 (1994)
In The Beginning / Hung On The Wings / Unreal Moon / In Veiled Language / The Pain Amplifier / A Song By The Way / Verses In The Fire / The Last Orgy / Strange Things Happen At Night / The End (Of The Outro)

MZ 412 (NORWAY)
Line-Up: Kremator Nordvargr, Ulvtharm, Drakhon

Previously an industrial band known as MASCHINZIMMER 412 - releasing two albums 'Malfeitor' and 'Macht Durch Stimme' - this Norwegian group adopted a Black Metal stance, including the adoption of de rigeour corpsepaint in 1995.
The vinyl version of the second album was limited to exactly 412 copies.

Albums:
MALFEITOR, Cold Meat Industry CMI07 (1989)
MACHT DURCH STIMME, (199-)
IN NOMINE DEI NOSTRI SATANAS LUCIFERI, Cold Meat Industry CMI 35 (1995)
In Nomine Dei / Salvo Sonoris Morte / Herrotic Birth / Black Earth / Daemon Raging / God Of Fifty Names / Regie Satanas / Paedophia Cum Sadismus / Hail The Lord Of Goats
BURNING THE TEMPLE OF GOD, Cold Meat Industry CMI 41 (1996)
Deklaration Of Holy War / The Winter Of

Mourning / Feasting On Khristian Blood /
Taking The Throne / Burning (God's
House) / Submit And Obey / Nebulah
Frost / Vampir Of The North / De Ondas
Vandring
NORDIK BATTLESIGNS, Cold Meat
Industry CMI 66 (1999)
MZ 412 Introduktion / Algiz-
Konvergence Of Life And Death / Satan
Jugend / Der Kampf Geht Weiter / Satan
Jugend II: Global Konquering / Tyranor /
NBS Act I: Begravning / NBS Act II: 14W

NAER MATARON
(GREECE)
Line-Up: Aithir (vocals / drums), Morpheas (guitar), Lethe (keyboards)

Hellenic Black Metal band NAER MATARON, which includes erstwhile members of VORPHALACK, was created in 1994 as NAR MATARON. The band's two demos 'Tales Of The Twelve Gods' and 'The Awakening Of Ancient Greece' both included credits for Lord Alatoth ('Screams') and Morpheas on guitar and bass. With a line up change NAER MATARON cut a further promotional track 'The Great God Pan' which led to an album deal with Black Lotus Records.
Frontman Aithir quit on the eve of recording and was replaced by ORDER OF THE EBON HAND's Lethe on the drums.
Lord Alatoth departed following recording as Aithir was re-inducted as the band shifted Lethe to keyboards. Aithir also shared drumming duties with LEGION OF DOOM.

Albums:
UP FROM THE ASHES, Black Lotus (1998)
The Chosen Son / Faethon / Zephyrous / Zeus (Wrath Of The Gods) / The Silent Kingdom Of Hades) / The Great God Pan

NAGELFAR (GERMANY)
Line-Up: Jarder (vocals), Zorn (guitar), Sveinn (bass), Alexander Von Mielenwald (drums)

NAGELFAR's debut album 'Hünengrab Im Herbst' was produced by former HOLY MOSES guitarist Andy Classen.
Following NAGELFAR's second album 'Srongorrth' both vocalist Jarder and bassist Sveinn left. Drummer Alexander Von Mielenwald took over the lead vocal role as the band pulled in Harris for session bass duties.
The band's label Kettenhund folded prior to the release of a projected third album 'Virus West'.

Albums:
HÜNENGRAB IM HERBST, Kettenhund KHR001 CD (1998)
Seelenland / Schwanengesang / Hünengrab Im Herbst / Bilnis der Apokalypse / Srontgorrth (Das Dritte Kapitel) / Der Flug des Rahe

SRONTGORRTH, Kettenhund KHR002 CD (1999)
Kapitel Eins- Der Fruhling: Als die Tore Sich Öffnen / Kapitel Zwei- Die Sommer: Die Existenz Jenseits der Tore / Kapitel Drei- Der Herbst: Endzeit / Kapitel Vier- Der Winter: Trümmer / Kapitel Fünf- Wilkommen Zu Haus

NAGLFAR (SWEDEN)
Line-Up: Jens Rydén (vocals), Andreas Nilsson (guitar), Kristoffer Olivius (bass), Morgan Hansson (drums)

A Black Metal band with Thrash influences, NAGLFAR's ex drummer - Matte Holmgren - formed EMBRACING, releasing the 'I Bear The Burden Of Time' album in 1996 and would add vocals to the debut SKYFIRE demo 'Within Reach'. The AZURE 'Moonlight Legend' of 1998 also includes Holmgren on drums.
NAGLFAR's high profile second album sees Matthias Grahn taking on the drummers role from previous incumbent Morgan Hansson. The parting of ways with Hansson could be viewed as acrimonious bearing in mind that the band pointedly offer him no thanks on the album cover and declare their former sticksman to be "mad"!
Ryden issued his solo project DEAD SILENT SLUMBER's 'Entombed In The Midnight Hour' album in 1999.

Albums:
VITTRA, Wrong Again WAR 008 (1996)
As The Twilight Gave Birth To The Night / Enslave The Astral Fortress / Through The Midnight Spheres / The Eclipse Of Infernal Storms / Emerging From Her Weepings / Failing Wings / Vittra / Sunless Dawn / Exalted Above Thrones
DIABOLICAL, War Music WAR 0005 (1998)
Horncrowned Majesty / Embracing The Apocalypse / 12th Rising / Into The Cold Voids Of Eternity / The Brimstone Gate / Blades / When Autumn Storms Come / A Departure In Solitude / Diabolical: The Devil's Child

NAHASH (LITHUANIA)
Line-Up: Munis (vocals / guitar), Ramsas (bass), Vadimas (keyboards), Audrius (drums)

Black Metal band NAHASH debuted with the 1994 demo 'Nocticula Hecate'.

Albums:
WELLON AETERNITAS, Drakkar
Productions (1997)

NAMELESS (PORTUGAL)

Albums:
**THE OVERCOME OF PORTUGESE
BASTARDS**, Guardian Of Metal (1997)

N.A.O.S. (GREECE)

N.A.O.S. is a solo embarkation of Magus
Wampyr Daoloth, the driving force behind
such diverse acts as NECROMANTIA,
ROTTING CHRIST, DIABOLOS RISING,
THOU ART LORD and RAISM.

Singles/EPs:
Split EP, Dark Side (1996) (Split EP with
EN GARDE)
Iron Youth EP, Membrum Debile
Propaganda (1997)

Albums:
THE FIRST HARVEST, Itsemuhra Arts
(1995)
MELANCHOLIA, Cacophonous NIHIL 15
(1996)
The Storm From Wewelsburg / Occultica
/ The King Is Dead / To Hell With The
Devil / Shaman's Tears / I Bleed
(Stigmata Martyr) / Ourovoros / The
Devil's Maze / Iron Youth / The Vampire
Weeps
COMMUNION, Go Underground (1998)

NARGATROND (RUSSIA)
Line-Up: Kai Mathias Stahlhammer
(vocals), Lazar (guitar / bass / keyboards
/ drums)

NARGATROND multi instrumentalist
Lazar also busies himself with fellow
Black metal band ROSSOMAHAAR and
Doom Metal band STONEHENGE.
Vocalist Kai Mathias Stahlhammer
contributed lyrics to the ROSSOMAHAAR
album 'Imperium Tenebrum'.

Albums:
**CARNAL LUST AND WULVEN
HUNGER**, More Hate Productions (2000)
Moonchild / Carnal Lust And Wulven
Hunger / Across The Circles Edge / I
Saw Them Dying / Ixaxer (Mera De
Intimis Gentibus Libyne, De Lapide
Hexecontalitho) / The Coldness Of
Venus / Sweet Red Divine / Marl
Bennique / Let My Dreams Become Your
Nightmares / Saducismus Triumphatas

NASHEHRUM (ITALY)

Italian keyboard based Black Metal band
NASHEHRUM debuted with a 1994 demo
'Black Ritual Of Hearts Asportation'.

Singles/EPs:
**Remember The Shining Moons Of The
Black Autumns EP**, Maggot (1996)

NÅSTROND (SWEDEN)
Line-Up: Arganas, Agni Hotri, Karl

NÅSTROND debuted with the 1994 demo
'From A Black Funeral Coffin'.

Singles/EPs:
Digerdöden, Full Moon Productions
(1995)

Albums:
TOTESLAUT, Napalm (1996)
Xolot / En Sång Från En Pestbesmittal
Graw / Lord Of The Woods / Akhkharu
(The Grave Dweller) / Neuntöter / May
The Rotten Bones Absorb Life Again / A
Black Hearse Clad In Human Bones And
Skulls / Jai Ma Kali / Gravestench /
Toteslaut
AGE OF FIRE, Napalm (1997)
Prologue / Age Of Fire / Winged Phallus
(Ferocious Angel) / Womb Of Chaos /
The Four / Une Charogne / Consecration
Of The Flame / The Great Below /
Vanished From The World / The Red
Force (Of The Trapesoid) / Emancipation
/ Opening Of The Mouth / Epilog- The
Fifth Book Of Satan

NATTVINDENS GRÅT (FINLAND)
Line-Up: Teemu (speechs / guitar), Sami
(bass), Tuomas Holopainen (keyboards)
Tero (drums)

Fronted by ex DARKWOODS MY
BETROTHED man Teemu Kautonen.
NATTVINDENS GRÅT keyboard player
Tuomas Holopainen also shares his
creative energies with NIGHTWISH, an
outfit that released the 'Angels Fall First'
album on Spinefarm Records in 1998.
NATTVINDENS GRÅT got a deal after
only one demo, Där Svanar Flyger', and
have since offered Death Metal reliant on
strong melodies and, sometimes, unusual
instrumentation.
'A Bard's Tale' features the additional
talents of female vocalist Suvi and male
vocalist Wilsa. The band's logo,
incidentally, was drawn by Tom of
HELMEIM fame.

266

Kautonen issued a solo project album 'Songs Of Sin And Decadence' under the band name WIZZARD in 1999.

Albums:
A BARD'S TALE, Solistitium SOL 004 (1995)
Introduction / The Road Goes Ever On / The Echo / Skyfires Dance / Towards The Sea / Song Of The Tide Waves / A Lonely October Night / Stormwind The Soothsayer / Vagabond's Dusk
CHAOS WITHOUT THEORY, Solistitium SOL 012 (1997)
Sethian Seal / The Dance From Beyond / Sleep Eternal / In Gothic Archways / Thelemite / Sadoeroticart / Chaos Without Theory / Liquid Silent Dreams / Sorrow's Shroud

NAZXUL (AUSTRALIA)
Line-Up: Dalibor (vocals), Greg Morelli (guitar), Rev. Kriss Hades (guitar), Adrian Henderson (bass), Lachlan Mitchell (keyboards), Steve Hughes (drums)

Black Metal act NAZXUL issued the 1994 'Nazxul' demo and its follow up 'Hymn Of A Dying Moon' before cutting their debut 'Totem' album.
NAZXUL did not perform live until 1998 and would tour alongside IMPALED NAZARENE on their Australian dates. Vocalist Dalibor exited in favour of the red robed Morte but Dalibor would usurp his successor after one tour. Drummer Steve Hughes also lost his place to former FRONT END LOADER man Pete Kostic. Guitarist Rev. Kriss Hades is also a member of the notorious SADISTIK EXEKUTION.

Singles/EPs:
Vow Of Vengeance / Black See Sown / Apostasies Legions Arise, Xul! / Under The Signs Of Lifes Living End, Shock (1998) ('Black Seed Sown' EP)

Albums:
TOTEM, Vampire (1995)
Totem / Watching And Withering / I Awaken (Amongst Them) / Unearthed / Vernis Mysteriis / Hatred / Endless Reign Of Power / Distance Begins / Amidst The Hades / End / Eternum

NEBIRAS (MALAYSIA)
Line-Up: Agathos Daemon (vocals / guitar / drums) / Ominous (bass / guitar)

'Witching Metal' act NEBIRAS appeared to be a duo of Agathos Daemon and Ominous for their 1996 'Our Blood For His Glory' album. However, by the release of 'Into The Medieval Cults' the band transpired to be Faridz on bass and keyboards, Baron De Bellem on vocals and guitar and drummer Feanor.

Singles/EPs:
Sacrilegus, (199-)

Albums:
AS THE SKY TURNS BLACK, Dark Journey (1993)
OUR BLOOD FOR HIS GLORY, Dark Journey (1996)
INTO THE MEDIEVAL CULTS, (199-)

NEBULAR MYSTIC (NORWAY)

NEBULAR MYSTIC was created by former FORLORN IN SILENCE members vocalist Adhramalech and guitarist Morfahnus. Following two EPs NEBULAR MYSTIC folded when Adhramalech refounded FORLORN IN SILENCE.

Singles/EPs:
Taakeriket, (199-)
Frostlagt, (199-)

NEBULAR MOON (GERMANY)
Line-Up: Darius Widera (vocals), Andreas Caninberg (guitar), Ingo Haltermann (bass), Holger T. (keyboards), Stefan Hüls (drums)

NEBULAR MOON debuted with singer Andreas F. prior to Darius Widera taking the role for the self financed 'Mourning' album. The band came to the attention of Episode Records who re-released 'Mourning' with extra tracks. For these new songs ABBADON frontman Markus Esch performed vocals.
By October of 2000 Widera usurped Esch to resume his place for the 'Masterclone' album. Guest vocals came from Esch and Bjoern Goose of NIGHT IN GALES.

Albums:
MOURNING, Nebular Moon (1997)
Flames / Nevermore / Divine Agony / Pest / Mirror Of Truth / Escape / All Is Lost
MOURNING, Episode (1998)
Flames / Nevermore / Divine Agony / Pest / Mirror Of Truth / Escape / All Is Lost / My Cloud Eternity / Nightfall (A Moment Like Infinity) / Demons Of Time
OF DREAM AND MAGIC, Episode (1999)

Chapter I- Steeple Of Forgotten Knowledge: Gates Of Experience- Part I / Gates Of Experience- Part II / Chapter II- Dust Of Transience: My Cold Eternity / Schwarzengesang / Chapter III- Castle Of Oblivion: Dark Angel / Beyond The Sky / Chapter IV- Dark Dormant Desires: An Erotic Nightmare / Awakening In Black Thorns
MASTERCLONE, (2000)

NECROFEAST (HOLLAND)
Line-Up: Dagon (vocals), Centurion (all instruments)

Dutch Metal band NECROFEAST, founded by ex NIDHUG man Centurion, formed in 1995 and their first output was a two track demo featuring the songs 'doomed Christ' and 'The Blessing'.
The group's 1996 debut album features a cover of BATHORY's 'The Return Of Darkness And Evil'. NECROFEAST signed to Spanish label The Drama And Sin for the 2000 'Soulwinds' effort. The album included a take on the COUNTESS track 'Bloed In de Sneeuw'.
NECROFEAST's Krieger (also known as 'Centurion') also operates with FLUISTERWOUD, Polish act MORDEAOTH and WELTER.

Albums:
NECROFEAST, Creation Necromantical Mystical Productions (1996)
Hymn Of The Hordes / Time For Revenge / The Return Of Darkness And Evil / The Blessing / Doomed Christ / Northern Wrath / Outro
SOULWINDS, The Drama And Sin DAS004 (2000)
Slag Om Germania / Soulwinds In The Battle Sky / Runendans / Roep Oan De Raaf / A Sacrifice In Ingoi / Hymn- Spirit Of Death / Secrets Of The Shadowdancer / The Halls Of Glory Of Walhalla / Bloed In De Sneeuw / Ceumige Strijd Tegn Al Light En Leben

NECROMANTIA (GREECE)
Line-Up: Slow Death (vocals), Magus Wampyr Daoloth (vocals / bass), Divad (guitar), Baron Blood (8 string bass)

NECROMANTIA, fronted by the controversial figure of Magus Wampyr Daoloth (real name George Zaharopoulos) date back to their inception as a trio in late 1989. The band are unequivocal in their stance of blatant Satanism and although remaining

exceptionally heavy are eager to experiment with piano and saxophone. NECROMANTIA's first product, following a 1990 demo, was a split LP with another Greek act VARATHRON. The record was titled 'The Black Arts' on Black Power Records in 1992. The group added keyboard player Inferno later that year.
In 1993 the line-up was further enhanced by the addition of Yiannis- The worshipper of Pan (!) on Percussion, saxophone and flute.
NECROMANTIA signed to the adventurous French label Osmose Productions, releasing their debut full length album in 1994. A second album arrived in 1995.
Outside of NECROMANTIA Daoloth is involved in a plethora of Black Metal projects including DIABOLUS RISING, RAISM, THOU ART LORD with Sakis from ROTTING CHRIST and Gothmog of MORTIFY, N.A.O.S. and DANSE MACABRE in union with Sotiris of SEPTIC FLESH and ANCIENT RITES Gunther.
Daoloth also produced the 2000 'Rise From Within' album from all female Black Metal trio ASTARTE.

Singles/EPs:
Black Arts Leading To Everlasting Sins EP, Unisound (1992) (Split EP with VARATHORN)
La Mort (Live 1989), **Necromantia** (1995)
Shaman / Ancient Pride / For The Light Of My Darkness / Each Dawn I Die, Osmose Productions OPMCD 048 (1997) ('Ancient Pride' EP)

Albums:
CROSSING THE FIERY PATH, Osmose OPCD021 (1994)
The Vampire Lord Speaks / The Warlock / Last Song For Valdezie / Unchain The Wolf (At War) / Les Litanies De Satan / Lord Of The Abyss / Tribes Of The Moon.
SCARLET EVIL, WITCHING BLACK, Osmose Productions OPCD 036 (1995)
Devilskin / Black Mirror / Pretender To The Throne (Opus I: The Usurper's Spawn) / The Arcane Light Of Hecate / Scarlet Witching Dreams / The Serpent And The Pentagram / Pretender To The Throne (Opus II : Battle Of The Netherworld) / Spiritdance
IV: MALICE, Black Lotus BLRCD 015 (2000)
The Blair Witch Cult / Those Who Never Sleep / Disciples Of Sophia (The

Templars) / Murder, Magic And Tears / Invictus / Malice / Circles Of Burned Doves

NECROMASS (ITALY)
Line-Up: Ain Soph Aur (vocals / bass), J.C. Kerioth (guitar), Nachzerehmara (guitar), Black Wizard (drums)

NECROMASS guitarist Marco M also operates as a member of HANDFUL OF HATE.

Singles/EPs:
Connected Body Pentagram, Carnefication (1992) (7" single)
His Eyes, CNF (1993) (7" single)
Bhoma, Miscarriage (1995) (7" single)

Albums:
MYSTERIA MYSTICA ZOFIRIANA, Unisound (1994)
Night (Madness…Knowledge…Evil) / Necrobarathrum / Mysteria Mystica Zorifiana 666 / Exterior Circle / Sodomatic Orgy Of Hate / Black Mass Intuition (Atto 1: Introibo Ad Attare, Atto 2: Silver Reign) / Sadomasochist Tallow Doll / Into An Image Of Left
ABYSS CALLS LIFE, Dracma (1996)
(An Animal) Forever / Vibrations Of Burning Splendour / Into The Warmth Of Darkness / Bloodstorm Collide / Impure / Abyss Calls Life / A Serpent Is Screaming In The Abyss / Before To Obsess
CHRYSALIS' GOLD, Necromass (1998)

NECROMICON (SWEDEN)
Line-Up: Daniel (vocals), Nicklas (guitar), Stefan (guitar), Patrick (bass), Roger (keyboards), Robert (drums)

NECROMICON opened proceedings with the February 1994 demo 'When The Sun Turns Black' although the band had formed a year earlier. Following this inaugural tape bass player Hendrick took over guitar duties and Jonas filled the four string position. A further demo 'Through The Gates Of Grief' was cut before Hendrick's departure. Jonas moved over to guitar whilst Patrick joined on bass. NECROMICON also augmented their sound with the inclusion of keyboard player Roger.
After a string of live gigs Jonas was sacked. After the release of debut album 'Realm Of Silence' new guitarist Stefan joined the band.
NECROMICON member Baron De Samedi (Jonas?) would later join GATES OF ISHTAR before founding BATTLELUST.

Albums:
REALM OF SILENCE, Impure Creations (1996)
The Spawn Of Dracula / Gates Of Grief / Ages Unfold / Through The Darkness / In Blackened Robes / The Hateful One / Dreams Of The Ancients / Realm Of Silence
SIGHTVEILER, Hammerheart (1998)
Introduction / Gone Below / Homecomings / The Uprising / Veiled In Crimson / Endless Agony / In Desperation / Leaving Now / Ever After
PECCATA MUNDI, Hammerheart (2000)
Peccata Mundi / Heavens Of Hate… Fields Of Fire / The Find Of Alone / Voluptuous Womb / Awaiting The Long Sleep / Firebreeze / Lost Equilibrium / Suicide Caravan / Black Horsemen

NECROPHOBIC (SWEDEN)
Line-Up: Anders Strokirk (vocals / bass), Dave Parland (guitar), Tobbe Sidegard (keyboards), Joakim Sterner (drums)

Death Metal act created in 1989. NECROPHOBIC once included ex DARK FUNERAL guitarist Dave Parland in the ranks.
The band's initial demo, 'Slow Asphyxiation', sold a commendable 700 copies, prompting a 1991 three track tape entitled 'Unholy Prophecies', recorded at the ever popular Sunlight studios.
NECROPHOBIC's first commercial release came with an EP titled 'The Call' on U.S. label Wild Rags Records that featured ex CREMATORY vocalist Stefan Harrvik. A track also followed on a compilation album on Witchhunt Records. In late 1995 keyboard player Tobbe Sidegard joined fellow Swedes THERION and Parland quit in 1996 to concentrate on his solo outfit BLACKMOON.
1997's 'Darkside' album witnessed a fresh NECROPHOBIC line-up comprised of Tobbe Sidegard on vocals and bass, drummer Joakim Sterner and new guitarist Martin Halfdahn.

Singles/EPs:
Shadows Of The Moon / The Ancient Gate / Father Of Creation, Wild Rags WRR-NEC (1993)
Spawned By Evil / Die By The Sword / Nightmare / Enter The Eternal Fire, Black Mark BMCD 60 (1996) ('Spawned By

Evil' EP)

Albums:
THE NOCTURNAL SILENCE, Black Mark BMCD 40 (1993)
Awakening / Before The Dawn / Unholy Prophecies / The Nocturnal Silence / Shadows Of The Moon / The Ancients Gate / Sacrificial Rites / Father Of Creation / Where Sinners Burn
DARKSIDE, Black Mark BMCD 96 (1996)
Black Moon Rising / Spawned By Evil / Bloodthirst / Venasectio / Darkside The Call / Descension / Mailing The Holy One / Nifelhel / Christian Slaughter
THE THIRD ANTICHRIST, Black Mark BMCD 146 (2000)
Rise Of The Infernal / The Third Of Arrivals / Frozen Empire / Into Armageddon / Eye Of The Storm / The Unhallowed / Isaz / The Throne Of Souls possessed / He Who Rideth In Rage / Demonic / One Last Step Into The Great Mist

NECROPOLIS (UK)

Line-Up: Sven Olaffsen (vocals), Billy Liesegang (guitar), Trev Thoms (guitar), Keith More (guitar), Algy Ward (bass), Steve Clark (drums)

The debut album from Black Metallers NECROPOLIS is not all it seems. Drummer Steve Clark, previously with FASTWAY and mentor of Jazz Rock act NETWORK, assembled this band allegedly in an attempt to show the younger genre of Death Metal bands just how this kind of music should be performed. An odd contrast of styles were to make up NECROPOLIS with ex NINA HAGEN and JOHN WETTON guitarist Billy Liesegang, additional guitars from ASIA and ARENA man KEITH MORE, former TANK, DAMNED and ATOMGOD bassist Algy Ward and erstwhile HAWKWIND guitarist Trev Thoms.
The album, recorded in 1993, includes a guest session from ex MOTÖRHEAD and FASTWAY guitarist FAST EDDIE CLARKE.
Following recording of 'End Of The Line' Clark and Ward resumed activity with NETWORK for the 'Refusal To Comply' album.

Albums:
END OF THE LINE, Neat Metal NM021 (1997)
Victim / Samaritan / A Taste For Killing / Shadowman / 145 Speed Overload / The

Bitterness I Taste

NEFANDUS (SWEDEN)

Line-Up: Blackwinged (vocals), Belfagor (guitar / drums)

Amongst the purest of Black Metal acts NEFANDUS, although resisting commercial pressures, are a renowned force. Both Blackwinged and Belfagor also put their energies into a side project entitled HELLSENT.
Belfagor also is known for his other act OFERMOD in collusion with Mist of OPTHALMIA and Nebiros issuing a 7" single in 1996.

Albums:
THE NIGHTWINDS CARRIED OUR NAMES, Nexus NEX003 (1997)

NEGLECTED FIELDS (LATVIA)

Line-Up: Sergey (vocals), Herman (guitar), Sergey (bass), Karlis (drums)

Riga act previously titled CARRION with original drummer Kirill. A second drummer Alex became involved before CARRION folded in 1994. Founder members vocalist Sergey, guitarist Herman and bassist Sergey refounded the band rebilled as NEGLECTED FIELDS and with a new drummer Karlis, previously with SANCTIMONY.
In this new guise NEGLECTED FIELDS issued the demo cassette 'Sansara' prior to the departure of Karlis. Evil of HUSQVARN occupied the drumstool before the debut album 'Synthinity' for which Karlis made his return. Promoting the album saw support dates to MARDUK in Russia.
NEGLECTED FIELDS female singer Sandra would join HERESIARH.

Albums:
SYNTHINITY, Eldethorn (1997)
Spheres Rhapsody / Calm, Precious, Mad / Escatological / Ephemerae / Sansara / Synthinity / Living Structures / These Fires Thoughts / Fairy / Breathe
MEPHISTO LETTONICA, Scarlet (2000)
Solar / The Spider's Kiss / Whatever That Tempts / Feral Garden / Presentiment / The Human Abstract / Creaturesque / Once Caress Is Cold / Outro

NEGURA BUNGET (ROMANIA)

Line-Up: Hupogrammos Disciple (vocals / guitar), Spurcatu (guitar / bass), Negru (drums)

A genuine Transylvanian Black Metal act. NEGURA BUNGET began life as WICCAN REDE issuing the 1995 demo 'From Transylvanian Forests'. Early member keyboard player Ayvaz Valah Disciple had departed by the time of the first NEGURA BUNGET release 'Zirnindu Sa'. NEGURA BUNGET's 1998 'Sala Molska' EP saw the inclusion of guitarist Spurcatu.

Singles/EPs:
Suier De Solomonar / Sala Molska-Channeling Through Art Immortal / Din Afundul Adincului Intrupat, Bestial (1998) ('Sala Molska' EP)

Albums:
ZÎNINDU SA, Breath Of Life (1999)
Blaznit / Negrii / In Miaz De Negru / Din Afundul Adincului Nitrupat / Pohvala Hula / De Rece Singie / Dupre Reci Imbre / Vel Proclet
MAIASTRU SFETNIC, Bestial (2000)
Vremea Locului Sortit / In-Zicnirea Apusului / A Vint In Abis / Al Locului / Bruiestru / Plecaciunea Mortii

NEPHENCY (SWEDEN)
Line-Up: Martin Hallin (vocals / guitar), Adrian Kanebäck (guitar), Matthias Fredriksson (bass), Kim Arnell (drums)

Albums:
WHERE DEATH BECOMES ART, Black Diamond BDP 004 (1998)
Enchanted Bliss / Chain Of Command / Worshipped By The Mass / Imperial Dementia / Desolated / Tournament In Torment / Cursed / Hatred And Fantasies / The Meeting

NEPTUNE TOWERS (NORWAY)

Solo keyboard project from Fenris of DARKTHRONE and ISENGARD.

Albums:
CARAVANS TO THE EMPIRE ALGOL, Moonfog FOG002 (1994)
The Journey / The Arrival
TRANSMISSIONS FROM EMPIRE ALGOL, Moonfog FOG008 (1995)
First Communion. Mode: Direct / To Cold Void Desolation

NERGAL (GREECE)

Black Metallers NERGAL released a split single with fellow countrymen FUNERAL URN in 1994. The album 'The Wizard Of Nerath' was produced by Magus Wampyr Daoloth of NECROMANTIA.

Singles/EPs:
The Talisman Of Kioutha, Nergal (199-) (7" single)
The Middle Ages Return, Nergal (1993) (7" single)
De Vermis Mysteriis, Nergal (1993) (7" single)
Split, Nergal (1994) (Split single with FUNERAL URN)

Albums:
THE WIZARD OF NERATH, Unisound USR 016 (1995)
Timeless Father / My Soul, Blood, Will Be Dripping / The Wind Of Hate / Ljus Mörker / The Wizard Of Nerath / Katares / The Dream Of The Dragon / Frozen Forest / Sparagmos

NERGAL (SWITZERLAND)
Line-Up: Mike Burger (vocals / guitar), Gisela Imhof (bass), Nick (drums)

NERGAL began life as a death Metal band dubbed P.S.F. in 1989. The original trio comprised of frontman Mike Burger, bassist Beat Oswald and drummer Nick. Oswald exited and P.S.F. pulled in Peter Sarbuck for a demo 'Grotesque Ecstasy'. A name switch to NERGAL also witnessed a change to a Black Metal stance and the recruitment of former DAMNATORY and BERKAHAL bassist Gisela Imhof. The band's debut came with a split 7" single sharing vinyl with previous P.S.F. material.
NERGAL signed to the Colombian label Warmaster for a split album with Poles BUNDESWEHRA in 1993.

Singles/EPs:
Rites Of Beltane / , Wild Rags (1992) (Split 7" single with P.S.F.)

Albums:
NECROSPELL, Warmaster (1993) (Split EP with BUNDESWEHRA)
Necrospell / Rites Of Beltane / Summoning The Watchers (Of The Four Quarters) / Fountain (In Eternal Falls)

NHAAVAH (CZECH REPUBLIC)
Line-Up: Barbarud Hrom (vocals), Vlad Blasphemer (guitar)

NHAAVAH is a side project of MANIAC BUTCHER men Barbarud Hrom and Vlad

Blasphemer. The band's 1999 album was shared with German act KATHARSIS.

Albums:
KINGS OF CZECH BLACK METAL, (1998)
DETERMINATION-DETESTATION-DEVESTATION, Sombre (1999) (Split album with KATHARSIS)

NIDEN DIV. 187 (SWEDEN)
Line-up: Henke Forss (vocals), Leo Pignon (guitar), Jonas Albrektson (bass), Morth (drums)

An unashamed Black Metal trio founded in 1995 as a side project of A CANOUROUS QUINTET guitarist Leo Pignon, DAWN vocalist Henke Forss and THY PRIMORDIAL drummer Morth, NIDEN DIV. 187's first product was the 'Towards Judgement' demo. This tape secured a deal with Necropolis Records, who were keen to re-release the material on CD format.
A further THY PRIMORDIAL member, bassist Jonas Albrektson, was added to record the 'Impergium' album.

Singles/EPs:
Black Water / Reticence / A View In The Mirror Black / Towards Judgement, Necropolis 6665 (1996) ('Towards Judgement' EP)

Albums:
IMPERGIUM, Necropolis NR016 (1997)
Impergium / Genocide / Judgement Dawns / In The Twilight Of War / A View In The Mirror Black / The Execution / Funeral Pyres / Hate / Mass Burial Disorder / The End

NIFELHEIM (SWEDEN)
Line-Up: Hellbutcher Deathvomit (vocals), Morbid Slaughter (guitar), Tyrant Bestial Holocaust (bass), Demon Pounding Devestator (drums)

Teen Satanists NIFELHEIM came together in 1990, issuing the demo 'Unholy Death' in early 1993. Shortly after guitarist Morbid Slaughter departed.
The debut album features guest guitar contributions from DISSECTION's Jon Nodveidt and ex DISSECTION guitarist Jon Zwetsloot.
During 2000 bassist Tyrant and Hellbutcher joined PAGAN RITES for live shows.

Singles/EPs:
Unholy Death / The Devastation, Primitive Art (2000) (7" single)

Albums:
NIFELHEIM, Necropolis NR007 (1995)
The Devastation / Black Curse / Unholy Death / Possessed By Evil / Sodomiser / Satanic Sacrifice / Storm Of Satan's Fire / Witchfuck
DEVIL'S FORCE, Necropolis NR 022 (1997)
Deathstrike From Hell / The Final Slaughter / Desecration Of The Dead / Demonic Evil / Satanic Mess / Soldier Of Satan / Devil's Force / Hellish Blasphemy
SERVANTS OF DARKNESS, Black Sun BS22 (2000)
Evil Blasphemies / Sadistic Blood Massacre / Black Evil / Bestial Avenger / War Of Doom (Armageddon) / Scenarios Of Darkness / Infernal Desolation / Into The Morbid Black / Sacrifice To The Lord Of Darkness

NIGHT CONQUERS DAY (USA)
Line-Up: Mikael Bayusick (vocals / guitar), Justin (guitar), Tim (bass), John (keyboards), Gregg (drums)

NIGHT CONQUERS DAY was the progression of Mikael Bayusick's creative force following the demise in 1995 of BURIED BENEATH. At times the band has operated almost as a solo venture but latterly has enlisted SHADOWLORD members guitarist Justin and drummer Gregg.
Bayusick is not content to put all his energies into NIGHT BCONQUERS DAY and is also known for his other projects SHADOWCASTER, TEARSTAINED and INTO THE SUNLESS MERIDIAN.

Albums:
THE FIRST SNOWFALL, Hammerheart (199-)
Eastern Winds Mount The Virgin Winter (Introitus) / The First Snowfall / What Was And Never Shall Be Again / Banished From My Eyes / Snowmelting Requiem / The Storm Before The Calm / Nightfall's Promise / Footprints In The Snow Where The Wanderer Has Been
REBELLION IS THE ART OF SURVIVAL, Hammerheart (1999)
The Triumphant Night Conquers The Dying Day (Introitus II) / Mirror Gazing / The Perseverance Of Ignorance / Rebellion Is The Art Of Survival / Drawn Together In Magnetic Violet Trances /

272

Dream Sleep Sorcery / The Consequence Of Action

NIGHTFALL (GREECE)
Line-Up: Efthims Karadimas (vocals / bass), Mike Galiatsos (guitar), Chris Adamou (guitar), George Aspiotis (keyboards), Costas Savidas (drums)

NIGHTFALL first came to prominence with their 1991 demo 'Vanity', immediately prompting a deal from Holy Records. Promoting the debut album, 'Parade Into Centuries', NIGHTFALL supported PARADISE LOST in Athens during 1992.
The band would add keyboard player George Aspiotis in early 1993 to increase the depth of their music. In June of that year NIGHTFALL released a limited edition, red vinyl single titled 'Oh Black Queen, You're Mine'. All 1500 copies quickly sold out.
The impact made by their first album enabled NIGHTFALL to line up an extensive European tour during 1994 to promote their new 'Macabre sunsets' album and NIGHTFALL claimed a first by being the only Greek band to date to headline a European tour. Fellow Holy Records acts MISANTHROPE, CELESTIAL SEASON and SADNESS supported.
Having released 'Eons Aura' and 'Athenian Echoes' during 1995 NIGHTFALL would return in 1997 with the provocatively titled 'Lesbian Show'.

Singles/EPs:
Oh Black Queen, You're Mine / As Your God Is Failing Once Again / Enormous (The Anthem Of Death), Holy (1993)

Albums:
PARADE INTO CENTURIES, Holy HOLY01 (1992)
Thoughts / Domestication Of Wildness / Vanity / The Passage / In God They Trust / For My Soul, When The Dark Falls Into... / Immaculate (Enslaved By Need) / Birth / Crying Out The Fear Within / Domestication Of Wildness (Long Version)
MACABRE SUNSETS, Holy HOLY04 (1994)
H POLID C EALW / Precious (All My Love Is Lost) / As Your God Is Failing Once Again / Macabre Sunsets / Bitterness Leads Me To My Saviour Death / Mother Of All Gods, Mother Of Mine / Poetry Of Death / Enormous (The

Anthem Of Death) / As Your God Is Failing Once Again (Original Version)
EONS AURA, Holy HOLY (1995)
Eroding / Ardour I Was / Until The Day God Helps Us All / Thor
ATHENIAN ECHOES, Holy HOLY14 (1995)
Aye Azure / Armada / Ishtar (Celebrate Your Beauty) / The Vineyard / I'm A Daemond / Iris (And The Burning Aureole) / My Red, Red Moon (Emma O) / Monuments Of It's Own Magnificence
LESBIAN SHOW, Holy HOLY 28 CD (1997)
Lesbian Show / Aenon / Dead Woman, Adieu / The Secret Admirer / My Own Troy / The Fleshmaker / Death Star / Cold Bloody Killer / Lashed August Reign
DIVA FUTURA, Holy (199-)
Master, Faster, Sweet Disaster / Sin / The Sheer Misfit / Diva / Licked One's Iced Lips / Picture Me / Some Deaths Take For Ever / Lowve / Ceaseless / My Traitor's Kiss / Pleasure

NIGHTHATRED (RUSSIA)
Line-Up: Eternus (vocals / bass), Besheniy Topor (guitar), Dark Diamond Drums)

Moscow Black Metal act created in 1997 as NIGHT CAME WITH THE WIND by the erstwhile RAROG trio of vocalist / bassist Eternus (also known as 'Arutunian Artem'), guitarist Besheniy Topor and drummer Dark Diamond. A second guitarist, Blackstorm, was added to the ranks later the same year but with his swift departure the band evolved into NIGHTHATRED.
The band's first outing was the 1998 demo tape 'First Fiend Figures'.

Albums:
HELL'S BLOOD, (1999)

NIHILI LOCUS (ITALY)

Turin Black Metal act NIHILI LOCUS issued a demo tape 'Advesperascit' following their 1992 single. NIHILI LOCUS keyboard player Mysticall also works with NECROMASS and TAROT.

Singles/EPs:
Sub Hyersolyma, Obscure Plasma (1992)

Albums:
AD NIHILUM RECIDENT OMNIA, Boundless (1995)

NIRNAETH (POLAND)

Albums:
NAUDH EN NIRNAETH, Abstract Emotions (1999)
Lucifer I / Lucifer II / Lucifer III / Kain I / Kain II / Kain III / Wirez Wlast I / Wirez Wlast Ii / Wirez Wlast III

N.M.E. (USA)
Line up- Brian Llapitan (vocals), Kurt Struebing (guitar), Scot Tinsley (bass), Steve Meier (drums)

Infamous Black Metal band N.M.E. debuted with a 1985 demo 'Machines Of War'. One of the band members was reportedly jailed for killing his own mother.

Albums:
UNHOLY DEATH, LSR (1985)
Of Hell / Thunder Breakspace / Louder Than Hell / Black Knight / Evil Dead / Speed Kilz / Stormwarning / Blood And Souls / Decadent Mayhem / Unspeakable / Brick Wall / Warrior / Lethal Dose / Acid Reign

NOCTE OBDUCTA (GERMANY)
Line-Up: Torsten H. (vocals), Marcel Va. Traumschäuder (guitar / keyboards), Shin (bass), Steffen Emanson (keyboards), Matthias R. (drums)

NOCTE ABDUCTA include AGATHODAIMON's rhythm section of bassist Sathonys and drummer Matthias R.. The latter would also deputize for BLUTTAUFE during 1999.

Albums:
TAVERNE, Grind Syndicate Media (1999)
Hexer (Verflucht) / Prinzessin Der Nachtschatten / Die Ratlen Inm Gernäuer / November / Taverne / In Erinnerung An Herbststürme
LETHE- GOTTVERRECKTE FINSTERNIS, (2000)
Im Bizarren Theater / Eine Teichoskopie / Begraebnisvermaehlung / Lethe Teil I / Konig Der Finsternis- Phiala Vini Blasphemiae / Lethe- Teil II / Solange Euer Fleisch Noch Warm Ist Der Erste Frost / N.D.

NOCTES (SWEDEN)
Line-Up: Jöhan Lonn (vocals), Holger Thorsin (guitar), Pasi Lundegard (guitar), Asa Rosenberg (bass), Carl Leijon (keyboards), Hugo Thorsin (drums)

NOCTES previously operated under the name of CONCEALED. A continuing series of line up changes afflicted CONCEALED to such a degree that band opted for a name change to NOCTES. The band's debut album was recorded at the renowned Sunlight studios in late 1996. Following recording of 'Pandemonic Requiem' frontman Jöhan Lonn relinquished bass duties to new member Asa Rosenberg.

Albums:
PANDEMONIC REQUIEM, No Fashion NFR025 (1998)
Twilight Elysium / Reverie / Attila / Purgatory Temptations / Hokmah Nisthara / Butterfly / In Silence / Winterdawn / Lamia / Orphean Horizons / Outra
VEXILLA REGIS PRODEURT INFERNI, (199-)
Mirrorland / Frozen To Sleep / Demonica / A Demon From Within / Vexilla Regis Prodeurt Inferni / The Lost Garden / Darkside Whispers / The Dream Dominion / Persephone / Carnifax / De Profundis Clamavi

NOCTI VAGUS (GERMANY)

NOCTI VAGUS was previously known as NORDWIND under which title a brace of demos was issued.

Albums:
VENTURE IN SOMBRE PASSION, Solistitium SOL028 (1997)
In The Deepest Depths Grows The Greatest Flower Of Tomorrow / Astral Revealers Of The Hidden Secrets / Venture In Sombre Passion / Rising Of A Nonexistence / To Be Lost In Space And Time / Seen Through Black Eyes / Face Reality / Waves Of Undimensional Seas

NOCTUARY (USA)

Born out of the early 90's extreme Metal band SUMMONED. NOCTUARY's 2000 album 'When Fires Breed Blood' included session lead guitar from EVIL DEAD and DEATH veteran Albert Gonzales, vocals from James Reyes and drums from Rob Alaniz. The mini album release on Largactyl Records is a CD pressing of NOCTUARY's 1996 demo 'Where All Agony Prevails'.
Former NOCTUARY man Daren Winn would join RAVENS OVER GOMORRAH.

Albums:
FOR SALVATION..., Lost Disciple
LDR004 (1999)
Funeral Ceremony / For Salvation… /
Forever Shrouded Within This World /
Sorrow In Wilder Darkness / Eternal
Nightmare / The Once Forgotten Past /
Lost In Illusions / Consumed By Fear /
Black Bleeding Soul / Cast Into The
Brooding Shadow / Journey To The Lost
Kingdom
WHERE ALL AGONY PREVAILS,
Largactyl LR001 (2000)
Funeral Ceremony / Where All Agony
Prevails / Black Angels Return / Eternal
Nightmare / His Majesty Of The
Shadows / Nocturnal Sanctuary
WHEN FIRES BREED BLOOD, Lost
Disciple LDR010 (2000)
Chapter I- "The Fires Burning Cold":
Clouds Donning The Black Sky, … And
Hate Embraced The Night / Chapter II-
"A Call To Arms": Legions March Into
Unearthly Realms / Chapter III- "The
Battles": Vengeance Before Valour, A
Tears Descent From Heaven / Chapter
IV- "A Victory Celebration": At journeys
End / Chapter V- "The Rebirth"

NOCTURNAL BREED (NORWAY)
Line-Up: Ben Hellion (guitar), Archon
(guitar), Andy Michaels (drums)

Although Scandinavia threw up a
confusion of side project acts in the late
90s put together by various Black Metal
musicians made good, NOCTURNAL
BREED boast more pedigree than most.
A distinctly old style Death Metal
offering performed by members of
DIMMU BORGIR, LORD KAOS,
SATYRICON, COVENANT and
GEHENNA. NOCTURNAL BREED
debuted in 1998 with the 'Aggressor'
album.
NOCTURNAL BREED had in fact been
operating much earlier than this with a
pre DIMMU BORGIR founding member
Erkjetter Silenoz on guitar going under
the stage name of Ed Dominator.
Guitarist Archon also has credits with
MALEFICUM and his own project
ARCHON.

Albums:
AGGRESSOR, Hammerheart (1998)
Rape The Angels / Frantic Aggressor /
Maggot Master / Nocturnal Breed /
Death- evil dead / Metal Storm Rebels /
Dead Dominions / Alcoholic Rites /
Revelation 666 / Blaster / Locomotive

Death
TRIUMPH OF THE BLASPHEMER,
(199-)
Triumph Of The Blasphemer /
Screaming For A Leather Bitch / I'm
Alive / Frantic Aggressor / Evil Dead
NO RETREAT- NO SURRENDER, (199-)
The Artillery Command / Thrash The
redeemer / Warhorse / Killernecro / No
Retreat- No Surrender / Beyond Control
/ Sodomite / Fists Of Fury / Under The
Blade / Roadkill Maze / Possessed /
Armageddon Nights / Insane Tyrant

NOCTURNAL WINDS (FINLAND)
Line-Up: Jani Loikas (vocals / bass), Juha
Prnnanen (guitar), Miika Luolajan-
Mikkola (guitar), Ville Matilainen (drums)

Albums:
EVERLASTING FALL, Aftermath Music
(1999)
Maid From The Abyss / Touch Me / Frost
Divine / Son Of The Winterstorm /
Warrior Of Light / My Angel / Spiritdance

NOCTURNAL WORSHIPPER
(BRAZIL)
Line-Up: Thuringwthal (vocals), Katarus
(guitar), Amazarak (guitar), Hofgodhar
(bass), Radagast (drums)

Brazilian Black Metal act NOCTURNAL
WORSHIPPER debuted with a demo
entitled 'The Lords Of Occultism'. The
band, initially a trio of vocalist / guitarist
Wizard, bassist Hofgodhar and drummer
Adramelch, would undergo a dramatic
transformation leading up to the debut
album 'Return Of The Southern Tyrants'
with only Hofgodhar surviving.

Singles/EPs:
Into The Forests Of The Past /
Ceremonial Circle / Fury Of Demonic
Harvest, Heavy Metal Rock (1995)
('Ceremonial Circle' EP)

Albums:
**RETURN OF THE SOUTHERN
TYRANTS**, Demise DO22 (2001)
Ave Satani / Old Mist Of Funeral Empire
/ Prince Of Death / A Tomb In The
Satanist Hill / Fury Of Demonic Harvest /
Ancient Flames Of Darkness / The Altar

NOKTURNAL MORTEM (UKRAINE)
Line- Knjaz Varggoth (vocals / guitar),
Sataroth (keyboards), Saturious
(keyboards), Xaarquarth (bass),
Munruthel (drums)

NOKTURNAL MORTEM evolved from the 1991 vintage Black Death Metal act SUPPURATION. This early act featured frontman Knjaz Varggoth, bassist Xaarquarth and drummer Munruthel. Following the issue of SUPPURATION's 1992 album 'Ecclesiastical Blasphemy' the band invited new members Sataroth and guitarist Wortherax prior to folding.

A new act entitled CRYSTALINE DARKNESS sprang up which saw Varggoth and Munruthel in alliance with guitarist Karpath. This band in turn evolved into NOCTURNAL MORTUM in 1994 by unifying with Wortherax once again and with the adoption of a raw pure Black Metal direction added the 'K' to the title to become NOKTURNAL MORTUM.

A debut 'Lunar Poetry' was released after which Wortherax left and former colleague Karpath filled the gap as Saturious was added to provide further keyboard depth.

Both Saturious and Karpath also contributed to the debut album 'Vozradujsja, Zemlja!' from Slavonic war metal band ANTHROPOLATRI.

Albums:
LUNAR POETRY, Morbid Noizz (1997)
Tears Of Paganism / Lunar Poetry / Perun's Celestial Silver / Carpathian Mysteriuous / … And Winter Becomes / Ancient Nation / The Grief Of Orianna / Sorrow Of The Moon / Autodafe-Barbarian Dreams
GOAT HORNS, The End TE003 (1997)
Black Moon Overture / Kuyaviya / Goat Horns / Unholy Orathania / Veles; Scrolls / Kolyada / Eternal Circle
TO THE GATES OF BLASPHEMOUS FIRE, The End TE6661 (199-)
Bestial Summoning / To The Gates Of Blasphemous Fire / On The Moonlight Path / The Hands Of Chaos / Under The Banner Of The Horned Kniaz / The 13th Asbath Celebration / Cheremosh / The Forgotten Ages Of Victories
NECHRIST, Last Episode CD 5 7066 20 561 (2000)
The Funeral Wind Born In Oriana / Night Before The Fight / Black Raven / The Call Of Aryan Spirit / The Child Of Swamps And Full Moon / Death Damnation / In The Fire Of The Wooden Churches / Jesus Blood / Nechrist- The Dance Of Swords / Peruh's Celestial Silver

NON SERVIAM (SWEDEN)
Line-Up: Amon (vocals), Janos (guitar), Anders Nyander (guitar), Tyr (bass),

Magnus Emilsson (drums)

Named after a collection of Latin poems NON SERVIAM, fronted by Amon (real name Rikard Nilsson), came to the fore with their first demo 'Between Light And Darkness'. Further tapes included 1997's 'The Witches Sabbath' and its follow up 'The Witches Sabbath: The Second Vision' securing a deal with Invasion Records.

Guitarist 'Janos' is in reality Daniel Andersson, also a member of HELLSPELL. Bass player 'Tyr' is in fact Chrille Andersson who also has credits with MORTUM and HELLSPELL.

Albums:
BETWEEN LIGHT AND DARKNESS, Invasion IR030 (1997)
Queen Of Beauty / Satan's Spree / Melody Of Grief / Face Behind The Mirror Wall / The Enchanting Dance Of Mischief / Obscurity Unveiled / Temptation Of Blood / Sins And The Embracing Of Shades / Infernal Spirit / Sense Of Withering / Between Light And Darkness / The Witches Sabbath / Throne Of Mendes
NECROTICAL, (199-)
The Heretic / Possessed / Hatred Unleashed / Arch Angel / Which Eternal Lie / From Chaos To Pain / Haunted Domains / Inherited Blood / Incarnation (Of Evil) / Bringers Of Total Death / Sex, Religion, Suicide

NORTH (POLAND)

Black Metal group NORTH released a string of demo recordings before their debut 1995 album 'Thorns On The Black Rose'. The band's first attempt was the 1993 demo 'As My Kingdom Rises'.

The 1996 'Jeseinne Szepty' album was a split album combined with SACRILGIUM.

Albums:
THORNS ON THE BLACK ROSE, Astral Wings (1995)
The Heretic Kingdom / As Heretics Return / Purity Of The Tyrants / December Thought / Ages Of The Reign / Thorns Of The Black Rose / In The Circle Of Kings
JESEINNE SZEPTY, Black Arts (1996) (Split album with SACRILIGIUM)

NORTHLAND (POLAND)

Black Metal band NORTHLAND released

276

two demos in 1994's 'The Battle Into The Deep Dark Forest' and 'Smiere To Nienwisc' the following year. The first album 'Czernoboh' translates as 'Black God'.

Albums:
CZERNOBOH, Astral Wings (1996)

NOTRE DAME (FRANCE)
Line-Up: Vampirella (vocals), Jean Pierre De Sade (guitar), Mannequin De Sade (bass), Snowy Shaw (drums)

A 'Horror' Metal band assembled by drummer Snowy Shaw, better known for his work with MERCYFUL FATE and KING DIAMOND. Shaw's first side project outside of the KING DIAMOND confines was ILLWILL. However, this band would quickly lead to the formation of NOTRE DAME made up of Shaw's one time girlfriend and dancer Vampirella together with the brothers Mannequin and Jean Pierre De Sade from Death Metal band BLOODGROUP.
Ironically NOTRE DAME would debut with a track 'Into The Coven' included on a MERCYFUL FATE tribute album. This recording featured MERCYFUL FATE guitarist Michael Denner as guest. The band's debut proper came with the 'Coming To A Theatre Near You' EP on Head Not Found Records. The impact made by this release led in turn to a deal with the French Osmose Productions concern.
1999 saw a split single 'Abbatoir, Abbatoir Du Noir' shared with FORGOTTEN SILENCE. A much sought after rarity this release was limited to 555 copies.

Singles/EPs:
The Bell Of Notre Dame / Vlad The Impaler / A Misconception Of The French Kiss / Daughter Of Darkness / Sisterhood, Head Not Found HNF060 (1997) ('Coming Soon To A Theatre Near You' EP)
Abbatoir, Abbatoir Du Noir, (1999) (Split single with FORGOTTEN SILENCE)
La Croix Rouge / Abbatoir, Abbatoir Du Noir (Live), Osmose Productions OP CDS 096 (2000)

Albums:
NIGHTMARE BEFORE CHRISTMAS, Osmose Productions OPCD 091 (1998)
When You Wish Upon A Star… / Frost / Le Nostradamus De Notre Epoqué / A Scrooge Tale / Black Birthday (Hip Hip Hooray) / X-Masquerade / 1999 / Doom
LE THEATRE DU VAMPIRE, Osmose Productions OPCD 086 (1999)
Le Theatre Du Vampire / Bouffoon Bloody Bouffoon / Vlad The Impaler / I Bring Nosferatu You / A Sleighride Through Transylvanian Winterland / Dusk / Sabbat / Faust- The Ghostwriter / Black Birthday (Hip Hip Hooray) / Sisterhood / Spiderella's XXX

NOX INTEMPESTA (GERMANY)
Line-Up: Tyrann (vocals), Mordra Coldstone (guitar), Monastir (bass), Holocaust (bass)

Berlin Black Metal. NOX INTEMPESTA members Tyrann and Mordra Coldstone are also members of ARATHORN. Skoell of ARATHORN also sessions for the band on studio work.
NOX INTEMPSTA debuted with the demos 'A Grim Red Kiss In Transylvania' and 'Majestic Scarlet Moon'. Initially the band incorporated keyboards into their sound but dropped the ivories in an attempt to pursue a rawer form of Black Metal. The band has scored impressive support slots to MAYHEM in 1998

Albums:
DIE LIEDER VON TOD UND EWIGKEIT, Folter (1997)
Untrodden Shall Be The Path To The Marble Planet / Schreie Einer Wölfin / A Sylph Lost In A Sullen Slumber / Luna Uestthetica
DE VERMIS MYSTERIIS, Folter (1998)
DAMNANUS DOMINUM, Folter (1998)
Die Erhabere Dreifaltigkeit Des Leidens / Oh Herrlichkeit, Du Glanz Des Totenthrones / In Clairvoyant Flesh / Goldstone Sacrificial… / Damnanus Dominum / Krone Meiner Todessalburg / De Bermis Mysteriis / Abomination Jugglers / Impressionen Eines Sterberden / Speculum Spagyria Satana

NOX MORTIS (GERMANY)

Founded in 1993 NOX MORTIS released the 'Epitaph' and 'Wald Der Angst' demos before recording their 1996 debut album. A mixture of 'Dark Wave' and Metal, Prophecy Records were the label who showed the greatest interest in snapping the group - whose keyboard player has been a church organist for eight years - up for their album deal.

Albums:
IM SCHATTEN DES HASSES, Prophecy Productions PRO 002 (1996)
Intro / Inm Schatten Des Hasses / Lost In Selfhate / Horizon Of Shadows / Castle Of Eternity / Choirs In Trance / Outro
7 LIES, Prophecy Productions (1999)
I'm Floating / Thoughts / In The Grey Of The Clouds / 3.31 PM / Parabel Chiflrierter Instrumelisiering / Why I Need The Light / From Sorrow To Sun / Totentanz Im Blut / Wired Notes / Have You Ever Seen / Free Like Never Before

NUNSLAUGHTER (Pittsburgh, USA)
Line-Up: Don Of The Dead (vocals / bass), Megiddo (guitar), Insidious (bass), Jim Sadist (drums)

A notorious name in Death and Black Metal circles. NUNSLAUGHTER, not noted for their subtlety, date back to the late 80's with an initial incarnation of bassist Don Of The Dead, guitarist Jer The Butcher, vocalist Gregoroth and drummer Behemoth Bill. This line up cut the opening 'Ritual Of Darkness' cassette. Both Butcher and Behemoth would exit signalling a prelude to a turbulent career for the band as membership ebbed and flowed with each successive release. NUNSLAUGHTER's second demo 'The Rotting Christ' saw the inclusion of guitarist Rick Rancid and drummer John Sicko.
1991 saw the departure of both Sicko and Gregoroth and the emergence of new drummer Vlad The Impaler as Don Of The Dead took over lead vocal duties for the provocative demo 'Impale The Soul Of Christ On The Inverted Cross Of Death'.
In 1993 the inaugural demo 'Ritual Of Darkness' was bootlegged in Brazil on a 7" single. Meantime NUNSLAUGHTER laid down a fourth demo 'Guts Of Christ' with predictably another skinsman Mark Perversion.
By 1995 NUNSLAUGHTER reconvened the original founding trio of Don, Gregoroth and Butcher. Along with drummer Jim Sadist another session 'Face Of Evil' was issued. The line up did not stay the course though and soon new faces included bass player Chris 213 and guitarist Blood for a split 7" single with BLOODSTICK in 1997. This would herald a NUNSLAUGHTER tradition as further shared singles quickly surfaced shared with CRUCIFER, DECAPITATOR and female act DERKETA.
Later members include guitarist Megiddo

and bassist Insidious.

Singles/EPs:
Burn In Hell / Hell's Unholy Fire / Death By The Dead / Killed By The Cross / I Am Deaths, (1990) ('Killed By The Cross' 7" single)
Inri / Power Of Darkness / Sacrifice, (1997) (Split 7" single with BLOODSTICK)
Emperor In Hell / Demon's Gate / Bring Me The Head Of God, (1998) (Split 7" single with DECAPITATOR)
If The Dead Could Speak / Devil Meat / Black Beast, (1998) (Split 7" single with CRUCIFER)
Church Bizarre / Midnight Mass / It Is I / Poisoned Priest, (1998) ('Blood Devil' 7" single)
Black Horn Of The Ram / The Devil / murder By The Stake, Evil dreams (1999) (split 7" single with DERKETA)

Albums:
HELL'S UNHOLY FIRE, Revenge Productions (2000)
Burn In Hell / Killed By The Cross / Death By The Dead / Perversion Of Gore / The Dead Plague / Cataclysm / Burning Away / Nun Slaughter / Blasphemy / Seas Of Blood / Altar Of The Dead / Satanic / Blood For Blood / Impale The Soul Of Christ On The Inverted Cross Of Death / I Am Death / Hells Unholy Fire

OATHEAN (SOUTH KOREA)

OATHEAN were previously titled ODIN upon their formation in 1993.

Albums:
THE EYES OF TREMENDOUS SORROW, (1998)
Intro / The Last Elegy For My Sad Soul / Transparent Blue Light- So Too Much Tearful... / In Fear With Shiver / Frigid Space / The Eyes Of Tremendous Sorrow / The Rotten Egg Smell On My Belly / Punishment Of Being Alone- It's Cruel Strength Breaks Me Away

OBERON (SWEDEN)
Line-Up: Oberon, Randi Wedvich (vocals), Roger Egseth (drums)

Although essentially a solo project of Oberon, additional musicians on the album include vocalist Randi Wedvich and drummer Roger Egseth. OBERON first came to attention with the demo 'Through Time And Space'. A second tape 'Lily White' followed in 1995.

Albums:
OBERON, Prophecy Productions PRO 004 (1997)
Stay / The Nightingale / Out From A Deep Green Emerald Sea / L.I.T.L.O.T.W. / Lily White

OBSCURATION (FRANCE)

Albums:
THE FIFTH SEASON, Obscuration (1997)

OBSCURITY (SWEDEN)
Line-Up: Daniel Vala (vocals / bas), Jorgen Linde (guitar), Jan Johansson (guitar)

OBSCURITY were one of the forerunners of the Swedish Black Metal scene issuing two highly influential demos in 1985's 'Ovation Of Death' and the following year's 'Damnation's Pride'. During the 90's this material would be re-released on vinyl and CD format.
Frontman Daniel Vala is now a much in demand artist designing many Rock album covers.

Singles/EPs:
Damnations Pride, To The Death (1997) (7" single)

Albums:
DAMNATION'S PRIDE, Scarlet (1997)
Graves Of rebirth / Damnation's Pride / Mortal Remains / Demented / In The Watches Of The Night / Fallen Arches / Across The Holocaust / Excursion To Eternity / Spiritual Entity / Celestial Conquest / The Condemnation / Unblessed Domain

OBSECRATION (GREECE)
Line-Up: Kostas Dead (vocals), Manolis (guitar), John (guitar), Spiros Ruthren (bass), Alexandros (drums)

Formed in 1991 rooted in the Death Metal acts PARAKMI, MORBID ILLUSION and CURSE. The duo of vocalist Kostas Dead and drummer Jim first forged an alliance in 1989 with the band PARAKMI. This unit would evolve into MORBID ILLUSION with the inclusion of INSANITY bassist Nectarios and guitarist John from NECROMANCY.
In 1990 another name change occurred this time to CURSE as new faces bassist Billy and guitarist Apostolis were welcomed. In 1991 the final name switch came as CURSE became OBSECRATION with Billy switching instruments to bass as Nectarios returned to take over the guitarist's role for the debut demo 'Petrified Remains'. However, the group lost Nectarios in July as he departed to fulfill his national service obligations. In September OBSECRATION plugged the gap by enlisting ex AVATAR members guitarist Nick and bassist Sotiris for their first gig. Predictably the line up fractured once again with Billy joining EPIDEMIC and both Nick and Sotiris leaving.
1992 witnessed further changes with the return of Billy and Sotiris as well as new guitarist John for the second demo session 'The Morning Of The Ghoul'. Further live work ensued utilizing the services of erstwhile BLOOD COVERED drummer Angelos to promote the band's first commercial release the 'Oblivious' EP on Molon Lave Records. By March the bass position was temporarily in the care of Spiros from SEPTIC FLESH prior to Leftiris assuming the role.
OBSECRATION cut their full length debut album 'The Inheritors Of Pain', produced by Magus Wampyr Daoloth of

NECROMANTIA, for the Dutch Hammerheart label with unsurprisingly a revised line up comprising of Kostas Dead, guitarists Spiros N. and Billy, bassist Spiros Ruthren and drummer Paul OBSECRATION's line up ebbed and flowed thereafter with John rejoining replacing Spiros N. before he and brother Paul bailed out. By 2000 former LEPROSY members guitarist Manolis and drummer Alexandros were involved. Kostas would become a founder member of TERRA TENEBRAE but would depart prior to recording of their 'Subconscious' album.

Singles/EPs:
Oblivious, Molon Lave (1993)

Albums:
THE INHERITORS OF PAIN, Hammerheart (1995)
The Inheritors Of Pain Part I / Horror In The Gothic Genie's Game / For The King Of This World / … The Usurper From Darkness / Suffering Under The Unnamable Shade / The Serenity Of The Crystal Sentiments / Offsprings Of The Black Dimensions / The Inheritors Of Pain Part II
OCEANUM OBLIVIONE, Invasion INV015 (2000)

OBSIDIAN GATE (GERMANY)

Although OBSIDIAN GATE prefer to remain anonymous members Marco and Marcus guested on the debut AD INFERNA album.

Albums:
THE NIGHT SPECTRAL VOYAGE, Skaldic Art Productions (1999)
As The Void Opens (Introduction Opus) / When Death Unchains The Spectre / The Obsidian Eternity And Anguish / For The Infinite Forge Of Time / The Bethorian Shrine / Invoke The Dragon Constellation

OBTAINED ENSLAVEMENT
(NORWAY)
Line-Up: Pest (vocals / bass), Døden (guitar), Heks (guitar), Torquemada (drums)

A Black Metal band with Grindcore influences founded during 1989. OBTAINED ENSLAVEMENT started life as a trio of vocalist Pest (Thomas Kronenes), guitarist Døden (Ove Saebo)

and drummer Torquemada. Three years later second guitarist Heks (Heine Salbu) was added for the demo 'Out Of The Crypts'.
OBTAINED ENSLAVEMENT issued their debut 1994 album 'Centuries Of Sorrow' on Likstøy Music. The record was picked up by the Effigy label the following year for wider distribution. During the interim between albums Pest would session for the notorious Black Metal institution GORGOROTH appearing on the 1996 album 'Antichrist True Norwegian Black Metal'.
Sophomore effort 'Witchcraft' saw the inclusion of bassist Tortur although his position was short-lived. T. Reaper of MALIGNENT ETERNAL and GORGOROTH took the place for the band's Napalm Records debut 'Soulblight'. Keyboards were handled by Morrigan of AETURNUS.

Albums
CENTURIES OF SORROW, Effigy EFFI 002 (1995)
Desecration Of My Soul / As I Slowly Fade / Dark Holiness / Symbolic / Unblessed / Haze Of Knowledge / Centuries Of Sorrow / Pure... Sorrow
WITCHCRAFT, Wounded Love WLR 013 (1997)
Mono: Prelude Funebre / Di: Velts Of Wintersorrow / Tri: From Times In Kingdoms / Tetra: Witchcraft / Penta: Warlock / Hexa: Torned Winds From A Past Star / Hepta: Carnal Lust / Octa: The Seven Witches / Nona: O'Noccurne
SOULBLIGHT, Napalm (1998)
A Black Odyssey / The Dark Night Of The Souls / Soulblight / Nightbreed / Voice From A Starless Domain / The Goddess' Lake / Charge
THE SHEPHERD AND THE HOUNDS OF HELL, Napalm (2000)
Scrolls Of The Shadowland / Ride The Whore / Lucifer's Lament / Millenium Beast (Awaiting The Feast) / Stepping Over Angels / The Shepherd And The Hounds Of Hell / Utopia Obtained

OCCULT (HOLLAND)
Line-Up: Rachel Heyzer (vocals), Sephiroth (vocals), Leon Oennings (guitar), Richard Ebish (guitar), Sjors Tuithof (bass), Erik Fleuren (drums)

A leading Black Metal act from the Netherlands. Vocalist Sephiroth is ex BESTIAL SUMMONING. He would later drop the corpsepaint and revert to his real

name of Maurice Swinkle.
OCCULT vocalist Rachel Heyzer was previously a member of Death Metal band PATHOLOGY.

Albums:
PREPARE TO MEET THY DOOM, Foundation 2000 FDN 2010-2 (1994)
Leader In The War / The Black Are Rising / After Triumph / Prepare To Meet Thy Doom / And Darkness Shall Begin / Almighty Horde / Whispering Tear / The Nazarene Whore / Elements In Black / Quest For The Spirit
THE ENEMY WITHIN, Foundation 2000 FDN 2014-2 (1996)
Souls / Inquisition Of The Holy / Crossing The Boundaries (Of Life And Death) / Selfbetrayed / Twisted Words (My Darkest Emotions) / Through Dark And Light I Dwell / One Way Out / Passive Relations / Eyes Of Blood / Until The Battle / Delusion
OF FLESH AND BLOOD, Massacre (1999)
Intro / Parasite / Dreamsweeper / Stolen / Killing Breed / Ritual Of Demise / Downfall Of Deity / Oath In War / Doomsday Destroyer / Dead Man Walking / Vow Of Retaliation / Dormant Till Dusk / Creatures Of The Night

OCTINIMOS (SWEDEN)

Fredrik Söderlund of OCTINIMOS is also an active musician in PUISSANCE, PARNASSUS and ALGAION.
The OCTINOMOS project first came to the fore with the 1994 demo 'As Long As Evil Stars…'.

Albums:
ON THE DEMIURGE, Fullmoon IFR 003(1995)
The Ground Shall Sorrow Be / Slaves / Awaiting The Ungod / Into The Shadows / Beyond Salvation / As All Is Lost / On The Demiurge / Moribound World / Star Of The Apocalypse / Les Nuit Fauvres
WELCOME TO MY PLANET, Hammerheart (2000)
Nuclear Blitz / Divine Terror / Atomic Night / World Pulverization / Totalitarian Might / Plutonium Love / Genocide Mass

OCTOBER TIDE (SWEDEN)
Line-Up: Jonas Renske (vocals / drums), Fredrik Norrman (guitar / bass)

OCTOBER TIDE are the outfit created by KATATONIA's vocalist Jonas Renske,

also known under his stage name of 'Lord Seth'.
Renske involved himself in the BLOOD BATH Black Metal supergroup in 2000 alongside his KATATONIA band mate guitarist Blackheim, OPETH's Mikael Akerfeldt and EDGE OF SANITY's Dan Swanö.
OCTOBER TIDE's 1999 album 'Grey Dawn' found Renske in collaboration with Morten of A CANOUROUS QUINTET.

Albums:
RAIN WITHOUT END, Vic VIC003 (1997)
12 Days Of Rain / Ephemeral / All Painted Cold / Sightless / Losing Tomorrow / Blue Gallery / Infinite Submission
GREY DAWN, Avantgarde (1999)
Grey Dawn / October Insight / Sweetness Dies / Heart Of The Dead / Floating / Lost In The Dark- And The Gone / Into Deep Sleep / Dear Sun

ODES OF ECSTASY (GREECE)
Line-Up: Dimitrus Bikus (vocals / guitar), Nikos Baltas (guitar), Christina Miniati (vocals), Joseph Nikou (bass)

ODES OF ECSTASY debuted with a 1995 demo session 'Theogony'. At this formative stage the band comprised of frontman Dimitris Bikus, guitarist Dimitris Panyiotidis and bassist Joseph Nikou.
A second cassette in 1996 'Aetheastic Emotions', which included a version of BLACK SABBATH's 'Paranoid', saw female vocals from Christina Miniati. Panyiotidis was supplanted by Nikos Baltas for the inaugural album 'Embossed Dream In Four Acts'.

Albums:
EMBOSSED DREAM IN FOUR ACTS, The End TE005 (1999)
Autumn's Grief (Prologos) / The Total Abscence Of Light (Act I) / Faithless (Act II) / War Symphony (Act III) / Garden Of Temptation (Act IV) / Vampire Hunters (Epilogos)

ODIUM (NORWAY)
Line-Up: Sectdamon (vocals / guitar), Charon Martyras (guitar), Demariel (bass), Bastadon (keyboards), Anders Eek (drums)

ODIUM drummer Anders Eek also has impressive credits with FUNERAL, MYRSKOG and THE FLESH. Frontman Sectdamon (Odd Tony) has credits as drummer for MYRSKOG.

Albums:
THE SAD REALM OF THE STARS,
(199-)
Winterpath / Towards The Forest
Horizon / Palace Of Forgotten Dreams /
The eternal Nightfall / The Sad Realm Of
The Stars / Northern Flames / Through
The Sorrowfilled Forest / The Brightness
Of The Weeping Kingdom / Riding The
Starwinds
HÅRT MOT HÅRT, (199-)
Hårt Mot Hårt / Res Dig Upp / Då Ska
Packet Kastras Ut / Dom Kan Aldrig
Stoppa Oss / Sjrka Begår / Kravaller /
Brinn Avskum / Den Sista Slakten /
Knarkarjävtar / Från Musik Till Handling /
Härjat Land / Ondskars Techen / Martyr /
Vår Ära Hefer Trohet

ODIUM (RUSSIA)

A solitary Black Ambient project of
Crudelis.

Albums:
CLOTTED NONSENSE, Coronach
(1999)
Dismal Mood / The Dream / Hidden
Meaning / Underwater / Being's Futility /
A Posteriori / Cosmic Bursts / Outro
MY PERFECT FUNERAL, Coronach
(2000)
Coronach / Brooding / Diabolical Rave /
Delirium / As Salat / Insomnia Medicine /
My Perfect Funeral

OLD FOREST (UK)
Line-Up: Kobold (vocals / keyboards),
Beleth (guitar / bass), Grond (drums)

Albums:
INTO THE OLD FOREST, Mordgrimm
GRIMM 8 CD (1999)
Ground (Hammer Of The Underworld) /
Death In The Cemetery / To Haunt The
Old Forest / Hymn Of The Deep /
Glistening / Where Trees Are Weathered
/ Shadow Whispers / Become The Gods
Of War

OLD FUNERAL (NORWAY)

Quite an illustrious name in the annals of
Black Metal. The early 90's Death Metal
act OLD FUNERAL boasting latter day
members of premier acts including Ali
Gator, Abbath Doom Occulta of
IMMORTAL, Demonaz Doom Occulta
(Harald Naevdal) of IMMORTAL, John
Tonsberg of HADES ALMIGHTY and
even Varg Vikernes later of BURZUM

infamy. OLD FUNERAL was in fact a side
project of Vikernes' main act at the time
SATANEL.
Ali Gator, (real name Tore Brathseth)
known for his endeavours with the
underground 'Slayer' magazine much
later resumed musical activity with the
spoof act DESEKRATOR.
The old tapes were dusted down for
release by the Dutch Hammerheart
concern. Vikernes himself as apparently
dismissed OLD FUNERAL as 'Boring"!

Albums:
THE OLDER ONES, Hammerheart
(1999)
Abduction Of Limbs / Annoying
Individual / Skin And Bone / Haunted /
Incantation / Devoured Carcass / Alone
Walking / Lykternenn / Into Hades / My
Tyrant Grace / Devoured Carcass (Live)

OLD MAN'S CHILD (NORWAY)
Line-Up: Grusom (vocals / guitar /
keyboards), Jardar (guitar), Brynjard
Tristan (bass), Tjodalv (drums)

Norwegian quartet OLD MAN'S CHILD
were formed in 1993 by frontman Grusom
(real name Tom Rune Andersen) and
drummer Åkesson Tjodalv, the latter also
doubling up as skinsman for DIMMU
BORGIR. This pairing would operate as
REQUIEM from their 1989 inception until
1994 when the name switch to OLD
MAN'S CHILD occurred.
The group's debut album featured guest
appearances from members of DIMMU
BORGIR and MINAS TIRITH. Material
recorded before the album and had
consequently not made the cut were later
released as 'In The Shades Of Life'
during 1996. The same year Tjoldav
decamped to join DIMMU BORGIR as a
permanent member.
Following the appearance of the 'odds n'
sods' collection the group would part
company with bassist Tristan and replace
him with Gonde.
The band continued to evolve with
Grusom confusingly opting to change his
name to Galder as OLD MAN'S CHILD
undertook a European tour alongside
SACRAMENTUM and ROTTING
CHRIST. These dates witnessed the
departure of Gonde and Tony in favour of
drummer Sarke and bassist Blodstrup,
active members of TULUS.
OLD MAN'S CHILD's 1998 album 'Ill
Natured Spiritual Invasion' had the
esteemed DEATH and DARK ANGEL

282

drummer Gene Hoglan sessioning. Galder recorded all other instrumentation. The 'Satanic Assault' tour of January 1999 saw the employment of CROWNFALL and SENSA ANIMA guitarist Cyrus (real name Terje Andersen).

The 'Revelation 666' album was recorded with a predictably all new line up comprising of Glader, guitarist Jarder, former VANAHEIM bassist Memnock and drummers Tjodalv and Grimar. Touring in May found the band on the road on a multi band package alongside GORGOROTH, NIGHT IN GALES, KRISIUM and SOUL REAPER. Drums were handled by Trym of EMPEROR whilst keyboards were supplied by ALSVARTR's Vivandre.

Galder departed in August 2000 to join DIMMU BORGIR.

Memnock and Cyrus joined Tjovald's new act SUSPIRIA in 2000. Cryus also undertook live work with SATYRICON for their 'Rebel Extravaganza' tour.

Albums:
BORN OF THE FLICKERING, Hot Shagrath 003 (1995)
Demons Of The Thorncastle / Swallowed By Buried One / Born Of The Flickering / King Of The Dark Ages / On Through The Desert Storm / Christian Death / Funeral, Swords And Souls / The Last Chapter / ...Leads To Utopia / The Old Man's Dream
IN THE SHADES OF LIFE, Hot Shagrath 005 (1996)
St. Aiden's Fall / Seeds Of The Ancient Gods / Manet Sorgfull Iggjenom Skogen / The Old Man's Child / Og Jeg Iattok Dodsrikets Inntog
THE PAGAN PROSPERITY, Century Media 77183-2 (1997)
The Millenium King / Behind The Mask / Soul Possessed / My Demonic Figures / Doommaker / My Kingdom Will Come / Return Of The Night / Creatures / What Malice Embrace
ILL NATURED SPIRITUAL INVASION, Century Media 77219-2 (1998)
Towards Eternity / The Dream Ghost / Demoniacal Possession / Fall Of Man / Captives Of Humanity / My Evil Revelations / The Servant
REVELATION 666, Century Media 77282-2 (2000)
Phantoms Of Mortem Tales / Nominus Nocturna / In Black Endless Void / Unholy Vivid Innocence / Passage To Pandemonium / Obscure Divine

Manifestation / World Expiration / Into Silence Embrace

OLEMUS (AUSTRIA)
Line-Up: Robert Bogner (vocals / guitar), Simon Öller (guitar), Gernot Fuchs (bass), Markus Reischl (keyboards), Roland Kössler (drums)

Originally created in September 1993 under the name of GODLESS. By 1995 the teenage act, losing guitarist Zillner Andreas, had evolved into OLEMUS for a debut demo 'Learning To Die' and shows supporting CRADLE OF FILTH.
The vacant guitarists position was filled by Ganser Jürgen as OLEMUS also pulled in keyboard player Markus Reischl for a second tape entitled 'Blind'. Shortly after recording Jürgen decamped.
With the release of the first CD 'Bitter Tears' vocalist Robert Bogner added guitar to his duties as Gernot Fuchs was enlisted on bass. However, the line up problems continued to beset OLEMUS when both Fuchs and Reischl exited. The band soldiered on with fresh faces guitarist Eugen Baumann and bassist Markus Koblbauer.
The 1998 release 'Psycho-Path' witnessed yet another incarnation of the group with Manuel Barer on bass and Vera Silbereisen on keyboards.

Albums:
BITTER TEARS, N.S.M. NSM001 (1996)
Innocent And Wretched / Bitter Tears / Dreaming / Forever Gone / Scarred For Life / Scourge Of Seclusion / Slave Of Arrogance / Bastards / Ole-Mus
PSYCHO-PATH, (1998)

OLETHRIDRIGMA (GREECE)

Albums:
IRON PALM, (1999)

OMINOUS (SWEDEN)
Line-Up: Anders (vocals), Soren (guitar), Johan (guitar), Dan Johansson (bass), Thomas (drums)

Albums:
THE SPECTRAL MANIFEST, Holy HOLY56CD (2000)
A Piece Of Humanity / Cry For Dawn / Soon To Be Broken / Forever Remains True / Crossing Boundaries / Drained By A Soul / Keep In Graceful Memory / Center Of Gravity / Object Of Lust / Frequent Redemption

ON THORNS I LAY (GREECE)

Line-Up: Steven Kintzoglou (vocals), Chris Dragamestianos (guitar / keyboards), Jim (bass), Fotis (drums)

Previously known as PHLEBOTOMY (and originally a trio with Steven handling drums as well as lead vocals) during this time they released the demo 'Beyond The Chaos' in March 1992 and the limited edition EP 'Dawn Of Grief'.

The band adopted the new title of ON THORNS I LAY at the same time they added drummer Fotis in February 1992. And, in early 1994, the group recorded the 'Voluptuous' demo, inciting interest from Holy Records. A deal would follow.

The sophomore effort 'Orama' was a concept album based on the legend of Atlantis.

Albums:

SOUNDS OF BEAUTIFUL EXPERIENCE, Holy HOLY12CD (1995)
Voluptuous Simplicity Of The Line / All Is Silent / A Sparrow Dances / Cleopatra / A Dreamer Can Touch The Sky / Rainy Days / Sunrise Of A New Age / One Thousand Times / TAXIDI NOSTALGIAS
ORAMA, Holy HOLY29CD (1997)
Atlantis I / The Songs Of The Sea / Oceans / In Heaven's Island / Atlantis II / Atlantis III / If I Could Fly / Aura / The Blue Dream
CRYSTAL TEARS, Holy HOLY 44CD (1999)
Crystal Tears / My Angel / Obsession / Crystal Tears (Loosing Her) / Ophelia / Eden / Enigma / Midnight Falling / All Is Silent / Feelings
FUTURE NARCOTIC, Holy (2000)
Infinity / Future Narcotic / The Threat Of Seduction / Freed Her Lust / Love Can Be A Wave / Ethereal Blue / Heaven's Passenger / Desire / Back To That Enigma / The K Song

OPERA IX (ITALY)

Line-Up: Cadeveria (vocals), Ossian (guitar), Vlad (bass), Lunaris (keyboards), Flegias (drums)

OPERA IX were started as a one man project by guitarist Ossian. Later additions included female vocalist Cadeveria, Vlad on bass and NECRODEATH's vocalist Flegias on drums. Completing the line up was Lunaris.

OPERA IX made their first impression with the 1993 EP 'The Triumph Of Death'

before signing to Shiver Records for the 'Sacro Culto' album of 1998 and a video 'Live In Babylonia' the following year.

The 2000 album sees a cover of BAUHAUS's 'Bela Lugosi's Dead' and IRON MAIDEN's 'Rime Of The Ancient Mariner'.

Singles/EPs:
The Triumph Of Death, Wimp (1993)

Albums:
THE CALL OF THE WOOD, Miscarriage (1995)
Alone In The Dark / Esteban's Promise / The Call Of The Wood / Al Azif / Sepulcro
SACRO CULTO, Shiver (1998)
The Oak / Fronds Of The Ancient Warlust / The Naked And The Dance / Cimmeries / My Devotion / Under The Sign Of The Red Dragon
THE BLACK OPERA: SYMPHONIAE MYSTERIORUM IN LAUDEM TENEBRARUM, Avantgarde (2000)
The First Seal / Beyond The Black Diamond Gates / Carnal Delight In The Vortex Of Evil / Congressus Cum Daemone / The Magic Temple / The Sixth Seal / Bela Lugosi's Dead

OPETH (SWEDEN)

Line-Up: Mikael Åkerfelt (vocals / guitar), Peter Lindgren (guitar), Martin Mendez (bass), Martin Lopez (drums)

Another in the long list of albums produced by EDGE OF SANITY's Dan Swanö. Vocalist / guitarist Mikael Åkerfelt and drummer Anders Nordin are ex ERUPTION. Starting life influenced by the rawer Black Thrash acts OPETH have steadily matured into more melancholic landscapes with each successive release.

The late 80's act ERUPTION had featured Åkerfeldt, Nordin, guitarist Nick Döring and bassist Stephan Claesberg. When singer David Isberg's previous band OPET had floundered when the main mass of members split off to create CROWLEY the two parties combined to reforge the act subtly retitled OPETH.

Second guitarist Andreas Dimeo was recruited for OPETH's debut gig supporting THERION. However, shortly after both Dimeo and Döring decamped quickly after. The former CRIMSON CAT duo of Kim Pettersson and Johan De Farfalla plugged the gap for a second show but the pair would also drift off and more significantly Isberg left for pastures new in LIERS IN WAIT. Åkerfeldt took the lead vocal role as he rebuilt the band with Nordin and bassist Stephan Guteklint. Securing a deal with the British Candlelight Records label the debut album 'Orchid' was cut using previous member De Farfalla on session bass. Gigs followed including a British show alongside VED BUENS ENDE, HECATE ENTHRONED and IMPALED NAZARENE.

OPETH's second album was promoted with a support slot to MORBID ANGEL in the UK and to CRADLE OF FILTH in Europe. Following these dates both Nordin and De Farfalla made their exit Akerfeldt teamed up with Swanö, KATATONIA's Blackheim and Jonas Renske to create side project BLOOD BATH in 2000.

Albums:
ORCHID, Candlelight CANDLE 010CD (1995)
In Mist She Was Standing / Under The Weeping Moon / Silhouette / Forest Of October / The Twilight Is My Robe / Requiem / The Apostle In Triumph
MORNING RISE, Candlelight CANDLE 015 (1996)
Advert / The Night And The Silent Winter / Nectar / Black Rose Immortal / To Bid You Farewell
MY ARMS, YOUR HEARSE, Candlelight CANDLE 025CD (1998)
Prologue / April Ethereal / When / Madrigal / The Amen Corner / Demon Of The Fall / Credence / Karma / Epilogue
STILL LIFE, Peaceville (1999)
The Moon / Godhands Lament / Benighted / Moonlapse Vertigo / Face Of Melinda / Serenity Painted Death / White Cluster
BLACKWATER PARK, Peaceville (2001)
The Leper Affinity / Bleak / Harvest / The Drapery Falls / Dirge For November / Funeral Portrait / Patterns In The Sky / Blackwater Park

OPTHALAMIA (SWEDEN)
Line-Up: Legion (vocals), It (guitar), Night (bass), Winter (drums)

Formed by It (real name Tony Särkää) in 1989 under the name of LEVIATHAN, It was later to create ABRUPTUM and VONDUR.
OPTHALAMIA's debut album had guest lead vocals from Shadow, in reality DISSECTION vocalist Jon Nödtveidt. Bass was supplied by Mourning (real name Robert Ivarsson).

OPTHALAMIA drummer Winter (real name Benny Larsson) is also a member of EDGE OF SANITY and PAN-THY-MONIUM. Bassist Night (real name Emil Nödtveidt) now plays with SWORDMASTER.
OPTHALAMIA vocalist All - who also fronts VONDUR - replaced Legion (real name Erik Hagstedt) who quit to front MARDUK.

With the apparent disappearance of It and the jailing for murder of Shadow it seemed OPTHALAMIA's career was over but the band re-emerged in 1998 for the 'Dominion' album, a concept affair based on Shakespeare's 'Macbeth'! The other 1998 release 'A Long Journey' is in fact a re-recording of the debut album with extra tracks including a VENOM cover.

Albums:
A JOURNEY IN DARKNESS, Avantgarde AV003 (1994)
A Cry From The Halls Of Blood - Empire Of Lost Dreams / Enter The Darkest Thoughts Of The Chosen - Agonys Silent Paradise / Journey In Darkness - Entering The Forest / Shores Of Kaa-Ta-Nu - The Eternal Walk Pt II / A Lonely Soul - Hymn To A Dream / Little Child Of Light - Degradation Of Holyness / Castle Of No Repair - Lies From A Blackened Heart / This Is The Pain Called Sorrow - To The Memory Of Me / I Summon Thee Oh Father - Death Embrace Me
VIA DOLOROSA, Avantgarde AV013 (1995)
Intro - Under Ophthalamian Skies / To The Benighted / Black As Sin, Pale As Death / Autumn Whispers / After A Releasing Death / Castle Of No Repair (Part II) / Slowly Passing The Frostlands / A Winterlands Tear / Via Dolorosa / My Springnights Sacrifice / Ophthalamia / The Eternal Walk (Part III) / Nightfall Of Mother Earth / Summer Distress / Outro - Message To Those After Me / Death Embrace Me (Part II) / A Lonely Ceremony / The Eternal Walk / Deathcrush
TO ELISHA, Necropolis NR013 (1997)
A Cry From The Halls Of Blood- Empire Of Lost Dreams (1991 demo) / A Lonely Ceremony- The Eternal Walk (1990 rehearsal) / Journey In Darkness-Entering The Forest (Rehearsal) / Castle Of No Repair- From A Blackened Heart (1991 demo) / Shores Of Kaa Tu Nu-The Eternal Walk Part II (1991 demo) / Nightfall Of Mother Earth- Summer

Distress (1994 rehearsal) / Enter The Darkest Thoughts Of The Chosen-Agony's Silent Paradise (1992 version) / Deathcrush (Rehearsal) / Sacxrifice (Rehearsal) / I Summon Thee Father-Death Embrace Me (1991 demo)
DOMINION, No Fashion NFR024 (1998)
A LONG JOURNEY, Necropolis (1998)

ORDER FROM CHAOS (USA)
Line-Up: Pete Helmkamp (vocals / bass), Chuck Keller (guitar)

ORDER FROM CHAOS debuted in 1988 with the 'Inhumanities' and 'Crushed Infamy' demos. Following the debut single 'Will To Power' on the Putrefaction label a further demo 'Alienus Sum' was issued.
The 1994 'Plateau Of Invincibility' album included two VENOM cover versions. In 1998 Osmose Productions re-released the 'Stillbirth Machine' recordings as a split album shared with CRUSHED INFAMY.
Chuck Keller founded VULPECULA whilst Pete Helmkamp created ANGEL CORPSE.

Singles/EPs:
Will To Power, Putrefaction (1990) (7" single)
Jericho Trumpet, Gestapo (1994) (7" single)
Into Distant Fears (Live), Eternal Darkness (1994) (7" single)
Pain Lengthens Time (Live), (1994) (7" single)

Albums:
STILLBIRTH MACHINE, (1991)
Aion / The Edge Forever / Power Elite / Iconoclasm Conquest / Forsake Me This Mortal Coil / Stillbirth Machine / Blood And Thunder / As The Body Falls Away
PLATEAU OF INVINCIBILITY, Shivadarshana (1994)
Plateau Of Invincibility / Nuctemeron / Dead Of The Night- Senile Decay / Stillbirth Machine (Live) / Plateau Of Invincibility (Live)
DAWNBRINGER, Shivadarshana (1994)
AND I SAW ETERNITY, Ground Zero (1996)
The Edge Of Forever / Webs Of Perdition / Imperium / De Stella Nova
AN ENDING IN FIRE, Osmose Productions (1998)
Dawnbringer Invictus / Tenebrae / The Sign Draconis / Plateau Of Invincibility / The Angry Red Planet / there lies Your

Lord, Father Of Victories / Nucleosynthisis / De Stella Nova / An Ending In Fire

ORDO ROSARIUS EQUILIBRIO (SWEDEN)

ORDO ROSARIUS EQUILIBRIUM was founded by ARCHON SATANI members Thomas Petersson and Mikael Stavöstrand. As Petersson set up ORDO ROSARIUS EQUILIBRIUM Stavöstrand opted to concentrate on ARCHON SATANI and his other act INAANA.

Albums:
REAPING THE FALLEN... THE FIRST HARVEST, Cold Meat Industry (1995)
THE TRIUMPH OF LIGHT.. AND THY THIRTEEN SHADOWS OF LOVE, Cold Meat Industry (1997)
CONQUEST, LOVE AND SELF PERSEVERENCE, Cold Meat Industry (1998)
MAKE LOVE AND WAR: THE WEDLOCK OF ROSES, Cold Meat Industry (2000)
Beloved Kitty And The Pierced Bolts Of Amor / Ashen Like Love, And Black Like The Snow / Passing Eyes In Mimer's Well / Hunting For The Black September / Flowers And Moonshine In My Garden Of Eden / Liebe Utopia, On Weaves Of Silken Carnage / Make Love And War / Never Before At The Beauty Of Spring / Ode To The Beloved And Impaired

OSCULUM INFAME (FRANCE)
Line-Up: Vlad Drakul (vocals), Drac Vortigern (guitar), Gorthaur (bass), Arkdae (keyboards), Malkira (drums)

Now deceased Black Metal merchants OSCULUM INFAME debuted with the 1994 demo 'Scorn The Mortified Deceiver' quickly followed by the illustrious 'Sadomastic Impure Artgoat'. Initially the trio credited themselves as vocalist Sidragasun, guitarist Se Irim Abrahel and bass player Isacaron.
During 1995 the band drafted drummer Beleth but by the time of the debut album OSCULAM INFAME's rhythm section was bolstered with CHEMIN DE HAINE drummer Malkira and keyboard player Arkdae of DARK SANCTUARY and BEKHIRA. The original band members also used this opportunity to adopt new pseudonyms of Vlad Drakul, Gorthaur and Drac Werevolf (later Drac Vortigern).. OSCULAM INFAME would ultimately fold

with Drakul and Gorthaur remaining together in BLUTORDEN.

Albums:
DOR-NU-FAUGLITH, Mordgrimm (1997)
A Prelude To Dor-Nu-Fauglith / Under The Sign Of The Beast / Vampyric Warmaster (Part II) / Dark Wickedness / When Iron Has Been Blended With Blood / The Nine Ghosts Of The Ring Of Power / Kein Entkommen / Whisper Of The Witch / Among Mist And Shadows…
THE BLACK THEOLOGY, Mordgrimm GRIMM 7 MCD (1999)
Rising In The Glorious Dawn Of Satan / On The Throne Of The Darkest Domain / When The Signs Allow / The Black Theology

OSSUARY INSANE (Eagan, MN)

Albums:
DEMONIZE THE FLESH, Galdre (1998)
Fallen To The pits / Inverted In Darkness / Summoned To Death / Imprecari / The Olde Ragged Cross / Von Pagen Blut / Blaspheme Unto Rebirth / Excruciate With Flames / From Beneath The Blood (Remix) / Siummoned To Death (Remix) / Blaspheme Unto rebirth (Remix)

OTYG (SWEDEN)
Line-Up: Vintersorg (vocals / guitar), Cia (vocals / violin), Mathias (guitar), Daniel (bass), Samuel (mouth harp), Stefan (drums)

Folk Black Metal incorporating violins, willow flutes, mouth harp and flute. OTYG were previously known as BLACK BURNING EVENING.
As OTYG they re-debuted with a demo titled 'Bergtagen' which featured female vocals from Sara. A second better distributed demo 'Galdersang Till Bergfadern' emerged in 1996 which saw the departure of Sara and violinist Cia taking her role for vocal parts.
The 1999 album 'Sagovindersboning' includes a radical rework of DIO's 'Holy Diver'!
Frontman Vintersorg, besides being frontman for HAVAYOTH, also runs his own project aptly titled VINTERSORG.

Albums:
ÄLVEFÄRD, Napalm NPR042CD (1997)
Huldrun / I Trollberg Och Skog / Älvadimmans Omdaning / Ulvskrede / Fjällstrom / I Höstlig Räkt / Myrdingar-Martyrium / All Fader Vite /

Fjälldrottningens Slott / Trollpiskal / Ödermarksblod / Draugen / Skymningsdans
SAGOVINDERSBONING, Napalm (1999)
Trollslottet / Vilievandring / Galdersbesjurgen / När Älvardrottningen Krons / Bächahästen / Årstider / Mosstrun Kolnar / Vättar Och Jättar / Holy Diver / Lövjerskan / Varulvsnatt / Gygraloch

OUIJA (SPAIN)

Black Metal band OUIJA remain somewhat of a mystery. Record company Relapse have thus far refused to reveal the identities of the band members or the group's country of origin. The 1997 album cover was designed by Joe Petagno, famous for designing the classic MOTÖRHEAD logo.

Albums:
RIDING INTO THE FUNERAL PATHS, Repulse RPS 024 CD (1997)
When The Sun Shall Die / Crossing The Seventh Gate / Unbridled Transylvanian Passion / Hear The Call Of The Wolves (Fullmoonlight Lovers) / Before A Possible Relapse / In The Witching Midnight / Riding Into The Funeral Paths / Holocaust In Heaven

OVERFLASH (SWEDEN)
Line-Up: Devo (vocals / guitar / bass), Dan Swanö (drums)

A Death Metal project from CARDINAL SIN's Magnus 'Devo' Andersson (also a former member of MARDUK), the album involved the ever busy EDGE OF SANITY vocalist Dan Swanö filling a drumming role.

Albums:
THRESHOLD TO REALITY, MNW ZONE MNWCD 257 (1993)
Total Devastation / Enter Life Between / Land Beyond / Future Warrior / Nuclear Winter / Life Converter / Infinity (Journey I) / Strange Environment (Journey II) / The Evolution / Threshold To Reality

OXIPLEGATZ (SWEDEN)

A one man undertaking by ex AT THE GATES man Alf Svensson, contributing vocalists to the project included Uno Bjurling (vocalist with Svensson's Punk outfit ORAL), Håkan Bjurgvist and Sara Svensson.

Alf Svensson had originally formed GROTESQUE with Tomas Lindberg, Kristian Wahlin and Thomas Eriksson. The quartet released an EP entitled 'Incantation' before splitting due to personal differences.

While Wahlin proceeded to form LIERS IN WAIT, Svensson and Lindberg put AT THE GATES together, although Alf Svensson would ultimately choose to leave the group in order to pursue his other musical avenues.

The 1997 release, 'Worlds And Worlds', includes a track entitled 'Graveyard Dream' that was originally written in 1990 for GROTESQUE.

Albums:

FAIRYTALES, Fairytale FTCD 001 (1995)
Starseed / Fairytale / Northern Stars / His Time Has Come / I See It Now… / Dark Millenium (There Shall Never Be Another Dawn) / Conclusion / Lust For Life / Numb / Departure / Vision / Adrift / Oh No…

WORLDS AND WORLDS, Adipocere FTCD003 (1997)
Battle Of Species / First Contact - Conflict / Aftermath / Quest / Graveyard Dream / Usurpers / The End Is Nigh / Abandon Earth / Journey

SIDEREAL JOURNEY, (1999)
A Black Hole Is Swallowing The Sun / They Learned Of Its Existence / For Persistence / Bringer Of Obliteration / Into Nowhere / For Persistence / So It's Our Final Hour / The Light From The Perishing Sun / Ahead- The Universe! / No Longer Will We Be The Meek Ones / How Could We Ever Know / Head For That Star / As One Surveys This Ocean / The Londrive A Silent Vibration / Several Planet In Orbit / Enemies!? / Once More Proven- We Are Not Alone / Lightspeed- Flung Into Hyperspace / No Clue To Where This Jump Is Taking Them / Breathless / Turning Up The Power, Accelerating Again / This Time Passage Was Violent / Rings, Spread Like Rippled Water / They Stare Unblinking / Eternal Night / How Many Worlds / These Beings Failed And Perished / Ahead Once More / This Journey Has Taken Us / The Moon Was Land In Orbit / Can This Be What We Hore For / Teraform- Alter The Environment / And So One Day The Sleepers Awaken

PAGAN ALTAR (UK)
Line-Up: Terry Jones
(vocals), Alan Jones (guitar),
Trevor Portch (bass), Brian
Cobbold (drums)

Albums:
PAGAN ALTAR VOLUME ONE, (1982)
Pagan Altar / In The Wake Of Armadeus
/ Judgement Of The Dead / The Black
Mass / Night Rider / Acoustics /
Reincarnation
LORDS OF HYPOCRISY, (198-)
Lords Of Hypocrisy / The Masquerade /
Witches Pathway / Armageddon / The
Aftermath / The Interlude / March Of The
Dead
MYTHICAL AND MAGICAL, (198-)
Flight Of The Witch Queen / The
Sorcerer / Rising Of The Dark Lord / Lily
Maid Of Astloat / Dance Of The Druids /
The Erl King / Salron's Henchmen
NEVER QUITE DEAD- LIVE, (198-)
Lords Of Hypocrisy / Flight Of The Witch
Queen / Judgement Of The Dead / The
Black Mass / Armageddon / The
Interlude / Reincarnation

PAGAN HELLFIRE (CANADA)

Based in Nova Scotia, PAGAN
HELLFIRE is the solo venture of one
Incarnatus. The band had originally
included bassist Blackthorn for a series of
three demos 'Everlasting Funerals'.
'Honor Black War' and 'Outlander'. These
latter two tapes were scheduled for a CD
release by an American label but this
project floundered. Undaunted Incarnatus
released a new set of songs for the album
'A Voice From The Centuries Away'.
PAGAN HELLFIRE has contributed a
version of 'Frijos Einsames Trauern' for a
BURZUM tribute album.

Albums:
**A VOICE FROM THE CENTURIES
AWAY**, Pagan Hellfire (2000)
March Of Incarnatus / The Collapsing
Pillars Of Humanity / Light In The Hours
Of Dusk / The Enlightened Place / A
Time To Depart / A Space Below The
Earth / Wolfland

PAGANIZER (SWEDEN)

PAGANIZER's demo 'Stormfire' would
later be pressed onto CD as a shared
album with Singapore act ABBATOIR.
Vocalist / guitarist Rogga would aid

BLODSRIT on drums.
PAGANIZER evolved into CARVE.

Albums:
STORMFIRE, (199-) (Split album with
ABBATOIR)
DEADBANGER, Psychic Scream (1999)
Branded By Evil / The Mask Of Evil /
Deadbanger / Heads Of The Hydra /
Storms To Come / Time To Burn /
Sinners Burn / Into The Catacombs /
Phantoms / Metal Crusade
STILLBORN REVELATIONS, Psychic
Scream (2001)

PAGAN RITES (SWEDEN)
Line-Up: Unholy Pope (vocals), Fiend
(guitar), Black Agony (guitar), Lord Of The
Deeps (bass), Sexual Goatlicker (drums).

Vocalist 'Unholy Pope' (real name
Thomas Karlsson and an ex AUTOPSY
TORMENT member) and bassist 'Black
Agony' (real name Adrian Letelier) joined
TRISTITIA after the single release.
PAGAN RITES were still a going concern
in 2000 but surviving through constant
line up ructions. The band, now fronted
by Karlsson now billing himself Devil Lee
Rot, pulled in guitarist Angerboder of THE
ANCIENTS REBIRTH and NIFELHEIM
bassist Tyrant.
Drummer Sexual Goatlicker would
decamp with haste necessitating the
recruitment of another NIFELHEIM man
Hellbutcher.

Singles/EPs:
Flames Of The Third Antichrist /
Sodomy In Heaven, Stemra STEMA002
(1993)

Albums:
PAGAN RITES, Warmaster WAR008
(1996)
Frost / Lord Of Fire / Crucified In Flames
/ Pagan Rites / Unholy Ancient War /
Metal King / Images Of The Moon /
Return To The Lake Of Fire / Hail
Victory! / Heathen Land / Domain Of The
Frozen Souls / Land Beyond Our
Dreams / Pagan Metal / Winter Grief /
Once Upon A Time / Under The Church /
Blood Of My Enemies

PANDEMONIUM (ITALY)
Line-Up: Daniel Reda (vocals), Alex Niall
(guitar), Ragman (guitar), Lorenzo Zirilli
(bass), Simone Barbieri (drums)

AND THE RUNES BEGAN TO PRAY,
(1999)
The Alchemist / Birth Of The Fallen Angel
/ Sabbath Day / Wings Of The Wind / The
Dark Before… / The War Of Races / …
The Light / Love Warmer / Pandemonium
/ The Alchemist (Piano version)

PANDEMONIUM (POLAND)

Albums:
THE ANCIENT CATATONIA, Baron
(1994)
The Majesty / Memories / Different Parts
/ The Black Arts / Winter / Might Is Right
/ Morbid Gods / Unholy Existence /
Seven Signs

PAN.THY.MONIUM (SWEDEN)
Line-Up: Derelict (vocals), Aag (guitar),
Mourning (guitar), Day Dissyraah (bass),
Winter (drums)

PAN.THY.MONIUM is one of many
project ventures pursued by EDGE OF
SANITY vocalist Dan Swanö. With
PAN.THY.MONIUM Swanö played guitar
under the disguise of 'Aag'. EDGE OF
SANITY drummer Benny Larsson also
contributed, going under the pseudonym
of 'Winter' (Larsson drums for
OPTHALMIA under the same guise),
whilst vocalist 'Derelict' is in reality
DARKIFIED frontman Robert Karlsson.
During 1997 guitarist Mourning left to join
ASHES, appearing on their debut 'Death
Has Made It's Call' album the same year.
Ironically, Robert Karlsson later became a
permanent frontman for EDGE OF
SANITY for their 'Cryptic' album, ousting
Swanö.

Singles/EPs:
The Battle Of Geeheeb / Thee-Pherenth
/ Behrial / In Remembrance, Relapse CD
6936-2 (1993) ('Khaoohs And Kon-Fus-
Ion' EP)
I / II / III / Vvoiiccheeces / IV, Avantgarde
AV008 (1994) ('Dream II' EP)

Albums:
DAWN OF DREAMS, Osmose
Productions OPCD006 (1992)
KHAOOHS, Osmose Productions
OPCD014 (1993)
I Manens Sken Dog En Skugga / Under
Ytan / Jag & Vem / Lava / Lömska Försat
/ I Vindens Väld / Klieveage / Ekkhoeece
III / Khaoohs I / Utsikt / Khaoohs II

PANZERCHRIST (DENMARK)
Line-Up: Lasse Hoile (vocals), Jes
Christiansen (guitar), Finn Henriksen
(guitar), Nikolaj Brink (bass), Michael
Enevoldsen (drums)

A brutal Death Metal / Grindcore quintet
from Aarhus. PANZERCHRIST include ex
ILLDISPOSED drummer Michael
Enevoldsen in the line-up. Later line ups
had female bassist Karina Bundgaard
taking the place of Nikolaj Brink. The
band name was inspired by the
DARKTHRONE album 'Panzerfaust'.
A six track 1995 demo led to a record
deal. Guitarist Jens Christensen was
added to the group prior to recording of
the '6 Seconds To Kill' album. However,
the band would split with only Enevoldsen
and frontman Lasse Hoile surviving. New
recruits for the 'Outpost Fort Europa'
record were guitarists Rasmus Nørland
and Kim Jensen and bassist Karin B.
Nielsen.
ILLDISPOSED man Bo Summer joined
the band for 2000's 'Soul Collector'. The
album, sung in German, comprised
entirely of songs devoted to second world
war German panzers!
An ex PANZERCHRIST guitarist F.
Conquer would go on to the infamous 122
STAB WOUNDS and join Norwegian
Black Metal band A WINTER WITHIN
during 2000.

Albums:
6 SECONDS TO KILL, Voices Of Wonder
SE003CD (1996)
OUTPOST FORT EUROPA, Serious
Entertainment (1999)
SOUL COLLECTOR, Mighty Music
(2000)
Das Leben Will Gewonnen Sein / Y2Krieg
/ Der Panzertöter / Panzergrenadier /
Schwarz Ist Unser Panzer (Ich Hatt Einen
Kamaraden) / Unsere Höchste Ehre / Kalt
Wie Der Finsternis / Zum Gegenstoss

PARADIGMA (NORWAY)
Line-Up: Tom Erik Evensen (vocals /
guitar), Tom Kvalsvoll (guitar), Chris
Eidskrem (bass), Zilla (keyboards), K.J.
Lervag (drums)

A Norwegian Doom Metal band that
debuted with the 1993 demo 'As Autumn
Dies'. PARADIGMA's 'Skadi' EP includes
a version of the RUSH classic 'Witch
Hunt'. Tom Kvalsoll would add guest
vocals to noted British act ESOTERIC's
'Metaporphogenesis' EP.

Both bassist Chris Eidskrem and Tom Erik Evensen would leave the fold with the bass position being taken over by FUNERAL's Einar Frediriksen in 1997.

Singles/EPs:
Best Regards (Astral Version) / Half / Witch Hunt / Agonized / Come Winter (The Skadi Interpretation), Head Not Found HNF 021 (1996) ('Skadi' EP)

Albums:
MARE VERIS, Head Not Found HNF 008 (1995)
Come Winter / Best Regards / Inner Chanting / One Away From Paradise / Sleep / The Shadow / Terra Mater / Journey's End / When The Storm Comes Down
THE BECKONING OF LAST LIGHT, Head Not Found HNF049CD (1999)
Severance / Bleed / Of Fragile Essence / October / A Pilgrim's Yoke / The Beckoning Of Last Light / Woodtemple / At The Crossroad / Withdrawn / Bort / Heathenesse

PARAGON BELIAL (GERMANY)
Line-Up: Andras (vocals / bass), Ralph (guitar), Zahgrurim (drums)

PARAGON BELIAL were a band featuring former BETHELHEM singer Classen (Andras). This, in spite of reports of his death!
Andras would later reunite with former BETHLEHEM drummer Rolf in September of 1997 to found DARK CREATION.

Albums:
HORDES OF THE DARKLANDS, Folter (1996)
Intro / Coming Of A New Dynasty / Black tears Of Diabolical Rage / Shadow Grave / Horns Of Reprisal / Cradle Of Blood / Necromancer Of The Dark Valley / Verdelet (Master Of Zeremonies)

PARNASSUS (SWEDEN)

A solo project ALGAION and PUISSANCE man Fredrik Soderlund. The industrious individual, who also formed part of one of the earliest Black Metal bands OCTINIMOS, also operates the Industrial act STATE RESEARCH BUREAU and also VALKYRIA.

Albums:
IN DOLORIAM GLORIA, Secula

Delenda (1995)
In Dolorium Gloria / Void Of All Desires / To The Wither And Die / The First Of Seraphs / Cum Trist Issimo Dolore / Receive My Dying Spirit / In The Purlieus Of Light / The End Of Time Am I
LET THE STARS FALL AND KINGDOM COME, Secula Delenda (1997)
Introduction / Cling To Your Life As I Take Them / The Hate I Have For Mankind / Let The Stars Fall And Kingdom Come / Rape This Mortal Earth / Array Of Desolation / Bow Down To Your Master / Turn All Earth Into ashes / Crush Thy Grape Called Tellus / I Bid You Farewell

PAVOR (GERMANY)
Line-Up: Claudio Schwartz (vocals), Armin Rave (guitar), Holger Seebens (guitar), Rainer Landfermanns (bass), Michael Pelkowski (drums)

Bassist Rainer Landfermanns performed guest lead vocals on BETHLEHEM's second album 'Dictus Te Necare'. Drummer Michael Pelkowski also has issued an album from his side project BEYOND NORTH.

Albums:
A PALE DEBILITATING AUTUMN, Imperator GRIM 001(1995)
A Pale Debilitating Autumn / Total Warrior / Corpses / Careworn / Pavor / Imperator Of An Ashen Bane / Fucked By Darkness / Symbols Of Depravity.

PAZUZU (AUSTRIA / CANADA)
Line-Up: Pazuzu (vocals), Trifixion Of The Horned King (vocals), Empress Lilith (vocals), Minh Ninjao (vocals), Silenius (vocals / keyboards), Protector Of All Endless Sleeps (vocals / keyboards)

PAZUZU involves the ever busy WERWULF, PERVURTUM and TRIFIXION member Trifixion Of The Horned King on vocals.
'Pazuzu' turned out to be Canadian native Ray Wells. As well as busying himself with PAZUZU Wells issued a 1998 album 'Malice In Wonderland' by his other project act RAVENTHRONE.
PAZUZU cut 'Living In Fear' for the 2000 KREATOR tribute album 'Raise The Flag Of Hate'.

Albums:
AND ALL WAS SILENT..., Head Not Found HNF004 (1995)
Prologue / And All Was Silent /

Incantation Of The Firegod / La Baronese Et Le Demon / Baptism Of Infant Flesh / The Urilia Abomination / The Churning Seas Of Absu / Beneath The Bowels Of The Earth / Ask My Dying Soul / The Crusades / Der Mond Ward Der Ende Neue Sonne / Invocation Of The Ninib Gate / Forgotten Scrolls / Epilouge
AWAKEN THE DRAGON, Dark Matter (1997)
Awaken The Dragon- Millenium Two / The Fire Emperors / Bal Of Thieves / Roharre Ds Rhves (Baronesse Chapter II) / The Messenger And The Spiritworld / The King Of Vermin / Verfall / Until The Sun Returns / In A Tavern / Pazuzu / Im Mordscheim (Die Tragihdas Todes) / Outro
III- THE END OF AGES, Avantgarde (1999)
Somber Arrival- The Introduction / Schaden Des Zorns / Passages / An Antidote For God / Epic / Eclipse: Final Clash Of Swords / Saturn's Somber Moons… (The Voyage) / Harpsichord And Percussion Interlude / The weeping Willow (Out Of Body Experience) / Das Reich Der Magie… / The Haunted City / La Fin De L'Ete / Hallucination / Death Of An Infant / Reawakening- The Conclusion

PECCATUM (NORWAY)
Line-Up: Ihsahn, Ihriel, Lord PZ

Avantgarde Norwegian trio made up of EMPEROR frontman Ihsahn, his girlfriend Ihriel and his brother Lord PZ. The 2000 EP 'Oh, My Regrets' includes a cover of JUDAS PRIEST's 'Blood Red Skies'.
 Ihsahn also busies himself with THOU SHALT SUFFER.

Singles/EPs:
Oh My Regrets / Blood Red Skies, Candlelight (2000)

Albums:
STRANGLING FROM WITHIN, Candlelight (1999)
Where Do I Then Belong / Speak Of The Devil / The Change / The Song Which No Name Carry / The Sand Was Made Of Mountains / I Breathe Without Access To Air / The World Of No Worlds / And Pray For Me / An Ovation To Art
AMOR FATI, Candlelight (2000)
One Play, No Script / No Title For A Cause / Murder / A Game Divine? / Untitled I / Rise, Ye Humans / Between The Living And The Dead / Untitled II /

The Watchers Mass Part I / The Watchers Mass Part II

PENATRALIA (GERMANY)
Line-Up: Daniel Droste (vocals / guitar), Bianca Eyermann (vocals), Christian Hector (guitar), Felix Gramling (bass), Daniel Fischer (keyboards), Christopher Merzinsky (drums)

Albums:
TRIBUTE TO THE MOON, (199-)
Mother Moon / En Erighet Av Kulda / Levthans Feuer / Dark Haze / Penatralia
CARPE NOCTEM: LEGENDS OF FULLMOON EMPIRES, Last Episode (1998)
The Arrival / En Evighet Av Kulde / Mother Moon / … And Reverence Will Be Levthans Feuer / Escape / Penatralia / Forest / Dark Haze / The Dark
SEELENKRANK, Last Episode LEP060CD (2000)
Intro / The Doctor / Tumortod / Legion / Drink Or Drown / Never Bow To None / Total Eclipse Of The Mind / Seelenkrank / Dead Girls Boogie (The Living Dead)

PENITENT (NORWAY)
Line-Up: Beastus Rex, Azgoth

Stavanger's PENITENT is centred on multi instrumentalist and poet Beastus Rex (real name Karsten Hamre). Drums are supplied by Azgoth, otherwise known as Asbjörn Log.
Hamre also has concerns with side projects ARCANE ART and VEILED ALLUSIONS.

Albums:
MELANCHOLIA, Cold Meat Industry CMI 39 (1996)
Prologue / In The Infinity / Silence / The Path I Follow / The Dance Of Demons / The Undertaker / Possessive Thought / The Black Lake
THE BEAUTY OF PAIN, Draenor Productions DPR001 (1997)
Autumn Is The Beauty Of Pain / Black Is The Sun Shining / Into The Great Inferno / A Mourning Bridge Over A River Of Tears / Necropolis / My Secret Garden
AS LIFE FADES AWAY, Draenor Productions DRR003 (1998)
Entering The Gate / The Birth Of My Funeral / I Die And Become / The Shadow Of Sorrow / Into The Vast Eternity / A Last Temptation
ROSES BY CHAOS SPAWNED, (1999)
Voices In The Night / A Bleeding Heart Of

Desire / In Mortal Fear (Life And Death Part I) / The Arcane Epitaph / Ancient Despair / In Mortal Fear (Life And Death Part II) / The Endless Spheres

PENTACLE (HOLLAND)
Line-Up: Wannes (vocals / bass), Axeweilder (guitar), Mike (guitar), Marc (drums)

Created as a Black Metal quartet in 1989 PENTACLE's first product was the 1992 demo tape 'Caressed By Both Sides', which featured four original tracks plus a version of HELLHAMMER's 'The Reaper'. A further demo, 'Winds Of The Fall', was issued in 1993 as the band gained live experience opening for ASPHYX, ANATHEMA, SAMAEL and ANCIENT RITES.
The band's growing exposure led to a track, 'A Dance Beyond', on the 1994 DSFA Records compilation album 'Paradise Of The Underground' shortly followed by the debut single 'Exalted Journey'.

Singles/EPs:
Exalted Journey, Midian Creations (1995)
Black Heart / A Serpent In Blood Red / The Flame's Masquerade (Her Sun Is The Moon) / Adoring An Endless Dawn, Displeased D00047 (1996) ('The Fifth Moon' EP)

THE PENTAGRAM (TURKEY)
Line-Up: Hakan (vocals / guitar), Demir (guitar), Tarkan (bass), Cenk (drums)

Albums:
ANATOLIA, Raks 97 34 Ü 1036 (1997)
Anatolia / 1'000 In The Eastland / Dark Is The Sunlight / Gündüz Gece / Stand To Fall / Give Me Something To Kill The Pain / Welcome The End / Anatolia / On The Run / Time / Behind The Veil / Fall Of A Hero

PERISHED (NORWAY)
Line-Up: Bathyr (vocals), Ymon (guitar), Ihizahg (guitar), Bruthor (bass), Knut Erik Jensen (keyboards), Jehmod (drums)

Death Metal band PERISHED were created in 1991. Demo tapes 'In Hoc Signo Vinces' and 'Through The Black Mist' followed upfront of a 1996 EP for Solistitium Records.
The debut album 'Kark' sees sessions from Tom Arild Johansen and Knut Erik

Jensen.
PERISHED drummer Jehmod would join BLACKTHORN.

Singles/EPs:
Kald Som Aldri For / Gjennom Skjoerende Lys, Solistitium SOL008 (1997)

Albums:
KARK, Solistitium SOL022 (1998)
Introduksjon / Imens Vi Verter... / Stier Til Visdoms Krefter / På Nattens Vintervinger / Iskalde Strømmer / ... Og Spjuta Fauk / Befri De Trolske Toner / Renheten Og Gjenkomsien

PERVERTUM (AUSTRIA)
Line-Up: Cromm (vocals), Yog Sototh (guitar), Necros (guitar), Aisthasis (bass), Trifixion Of The Horned King (drums)

PERVERTUM feature the bizarrely named Trifixion Of The Horned King, who also figures in WERWULF, PAZUZU and his own side project TRIFIXION. He is also an ex member of SUMMONING, leaving that band claiming they were not heavy enough!

Albums:
CREATURE OF UNGOD, Lethal LRC 19 (1995)
Gott Ist Im Chaos Gestorben! / Back To Times Of Erian / Christ / Unfulfilled Promise / Creature Of Ungod / ...And the Sycophant / Gather / Glade Of Darkness / Chaos / Chaos Reprise

PESSIMIST (USA)
Line-Up: Ralph Runyan (vocals / bass), Kelly McLachlin (guitar), Bill Hayden (guitar), John Gordon (drums)

Self styled 'Dungeon Metal' act PESSIMIST trace their history as far back as 1989 when guitarist Kelly McLachlin, a veteran of RESISTANCE, DEATH FORCE and Grindcore act DEMOLITION cut the 'Tunnel Vision' demo. McLachlin had previous to founding PESSIMIST been involved with the Tampa, Florida act CAULDRON which featured a pre ICED EARTH Matt Barlow.
PESSIMIST laid down a second demo session 'Dark Reality' during 1993 but were assailed by constant line up changes. Rob Kline was pulled in on second guitar as the promotion release 'Let The Demons Rest' secured a deal with Lost Disciple Records.

Latter day PESSIMIST recruits include former FEAR OF GOD men guitarist Bill Hayden and drummer John Gordon with frontman Ralph 'Reaper' Runyan, previously a member of New Jersey's CORRUPTURE.
Dave Brenzeal of TROKKAR would later take the drum stool.

Singles/EPs:
Absence Of Light, Wild Rags (1995)

Albums:
CULT OF THE INITIATED, Lost Disciple (1998)
The Stench Of Decay / Let The Demons Rest / Cult Of The Initiated / Drunk With The Blood Of The Saints / Dungeonlorde / Pyrosexual / Innocence Defiled / Unholy Union
BLOOD FOR THE GODS, Lost Disciple (1999)
Century Of Lies / Unspeakable Terror / Psychological Autopsy / Demonic Embrace / Mers Rea / Whore Of The Undead / Unborn (Father) / Tunnel Rats / Wretched Of The Earth

PHLEBOTOMY (GREECE)

PHLEBOTOMY later adopted the new title ON THORNS I LAY, recording an album for Holy Records to follow up the 'Dawn Of Grief' record issued in 1994.

Albums:
DAWN OF GRIEF, Holy (1994)

POCCOLUS (LITHUANIA)
Line-Up: Ramunas Personis (vocals / guitar / keyboards), Raimondas Ramonus (bass), Andrius Simkunas (drums)

Black Metal act POCCULUS debuted with the 1993 demo 'Kingdom Of Pocculus'.

Albums:
POCCULUS, Hammerheart (1996)
Werewolves / While The Fires Burn / Fire Rises Over The Oaks / Begeyte Pecolle / They Will Come… / Whispers Of The Autumn's Wood / That Will Be A Hour Of My Triumph / Strike, Medeine, Strike

POSSESSED
(San Francisco, CA, USA)
Line-Up: Jeff Beccara (vocals / bass), Larry LaLonde (guitar), Mike Tarrao (guitar), Mike Sus (drums)

One of the instigators of the Bay Area Thrash scene. Founded as teenagers during 1983 POSSESSED were originally fronted by singer Barry Fisk. Tragedy struck the band early in their career though when Fisk committed suicide.
With Jeff Beccara replacing Fisk the band, including guitarists Mike Tarrao and Brian Montana with drummer Mike Sus, cut a 1984 demo which excited the interest of Metal Blade Records. The label gave an inclusion to POSSSESSED's 'Swing Of The Axe' to their 'Best Of Metal Massacre' compilation but did not sign the band up for an album.
This honour fell to Combat Records although not before Montana was fired, apparently for disagreeing with the bands image of leather, studs and inverted crosses. Larry LaLonde took his place for the debut 'Seven Churches'.
POSSESSED toured Europe with VOIVOD in 1986. The 'Beyond The Gates' album, produced by Carl Canedy of THE RODS, came wrapped in a lavish fold out sleeve, a rare extravagance for a Thrash act.
The follow up mini album 'The Eyes Of Horror' was produced by none other than guitar guru JOE SATRIANI and found the group mellowing out slightly.
POSSESSED fractured leaving Tarrao to carry on the name. LaLonde would join BLIND ILLUSION then create the offbeat but commercially successful PRIMUS. Beccara suffered the misfortune of being shot by two drug addicts and was paralyzed from the waist down.
POSSESSED resurfaced in 1992 comprising of Tarrao, guitarist Mark Strausberg, bassist Bob Yost and drummer Walter Ryan. The band supported MACHINE HEAD the same year and cut a three song demo. POSSESSED's last incarnation came in 1993. Former POSSESSED guitarist Mike Hollman joined hardcore merchants PRO-PAIN in 1994.
Ryan joined MACHINE HEAD. Torrao later forged IKONOCLAST.
Although their career was short the band's music is now held in high regard in particular by today's Black Metal legions.

Albums:
SEVEN CHURCHES, Roadrunner RR 9757 (1985)
Exorcist / Burning In Hell / Seven Churches / Holy Hell / Fallen Angel / Pentagram / Evil Warriors / Satan's

Curse / Twisted Minds / Death Metal
BEYOND THE GATES, Under One Flag
FLAG 3 (1986)
Heretic / Tribulation / March To Die /
Phantasm / No Will To Live / Beyond
The Gates / Beast Of The Apocalypse /
Séance / Restless Dead / Dog Fight
THE EYES OF HORROR, Under One
Flag FLAG 16 (1987)
Confessions / My Belief / The Eyes Of
Horror / Swing Of The Axe / Storm In My
Mind

PRIMARY SLAVE (UK)
Line-Up: Mark Gilltrow (vocals / guitar),
Paul Allender (guitar), David Pallser
(bass), Mark Royce (keyboards), G.
(drums)

Originally titled LILLITH and created by
ex CRADLE OF FILTH and BLOOD
DIVINE guitarist Paul Allender and former
ENTWINED keyboard player Mark
Royce. Vocalist / guitarist Mark Giltrow is
ex CENOBITE.
Prior to recording the debut album
Allender quit to rejoin CRADLE OF
FILTH, his place being swiftly taken by
Lee Dunham.

Albums:
DATA PLAGUE, Visible Noise (2000)
Spasm / Electric Dream State / Slide /
Re-Wire / D.E.F. / Lifelike / Jagd2 /
Silicone / A Way To Be Religious

PRIMIGENIUM (SPAIN)
Line-Up: Smaug, Alhaz, Nebulath (bass)

Founded in 1992 by Smaug and Alhaz
PRIMIGENIUM's debut demo included
session bass from "The Caller". Nebulath
took the four string position but would
depart in 1999.

Singles/EPs:
Feeling At One With The Night / The
Cold, The Emptiness / As Eternal As The
Night / Art Of War- Outro, Wild Rags
(1996) ('As Eternal As The Night' EP)

Albums:
ART OF WAR, Full Moon Productions
(1997)
Ridden Into Battle / Embrace Me
Darkness / Black Sword Of Vengeance /
Shall The Forest Open For Us / … And
Jesus Wept? / Anachronism / Pact Of
Solitude / Enemy / Dragons Tears-
Epilogue

PRIMORDIAL (IRELAND)
Line-Up: Alan 'Naihmass Nemtheanga'
Averill (vocals), Ciaran Mac Uiliam (guitar
/ keyboards), Pol Mac Amhlaidh (bass),
D. Mac Amhlaidh (drums)

Pagan Death Metallers PRIMORDIAL,
who came to the fore with their 'Dark
Romanticism' demo, are heavily reliant
on Celtic imagery and influences. The
split single with Sweden's KATATONIA
features the band's 1993 demo 'To Enter
Pagan'.
For live work PRIMORDIAL drafted
ARCANE SUN guitarist Feargal.

Singles/EPs:
To Enter Pagan, Misanthropy (1996)
(Split EP with KATATONIA)
The Calling / Among The Nazarene / The
Burning Season / And The Sun Set On
Life Forever, Hammerheart (1999) ('The
Burning Season' EP)

Albums:
IMRAMA, Cacophonous NIHIL 08 (1995)
Fuil Arsa / Infernal Summer / Here I Am
King / The Darkest Flame / The Fires... /
Mealltach / Let The Sun Set On Life
Forever / To The Ends Of The Earth /
Beneath A Bronze Sky / Awaiting The
Dawn...
A JOURNEYS END, (199-)
Graven Idol / Dark Song / Autumn's
Ablaze / Journeys End / Solitary Mourner
/ Bitter Harvest / On Aistear Deirneach
SPIRIT THE EARTH A FLAME,
Hammerheart (2000)
Spirit The Earth Aflame / Gods To The
Godless / The Soul Must Sleep / The
Burning Season / Glorious Dawn / The
Cruel Sea / Children Of The Harvest / To
Enter Pagan

PROFANATICA (USA)
Line-Up: Aragon Amori (vocals), Paul
Ledney, Brett Makowski (guitar)

One of the more illustrious names on the
American Black Metal scene.
PROFANATACA, an extremely brutal and
intentionally primitive act, debuted with
the 'Putrescence Of…' demo.
PROFANATICA was assembled by
former INCANTATION personnel Aragon
Amori, Paul Ledney and Brett Makowski.
Previous trio INCANTATION both Amori
and Makowski had been members of
BLOOD THIRSTY DEATH whilst Ledney
had been involved with REVENANT and
G.G. Allin's CONNECTICUT

COCKSUCKERS.
A sophomore PROFANATICA product 'Broken Throne Of Christ' led to a deal with After World Records. PROFANATACIA gave their fans more than they had bargained for when copies of the debut single 'Weeping In Heaven' came complete with genuine smears of group members blood and semen! Makowski had been replaced with John Gelso signaling the start of numerous fluctuations in the guitar department.

The equally notorious EP 'As Tears Of Blood Stain The Altar Of Christ' quite uniquely for a Black Metal band featured the corpsepainted group members baring all! PROFANATICA would also cut a split single with Colombian band MASACRE. The band united with guitarist Wicked Warlock Of Demonic Blasphemy managing one solitary gig before disbanding. An album was rumoured to have been recorded entitled 'The Raping Of The Virgin Mary' but according to stories the tapes were deliberately destroyed.

Aragon Amori later founded CONTRIVISTI, Hardcore act SEALED WITH A FIST and involvement with DEMONIC CHRIST on the 1993 demo 'Deceiving The Heavens' but would die prematurely in 1996. PROFANATICA's last guitarist Wicked Warlock Of Demonic Blasphemy would retitle himself Ixithra to create DEMONCY.

Ledney HAVOHEJ in 1993. Although this project folded it would be resurrected in 2000.

Rare PROFANATICA tapes surfaced in 1999 as part of a split EP with Singapore Black Metal band IMPIETY.

<u>Singles/EPs:</u>
Weeping In Heaven / Heavenly Father, After World (1991) (7" single)
Scourging And Crowning / Final Hour Of Christ, After World (1992) (7" single)
Spilling Holy Blood / Final Hour Of Christ / Weeping In Heaven / I Arose, Osmose (1992) ('Tormenting Holy Flesh' Split EP with MASACRE)
Raping Of Angels / Final Hour Of Christ / Of Pestilence, Osmose OPCD05 (1993) (7" single) ('As Tears Of Blood Stain The Altar Of Christ' EP)
Weeping In Heaven (Rehearsal 1991) / Crucifixion Wounds (1992 demo) / Mary (1992 demo), Samhain (1999) ('Unholy Black Death' EP Split with IMPIETY)

PROFANE CREATION (BRAZIL)
Line-Up: Ciro Voohers (vocals), Rochester Cypher (guitar / bass), Roger Cypher (drums)

Black Metal Brazilians PROFANE CREATION first issued two demos in 1994's 'Supremacy' and the 1996 effort 'In Name Of Supreme Black Arts'. The debut album 'Nema' was a shared affair with Americans INQUISITION.

<u>Albums:</u>
NEMA, Sylphonium (1997) (Split album with INQUISITION)

PROFANUM (POLAND)
Line-Up: Geryon, Vlad Ysengrimm, Lord Reyash

Black Metal group PROFANUM date back to 1993 releasing the demo 'Under The Black Wings Of Emperor' the following year. This tape secured a deal with Polish label Astral Wings for the debut album. PROFANUM also contributed a track to the Cyclonic Records compilation album 'Under The Pagan Moon'.

<u>Albums:</u>
FLOWERS OF OUR BLACK MISANTHROPY, Astral Wings (1996)
Tears Of Chors / Gates Of Armageddon / Song Of The Mist (Part I: Wolfenthirst) / Into The Beginning Of Eternal Wisdom / The Gathering Of Funeral Gods / Songs Of The Mist (Part II: Serpent Garden) / Unspoken Name Of God / Under Black Wings Of Emperor / 666
PROFANUM AETURNUM: EMINENCE OF SATANIC IMPERIAL ART, Pagan Moon CD 011 (1998)
The Descent Into Medieval Darkness / Conquering The Highest Thrones In Universe / The Serpent Crown / Raven Singing Over My Closed Eyes / Journey Into The Nothingness

PROPHANITY (SWEDEN)
Line-Up: Mathias Jarrebring (vocals), Christer Olsson (guitar), Robert Lindmark (bass), A.W. Malmström (drums)

Black Metal crew PROPHANITY first issued a demo in 1994. A second set of tapes followed the same year titled 'Messenger Of The Northern Warrior Host'.

After the single release in 1995 PROPHANITY put together a 1997 demo titled 'The Battleroar'.

Singles/EPs:
I Vargans Tekken, Voice Of Death (1995)

Albums:
STRONGER THAN STEEL, (199-)
Armed To The Teeth / Walking Through
Fire / Beast Of The North / Fate Of The
Gods / The Battleroar / … To Hargatyr /
Towards The Sinister Realms / Awaiting
Your Valkyries Arrival

PROSCRIPTOR (USA)

Solo outing by renowned ABSU vocalist /
drummer Proscriptor McGovern.
The album's theme is based around
Proscriptor's supposed astral travels
during the 13th century. The album title is
a metaphor for Proscriptor himself- Venus
being his zodiacil sigil Gemini whilst
Bellona translates as 'War God'.
'The Venus Bellona' was released in two
different formats. The American version,
on Dark Age Productions, is a double
vinyl album with unique artwork.

Albums:
THE VENUS BELLONA, Cruel Moon
(1997)
An Initium For You / I Am The One / Our
Blood And Veins From The McGovern
Regiment / Hi Ri Ri Tha E Tighinn / Lady
Day Eve / Madeleine / Kiss Of Shame /
Tractus / My Legacy: A Crysknife /
Serpentine Of Six-Fold Stars / The
Barren Stone Of Lughnasadh / Far Away
From Balkan Hill / De La Fletus Des
Athroll (After The Massacre Of Glencoe)
Part II / Chomere! / Commanding The
Dragon Of Keppoch / Ground's Afire /
Defeat / We Raise Our Silver Goblets In
Triumph / We Procured The Non-
Existence Of Xalteun / Finem Habere:
Flames For You- I Ran (So Far Away)

PSYCHONAUT (USA)

PSYCHONAUT is the outlet of for tribal
ritualistic music of Michael Ford (a.k.a.
'Nachttoter') of Black Metal bands
SORATH, BLACK FUNERAL,
DARKNESS ENSHROUD and the
current Dark Industrial act VALEFOR.
Although the album 'Liber Al Vel Legis',
Ford's musical interpretation of Aleister
Crowley's 'Book of the law', was recorded
in 1999 it did not see a commercial
release until 2001.
PYCHONAUT's 'The Witches Sabbath'

album was an ambitious concept based
on the works of Austin Osman Spare
utilizing tape loops and woodwind. The
1999 'Pylon Of Daath' recordings were
issued in the extremely limited form of a
cassette run of a mere 131 copies.
2000 saw the addition of female vocalist
Davcina and keyboard player The Fallen.

Singles/EPs:
Zos Vel Thanatos / Lunar Emanations,
Ajna (1999) (7" red vinyl single)

Albums:
THE WITCHES SABBATH, Althanor
(1999)
Fornications Benedictus / Evocation /
Prayer Of Communion / Prayer Of
Adoration / The Affirmation Creed /
Leburah / Bacchanel / Light's Black
Majesty / Fohat / Hymn To Pan
PYLON OF DAATH, Live Bait Recording
Foundation (1999) (Cassette release)
Thanatos And The Death Posture /
Ophidian Dream / Zos Vel Thanatos
(Poisoned Cup Of Ers mix) / OhZvN /
Between Nether Neither / Sabbat And
Dreaming / I And The Hidden /
Nekronaut / Quadrig A Sexualis / Nuit
And The Manifestation Of The Woman
Divine / Pylon Of Daath
**LIBER AL VEL LEGIS: THE MUSICAL
EMBODIMENT OF ALEISTER
CROWLEY'S 'THE BOOK OF THE
LAW'**, Althanor (2001)
The Manifestation Of Nuit / The Winged
Globe / Blue Lidded Daughter Of Sunset
/ Love Is The Law- Love Under Will /
Serpent Flame / The Hiding Of Hadit /
Servants Of The Star And Snake / A
Greater Feast Of Death / Prophet Of Ra-
Hoor-Khuit / Emblems Of Death /
ABRAHADABRA / Hadit Your Light / Lust
And Worship Of The Snake / The Light
Is In Me (Lucern Fero) / The Scarlet
Woman / Do What Thou Wilt Shall Be
The Whole Of The Law
STEALING THE FIRE FROM HEAVEN,
(2001)

PUISSANCE (SWEDEN)
Line-Up: Henry Moller, Fredrik Soderlund

PUISSANCE man Fredrik Soderlund is
also a member of ALGAION,
PARNASSUS and OCTINIMOS. Henry
Moller is unique among electronic Death
band members having been declared
clinically insane!!!
Moller also operates ARDITI along with
ALGAION's Martin Bjorkman.

Albums:
LET US LEAD, Cold Meat Industry CMI 42 (1996)
Burn The Earth / Control / To Reap The Bitter Crops Of Hate / Behold The Valiant Misanthropist / Dance In The Sulphar Garden / March Of The puissant / Global Deathrape / Whirlpool Of Flames
BACK IN CONTROL, Cold Meat Industry CMI 58 (1997)
Actinum / Evolution / Love Incinerate / Bloodwed / Command And Conquer / Artificial Sun / Stagnate And Perish (Resculptured) / Totalitarian Heights
HAIL THE MUSHROOM CLOUD, (199-)
Act I / Act II / Act III / Act IV
MOTHER OF DISEASE, (199-)
Light Of A Dead Sun / Reign Of Dying Angels / Mother Of Disease / In Shining Armour / Post Ruin Symphony / Core Of Revelation / Human Error / The Voice Of Chaos
WAR ON, (199-)
Control / Erlangen / Totalitarian Heights / For The Days Of Pestilence / Burn The Earth / In Shining Armour / Light Of A Dead Sun / Command And Conquer
TOTAL CLEANSING, Regain BLOOD 010 (2001)

PYRAMID (SPAIN)
Line-Up: Javier Cespedes (vocals),

Albums:
PYRAMID, Arise (1999)
THE IMMACULATE LIE, Locomotive Music (2000)

PYREXIA (USA)
Line-Up: Darryl Wagner (vocals), Tony Caravella (guitar), Guy Marchais (guitar), Chris Basile (bass), Mike Andrekio (drums)

A Deathcore unit with blasphemous overtones. Guitarist Guy Marchais would later join INTERNAL BLEEDING and CATASTROPHIC.

Singles/EPs:
Hatred And Disgust / Bludgeoned By Deformity / The Enshrined, (199-) ('Hatred And Disgust' EP)

Albums:
SERMON OF MOCKERY, Drowned (1993)
Sermon Of Mockery / Resurrection / Abominat / The Uncreation / God / Demigod / Inhumanity / Lithurgy Of Impurity

QUORTHORN
(SWEDEN)

Quorthorn is the enigmatic mentor and driving force behind cult outfit BATHORY. Quorthon's second album, a double album affair, saw the man exploring distinctly poppier territory.

Singles/EPs:
Not More And Never Again / Feather / Boy in The Bubble, Black Mark BMCD 666-9 (1994) (Promotion release)

Albums:
ALBUM, Black Mark BMCD 666-9 (1994)
No More And Never Again / Oh No No / Boy / Major Snooze / Too Little Much Too Late / Crack In My Mirror / Rain / Feather / Relief / Head Over Heels
PURITY OF ESSENCE, Black Mark BMCD 666-13 (1997)
Rock n' Roll / I've Had It Coming My Way / When Our Day Is Through / One Of Those Days / Cherrybutt And Firefly / Television / Hit My Head / Hump For Fun / Outta Space / Fade Away / I Want Out/ Daddy's Girl / Coming Down In Pieces / Roller Coaster / It's Ok / All In All I Know / No Life At All / An Inch Above The Ground / The Notforgettin' / Deep / Label On The Wind / Just The Same / You Just Got To Live

RAGNAROK (NORWAY)
Line-Up: Thyme (vocals), Rym (guitar), Jerv (bass), Jontho Pantera (drums)

RAGNAROK maintain that they are true practicing Satanists. The 'Arising Realm' album features DIMMU BORGIR's Shagrath on keyboards. The band added OVERLORDS man Sander on second guitar. Vocalist Thyme departed following the third album 'Diabolical Age' as RAGNAROK persevered with Caligula of DARK FUNERAL deputizing.
RAGNAROK members guitarist Rym (Øyvind Trindborg) and drummer Jontho Pantera (John Thomas Bratland) along with second guitarist Sanders also form part of ex MAYHEM vocalist Stian Johansen's Gothic Rock project SHADOW DANCERS.
Besides RAGNAROK both Rym and Jontho also operate with CROWHEAD.

Albums:
NATTFERD, Head Not Found (1995)
Intro / Pagan Land / Age Of Pride / From The Darkest Deep / Daudens Natt / The Norse Winter Demon / Hammerens Slag / Minner Om Svunne Tider / Ex Vinterland I Nord / Ragnarok / Nattferd -Outro
ARISING REALM, Head Not Found (1997)
Intro / God Is Wasted / Searching For My Dark Desire / En Verden Av Stein / Time Before Birth Of Light / My Hate Is His Spirit / My Refuge In Darkness / The Reflection From The Starworld Above / The Fall Of Christianity / The Predicted Future / For The World I Am Blinded / Outro
DIABOLICAL AGE, Voices Of Wonder (2000)
It's War / Nocturnal Spheres / Diabolical Age / Certain Death / The Heart Of Satan / Devastated Christ / The Key Is Turned For The 7th time / Post Ludium

RAGNAROK UK (UK)
Line-Up: Deörth (vocals / bass), Stenfalt (guitar), Ashrath (guitar / fiddle), Senrith (keyboards)

Durham based Pagan Metallers formed in 1988 as a duo of vocalist/bassist Deörth and guitarist Morgoth. Added drummer Cernunnos and released two demo tapes, 'Ragnarok' and 'Völuspa' in 1991. Both Morgoth and Cernunnos quit and in

came female guitarist Moon.
A further album length demo, 'Beloved Of The Raven God', came out in 1995. Shortly after the band recruited guitarist Stenfalt and keyboard player Senrith as Moon departed. Her position was taken by Ashrath.
The band's profile suffered due to the existence of a Scandinavian outfit also titled RAGNAROK.
The second album 'Domgeorn' sees Deörth and Stenfalt accompanied by David Youll on keyboards, Phil Tyler on fiddle, Giovanna Fella on vocals, Sean Barry on Celtic harp and Richie F. Ewok on percussion.

Albums:
TO MEND THE OAKEN HEART, Neat Metal NM018 (1996)
Haeled Under Heofenum / Rekindling An Old Flame / ... And The Earth Shall Be Holy / Arose By Another Name / Passion To a Golden Dawn / Where Once Ravens... / Fortuna Imperatrix Mundi / Heartfire And Forge / To Mend The Oaken Heart
DOMGEORN, Eldethorn ELD 007 (1999)
Be Him To Bresnagod Gaels / Wodnesuno / Bonne Waeron We Haeles / Sigrleos / Ni Fuil An Sabras Ajragad Deas / To Walhealle / I Hear The Mountain / Legion Of Death / Hlijescleos / Samhain / John Barleycorn / To Aestreow / Beloved Of The Raven God

RAINMAKER 888 (UK)
Line-Up: Zakk Bajjon (vocals / bass), Rishi Mehta (guitar), Ryk Swillo (guitar), Benjamin Ryan (keyboards), Mark Cooper (drums)

Late 90's act previously titled CROWFOOT. RAINMAKER 888 are fronted by former WITCHFINDER GENERAL, BAJJON and LIONSHEART leader Zakk Bajjon.
Also included are guitarist Rishi Mehta, who boasts a spell in CRADLE OF FILTH in 1994, erstwhile CRADLE OF FILTH and BLOOD DIVINE keyboard player Benjamin Ryan and ex INCARCERATED drummer Mark Cooper.
Bajjon has also produced early albums for CRADLE OF FILTH.

RAISE HELL (SWEDEN)
Line-Up: Jonas Nilsson (vocals / guitar), Torstein Wickberg (guitar), Niklas Sjostrom (bass), Dennis Ekdahl (drums)

RAISE HELL
Photo : Martin Wickler

Drummer Dennis Ekdahl also drums for SINS OF OMISSION.

Albums:
HOLY TARGET, Nuclear Blast (1998)
The March Of Devil's Soldiers / Raise The Dead / Beautiful As Fire / Holy Target / Legions Of Creeps / The Red Ripper / Black Visions / Mattered Out / Superior Powers
NOT DEAD YET, Nuclear Blast NB 443-2 (2000)
Dance With The Devil / Babes / Back Attack / Devilyn / Not Dead Yet / No Puls / User Of Poison / He Is Coming / Soulcollector

RAISM (GREECE)

RAISM is the side project of DIABLOS RISING man Magus Wampyr Daoloth together with Mika X6X Alienseed (a.k.a. Mika Luttinen of IMPALED NAZARENE).

Albums:
THE VERY BEST OF PAIN, Kron-H KRON-H 4MCD (1996)
Chasphere / Killing Machine / Les 120 Journees De Sodome (A Velvet Ballad For De Sade) / Alienation / What Kind Of Hell Is This Anyway?

RAKOTH (RUSSIA)

Line-Up: Rustam (vocals), Dy (guitar), Sergey (guitar), Den (bass), Leshy (drums)

Obrinsk based band rooted in the 1996 act BEDEVIL founded by vocalist Fascist, guitarist Ilya and drummer Leshy. BEDEVIL later augmented their sound with the addition of former DISSINTER bassist Rustam, bass player Miguel The Blind and shortly thereafter evolved into RAKOT. A further subtle change to RAKOTH saw the enrollment of Black on vocals.

In early 1997 Rustam parted ways with the band which promptly collapsed as Fascist, Ilya and Ilya created a fresh act titled GORBUG. However, within months Rustram had resurrected the name RAKOTH with singer Black and new members Den and guitarist Dy from Rustam's former Death Metal band DISSINTER. Drummer Leshy would also rejoin in time for the demo 'Dark Ages Chronicle'. Following these recordings Leshy upped and left to reunite with his erstwhile colleagues Fascist and Ilya in TEMNOZOR. In this new band Fascist became Tuuv whilst Ilya adopted the pseudonym of Vuulko.

Rustram also has a side project titled UNBRAL PRESENCE.

Albums:
PLANESHIFT, Code 666 (2000)
Planeshift / Fear (Wasn't In The Design) / Noldor Exodus / The Dark Heart Of Uukrul / Og' Bend / Planeshift / Gorthaur Alendil / Mountain God / The Unquiet Grave

RAMPAGE (Augusta, GA, USA)

Line-Up: Lord Vic Naughty (vocals / guitar), Earwhig Ringworm (guitar), Tom Coffinsmasher (bass), Paul Bearer (drums)

Georgia's schizophrenic Death Metal band RAMPAGE have proved an elusive beast to categorize. Many albums are deliberately humorous whilst increasingly latter day albums are deadly serious affairs, in particular the overtly Black Metal 'Bellum Infinitium' concept outing.

The Band's first attempt at a formation was as far back as 1989 with Lord Vic Naughty on bass, Paul Bearer on guitar and Sexxxual Rush (real name Ben) on vocals. This unit soon disbanded and it would not be until 1995 when Lord Vic and Bearer, the latter now on drums, reunited. In 1997 the mini album 'Misogyny- Thy Name Is Woman' was issued followed shortly after by the full length 'This End Up'. Although a less tongue in cheek affair 'This End Up' would still obviously mimic POSSESSED's infamous logo and include an irreverent take on 'Jailhouse Rock'.

In 1998 RAMPAGE undertook the 'Gore To Your Door' in alliance with GORTICIAN. For these shows Lord Vic pulled in guitarist X Re, bassist Sven Hemlock and drummer Aldo Eniwan. Predictably the band would break up while on the road with roadies taking over musical duties in order to fulfill the dates. Lord Vic would combine RAMPAGE with FESTERING SORE for a split EP including original 'Doom Metal' along side takes on VENOM's 'Leave Me In Hell' and IMMORTAL's 'Unsilent Storms In The North Abyss'. An admittedly 'fake' live album 'Cummin' Atcha Live, with suitably pornographic cover photograph, followed before recording of the ambitious 'Bellum Infinitium'. Despite being a weighty affair the album would include versions of the KISS classic 'War Machine' and DARKTHRONE's 'In The Shadow Of The Horns'.

Besides RAMPAGE Lord Vic has scored production credits with MEGIDDO, FESTERING SORE and EYES OF LIGEIA. The man also operates the spoof Metal Rap band THE GUYS WHO WEAR BLACK TOO MUCH in collaboration with GORTICIAN's High C. Further split albums are planned for 2001 including unions projected with MEGIDDO, CHERNOBOG and ENBILULUGUGAL although reportedly RAMPAGE is now purely a Lord Vic solo venture now.

Singles/EPs:
Doom Metal / Leave Me In Hell / Unsilent Storms In The North Abyss, Unsung Heroes (1999) (Split EP with FESTERING SORE)

Albums:
MISOGYNY- THY NAME IS WOMAN, Unsung Heroes (1998)
The Wigglesnake Blues / Kill Ya Tonite / Deadrot / The Round Mound Of Rebound / Cocksucker / Deathcrush / Bloody Leg (The Wifebeatah Mix)
THIS END UP, Unsung Heroes (1998)
Bloody Leg / Burn In Hell / Ticket To Hell / Satanic Symphonies / Satanic Death / Heavens Gate / The Sceptre / Rampage / The Gates Of The Abyss / Six Bells At

Midnight / Eye Of The Hellstorm / Jailhouse Rock '98 (The Emperor Mix) Witches Sabbath XXX
CUMMIN' ATCHA LIVE, Unsung Heroes (1999)
Bloody Leg / Born In Hell (On The Bayou) / Deadrot / Satanic Death / The Gates Of The Abyss / Cocksucker / Buried Alive-Money For Nothing' / Six Bells At Midnight / Rampage / Ticket To Hell / The Round Mound Of Rebound / Twisted Minds / Storm Over Avalon / Wanderlust
BELLUM INFITIUM, Unsung Heroes (2000)
Up From The Depths- Rainbow Skies / Sisters Of Death / Storm Over Avalon / The Wakening- Soulsword / Excalibur / Nemesis / The Vow / The Final Day- Into The Great Beyond- Orbis Tertius / War Machine / In The Shadows of The Horns

RAM ZET (NORWAY)
Line-Up: Eric Hawk (vocals), H. Ram Zet (guitar), Solem (bass), Aud (fiddle), Kent (drums)

A Black Metal act that experiments with pushing the boundaries of the genre. Borne out of a 1998 solo project of H. Ram Zet the band later evolved with the inclusion of bassist Solem, fiddle player Aud, drummer Kent and erstwhile ARTCH vocalist Eric Hawk.

Albums:
PURE THERAPY, Spikefarm NUALA 009 (2000)
The Fall / King / For The Sake Of Mankind / Eternal Void / No Peace / Kill My Thoughts / Sense / Through The Eyes Of The Children

RAVEN (NORWAY)

Albums:
F.M: LIKE VIRGINSPIT, No Colours NC 015CD (1998)
F.M. (Part I) / F.M. (Part II) / F.M. (Part III) / F.M. (Part IV) / Misanthropic Black Metal

RAVENTHRONE
(AUSTRIA / CANADA)
Line-Up: Engelmacher (vocals), Ray Wells (guitar / bass)

Side project act of PAZUZU's Ray Wells. The 1998 album 'Malice In Wonderland' is produced by PUNGENT STENCH man Martin Shirenc.

MALICE IN WONDERLAND, Avantgarde
AV030 (1998)
Intro / Obsidian Horizon (The Infinite
Azure) / Raventhrone / Malicia The Third
(Empress Of Insomnia) / Malice Garden
/ Ode To all Brave / The Three Faced
King Of Dominion One / The Stargazer
(Chastize The Absolute) / Crepsucle /
Vision Dementia / Final Farewell (A
Voyage In Cm)

REBAELLIUN (BRAZIL)
Line-Up: Marcello Marzari (vocals / bass),
Ronaldo Lima (guitar), Fabiano Penna
(guitar), Sandro M. (drums)

Death Metal band led by guitarist Fabiano
Penna founded as BLESSED in 1996.
REBAELLIUN have opened for MYSTIC
CIRCLE and LIMBONIC ART.
In 2000 REBAELLIUN formed part of the
'No Mercy' Festivals across Europe
together with VADER, FLESHCRAWL
and VITAL REMAINS.

Albums:
BURN THE PROMISED LAND, (1999)
At War / And The Immortals Shall Rise /
Killing For The Domain / Spawning The
Rebellion / Flagellation's Of Christ (The
Revenge Of King Beelzebuth) / Hell's
Decree / The Legacy Of Eternal Wrath /
Burn The Promised Land / Triumph Of
The Unholy Ones

RED HARVEST (NORWAY)
Line-Up: Jimmy Bergsten (vocals /
guitar), Jan F. Nygard (guitar), Thomas
Brandt (bass), Cato Bekkevold (drums)

Oslo's RED HARVEST kicked off their
career with distinct Thrash Metal leanings
but had introduced Industrial elements
with each successive release. The band
debuted with the demos 'Occultia' and
'Psychotica'. The band's sixth album
'Cold Dark Matter' features
DARKTHRONE's Fenriz as guest
musician.
By 1995 RED HARVEST guitarist Jan F.
Nygard had departed and the group had
added guitarist Ketil Eggum and
keyboard player Lars R. Sorensen.
Drummer Cato Bekkevold also has
credits with DEMONIC.

Singles/EPs:
The Harder They Fall / Enlighten The Child
/ Dream Awake / Tears, Voices Of Wonder
046 (1995) ('The Maztür Nation' EP)

Albums:
NO MINDS LAND, Black Mark BMCD 19
(1991)
The Cure / Righteous Majority / Acid /
No Next Generation / Machines Way /
(Live And Pay) The Holy Way /
Crackman / Face The Fact
**THERE'S BEAUTY IN THE PURITY OF
SADNESS**, Voices Of Wonder 039 C
(1994)
Wounds / Naked / Resist / Mindblazt /
Mastodome / Shivers / (?) / Mother Of All
/ Alpha Beta Gamma L.E.A.K. / Sadness
/ The Art Of Radiation
HYBREED, Voices Of Wonder (1996)
Maztür Nation / The Lone Walk / Mutant
/ After All... / Ozrham / On Sacred
Ground / The Harder They Fall /
Underwater / Monumental / In Deep /
The Burning Wheel
NEW RAGE WORLD MUSIC, Voices Of
Wonder (1999)
Ad Noctum / Move Or Be Moved
(Preview) / Swallow The Sun / Pity The
Bastard / Concrete Steel Vs. The Brain
(PTB Remix)
COLD DARK MATTER, Nocturnal Art
(2000)
Omnipotent / Last Call / Absolut
Dunkelheit / Cold Dark Matter / Junk-O-
Rama / Fix Hammer Fix / The Itching
Scull / Death In Cyborg Era / Move Or
Be Moved

REGREDIOR (LITHUANIA)
Line-Up: Marius (vocals), Rytis (guitar),
Tomas (bass), Linas (drums)

Death Metallers debuted with the demo
tape 'Born In A Coffin'. REGREDIOR split
after the 'Forbidden Tears' effort with
vocalist Marius joining GHOSTSTORM.

Singles/EPs:
Touched By Thanat, (1995)

Albums:
FORBIDDEN TEARS, Shiver SHR 010
(1995)
Reflection Of The Shadows Age /
Hungry Ghost / Forbidden Tears /
Touched By Thanat / Return To The
Kingdom Of Mandragora

REIGN OF EREBUS (UK)
Line-Up: Chthonian (vocals / bass),
Crucem (guitar), Ewchymlaen
(keyboards), Malleus (drums)

Hampshire based Black Metal band.
REIGN OF EREBUS lost drummer

Samoth V. shortly before recording the debut album with a replacement being found in former SEASONS END man Malleus.
Previous to adopting their mythical pseudonyms REIGN OF EREBUS were more commonly known as singers Scott and Emma, guitarist Pete, bassist Mike, keyboard player Natasha and drummer Stuart. An early guitarist Chris was replaced by Colin who in turn was usurped by former HECATE ENTHRONED guitarist Paul Massey for the demo 'Of Blackest Magic And Deepest Dreams'.
Female keyboard player Lamier Van Der Weyers also exited making way for Ewchymlaen of ACOLYTE'S RUIN.

Albums:
OF BLACKEST MAGICK, Blackend (2000)

REX INFERI (ITALY)
Line-Up: Maurizio Samori (vocals / guitar), Flavio Portolano (bass / keyboards), Franco Bonassi (drums)

Albums:
THE DAMAGE HAS BEEN GONE, LM (1986)
Lost In Oblivion / Destroyer / Warriors Of The Sea / Axeman In Black / Metal Possession

RIGER (GERMANY)
Line-Up: Ingo Tauer (vocals), Nicola Jahn (guitar), Peter Patzelt (guitar), Jan Kersten (bass), Roberto Liebig (keyboards), Stefan Schiek (drums)

Frankfurt Black Metal act opened up the proceedings with the 1996 demo 'Die Belagerung'. Keyboard player Roberto Liebig created a side project DORU to issue the 2000 album 'Falscheit'.

Albums:
DERWANDERER, CCP (1998)
HAMINGJA, CCP (2000)
Prolog / Krieg / Mit Goettlicker Hand / Hamingja / Welk / 6 / Hexenhammer / Othala / Totensonett / Grendel

RINGNEVOND (NORWAY)
Line-Up: Darkjött (vocals), Görin (guitar), Elvorn (guitar), Revrod (keyboards)

Albums:
NATTVERD, Edgerunner EDGE001 (1999)

Jøkulvinter / Gudefall / Trollsyn / Åsgårdreien / Mellon De Høye Tinde / Mellom Sier / Efterklang / Frostmorgenhildring / Drapskvad / Skugger Over Skymningsskog / La Pesten Herge

RITUAL (USA)
Line-Up: Robert Nusslein, Mike Parch

Black Metal act came to the fore with the 1993 demo 'Goat Prophecies' followed up by 1994's 'Blackest Of Evil And Mysticism'. RITUAL member Robert Nusslein has allegedly been imprisoned for various crimes and released under medical supervision.

Albums:
THE SUMMONING, Wild Rags (1994)
Intro / Pagan Warfare / In The Forest / Visions Of Souls Once Lost / Blood Moon / Journey Into The Frozen Wasteland / Ancient God Of Winter / Hail The Dark Lord / Dark Cathedrals
CRIMINAL BLACK METAL, Wild Rags (1995)
DEMONIC WINTER METAL, Wild Rags (1997)
Where The Rivers Run Blood / Infernal Whirlwinds / Nuclear Crucifixion / Undying / Where Witches And Warlocks Gather / Dark Emptiness / Heathen Holy War / Stalking The Christian God / Untitled
SOLDIERS UNDER SATAN'S COMMAND, Wild Rags (1998)
Kill, Maim, Destroy / Steamroller / Triumph Of The Teutonic / Wars / Soldiers Under Satan's Command / Death Machine / The Mysterious Portals / Elucidarium (Honorious Of Satan) / Infinite Eyes

ROK (AUSTRALIA)
Line-Up: Rok (vocals). Princess Hellfucker (guitar), The Imposter (bass), Hellaxe Shothammer (drums)

Solo band of SADISTIK EXEKUTION vocalist Rok. Alongside Rok, guitarists Princess Hellfucker and Imposter various credited musicians on the 2000 'Burning Metal' album include guitarist King Pest III and drummers and Thunderblood, Sloth and Kunthammer.

Albums:
THIS IS SATANIK, (1998)
Vokalik Vomitation / Bulk And Ferocity / Heinkel Hellfukker / The Butcher Of

Baghdad / Fukked / The Fall Of The Macedonian Empire / Shit City / Multidimensional Mentality / Pestilence Of Insanity Backwards
BURNING METAL, Modern Invasion MIM 7330-2CD (2000)
Hell / Warpower / Born In Fire / Roadkill / Satanik Slut / Black Leather / Vampire / Funeral Guts / Sex And Lust Hells Angels / The Kurse / Satanika 6000 / Backwards Message

ROOT (CZECH REPUBLIC)
Line-Up: Jiri Valter (vocals / bass), Dan Janacek (guitar), Rene Kostelnak (drums)

Extremely popular act in the Czech Republic. Mainman Jiri Valter, happy to admit to being nearly 50 years old, is more popularly known as 'Big Boss' whilst guitarist Dan Jacek goes under the title 'Blackie'. ROOT emerged with a series of demo tapes beginning with the 1986 effort 'War Of Rats' followed by 1987's 'Reap Of Hell', 1988's 'Messengers Of Death' and 1989's 'The Trial'.
Drummer Rosta Mozga was replaced by Rene Kostelnak for 1992's 'Hell Symphony' album. ROOT's 2000 line up comprised of Big Boss, Blackie, second guitarist Ashok, bassist Igor and drummer Evil.
Big Boss operates his own solo project fittingly named BIGG BOSS having released two albums to date with 1994's 'Q7' and 1998's 'Belial's Wind'.
Guitarist Blackie is more industrious spreading his talents into many projects including CRUX (along with Evil on drums), VYLET, CALES and ENTRAILS. The latter three outfits have all released albums.

Singles/EPs:
666 / 7 Black Horsemen, Zeras (1990) (7" single)

Albums:
ZJEVENI, Zeras (1990)
Intro / Zjeveni / Aralyon / Vyslech / Upaleni / Pisen Pro Satansa / 666 / 7 Cernych Jezdcu / Demon / Znameni / Cesta Zkazy / Hrbitou
HELL SYMPHONY, Cacophonous NIHIL 11 (1992)
Beelzebub / Belial / Lucifer / Abaddon / Asmodeus / Satan / Leviathan / Astaroth / Loki / The Prayers (T. Raudelaire) / The Oath / Satan's March
THE TEMPLE IN THE UNDERWORLD,

Monitor 0100864331 (1994)
Intro / Casilda's Song / The Temple In The Underworld / Aposiopesis / The Solitude / Voices From… / The Wall / The Old Ones / Message / My Name… / My Deep Mystery / Freebee
KÄRGERÄS, Metal Age (1996)
Lykorian / Kärgeräs Proluge / Kärgeräs / Prophets Song / Rulbräh / Rodäxx / Old Man / Old Woman / Equirhodout-Grandiose Magus / Dygon- Sexton / Trygän- Sexton / Dum Vivimus, Vivimus
THE BOOK, Redblack (1999)
The Book / The Mystical Words Of The Wise / The Curse- Darron / Why / Corabeau Part I / Corabeau Part II / The Birth / Lykorian / The Message Of The Time / Remember Me! / Darkoutro… Toccato- Prestissimo Molto

ROSSOMAHAAR (RUSSIA)
Line-Up: Lazar (vocals), Ixxaander (guitar), Kniaz (bass), Maiden (keyboards), Sigizmund (drums)

ROSSOMAHAAR first emerged with the 1998 demo cassette 'Grotesque' in 1998. Main man Lazar is also a member of ambient dark wave project NARGATROND and Moscow Doom Metal act STONEHENGE. Although the 'Grotesque' session was completed as a solo project of Lazar bass player Baalseguothsarius of STONEHENGE became involved in ROSSOMAHAAR during 1998.
The 2000 album 'Imperium Tenebraum' sees lyrics from Kai Mathias Stahlhammer of NARGATROND. Originally released by the domestic CDM label ROSSOMAHAAR secured a deal with the American Rated X concern for releases outside of Russia.
ROSSOMAHAAR evolved into a full band line up in 2000 comprising of Lazar, guitarist Ixxaander, bassist Kniaz, keyboard player Maiden and drummer Sigizmund.

Albums:
IMPERIUM TENEBRARUM, Rated X (2000)
Into The Domain Beyond All Horizons / Mists Of Eternity / The Spectral Prophecy / The Forlorn Existence Of Soul Divine / … Of Shadows Exaltation (When Night Blackens With Storm) / Imperium Tenebrarum / Portals Of Chaos (The Final Transmigration)
QUARITE LUX IN TENEBRIS (EXPLORING THE ETERNAL

WORLDS), Rated X (2001)

ROTTING CHRIST (GREECE)
Line-Up: Sakis 'Necromayhem', (vocals / guitar), Jim 'Mutilator' (bass), Themis 'Necrosauron' Kostas (drums)

ROTTING CHRIST, being founded in 1987, are the foremost of Greek black metal acts. In their earliest incarnation ROTTING CHRIST were very much in the Grind style as amply displayed on their split single shared with SOUND POLLUTION.
Following the 1989 'Satanas Tedeum' demo the band secured a deal with Norwegian label Deathlike Silence but this venture was curtailed when label boss Euronymous, also a member of MAYHEM, was murdered by BURZUM main man Count Grisnackh. A further split single, shared with MONUMENTUM, was also issued at this time.
Undaunted ROTTING CHRIST self financed a mini album 'Passage to Arcturo' the band signed to French label Osmose Productions releasing the well received 'Thy Mighty Contract' album. Toured with BLASPHEMY and IMMORTAL on the quaintly dubbed 'Fuck Christ' tour.
ROTTING CHRIST split from Osmose in an ugly war of words signing to Greek label Unisound. As well as recording a new album Unisound also pressed up their 1989 demo 'Satanas Tedeum' onto vinyl. ROTTING CHRIST toured Mexico in 1995.
The band's debut for German label Century Media 'Triarchy Of Lost Lovers' was produced by ex HOLY MOSES guitarist Andy Classen. The digipack version included three KREATOR cover versions.
ROTTING CHRIST brought in two new recruits for the 1997 album 'A Dead Poem' Andreas on bass and Payanotis on keyboards. The record was produced by SAMAEL keyboard player Xy and features MOONSPELL vocalist Fernando Riberio on the track 'Among Two Storms'. Touring in Europe found the band sharing a package billing with OLD MAN'S CHILD and HECATE ENTHRONED.
Century Media re-released the 'Thy Mighty Contract' album in 1997 featuring two previous rare single cuts 'Visions Of The Dead Lover' and 'The Mystical Meeting'.
Sakis guested on the 1999 album from SWAN CHRISTY 'Today Died Yesterday'. The man is also involved in THOU ART

LORD, a collaboration featuring Magus Wampyr Daoloth of NECROMANTIA and Gothmog of MORTIFY.

Singles/EPs:
The Other Side Of Life, (1987) (Split single with SOUND POLLUTION)
Split EP, Obscure Plasma (1991) (Split EP with MONUMENTUM)
Passage To Arcturo EP, Decapitated DEC003 (1992)
Visions Of Dead Lovers / The Mystical Meeting, Osmose Productions (1993) (7" single)
Rotting Christ EP, Osmose Productions OPEP004 (1993)
The Hills Of The Crucification / Feast Of The Grand Whore / The Nereid Of Esgaldum / Restoration Of The Infernal Kingdom / The Sixth Communion, Unisound USR 015 (1995) ('Satanas Tedeum' EP)

Albums:
PASSAGE TO ARCTURO, Decapitated DEC003 (1991)
Intro - Ach Golgotha (The Small One In The Cross) / The Old Coffin Spirit / The Forest Of N'Gai / The Mystical Meeting (Sevlesmeth Esoth Spleh Dog) / Gloria De Domino Inferni / Inside The Eye Of Algond
THY MIGHTY CONTRACT, Osmose Productions OPCD012 (1993)
The Sign Of Evil Existence / Transform All Suffering Into Plagues / Fgmenth, Thy Gift / Dive The Deepest Abyss / Exiled Archangels / His Sleeping Majesty
NON SERVIAM, Unisound USR012 (1995)
The Fifth Illusion / Wolfera The Chacal / Non Serviam / Morality Of A Dark Age / Where Mortals Have No Pride / Fethroesforia (Instrumental) / Mephesis Of Black Crystal / Ice Shaped God / Saturn Unlock Avey's Son
TRIARCHY OF THE LOST LOVERS, Century Media 77138-2 (1996)
King Of A Stellar War / A Dynasty From The Ice / Archon / Snowing Still / Shadows Follow / One With The Forest / Diastric Alchemy / The opposite Bank / The First Field Of Battle
A DEAD POEM, Century Media 77166-2 (1997)
Sorrowful Farewell / Among Two Storms / A Dead Poem / Out Of Spirits / As If By Magic / Full Colour Is The Night / Semigod / Ten Miles High / Between Times / Ira Incensus
THE MYSTICAL MEETING, Century

Media (1997)
Tormentor / Flags Of Hate / Pleasure To
Kill / Visions Of The Dead Lovers / The
Mystical Meeting
SLEEP OF THE ANGELS, Century
Media (199-)
Cold Colour / After Dark I Feel /
Victoriatus / Der Perfeckte Traum / You
My Flesh / The World Made End / Sleep
The Sleep Of Angels / Delusions /
Imaginous Zone / Thine Is The Kingdom
KHRONOS, Century Media (2000)
Thou Art Blind / If It Ends Tomorrow / My
Sacred Path / Aeturnatas / Act Of Sin /
Lucifer Over London / Law Of The
Serpent / You Are I / Khronos / Fadeless
/ Time Stands Still / Glory Of Sadness /
After Dark I Feel

ROUTE NINE (SWEDEN)
Line-Up: Dan Swanö (vocals / guitar /
bass / keyboards), Anders Jacobsson
(drums)

ROUTE NINE is a side project of
NECRONY and EDGE OF SANITY
members. Swanö is a noted producer on
the Swedish metal scene as well as being
a member of PAN-THY-MONIUM,
UNICORN and NIGHTINGALE.

Singles/EPs:
**Before I Close My Eyes Forever (Part
1)** / Before I Close My Eyes Forever (Part
2), Inorganic ORGAN001 (1995)

RUDRA (SINGAPORE)
Line-Up: Kathi (vocals / bass), Alvin
(guitar), Bala (guitar), Shiva (drums)

Named after the Hindu God of destruction
and created as RUDHRA in 1992 as a
Death Black Metal trio of vocalist / bassist
Kathi, guitarist Bala and drummer Shiva.
The band would feature on numerous
compilation albums including 'Battle Of
The Bands', 'Made In Singapore' and
'The Birth Of Death', RUDHRA issued
their own demo 'The Past' in 1994.
The band would fold in 1996 but Kathi
and Shiva pulled the act back together
newly billed as RUDRA by the end of the
year with new guitarist Alvin. MANIFEST
guitarist Burhan would fill in on a
temporary basis until the resumption of
duties from Bala.

Albums:
RUDRA, Candlelight (1998)
Obeisance / Bliss Divine / Black /
Mahamaya / The Ancient One / Atman /

War Legion / For The Dying / Sin No
War (demo) / Ananda (Demo)
METAL LEGION, Candlelight (1998)

RUINATION (LITHUANIA)
Line-Up: Donatas Abrutis (vocals), Ainius
Staneika (guitar), Saulius Vinslovas
(guitar), Andrius Kraskauskas (bass),
Vytautas Diskevicius (keyboards),
Vytenis Beinortas (drums)

Vilnius act RUINATION started life in a
Death / Doom mode but soon switched to
a more concentrated Black attack after
supporting DEICIDE in their home town.
After signing with Spanish label Goldtrack
the band cut their debut album 'Visionary
Breed' with producer Peter Tägtgren of
HYPOCRISY in Sweden. Support gigs to
promote the album included Lithuanian
guest slots to both HYPOCRISY and
APOCALYPTICA.
Tägtgren would also produce the
sophomore 'Xura' album.

Albums:
VISIONARY BREED, Goldtrack (1998)
My Soul's Enchantment / Back Of
Dreams / Loss Of Hopes / End Of
Prayer / Autumn's Blaze / Never / Listen
To The Wind / The Key / My Life, My
Cross / I Found The Feelings / A Lover /
From Your Eyes / Dead Loss Spring .
Just A Joke / Me Kosdykumos
XURA, (1999)
Eject II / Souls On Fire / Trust Again /
Long Way / World In Stain / Xura (The
Lord Of Pleasures Unattached) / For
Ever Descending / Dreamfield / Don't
Take My Name In Vain

RUNEMAGICK (SWEDEN)
Line-Up: Nicklas Rudolfsson (vocals /
guitar), Fredrik Johnsson (guitar), Peter
Palmdahl (bass), Jonas Blum (drums)

Side project of the ever industrious
Nicklas Rudolfsson of SWORDMASTER,
SACRAMENTUM and DEATHWITCH.
RUNEMAGICK came together in 1990
originally with the 'Fullmoon Sodomy'
demo. Early live gigs found
DISSECTION's Johan Norman and
DECAMERON's Alex Losbäck in the fold.
RUNEMAGICK was put on hold in 1993
as Rudolfsson's time was allotted to other
acts.
In 1997, with a gap in his schedule,
Rudolfsson resurrected RUNEMAGICK
pulling in ex DISSECTION bassist Peter
Palmdahl, guitarist Fredrick Johnsson

and drummer Jonas Blum.
Blum is also skinsman for GRIEF OF
EMERALD featuring on their 'Malformed
Seed' album.

Albums:
THE SUPREME FORCE OF ETERNITY,
Century Media 7935-2 (1998)
At The Horizons End / The Black wall /
When Death Is The Key / For You, My
Death / Curse Of The Dark Rune /
Nocturnal Creation / The Supreme Force
/ Sign Of Eternity (Part II)
ENTER THE REALM OF DEATH,
Century Media (1999)
Hymn Of Darkness / Enter The Realms
Of Death / Longing For Hades / Dwellers
Beyond Obscurity / Abyss Of Desolation
/ Beyond (The Horizon's End) / Dethrone
The Flesh / The Portal Of Doom /
Dreamvoid Serpent / The Call Of Tombs
/ Lightworld Damnation / Dark
Necroshades
RESURRECTION IN BLOOD, Century
Media (2000)
Resurrection Of The Dark Lord / Reborn
In Necromancy / Death Collector / Dark
Dead Earth / Lord Of The Grave / Choir
Of Hades / Resurrection In Blood / Hail
Death / Dominion Of The Necrogods /
Demonstrosity / The Gates Of Hades /
Return Of The Reaper / Celebration Of
Death

SABAOTH (PARAGUAY)
Line-Up: Zethineph (vocals / keyboards), Zethyas (guitar / bass), Lord Norack (drums)

Black Metal band SABAOTH released two demos 'Dentro Del Culto' in 1993 and 1994's 'Southern Twilight' before recording their debut eponymous album.
Three years later SAAOTH issued the sophomore 'The Windjourney'. Drummer Lord Norack opting for the new pseudonym of simply 'The N.'
SABAOTH guitarist Zethyas also operates an electronic theatric side project EYESIGHT.

Albums:
SABAOTH, Stormsouls SO5 (1996)
Martyrium / Labyrinth Of Remembrance / Offering Ritual / Where Everything Is Born (Southern Lands) / Time No Longer Exists / Star Shaped Sky / The Wanderer
THE WINDJOURNEY, Icarus ICARUS 05 (1999)
The Thorn And The Relief / DB (On The Horizon Of My Dreams) / Soul / Fragile / I Have Been Asleep / Wishes / The Rain Never Comes / Just Like Drops In The Sea / Blue Seasons / The Windjourney

SABBAT (JAPAN)
Line-Up: Gezol (vocals / bass), Temis Osmond (guitar), Zorugelion (drums)

Extremely Primitive and raw Black Metal band. In keeping with Japanese stereotypes SABBAT are seemingly armed with an inexhaustible work ethic. However, their industry is tempered by the fact that most of their releases are issued in strictly limited amounts as low as 100. Indeed, SABBAT's first four albums were restricted to a mere 500 copies.
SABBAT formed in 1983 with a line up of frontman Gezol, guitarists Elizaveat and Ozny with drummer Valvin. The band had previously been titled EVIL with singer Toshiya but upon his departure the title SABBAT was adopted. In 1985 Valvin departed to be superseded by Samm (sometimes known as 'Gero'). Ozny left the following year trimming SABBAT down to a trio.
In 1989 SABBAT united for a one off gig and tried out the services of vocalist Possessed Hammer and guitarist Barraveat.
Further ructions witnessed the departure of Samm in 1990 being replaced by Zorugelion. Temis Osmond took the guitarists position in 1991 in time for the 'Bloody Countess' demo sessions.
The 1994 compilation of re-recorded early material 'Black Up Your Soul' included a version of 'Satan's Serenade' by English NWoBHM band QUARTZ. The same year SABBAT contributed a bilingual version of 'Black Fire' and a remix of 'Satanic Rites' to the compilation 'Far East Gate In Inferno'.
1995 saw SABBAT revisiting more old songs for the album 'For Satan And Sacrifice'. They also chose another NWoBHM cover version, this time 'Kiss Of Death' by SATAN. The band proved that they had a sense of humour by re-recording their earlier 'Panic In The Head' retitled and with new lyrics as 'Baby Disco Is Fuck' as part of their contribution to the infamous 'Headbangers Against Disco' EP alongside GEHENNAH, BESTIAL WARLUST and INFERNO.
SABBAT are noted for their run of international flavoured 'Harmageddon' series of singles which comprise songs in different languages including rather novelly a Swahili version of 'Black Fire'! The 'South American Harmageddon' outing was made up exclusively of cover versions of fellow Japanese artists JURASSIC JADE and SACRIFICE.
The 1999 'Live Panica' and 2000's 'Live Revenge' albums were both limited to 100 copies. 2000 also saw SABBAT cutting their take of Italian 80's Thrash act BULLDOZER's 'Whisky Time' on a split tribute single shared with IMPERIAL.

Singles/EPs:
Black Fire / Mion's Hill, Evil 666-01 (1985) ('Sabbat' 7" single)
Satanic Rites / Curdle The Blood / Poison Child, Evil 666-02 (1987) ('Born By Evil Blood' 7" single)
Welcome To Sabbat / Crest Of Satan / Children Of Hell / Darkness And Evil, Evil 666-03 (1988) ('Desecration' 7" single)
Hellfire / Immortality Of The Soul, Evil 666-04 (1989) ('The Devil's Sperm Is Cold' 7" single)
Possessed The Room (Kanashibari) / Sacrifice Of Angel / Crying In Last, Evil 666-05 (1990) ('The Seven Deadly Sins' 7" single)
All Over The Desolate Land / Blacking Metal / Witch's Mill / Rage Of The Mountains, Holycaust SIN001 (1994) ('Sabbatical Devilucifer' EP)
Satanican / Gok Kan Ma, Merciless MREP004 (1997) (7" single) ('European

Harmageddon' 7" single) (German release)
Bleeding From The Ear / Reek Of Cremation (Live) / Jumu, Primitive Art PAR 014 (1997) ('Scandinavian Harmageddon' 7" single) (Swedish release)
Sabbat / Snow Woman, View Beyond VB0018 (1998) ('East European Harmageddon' 7" single) (Czech release)
The Well Of Krath (Kanashibari 6) / Another Collector (Dwelling II), Holycaust S810 (1998) ('American Harmageddon' 7" single) (USA release)
Takaightenshow / Rinnereighshi, Evil J001ER666-HS6 (1998) ('Asian Halmageddon' 7" single) (Chinese release)
Black Fire (Swahili version) / Splatter '98, Mganga UCHAIVI001 (1998) ('African Harmageddon' 7" single) (Tanzanian release)
Satanic Rites (Live) / Disembodys To The Abyss (Live) / Curdle The Blood (Live) / Dead March (Live), Way Of Life WOLR1 (1999) ('Oceanic Harmageddon' 7" single) (Australian release)
Terror Beast / Hello Darkness / Destroy-Witch Hunt / Friday Nightmare, Mega Thrion MTSS1 (1999) ('South American Harmageddon' 7" single) (Brazilian release)
Angel Of Destruction / Satan Bless You / Kamikaze Bomber / Darkness And Evil, View Beyond (1999) ('sabbatical Demonslaught' Czech release)
Incubus Succubus / Possessed Hammer (Tribute To Possessed Hammer) / Whisper Of Demon '99, Sadistic Sodomizer SS-001 (2000) ('Sabbatical Magicurse- Baltic Harmageddon' 7" single) (Latvian release)
Whisky Time, Warlord (2000) (Split 7" single with IMPERIAL)
Envenom Into The Witch's Hole / Ghost Train, Hibernia Productions HB02V (2000) ('Iberian Harmageddon' 7" single) (Portuguese release)
Elixir De Vie (Nouvelle version) / Les Flammes De L'Enfer ('Hellfire' Version Francais), EAL Productions (2000) ('French Harmageddon' 7" single) (French release)

Albums:
ENVENOM, Evil 666-06 (1991)
Bewitch / The 6th Candle / Satan Bless You / Evil Nations / Devil Worship / Reek Of Cremation / Deathtemptation (Kanashibari Part II) / King Of Hell / Eviler / Carcassvoice / Deadmarch / Reminiscent Bells

EVOKE, Evil 666-07 (1992)
Dance Du Sabbat / Envenom Into Witch's Hole / Godz Of Satan / Total Necro… / Torment In The Pentagram / Beyond The River / The Whisper Of Demon / Hellhouse / The Curse Of Pharaoh / Metalucifer And Evilucifer
DISEMBODY, Evil 666-08 (1998)
The Seven Crosses Of Damnation / Bird Of Ill Omen / Metamorphosis / Diabolicalborn / Unknown Massacre / Evoke The Evil / Flower's Red / Reversed Bible / Hungarian Death No. 5 / Ghost In The Mirror
FETISHISM, Evil 666-09 (1994)
Disembody In The Abyss / In Satan We Trust / Satan Is Beautiful / Sausine / Elixir De Vie / Lost In The Grave / Burn The Church / Ghost Train / The Exorcism / Evanescent Quietude
BLACK UP YOUR SOUL, Evil 666-0A (1994)
Welcome To Sabbat / Black Fire / Poison Child / Rage Of The Mountains / Possessed The Room / Darkness And Evil / All Over The Desolate Land / Satan's Serenade / Mion's Hill / Black Fire / Hellfire / Bird Of Ill Omen / Danse Du Sabbat / Envenom Into The Witch's Hole / Carcassvoice / Bewitch
LIVE IN BLOKULA, Evil 666-00B (1995)
The Seven Crosses Of Damnation / Satan Bless You / Possessed The Room- Dead March / Bird Of Ill Omen / Reversed Bible / Evoke The Evil / Evil Nations / Total Necro… / Envenom Into The Witch's Hole / Disembody To The Abyss / Satan Is Beautiful / Hellfire / Ghost In The Mirror / Black Fire
FOR SATAN AND SACRIFICE, Evil 666-0C (1995)
Witch's Mill- Curdle The Blood / Satanic Rites- Crest Of Satan / The Egg Of Dapple / Acid Angel / Immortality Of The Soul / Gideon / Kiss Of Death / Mion's Hill / Sodoomed / Disembody To The Abyss / Unknown Massacre / Whisper Of Demon / Satan Bless You / Remiscent Bells
BLOODY COUNTESS, Holycaust SIN002 (1996) (USA release)
Splatter / Satan's Night / Bloody Countess / Panic In The Head / Madara No Tamago / Poison Child / Children Of Hell / Kanashibari Part 1 / Bloody Countess
THE DWELLING: THE MELODY OF DEATH MASK, Evil 666-10 (1996)
The Swelling- Melody Of The Death Mask
LIVE 666- JAPANESE
HARMAGEDDON, Evil 666-HS1 (1996)
In Satan We Trust / Total Necro… / Beyond The River / Satan Bless You /

Bird Of Ill Omen / Mion's Hill / Black Fire
LIVE CURSE, Heavy Metal Super Star
HMSS CD001 (1999)
Satanic Rites / Curdle The Blood / Crest
Of Satan / Poison Child / Immortality Of
The Soul / Devil's Sperm Is Cold / Black
Fire / Mion's Hill / Intro: Welcome To
Sabbat / Poison Child / Children Of Hell /
Black Fire / Immortality Of The Soul /
Mion's Hill
SABBATICAL RITES, Iron Pegasus IP04
(1999) (German release)
Black Fire / Mion's Hill / Satanic Rites /
Curdle The Blood / Poison Child (Mix) /
Darkness And Evil (Full version) /
Welcome To Sabbat / Crest Of Satan /
Children Of Hell / Immortality Of The
Soul (Mix) / Hell Fire (Mix)
KARISMA, Iron Pegasus IP05 (1999)
(German release)
Karisma / Bowray Samurai (Samurai
Zombies) / Orochie / Harmageddon /
Makutsu (Den Of Hades) / Okiko Ningyo
(Okiku Doll Of The Devil) / Yoochuu
(Japanese Revelation)
LIVE KINDERGARDEN, Heavy Metal
Super Star HMSS CD-02 (1999)
Welcome To Sabbat / Black Fire / Hell
Fire / Possessed The Room / dead
March / Envenom Into The Witch's Hole
/ Beyond The River / Evil Nations /
Satan Bless You
LIVE PANICA, Heavy Metal Super Star
HMSS CD-03 (1999)
Welcome To Sabbat / Panic In The Head
/ Wolfman / Splatter / Bloody Countess
LIVE DEVIL, Heavy Metal Super Star
HMSS CD-03 (2000) (Promotion release)
Sabbat Tribes / Gok Kan Ma / The
Seven Crosses Of Damnation / Satan
Bless You / Evil Nations / Whisper Of
Demon / Evoke The Evil / Panic In The
Head / Mion's Hill / Black Fire /
Darkness And Evil
SATANSWORD, Iron Pegasus IP010
(2000) (German release)
Charisma / Angel Of Destruction / Kiss Of
Lilleth / Death Zone / The Gate / Dracula /
Nekromantik / Jealousy Carnage
LIVE REVENGE, Heavy Metal Super
Star HMSS CD-05 (2000)
Black Fire XX / Splatter / Children Of
Hell / Black Fire / Gok Kan Ma /
Immortality Of The Soul / Kanashibari /
Poison Child / Mion's Hill

SABBAT (UK)
Line-Up: Martin Walkyier (vocals), Andy
Sneap (guitars), Frazer Craske (bass),
Simon Negus (drums)

SABBAT -A Nottingham based 'Satanic

Opera' styled quartet - formed in June
1985 from a previous act titled HYDRA.
The Line up for HYDRA featured vocalist
Martin Walkyier, guitarist Adam Ferman,
bassist Frazer Craske and drummer Mark
Daley. This quartet soon added second
guitarist Andy Sneap, but Ferman and
Daley quit and a name change to
SABBAT was agreed.
SABBAT were noted for their onstage
theatrics (heavily influenced by another
Nottingham act HELL) and the creative
lyrical talents of Walkyier. The band
debuted live at a young offenders institute
in Doncaster before recording their
'Fragments Of A Faith Forgotten' demo
that gained the band much critical praise
and ultimately led to a deal with
Germany's Noise Records. Once offered
the deal SABBAT had to wait for guitarist
Andy Sneap to turn 18 before they could
sign the contracts!
The first commercially available record
was a flexi disc for 'White Dwarf'
magazine entitled 'Blood For The
Bloodgod', produced by ex HELL and
PARALEX guitarist Kev Bower.
SABBAT's debut album 'History Of A
Time To Come' launched the band onto
the forefront of the British Thrash Metal
scene with Walkyier's distinct pagan
themes interwoven into it's impressive
epic songs. The album went on to sell in
excess of 60'000 copies.
SABBAT played both Dynamo and
Eindhoven festivals in 1988 as part of a
very successful European tour. Shortly
after, SABBAT added second guitarist
Simon Jones - previously known as Jack
Hammer from HOLOSADE- to replace
touring guitarist Richard Scott (on loan
from NO EXCUSE), who accompanied
the band on the European tour.
The group's second album,
'Dreamweaver', produced by Roy
Rowland, was an opportunity for Walkyier
to really let his imagination fly as SABBAT
launched the crucial release in the form of
a concept based on the Brian Bates book
'The Way Of Wyrd'. SABBAT
subsequently toured Europe heavily,
including support dates to MANOWAR in
Spain.
Surprisingly, Walkyier and Craske quit
after internal disputes and the vocalist
went on to form the highly successful and
industrious Folk Rock act SKYCLAD,
whilst Craske opted out of the music
business returning to a printing career.
American vocalist Richie Desmond (who
had previously been guitarist in CELTIC
FROST for a very short period) joined

SABBAT in 1990. The band's line up at this point comprised of Sneap, Desmond, guitarist Neil Watson and bassist Wayne Banks. However, both record company and fans were not impressed with the resulting album 'Mourning Has Broken' which sorely lacked Walkyier's more innovative input.

Noise dropped the band and, after two disastrous British dates, Sneap pulled the plug on the tour and the band. Negus joined skinheads SKREWDRIVER then local act GLORY BOYS. Sneap and Banks went on to form GODSEND. As GODSEND dissolved after a batch of demos Sneap began carving out a niche for himself in the production role making quite a name for himself with some high profile bands such as STUCK MOJO and MACHINE HEAD.

In 1995 there were rumours of a SABBAT reformation between Walkyier and Sneap, but this came to nothing.

SABBAT reared it's head again though in 2000 when Britain's leading Black Metal exponents CRADLE OF FILTH covered 'For Those Who Died' with Walkyier providing guest vocals.

As 2001 dawned an announcement was made that a band entitled RETURN TO THE SABBAT was planned for a one off live show comprising of Walkyier, Craske, Jones in alliance with former TALION guitarist Pete Wadeson and SKYCLAD and UNDERGROOVE drummer Jay Graham.

Singles/EPs:
Blood For The Blood God, Games Workshop (1988)
Wildfire / The Best Of Enemies (Wulf's Tale), Noise (1989) (Flexidisc)

Albums:
HISTORY OF A TIME TO COME, Noise N0098 (1988)
Intro / A Cautionary Tale / Hosanna In Excelsis / Behind The Crooked Cross / Horned Is The Hunter / I For An Eye / For Those Who Died / A Dead Man's Robe / The Church Bizarre
DREAMWEAVER – REFLECTIONS OF OUR YESTERDAYS, Noise N0132 (1989)
The Beginning Of The End / The Clerical Conspiracy / Advent Of Insanity / Do Dark Horses Dream Of Nightmares? / The Best Of Enemies / How Have The Mighty Fallen? / Wildfire / Mythistory / Happy Never After
MOURNING HAS BROKEN, Noise

N0162-2 (1991)
The Demise Of History / Theological Void / Paint The World Black / Dumbstruck / The Voice Of Time / Dreamscape / Without A Trace / Mourning Has Broken

SACRAMENTAL SACHEM
(HOLLAND)
Line-Up: Maril (vocals), Michiel (guitar), Ronald (bass), Mario (keyboards), Luciano (drums)

A Melodic Black / Doom Metal act.

Singles/EPs:
The Dolcinites Were Wrong, (1995)

Albums:
RECRUCIFICTION, Lowland (1995)
Pure And Simple / Feel My Hate / Bloody Cages / Recrucifiction / Choice Is Yours / Mind Vs. Mind / Selfish World

SACRAMENTUM (SWEDEN)
Line-Up: Nissé Karlen (vocals), Anders Brolycke (guitar), Johan Norrrman (guitar), Freddy Andersson (bass), Niklas Rudolfsson (drums)

A Death Metal five-piece, SACRAMENTUM's vocalist Nissé Karlen was previously with RUNEMAGICK.
Karlen formed the group as TUMULUS and recorded a demo in 1993 entitled 'Sedes Imporium'. In 1994 the group released their self-produced promo EP, 'Finis Maloum' later released by Adipocere Records.
However, after the departure of bassist Freddy Andersson, Nissé doubled up on bass whilst former DECAMORAN and DISSECTION guitarist Johan Norrman also played in the group for a period before he quit and was replaced by Anders Brolycke.
The SACRAMENTUM album, 'Far Away From The Sun', was produced by EDGE OF SANITY mainman Dan Swanö.

Singles/EPs:
Moonfog / Travel With The Northern Winds / Devide Et Impera / Pagan Fire / Finis Malorum (Outro), Northern Production EVIL001 (1994) ('Finis Malorum' EP)

Albums:
FAR WAY FROM THE SUN, Adipocere AR034 (1994)
Fog's Kiss / Far Away From The Sun / Blood Shall Be Spilled / When Night

Surrounds Me / Cries From A Restless Soul / Obsolete Tears / Beyond All Horizons / The Vision And The Voice / Outro- Darkness Falls For Me / Far Away From The Sun (Part Two)
THE COMING OF CHAOS, Century Media 77178-2 (1997)
Dreamdeath / … As Obsidian / Awaken Chaos / Burning Lust / Abyss Of Time / Portal Of Blood / Black Destiny / To The Sound Of Storms / The Coming Of Chaos
THY BLACK DESTINY, (199-)
Iron Winds / The Manifestation / Shun The Light / Demoneaeon / Overlord / Death Obsession / Spiritual Winter / Raptures Paradise- Peccata Mortali / Weave Of Illusion / Thy Black Destiny

SACRED SIN (PORTUGAL)
Line-Up: José Costa (vocals / bass), Rui Dias (guitar), Antonio Pica (guitar), Carlos A.C. (keyboards), Eduardo 'Dico' (drums)

Death Metallers SACRED SIN were created by erstwhile members of NECROPHILIAC, MASSACRE and SILENT SCREAM. The band toured Portugal in summer of 1993 promoting their 7" EP 'The Shades Behind'. The full length album 'Darkside' led to festival appearances. Other shows would include supports to MANOWAR, TIAMAT, NAPALM DEATH and SENTENCED.
A second pressing of 'Darkside' included a live EP and SACRED SIN's work ethic paid off when they inked a deal with major label BMG.
The 'Eye M God' album was to provide SACRED SIN, now with ex DISAFFECTED man Quim Aries on drums, with a European tour support to MALEVOLENT CREATION.

Singles/EPs:
The Shades Behind, Slime (1992)

Albums:
DARKSIDE, Musica Alternavata MA001 (1993)
Darkside / In The Veins Of Rotting Flesh / Ode To My Crucifying Lord / Deliverance / The Chapel Of The Lost Souls / Requiem...For Mankind / Gravestone Without Name / Suffocate In Torment / Life - A Process Revealed / Terminal Collapse / A Monastery In Darkness / The Shades Behind
EYE M GOD, Dinamite DT 95012 (1995)
Intro / Evocation Of The Depraved / Inductive Compulsion / Eye M God / Death-Bearing Machine / The Nighthag

(Nocturnal Queen) / One With God / Guilt Has No Past / A Human Jigsaw / Link To Nothingness / Dead Mind Breed / The Endless Path Of Hecate
ANGUISH… I HARVEST, (199-)
Ghoul Plagued Darkness / Thirteenth Moon / Lead Of Insects / Firethrone / Profane / (Hope) Still Searching / Aghast / Astral / Feathers Black / The Shining Trapezoid

SACRILEGE (SWEDEN)
Line-Up: Michael Andersson (vocals), Daniel Svensson (vocals / drums), Daniel Dinsdale (guitar), Richard Bergholtz (guitar), Daniel Kvist (bass)

SACRILEGE vocalist Michael Andersson would depart prior to recording of the second album 'The Fifth Season' necessitating drummer Daniel Svensson to take the role.
Svensson joined premier Death Metal band IN FLAMES as drummer during 1998.

Albums:
LOST IN THE BEAUTY YOU SLAY, Black Sun (1996)
Frozen Thoughts / Beyond The Gates Of Pain / Without Delight / Crying Statues Of Paleness And Ice / Fettered In Shackles Of Light / Lost In The Beauty You Slay / Silence In A Beloved Scream / Torment Of Life / Initio Silentium Noctis
THE FIFTH SEASON, Black Sun BS013 (1997)
Summon The Masses And Walk Through Fire / Sweet Moment Of Triumph / Nine Eyes Of Twilight / Feed The Cold / Fifth Season / Moaning Idiot Heart / Dim With Shame / Seduction Nocturne / In Winter Enticed / Sorc

SACRILEGIUM (POLAND)
Line-Up: Nantur (vocals / bass), Suclagus (guitar), Thoarinus (drums)

A well known band back home in Poland, Black Metallers SACRILEGIUM have yet to breakthrough on the International market. The band bowed in with a 1994 demo 'Sleeptime'.
After their debut album 'Wicher' (translated as 'Stormwind') SACRILEGIUM recorded a split album with NORTH for Dutch label Black Arts.

Singles/EPs:
Sleeptime EP, (1996)

WICHER, Last Epitaph LEP 005 (1996)
W Dolinie Rwacych Potokow / Spiew
Krukow Czarnych Cieni / Wilczy Skowyt
/ W Rogatym Majestacie Snu /
Zagubiona Ciemnosc / Wicher Falami
Ognia / Szept Nocy

SADISTIC NOISE (GREECE)

Singles/EPs:
The Crush Of Heaven, Molon Lave
(1995)

Albums:
A DECADE IN THE GRAVE, Seven
(1999)

SADISTIK EXEKUTION
(AUSTRALIA)
Line-Up: Rok (vocals), Rev. Kriss Hades
(guitar), Dave Slave (bass), Sloth (drums)

SADISTIK EXEKUTION toured Europe
on a package bill with ABSU and
IMPALED NAZARENE in 1995.
Former SADISTIK EXEKUTION drummer
Mechanic joined the mysterious
'Macedonian' act BALTAK. Guitarist Rev.
Kriss Hades also performs with NAZXUL.
Vocalist Rok has issued two albums by
his eponymous solo band ROK namely
'This Is Satanik' and 'Burning Metal'.

Singles/EPs:
Proxima Centauri / Demon With Wings,
Osmose Productions OP 037 (199-)

Albums:
THE MAGUS, (1988)
WE ARE DEATH... FUCK YOU, Osmose
(1994)
Suspiral / Burnt Offering / Internal Klok /
Mathematikus / Electrokution / Lest We
Forget / Evoke War Vomit / Astral Abortis
/ Ipsissimus / Hades Valley
KAOS, Osmose Productions (1999)
Ultra Maximizer Of Agony / Dejekta
Infinitus / Volkanik Violence / Burning
Blasphemy / Demon With Wings II /
Voltage By Sadism / Horror Inferno /
Sadistik Electrokution / The Return Of
Proxima / Korpse On The Grave /
Fukked Up And Burned

SAD LEGEND (KOREA)
Line-Up: Naamah (vocals / drums),
Young-Woo Kwon (guitar), Eun-Hyung
Kang (guitar), Hang-Hyun Lee (bass)

Albums:
SAD LEGEND, Hammerheart (1998)
Han / Dawn Of Despair / Nocturnal Cries
Of Agony / Utter Emptiness On The
Dusk fallen Lake / Reak Of The Soulless
/ Reincarnation / A Funeral In Solitude

SADNESS (SWITZERLAND)
Line-Up: Steff (vocals / guitar), Chiva
(guitar / keyboards), Erik (bass), Gradel
(drums)

Following the first SADNESS demo,
merely titled 'Y', in 1990 bassist Erik
departed to join ALASTIS. His place was
taken by Andy and a further demo,
'Eodipus', was released.
SADNESS signed to the Polish label
Mystic Records for the 'Evangelion'
album and toured Poland alongside
BEHEMOTH, ASGARD, COLD PASSION
and LIMBONIC ART.
'Danteferno' was produced by former
CELTIC FROST bass player Martin E.
Ain.
In 1997 Chiva debuted his side project
act CHIVA with the 'Oracle Morte' album.

Albums:
AMES DE MABRE, Witchhunt WIHU
9313 (1994)
Ames De Marbre / Lueurs / Tristessa /
Opal Vault / Tears Of Sorrow / Red
Script / Antofagasta
DANTE FERNO, Godhead GOD020
(1996)
Danteferno / The Mark Of The Eldest Son
/ Tribal / Delia / Below The Shadows /
Shaman / Aphrodites Thorns / Talisman
EVANGELION, Mystic Radio 99 (1998)
Mr. Faust / Heretic / Dias De Las
Muertes / Nosfera / Tears Of Sorrow
(remastered) / Danteferno (remastered) /
Red Script (demo version 1990)

SALACIOUS GODS (HOLLAND)
Line-Up: Staekelhorn (vocals), Strid
(guitar), Lezelzweard (guitar),
Nevhelnoasle (bass), Gra Blackswamp
(keyboards), Draeleor (drums)

SALACIOUS GODS started life billed as
PROFANATICA. Switched title to
SALACIOUS GODS following the 1999
demo 'The Slumbering Silence'.
Guitarist Strid, who also involves himself
with OBSCURA NEBULA, LUGUBRE
and STRID, left in October 2000.

Albums:
ASKENGRIS, Cold Blood Industries

(1999)
My Effigy, Unfurled And Withered / Blazeheart / Firestorm / The Draft That Scourges The Innocence Of Ages / Everlasting Winter Breeze / Mellow Dance Within The Wicked Circle / Salacious Gods / Askengris

SALEM (ISRAEL)
Line-Up: Ze'eb Tanaboim (vocals), Lior Mizrachi (guitar), Giora Hirsch (guitar), Michael Goldstein (bass), Amir Neubach (drums)

An Israeli Black Doom Metal band that trace their history back to the very roots of Black Metal in the mid 80's. Frontman Ze'eb Tanaboim was in correspondence with the late MAYHEM mentor Euronymous in regards to releasing a SALEM record on his Deathlike Silence label. Tanaboim was also in communication with Euronymous's arch rival and eventual murderer Varg Vikernes of BURZUM although on less salubrious terms. Allegedly Vikernes posted a nail bomb to Tanaboim after the SALEM man had offered to shoot him for derogatory comments against Jews.
The corpse paint bedecked SALEM, with new drummer Amir Neubach, emerged once more with the 1992 demo 'Millions Slaughtered'. Other founder members included Tanaboim, guitarists Lior Mizrach and Giora Hirsch with bass player Mikael Goldstein. These tapes were included as part of the band's first release for Morbid Records 'Creating Our Sins'.
SALEM's third release, the Colin Richardson produced 'Moment Of Silence', saw a drift into Gothic territory and the loss of Hirsch and Neubach. The album included an ambitious version of PINK FLOYD's 'Set The Controls For The Heart Of The Sun'. New drummer was Niv Nakov

Albums:
CREATING OUR SINS, Morbid (1994)
Masquerade In Claustrophobia / Creating Our Sins / Old Wounds / Millions Slaughtered / Children Don't Fight / Execution / Necromancy / Fields Of Death / Voices From Hell / Fucking Maniac / Old Wounds / Emotional Demands / Slow Death / Children Don't Fight / Fields Of Death
KADDISH, Morbid (1995)
The Fading / Above The Ground / Eyes To Match A Sul / Kaddish / Fear Of The

Future / Dying Embers / Desert Prayer / The Edge Of The Void / Ha'ayana Bo'eret / The One That No One Knows
MOMENT IN SILENCE, BNE (1998)
Moment In Silence / Winter's Tear / Hour Glass / Flames / Set The Controls For The Heart Of The Sun / In Another Dimension / The Worst To Come / An Unwanted Guest / Symbiosis / Eyes To Match A Soul / Who Will Comfort Me Now?

SALEM ORCHID (UK)
Line-Up: Jason Mendonca (vocals / guitar), Stephen Wood (guitar), David Gray (bass), Dan Temple (drums)

Singles/EPs:
Sempiternal Suffering / The Nirvana Of Agony, Salem Orchid (1992)

SAMAEL (SWITZERLAND)
Line-up: Vorphalack (Vocals / guitar), Masmisiem (bass), Xytraguptor (drums)

Proud to be recognized as one of the gloomiest bands in Europe. Over a series of finely crafted albums SAMAEL have built up an enviable reputation for quality Metal with a unique touch. SAMAEL heralded their arrival with the 1987 demo recording titled 'Into The Infernal Storm Of Evil'.
Swiss act SAMAEL's 1989's 'Medieval Prophecy' mini album featured a cover of HELLHAMMER's 'The Third Of The Storm'. SAMAEL's next release in 1990 was the demo tape 'From Dark To Black'. The 'Rebellion' mini album boasted a cover of ALICE COOPER's 'I Love The Dead'.
The group added keyboard player Rudolphe H. for live dates in 1995 with SENTENCED and for the recording of 1996's ' Passage' all drum parts were programmed and Xytraguptor (later simply 'Xytra') assumed a new role as keyboard player. A second guitarist, Khaos from French Death Metallers GORGON, was also brought in for recording and live dates.
SAMAEL's 'Worship Him' album went on to sell over 10,000 copies in Europe. The follow up 'Blood Ritual' was produced by GRIP INC.'s Waldemar Sorychta.
For 'Ceremony Of Opposites', produced by Sorychta once again, SAMAEL added keyboard player Rudolphe H.
SAMAEL's 1996 album 'Passage' would be re-released two years later with ambient classical remixes of all tracks by

314

SAMAEL
Photo : Martin Wickler

Xystra. 199's 'Eternal' was widely acknowledged to be a classic of the genre.

<u>Singles/EPs:</u>
Medieval Prophecy, Necrosound (1989)
Rebellion / After The Sepulture / Into The Pentagram / I Love The Dead / Static Journey, Century Media 77099-2 (1995) ('Rebellion' EP)

<u>Albums:</u>
WORSHIP HIM, Osmose Productions OPCD001 (1991)
Sleep Of Death / Worship Him / Knowledge Of the Ancient Kingdom / Morbid Metal / Rite Of Cthulhu / The Black Face / Into The Pentagram / Messengers Of The Light / Last Benediction / The Dark
BLOOD RITUAL, Century Media CM97372 (1992)
Epilogue / Beyond The Nothingness / Poison Infiltration / After The Sepulture / Macabre Operetta / Blood Ritual / Since The Creation / With The Gleam Of Torches / Total Consecration / Bestial Devotion / Until The Chaos
SAMAEL 1987-1992, Century Media 77085-2 (1993)
Epilogue/ Beyond The Nothingness / Poison Infiltration / After The Sepulture / Macabre Operetta / Blood Ritual / Since

The Creation / With The Gleam Of Torches / Total Consecration / Bestial Devotion / ...Until The Chaos / Sleep Of Death / Worship Him / Knowledge Of The Ancient Kingdom / Morbid Metal / Rite Of Cthulhu / The Black Face / Into The Pentagram / Messengers Of The Light / Last Benediction / The Dark
CEREMONY OF OPPOSITES, Century Media CD 77064-2 (1994)
Black Trip / Celebration Of The Fourth / Son Of Earth / 'Til We Meet Again / Mask Of The Red Death / Baphomet's Throne / Flagellation / Crown / To Our Martyrs / Ceremony Of Opposites
PASSAGE, Century Media 77127-2 (1996)
Rain / Shining Kingdom / Angel's Decay / My Saviour / Jupiterian Vibe / The Ones / Liquid Souls / Moonskin / Born Under Saturn / Chosen Race / A Man In Your Head
EXODUS, Century Media 77210-2 (1998)
Exodus / Tribes Of Cain / Son Of Earth / Winter Solstice / Ceremony Of The Opposites / From Malkuth To Kether
PASSAGE/XYSTRA, Century Media (1998)
Rain / Shining Kingdom / Angel's Decay / My Saviour / Jupiterian Vibe / The Ones / Liquid Souls / Moonskin / Born Under Saturn / Chosen Race / A Man In Your Head / Regen / Glanzednes Königreich / Des Engels Untergang / Jupiterianische Schwingungen / Die Volter Kamen / Der Stamm Kains / Mondhaut / Mein Retter / Wintersonnenwerde / Ein Mensch Im Kopf
ETERNAL, Century Media (1999)
Year Zero / Ailleurs / Together / Ways / The Cross / Us / Supra Karma / I / Nautilus And Zeppelin / Infra Galaxia / Berg / Radiant Star

SAMAIN (AUSTRALIA)
Line-Up: Warren Hatley (vocals / bass), Nick Bell (guitar), Liam Stone (drums)

<u>Albums:</u>
INDOMITUS, Nightmare (1996)
Heralding The High King / Mac An Earraich Uaire Ri Caige / Stormclouds Gather / Lament / Fianna / Tir Na Noc / The Red Field / A Pagan Funeral / Seeking The Way / Beyond The Waves

SANCTIFICA (SWEDEN)
Line-Up: Hubertus Liljegren (vocals/ guitar), Henrik (guitar), Jonathon (bass), Aron (keyboards), Daniel (drums)

A Christian Black Metal band? Fronted by Hubertus Liljegren, brother of Christian Liljegren of noted Christian Hard Rock act NARNIA, SANCTIFICA include OBSECRATION man Jonathon on bass guitar.

The band's debut demo 'In The Black Midwinter' was produced by NARNIA's Carl Johan Grimmack whilst NARNIA's keyboard player Martin Olaesson would deputize for SANCTIFICARA for a period.

Albums:
SPIRIT OF DUTY, Little Rose Productions (2000)
Riket / The Dark Desires / Released For From Pain / Spirit Of Purity / Alhårskaren / Landscape / The Dark Embrace Of Night / The Wanderer

SANCTUM (UK)
Line-Up: Brad Cranwell (vocals / keyboards), Matt Howe (guitar), Cherry (guitar), Bradless (bass), Shirty (drums)

An English Black Metal band.

Albums:
RAPED OF YOUR RELIGION, Lethal LRC 004 (1993)
Parasite / Inner Depraving / Overcasting The Truth / Emission / Dimension Of The Mind / Our Violent World / Raped Of Your Religion / To Wither Away

SARCOPHAGUS (De Kalb, IL, USA)
Line-Up: Andrew Jay Harris (vocals / guitar), Daniel Guenther (guitar), Marcus Matthew Kolar (bass), Duane Timlin (drums)

Blasphemous Death Metal band SARCOPHAGUS are in fact yet another outlet for the creative forces of Andrew Jay Harris, more commonly known as Akhenaten of JUDAS ISCARIOT and WELTMACHT alongside Lord Imperial of KRIEG. Harris also owns Breath Of Night Records and has issued the one off JESUS FUCKING CHRIST single 'Unalive At Golgotha'.

Debuted with the demo 'Cursed Are The Dead' in 1991. At this point the band comprised of Harris, bassist Marcus Matthew Kolar, vocalist Frank Drago, guitarist Michael Matejka and drummer Paul Bruneau. A stream of demos followed including 'Sarcophagus' in 1993 (bootlegged on a 7" single the following year), 'Der Ubermensch' and 'Apathy' in 1995. By 1994 though SARCOPHAGUS

was down to a duo of Harris and Kolar.
A projected album on the Interment label to be titled 'Thirteen Songs' was announced but never released. 1997 saw SARCOPHAGUS up to full band strength with the enlistment of guitarist Daniel Guenther and FOREST OF IMPALED drummer Duane Timlin.

One of Harris' side concerns WELTMACHT also includes Timlin under the pseudonym of Cryptic Winter.

Akhenaten would relocate to Germany for later JUDAS ISCARIOT releases and would also become live bass player for the infamous Czech Black Metal act MANIAC BUTCHER.

Albums:
DEADNOISE, (1994)
Banned From The Altar / From The Cross / Masquerade / Mental Atrocities / Black / The Absence
FOR WE... WHO ARE CONSUMED BY DARKNESS, Pulverizer PRCD001 (1996)
Godless / Our Black Autumn / Die Totenmaske / Fuck Pig / Agony's Tale / Wrath / Damned Below Judas / Si Piangiamo Or Dunque Uniti / Breath Of Night
SARCOPHAGUS- DEADNOISE-UBERMENSCH, Pulverizer (1996)
Sarcophagus / Human Machines / Morbid Dreams / Banned From The Altar / From The Cross / Masquerade / Mental Atrocities / Black / The Absence / Die Totenmaske / Fuck Pig / Si Piangiamo Or Dunque Uniti / Ubermensch
REQUIEM TO THE DEATH OF PASSION, Nightfall (1997)
From The Ruin Of Paradise / The Dark Lord Of Impurity / Requiem To The Death Of Passion / In Silent Death / Of Fire Surrounding All The Heavens / Bastard Sons Of Ignorance / Infernal Supremacy / The Pagan Battlefield

SARGATANAS (MEXICO)
Line-Up: Anathema's God (vocals / bass), Lord Sargatanas (guitar), Astaroth (guitar), Lord Baalberith (drums)

SARGATANAS date back as far as 1986. Originally a trio of guitarist Lord Sragatanas, vocalist / bassist Jorge and drummer Miguel the band would relocate from Monterey Nuero Leon to Guadalajara totally revamping the line up. Sargatanas rebuilt the band with Manuel H on vocals and bass and Urantial's Emperor on drums. However,

Anathema's God took the four string position in time for initial recordings of 'The Enlightenment' in 1996. Astaroth would be added on second guitar. 'The Enlightenment' includes a spirited cover of POSSESSED's 'Satan's Curse'. December of 1999 witnessed Lord Baalberith assuming the drummer's role.

Albums:
SARGATANAS, Wild Rags (1995)
THE ENLIGHTENMENT, Conquistador CORTÉS003CD (1999)
Eternal Darkness / Fear And Suffering / The Proclamation / Diatribe Of The Cult / Ritual Of The Advent / Satan's Curse / Satanist / Veneration Of The Black Mark At The Dark Ancestral Forest / Doom Of Fire / Sargatanas / Blessed Are The Sons Of The Black Flame / The Enlightenment

SARNATH (FINLAND)
Line-Up: Peter Taranish (vocals / bass), Antti Kamppuri (guitar), Mika Matveinen (guitar), Juha Hirvonen (drums)

The 'Cosmopolitan' EP from Finns SARNATH introduced this Black Metal troupe in 1993 before a split album with NOMICON appeared and a full blown debut in 1996 entitled 'Overshine'.
The 1996 line up of SARNATH included vocalist Lasse Pykko and bassist Antti Hekkila.

Singles/EPs:
The Divine Path / Wings Of Trinity, Regress, (1995) ('Cosmopolitan' EP)

Albums:
NORTHODOX, Shiver SHR011 (199-) (Split LP with NOMICON)
In The Flames Of Midsummer Pyre / Silence Of The Lambs / Covenant / Walking Through Her Shrine / The Fantome Reign (Kali Yuga) / Marian Luostari
OVERSHINE, Shiver (1996)
Streams Of Belief / Fallen Pretender / Annuiation / Mountains Of Norway / Forever Father / Northodox / The War Was Built To Play / Tower Of Rising Moons / Bow Again
LIFE, LIES, Shiver (1999)

SATANARCHY (SWEDEN)

SATANARCHY, founded in late 2000, comprise an all star Black Metal cast from GEHENNAH, RISE AND SHINE and FURBOWL.

Albums:
DISGRACEFUL WORLD, Primitive Art (2001)

SATANIC SLAUGHTER (SWEDEN)
Line-Up: Toxine (vocals), Ztephan Dark (vocals / guitar), Patrick Jensen (guitar), Richard (guitar), Goat (bass), Mique (drums)

SATANIC SLAUGHTER are one of Scandinavia's older Black Metal acts having formed in 1985. Previous to this date the band went under the politically incorrect name of EVIL CUNT. Of the original line up only guitarist Ztephan Dark remains. Original bassist Goat became a pyromaniac and now resides in a mental hospital!
SATANIC SLAUGHTER released their demo 'One Night In Hell' during 1988. Vocalist Moto was replaced by Andy. In December of the following year the band was put on ice as Dark was imprisoned, convicted of assault. The man would later join MORBIDITY, CRUZIFIED ANGEL and MORGUE.
The band got back together in 1992 with members of SÉANCE, including vocalist Toxine, drummer Mique and guitarists Patrick Jensen and Richard were involved.
However, in 1997 SATANIC SLAUGHTER collapsed yet again, this time due to time honoured musical differences. Dark resolved himself to pick up the pieces with all the other ex members creating the high profile act WITCHERY. Jensen also became a member of THE HAUNTED.
In 1999 SATANIC SLAUGHTER brought in former TRIUMPHATOR drummer Martin Axenroth to replace previous incumbent Robert Eng. The 2000 line up comprised of Dark, Axenroth, guitarist Christian Ljungberg, vocalist Andreas Deblén and bassist Filip Carlsson.

Albums:
SATANIC SLAUGHTER, Necropolis NR004 (1995)
Immortal Death / Forever I Burn / Dark Ritual / Into The Catacombs / Breath Of The Serpent That Rules The Cold World / On Black Wings / Nocturnal Presence / Legion Of Hades / Divine Exorcism / I'll Await My Lord / Embraced By Darkness / Domine Lucipheros
LAND OF THE UNHOLY SOULS, Necropolis NR014 (1997)

Intro / Hatred Of God / Servant Of Satan / Satanic Queen / Demons Feast / Forever I Burn / Legion Of Hades / Breath Of The Serpent That Rules The Cold World / Immortal Death / Land Of The Unholy Souls / One Night In Hell / Dark Ritual / Forever I Burn
AFTERLIFE KINGDOM, Loud n' Proud LNP012 (2000)
The Arrival- Afterlife Kingdom / Nocturnal Crimson Nightmare / When Darkness Prevails / Divine Repulsion / Through The Dark Profound / Autumn / Ad Noctum / Flag Of Hate

SATAN'S HOST (USA)
Line-Up: Leviathan Thisiren (vocals), Stan Patrick Evil (guitar), Belial (bass), D. Lucifer Stele (drums)

SATAN'S HOST vocalist Leviathan Thisiren is none other than Harry Conklin who, under the new nom de guerre of 'The Tyrant' went on to front Heavy Metal band JAGPANZER and later (under his real name) trad rockers RIOT for just one gig.

Albums:
METAL FROM HELL, Web (1986)
Prelude: Flaming Host / Black Stele / In The Veil / Metal From Hell / King Of Terror / Strongest Of The Night / Standing At Death's Door / Hell Fire / Souls In Exile

SATARIEL (SWEDEN)
Line-Up: Par Johansson (vocals), Mikael Grankvist (guitar), Magnus Alakangas (guitar / keyboards), Mikael Degerman (bass), Robert Sundelin (drums)

SATARIEL was a 1993 union of erstwhile members of defunct outfits BEHEADED and DAWN OF DARKNESS namely vocalist Pär Johansson on vocals, guitarist Maguns Alakangas and bassist Mikael Degerman. A later recruit was guitarist Mikael Grankvist for the debut demo 'This Heavens Fall'. SATARIEL added Mats Ömalm after this recording but his exit followed swiftly after.
1995 also saw the departure of Grankvist. Further changes apparent on the second session 'Hellfuck' included the addition of guitarist Fredrik Andersson and drummer Andreas Nilzon. By 1996 Nilzon was out of the picture and Robert Sundelin took the drum stool position. However, SATARIEL was put on ice for a lengthy period when both Sundelin and Degerman undertook their military service.
When SATARIEL reformed Grankvist too was back in the fold for the debut album 'Lady Lust Lilith' on Pulverized Records. SATARIEL guitarist Mikael Grankvist also operates in THE MOANING. Drummer Robert Sundelin is a member of NECROMONICON.
Between 1993 and 1995 Johansson also put time into his side project BELSEMAR releasing the demos 'De Svarta Gudarnas Sömn' and 'Epistles Of Pain'.
Not to be confused with the theatric Russian band of the same name that issued the album 'The Queen Of The Elves Land'.

Albums:
LADY LUST LILITH, Pulverized (1998)
Devils Dozen XIII / The Well Of The Artist / Four Moons Till Rising / The Span Of The Shadows / Lady Lust Lilith / The Great Necropolis- Baphomet Erected / Behind What's I / They're Sheep To Be Slain / A Vision Of An Ending / Greeting Immortality
PHOBOS AND DAIMOS, Hammerheart (2001)

SATHANAS (USA)
Line-Up: Paul Tucker (vocals / guitar), Bill Davidson (bass), Jim Baker (drums)

SATHANAS date back to 1988 and the 'Ripping Evil' demo session. However, SATAHANAS folded various as members joined ACHERON whilst Tucker founded BATHYM for the 1990 'Into Darkness' demo and the 7" single 'Demonic Force'. By 1994 Tucker was ready to resurrect SATHANAS pulling in bassist Bill Davidson and drummer Jim Baker. A series of false starts with various labels going bankrupt eventually led to Alex Kurtagic's Conquistador label for release of the 'Armies Of Charon' album.
A split album 'Destroying All Hopes' was shared with CHRISTIAN CARRION.
Baker would decamp leaving Davidson to put down drums on a track included on a free CD given away with 'Pit' magazine.

Singles/EPs:
Ripping Evil, Reaper (1994)

Albums:
BLACK EARTH, Metal Merchant (1997)
ARMIES OF CHARON, Conquistador CORTÉS002CD (1999)
Intro / Armies Of Charon / Servant To The Ungod / Exorcism / Palace Of Belial

/ Resurrect / Before The Throne / Into Darkness / Devoured By The Beast / Prophecy Unfolds / Writhe In Sin

SATURNUS (DENMARK)
Line-Up: A.G. Jensen (vocals), Kim Larsen (guitar), Brian Hansen (bass), Anders Ro Nielsen (keyboards), Jesper Saltoft (drums / keyboards)

A Danish Doom / Death band initially titled ASSESINO. The band can trace it's history back to the 1991 union of vocalist Thomas A.G. Jenson, guitarists Kim Sindahl and Christian Brenner, bass player Brian Hansen and drummer Pouli Choir as ASSESINO.
The band actually split but reunited with fresh recruit Jesper Saltoft. A period of flux ensued with Sindahl decamping and guitarist Michael Andersen and keyboard player Anders Ro Nielsen being drafted. At this stage the unit opted for the new title of SATURNUS.
1994 saw the inclusion of guitarist Kim Larsen and the following year the exit of Andersen. A support gig to Britain's doom mongers MY DYING BRIDE made a weighty impression on the band who acknowledge their shift in style to a gloomy, melancholic style from this juncture.
SATURNUS cut their debut album 'Paradise Belongs To You' for the Euphonious label which included new drummer Morten Skrubbeltrang. Promoting the album SATURNUS ambitiously employed an 8 piece choir for live gigs.
After a mini album 'For The Loveless Lonely Nights' a switch in drummers had Peter Poulsen joining in time for the Flemming Rasmussen produced 'Martyre' album.
SATURNUS suffered further internal strife in 1999 with new enlistees being drummer Morten Plenge, guitarist Tais Pedersen and bassist Peter Heede.
Both Larsen and Nielsen sessioned on BLAZING ETERNITY's debut album of 2000.

Albums:
PARADISE BELONGS TO YOU, Euphonious PHONI 005 (1996)
Paradise Belongs To You / Christ Goodbye / As We Dance The Path Of Fire And Solace / Pilgrimage Of Sorrow / The Fall Of Nakkiel (Nakkiel Has Fallen) / Astral Dawn / I Love Thee / The Underworld / Lament For This Treacherous World
FOR THE LOVELESS LONELY NIGHT, Euphonious (1998)
Starres / For Your Demons / Thou Art Free / Christ Goodbye (Live) / Rise Of Nakkiel (Live) / Consecration
MARTYRE, Euphonious (2000)
Inflame Thy Heart / Empty Handed / Noir / A Poem (Written In Moonlight) / Softly On The Path You Fade / Thou Art Free / Drown My Sorrow / Lost My War / Loss (In Memorium) / Thus My Heart Weepeth For Thee / In Your Shining Eyes

SATYRICON (NORWAY)
Line-Up: Satyr (vocals), Haarvard (guitar) Vegard (bass), Carl Michael Eide (drums)

Arch self proclaimed Antichrists SATYRICON, founded by drummer Carl Michael Eide in September 1991, ply Black Metal with some unique twists.
At the time of forming frontman Satyr was a mere fifteen years old and the group debuted in 1993 with a self titled demo tape. SATYRICON's subsequent 1994 demo 'The Forest Is My Throne' was later issued as a split CD with ENSLAVED.
Following the second demo guitarist Haarvard departed and Satyr would take over his role in the band and later issued a solo album, 'Fjelltronen', under the project title of WONGRAVEN.
1994's 'The Shadow Throne' album featured Samoth from EMPEROR on bass, but as he was forced to serve a prison sentence was replaced by Kveldulv.
1995 found Frost involved with the ZYKLON B project for the 'Blood Must Be Shed' album working alongside Aldrahn of DØDHEIMGARD and EMPEROR men Ihsahn and Samoth.
SATYRICON pulled in Daniel Olaisen for live guitar work and toured Europe on a bill alongside DISSECTION and GORGOROTH in 1996. Ex SATYRICON member Carl-Michael Eide departed first to ULVER then VED BUENS ENDE. Eide is an industrious figure on the Black Metal scene also contributing to AURA NOIR and INFERNÖ although billing himself 'Aggressor'.
The 1997 EP gave fans a diverse view of SATYRICON. The track 'The Dawn Of A New Age' was given an Industrial remix by Apoptygma Berzerk and further Industrial treatment was given to a cover version of MOTÖRHEAD's 'Orgasmatron'.
1999 found SATYRICON branching out into ever more experimental areas with

SATYRICON Photo: Martin Wickler

the 'Rebel Extravaganza' album. Featured guests were as diverse as DARKTHRONE's Fenriz, THORNS Snorre, Norwegian trance artist Ra and actress Trine Svensson.

Olaisen and Tchort both decamped from the line up to found BLOOD RED THRONE. Olaisen later assembled SCARIOT for the album 'Deathforlorn'.

In 2000 Wongraven was involved in the all star Black Metal side project EIBON. Debuting with a low profile track on the 'Moonfog 2000' compilation EIBON had Wongraven alongside MAYHEM's Maniac, DARKTHRONE's Fenriz, NECROPHAGIA's Kiljoy and even PANTERA frontman Phil Anselmo.

Following headline shows in Europe with guests BEHEMOTH and HECATE ENTHRONED the band supported PANTERA on their 2000 European dates. SATYRICON included former EMPEROR bassist Erik with SPIRAL ARCHITECT's Steinar Urdesen and OLD MAN'S CHILD and SUSPERIA Cyrus on guitar for touring duties.

Singles/EPs:
The Dawn Of A New Age / Orgasmatron / Night Of Divine Power / Forkhekset (Live), Nuclear Blast NB CD 261-2 (1997) ('Megiddo- Mother North In The Dawn Of A New Age' EP)

A Moment Of Clarity / I.N.R.I. / Nemesis Divina (Clean Vision mix) / Blessed From Below: Melancholy, Oppression, Longing, Nuclear Blast NB 396-2 (1999) (Intermezzo II' EP)

Albums:
DARK MEDIEVAL TIMES, Moonfog FOG 001 (1994)
Walk The Path Of Sorrow / Dark Medieval Times / Skyggedens / Min Hyllest Til Vinterland / Into The Mighty Forest / The Dark Castle In The Deep Forest / Taakeslottet
THE SHADOWTHRONE, Moonfog FG003 (1995)
Hvite Krist Død / In The Mist By The Hills / Woods To Eternity / Vikingland / Dominions Of Satyricon / The King Of The Shadowthrone
THE FOREST IS MY THRONE, Moonfog FOG009 (1996) (Split LP with ENSLAVED)
Black Winds / The Forest Is My Throng / Min Hyvisst Til Vingrland / The Night Of The Triumphator
NEMESIS DIVINA, Moonfog FOG012 (1996)
The Dawn Of A New Age/ Forhekset / Mother North / Du Som Hater Gud / Immortality Passion / Nemesis Divina / Trancendental Requiem Of Slaves
REBEL EXTRAVAGANZA, Nuclear Blast

(1999)
Tied In Bronze Chains / Filthgrinder / Rhapsody In Filth / Havoc Vulture / Prime Evil Renaissance / Supersonic Journey / End Of Journey / A Moment Of Clarity / Down South, Up North / The Scorn Torrent

SCARIOT (NORWAY)
Line-Up: Bernt Fjellestad (vocals), Ronni Thorsen (vocals), Daniel Olaisen (guitar), Anders Kobro (drums)

SCARIOT was created by erstwhile SATYRICON guitarist Daniel Olaison and Anders Kobro of IN THE WOODS and CARPATHIAN FOREST. Also featured was TRAIL OF TEARS "growling" vocalist Ronnie Thorsen and "clean" vocals courtesy of Bernt Fjellstad with session members guitarist Hugo Isaksen and bassist Bonne Thorson.

After the debut album 'Deathforlorn' SCARIOT trimmed down to a duo of Olaisen and Thorsen. The band by early 2001 had been brought back up to strength with Olaisen joined by guitarist Frank Orland, vocalist Inge J. Tobiassen, bassist Stefan Schulz and drummer Freddy Bolso.

Olaisen also operates BLOOD RED THRONE with former SATYRICON and EMPEROR member Tchort.

Albums:
DEATHFORLORN, Demolition DEMCD 017 (2000)
Crimson Tears / Sister / The Bad Man / Within / False Power / Resurrection / Remains Of Dreams / Cruisin'

SCHALIACH (NORWAY)
Line-up: Peter Dalbekk (vocals / guitar), Ole Børud (guitar / bass / drums)

Despite the typically Black Metal logo and undoubted extremities of their music SCHALIACH are not all they seem. Founded by Ole Børud of EXTOL the band is in fact a Christian self styled "Unblack" Metal band.

Albums:
SONRISE, Pleitegeier PGD 7970 (1997)
The Last Creed / You Maintain / In Memorium / A Fathers Mourning / A Whisper From Heaven / On A Different Day / Coming Of The Dawn / Sonrise

SCHEITAN (SWEDEN)
Line-Up: Pierre Törnvist (vocals / guitar /

bass), Oskar Karlsson (drums)
A Black Metal project formed by THE EVERDAWN vocalist Pierre Törnkvist and THE EVERDAWN and GATES OF ISHTAR drummer Oskar Karlsson, both had originally recorded only one track to find a suitable label for the project but, in the end, an entire conceptual record was cut for Invasion Records.

Törnkvist, a former member of DECORTICATION, also opted to reform side band THE EVERDAWN. Törnkvist also operates in THE MOANING.

Albums:
TRAVELLING IN ANCIENT TIMES, Invasion I.R. 024 (1996)
October Journey / Autumn Departure / Riding The Icewinds / December At Fullmoon / In Battle With Angels / Leaving The Mortals / Devastating Heaven / Portals Of Might
BEZERK 2000, (1998)
Raincoat / Exitways / Soulside / Sad To Say / V / Terror / Bombraid Over Wastelands / Bezerk 2000 / The Scheitan
NEMESIS, Century Media (1999)
Fury Flow / Psyched / Black Rain / Marionette / Forgive Me / A Silent Hum / Ways / My Isle / Emergency

SEANCE (SWEDEN)
Line-Up: Johan (vocals), Patrick Jensen (guitar), Tony (guitar), Bino (bass), Mique (drums)

SEANCE came into being from an amalgamation of two Linköping acts ORCHRIST (who released the 1989 demo 'Necromonicon') and TOTAL DEATH in 1990, the band name SEANCE coming from an ORCHRIST song title.

December 1990 saw the first SEANCE gig, with the Swedes playing alongside MERCILESS and TOXAEMIA.

The group's first demo, 'Levitised Spirit', was released in 1991and gained the band a deal with Black Mark Records. After their release of the 'Forever Laid To Rest' album bassist Bino (real name Christian Karlsson) lost his place to ex MORGUE man Rickard Limfeldt.

When SEANCE dissolved various members founded trad Metal act WITCHERY. As well as WITCHERY drummer Mique, vocalist Toxine and guitarists Patrick Jensen and Richard also performed in SATANIC SLAUGHTER.

Jensen formed THE HAUNTED with

321

former AT THE GATES personnel.

Albums:
FOREVER LAID TO REST, Black Mark BMCD 17 (1992)
Who Will Not Be Dead / Reincarnage / Blessing Of Death / Sin / Haunted / Forever Laid To Rest / Necromonicon / Wind Of Gehenna / Inferna Cabballa
SALT RUBBED EYES, Black Mark BMCD 44 (1994)
Soulerosion / 13th Moon / Saltrubbed Eyes / Controlled Bleeding / Angelmeat (Part II) / Til Death Do Us Join / Sanctum / Skinless / Hidden Under Scars

SEAR BLISS (HUNGARY)
Line-Up: Andras Nagy (vocals / bass), Janos Barbarics (guitar), Csaba Csejtei (guitar), Winter (keyboards), Gergely Szücs (keyboards), Zoltan Csejtei (drums)

Szombathely based SEAR BLISS are a Gothic / Black Metal band.
SEAR BLISS first arrived on the Metal scene with their 'Pagan Winter' demo tape of April 1995, leading directly to a record contract with Two Moons Records. During early 1997 SEAR BLISS promoted the subsequent 'Phantoms' album with shows in Europe opening for MARDUK and TSATTHOGGA.
With SEAR BLISS making serious strides Two Moons re-released the 'Pagan Winter' demo on CD adding bonus tracks to make up the 1997 release. However, subsequent touring highlighted divisions within the band unit and keyboard player Winter departed to give more concentration to his solo projects ARUD and FOREST SILENCE.
SEAR BLISS also pulled in new members guitarist Viktor Max Scheer and drummer Zoltan Schönberger.

Albums:
PHANTOMS, Two Moons TM1201-2 (1996)
Far Above The Trees / Aeons Of Desolation / 1100 Years Ago / As The Bliss Is Burning / Land Of The Phantoms / Beyond The Darkness / With Mournful Eyes
THE PAGAN WINTER – IN THE SHADOW OF ANOTHER WORLD, Two Moons TM 1202 2 (1997)
Ancient / The Pagan Winter / … Where Darkness Always Reigned / Twilight / In The Shadow Of Another World
THE HAUNTING, Two Moons TM 1205 2 (1998)

Tunnels Of Vision / Hell Within / Land Of Silence / Unholy Dance / Soulless / The Haunting / Left In The Dark

SELEFICE (GREECE)
Line-Up: Miltos Jalagiannis (vocals / guitar), Petros Milhopoulos (guitar / keyboards), Dimitris Vrahidis (bass), Vaggelis Kalergis (drums)

Albums:
WHERE IS THE HEAVEN, Molon Lave (1991)
'Utopia' Intro / I Was Born In Darkness / Die / The Duty Of Lie / The Prayer / Nothing But Freedom / I Will Die By Evil Ways / Where Is The Heaven / (Outro) Years Of Emptyness

SEPTIC CEREMONY (AUSTRIA)
Line-Up: Roland (vocals / guitar), Thomas (guitar), Michael (keyboards), Thomas (bass), Gerald (drums)

SEPTIC CEREMONY were previously known as LEVIATHAN.

Albums:
DIABOLOS REBELLION, CCP 100 189-2 (1998)
Septic Silence / Screams In A Faithless Time / Tears About… / Apocalyptical Visions / The Symphonie Of The Diabolos Rebellion / In Breathless Sleep

SEPTIC FLESH (GREECE)
Line-Up: Spiros (vocals / bass), Chis Antoniou (guitar), Sotiris (guitar), Kostas (drums)

SEPTIC FLESH describe themselves as "Dreamy Emotional Death" and the band first made their mark with the track 'Melting Brains', which appeared on numerous compilation albums.
In early 1991 this was capitalized on by the 5 track demo 'Forgotten Path'. The tape sold well, shifting 800 copies. Their debut vinyl came in the form of the mini album 'Temple Of The Lost Race', which surfaced in early 1992.
A further demo, this time highlighting their talents on the solitary track 'Morpheus-The Dream Lord' secured a deal with Holy Records. In early 1993 Spiros would deputize for OBSECRATION.
Sotiris teamed up with Gunnar Theys of ANCIENT RITES and the industrious Magus Wampyr Daoloth of NECROMANTIA to forge the DANSE MACABRE project but bowed out before

completion.

SEPTIC FLESH's 1998 release 'A Fallen Temple' found the band re-recording their debut effort and adding new songs. Toured Europe as headliner in the spring of 1999 with support from MISANTHROPE and NATRON. Antoniou issued a self titled side project album CHAOSTAR in 2000. All the members of SEPTIC FLESH contributed. The 2000 release 'Forgotten Paths' is a collection of early demos.

Spiros also involves himself in the THOU ART LORD side concern.

Albums:
TEMPLE OF THE LOST RACE, (1992)
Erebus / Another Reality / Temple Of The Lost Race / Setting Of The Two Suns
MYSTIC PLACES OF DAWN, Holy HOLY05 (1994)
Mystic Places Of Dawn / Crescent Moon / Return To Carthage / The Underwater Garden / Pale Beauty Of The Past / Chasing The Chimera / Behind The Iron Mask / (Morpheus) The Dream Lord / Mythos- Part One: Elegy, Part Two: Time Unbounded
ESOPTRON, Holy HOLY13 (1995)
Breaking Of The Inner Seal / Esoptron / Burning Phoenix / Astral Sea / Rain / Ice Castle / Celebration / Succubus Priestess / So Clean, So Empty / The Eyes Of The Set / Narcissism
OPHIDIAN WHEEL, Holy (1997)
The Future Belongs To The Brave / The Ophidian Wheel / Phallic Litanies / Razor Blades Of Guilt / Tarturus / On The Topmost Step Of The Earth / Microcosmos / Geometry In Static / Sharmanic Kite / Heaven Below / Enchantment
A FALLEN TEMPLE, Holy (1998)
Brotherhood Of The Fallen Knights / The Eldest Cosmonaut / Marble Smiling Face / Underworld Act I / Temple Of The Last Race / The Crypt / Setting Of The Two Suns / Erebus / Underworld Act II / The Eldest Cosmonaut (Dark version)
REVOLUTION DNA, Holy (1999)
Science / Chaostar / Radioactive / Little Music Box / Revolution / Nephilim Sons / DNA / Telescope / Last Ship To Nowhere / Dictatorship Of The Mediocre / Android / Arctic Circle / Age Of A New Messiah
FORGOTTEN PATHS (THE EARLY DAYS), Black Lotus BLRCD 017 (2000)
Intro / Power Of The Dark / Melting Brains / Unholy Ritual / Curse Of Death / Forgotten Path / Outro / Power Of The Dark (Live) / Forgotten Path (Live) / Melting Brains (Live)

SEPTIC GRAVE (SWEDEN)
Line-Up: Daniel Engman (vocals), Fredrik Hjärström (guitar), Robert Lindmark (bass), Jörgen Björnström (drums)

SEPTIC GRAVE bass player Robert Lindmark would join PROPHANITY during 1996.

Singles/EPs:
Caput Mortam, Midnight Sun MSR3 (1995)

SERPENT OBSCENE (SWEDEN)
Line-Up: Erik Tormentor (vocals), Nicklas Eriksson (guitar), Johan Thorngren (guitar), Jonas Eriksson (drums)

Albums:
SERPENT OBSCENE, Necropolis (2000)
Devastation / Serpent Prophecy / Sadistic Abuse / Rapid Fire / Pestilent Seed (The Plague) / Evil Rites / Morbid Horror / Violent Torture / Act Of Aggression

SETH (FRANCE)
Line-Up: Vicompte Vampyr Arkames (vocals), Heimothn (guitar), Faucon Noir (bass), Alsvid (drums)

Black Metal band SETH's 2000 album 'War Vol. III' was recorded in collaboration with Italians CULTUS SANGUINE and includes a cover of the CULTUS SANGUINE track 'The Calling Illusion' and more adventurously DEPECHE MODE's 'Behind The Wheel'.

Singles/EPs:
Until The End / The Forest Of The Damned (Forever Lost) / The Chemerical **Quest**, A.M.S.G. (1997) ('By Fire, In Power, Shall be' EP)

Albums:
LES BLESSURES DE L'AME, (1998)
La Quintessence Du Mal / Hymne Au Vampire (Acte I) / Hymne Au Vampire (Acte II) … Vers Une Nouvelle Eve / Le Cerdede La Renaissance / Les Silences D'Outre- Tombe / Dans Les Yeux Du Serpent / … A La Memoire De Nos Freres
L'EXCELLENCE, (2000)
Die Weihe / Let Me Be The Salt In Your Wound / Bastard Beast / Acid Christ / Corpus Et Anima / Legions Spirituelle Damnatrice / L'Excellence / Leave This Planet
WAR VOL. III, Season Of Mist (2000)
(With CULTUS SANGUINE)

Corpus Et Anima / Les Services De La Peste / The Calling Illusion / Behind The Wheel

SETHERIAL (NORWAY)
Line-Up: Kraath Zaahr Raath (vocals), Chorozon (guitar), Thorn (bass), Lord Alastor Mysteriis (drums)

A Swedish Black Metal band created in 1993. SETHERIAL's inaugural line up comprised of guitarist Mysteriis and bassist Devothan together with vocalist Kheeroth and drummer Zathanel. Shortly after bassist Thorn was added to the ranks from EGREGORI as Devothan shifted duties to second guitar.

Kheeroth was then ousted in favour of another EGREGORI member singer Kraath Zaahr Raath for the demo 'A Hail To Faceless Angels' and the 7" single 'For Dem Mit Blod'.

Signing to Napalm Records SETHERAIL cut their first album 'Nord' for 1996 release after which Zathanel decamped to join SORHIN. Mysteriis plugged the gap by switching from guitar to drums before Lord Moloch took the role. Zathanel, besides his activity with SORHIN, would, along with ex member Kheeroth, join a resurrected version of MIDVINTER.

1996 found outside activity for Mysteriis and Lord Moloch forging the "War Metal" act IN BATTLE.

Mysteriis would deputize in fellow Black Metal band IMPERIAL during 1997 and with Kraath and ex IMPERIAL members would create HELVETE as a side project. Mysteriis still retains links with erstwhile IMPERIAL personnel as session drummer for DIABOLICUM.

A collaboration with strong SETHERIAL connections emerged in 1999 titled BLACKWINDS. Lord Kraath and Lord Alastor Mysteriis united with erstwhile drummer Zathanel (now on bass) for a three track EP.

Apparently SETHERIAL have suffered the ultimate indignation for a Black Metal band with Mysteriis being accused of a being a Christian. The man vigorously denies this!

Singles/EPs:
For Dem Mit Blod, Arte De Occulta (1995)

Albums:
NORD, Napalm (1996)
In The Still Of A Northern Fullmoon /

Morkrets Tid / Over Det Blodtackta Nord / I Kattens Famn / For Dem Mitt Blod / I Skuggors Dunkla Sken
LORDS OF THE NIGHT REALM, Napalm (1998)
Satan's Realm / Shades Over Universe / Into Everlasting Fire / Summon The Lord With Horns / Diabolus Enum / Enthroned By Dusk And Shadows / Through Sombre Times / Lords Of The Nightrealm
HELL ETERNAL, (1999)
Towards Thy Realm / Shadows Of The Throne / Hell Eternal / The Aeschma Deava / The Sign Of The Wrath Awakes / The Nightrealm / The Guardians Of The Gates Of Flame

SHADOWCASTER (USA)

SHADOWCASTER guitarist Mikael Bayusick also operates the side project INTO THE SUNLESS MERIDIAN. His main focus is NIGHT CONQUERS DAY. SHADOWCASTER was conceived as an electronic atmospheric experiment testing the waters with the 1994 demos 'My Love Affair With Death And Melancholy' and 'To Gather My Thoughts Among The Sleeping Summer Spires'.

Albums:
ABANDONMENT, Unisound USR 25 (1996)
Wisdom Is My Misery (Melancholia's Caress) / Abandonment / In The Darkest Reaches Of A Distant Cavern At The Very Depths Of A Great And Silent Lake / We Are The Elite (Into En Abstract View Of A Sail) / Ereskingals Gift (The Descent Of Innanna Part II- The Ascension) / The Shadowcaster / Prolonged Aftermath, The Salitude (Fearless And Surreal, 3rd Movement) / My Summoning Of The Darkest Princess / I Am Truly Free: The Blackness Within
TEMPTATION, Wild Rags RR113 (1999)
PSYCHELECTRONIC EXPERIENCE, Wild Rags RR114 (1999)

SHADOW DANCERS (NORWAY)
Line-Up: Stian Johansen (vocals), Rym (guitar), Sanders (guitar), Joy B. (bass), Jontho Pantera (drums)

Although SHADOW DANCERS are Gothic Rock in style the band membership is firmly entrenched in Black Metal folklore led as they are by vocalist Stian Johansen, better known as Occultus of MAYHEM.
Johansen, a member of THY

ABHORRENT, had been editor of 'Sepulchral Noise' fanzine and an employee of the late Euronymous at his infamous 'Helvete' store when he bravely filled the awning chasm in the MAYHEM ranks left after the suicide of Dead. Johansen's stay was short and after a matter of weeks he exited to found PERDITION HEARSE.

SHADOW DANCERS was founded in collusion with RAGNAROK members guitarist Rym (Øyvind Trindborg) and drummer Jontho Pantera (John Thomas Bratland) along with second guitarist Sanders and bassist Joy B.

Besides RAGNAROK both Rym and Jontho also operate with CROWHEAD.

Albums:
EQUILIBRIO, (1999)
In The Heart Of America / Tears From Heaven / Son Of Aequilibrium / The Wasp / The Island / Sherwood Life / The Glum Comedy / Revelation / My Fate / When It's All Over / Beyond Death

SHADOW PROJECT (USA)
Line-Up: Rozz Williams (vocals / guitar), Eva O (vocals / guitar), Jill Emery (bass), Paris (keyboards), Pete Tomlinson (drums)

A satanic Gothic offshoot of CHRISTIAN DEATH led by the late Rozz Williams and wife Eva O.

Albums:
DREAMS FOR THE DYING, Fire Music (1992)
Static Jesus / Days Of Glory / Funeral Rites / Zaned People / Thy Kingdom Stalker / Holding You Close / Lord Of The Flies / The Circle And The Cross

SHADOWSEEDS (SWEDEN)
Line-Up: Daemon Deggial (vocals / keyboards), Petra Aho (vocals), Daemon Kajghal (guitar / bass / drums)

Albums:
THE DREAM OF LILITH, Dark Age DARKAGE001 (1995)
Dream Of Lilith / The Hidden God / Thy Shrouded Wings / Lion Serpent Sun / Baptized In Blood / Dreaming In Ecstasy / Dark Night Of The Soul / Daemon Est Deus Inversus / Shadowseeds

SHAMASH (MEXICO)
Line-Up: Alejandro Barrera (vocals / guitar), Alejandro Penaloza R. (guitar),

Oscar Prior (bass), Mauricio Delgado (keyboards), Carlos Velazquez (drums)

Albums:
ETERNAL AS TIME, Oz Productions CDOZ010 (199-)
Eternal As Time / Empire Of The Sun / Where Every Tear Weaked The Sky / Where The Hate Becomes / Among The Fire And Blood / The Silence / The Divine Oversight / The Whispers Of The Darklight

SHAPE OF DESPAIR (FINLAND)
Line-Up: Azhemin (vocals), N.S. (vocals), J.S. (guitar), T.U. (bass)

SHAPE OF DESPAIR is a Doom act assembled by members of THY SERPENT and BARATHRUM. The band, originally assembled in 1995, was initially titled RAVEN issuing the 1998 demo tape 'Alive In The Mist'.
The act became SHAPE OF DESPAIR in 1999 with the addition of THY SERPENT man Azhemin and female singer N.S.

Albums:
SHADES OF..., Spikefarm NUALA 005 (2000)
... In The Mist / Woundheir / Shadowed Dreams / Down Into The Stream / Sylvan Night
ANGELS OF DISTRESS, Spikfarm (2001)

SHEMHAMFORASH

Albums:
LUCIFERI OMNIS YSIGHDA WITH DOLOR ANTE LUCERN DARK OPERA, (2000)

SHINING OF KLIFFOTH
(AUSTRIA / RUSSIA)
Line-Up: Christof Niederwieser (vocals), Dimitriy (vocals), Miralem (guitar), Eveline (keyboards), Evgeniy (drums)

SHINING OF KLIFFOTH feature KOROVA and ANGIZIA vocalist Christof Niederwieser. The 2000 album 'Twilight Of Sehemeah' includes a cover version of KING DIAMONDS 'Welcome Home'.

Albums:
SUICIDE KINGS, (199-)
All Is Blind / Suicide King / Moonlight Bizarre / In Ice Thin Lucid Airs / Atomic 666 / After Apocalypse
TWILIGHT OF SEHEMEAH, Last

Episode LEP055CD (2000)
Intro / Hellwards Into The Infernal / Luciferian Landscapes / Under The Sunshield / The Rose Of Clotted Light / Dark Spheres Of Aziluth / Purgatory / Evocation Of Sitael / Im Schoss Der Erde / Binah / Welcome Home

SHUB NIGGURATH (MEXICO)
Line-Up: Arturo Alvarez (vocals), Julio Viterbo (guitar / bass / keyboards), Oscar Clorio (drums)

Albums:
EVILNESS AND DARKNESS PREVAILS, Gutteral (1995)
Lying The Dormant Awaits / Zatanazombie (Demoniacal Tribute) / Thy Black Dawn (The Execrable Damnation For The No Tomorrow) / Nightmares From Beyond / The Ninth Revelation (Part I) / Demons Conjuration / Legions From Absu
THE KINGLIKE CELEBRATION: (THE FINAL AEON ON EARTH), Oz Productions (1997)
The Only One Astral Being / … From The Stars Nyarlatholep / Sub-Human Immortality / Abominations Of Ancient Gods / Inameable Evokation / Inside The Labyrinth Of Illusion / Legions Of Absu / Royal Demon

SIEBENBÜRGEN (SWEDEN)
Line-Up: Kicki Höijertz (vocals), Lovisa Hallstedt (vocals), Marcus Ehlin (guitar), Fredrick Brockett (bass), Anders Rosdahl (drums)

SIEBENBÜRGEN date to 1994 and the inaugural duo of vocalist / guitarist Marcus Ehlin and drummer Anders Rosdahl. Later recruit was bassist Fredrick Brockett in time for the demo 'Ungentum Pharelus'.
Female vocalist Lovisa Hallstedt was enlisted for the album recordings.

Albums:
LORIEA, Napalm NPR030CD (1997)
Vampyria / Nattens Väv / Mardröm / Ungentum Pharelus / Om Hösten Död / Loreia / Att Dricka Nagons Blod / Vittring Av Liv / Morgataria / Dödens Sömn
GRIMJAUR, Napalm (1998)
Grimjaur / Vintervila / Nattskräcken / Slottet Auragon / För Mig… Ditt Blod Utgsjutet / Dödens Svarta Fana / Luna Luciferi / I Döden Fann Hon Liv / Vargablod / Ibi Cubavit Lamsa
DELICTUM, Napalm NPR 075 (2000)

Delictum / Majesties Infernal / Storms / Thou Blessed Be By Night / As Of Sin / La Vande / Begravd / Thy Sister Thee Crimson Wed / Opacitas (Queen Of The Dark) / A Dream Of Scarlet Nights / Oculas Malus

SIGH (JAPAN)
Line-Up: Mirai, Shinichi, Satoshi (drums)

Extreme Japanese act SIGH founded in 1989 are noted for having their first album release issued on Euronymous' Deathlike Silence label prior to the Black Metal mentor's untimely death at the hands of Count Grisnackh.
SIGH issued two demos in 1990 'Tragedies', with drummer Kazuki, and 'Desolation' leading to a single release with German label Wild Rags and their first album 'Scorn Defeat' for the aforementioned Norwegian label Deathlike Silence.
Following the murder of Euronymous SIGH contributed a track to a VENOM tribute album and committed recordings to a split EP with KAWIR, including the VENOM cover 'Schizo', before being signed by British label Cacophonous. A cassette release entitled a tribute to Venom' was also issued comprising of seven live VENOM cover versions.
The 2000 album 'Scenario IV: Dread Dreams' has SIGH utilizing English language lyrics from various singers including DECEASED's King Fowley, NECROPHAGIA's Killjoy and RITUAL CARNAGE's Damien Montgomery.
Mirai and Shinichi also have a side band CUTTHROAT with members of ABIGAIL.

Singles/EPs:
The Knell / Desolation / Taste Defeat, Wild Rags (1992) ('Requiem For The Fools' EP)
Suicidigonic / Schizo, (1994) (Splt EP with KAWIR)

Albums:
SCORN DEFEAT, Deathlike Silence Anti-Mosh 007 (1993)
A Victory Of Dakini / The Knell / At My Funeral / Bundali / Ready For The Final War / Weakness Within / Taste Defeat
INFIDEL ART, Cacophonous (1995)
Isuna / The Zombie Terror / Desolation / The Last Elegy / Suicidogenic / Beyond Centuries
GHASTLY FUNERAL THEATRE, Cacophonous (1997)
Intro- Souhki / Shingontachkawa /

Domain Seman / Imiuta / Shikigami / Outro- Higeki
HAIL HORROR HAIL, Cacophonous (1997)
Hail Horror Hail / 42 49 / 12 Souls / Burial / The Dead Sing / Invitation To Die / Pathetic / Curse Of Isanagi / Seal Of Eternity
SCENARIO IV: DREAD DREAMS, Cacophonous NIHIL34CD (1999)
Diabolic Suicide / Infernal Cries / Black Curse / Iconoclasm In The Fourth Desert / In The Mind Of A Lunatic / Severed Ways / Imprisoned / Waltz: Dead Dreams / Divine Graveyard

SILENT STREAM OF GODLESS ELEGY
(CZECH REPUBLIC)
Line-Up: Petr Stanek (vocals / guitar), Michal Hajda (guitar), Kiril Chlebnikov (bass), Zuzana Zamazalova (violin), Pavla Lukasova (violin cello), Radek Hajda (drums)

A Doom band laced with Pagan imagery and adventurous enough to include violins and cellos alongside the expected modern day arsenal. The act was founded by the Hajda brothers guitarist Michal and drummer Radek along with bassist Filip Chudy, frontman Petr Stanek and violinist Zuzana Zamazalova in 1995. SILENT STREAM OF GODLESS ELEGY debuted with the promotional tape 'Apotheosis' capitalized on by 1996's 'Amber Sun'. A second violinist Ski was added after the debut album 'Iron'.
Following the sophomore 'Behold The Shadows' outing Chudy lost his place to Kiril Chlebnikov and the 16 year old Pavla Lukasova took Ski's position

Albums:
IRON, Leviathan (1996)
Ugly Jewel / Passion And Desire / Iron Mask / Last… / Desolated Remains / Only Stream / Crying Haven / Burned By Love To Christ / Bittery Sweet / Naked Susan / Amber Sea / Apotheosis
BEHOLD THE SHADOWS, Redblack (1998)
Wizard / Garden / The Last Place / Old Woman's Dance / When Sun Rises For The Last Time / Summoning Of The Muse / Ghost / Embrace Beyond / Black Tunnel / Shadow / Cantara / I Come And Stand At Every Door
THEMES, Redblack (2000)
Lovin' On The Earth / We Shall Go / My Friend… / Theme I / In Bone Frames /

Theme II / Flowers Fade Away / Eternal Cry Of Glory / Theme III / Il Tsohg / Winter Queen / Hrob (The Grave)

SINERGY (USA / FINLAND)
Line-Up: Kimberley Goss (vocals), Alexi Laiho (guitar), Roope Latvala (guitar), Marco Hietala (bass), Erna Siikavarta (keyboards), Tommi Lillman (drums)

Metal band founded by former CRADLE OF FILTH and DIMMU BORGIR keyboard player Kimberley Goss. Bass was in the hands of Sharlee D'Angelo, a veteran of MERCYFUL FATE, WITCHERY and ARCH ENEMY. The band's original drummer was Ronny Milianowicz whilst guitars came courtesy of THY SERPENT, IMPALED NAZARENE and CHILDREN OF BODOM man Alex Laiho. SINERGY debuted live supporting METALIUM and PRIMAL FEAR in Europe during 1999.
SINERGY adopted a fresh line up for the second album 'To Hell And Back'. Joining Goss were TAROT bassist Marco Hietala, TO DIE FOR drummer Tommi Lillmann and WALTARI guitarist Roope Latvala. The album included a twisted cover of the BLONDIE hit 'Hanging On The Telephone'.
As Laiho's commitments to the increasingly successful CHILDREN OF BODOM for live work SINERGY pulled in second guitarist Peter Huss.
Milianowicz created DIONYSUS in 2000 with LORD BYRON and LUCA TURILLI vocalist Olaf Hayer and NATION members Johnny Öhlin and bassist Magnus Norberg.

Albums:
BEWARE THE HEAVENS, Nuclear Blast (1999)
Venomous Vixens / The Fourth World / Born Unto Fire And Passion / The Warrior Princess / Beware The Heavens / razor Blade Salvation / swarmed / Pulsation / Virtual Future
TO HELL AND BACK, Nuclear Blast NB 503-2 (2000) **27 GERMANY**
The Bitch Is Back / Midnight Madness / Lead Us To War / Laid To Rest / Gallowmere / Return To The Fourth World / Last Escape / Wake Up In Hell / Hanging On The Telephone

SINISTER (HOLLAND)
Line-Up: Mike (vocals), Ron (guitar), Andre (guitar), Aad (drums)

SINISTER formed in 1988 as a trio of Mike, Ron and Aad adding bassist Corzas in early 1989. This line up released the 'Perpetual Damnation' demo. Sales of the tape were strong and SINISTER toured supporting ENTOMBED and DISHARMONIC ORCHESTRA.
Corzas left in May 1991 and bass duties were handed over to SEMPITERNAL DEATHREIGN's Frank Faase. Another line up shuffle saw Ron moving over to bass as SINISTER added second guitarist Andre.
Their second demo had secured enough interest to land a deal with Nuclear Blast. The band had also released three singles, one a split EP with MONASTERY, and appeared on a compilation album in the interim. In 1991 SINISTER toured as support to ATROCITY. More touring opened up 1992 as SINISTER gained a valuable support slot to MORGOTH.
A deal was struck with Nuclear Blast Records with debut album 'Cross The Styx' being produced by ATROCITY's Alexander Krull. The band toured to promote 'Cross The Styx' by opening for DEICIDE, ENTOMBED, CANNIBAL CORPSE and ATROCITY among others. SINISTER's second album, 'Diabolical Summoning', was produced by Colin Richardson, with a third album appearing in 1995 entitled 'Hate'.
Mike and Aad founded HOUWITZER in 1999 for the 'Death But Not Buried' album.

Singles/EPs:
Sinister, Sicktone 3 (1991) (Split 7" with MONASTERY)
Putrefying Remains / Spiritual Immolation, Witchhunt 9103 (1991)
Compulsory Resignation, Seraphic Decay 019 (1992)
Bastard Saints / Reborn From Hatred / Rebel's Dome / Cross The Styx / Epoch Of Denial, Nuclear Blast NB183 (1996) ('Bastard Saints' EP)

Albums:
CROSS THE STYX, Nuclear Blast NB 061-2(1992)
Carnificinia Scelesta / Perennial Mourning / Sacramental Carnage / Doomed / Spiritual Immolation / Cross The Styx / Compulsory Resignation / Corridors To The Abyss / Putrefying Remains / Epoch Of Denial / Perpetual Damnation / Outro

DIABOLICAL SUMMONING, Nuclear Blast NB081 (1993)
Sadistic Intent / Magnified Wrath / Diabolical Summoning / Sense Of Demise / Leviathan / Desecrated Flesh / Tribes Of The Moon / Mystical Illusions
HATE, Nuclear Blast NB 131-2 (1995)
Awaiting The Absu / Embodiment Of Chaos / Art Of The Damned / Unseen Darkness / 18th Century Hellfire / To Mega Therion / The Cursed Mayhem / The Bloodfeast
AGGRESSIVE MEASURES, Nuclear Blast (1998)
The Upcoming / Aggressive Measures / Beyond The Superstition / Into The Forgotten / Enslave The Weak / Fake Redemption / Chained In Reality / Emerged With Hate / Blood Follows The Blood

SINS OF OMMISSION (SWEDEN)
Line-Up: Toni Kocmut (vocals / guitar), Martin Persson (guitar), Thomas Fallgren (bass), Dennis Ekdahl (drums)

SINS OF OMMISSION, founded by ex members of acts such as BESERK, METEPSYCHOSIS and MOURNFUL, initially comprised of singer Toni Kocmut, guitarists Martin Persson and Johan Paulsson, bass player Thomas Fällgren and drummer Dennis Ekdahl.
In 1997 Paulsson made his exit and his position was covered by RAISE HELL's Jonas Nilsson.
SINS OF OMMISSION added former A CANOUROUS QUINTET vocalist Martin Hansen as Kocmut reverted to simply guitar.
Drummer Dennis Ekdahl also performs with RAISE HELL whilst both Persson and Kocmut session on albums by THYRFING.

Albums:
THE CREATION, Black Sun (1999)

SIRIUS (PORTUGAL)
Line-Up: Lord Gornoth (vocals), Draconiis (guitar), Barzh (guitar), Vukodlack (bass / drums)

One of the more lauded names on the Black Metal scene. The heavily keyboard driven debut 'Aeons Of Magick' album, released on Samoth of EMPEROR's Nocturnal Art Productions label, has received almost universally glowing reviews.
SIRIUS was created by former

TWILIGHT members guitarist Draconiis, Raven and Vukodlack. The act announced their arrival with the demo 'The Eclipse (the Summons Of The Warriors Of Armageddon)'. Guitarist Barzh and drummer Flame were added in October of 1998.

Albums:
AEONS OF MAGICK, Nocturnal Art Productions (2000)
Sidereal Mirror / The Collapsing Spheres Of Time / Ethereal Flowers Of Chaos / The Stargate / Travellers Of The Stellar Oceans / Aeons Of Magick / Beyond The Scarlet Horizons

SKYFIRE (SWEDEN)
Line-Up: Henrik Wenngren (vocals), Andreas Edlund (guitar), Martin Hanner (guitar), Jonas Sjögren (bass), Tobias Björk (drums)

Höör based SKYFIRE featured erstwhile NAGLFAR drummer Mattias Holmgren on lead vocals for their inaugural 1998 demo 'Within Reach'. Henrik Wenngren of MORNALAND took over for the subsequent 'The Final Story' effort and the debut album 'Timeless Departure'.

Albums:
TIMELESS DEPARTURE, Hammerheart (2001)
Intro / Fragments Of Time / The Universe Unveils / Skyfire / Timeless Departure / Breed Through Me, Bleed For Me / Dimensions Unseen / By God Forsaken / From Here To Death

SKYFORGER (LATVIA)
Line-Up: Rihard (vocals / guitar), Peter (vocals / guitar), Edgar (vocals / bass), Imant (vocals / drums)

SKYFORGER, named after a mythological God, was created by erstwhile GRINDMASTER DEAD members guitarist Peter, bassist Edgar and drummer Imant. Fourth member Rihard was enrolled later to complete the line up. SKYFORGER's 2000 album 'Latvian Riflemen' is a historical concept album relating the story of Latvian recruits in the Russian army during the first world war.
SKYFORGER blend Metal with traditional Folk instruments.

Albums:
KAUJA PIE SAULES, Mascot (1998)

Zviegtin Zviezda Kara Zirgi / Kauja Pie Saules 1236 / Sewchu Ozols / Viestarda Ciinja Pie Mezhotnes / Kurshi / Kaleejs Kala Debesiis / Kam Puushati Kara Taures / Kauja Garozas Silaa 1287 / Sveetais Ugunskrusts
LATVIAN RIFLEMEN, Mascot M70482 (2000)
Latvian Riflemen / Battle Of Plakani, Battle Of Veisi / The March Of 1916 / Death Island / Six Days Of Madness / Colonel Briedis / In The Tirelis Swamp / Be Like A Man / In Life's Darkest Hour

SLAYER (Huntington Beach, CA, USA)
Line-Up: Tom Araya (vocals / bass), Kerry King (guitar), Jeff Hannemann (guitar), Paul Bostaph (drums)

SLAYER are without question the most sinister of the acts to break out onto the world stage from the early eighties American thrash phenomena. With an unwillingness to compromise they have seemingly defied all the odds to place themselves in the position of regular chart breakers.
SLAYER's music is unrelentingly intense, initially fuelled by drummer DAVE LOMBARDO (Often voted as the 'World's best drummer' in many Metal mags), the mainstay lethal twin guitars of Kerry King and Jeff Hanneman together with the almost inhuman vocals of bassist Tom Araya (a former hospital respiratory therapist). This union made SLAYER not only mould-breakers but an act faithfully plagiarized by countless lesser bands. Lyrically they are unafraid to venture into the realms of the most despicable and overtly controversial. Satanism and Nazism are familiar territories for SLAYER.
Initial recordings were marred by inadequate production and thus universally dismissed as derisory by the world's rock media. Even hardened thrash fans found SLAYER's inaugural bursts of speed noise, when compared with rising stars such as MEGADETH, ANTHRAX and METALLICA, difficult to stomach.
Founded in 1981 by uniting former SABOTAGE drummer Lombardo, King and Araya from QUITS and Hanneman SLAYER, originally titled DRAGONSLAYER. At first they pursued a traditional heavy metal stance musically but debuting with the fast track 'Aggressive Perfector' on the 'Metal Massacre IV' compilation album on Metal Blade Records persuaded the band to

adopt a more intense leaning. A three track demo tape followed comprising of 'Fight 'Til Death', 'Black Magic' and 'The Antichrist' which rapidly became a much traded item on the underground metal scene.

King teamed up with fellow Los Angeles speed metal band MEGADETH performing live gigs on a temporary basis. During this period of flux Lombardo was briefly supplanted by drummer Bob Gourley, later to join DARK ANGEL then create POWERLORD.

Brian Slagel, Metal Blade mentor, was quick to notice the reaction and duly signed the band up putting them in the studio to record 'Show No Mercy' whilst Lombardo graduated from high school. The press hated proclaiming into an unintelligible mess it but it still sold.

The band got out on the road, even putting in an English appearance at London's Marquee club, before setting off on the "Haunting North America' tour. SLAYER's no compromise approach saw them using inverted crosses onstage and King wearing leather armbands encrusted with nails.

With second album 'Hell Awaits' SLAYER provided ample defiance to those that sneered with the music easily equal in ferocity to the debut. SLAYER were clawing their way up and the British rock magazine 'Metal Forces' readers poll was a case of SLAYER sweeping the board gaining honours for best band, best live band, best album and best drummer.

SLAYER began to make serious headway when Rick Rubin, Owner and producer of Def Jam Records, signed the band in 1986. First fruits of this liaison was the 28 minute 'Reign In Blood' opus, a pure thrash album that took the genre to new levels of extremity. Quite incredibly the album was to break into the American Billboard top album 100 charts, the first of many.

'Reign In Blood' also embroiled SLAYER into political condemnation almost immediately for the lyrics to the opening track 'Angel Of Death'. The song dealt with the infamous SS Auschwitz extermination camp doctor Joseph Mengele and many were quick to accuse SLAYER of fascist sentiments. The mighty CBS corporation, distributors of Def Jam, refused to handle the album.

The band retorted that this was merely an observation and not a belief, citing that Araya himself was far from being an all American white boy. The obviously Ayran Hanneman compounded the problem however by frequently wearing SS collar patches, iron crosses and insignia in photos and by adorning one of his guitars with cuff titles of notorious SS panzer divisions such as 'Totenkopf' and 'Das Reich'. SLAYER's tour T-shirts of the time proudly declared that the band were 'Slaytanic Wehrmacht' and featured a skull encased in a World War II German helmet. SLAYER seemed quite content to be stoking up their reputation as number 1 bad boys.

The band provoked further adverse reaction by their use of a new logo, a nazi eagle with the swastika replaced with the SLAYER logo. The furore over 'Angel Of Death' was so great that British distributor Geffen, owned by the Jewish entrepreneur David Geffen, dropped the album from their schedules. Ironically Geffen had been quick to capitalize on SLAYER's dumping by CBS earlier.

SLAYER heralded their first celluloid performance captured at New York's Studio 54 club alongside EXODUS and VENOM for 'The ultimate revenge' video. SLAYER, on the 'Reign In Pain' tour for the first time enjoying the comforts of a tour bus, toured America with OVERKILL before European dates with openers MALICE. Such was the headliner's extreme loyalty that MALICE were very often the subject of ugly scenes, having to endure booing and, sadly, more often than not, spitting.

With the band's burgeoning popularity former label Metal Blade were quick to capitalize releasing 'Live Undead', a picture disc live album with tracks culled from 1984 American shows.

Between albums and whilst in the midst of an American tour Lombardo announced he was quitting in December 1986. Rumours circulated that the cause of the split was an argument over Lombardo's wife being on the road. Nonetheless, SLAYER continued with substitute T.J. Scaglione of WHIPLASH. As the tour rolled on SLAYER hooked up with W.A.S.P., an ill fated union that witnessed a bitter war of words between the two bands as to which act viewed itself as selling the more tickets.

SLAYER were back in the headlines once more in 1987 for all the wrong reasons when they pulled out of a headlining slot at the prestigious Aardschock Festival in Holland at the eleventh hour. A great degree of ill feeling was generated until the band explained that with the cancellation of METALLICA (due to the death of Cliff Burton) SLAYER had no intentions of performing but their agency had neglected to inform the relevant parties.

With the band's burgeoning popularity former label Metal Blade were quick to capitalize releasing 'Live Undead', a picture disc live album with tracks culled from 1984 American shows.

Lombardo, who during his sabbatical had turned down the opportunity to join MEGADETH, was enticed back into the band in April 1987 in time to record the next album. The reinstated drummer did however nearly miss a batch of British dates when his work permit had been refused.

SLAYER plugged the gap between albums by covering IRON BUTTERFLY's 'In A Gadda Da Vida' for the movie soundtrack 'Less Than Zero'.

1988's 'South Of Heaven', which saw SLAYER slowing the pace somewhat and included a cover of JUDAS PRIEST's 'Dissident Aggressor', gave SLAYER increased sales yet again. With the band seemingly attempting to extricate themselves from their previous black metal trip oddly Rubin was to insist that the word 'Satan' appear on the record and at the last minute Araya reworked the lyrics to 'Read Between The Lies' to include a reference to ol' Nick.

American dates kicked off with support from NUCLEAR ASSAULT then SLAYER finally got the opportunity to play the major American arenas at the end of 1988 when they were invited to join JUDAS PRIEST as guests.

SLAYER took a lengthy break of some two years after the world tour during which time they severed ties with their British record company London Records. SLAYER had been far from amused when the single 'Mandatory Suicide' had been released on the very last date of the British tour.

1990 saw SLAYER in what some envisaged as an unholy union on the 'Clash Of The Titans' festival touring package. Three out of 'The big four', SLAYER, MEGADETH and ANTHRAX teamed up for a series of monumental shows across arenas in America and Europe. For the stateside dates ALICE IN CHAINS opened whilst the eighteen shows in Europe ANTHRAX were supplanted by SUICIDAL TENDENCIES and TESTAMENT opened.

One result of these dates is that Araya was invited to guest on ALICE IN CHAINS 'Dirt' album. His contribution comes in the form of a Slayeresque scream on an untitled track.

In May 1992 Lombardo quit for good. His first project being recording with VOODOO CULT then the formation of GRIP INC. with VOODOO CULT guitarist Waldemar Sorychta, a band that has released two albums to date. Lombardo's substitute was ex FORBIDDEN man Paul Bostoph.

During 1994 SLAYER teamed up with gangster rapper ICE T to cut a track for the soundtrack to the movie 'Judgement Night', a cover of British punk act THE EXPLOITED's 'Disorder'.

SLAYER shot back to their previous status with 'Divine intervention' in 1995. The album blasted into the Billboard top 100 at an incredible number 8 and the band geared up for a world tour with openers BIOHAZARD and MACHINE HEAD prior to a fourth on the bill showing at the 'Monsters of rock' festival headlined by METALLICA.

'Divine Intervention' was quick to achieve gold sales status and SLAYER's longevity was confirmed when 'Reign In Blood', 'South Of Heaven' and 'Seasons In The Abyss' were all confirmed gold too.

The subsequent tour had SLAYER appearing on an all star 'Monsters Of Rock' bill in South America alongside KISS and BLACK SABBATH.

SLAYER paid homage to their musical heroes in 1996 by cutting the 'Undisputed Attitude' (originally titled 'Selected And Exhumed') album made up of favourite punk tunes and three SLAYER original compositions including the more metal orientated 'Gemini' and 'D.D.A.M.M.'. Songs covered included those by T.S.O.L., England's G.B.H., and no less than three MINOR THREAT tracks. The Japanese version added SUICIDAL TENDENCIES 'Memories Of Tomorrow'. The event was marred for the band though when after recording Bostoph made his exit to concentrate on a jazz career. Drummerless SLAYER were forced to cancel South American and European tours.

Coincidentally while SLAYER were offering tribute to their mentors a series of Swedish compilation albums 'Slaytanic Slaughter' were released were Scandinavian acts covered their favourite SLAYER song.

SLAYER resumed activity with the addition of erstwhile TESTAMENT drummer John Dette, however his tenure was fleeting as Bostoph was reinstated, Dette returning to the TESTAMENT camp.

In his time away from the band Bostoph had formed THE TRUTH ABOUT SEAFOOD (and a stint with TESTAMENT!).

1996 also found the band pushed back into the public arena once more although unwittingly when the band's music was cited in a lawsuit as being a direct influence on the 1995 murder of a 15 year old girl. The teenager was kidnapped, tortured and killed by three members of a Black Metal band HATRED. The prosecution alleging that the band members were influenced by and inspired by SLAYER's lyrics from the track 'Necrophiliac'. The findings of the court were due to be heard in 2001.

Undeterred SLAYER came up with new product in 1998 with the 'Diabolus' album and appeared on the bill of the 'Ozzfest show' at Milton Keynes during June. The group had been scheduled to appear on the American dates but the spot on the bill eventually went to MEGADETH.

In 1999 SLAYER teamed up with Berlin Techno-Punks ATARI TEENAGE RIOT to mould the track 'No Remorse (I Wanna Die') for the 'Godzilla' movie soundtrack.

2000 saw SLAYER contributing their take on 'Hand Of Doom' for the BLACK SABBATH tribute album 'Nativity In Black 2'. Araya has also been writing material with Max Cavalera of SOULFLY, the track 'Terrorist' being featured on SOULFLY's 2000 album. Not to be outdone King features a guest guitar solo on the cut 'Goddamned Electric' from PANTERA's 2000 album 'Reinventing The Steel'.

SLAYER included the track 'Bloodline' on the movie soundtrack album 'Dracula 2000'.

Singles/EPs:
Haunting The Chapel / Chemical Warfare / Captor Of Sin, Roadrunner RR 1255087 (1984)
Criminally Insane / Aggressive Perfector / Post Mortem, London LONX 133 (1987) 64 UK
South Of Heaven / Mandatory Suicide / In A Gadda D Vida, London LONX 201 (1988)
Seasons In The Abyss (Live) / Aggressive Perfector (Live) / Chemical Warfare (Live), Def American DEFAC 9 (1991) 51 UK
Ditto Head / Serenity And Murder, American ALASKA1 (1995) (USA promotion)
Witching Hour / Ditto Head / Divine Intervention, American 74321 38325-2 (1996) (Free CD single with 'Undisputed Attitude' album)
Serenity In Murder / Raining Blood / Dittohead / South Of Heaven, Def American 74321262347 (1995)
Serenity In Murder / At Dawn They Sleep / Dead Skin Mask / Divine Intervention, Def American 74321262342 (1995) (CD single)
Serenity In Murder / Angel Of Death / Mandatory Suicide / War Ensemble, Def American 74321312482 (1995) (CD single)
Abolished Government / Superficial Love, Sub Pop SP368 (1996) (Split single with T.S.O.L.)
Bitter Peace, American (1998) (Promotion release)

Albums:
SHOW NO MERCY, Roadrunner RR 9868 (1984)
Evil Has No Boundaries / The Anti-Christ / Die By The Sword / Fight Till Death / Metalstorm / Face The Slayer / Black Magic / Tormentor / The Final Command / Crionics / Show No Mercy
HELL AWAITS, Roadrunner RR 97951 (1985)
Hell Awaits / Kill Again / At Dawn They Sleep / Praise Of Death / Necrophiliac / Crypts Of Eternity / Hardening Of The Arteries
REIGN IN BLOOD, London LONPP 34 (1986) **47 UK, 94 USA**
Angel Of Death / Piece By Piece / Necrophobic / Jesus Saves / Altar Of Sacrifice / Criminally Insane / Reborn / Epidemic / Post Mortem / Raining Blood
LIVE UNDEAD, Roadrunner RR 9574 (1987)
Black Magic / Die By The Sword / Captor Of Sin / The Antichrist / Evil Has No Boundaries / Show No Mercy / Aggressive Perfector / Chemical Warfare
SOUTH OF HEAVEN, London LONLP 63 (1988) **50 SWEDEN, 25 UK, 57 USA**
South Of Heaven / Silent Scream / Live Undead / Behind The Crooked Cross / Mandatory Suicide / Ghosts Of War / Cleanse The Soul / Read Between The Lies / Dissident Aggressor / Spill The Blood
SEASONS IN THE ABYSS, Def American 84968712 (1990) **47 SWEDEN, 18 UK, 40 USA**
War Ensemble/ Blood Red/ Spirit In Black/ Expendable Youth/ Dead Skin Mask/ Hallowed Point/ Skeletons Of Society/ Temptation/ Born Of Fire/ Seasons In The Abyss
DECADE OF AGGRESSION-LIVE, Def American 5106052 (1991) **29 UK**

332

Hell Awaits / The Anti-Christ / War Ensemble / South Of Heaven / Raining Blood / Altar Of Sacrifice / Jesus Saves / Dead Skin Mask / Seasons In The Abyss / Mandatory Suicide/ Angel Of Death / Hallowed Point / Blood Red / Die By The Sword / Black Magic / Captor Of Sin / Born Of Fire / Post Mortem / Spirit In Black / Expendable Youth / Chemical Warfare / Black Magic

DIVINE INTERVENTION, American 74321236771 (1994) **15 UK, 8 USA**
Killing Fields / Sex, Murder, Art / Fictional Reality / Dittohead / Divine Intervention / Circle Of Beliefs / SS III / Serenity In Murder / Two-Thirteen / Mind Control

UNDISPUTED ATTITUDE, American 74321357591 (1996) **31 UK, 34 USA**
Disintegration- Free Money / Verbal Abuse- Leeches / Abolish Government-Superficial Love / Can't Stand You / D.D.A.M.M. / Guilty Of Being White / I Hate You / Filler- I Don't Want To Hear It / Spiritual Law / Sick Boy / Mr. Freeze / Violent Pacification / Richard Hung Himself / I Wanna Be Your God / Gemini

DIABOLUS IN MUSICA, American 4913022 (1998) **27 UK, 31 USA**
Biter Peace / Stain Of Mind / Love To Hate / Death's Head / Screaming From The Sky / Overt Enemy / Scrum / In The Name Of God / Perversions Of Pain / Desire / Point

THE SOIL BLEEDS BLACK (USA)

Line-Up: Mike Riddick, Mark Riddick, Eugenia Houston, Amanda Blickos

Occult Mediaeval act centred upon twins Mike and Mark Riddick and two female singers Eugenia Houston and Amanda Blickos, the latter also contributing flute. Bard Algol of CERNUNNOS WOODS contributes lyrics.

THE SOIL BLEEDS BLACK emerged with a brace of well received cassettes entitled 'Summon The Dragons Of Wyth' and the ambitious 'Because The World Is So untrue, I Go My Way So Full Of Rue'. These two tapes would be combined for the first album release 'The Kingdom And It's Fey'.

Mike Riddick is also a member of MOONROOT alongside Proscriptor McGovern of ABSU. Other side activities include the ambient project DRAGONWYND and the eclectic YAMATU. Both brothers also devote time to a fourth band 15 DELIGHTS OF DIONYSUS.

Albums:
THE KINGDOM AND IT'S FEY, Cruel Moon International (199-)
Odde Feormie / Bite Irena, Wide Feran / The Village Courtyard / Annwyfn / At That Fiery Pond / Burh Stede Beated / Behold Thou My Crest / To Thy Queen / Atop Mount Snowdon / Fig And Jig In The Miller's Tavern / The Charm Of Making / Ecce, Victoria / Redivivus 'Ole Norwich, The Triumph Of Hormane / Dragone Arte / Dance O' Lord And Lady / He Shall Be King / A Hymn To Dechtire / Because The World Is So Untrue, I Go My Way So Full Of Rue / Adieu, And Off To Battle / The Stolen Princess Sleeps / Summoning The Dragons Of Wyth / The greenest Hilltop / Distillation Of Lady Luna In The Vessel / Homonucleus / They Take Their Own Path Home

MARCH OF THE INFIDELS, Draenor (199-)
Sound The Trumpet / In Days Of Victory / The Journey Is Not Yet Over / Autumn Call / Woodnymphs In The Hazel Patch / Ceilidh / The Bog / We Wave Our Flags In Triumph / Meade For All (In The Pub) / Preparations For The Royal Feast / Avalon (Shores And Seas) / Our Flames Have Never Died / The Bard's Tale / The Kingdom Thereafter / Leave Now Soldier / Armed To The teeth

MAY THE BLOOD OF MANY A VALIANT KNIGHT BE AVENGED, Draenor (199-)
This Is A Tale…/ Enter The Green Knight / To Strike One Stroke For Another / A Twelvemonth Of Fear For The Coming Year / Rejoice / Victory Is Mine! / Foreshadow / Now Sets Off A Noble Knight / Sorrow With Summer Comes / Sir Gawain Bores His Emblem Bright / Across Country He Rides For The Table Round / A Castle Most Comely / We Welcome Thee, Sir Gawain / There Was Meat, There Was Mirth, There Was Much Joy / The Good Host's Deal / The Lord, His Host, Leads The First Hunt / Fair Passtimes They Pursue / she Kisses The Knight So True / With Many A Brave Blast They Boast Their Prize / sweet Melody / Gallant And True Is The Sir Gawain Still / Off To The Wood Away / Gracious Gawain Gives Thanks… / Now The New Year Draws Near / In His Richest Raiment / That Princely Steed / Warning From The Man That Rode Nearby / The Chapel Green / What A Place Accursed / Strike Once More / Sir Gawain And The Green Knight / The Green Knight Falls At The Third Throw / Hony Soyt Qui Mal Pense / Gawain Sets Out Anew

SOLACE IN THE SHADOWS
(PA, USA)
Line-Up: John Sheldon (vocals / guitar), Matt Moore (guitar), Jason Conrad (bass), Hugh Morretta (keyboards), Patrick Battaglia (drums)

SOLACE IN THE SHADOWS was created in 1996 by former ARMAGEDDON members. Guitarist Matt Moore and drummer Patrick Battaglia would forge INNOCENCE FALLEN in 2000 with former EVIL DIVINE members. This act would evolve back into EVIL DIVINE for the 'Dawn Before The Dawn' album with the re-enlistment of original frontman J. Demonic.

Albums:
OF DARKNESS IN ANGELS, (199-)
The Netherblaze / Haunting Purity's Gates / By Night We Burn / Devil's Kiss / Blood And Tears Adorn Our Embrace

SOLEFALD (NORWAY)
Line-Up: Cornelius (vocals / guitar / bass), Lazare (drums)

A rare attempt at Black Metal humour. SOLEFALD describe their music as "Red music with black edges". Vocalist Cornelius has credits with MONUMENTUM and a solo project entitled PERSONA. Drummer Lazare (Lars Are Nedland) has credits with BORKNAGER and CARPATHIAN FOREST.
Live work employed the use of guitarist John E, drummer Tarald. and DIMMU BORGIR man Jens Peter on bass.

Albums:
THE LINEAR SCAFFOLD, Avantgarde Music (1997)
Jemlor / Philosophical Revolt / Red View / Floating Magenta / The Macho Vehicle / Countryside Bohemians / Tequila Sunrise / When The Moon Is On The Wave
NEONISM, Avantgarde (1999)
Flourescent (The Total Orchestra) / Speed Increased To Scaffold / CK 11 Chanel. No. 6 / Proprietors Of Red / A Motion Picture / Omnipolis / Bacpacka Baba / Third Personal Plural / 04.34 PM / The New Timelessness

SOLHVERV (DENMARK)
Line-Up: Thomas F. Jørgensen (vocals / guitar), Martin F. Jørgensen (vocals / bass / keyboards), Erik E. Marcussen (drums)

A Danish Black Metal band.

Albums:
TÅGERNES ÅRTUSINDE, Euphonious PHONI 004 (1995)
Tågernes Årtusinde / Helvedeskedlen / Ur - Tidens Ekko / Månens Skygge / Blodig Haevn / Under Dodens Grumme Svøbe / Gravkammerets Gru / Alt Ondt Skal Komme Fra Norden / Glams Øjne

SÓLSTAFIR (ICELAND)
Line-Up: Albjörn Tryggvason (vocals / guitar), Svavar Austmann (bass), Gudmundur Óli Pálmason (drums)

SÓLSTAFIR was created in the early 90's by the duo of Albjörn Tryggvason and bass player Halldór Einarsson. The band first emerged with the 1994 demo 'I Nordri' which led to a deal with Czech label View Beyond for the 'Til Valhallar' EP. Guest vocals on these recordings came from Sindre of ANCIENT OF DAYS. A promotional release in 1997 had Kola of DARK HERESY on vocals but despite progress Einarsson left for a new life in Australia. His replacement was Svavar Austmann.
SÓLSTAFIR drummer Gudmundur Óli Pálmason sessioned on POTENTIAM's 1999 album 'Balsyn'.

Singles/EPs:
Til Valhallar, View Beyond (1997)

SOLSTICE (UK)
Line-Up: Simon Matravers (vocals), John Piras (guitar), Rich 'Militia' Walker (guitar), Chaz Netherwood (bass), Lennart 'Lentil' Roomer (drums)

SOLSTICE included former SHIP OF FOOLS guitarist John Piras. The band toured with YEAR ZERO and COUNT RAVEN in 1994. Ex IRONSIDE drummer Sean Steels joined the band in early 1995. Matravers was replaced in August 1995 by American WHILE HEAVEN WEPT singer Tom Phillips.
Confusion reigned in the SOLSTICE camp during 1997 as their 'Halycon' album, originally recorded for Stormstrike Records, was sold to the Godhead label and then to Black Tears.
By the 1998 album though SOLSTICE were fronted by Morris Ingram joining the ranks of Netherwood, guitarist Hamish Glencross and drummer Rick Budby.
SOLSTICE men drummer Sean Steels and guitarist Hamish Glencross joined the

ranks of MY DYING BRIDE in 1999. Back in America Phillips issued the debut WHILE HEAVEN WEPT album 'Sorrow Of The Angels' in 1999.
Guitarist John Piras went on to greater recognition in CRADLE OF FILTH renaming himself Gian Pyres.

Albums:
LAMENTATIONS, Candlelight 007 (1994)
Lamentations IV / Neither Time Nor Tide / Only The Strong / Absolution Extremis / These Forever Bleak Paths / Empty Lies The Oaken Throne / Last Wish / Wintermoon Rapture / The Man Who Lost The Sun / Ragnorak
HALYCON, Black Tears (1997)
NEW DARK AGE, Misanthropy (1998)
New Dark Age- The Sleeping Tyrant / Cimmerian Codex / Alchemiculte / Hammer Of Damnation / The Anguine Rose / Blackthorne / The Keep / Cromlech / New Dark Age II- Legion XIII

SONGE D'ENFER (BRAZIL)
Line-Up: Fog (vocals / guitar), Hofgodhar, Lia, Reston (drums)

SONGE D'ENFER was founded by former GENETIC DEFORMATION frontman Fog. Following the debut release 'Visions In The Forest' the band lost bassist Lechis and Haschcloud opted to become a roadie rather than a band member. New draftees were former NOCTURNAL WORSHIPPER man Hofgodhar and erstwhile QUINTESSENCE member Lia.
SONGE D'ENFER shared a split album with fellow Brazilians MIASTHENIA.

Albums:
MY VISION IN THE FOREST, Bhe (1997)
VISIONS OF NOCTURNAL TRAGEDIES, (2000) (Split CD with MIASTHENIA)
Intro / Visions Of Nocturnal Tragedies / Et Videt Quod Esset Bonum / My Lady Princess Of Hell- Conjuration To Gorgon / My Visions In The Forest / Embrace The Fire

SONICHAOS AEON (GREECE)

Albums:
HEAVY METAL ANTICHRIST, Invasion Music INV016 (1999)

SORATH (CZECH REPUBLIC)
Line-Up: Admirerforestrae (vocals / guitar), Francis Empty (guitar), Martin Tree (bass), Ottar Distress (drums)

Pilsen based Black Metal band SORATH issued a 1995 split album shared with unholy Czech companions UNCLEAN. Previous to this SORATH had issued the demos '666 The Awakening' in 1993 and 'Voices' in 1995.
The band co-exist with MYTHOPEIA, indeed, SORATH was borne out of the earlier incarnation MYTHOPEIA-KINGDOM OF FROST when mainman Heon Ostamon was drafted into his military service. During the interim vocalist / guitarist Admirerforestrae, guitarist Francis Empty, bass player Martin Tree and drummer Ottar Distress forged SORATH.
Upon Ostamon's release from the Czech army the former band was resurrected as MYTHOPEIA with Ostamon on keyboards joined by Admirerforestrae, Empty, Tree and Distress with fresh members Asura Godwar Gorgon's Ray on vocals and third guitarist Johannes Rhodostauroticus R.C. However, SORATH also continued.
MYTHOPEIA issued the demo 'Haaramonia In Microcosmos' and contributed the track 'It Is Blood Of My Veins' to the 'Breath Of Doom' compilation album prior to Tree decamping from both acts. MYTHOPEIA enrolled bass player Lucas whilst the gap in SORATH was filled by Mar Markoon. Later Markoon would replace Gorgon's Ray as singer of MYTHOPEIA.

Albums:
SORATH, Pussy God (1995) (Split album with UNCLEAN)

SORATH (USA)

Black Metal band SORATH included the teenage Baron Von Abaddon of BLACK FUNERAL, VALEFOR and DARKNESS ENSHROUD. Previous to the 1994 single SORATH had issued 'The Forest Of Winter' demo, the quaintly titled 'Sodomizing Jesus Christ' followed by 'Ancient Dead'.
Abaddon (real name Michael Ford) also goes under the titles of 'Nachtotter' and 'Talnagraph 108'.

Singles/EPs:
The Horns Of The Goat, Sorath (1994)

SORCERY (SWEDEN)

Satanic Death Metal. SORCERY guitarist Peter Lake would later surface as a member of THEORY IN PRACTICE and RIVENDELL. Bass player Daniel Bryntse's later labarinthyne activities included WITHERING BEAUTY, WINDWALKER, MORRAMON and Doom Metal band FORLORN. The SORCERY 'Bloodchilling Tales' album was re-released in 1999 bu No Colours Records.

SORG (NORWAY)
Line-Up: Karl Ø. Langedahl (vocals), Aslak Janitz (guitar), Knut E. Bakkevold (guitar / keyboards), Bjorn A. Johansen (bass), Øyvind Karlsen (drums)

SORHIN (SWEDEN)
Line-Up: Nattfursth (vocals / bass), Eparygon (guitar), Zathanel (drums)

Black Metal band SORHIN feature ex SETHERIAL and MIDVINTER drummer Zathanel. SORHIN, then with drummer Shamaatae of ARCKANUM as session man, first offered a 1993 demo 'Svarta Själars Vandring' followed by a further effort in 1995 'I Fullmånens Dystra Sken'. The 1998 album was produced by HYPOCRISY's Peter Tägtgren. For the 2000 album 'Apokalypsens Ängel' the band split away from Near Dark Records

and issued the record on their own Svartvintras label.

SORT VOKTER (NORWAY)

A project of THOU SHALT SUFFER, PECCATUM and EMPEROR man Ildjarn.

SOULGRIND (FINLAND)
Line-Up: Jussi Heikkinen, Ceasar T. Launonen (vocals), Luopio (keyboards), Agathon Frosteus (drums)

The extra curricular project of TENEBRAE's Jussi Heikkinen. The man works constantly in collaboration with other Death Metal musicians on the albums issued under the SOULGRIND banner. For example, 'Ladit AD 1999: Bihttpotp' was recorded with DEMENTIA's Roope Latvala, Juke Eräkangas, Sauli Kivilahti, Henrick Laine and Kirsi Reunenen (female vocals).

For the 1998 'Whitsongs' release Heikkinen employed drummer Agathon Frosteus of THY SERPENT, BARATHRUM, NOMICON and GLOOMY GRIM, keyboard player Luopio of THY SERPENT whilst vocalist Ceasar T. Launonen is a NOMICON, WALHALLA and GLOOMY GRIM member. The album also sees contributions from female vocalist Whisper, also of GLOOMY GRIM.

Besides SOULGRIND Heikkinen is an active participant in GLOOMY GRIM, WALHALLA and FIRE TRANCE 666.

The 1999 'Kalma' album sees guest guitar from one Warhammer Newborn.

Singles/EPs:
Santa Sangra EP, MMI (1993)
Black Orchid / In My Darkest Sabbath / Anal Christ Pose, MMI (1995)

Albums:
LA MATANZA, EL HIMMO PAGANO, MMI M.M.I. 011 CD (1994)
Summoning / Kuoto / Santa Sangre / La Matanza, El Himmo Pagano / Black Abyss, Deep Enterium / Dark Misty Trail / Inner Chain Of Perversions / The Pit/ Virginity, A Sanctum Of The Red / Ainomonus (Outro)
LUST AND DEATH IN TUONELA A.D. 1999: BLACK INDUSTRIALHOLOCAUST THROUGH THE PANDEMONIUM OF THE BIZARRE, MMI M.M.I. 020 (1995)
Introitus Nostrodamus 1999 / Black Orchid / Darkseed Lust / As Shadows Whisper The Shine / Shamanic Ecstasy / Spin Of Life / The Pandemonium Of The Bizarre / Immortal Desire / Industrial Holocaust (Inferia) / The End Of All
WHITSONGS, Icarus (1998)
Yermi / The Girl And The Boyar's Sun / Oterma And Katerma / Tumma / Revenge / Maids Of Hiss / Bwe Cross / The Dark One / Tuoni's Eyes / The Song Of Mantsi / Thalempe / The Serf's Son / Tuuri
KALMA, Holy HOLY048CD (1999)
Kalma / Goatride / Secrecy Supreme / Remembrance Through Deep Red Masquerade / Cage / Across The Field Of Thought / Seed (A Sermon In Stone) / Black Lust / Harsh Mother Time / Pagan Pride

SOULLESS (BRAZIL)

Albums:
LIFE EXTINCTION, (199-)

Dismal Atmosphere / Spiritual End / Life Extinction / Way To Nowhere / Erase The Future / Soulless / Morality
JOURNEY OF SOULS, Brazil (2000)

SOUL REAPER (SWEDEN)
Line-Up: Christoffer Hjertén (vocals), Johan Norman (guitar), Stefan Karlsson (guitar), Mikael Lang (bass), Tobias Kjellgren (drums)

Originally titled REAPER and forged by two erstwhile members of DISSECTION drummer Tobias Kjellgren and guitarist Johan Norman. Original second guitarist Mattias Eliasson would relinquish his post to Christoffer Hermansson for recording of the 'Written In Blood' album. Hermansson in turn exited in favour of Stefan Karlsson.

Albums:
WRITTEN IN BLOOD, Nuclear Blast NB 403-2 (2000)
Darken The Sign / Written In Blood / Satanized / Seal Of Degradation / Ungodly / Subterranean Night / Labyrinth Of The Deathlord

SOUL SEARCH (AUSTRIA)
Line-Up: T.K. (vocals / guitar), K.P. (guitar), S.B. (bass), E.O. (drums)

An Anonymous Salzburg based Doom band that have progressed, according to the band, from 1991 Gothic Doomsters through Folk-Doom with the 1994 'Die Essenz' EP to an amalgam of epic Doom Metal and ambience.

Singles/EPs:
Untapped Horizons / In Earth / Star Chamber / Fruit Of The Doom, Soulsearch (1994) ('Die Essenz' EP)

Albums:
NATURE FALLS ASLEEP, (1992)
GWYNEDD- THE ETHNIC TRUTH, Serenades SR012 (1997)
Neumondblut (The Principle Of Womanhood) / Feldfeuer (Fires Of The Womb) / Ahnenstahl (The Synonym For The Godly Mystery) / Schwarze Erde (The Guilt Of Blood) / Ährenschuld (Breathing The Land) / Kundgebung / Rabenhorst (Last Days Of A Bloodless Land)

SOURCE OF TIDE (NORWAY)
Line-Up: Lord PZ (vocals), Pendragon (guitar), Taranis (guitar), Targenor (bass),

Consecrator (keyboards)

SOURCE OF TIDE is led by Lord PZ who along with EMPEROR's Ihsahn also comprise PECATTUM. The band actually started prior to the inclusion of Lord PZ billed as NOME COUNCIL issuing the 'Rock Vs. Art' project album 'Dawn Of Tides' in 1997 in collusion with painter Knut. M. Nesse.
The initial 1996 line up included former BLACKWIND and PRIVITATION keyboard player Cosmocrator, ex BYZANTIUM guitarist Pendragon (real name Jostein Thomassen), vocalist Sven Torre Dammen, guitarist Atle Hoidalen, bassist Geir Hovland and drummer Goran Flatin.
The band hit internal problems resulting in only Pendragon and Consecrator surviving. New additions were former EVERFLOOD and PRIVITATION bassist Targenor and guitarist Taranis.
Pendragon also sessions for PECCATUM. Cosmocrator sessions as bassist for ZYKLON.

Albums:
RUINS OF BEAUTY, Candlelight (2000)
Raven Goddess / Symphony Of The Sovereign / The Awakening (Ode To The Art Of Self Destruction: Part I) / Chains Of Mythic Fantasy / Autumn Leaf / Final Battle (Ode To The Art Of Self Destruction: Part II) / Ye Memories Of Sad Rebirth / Who am I?

STENTORIAN (HOLLAND)
Line-Up: Arne Sunter (vocals), Jeffrey Brugman (guitar), Paul Hendriksen (guitar), Paul Noomen (bass), Martijn Peters (drums)

Arnhem's STENTORIAN appeared on two compilations albums during 1993; Displeased Records' 'Against All Gods' and DSFA Records 'Resurrection Of Reality'. The group later toured Holland opening for GOREFEST, THERION, EXHORDER and DEADHEAD.

Albums:
GENTLE PUSH TO PARADISE, Jaciberg JR CD001 (1996)
This Jericho Dance / Collapsed At The Crossing Path / Man From The Forest / July The 24th / Into The Deep / The Loss / Weltschmewrz / Romancing The Lost Love

STONE TO FLESH (AUSTRIA)
Albums:
SOME WOUNDS BLEED FOREVER, CCP CCP 100206-2 (2000)

STORM (NORWAY)
Line-Up: Kari Rueslatten (vocals), S. Wongraven (vocals / guitar / bass), Herr Nagell (vocals / drums)

STORM was formed by members of EMPEROR, SATYRICON and DARKTHRONE in 1994.
The group released the debut album, 'Nordavind', in 1995 and the record featured adaptations of old Norwegian Folk songs recorded multitude of acoustic instrumentation.
Vocals were supplied by ex THE 3RD AND THE MORTAL vocalist Kari Rueslatten, although S. Wongraven and Herr Nagell also contributed vocals adding a good deal of diversity to the material.

Albums:
NORDAVIND, Moonfog FOG 004 (1995)
Innferd / Mellom Bakkar Og Berg / Haavard Hedde / Villemann / Naggelstev / Oppi Fjellet / Langt Borti Lia / Lokk / Norgsgard / Utferd

STORMLORD (ITALY)
Line-Up: Cristiano Borchi (vocals), Piereangelo Giglioni (guitar), Francesco Bucci (bass), Fabrizio Cariani (keyboards), David Folchitto (drums)

Founded as a Power Metal trio in 1991 STORMLORD debuted with the demo 'Black Knight' the following year. A deal with Metal Hearse Productions led to the inclusion of the track 'Cataclysm' on the compilation album 'Dawn Of Gods'.
By 1997 STORMLORD could boast seven members and cut the EP 'Under The Sign Of The Sword' and another appearance on volume two of 'Dawn Of Gods'. Touring in Italy found STORMLORD sharing stages with ATROCITY, OVERKILL and the infamous DEATH SS.
The band then trimmed down to 5 members with bassist Maffeitor Fabban making way for Francesco Bucci as a deal was signed with German label Last Episode for the 'Supreme Art Of War' album.
A European tour with MYSTIC CIRCLE and GRAVEWORM ensued prior to the

recruitment of keyboard player Simore Scazzocchio.

Singles/EPs:
Under The Sign Of The Sword / Riding The Sunset / The Scarlet Kingdom, Metal Horse (1997)
Where My Spirit Forever Shall Be / Sir Lorial / War- The Supreme Art, (199-)

Albums:
SUPREME ART OF WAR, Last Episode (1999)
Where My Spirit Forever Shall Be / A Descent Into The Kingdom Of The Shades / Sir Lorial / Age Of The Dragon / War- The Supreme Art / Immortal Heroes / Of Steel And Ancient Might

STRID (NORWAY)

Solo "Alcoholocaustic War Black Metal" act STRID opened with the 1993 demo 'End Of Life'. Multi instrumentalist Strid was also guitarist with SALACIOUS GODS until October 2000.
Other Strid endeavours include OBSCURA NEBULA and LUBUBRE,

Singles/EPs:
Det Hviskes Blant Sorte Vinder, (1995)
Nattvandring, Malicious Records (1995)

STRIGASKOR NO.42 (ICELAND)

Albums:
BLOT, (1995)

SUFFERING (NORWAY)
Line-Up: Jan Sorensen (vocals / bass), Ivar Gundersen (guitar), Ole Morten Persen (guitar), Ivar Arnes (drums)

A Black Metal act that have the honour of being the debut release for the now defunct Arctic Serenades label.

Albums:
SOWING THE SEEDS OF SUFFERING, Arctic Serenades SERE 001 (1994)
Visions / Suffering Soul / Endless Journey / Dream Of Darkness / The Age Of Darkness / The Seeds Of Eternal Suffering

SUICIDAL WINDS (SWEDEN)
Line-Up: Peter Haglund (guitar)

SUICIDAL WINDS also have a split EP shared with BESTIAL MOCKERY to their credit.

Albums:
WINDS OF DEATH, No Colours (1999)

SUIDAKRA (GERMANY)
Line-Up: Arkadius Antonik (vocals / guitar), Marcel Schoenen (guitar), Daniela Voigt (bass), Stefan Moller (drums)

Folk Black Metal band heralded their arrival with the 1995 'Dawn' demo. SUIDAKRA's 2000 album 'The Arcanum' included a cover version of SKYCLAD's 'The One Piece Puzzle'.

Albums:
LUPINE ESSENCE, Suidakra (1997)
Banshee / Dragon Tribe / Heresy / Sheltering Dreams / Havoc / Warpipes Call Me / … And A Minstrel Left The Mourning Valley / Internal Epidemic
AULD LANG SYNE, Last Episode (1998)
Auld Lang Syne / Hall Of Tales / A Menhirs Clay / And Another Cist Looms / An Dúdlachd / Tuatha Dé Danaan / Jeremiad / The Fall Of Tarra / Enticing Slumber / Calm…
LAYS FROM AFAR, Last Episode (1999)
A Darksome Path / Chants Of Lethe / The Well Of Might / The Hidden Quest / Morrigan / Peregrin / Wasted Lands / Stayed In Nowhere / Aime / Lays From Afar / Foggy Dew
THE ARCANUM, Last Episode LEP 056 (2000)
Wartunes / Last Fortress / Dragonhead / Rise Of Taliesin / Res In Silence / Gates Of Nevermore / Serenade To A Dream / The Arcane Spell / The One Piece Puzzle

SUMMON (USA)
Line-Up: Xaphan (vocals / guitar), Ankharu (guitar), Necromodeus (bass), Anbrusius (drums)

Michigan band SUMMON evolved from the hotly tipped MASOCHIST. When MASOCHIST founder member Tchort was ejected from the band (to found WIND OF THE BLACK MOUNTAINS) the remaining members reforged the act as SUMMON.
The debut SUMMON album 'Baptized By Fire', which includes drummer Astaroth, has a cover version of MAYHEM's perennial 'Deathcrush'.
Vocalist Xaphan (Sean) also has credits with LUCIFER'S HAMMER.

Albums:
BAPTIZED BY FIRE, Baphomet (199-)

Sons Of Wrath / Visions Of Apocalyptic Grace / Baptized By Fire / The Silence Of Chaos / Dark Descent Of Fallen Souls / Realm Of No Return / Bring Black Desire / Beyond The Gates Of Scora / Eve Of Anti Creation / Eternal Darkness

DARK DESCENT OF FALLEN SOULS, Grinding Peace (1996)
Intro / Dark Descent Of Fallen Souls / Enter Into Eternal Oath / Eve Of Anti-Creation / Beyond The Gates Of Storm / Necromantic Lust / Under The Midnight Shadows / The Silence Of Chaos / Tales Of Immortality / Sorrows Of Moonlight Night / Outro- Tranquil Deed

SUMMONING (AUSTRIA)
Line-up: Protector (vocals / guitar / keyboards), Silenius (vocals / bass), Trifixion (drums)

A side project of ABIGOR vocalist / bassist Silenius founded during 1993, SUMMONING's debut album is a conceptual Black Metal orchestral slant on Tolkein's 'Lord Of The Rings'. Further albums became increasingly ambient in their approach.
Drummer Trifixion announced that the music was not aggressive enough for his liking and promptly left after the debut, forging his own act TRIFIXION in 1995 and releasing the 'The First And Last Commandment' album.
Trifixion also involves himself with other acts PAZUZU and WEREWOLF. Silenius has an outside interest in KREUZWEG OST with HOLLENTHON man Martin Shirenc.
A further offshoot emerged in 2000 when Protector and Silenius forged ICE AGES in 2000.

Albums:
LUGBURZ, Napalm NPRO10 (1994)
Grey Heavens / Beyond Bloodred Horizons / Flight Of The Nazgul / Where Winters Forever Cry / Through The Valley Of The Frozen Kingdom / Raising With The Battle Orcs / Master Of The Old Lure / Between Light And Darkness / The Eternal Lands Of Fire / Dragons Of Time / Moondance
MINAS MORGUL, Napalm NPR 018 (1995)
Soul Wandering / Lugburz / The Passing Of The Grey Company / Morthond / Marching Homewards / Orthanc / Ungolianth / Dagor Bragollach / Through The Forest Of Dol Guldar / The Legend Of The Master Ring/ Dor Daedeloth

DOL GULDUR, Napalm NPR 024 (1996)
Ungbands Schmieden / Nightshade Forests / Elfstone / Khazad Dum / Kôr / Wyrmvater Glaurung / Unto A Long Glory... / Over Old Hills
NIGHTSHADE FORESTS, Napalm (1997)
Mirkwood / Kortiron Among The Trees / Flesh And Blood / Habbanan Beneath The Stars
STRONGHOLD, Napalm (1999)
Rhun / Long Lost To Where No Pathway Goes / The Glory Disappears / Like Some Snow White Marble Eyes / Where Hope And Daylight Die / The Rotting Horse On The Deadly Ground / The Shadow Lies Frozen On The Hills / The Loud Music Of The Sky / A Distant Flame Before The Sun

SUNCHARIOT (RUSSIA)

Rostov on Don Black Metal unit led by singer Stanislav Ivanoff. SUNCHARIOT includes erstwhile members of SACRIFICED and FUNERAL SPEECH. The 1998 album 'Betrayed Light Of Fertile Ground' album was released in the West by the Canadian Soundscape Music label.

Albums:
BETRAYED LIGHT OF FERTILE GROUND, Soundscape Music (1998)
Mother Ground / Only One Branch Of Dullness / Carrion / ... Of Those, Whose Walls Return To Life After The Long Oblivions / Bopohbi

SURRENDER OF DIVINITY (THAILAND)
Line-Up: Whathayakorn (vocals), Monchai (guitar), Settha (bass), Paritat (drums)

Albums:
ORIENTAL HELL RHYTHMICS, Psychic Scream (2001)

SUSPIRIA (NORWAY)
Line-Up: Athera (vocals), Cyrus (guitar), Elvor (guitar), Memnock (bass), Tjodalv (drums)

A much anticipated Black Metal amalgam boasting heritage linked with such premier acts like DIMMU BORGIR, SATYRICON and OLD MAN'S CHILD. Originally titled SEVEN SINS the band was first mooted by drummer Åxelsson Tjoldav, a veteran of OLD MAN'S CHILD

340

SUSPERIA Photo : Nuclear Blast

and DIMMU BORGIR. Upon leaving DIMMU BORGIR in March 1999 Tjoldav sessioned for OLD MAN'S CHILD once again for their 'Revelation 666' album. In August of the same year a meeting with erstwhile SENSA ANIMA, OLD MAN'S CHILD and SATYRICON guitarist Cyrus and former MORTEM and ARCTURUS vocalist Athera (Marius Vold) prompted the formation of SEVEN SINS.

The band unit was brought up to strength with the addition bassist Memnock and second guitarist Elvorn for the demo 'Illusions Of Evil'. Memnock's history includes stints with METADOX, POWERHUNT, VANAHEIM and yet again OLD MAN'S CHILD.

SUSPERIA debuted live in Oslo supported by ALSVARTR and RAGNAROK.

DIMMU BORGIR keyboard player Mustis sessions on the 'Predominance' album.

Albums:
PREDOMINANCE, Nuclear Blast (2001)

SVARTAHRID (NORWAY)

SVARTAHRID comprise of MACTÄTUS keyboard player Forn and erstwhile MACTÄTUS bassist Istar. Later additions were bassist Illvaster and keyboard player Bjorn Andre.

Albums:
FORTHCOMING STORM, Napalm NPR 071 (2000)
Atter Et Rike / Faustbitten / Lagnaden / Forthcoming Storm / Sjelefall / Under Den Enoydes Trone / Herskende I Blod / Stier Av Hat / Gods Of War / Lords Mystery
AS THE SUNRISE FLICKERS, Napalm (2000)

SVARTSYN (SWEDEN)
Line-Up: Ravn (vocals), Kolgrim (guitar), Jonas (bass), Draugen (drums)

Self styled 'Satanic cursed Black Metal' act SVARTSYN's first product was the 1996 demo tape 'A Night Created By Shadows'. The band had been formed as INCITATUS by vocalist Ravn, guitarist Heike and bassist / drummer Jonas. Promotion for the debut album 'The True Legend' had the band on tour in Europe with DESASTER Poland's BEHEMOTH. Following these dates guitarist Surth relinquished his position to Kolgrim. SVARTSYN include former DARK FUNERAL drummer Draugen in the ranks.

Albums:
THE TRUE LEGEND..., Folter (1996)
Goatthrone / The True Legend / Tearing Your Soul / The Snake In The Garden Of Eden / Into The Ghoul Haunted Forest Where The Winter Was Eternal / Under The Devil's Moon / A Cursed Blaze For The Caster / The Shadow Is Painting My Eyes
HIS MAJESTY, Sound Riot SRP06 (2000)
Apocalyptic Prophecy / Dungeons / Tunnels Of His Majesty / It Breathes / Necromantic Flesh / I'm Cleopatra's Killer

SWORDMASTER (SWEDEN)
Line-up: Andreas Bergh (vocals), Emil Nödtveidt (guitar), Kenneth Gagfner (bass), Tobias Kjellgren (drums)

SWORDMASTER date to 1993 and their foundation by guitarist Nightmare (real name Emil Nödtveidt). Nightmare also plays with OPTHALAMIA and is the brother of the imprisoned DISSECTION mentor Jon.

Following the mini album release on Florida's Full Moon Productions, drummer Tobias Kjellgren joined DECAMERON. He would eventually rejoin DISSECTION for their December 1995 European tour. His temporary replacement in SWORDMASTER was another ex DISSECTION member, Ole Öhman.

The 'Wrath Of Time' mini-album was re-released on vinyl format in 1996, limited to 1000 copies and with two extra tracks; 'Metallic Devastation' and 'Claws Of Death (Conspiracy)'. The band signed to Osmose Productions the same year but would start to draw themselves away from Black Metal with each successive release.

Presently the band are credited as vocalist Whiplasher, guitarists Nightmare and Beast Electric, bassist Thunderbolt and drummer Terror.

Singles/EPs:
Wraths Of Time / Upon Blood And Ashes / Conspiracy- Preview / Outro, Full Moon Productions FMP004 (1995) ('Wraths Of Time' EP)

Albums:
POST MORTEM TALES, Osmose Productions OPCD055 (1997)
Indeathstries- The Master's Possession / Crust To Dust / Postmortem Tales / Past Redemption / Claws Of Death / Blood Legacy / The Serpent Season / Metallic Devastation / Black Ace
DEATHRAIDER, Osmose Productions (1999)
Deathraider 2000 / Firefall To The Fireball / Necronaut Psychout / Iron Corpse / Stand For The Fire Demon
MORIBUND TRANSGORIA, Osmose Productions OPCD084 (1999)
Deathspawn Of The Eibound / Towards The Erotomech Eye / The Angel And The Masters- Metalmorphosis- The Secret Of Cain / Sulphar Skelethrone / Moribund Transgoria / Doom At Motordome / The Grotesque Xtravaganza

SYMAWRATH (SPAIN)
Line-Up: Baron Saggitar (vocals), The Hunter (guitar), Zorn (guitar), Rex M. (keyboards), Malice (drums)

SYMAWRATH was a union of erstwhile members of MYSTHICAL and MAJESTIC MIDNIGHT vocalist Baron Saggitar, guitarist The Hunter and keyboard player Abyss Musician. Later entrants were guitarist Zorn and drummer Malice with ASGAROTH's Mythral C. deputizing on bass guitar.

SYMAWRATH debuted with a track included on a free CD given with issues of Spanish Metal magazine 'Necromance'

which led to a shared album with Basque act OMINOUS.

Rex M. would later supplant Abyss Musician on keyboards.

Albums:
DRAMATIS PROFILE, Donosti Rock (1999) (Split album with OMINOUS)
Cosmic Incense Contemplating The Poisoned Dance / Velum Artis / Vampirical Lascivious Passion
SCAEN I: INCESTUOUS OVERTURE IN THE CRYSTAL AUDITORIUM, Abstract Emotions (1999)
Onyric Conspiracy / Misanthropic Criminal In The Iron Scorpion / Masquerotica In Crescendo (Woman, Goddess, Perverse...) / Clandestine Laberinthic Bizarre / Vampirical Lascivious Passion / Hierarchical Whore's Charm (Phantasmagorical Aphrodisiac) / My Epigraph's Horror

T

TAAKE (NORWAY)

TAAKE is the solo vehicle of ex THULE member U. Hoest with session drummer Tundra of FROSTMOON and TUNDRA.

Albums:
NATTESTID SER PORTEN VID, Avantgarde (1999)
Part I / Part II / Part III / Part IV / Part V / Part VI / Part VII

TAETRE (SWEDEN)
Line-Up: Jonas Linblad (vocals / guitar), Dan Yael (guitar) Conny Vandling (bass), Kalle Pettersson (drums)

TAETRE vocalist Jonas Linblad also goes under the stage surname of 'Linblood'. TAETRE's debut 1998 album 'The Art' was produced by KING DIAMOND guitarist Andy La Rocque. The 1999 album 'Out Of Emotional Disorder' includes a cover version of the ROLLING STONES classic 'Paint It Black'.
TAETRE have toured as support to DISSECTION, LUCIFERION and DARK TRANQUILITY.
Linblad is also a member of Black Deathsters THORIUM.

Albums:
THE ART, Diehard RRS 963 (1998)
Intro: Entrance 666 / My Lament / Prince Of Many Faces / The Art / When Winter Came / Lifeplague / Labyrinth / The Halls Have Eyes / Into The Dawn / Outro: The Return
OUT OF EMOTIONAL DISORDER, Diehard RRS965 (1999)
Intro / Die With Me / The Bitter Withering / Your Illusion Unmasked / Poisoned An Epitaph Cavern / Nightbreed / Departure Suicide / Paint It Black / Outro

TALES OF DARKNORD (RUSSIA)
Line-Up: Anton Shirl (vocals / bass), Alex Kantemirov (guitar), John Kuznetson (drums)

Volgograd's TALES OF DARNORD was founded in 1991 by guitarist Alex Kantemirov. The band has issued a steady stream of demo cassettes over the years starting with 1992's 'Obliteration Allegory'. Later titles included 'Blackened Skies Remain' and 'Tragedy' in 1993 with 'Unearthly Agitator' in 1995.

Albums:
ENDLESS SUNFALL, R.I.P. Productions (1997)
DISMISSED, More Hate Productions MHP002-02 (2000)
Nonsense / Dismissed / Dirge / Everyday Eternity / Nothing More Except Circulation / Really Rich Grave

TARAMANTIA (SWITZERLAND)

A solo project from one David Hera, TARAMANTIA is known to feature several guest musicians. The 'Dark Are The Veils Of Death' offers contributions from Roger Baumer.

Singles/EPs:
To Embrace Forlorn / Dream Force (Baldr's Draumar), Darken Art (199-), ('Dark Are The Veils Of Death' EP, Split 7" single with AZRAEL. Limited edition of 500 copies only)

TARANIS (POLAND)

Albums:
FAUST, (1995)

TARTAROS (NORWAY)

Solo album project by EMPEROR's live keyboard player Charmand Grimloch.

Albums:
THE GRAND PSYCHOTIC CASTLE, Necropolis (1997)
Intro / Darkred Light Upon The Bomos / Images Of Mystic Sphere / Tunes Towards The Empyreum / The Grand Psychotic Castle
THE RED JEWEL, Necropolis NR042 (1999)
The Lamentable Sonata / The Ruby Mine / A Shape In Fair Disguise / Storm Of Terror / Into The Faculty Of Wonderful Secrets / The Red Jewel / The Intense Domain Of Grievousness / The 5th And The Hysteric

TATIR (GREECE)
Line-Up: Hierphant (vocals), Necrolord (guitar), Filid Of Carpathian Forest (drums)

Raw and primitive Black Metal act TATIR issued two highly praised demos 'Dark Autumn Nights' and 1996's 'Fons Acheroni'. Guitarist Necrolord also operates GOATTHRONE with Voreas of DRUTENTUS.

TEARS OF CHRIST (ITALY)

Sassari based TEARS OF CHRIST is a Black Metal side project of CALVARY members.

Singles/EPs:
Within My Forgotten Woods Of Misery, Dawn Of Sadness (1996)

TEMPERANCE (SWEDEN)
Line-Up: Fredrik Ernroth (vocals / guitar), Malena Bengtsson (bass), Johan B-Häng Erneroth (drums)

Singles/EPs:
One Foot In The Grave / Left Inside, Shiver SHR001 (1993)

Albums:
KRAPAKALJA, Shiver SHR015 (1995)
Land Of The Brave / Only For Eyes / Vem Vet Vad / Dimension Unknown / Dimension Complete / Deep Down And All Alone / Krapakalja / Wrecked Lives

TENEBRE (SWEDEN)
Line-Up: Kalle Metz (vocals), Franco Bollo (guitar), Fredrik Täck (guitar), Richard Lion (bass), Andreas Albin (drums)

Self Styled 'Evil' Metal band created by former FLEGMA members vocalist Kalle Metz and bassist Richard Lion along with ex FUNHOUSE guitarist Fredrik Täck and drummer Joel during 1996.
The opening release 'XIII" saw FUNHOUSE guitarist Martin as session player but Lukas Sunesson took the role on a more permanent basis shortly after. TENEBRE rounded off the year contributing two tracks 'Halloween II' and 'Vampira' to a MISFITS tribute album.
TENEBRE's second record 'Grim Ride' only saw a limited European release. 1999 saw the departure of Joel and the recruitment of ex EMBRACED man Andreas Albin on the drum stool. Another change saw Sunesson exiting (the band claimed he was 'fat'!) with Franco Bollo (a.k.a. Jan Gajdos of FUNHOUSE) assuming the role.
TENEBRE's 2000 album, the deliberately mis-spelled 'Mark Ov The Beast', includes a guest performance from Steve Sylvester from cult Italian band DEATH SS.

Singles/EPs:
Halloween, RHCDM2 (1997)
Cultleader, RHCDM3 (1997)
Tombola Voodoo Master / Terror, (1999)

Albums:
XIII, RHCD3 (1997)
Thirteen / I / Taste My Sin / A Cross On Your Door / Tenebre / Rites Of Passage II / Dead But Dreaming / Moth To The Flame / No Wrong / Thunrida / The Case Of Charles Dexter Ward / Buried And Forgotten / March Of The Dying Angel
GRIM RIDE, (1998)
Demon / No Time For Pain / The Call / Demonicus Ex Deo / Like A Needle / Soulbleed / When Razors Cry / Love 666 / Scarecrow / Without / Darkness Bound
MARK OV THE BEAST, Regain RR0010-009 (2000)
Harvester Of Souls / Tombola Voodoo Master / Mark Ov The Beast / I Am Your Ritual / God Speaks In Tongues / Putana Satana / Gone With The Wind / The Undertaker / Come To season / Thy Darkness Come / Alignment

TERRA TENEBRAE (GREECE)
Line-Up: Gothmog (vocals), Vassilis (guitar), Baron Blood (bass)

Black Metal act created by personnel from THOU ART LORD, VANITY and NECROMANTIA. The band was originally fronted by Kostas of OBSECRATION but in 1998 Gothmog of THOU ART LORD took the role.
8 string bass player Baron Blood is in fact a moonlighting Makis of NECROMANTIA.

Albums:
SUBCONSCIOUS, Black Lotus BLRCD 010 (1999)

THA-NORR (GERMANY)
Line-Up: Hendrik Poppe, Marko Sklenarz

THA-NORR debuted their own brand of unholy Black Metal with the 1994 demo 'Assault On Aerie'.

Albums:
WOLFENZEITALTER, Nazgûl's Eyrie Productions NEP007CD (1995)
Tears For All Those Who Died / Calling Forth The Spirits Of The Elements / Sathanas, Triumphator! / Assault On Aerie / Bowels Of My Beloved Earth / Wolfenzeitalter / The Fortress Will Fall / Fegefeuer / Weltschmerz / Tyrant Of The New Aeon

THEATRE OF THE MACABRE
(MN, USA)
Line-Up: Le'Rue Delashay (vocals / guitar), Erisichthon (guitar), Antaeus (bass), Umbruskus (drums)

THEATRE OF THE MACABRE released two demos 1996's 'Tales Of Tragedy' and the 2000 'Bathed In Blood Of Angels'. The period between these two sessions was spent on ice as frontman Le'Rue Delashay founded LORDES OF ALL DESIRES for the 1998 album 'Crowned In Blasphemy'. THEATRE OF THE MACABRE reconvened with Delashay enlisting DEMONICON drummer Umbruskus.
Guitarist Erisichthon would depart following the release of the debut album. Bass player Antaeus also left the fold as the band announced he was sacked for attempting to stab another band member! Erstwhile LORDES OF ALL DESIRES member Malmstorm was enlisted during 2000.

Albums:
A PARADISE IN FLESH AND BLOOD, Root Of All Evil (2000)
A Prelude Unto Infernal Resurrection / A Paradise In Flesh And Blood / Bathed In The Blood Of Angels / Bequeathed Archaic Love / Forsaken In The Garden Of Earthly Delights / What Wicked Web She Weaves / Enraptured By Temptation / Through The Eyes Of The Serpent / Enthroned In The Halls Of Martyrdom / A Distant Thunder / Storm Giants / Cathedral Of Chaos

THEATRES DES VAMPIRES
(ITALY)
Line-Up: Lord Vampyr (vocals), Scarlet (vocals), Justine (vocals), Strigoi (guitar), Incubus (guitar), Blaut Sauger (bass), Necros (keyboards), Blasfemator (drums)

Italian Black Metal exponents THEATRES DES VAMPIRES debuted with the demo recording 'Nosferatu, Eine Symphone Des Gravens'.

Albums:
VAMPYRISME, NECROPHILIE, NECROSADISME, NECROPHAGIE, Gardens Of Grief (1996)
Intro- Twilight Kingdom / The Land Beyond The Forest / Reborn In The Wood / Ancient Vampires / Woods Of Vallachia / Within The Dark Domain / Upon The Darkest Mountain / While The

Snow Turns Red / Vlad The Impaler
THE VAMPIRE CHRONICLES, Alkaid (1999)
Preludium / Enthrone The Dark Angel / Thule / Throne Of Dark Immortals / Woods Of Vallachia Part II: The Revelation / When The Wolves Cry / Exorcism / Carpathian Spells / Cursed / The Coven
BLOODY LUNATIC ASYLUM, Blackened (2000)

THEMGOROTH (POLAND)
Line-Up: Asmodeus (vocals / guitar), Kiejstut (bass), Sammach (keyboards), Alkalon (drums)

An extreme outfit Polish underground kings THEMGOROTH mix Black Metal and Gothic influences to fine effect. The band recruited guitarist Sammach in October 1993 and debuted with a two track demo the following year.

Albums:
GATE TO THE UNKNOWN, Amber (1995)
The Initiate / Gate To The Unknown / Dead Valley / A Poet Inspired By Pain / In The Name Of...
HIGHWAY INTO THE UNKNOWN, (199-)
Highway Into The Unknown / A Poet Inspired By Pain / Is This You, Maybe? / Gate To The Unknown / Dead Valley / In The Name Of...

THERGOTHON (FINLAND)
Line-Up: Niko Sirkiä (vocals), Mikko Ruotsaainen (guitar), Sami Kaveri (guitar), Jori Sjöroos (drums)

THERGOTHON are renowned for releasing one of the most melancholic and bleak Doom albums of all time. The band first emerged with the 1991 demo 'Ftaghn-Nagh Yog Sothtoth'. Various members of THERGOTHON later formed THIS EMPTY FLOW, releasing a 1996 album 'Magenta Skycode'.

Albums:
STREAM FROM THE HEAVENS, Avant Garde Music AV001 (1995)
Everlasting / Yet The Watchers Guard / The Unknown Kadath In The Cold Waste / Elemental / Who Rides The Astral Wings / Crying Blood + Crimson Snow

THIRD MOON (AUSTRIA)
Line-Up: Wolfgang Rothbauer (vocals / guitar), Markus Miesbauer (bass /

keyboards), Magus Milan Pejak (drums)

Austrians THIRD MOON arrived in 1994 with a line up of singer Wolfgang Rothbauer, guitarist Mattias Larreder, bass player Markus Miesbauer and drummer Magus Milan Pejak. The latter would make way for Johannes Jungreithmeier.
Rothbauer and Jungreithmeier also have a side project entitled ELEMENT HATE in alliance with bassist Eugen Pagany of EMPYRE, PUNISHMENT and MORTICIAN.
Both Miesbauer and Pejak have credits with ASTAROTH. The drummer is also a veteran of SEPTIC CEREMONY and ESTATIC FEAR.

<u>Albums:</u>
GROTESQUE AUTUMNAL WEEPINGS, CCP 1001 74-2 (1997)
Grotesque Autumnal Weepings / Supreme Ancient Sanctum / Moonlight / Timeless Dissent / Monbluttraurer / Frozen Lunar Autumn / Velvet Thorns / Crimson Crescent
AQIS SUBMERSUS, Napalm (1999)
Atlantis / Scargod / The Spirits Wept / Aqis Submersus Prologue / Aqis Submersus / Farewell In Welkin Dust / Carrion / Transcend The Second Twilight / Transcend / Shadow / De Profundi
BLOODFORSAKEN, Napalm (2000)
Spiritual Icons / Catharsis In Azure / Fractured Abandonment / Fallen Skin Dimension / Buried Awakening / Costal Angels / Thirdmoon / Obsolete Scars / Captured / Grotesque Chapter / Thirdmoon- Outro

THIS EMPTY FLOW (FINLAND)
Line-Up: Jori Sjöroos (vocals / instruments), Augustus Mattila (bass), Niko Sirkiä (keyboards)

The intensely dismal Doom laden act THIS EMPTY FLOW feature ex members of THERGOTHON Jori Sjöroos and Niko Sirkiä. In 1996 the band added guitarist, and producer of debut album 'Magenta Skycode', Jukka Sillanpää to the line up. Sirkiä then departed as in 1997 keyboard player Hanna Kalske made her presence felt.

<u>Albums:</u>
MAGENTA SKYCODE, Avantgarde Music AV016 (1996)
Nowafter / Useless / Stream / Towards Distant / Snow Blind / Distress / (But I Am)

Still / Sweet Bloom Of Night Time Flowers
THREE EMPTY BOYS, Plastic Passion (1999)
Blear / Drops / Dive Nothing / To Drink Atlantic Dry / Angels Playground / Playground Of The Angels / Hello Spaceboy / Rebuilt Passage / Hunger / Abell / This Empty Boy
USELESS AND EMPTY SONGS, Plastic Passion (2000)
Useless (Trip To Mäntyluoto version) / One Song About Solitude / Everything-Nothing / Dubby / Of Blossom And Decay

THOKK (VA, USA)

THOKK is a side project of erstwhile GRAND BELIAL'S KEY and ANCIENT member Lord Kaiaphas.

<u>Albums:</u>
OF RAPE AND VAMPIRISM, Mordgrimm (1997)
First Evocation: i) Wolf-Hymn, ii) Falling In The White Tempest, iii) Of Rape And Vampirism, iv) The Witch Tower Of Ushanaad, v) In The Phantasmagoric Dimensions / Second Evocation: i) Abscend To Nightmare Chasms, ii) Come A Grimmer Presence, iii) Haunted By Saturnian Phantoms (Abducted In The Cosmic Bog)

THORIUM (DENMARK / SWEDEN)
Line-Up: Michael H. Anderson (vocals), Morten Ryberg (guitar), Allan Tvelebakk (guitar), Jonas Lindblood (guitar), Jesper Frost (drums)

The Danish / Swedish collaboration THORIUM boasts no less than three guitarists with bass duties reportedly delegated out to whichever one is the most drunk at the time! The band produced an outstanding Black Death Metal record but fell foul of their record company Diehard who relinquished the band's contract due to apparent Nazi lyrics. The situation was a huge misunderstanding and Diehard resigned the group.
Vocalist Michael H. Anderson, guitarists Morten Ryberg and Allan Tvelebakk are all erstwhile members of WITHERING SURFACE. Ryberg, a veteran of cult act ARISE, also plays with INFERNAL TORMENT.
Jonas Lindblood (Linblad) has credits with TAETRE whilst drummer Jesper Frost is known from INIQUITY.

OCEAN OF BLASPHEMY, Diehard RRS948 (1999)
Crest For War / Abomination Of God / Crypts Of Chaos / Impaled / Betrayed By God / Countless Ways To Die / Ocean Of Blasphemy / Desecrating The Graves / Dawn Of Flames / Lunatic Of God's Creation

THORNIUM (SWEDEN)
Line-Up: D. "Thyphenz" Munoz (vocals / guitar / bass / drums), Ulverheim (guitar)

Black Metal band THORNIUM debuted with a 1994 demo entitled 'Northstorm Of The Bestial Goatsign'.

Albums:
DOMINIONS OF THE ECLIPSE, Necromantic Gallery NGP 005-95 (1995)
The Desert Land Of Blackness / Emperor Of The Carpathians / De Som Pesten Drapde / Dominion Of The Eclipse / Det Svarte Riket / Enslaved By The Witches Eye / Helvetespsalm / Slottet I Skuggornas Mörker / Förmörkelsers Herravälde

THORNSPAWN
(San Antonio, TX, USA)
Line-Up: Blackthorn (vocals / drums), Swornghoul (guitar), Bolverk (bass), Lord Necron (guitar)

THORNSPAWN, created in 1993, first made a major impact upon the scene with the infamous demo 'Consecration Of Evil Flesh'. The bands early incarnation for the earlier 1996 'The Dacian Empire' tape, produced by Wrath of AVERSE SEFIRA, was a trio of Blackthorn, Swornghoul and Lord Necron. Bassist Gothmog was added to the ranks shortly after, supplanting Gnostic, but would make way for ex NECROVORE man Bolverk.
THORNSPAWN supported Black Metal veterans MAYHEM on their 2000 American tour.
Both Blackthorn and Lord Necron were announced as being part of the 2000 live incarnation of KRIEG.

Singles/EPs:
Blood Of The Holy, Taint Thy Steel / Master Of The Bloodfury, Profanation (1999) (7" single)
Empress From The Realms Of Blasphemy / Everlasting Siege Of The Necrosoldiers / Master Of The Bloodfury /

Empress From The Realms Of Blasphemy (Unreleased 1998 version), Baphomet (2001) ('Empress From The Realms Of Blasphemy' EP)

Albums:
BLOOD OF THE HOLY, TAINT THY STEEL, Baphomet (2000)
Blood Of The Holy, Taint Thy Steel / Man, Thy Name Is Satan / Storming The Heavens / Ancient Path / Bringer Of Malevolent Storms / Dominion Of Darkness / Thrones Of Susperia

THOR'S HAMMER (POLAND)

THOR'S HAMMER is a solo undertaking of GRAVELAND drummer Capricornus. The man also has another solitary venture entitled CAPRICORNUS which has issued the 7" single 'Stahlgewitter' on Wolftower Records.
Capricornus is also a veteran of INFERNUM and THY WORSHIPPER.

Albums:
FIDELITY SHALL TRIUMPH, Darker Than Black DTB 001 CD (1998)
Fidelity Shall Triumph / Don't Let Your Folk Forget / Atheosophia / Nine Steps To Eternity / Apothetai / Nothing But Hate / Sutr Ferr Sunnam

THORR'S HAMMER
(NORWAY / USA)
Line-Up: Runhild Gammelsäeter (vocals), Stephen O'Malley (guitar), Greg Anderson (guitar), James Hale (bass), Jamie Sykes (drums)

Despite the Norwegian album title THORR'S HAMMER are in fact a project band led by BURNING WITCH's Stephen O'Malley and GOATSNAKE's Greg Anderson. Female lead vocals are handled by the striking figure Ihsahn of EMPEROR's girlfriend Runhild Gammelsäeter.
Both O'Malley and Anderson also busy themselves with SUNNO.

Albums:
DOMMEDAGSNATT, Southern Lord (1999)
Norge / Troll / Dommedagsnatt / Mellom Gadgeme

THOU ART LORD (GREECE)
Line-Up: Gothmog (vocals), Necromayhem (guitar), Magus Wampyr Daoloth (keyboards), Lord Daemon (drums)

THOU ART LORD is a side project from ROTTING CHRIST guitarist Necromayhem, NECROMANTIA's Magus Wampyr Doalath and MORTIFY vocalist Gothmog. The collective heralded their presence with the 1993 demo 'The Cult Of The Horned One'. These tracks later being used for THOU ART LORD's debut 7" single on Molon Lave Records.
A third full length album was planned between Daoloth, Spiros of SEPTIC FLESH and Sakis of ROTTING CHRIST.

Singles/EPs:
Diabolu Archaes Legones, Molon Lave (1993)
In Blood We Trust EP, Molon Lave (1993) (Split EP with ANCIENT RITES)

Albums:
EOSFOROS, Unisound USR011 (1995)
For The Lust Of Lilith / Disciples Of The Black Sorcery / Eosforos Rex Infernus / Towers Of The Autumn Moon / A Call To Chaos (Kaos Keravnos Kybernetos) / Through The Eye Of The Hierophant / Warhammer / The Era Of Satan Rising
APOLLYON, Unisound (1996)
Hate Is Thicker Than Love / Prelude To Apocalypse / Wardance Of The Empress / He Whom The Gods Hath Feared / Societas Satanas / Excremental Magic / Moonscar / In Blood We Trust

THOU SHALT SUFFER (NORWAY)
Line-Up: Ihsahn (vocals / guitar) / Samoth (guitar), Ildjarn (bass), Thorbjorn (drums)

Another side project from Ihsahn of EMPEROR and PECATTUM. Although a more electronic based project than Ihsahn's priority act THOU SHALT SUFFER actually began life as an early 90's precursor to EMPEROR.
The 1991 line up of the band comprised of Ihsahn on vocals and guitar, Samoth on second guitar, Ildjarn on bass and Thorbjørn on drums. For the inaugural demo 'Into The Woods Of Belial'.
A single 'Open The Mysteries Of Your Creation' was released by Mexican label Distorted Harmony with Ronny on drums and Thorbjørn switched to bass. With the foundation of EMPEROR in the summer of 1991 THOU SHALT SUFFER was put on ice with Ildjarn later joining EMPEROR.
Ihsahn resurrected THOU SHALT SUFFER in the late 90's.

Singles/EPs:
Open The Mysteries Of Your Creation, Distorted Harmony (1991)

Albums:
INTO THE WOODS OF BELIAL, (199-)
Into The Woods Of Belial / I Seek The Path Of Obscurity / Chimera Dimension / The Goat Of A Thousand Young / Succumb To Vestigia Terrent / Painful Void Of Time / Spectral Prophecy / Into The Woods Of Belial / The Goat Of A Thousand Young / Chimera Dimension / I See The Path Of Obscurity (burp mix) / Obscurity Supreme
SOMNIUM, Candlelight (2000)
Somnium I / Somnium II / Somnium III / Somnium IV / Somnium V / Somnium VI / Somnium VII / Somnium VIII / Somnium IX / Somnium X

THRENODY (HOLLAND)
Line-Up: Rene Scholte (vocals / guitar), Erik Van De Belt (guitar), Henry McIlveen (bass), John Suyker (drums)

Dutch quartet THRENODY, founded in 1988, first released a 1990 demo, 'Ode To The Lamented', featuring original drummer Mark Van Bel. A further demo titled 'Profonation' scored a big impact on the underground Metal scene.
Having released the 'As The Heavens Fall' in 1995 the self-titled 1997 album saw a break up in ranks with only vocalist/guitarist Rene Scholte and bassist Henry McIlveen surviving. New members were guitarist Menno Gootje and former HIGHWAY CHILE, HELLOISE and VENGEANCE drummer Ernst Van Ee.
Van Ee was to depart and THRENODY drafted Richard Van Leuwen. After touring Van Leuwen also broke ranks to join FROZEN SUN.
For the 1997 eponymous album Van Ee was back on the drum stool on a session basis. The sticksman was to later issue a 2000 solo album credited to simply VAN EE.

Albums:
AS THE HEAVENS FALL, Massacre CD024 (1995)
Cries / Regrets / Dark Ages / Ode To The Lamented / As The Heavens Fall / Come For Me / Despair / The Elder / Supersession Of Breath / In Memorium
BEWILDERING THOUGHTS, Massacre MASS CD065 (1995)
Dare Restrain / Willful / Bewildering

Thoughts / Solitude / Fin De Siecle / Silence / Black Nazareth / Profanation / Autumn / Farewell
THRENODY, Massacre MASS PC0121 (1997)
None/ This Day / Vengeance / Shallow / Dead Man Progress / Instinct Of Pride / Your Truth / To Let Die / Loss Of Dreams / Revelations / Redemption / Outro

THROES OF DAWN (FINLAND)
Line-Up: Jani Heinola (guitar), Toni Jokinen (guitar), Matti Suomela (bass), Teemu Jokinen (drums)

Finnish Black Metal crew THROES OF DAWN heralded their arrival with the 1994 demo 'With The Northern Wind'. When drummer Teemu Jokinen was drafted for his military service the gap was filled by ENOCHIAN CRESCENT's Kai Hahts.

Albums:
PAKKASHERRA, Woodcut (1997)
Across The Loveless Horizon / The Night Belongs To Us / Pakkasherra / Watcher In The Tower / As A Spirit / Cosmic Seas / End Is Silence / Autumn Winds / Cold Goddess / Winter Romance
DREAMS OF THE BLACK EARTH, Woodcut (1998)
The Withering Goddess (Of Nature) / The Weeper / The Blackened Rainbow / Spring Blooms With Flowers Dead / Of Scarlet Skies Made / Titania / Where Once The Sun Rose / Dreams Of The Black Earth
BINDING OF THE SPIRIT, Wounded Love (1999)
The Last Rainbow Warrior Is Dead / The Warprophet Dreams / Binding Of The Spirit Unto Earth / The Hermit / Master's Garden / The Wanderer / On Broken Wings Of Despair / Stardestroyer

THROMDARR (FINLAND)

THROMDARR drummer Marko also lends his talents to BLIND REALITY, PARALYSIS and LET ME DREAM. THROMDARR members would also figure in SKEPTICISM.

Albums:
NORTHSTORM ARRIVES, Millenium Metal Music SOL029 (2000)
Northstorm Arrives / An Eclipse Over The Mountains / Eyes Of Crystal / Path Leads Over The Stone Bridge / Ravens

At The Lake / A Crown Of Black Thorns / Silver Throne / The Embrace Of Cold / By Thy Arrows

THRONE OF AHAZ (SWEDEN)
Line-Up: Fredrik 'Beretorn' Jacobsson (vocals), Marcus 'Whortael' Norman (guitar), Kalle 'Taurtheim' Bondesson (bass), Johan Mortiz (drums)

Umea based Death Metallers THRONE OF AZAZ formed in 1991 and initially comprised the duo of vocalist Beretorn and bassist Taurtheim.
The group was offered a deal by No Fashion Records after the release of the demo 'At The Mountains Of The Northern Storms' in 1992.
Prior to recording of the first album commenced original guitarist Peter was sacked due to musical differences and replaced by Nicklas 'Whortael' Svensson.
The group started work on the record in March 1993, but it was beset by problems and took almost a year to complete.
'Nifelheim' eventually emerged in early 1995, by which time 'Whortael' was superceded by Marcus 'Vargher' Norman. And, although he played on the album, drummer Johan Mortiz did not become a full member of the band until after it's release.
THRONE OF AZAZ returned to the studio in September 1995 in order to put 'On Twilight Enthroned' together, a record that would ultimately comprise eight tracks of hellish Black Metal. It also included a cover of the BLACK SABBATH anthem 'Black Sabbath'.
The group now listed themselves as: Veretorn (vocals), Varghar (guitar / keyboards) and Taurtheim (bass). Moritz still plays drums.
However, 'Varghar' Norman joined both ANCIENT WISDOM and BEWITCHED.

Albums:
NIFELHEIM, No Fashion NFR008 (1995)
Northern Thrones / An Arctic Star Of Blackness / Where Ancient Lords Gather / The Dawn Of War / Nifelheim / The Calling Blaze / A Winter Chant / The Kings That Were...
ON TWILIGHT ENTHRONED, No Fashion NFR016 (1996)
Fenris/ The Forlorn / With Shadow Wings / On Twilight Enthroned / Where Veils of Grief Are Dancing Slow / Let Blood Paint The Ground / Blackthorn Crown / Black Sabbath

349

THRONE OF CHAOS (FINLAND)
Line-Up: Mr. Kiljunen (vocals / guitar), Mr. Harmaja (guitar), Mr. Nora (bass), Mr. Sjoblom (keyboards), Mr. Laitenen (drums)

Albums:
FATA MORGANA, (199-)
MENACE AND PRAYER, Spikefarm NUALA 007 (2000)
From Clarity To Insanity / The Scaffold Scenario / Cold Bits Of Fire / Bloodstained Prophecy / Menace And Prayer / Synthetia / Opus Void / Divinity

THUNDERBOLT (POLAND)
Line-Up: Wrathyr (vocals), Paimon (guitar), Galan Dracos (bass), Uldor (drums)

Black Metal band THUNDERBOLT's debut album 'Black Clouds Over Dark Majesty' was a split affair with KATAXU. The band has been embroiled in controversy since it's inception in 1993 for both their religious and political views.
The band debuted with a demo 'Beyond Christianity' re-released the following year sharing space with KATAXU. Shortly after guitarist Durson was forced out and drummer Uldor was welcomed into the ranks for further recordings 'Black Clouds Over Dark Majesty'.
THUNDERBOLT's problems began when Uldor was imprisoned and other band members were accused of church burning.
Guitarist Paimon also divides his duties as guitarist for SWASTYKA and SELBSTMORD.

Albums:
BLACK CLOUDS OVER DARK MAJESTY, Cymphane AR001CD (2000) (Split album with KATAXU)
Initiation / Shadows Of The deepest Night / My Dark Imagination / Wilderness Of The Eternal Darkness / Moonglare / The Song Of Glory / Intro / My Name From The Forest / War / Roots Thunder / Nawia

THUNDRA (SWEDEN)
Line-Up: Harald Helgesson (vocals/ drums), Rune (guitar), Stein Sund (bass), Nils (keys)

THUNDRA are a Viking Metal side project of EINHERJER bassist Stein Sund and ex ENSLAVED drummer / vocalist Harald Helgesson

Albums:
BLOOD OF YOUR SOUL, Spinefarm (2000)
Infernal / Frozen Ground / Soulseeker / Blood Of Your Soul / Empreal Empress Of War / With Power And Might / Reborn / Raevenrealm

THUS DEFILED (UK)
Line-Up: Paul Carter (vocals / guitar), Jason Bushell (guitar), Sam Cottingham (bass), Nick Leggatt (drums)

Black Metal act THUS DEFILED was created in March 1992 by two ex UNHOLY DEFECATION members bassist Grant Saunders and guitarist Paul Carter.
The duo soon added ex BERSERKER drummer Nick Leggatt. and this line up released two demo tapes during 1993, namely 'Blasphemous Coven' in April and 'Enchanted By The Dark One' in August .
Grant Saunders was later replaced by ex FLESH bassist Sam Cottingham.

Albums:
THROUGH THE IMPURE DARK VEILS OF DAWN, Dark Trinity DTP001 CD (1995)
Wings Of Fallen Majesty / A Crimson Vision In The Glare Of Shadowfire / Prelude To Midnight / Under Blackening Horizons / Through The Impure Veil Of Dawn / Dreaming Beyond Dawnless Realms / Dominus Luciferi / Fear Us For We Are The Darkness / Darkness Rape The Tranquil Shore Of Eternity
WINGS OF THE NIGHT STORM, Dark Trinity (1997)
To Death That Which Again Shall Be / Rapture Of Twilight Burning / Angelblood- The Tears Of An Age Now Dead / Through Eyes Of Fire / Illumination Through Darkness- A Calling For The Chosen / Winters Dawn / Empire Of Souls Bleeding / On Ravenwings I Fly / The Final Fall Of The Light

THY GRIEF (NORWAY)
Line-Up: Kjetil Monsen (vocals / guitar), Kim Anders H. Johannesson (guitar), Christer Korsvold (bass / keyboards), Frode Gaustad (drums)

Bergen's THY GRIEF included AETURNUS and GORGOROTH drummer Vrolok as session drummer on their initial studio demo recordings 'A

Frozen Realm'. THY GRIEF's opening line up comprised of vocalist Roald, guitarists Ken and Kim Anders H. Johannesson with bassist Kjetil Monsen. Upon the demo release THY GRIEF's singer made an exit and Monsen added the lead vocal role to his duties. The band suffered further internal disputes shortly after leaving only Monsen and Johannesson to pick up the pieces. The revitalized THY GRIEF pulled in bassist Christer Korsvold and drummer Frode Gaustad for the album 'The Frozen Tombs of Mankind'. Korsvold would not stay the course and Monsen resumed the bass position.

Albums:
THE FROZEN TOMB OF MANKIND, Solistitium SOL014 (1997)
The Frozen Tomb Of Mankind / Blod Pa Himmelen / Into The Band Of Shadows / Twilight Shine Upon Majestic Mountains / Da Morket Omfavnet Meg / Nocturnal Eyes / In Spite Of Victory / Echoes From A Past Forgotten / Sorgens Klor

THY PRIMORDIAL (SWEDEN)
Line-Up: Isidor (vocals), N. Nilsson (guitar), J. Albrektsson (bass), Morth (drums)

THY PRIMORDIAL started life billed as CARCHAROTH. A name change to LUCIFER ensued before a further name switch to PRIMORDIAL. As PRIMORDIAL the band released a 1995 demo 'En Mörka Makters Alla'. Discovering the Irish act of the same name the Swedes opted finally for THY PRIMORDIAL.
A second demo 'Svart Gryning' ('Black Dawn') led to a 7" single release.
THY PRIMORDIAL's debut album was recorded for the American Gothic label and intended for a 1995 release. However, the release was shelved and the act signed to the Pulverised label for the 'Where Only The Seasons Mark The Path Of Time' effort. The album was produced by Tommy Tägtgren. Seeing THY PRIMORDIAL making strides on their own Gothic hastily issued the intended debut 'Under Iskall Trollmáne'.
The band is fronted by Isidor, otherwise known as Michael Andersson. Both Andersson and bass player J. Albrektssson are also members of INDUNGEON together with MITHOTYN / FALCONER personnel Karl Beckmann and Stefan Wienerhall.

Drummer Morth (real name Jocke Petersson) sessioned on UNMOORED's 'Kingdoms Of Grief' album.

Singles/EPs:
Thy Primordial, Paranoia Syndrome (1996)

Albums:
WHERE ONLY THE SEASONS MARK THE PATH OF TIME, Pulverised ASH 002CD (1997)
The Conquest / Av Ondskapens Natur / Svart Gryning / Forthcoming Centuries / Where Only The Seasons Mark The Path Of Time / Enrapture... Silence / Eristallikar Vinternatt / Hail Unto Thee... Who Travels Over The Heavens / Tronad Av Natten / Dödsskuggan
UNDER ISKALL TROLLMÁNE, Gothic GOTHIC003 (1998)
Mitt Sokandes Ritual / Den Ondes Klor / Under Iskall Trollmáne / Blodsgras / Fe Viskande Tradens Skog / Bortom Nattsvart Himmel / De Morka Maktes Alla / The Impression Of War / Morkets Faste
AT THE WORLD OF UNTRODDEN WONDER, Pulverised (1999)
For Fires To Burn / Once Of The Fortunes Throne / The Fatal Journey / At The World Of Untrodden Wonder / Departure- Away In Spirit / Amongst The Chosen Lost / The Burden Of Time / To Ruin And Decay / My Beloved Darkness / Revealed Throughout The Ages
THE HERESY OF AN AGE OF REASON, Pulverised (2000)
Ceased To Decay / Ex Opere Operatu / Disguised As Beings Of Light / The Heresy Of An Age Of Reason / Mere Are They... / Tyrannize / The Enigma And The Fall / The Dead Live- Shining Crown Of Light

THYRANE (FINLAND)
Line-Up: Blastmor (vocals / drums), Avather (guitar), Daemon (guitar), R. Grönholm (bass)

THYRANE began life as THORNMOON in 1994. Mentor Blastmor would recruit all new members in guitarist Avather, NOCTURNAL ARTS six stringer Daemon and bass player R. Grönholm as the band became THYRANE for the demo 'Black Harmony'. These sessions would eventually see the light of day as a 7" single release too.

351

Black Harmony / Sacrifices / Enthroned By Anti Christ / Satanic Ages Overture, (1997) ('Black Harmony' EP)

Albums:
THE SPIRIT OF REBELLION, (199-) Insidious Dream Of Inhuman Fear / Soulless And Broken / Chaotic Profane Phenomenon / Crushing Defeat Of The Triune Godhead / Thy World Inverted / Words Of The Prophet / Blindfolded **SYMPHONIES OF INFERNALITY**, Woodcut (2000) In The Shape Of A Demon / Satanist / Black Atmospheric Madness / Simphony Of Infernality / Envenomed Suicidal Angels / Crimson Halls Of Blood / Beneath The Banner Of The Unholy Satan's Cult / Devil Messiah

THY REPENTANCE (RUSSIA)

Albums:
URAL TWILIGHT AUTUMNALIAS, Undead Wood Productions (1996) Sorcery- Inseparable Story / Moon Roots Of War / Before The Awakening / Wizard And Witch / When The Sky Is Dark Yet / Griefwings Bloddrup / Cloudy Sign-Unholy Psalm / Flowers Of Triumphant (I Hate Them Again) / Drowned In Leaves / Ural Twilight Autumnalias / My Show Funeral Curtain- New Scene
THROUGH THE TWILIGHT EYES OF FROST, Undead Wood Productions (1997)
CONTROL SHOT OR HALLS OF READ, (1998) (Split album with NUCLEAR WINTER)
Hall Of Hate (The Global Coffin) / Hall Of Opposition (Apocalyptic Impression) / Hall Of Predestination (Falling Of The poisoned) / Hall Of Fire (The Song Of Ash And Dust) / Hall Of Zero (The Bullet's Blizzard) / Hall Of Might (Supreme Meaning Of Knowledge)

THYRFING (SWEDEN)
Line-Up: Thomas Väänanen (vocals), Patrick Lindgren (guitar), H. Svegsjö (guitar), Kimmy Sjolund (bass), Pete Lof (keyboards), Jocke Kristensson (drums)

Epic Viking Metal. THRYFING was founded by PANTHEON members vocalist Thomas Väänanen, guitarist Patrick Lindgren and bass player Kimmy Sjolund. For the debut demo session 'Solen Svartnar' ('Sun Turns Black') the band drafted second guitarist Vintras of

FUNERAL MIST. A second cassette 'Hednaland' led to a deal with the Dutch Hammerheart label and album 'Thyrfing' produced by Tommy Tägtgren and DISMEMBER's Fred Estby. Vintras would depart in favour of ANCIENT WINDS man H. Svegsjö. 1999 proved an important year for the group as it included their first series of European shows playing alongside NILE, VADER, CRYPTOPSY and SIX FEET UNDER. The band also performed at the Dynamo Festival in Holland.
Grim rune Productions would reissue the band's first demo on a 7" single leading up to the release of second album 'Valdr Galga'. Further touring on the European mainland had THYRFING sharing stages with SHADOWBREED and PRIMORDIAL.
Versions of THRYFING's 2000 album 'Urkraft' sees an inspirational cover version of GARY MOORE's 'Over The Hills And Far Away'. Gust vocals came courtesy of SINS OF OMISSION members Toni Kocmut with session guitars from Martin Persson.

Singles/EPs:
Solen Svartner I / Solen Svartner II / Slaget / … Ty Mörkret Skallfallen / Thyrfing, Grim Rune Productions (1999) ('Solen Svartner' EP)

Albums:
THYRFING, Hammerheart HHR016 (1998)
Raven Eyes / Vargavinter / Set Sail To Plunder / Ur Asken Ett Rike / Celebration Of Our Victory / A Burning Arrow / En Döende Mars Förbannebe / Hednaland / Wotan's Fire / Going Berserk
VALDR GALGA, Hammerheart HHR039 (1999)
Heading For The Golden Hall / Storms Of Asgard / From Wilderness Came Death / Askans Rike / Valdr Galga The Deceitful / Arising / Forever / A Moment In Valhalla / Mimer's Well / A Great Man's Return
URKRAFT, Hammerheart HHR061 (2000)
Mjölner / Dryckesväde / Sweoland Conquer / Home Again / The Breaking Of Serenity / Bdfärd / Ways Of A Parasite / Jord / The Slumber Of Yesteryears / Till Valfader Ungrammal

THY SERPENT (FINLAND)
Line-Up: Luopio (vocals / bass / keyboards), Azhemin (vocals /

keyboards), Sami Tenetz (guitar), Agathon Frosteus (drums)

A Doom Death Metal band THY SERPENT formed in 1992 as guitarist Sami Tenetz began recording rehearsal tapes followed by more professional sounding demos, including 1994's 'Frozen Memory'.

With interest from Spinefarm Records Tenetz opted to recruit band members to a project he had worked on single handedly up to that point. After a number of changes a stable group of musicians were found that enabled recording of 1996's 'Forest Of Witchery' meisterwerk to be commenced.

Oddly, Spinefarm has gone on record to state that THY SERPENT will never play live. Nevertheless, the 1998 album saw the inclusion of CHILDREN OF BODOM guitarist Alexi Laiho into the ranks.

Drummer Agathon Frosteus also operates with GLOOMY GRIM, NOMICON, BARATHRUM and SOULGRIND. Luopio would session for SOULGRIND's 1998 record 'Whitsongs' whilst keyboard player Azhemin would contribute to the 1999 SOULGRIND album 'Kalma'. Members of the band involved themselves with BARATHRUM for the 2000 side project act SHAPE OF DESPAIR issuing the 'Shades of...' album.

Singles/EPs:
Death EP, Spinefarm (2000)

Albums:
FOREST OF WITCHERY, Spinefarm SPI 36CD (1996)
Flowers Of Witchery Abloom / Of Darkness And Light / Traveller Of Unknown Plains / Only Dust Moves... / Like A Funeral Veil Of Melancholy / Wine From Tears
LORDS OF TWILIGHT, Spinefarm (1997)
Prometheus Unbound / The Forest Of Blåkulla / Ode To The Witches- Part IV / In Blackened Dreams / As Mist Descends From the Hills / Unknown / Epic Torment / In Blackened Dreams / Ode To The Witches- Part III
CHRISTCRUSHER, Nuclear Blast NB 327-2 (1998)
Chambers Of The Starwatchers / Curtain Of Treachery / Thou Bade Nothingness / Go Free The Wolves / Circles Of Pain / Christcrusher / Crystalmoors / Calm Blinking
DEATH, Spinefarm SPI102CD (2000)
Deathbearer / Wounds Of Death / Sleep In Oblivion / Parasites

THY WORSHIPPER (POLAND)

Polish Black Metal protagonists THY WORSHIPPER issued the 'Winterdream' demo in 1993. Drummer Capricornus would later figure in GRAVELAND and INFERNUM as well as solo ventures THOR'S HAMMER and CAPRICORNUS.

Albums:
POPIOL (INTROIBO AD ALTARE DEI...), Morbid Noizz (1996)

TIDFALL (NORWAY)
Line-Up: Rogon D. Blodgraat (vocals), Abraxas (guitar), Sorg (bass), Aftaneldr (keyboards), Zarthon (drums)

TIDFALL members drummer Zarthon and bassist Sorg are also included in the ranks of PASQUIL and also Death Metal band CRITERION. Not to be outdone guitarist Abraxas and keyboard player Aftaneldr operate side act ICON 44.

Albums:
CIRCULAR SYMPHONY, Nocturnal Art (2000)
In The Eyes Of Death / A Hidden Realm / Allured By Grief / Black Psychotic Darkness / Bloodact / Shining Serpent / In A Dark Dream / Empty Silence / Reflections / Hymn To Fall

TIERMES (FINLAND)
Line-Up: Jarkkko Toivonen (guitar), Jussi Saivo

Ambient Black landscapes. TIERMES' guitarist Jarkko Toivonen is ex UNHOLY. Jussi Saivo is a former member of F.

Albums:
TIERMES, Elfenblut (1997)

TODAY IS THE DAY
(Nashville, TN, USA)
Line-Up: Steve Austin (vocals / guitar), Bill Kelliher (bass), Brann Dailor (drums)

Trio TODAY IS THE DAY forté is apocalyptic notions woven into a distinctly Satanic tapestry of Black Metal based around the turning of the millenium. The band actually evolved through the hardcore / Indie scene signed as they were initially to Amphetamine Reptile

Records in 1992.

Frontman Steve Austin forged the debut line up in alliance with drummer Brad Elrod and bass player Mike Harrell in 1992 for the 'Supernova' EP. Further recordings emerged on a shared mini album with GUZZARD and CHOKEBONE and 1994's 'Willpower' and TODAY IS THE DAY also scored a valuable session on Radio One's John Peel show. Touring in 1996 saw the band on the road with NEUROSIS and EYEHATEGOD.

Austin revamped the band completely by drafting bassist Chris Reeser and drummer Mike Hyde for the groundbreaking 'Temple Of The Morning Star' opus.

The pivotal track with which the 'Temple Of The Morning Star' album revolves is actually a real Satanic ritual conducted by the Denver Temple Of The Morning Star cult overladen with music.

In 1999 the trio morphed once more with new faces being bassist Bill Kelliher and drummer Brann Dailor.

Austin produced the debut album from BANE 'It All Comes Down To This' adding guest vocals too. Other acts to benefit from Austin's production talents include CONVERGE and BURN THE PRIEST.

Singles/EPs:
I Bent Scared / Come Down And Get Scared, Amphetamine Reptile (1993) (split EP with COALESCE)
Clusterfuck, Amphetamine Reptile (1994)

Albums:
SUPERNOVA, Amphetimine Reptile (1993)
Black Dahlia / 6 Dimensia Satyr / Silver Tongue / Blind Man And Mystic Lake / Adult World / The Begging / The Kick Inside / Goose Is Cooked / Timeless / Rise / The Guilt Barber / Self Portrait / Untitled
WILLPOWER, Amphetimine Reptile (1994)
Willpower / My First Knife / Nothing To Lose / Golden Calf / Sidewinder / Many Happy Returns / Simple Touch / Promised Land / Amazing Grace
TODAY IS THE DAY, Amphetimine Reptile (1996)
Hai Piranha / Marked / Bugs Death March / A Man Of Science / Realization / Black Iron Prison / Mountain People / Ripped Off / The Tragedy / She Is In Fear Of Her Death / I Love My Woman /

Dot Matrix
TEMPLE OF THE MORNING STAR, Relapse RR 6964 (1997)
Temple Of The Morning Star / The Man Who Loves To Hurt Himself / Blindspot / High As The Sky / Miracle / Kill Yourself / Mankind / pinnacle / Crutch / Root Of All Evil / Satan Is Alive / Rabid Lassie / Friend For Life / My Life With You / I See You / Hermaphrodite / Temple Of The Morning Star- Sabbath Bloody Sabbath
IN THE EYES OF GOD, Relapse (1999)
In The Eyes Of God / Going To Hell / Spotting A Unicorn / Possession / The Color Of Psychic Power / Mayari / Soldier Of Fortune / Bionic Cock / Argali / Afterlife / Himself / Daddy / Who Is The Black Angel? / Martial Law / False Reality / The Russian Child Porn Ballet / The Cold Harshness Of Being Wrong Throughout Your Life / Honor / Worn Out / There Is No End
LIVE TILL YOU DIE, Relapse (2000)
The Color Of Psychic Power / Pinnacle / Feel Like Makin' Love / Temple Of The Morning Star / Wicked Game / Crutch / Ripped Off (Acoustic) / High As The Sky / In The Eyes Of God / Users / TDA / Blindspot / Why Don't We Do It In The Street / Afterlife / The Man Who Loved To Hurt Himself

TORGEIST (FRANCE)

Black Metallers TORGEIST opened proceedings with a 1994 demo 'Devoted To Satan'. The 1996 album was a split affair shared with fellow countrymen VLAD TEPES.

Albums:
BLACK LEGIONS METAL, Drakkar DKC003 (1996) (Split album with VLAD TEPES)
March Of Black Assemblies / Sweet Death / Flame Of Hate / My Soul For Your Victory / Bloody Tears / Time Of Sabbath

TORMENTOR (HUNGARY)

Line-Up: Attila Csihar (vocals), Attila Szigeti (guitar), Tamás Budai (guitar), Frakas György (bass), Machat Zsolt (drums)

The 1996 TORMENTOR album is in fact the band's 1989 demo. TORMENTOR vocalist Attilla Csihar brought the band back to the attention of contemporary Black Metal fans with his guest appearance with MAYHEM's De Mysteriis

Dom Stahanas' album.

Such was the interest raised in TORMENTOR due to the MAYHEM connection a bootleg CD of the band's 1988 demo 'Seventh Day Of Doom' was issued in 1996. Attila guested on ABORYM's 'Kali Yuga Bizarre' album in 1999 and lent his vocal attributes to EMPEROR's cover of 'Funeral Fog' for a MAYHEM tribute. The 2000 album 'Recipe Ferrum!' had TORMENTOR credited as vocalist Paprikajancsiharcsa Drattula (Attila Csihar), guitarist Mugambi Zoldud Bwana, bassist Kelempajszzénó Galóla and drummer Machat St. Zsoltar Motolla.

Albums:
SEVENTH DAY OF DOOM, (1988)
Damned Graves / Intro / Tormentor / Branded The Satan / Infinitive Darkness / Mephisto / Damned Grave / Live In Damnation / Seventh Day Of Doom
ANNO DOMINI, Nocturnal Art Eclipse 004 (1996)
Introduction / Tormentor I / Grauen / Elisabeth Bathory / Damned Grave / In Gate Of Hell / Transylvania / Tormentor II / Trance / Beyond / Apocalypse / Lyssa / Anno Domine
RECIPE FERRUM!, Avantgarde AV049 (2000)
Intro / Recipe Ferrum! / Iron Country / The Little Match Girl / Dracula / Cara Mia / Cult, Legend, Tales, Nation, Fun, Theatre, Joke: Paprika Jancsi Intro / Paprika Jancsi / Hany Istok / A Hêtszúnyú Kaponyányi Monyók / Sickness, Punishment Of The Evil Child- Brummactza / Hany Istok (Barlang mix) / A'Ordog- The Devil

TOTENNACHT (AUSTRIA)
Line-Up: Hagen (vocals), Said El Mahdi (guitar / keyboards), Cornelius Dix (keyboards)

TOTENNACHT is the Doom / Gothic Metal side project of WERWOLF vocalist Hagen complete with German lyrics and programmed drums.

Albums:
DER SCHWARZE PRINZ, Serpent Qui Danse SQD 01 (1996)
Der schwarze Prinz / Vampir des Herzens / Flammentor / Romantisches Sterben / Der Freudige Tote / Schrei / Tod ist Abstrakt / Der Komödiant / Von Zwergen und Riesen / Die neue Erde

TRAIL OF TEARS (NORWAY)
Line-Up: Ronni Thorsen (vocals), Helena Iren Michaeisen (vocals), Runar Hansen (guitar), Terje Heiseldal (guitar), Kjell Rune Hagen (bass), Frank Roald Hagen (keyboards),

Founded as NATT in 1994 TRAIL OF TEARS are an ambitious Black Metal act employing both male and female lead vocals. The band was wrought with perpetual line up challenges on the path to the debut album for Dutch label DSFA Records.
Original female singer Ales Vik exited in favour of Helena Irena Michaelsen upfront of the demo 'When Silence Cries'. Further changes saw drummer Vidar Uleberg on his way out in favour of Jonathon Perez and the augmentation of keyboards to the band courtesy of Frank Roald Hagen.
Following the demo release guitarist Michael Krumis decamped and in came Runar Hansen. Supporting the promotion of the 'Disclosure In Red' album TRAIL OF TEARS toured with guests GAIL OF GOD prior to further dates alongside TRISTANIA. November 1999 found TRAIL OF TEARS on the road with CALLENISH CIRCLE.
The recording of the second album 'Profoundemonium' witnessed the acrimonious split with Michaelsen as TRAIL OF TEARS handed over the position of lead female vocals to Cathrine Paulsen.
TRAIL OF TEARS vocalist Ronni Thorsen also forms part of SCARIOT, the band project assembled by IN THE WOODS drummer Anders Kobros and ex SATYRICON guitarist Daniel Olaisen.

Albums:
DISCLOSURE IN RED, DSFA DSFA1018 (1998)
When Silence Cries / The Daughters Of Innocence / The Day We Drowned / Mournful Pigeon / Swallowed Tears / Illusion? / Enigma Of The Absolute / Words Of The Fly / Temptress / The Burden
PROFUONDEMONIUM, Napalm NPR 084 (2000)
Countdown To Ruin / Driven (Through The Ruins) / Fragile Emotional Disorder / Profoundemonium / Sign Of The Shameless / In Frustration's Preludium / In Frustration's Web / Released At Last / Image Of Hope / Disappointment's True Face / The Haunted

TRELLDOM (NORWAY)
Line-Up: Graahl (vocals), Bjorn (guitar / bass),

Black Metal merchants TRELLDOM released a demo 'Disappearing Of The Burning Moon' prior to signing to Head Not Found Records for the 1995 debut album.
Guitarist Bjorn has credits with BETRAYER. Vocalist Graahl would later front GORGOROTH.

Albums:
TIL EVIGHET..., Head Not Found (1995)
Endlos Vandring Gjennom Evighet / Fullmaanens Hemmelightet / Disappearing Of The Burning Moon / Sannhet, Smerte Og Dod / Taake / Sunset / Chasms Of Solitude / Frosten Har Tint Mine Smerter / Til Evighet...
TIL ET ANNET..., (1998)
Vander Meg Mot Et Kommende / Slave Til Den Kommende Natt / Min Dod Til Ende / Til Et Annet / Til Is Skal Jeg Forbli / Svinfylking / Hoyt Oppe I Dypet / Son Ardreyri

TRIFIXION (AUSTRIA)
Line-Up: Trifixion Of The Horned King (vocals / bass / keyboards / drums), Yog Sototh (guitar)

A Black Metal solo project from WERWOLF, PAZUZU and former SUMMONING member Trifixion Of The Horned King. Pre commercially available recordings TRIFIXION had tested the waters with the 'Syndrome Of New Flesh' demo.
The Austrian's album was recorded with the aid of guitarist Yog Sototh.

Albums:
THE FIRST AND LAST COMMANDMENT, Lethal LRC 20 (1995)
Prologue / Prince Lucifer Here I Stand / Dreams Of Burning Churches / Faceless Souls / From Far Beyond His Land / Let The Feast Begin / Ascending Of The Empire / The First And The Last Commandment

TRISTANIA (NORWAY)
Line-Up: Vibeke Stene (vocals), Morton Veland (vocals / guitar), Anders H. Hidle (guitar), Rune Osterhus (bass), Einar Moen (keyboards), Kenneth Olsson (drums)

A much vaunted female fronted Dark Wave Gothic project TRISTANIA was created in late 1996. Keyboard player Einar Moen and guitarist Morten Veland were both previously with UZI SUICIDE. Vibeke Stene created side project GREEN CARNATION with EMPEROR's Tchort and Mitgliedern from IN THE WOODS.

Singles/EPs:
Sirene / Midwintertears / Pale Enchantress / Cease To Exist, Napalm NRR036 (1997) ('Tristania' EP)
Angina / Opus Relinque (Radio edit) / Saturnine, Napalm (1999) ('Angina' EP)

Albums:
WIDOW'S WEEDS, Napalm NPR041 (1998)
Preludium / Evenfall / Pale Enchantress / December Elegy / Midwintertears / Angellore / My Lost Lenore / Wasteland Caress / Postludium
BEYOND THE VEIL, Napalm (1999)
Beyond The Veil / Aphelion / A Sequel Of Decay / Opus Reinque / Lethean River / ...Of Ruins And A Red Nightfall / Simbelmyne / Angina / Heretique / Dementia

TRISTITIA (SWEDEN)
Line-Up: Thomas Karlsson (vocals), Luis Beethoven Galvez (guitar / bass / keyboards), Bruno Nilsson (drums)

Labeled as 'Extreme dark Doom' TRISTITIA evolved from a meeting in August 1992 between the half Chilean / half Swedish guitarist ("All true axes of darkness, hatred and madness") Luis Beethoven Galvez and vocalist ("Chants of death") Thomas Karlsson.
Galvez was a former member of PAGAN RITES along with Karlsson, although the latter had also worked with AUTOPSY TORMENT.
TRISITIA's first four track demo in 1993 featured 'Winds Of Sacrifice', 'Dancing Souls', 'Burn The Witch' and 'The Other Side'.
A second demo followed in 1994, once more boasting four tracks (in this instance 'Reminiscences Of The Mourner', 'Envy The Dead', 'Ashes Of The Witch' and 'Mark My Words'. It was only at this point that the band added drummer Bruno Nilsson and signed with French label Holy Records.
Nilsson was not in the group for long as he was to depart in favour of ex PAGAN

RITES drummer Adrian Letelier.

Albums:
ONE WITH DARKNESS, Holy
HOLY11CD (1995)
Sorrow / Kiss The Cross / One With
Darkness / Winds Of Sacrifice / Burn
The Witch / Hymn Of Lunacy / Ashes Of
The Witch / Dancing Souls / Adagio
1809 / Reminiscences Of The Mourner /
Dance Of The Selenites
CRUCIDICTION, Holy HOLY 21 CD
(1996)
Ego Sum Resurrectio / Christianic
Indulgence / Crudiction / Wintergrief /
Envy The Dead / Lioness' Roar / Mark
My Words / Gardenia / Final Lament
THE LAST GRIEF, Holy (2000)
Once Upon A Dawn... / In The Light Of
The Moon / Slaughtery / Evolic / Golden
Goddess Of Fire / Tears And Tequila /
Angelwitch's Palace / Memory's Garden
/ Instrumental Hollowcoast / MediEvil /
Under The Cross / Darknia: The Last
Grief

TRIUMPHATOR

TRIUMPHATOR (SWEDEN)
Line-Up: Tena (vocals / bass), Arioch
(guitar), Draugen (drums)

Black Metal that features members of
FUNERAL MIST and MARDUK. The
band was created in 1995 by frontman
Tena together with members of the band

BLASPHEMER. A demo, 'The Triumph Of
Satan', was cut prior to Tena completely
overhauling the band.
The 1999 version of TRIUMPHATOR that
figured on the 7" single 'The Ultimate
Sacrifice' comprised of Tena, FUNERAL
MIST guitarist Arioch and MARDUK
drummer Fredrik Andersson.
Latterly TRIUMPHATOR have enlisted
Draugen as drummer.

Singles/EPs:
Redeemer Of Chaos / Heralds Of
Pestilence, Mark Of The Devil (1999)
('The Ultimate Sacrifice' EP)

Albums:
WINGS OF ANTICHRIST, Necropolis
NR048 CD (2000)
Infernal Divinity / Conquered Light /
Heralds Of Pestilence / Burn The Heart
Of The Earth / Crushed Revelation /
Redeemer Of Chaos /. The Triumph Of
Satan / Goathorned Abomination

TROLL (NORWAY)

TROLL is a project band of KOVENANT
and ex DIMMU BORGIR bass player
Nagash (a.k.a. Lex Icon, real name Stian
Arnesen). In TROLL Nagash performs
vocals, guitar, bass, keyboards and even
drums. TROLL debuted with a demo in
1994 although Nagash had first started
work on the band when he was a mere 14
years old. Co conspirators with Nagash
("Crusher of mountains") at this stage
were vocalist Fafnir and guitarist
("Swinging of the battle axe") Glaurung.
It's follow up titled 'Trollstorm Øver
Nidingjuv' was re-released commercially
by Head Not Found Records although
TROLL had now become a purely solo
venture.
For the 2000 album 'The Last Predators'
MAYHEM and KOVENANT drummer
Hellhammer also guests as does
KOVENANT's Psy Coma (Thanatos).
Fafnir also made a re-appearance but
retitled 'Sinister Minister Twice'.

Singles/EPs:
Naar Hatten Endelig Er Hev / Trollstorm
Øver Nidingjuv / Over Daudens Kolde
Mark / I Et Hedensk Land, Head Not
Found (1996) ('Trollstorm Øver Nidingjuv'
EP)
Albums:
DREP DE KRISTNE, Damnation (1996)
Kristenhat / I Saler Av Stev / Trollberg /
Naar Solenblekner Bort / Troll Riket /

Med Vold Skal Takes Kristen Liv / Gud's Fall / Drep De Kristne
THE LAST PREDATORS, Voices Of Wonder (2000)
Bastards Last Breath / Fall Of The Marbled Galaxy / Seierens Stråler / Mending The Instincts / Colony XII-Inflict Mythical Mayhem / My Glance Into The Narrow Moon / Eye As In I / A.T.-The Last Riddle / The Last Predators / Freisevers Visjoner

TSATTHOGGUA (GERMANY)
Line-Up: False Prophet (vocals / bass), Nar Marratuk (guitar), Northwind (keyboards), Lightning Bolt (drums)

This German Black Metal band was formed in 1993 from the ashes of DISSECTION. In their previous manifestation as DISSECTION the band issued three demos starting with 1989's 'Maniac Depression' followed by 'Unrecognizable Human Form' in 1991 and finally 'Hyperboreer' in 1993.
Releasing a number of demos, including 'Siegesville', that found favour on the underground scene, the group played shows with THERION and ATROCITY before being signed by Osmose.
The group's debut album, 'Hosanna Bizarre', was released in early 1996. Touring the same year had the band on the road with MARDUK.

Singles/EPs:
Status Stürmer (Black Sun mix) / Courtesan May Slut (666 Joy edit), Osmose Productions (1999) ('German Black Metal' 7" single)

Albums:
HOSANNA BIZARRE, Osmose OP 035 (1996)
Heirs Of Fire / Dionysos' Ecstasy / Niemals Geboren / 2000 V Kum / Hosanna Bizarre / The Belief-The Lie / Intrude Into Immortality / Worm Of Sin / Seventh Solitude
TRANS CUNT WHIP, Osmose (199-)
Trans Cunt Whip / La O Tsatthoggua / Status Stürmer / To The Credo Of Inversion / Golden Shower / Endeavour To Pace / In Dope We Trust / Angel Of The Universe / Courtesan May Slut
EXTAZIA, Necropolis (1999)
Extazia / Halleluja Iudäa / 2000 V. Kum Part II / Ancient World Of Terror / Bondage Sisterhood / Of Gods And Stars / Lascivious Way Of Life / Melmoth In Providence / Orgies Of The Deranged

/ 23 Atlantia

T666 (AUSTRALIA)

Singles/EPs:
Comrades In Slaughter / Execute All Christians / Smash The Cross, (1999) ('Troops Of Satan' EP)

TSJUDER (NORWAY)
Line-Up: Nag (vocals / bass), Arak Draconiiz (guitar), Diabolus Mort (guitar), Draugluin (guitar), Anti Christian (drums)

Pure unadulterated no frills Black Metal band TSJUDER date back to 1993 and the union of guitarist Berserk and vocalist and bassist Nag. The following year Draugluin (real name Halvor Storrøsten) was added on guitar for the initial demo tape 'Vedferdensende'.
Berserk exited after the tape release as TSJUDER enrolled drummer Torvus for a second session 'Possessed'. Friction was still evident as Torvus was given his marching orders being supplanted by Desecrator. The band also enlisted American guitarist Diabolus Mort.
This line up cut the EP 'Throne Of The Goat' for Solistitium Records.
Blod of GEHENNA sessioned on drums for the debut album 'Kill For Satan'. TSJUDER also drafted ISVIND mainman Arak Draconiis on guitar.
Live work saw the addition of drummer Anti Christian.

Singles/EPs:
Throne Of The Goat / Dying Spirits, Solistitium SOL025 (1997)
Atum Nocumem, At War (1999)

Albums:
KILL FOR SATAN, Drakkar (1999)
The Daemon Gate / Necromancy / Lord Of Terror / Raping Christianity / Dying Spirits / Kill For Satan (The King's Bizarre) / Sodomising The Lamb (The King's Conquering) / Beyond The Gate (The King's Reign)

TULUS (NORWAY)
Line-Up: Blodstrop (vocals / guitar), Gottskalk (bass), Sarke (drums)

Influential Black Metal merchants TULUS date back to 1991. A series of demos including 1994's 'Samlerens Kammer' and 1995's 'Midvintermane' were issued prior to the debut album. Bassist Gottskalk has credits with MINAS

TIRITH.

Both frontman Blodstrup (real name Sverre Stokland) and drummer Sarke would opt to join OLD MAN'S CHILD in 1996 but TULUS carried on releasing a sophomore effort 'Mysterion' in 1998. Sarah Jezebel Deva of CRADLE OF FILTH added guest vocals.

The 1999 album, released on the Dutch Hammerheart label, had Sir Graanug taking the bass guitar role.

The 2000 compilation 'Cold Core Collection' comprise the first two albums, demo tracks and newly recorded cover versions of DAVID BOWIE's 'Space Oddity' and OBITUARY's 'Slowly We Rot'.

Albums:
PURE BLACK ENERGY, Hot (1996)
Grav / Samlerens Kammer / Tjern / Ulvemelk Og Trollsmer / Søstre Av Natten / Inskripsjon Etter Jordferd / Kaldt / Varg / Midtvintermåne / De Dødes Attest
MYSTERION, Hot (1998)
Dommes Fugi / Skugg Eskip / Gravstenskugge / Mysterion / Vetterels / Døderhulder / Skriket Fra Juvet / Evighetens Port / Mäne
EVIL 1999, Hammerheart (1999)
Mennesskefar / Tarantulus / Draug / Cyprianus / Dokkemaker / Salme / Blodstrup / Sjel / Dårskap Tilvisdom / Kviteheim
COLD CORE COLLECTION, Facefront (2000)
Grav / Samlerens Kammer / Tjern / Ulvemelk Og Trollsmer / Søstre Av Natten / Inskripsjon Etter Jordferd / Kaldt / Varg / Midtvintermåne / De Dødes Attest / Dommes Fugi / Skugg Eskip / Gravstenskugge / Mysterion / Vetterels / Døderhulder / Skriket Fra Juvet / Evighetens Port / Mäne / Søstre Av Natten / Varg / Kulde / Grav / De Dødes Attest / Samlerens Kammer / Varg / Midtvintermåne / Inskipsjorn Etter Jordferd / Tunge Dråper Fra Et Mørkt Hjerte / Slowly We Rot / Space Oddity

TUNRIDA (FINLAND)
Line-Up: Lord Adad (vocals / guitar), Baron Thoth (guitar), Arrakis (bass), Achernar (drums)

Albums:
HIERARCHY, Solistitium SOL026 (1997)
My Finest Hour / Pathways To Cosmos Opened / Est Sularus Oth Mithas / God Of Infamy, Lies And Fear / The Calling /

Preacher Of Immortality / Hierarchy Of The Cosmos / Astral Majesty Revealed / Your Second Coming

TUONELA (FINLAND)
Line-Up: Skred (vocals), I. Laitinen (guitar), Leka (bass), J. Lehtinen (keyboards), M. Lehtelä (drums)

TUONELA first developed in 1996 founded by I. Laitinen but would split mid career in acrimonious circumstances. Laitinen at first pulled in guitarist J. Jokinen and KHARON drummer M.K. in an as then unnamed band. With the departure of Jokinen the title TUONELA was adopted as vocalist / guitarist T. Ahonierri and bassist M. Parvianen were drafted in. The latter would soon make a hasty exit as did the next incumbent of the bass position M. Suominen. J. Lehtinen took the keyboard role but he too would bail out before the debut demo of 1997 'Metsän Pimennossa'.
In 1997 vocalist Skred, his bassist brother Leka and drummer Mortarr created MYRING. Mortarr was soon to depart this new act being replaced by Vidar.
TUONELA persevered and by 1999 J. Betlämäki was on drums with NOCTURN bassist J. Tolonen making up the rhythm section. A later line up saw the return of keyboard player Lehtinen and the recruitment of drummer M. Lehtelä.

Albums:
ASTRALS OF DISTANCE, (199-)
Astrals Of Distance / Incomprehensible Structure Of Absurdity / Snowcovered North / Obscure Agony / Aurora Borealis Beneath The Firmament / Final Verses Of Destint

TVANGESTE (RUSSIA)
Line-Up: Miron (vocals / guitar), Nicholas Kazmin (guitar), Vano Maioroff (bass), Victoria Koulbachnaia (keyboards)

A highly rated symphonic Black Metal act created in 1996 by vocalist / guitarist Miron (real name Michael Chirva) and guitarist Nicholas Kazmin. Later recruits were former DIS PATER and ROMOWE RIKOITO keyboard player Victoria Koulbachnaia and bassist Vano Maioroff from Death Metal act DIVERSION.
Singles/EPs:
Blood Dreams, (1998)

Albums:
DAMNATION OF REGIOMONIUM,

359

Valgaldar (2000)
From Nameless Oracle / Angels Retreat / Damnation Of Regiomonium / Thinking / Born To Be King Of Innerself

TWILIGHT (GREECE)
Line-Up: Hades Of Absu (vocals), Oinopion Ho Satyrus (guitar), Kataclysm (bass), Death Dealer (keyboards), Vongar (drums)

TWILIGHT was created by erstwhile OSCULAM INFAME singer Hades Of Absu. After numerous line up shuffles the band settled on a line up headed by Hades and featuring guitarist Oinopion Ho Satyrus, bassist Marder, keyboard player Death Dealer and drummer Nocturnal Wizard.
In 1996 a fresh rhythm section of bassist Kataclysm and drummer Vongar was recruited.

Albums:
AND WITH THE TWILIGHT THEY RETURN, Invasion Music INV004 (1999)

TWILIGHT OPERA (FINLAND)
Line-Up: Sauli Karkkunen (vocals), Mikko Kaipaine (guitar), Tony Natkki (guitar), Timo Puranen (keyboards), Timo Kollin (drums)

Black Metal with classical structures forged by former members of REMEMBRANCE and KATHARSIS.

Albums:
SHADOWS EMBRACE THE DARK, Cacophonous NIHIL 27 CD (1998)
Crown Of Thorns / Blessed To Forget / The Moon Is Your Lover / Darkness Is Thy Kingdom Part I / Queen Of The Night / Darkness Is Thy Kingdom Part II / Shadowdancer / Opera 666: The Whore / Wasted / Storms Of Silence
MIDNIGHT HORROR, Cacophonous NIHIL 35 CD (1999)
Pandemonium Bizarre / Burning Velvet Panquin / Passion's Delivery / Chaos And The Conquest / Night Beholds To Supreme Clandestine / Black Fire In The Chasm Of Rapture / Devastation Of Empyrean (Before The Dawn) / Engrossed By Carnal Lust / Midnightmare

TWIN OBSCENITY (NORWAY)
Line-Up: Atle Wiig (vocals / guitar / keyboards), Jo-Arild Toennessen (bass), Evilhomer (drums)

Black Metal band TWIN OBSCENITY was created in late 1991. The band issued a stream of demos with 1993's 'Ruins' and 'Behind The Castle Walls' leading up to the 'Revelations Of Glaaki' session.
Drummer Evilhomer is better known to his parents as Knut Naesje and also has credits with HATE DIVISION. During mid 1997 the band drafted MYRIADS members guitarist Alexander Twiss and vocalist Mona Undheim Skottere but by the summer of the following year the pair had departed to concentrate on their main act.

Albums:
WHERE LIGHT TOUCHES NONE, Head Not Found HNFO 26CD (1997)
Dark Millennium's End / When The Chains Are Broken / Enchanted By The Empress' Beauty / Like The Death Of A Sorceress / Tribute To Mortality / The Infernal Dance Of Prince Kaleth / Dreams Of A Holocaust Night / Revelations Of Glaaki / Where Light Touches None
FOR BLOOD, HONOUR AND SOIL, (199-)
In Glorious Strife / The Usurper's Throne / For Blood, Honour And Soil / Upon The Morning Field / The Wanderer / Riders Of The Imperial Guard / The Thrice Damned Legions / The 11th Hour / Lain To Rest By The Sword

TYRANT (JAPAN)

TYRANT included RITUAL CARNAGE man Damian Montgomery in the ranks before recording of the 'Under The Dark Mystic Sky' debut.

Albums:
UNDER THE DARK MYSTIC SKY, Pulverised ASH 004 CD (1998)
Prologue To Tragedy / Grudge Of Dannoura / Ghost Waltz / The God Of Winter / Vice / Into The Hades / Under The Dark Mystic Sky / Mirage Beneath The Black Moon

ULCUS (NORWAY)
Line-Up: Sture Dingsøyr (vocals / guitar), Stian Bakketeig (guitar), Jarle Kvåle (bass), Jørn Holen (drums)

ULCUS, previously titled ULCUS MOLLE, was borne in 1994 with a line up of vocalist / guitarist Sture Dingsøyr, guitarist Hektor, bass player Jarle Kvåle and drummer Jørn Holen. Before the band's self financed 'Roles' outing Hektor bailed out to be supplanted by WINDIR guitarist Stian Bakketeig. A later recruit was keyboard player Gaute Refsnes.

In January 1999 the band shortened the group title to ULCUS signing with the Belgian label Shiver for the 'Cherish The Obscure' album.

Albums:
ROLES, Ulcus Molle (1996)
As We Pass Away / Mindgames / The Ship Is Sailing / The Genuine Loss / Nell / Days Of Grey
MALICIOUS TRIUMPH, Ulcus Molle (1998)
Self Absorbed / Tears Complete / The Pain / Blood Dust / Malice
CHERISH THE OBSCURE, Shiver (2000)
Vortex Of Vengeance / Stigmatized / Carved In Stone / The Profound Power / Self Absorbed / Beastly Behaviour / Malice / New God / Closer To Hell / The Final Caress

ULVER (NORWAY)
Line-Up: Garm (vocals), Aismal (guitar), Aiwarikiar (drums), Haavard Skoll

A Satanic Black Metal act that stood out from the pack with their use of flute and acoustic instruments alongside the more familiar screams and grating guitars. ULVER (Norwegian for 'Wolves'), following the 1993 demo 'Vargnatt', debuted in 1995 with 'Bergtatt (translated as 'Mountain Taken').

Drummer Aiwarikiar (Erik Lancelot) has connections with URAK HAI and BURZUM and also sessions on flute for ARCTURUS.

The album relates the legend of abduction into the mountain netherworlds by the little people and it was followed in 1996 by 'Kveldssanger' ('Twilight Songs') which proved to be drastic about turn, being a mainly acoustic affair.

In 1996 former SATYRICON drummer

Carl Michael Eide joined ULVER although his tenure was brief. Eide left for VED BUENS ENDE and is an industrious figure on the Black Metal scene also contributing to AURA NOIR and INFERNÖ although billing himself 'Aggressor'.

1997's 'Nattens Madrigal' saw a return to full force, Satanic Black Metal woven around lyrical themes based on lycanthropy.

ULVER's frontman Garm, real name Kristoffer Rygg, is also a member of ARCTURUS and BORKNAGAR. Guitarist Aismal (real name Knut Magne Valle) would also join ARCTURUS.

Under the pseudonym of 'Trickster G' Garm guested on the ZYKLON 2000 album 'World Ov Worms', the side project of EMPEROR's Samoth and Trym in collusion with MYRSKOG's Destructor.

Singles/EPs:
Split EP, Necromantic Gallery (1994) (With MYSTICYM)
Of Wolves And Vibrancy / Gnosis / Limbo Central (There From Perdition City) / Of Wolves And Withdrawal, (2000) ('Metamorphosis' EP)

Albums:
BERGTATT, ET EVENTYR 15 CAPITLER, Head Not Found HNF005 (1995)
Troldskog Faran Vild / Svelon Gaagr Bag Vase Neod / Graaabuck Blov Huv Vaor Igon Stomme Lockor / Burgtatt- Mo I Agudwmrove
KVELDSSANGER, Head Not Found HNF014CD (1996)
Østenfor Sol Og Vestenfor Maane / Ord / Hoyfjeldsbilde / Nattleite / Kveldssang / Naturmystikk / A Cappella- Sielens Sang / Hiertets Vee / Kledt I Nattens Farger / Halling / Utreise / Sofu-Or Paa Allfers Lund / Ulvsblakk
NATTENS MADRIGAL: THE MADRIGAL OF THE NIGHT- NIGHT HYMNS TO THE WOLF IN MAN, Century Media 77158-2 (1997)
Wolf And Fear / Wolf And The Devil / Wolf And Hatred / Wolf And Man / Wolf And The Man / Wolf And The Moon / Wolf And Passion / Wolf And Destiny / Wolf And The Night
TRILOGIE, Century Media (1997)
THEMES FROM WILLIAM BLAKE'S THE MARRIAGE OF HEAVEN AND HELL, Jester (1999)
The Argument / The Voice Of The Devil / A Memorable Fancy / A Sons Of Liberty / Chorus

UNANIMATED (SWEDEN)
Line up- Micke Jansson (vocals), Jonas Melberg (guitar), Jonas Bohlin (guitar), Richard Cabeza (bass), Jocke Westman (keyboards), Peter Stjärnvind (drums)

UNANIMATED were created in 1989. The inaugural line up of the group found guitarists Chris Alverez and Jonas Melklberg teamed with Richard Cabeza on lead vocals and bass and ex MERCILESS drummer Peter Stjärvind.
By the time of their first demo tape, 'Firestorm', UNANIMATED had replaced Alverez with Jonas Bohlin, whilst Cabeza left for a time to join DISMEMBER as the band drafted in Micke Jansson on lead vocals and Daniel Lofthagen on bass.
Some versions of the first UNANIMATED album, 'In The Forest Of The Dreaming Dead', possess a cover of VENOM's 'Buried Alive'.
For the band's second album, 'Ancient God Of Evil', (a record hyped by No Fashion as one that took Death Metal into a new dimension) bass parts were once more handled by Cabeza, although he was still a full time member of DISMEMBER.
UNANIMATED split, with Stjärvind joining FACE DOWN.

Albums:
IN THE FOREST OF THE DREAMING DEAD, No Fashion NFR004 (1994)
At Dawn / Whispering Shadows / Blackness Of The Fallen Stars / Fire Storm / Storms From The Skies Of Grief / Through The Gates / Wind Of A Dismal Past/ Silence Ends / Moonlight Twilight / In The Forest Of The Dreaming Dead / Cold Northern Breeze
ANCIENT GOD OF EVIL, No Fashion NFR009 (1995)
Life Demise / Eye Of The Greyhound / Oceans Of Time / Dead Calm / Mirielle / The Depths Of A Black Sea / Ruins / Dying Emotions Domain / Die Alone

UNCLEAN (CZECH REPUBLIC)

Black Metal band UNCLEAN issued the 1995 demo 'Tam Kdesi V Hlubinach', translated as "There Is No Depth". The tape would also become the band's first commercial outing sharing space on a split CD with SORATH on the delightfully named Pussy God Records.
UNCLEAN guitarist Lord Unclean also performs as a member of the infamous MANIAC BUTCHER.

Albums:
TAM KDESI V HLUBINACH, Pussy God (1996) (Split album with SORATH)
TEN, KTERY SE VYHBA SVETHU, Pussy God (199-)

UNFOLDING (LUXEMBOURG)
Line-Up: Pol (vocals / guitar), Annabelle Saffron (vocals), Olli (guitar), Misch (bass / keyboards), Benny (drums)

Before becoming a Black Metal band UNFOLDING operated in more traditional Heavy Metal territory billed as ZEUS. The act became AUTUMN LEAVES as there music became progressively darker adding vocalist Miha Chinea. The final switch to full on Black Metal transpired with the departure of Chinea and guitarist Pol taking over lead vocal duties with back up from new member Annabelle Saffron.

Singles/EPs:
Enshroud The Light / Away / Unfolding / Needs Grown Apace, Unfolding (1999) ('Cimmerian Lands' EP)

UNGOD (GERMANY)
Line-Up: Infamist Of Tumulus (vocals), Ancient Blasphemic Grave Invocator (guitar), Angel Of Blasphemy (guitar)

A Black Metal act with plenty of old school Thrash influence to their sound. UNGOD made their presence felt with their 1993 demo tape titled 'Magicus Tallis Damnatio'. Following the debut album 'Circle Of The Seven Infernal Pacts' UNGOD released a brace of shared 7" singles combining forces with DESASTER and CABAL.
UNGOD issued a split album in 1997 shared with IMPENDING DOOM.

Singles/EPs:
Renaissance Of The Dark Arcade, Merciless (1995) (Split single with CABAL)
Split, Merciless (1995) (Split single with DESASTER)

Albums:
CIRCLE OF THE SEVEN INFERNAL PACTS, Merciless M.R. CD001 (1994)
Silence In The Golden Halls Of Endless Hope / Circle Of The Seven Infernal Pacts / Land Of Frozen Tears / Magicus Tulis Damnatio / Dark Winds Around The Throne Of Blood / Lost Beast Born In Darkness / A Journey Through Forgotten

Myth / The Grotesque Vision Of A Dying Moon / Black Clouds Beyond The Fullmoon
CONQUERING WHAT ONCE WAS OURS, Merciless (1997) (Split album with IMPENDING DOOM)
I Am The Chaos / Firestorm, Ashes, Genocide / Conquering What Once Was Ours / Via Reducta / Anatomy Of Human Destructivity

UNHOLY (FINLAND)
Line-Up: Pasi Aijö (vocals / bass), Jarkko Toivonen (guitar), Jade Muhli (guitar), Veer Vanhala (keyboards), Jan Kuhahen (drums)

Originally titled HOLY HELL and formed by vocalist / bassist Pasi and guitarist Jarkko in 1988, the group released the 'Kill Jesus' demo prior to a name change to UNHOLY.
The Finns' first recording under the new name was the 1990 demo 'Procession Of Black Doom' followed by a further tape, 'Demo 11.90'. The fourth demo, 'Trip To Depressive Autumn', in 1991 scored the band a deal with the Austrian Lethal Records.
UNHOLY's debut album 'From The Shadows', recorded in Vienna, proved a worthy success with strong sales across Europe. Sophomore effort, 'The Second Ring Of Power' with female vocals contributed by Merja Salmela, followed suit but during 1996 UNHOLY ground to a halt.
Guitarist Jarkko Toivonen later formed TIERMES, releasing a self titled album in 1997. However, the following year UNHOLY, with new member Veera Muhli on vocals and keyboards, was resurrected for the 'Rapture' album. The band added second guitarist Jade Vanhala in 1999 for live work.

Singles/EPs:
Stench Of Ishtar / Autumn / Creative Lunacy / The Trip Was Infra Green, Lethal (1992) ('Trip To Depressive Autumn' EP)
Albums:
FROM THE SHADOWS, Lethal LRC003 (1993)
Alone/ Gray Blow / Creative Lunacy / Autumn / Stench Of Ishtar / Colossal Vision / Time Has Gone/ The Trip Was Infra Green / Passe Tiemes
THE SECOND RING OF POWER, Avantgarde AV005 (1995)
The Second Ring Of Power / Languish

For Bliss / Lady Babylon / Neverending Day / Dreamside / Procession Of Black Doom / Covetous Glance / Air / Serious Personality Disturbance
RAPTURE, Avantgarde (1998)
Into Cold Light / Petrified Spirits / For The Unknown One / Wunderwerck / After God / Unzeitgeist / Deluge
GRACE FALLEN, Avantgarde (1999)
Of Tragedy / Immaculate / Daybreak / When Truth Turns Its Head / Wanderer / Reek Of The Night / Haoma / Seeker / Athene Noctua

THE UNHOLY
(Minneapolis, MN, USA)
Line-Up: Wade Laszlo (vocals / guitar), Chris Magras (bass), Tom Croxton (drums)

THE UNHOLY was borne out of Wade Laszlo's frustration with his then band ACHERON. Following recording of ACHERON's debut album 'Prophecies Unholy' he split to found THE UNHOLY in 1991 and was soon joined by other ACHERON members bassist Mark Belliel on bass and drummer Tom Croxton. For some time THE UNHOLY's rhythm section would share duties with both camps.
In 1992 Laszlo enlisted a fresh band comprising of bassist Chris Magras and drummer John Ryan for the demo 'Darkness Dawns'. Following the debut album 'Garden Of Sorrows' Ryan exited and original member Tom Croxton reassumed his old position.
In 1998 Croxton joined up with IMPALER whilst retaining links to THE UNHOLY. He also has a side project KREPITUS.

Albums:
GARDEN OF SORROWS, Kaleidoscope (1995)
Rite Of Spring / Raven Of Dispersion / Through My Hands / The Magician / Not Heaven Borne / The Tempter / Feast Of The Beast / Scyldings / History
TRINITY, Kaliedoscope (1997)
Hammer Of Thor / Lucifer's Flame / Jakarta / 13 / Aeon / Flawed / Wicca Rising
NIGHTSHADE, Scylding Music (1998)
Welcome To Hell / Night Of Time / Somewhere East Of Paradise / Maggot / Familiar / Lost Souls Lament / Succubus / Two Hours / Benediction
AS ABOVE SO BELOW, Scylding Music (1999)
Hammer Of Thor / Lucifer's Flame /

Jakarta / 13 / Aeon / Flawed / Wicca Rising / Welcome To Hell / Night Of Time / Somewhere East Of Paradise / Maggot / Familiar / Lost Souls Lament / Succubus / Two Hours / Benediction **ASH WEDNESDAY**, Scylding Music (1999)
Hexe / Bloody Earth / Osculam Infame / Goddamned / Lion Of May / Heaven's Burning / The Portrait / The Pact / Shrine / Raven Of Dispersion (Roots II Remake)

UNHOLY FLAMES (BRAZIL)

Albums:
CHRISTIAN DENIAL, Demise DMS004 (1998)
Through Of Dark Clouds / In The Death Short Of The Fall / Messenger Of Agony / Christian Denial

UNLORD (HOLLAND)

There are many myths surrounding UNLORD mainly due to the fact the band wish to remain totally anonymous with the exception of one Torgrim. UNLORD have been cited as German or even Icelandic in origin but are widely believed to be Dutch.

Albums:
SCHWARZWALD, Displeased (1997)
Inferno Bizarre / Uprising Hordes / Rivers Of Fire And Blood / Schwarzwald / Monarchy Dies / Heroism / Outburst Of Hate / Here Fire Burns / E Caha Di Beha / Messiah Noir / Blackbird / Thunderbuilder / Summoned Be Thy Flesh
GLADIATOR, Displeased D00066 (2000)
Into The Gates / Hell's Gates Are Opened / Swallow All Pride / Victory / Evil Spawn / Bloodgrief / Slavesend / Impaled Live / Hellbender / Crushed 'Til Death / Hymn Of The Gladiator

UNMOORED (SWEDEN)
Line-Up: Christian Älvestam (vocals / guitar), Rickard Larsson (guitar), Torbjorn Öhring (bass)

UNMOORED emerged with the 1995 demo 'Shadow Of The Obscure' issuing the later tape 'More To The Story Than Meets The Eye' prior to recording of the debut album 'Cimmerian'. Following this release drummer Niclas Wahlén decamped.
Still without a drummer the 2000 album 'Kingdoms Of Greed' would be sessioned

by Jocke Petterson, better known as Morth from THY PRIMORDIAL and also a veteran of DAWN and CRANIUM. Members billed on the recording were frontman Christian 'Evil Spice' Älvestam, guitarist Rickard 'Infernal Spice' Larsson and bassist Torbjorn 'Hellish Spice' Öhring.
Älvestamd and Petterson would also become members of Death Metal band SOLAR DAWN.

Albums:
CIMMERIAN, Pulverised (1998)
Trendmade Bitch / Now And Forever / Down At Zero / Blood By Tragedy / Here Today, Gone Tomorrow / Warsong / Solution .45 / Final State
KINGDOMS OF GREED, Pulverised (2000)
Feral Blaze / Tellurian Crown / Self Invoked / Torchbearer / Final State Part II (Last Entry) / Thrown Off The Scent / Milestone / In The Dark Midst Of Winter

UNPURE (SWEDEN)
Line-Up: Kolgrim (vocals / bass), Hräsvelg (guitar / drums)

Albums:
UNPURE, Napalm NPR011 (1995)
To The Ancients / Ashes With The Wind / Otherside Of The Sea / Call Of Doom Part I / Across With War / Arrival Of Chaos / A Forest Event: i) Behind The Mist, ii) The Eclipse / Lords Of War / Surrounded By Darkness / Outro
COLDLAND, Napalm NPR022 (1996)
Blacker Than Ever / Coldland / Full Of Hate / Cold Freezing Dark / Call Of Doom (Part II) / Horny Goats / Count Dracula / Frozen / All Dead / Valley Of Whirling Winds

URGEHAL (NORWAY)
Line-Up: Trondr Nefas (guitar), Ensifer (guitar), Chiron (bass), Jarl E. (drums)

The uncompromisingly brutal URGEHAL emerged with the 'Ferd' demo of 1994. 'Rise Of The Monument' followed in 1995 prior to signing to the No Colours label..

Albums:
ARMA CHRISTI, No Colours NC011 (1997)
Blood Hunt / The Night Armageddon Comes / Embraced By Cold / The Eternal Eclipse / Conjuring The Hordes Of Blasphemy / Maatte Blodet Flomme / Evocation Of The Satanic Ascendancy /

Dethronation Of God
MASSIVE TERRESTRIAL STRIKE, (199-)
The Sodomizer / Saturnize / Supreme Evil / Image Of The Horned King / Tellus Döed- Armageddons Svöepe / Apocalyptic Destruction / Flames Of Black Candles

USER NE (SPAIN)
Line-Up: Bossu Morbious El Tolerante (vocals), Xalen D Kharnash (vocals), Auxiliarum Cristianorum (soprano vocals), Pino (vocals), Trollberg (guitar), Josele (guitar), Hils Ver (bass), Ashkar (keyboards), X (pipes), Kyrtan (flute), Lupi (violin), Erdrop (percussion), Zamuel (drums)

Although undoubtedly and openly of Black Metal persuasion USER NE's music is infused with the legends and folklore of their pre Roman Iberian myths. USER NE employ a veritable arsenal of eclectic musicians in their bid to attain an authentic sound.
Piper Jow would depart in November 2000 to be replaced by the mysterious 'X'.

Albums:
NIBELUM DAS UHÖRT, (1999)
El Encuertro / La Llegada De Norbert / ...Y Quedó Sediada / Marchando Hacia Sumel / Continuará
NIBELUM DAS UHÖRT, War Is Imminent Productions (2000)
The Find / The Arrival Of Norbert / The Siege / On Way To Sumel / Zienfuegos / Days Of Another Times / Ofendor's Clan

USURPER (Atlanta, GA, USA)
Line-Up: Sterling Von Scarborough (vocals / bass), Danny Klein (guitar), Rich Fuscia (drums)

1993 act founded by former MORBID ANGEL and INCUBUS man Sterling Von Scarborough. USURPER only cut demos.

USURPER (Chicago, IL, USA)
Line-Up: Diabolical Slaughter (vocals), Rick 'Rigor' Scythe (guitar), Jon Necromancer (bass), Apocalyptic Warlord (drums)

Black Metal outfit USURPER, founded by former ARMAGEDDON members guitarist Rigor and vocalist Diabolical Slaughter, debuted with the 1994 demo 'Visions From The Gods'. Drummer

Apocalyptic Warlord retired from the band in March 1996. Following a period with a temporary sticksman former FUNERAL NATION and DISINTER drummer Dave Chiarella joined the fold renaming himself Dave Hellstorm.
USURPER toured Europe with ENTHRONED, HECATE ENTHRONED and later as guests to CRADLE OF FILTH supporting their 2000 album 'Necronemesis'. The album included guest vocals from ABSU mentor Proscriptor McGovern.
For live work USURPER's sound was fattened out by former ETERNAL HATRED and HATE ETERNAL guitarist Carcass Chris. Strangely the same individual USURPER had gone into a dispute with some years earlier when he had, according to some reports, claimed credits for work on earlier albums.

Albums:
DIABOLOSIS, Head Not Found (1997)
Hypnotic Void / Blood Passion / Fullmoon Harvest / Nulla Sallus Extra Eccelcium / Deep In The Forest / The Infernal Storm / Diabolosis / The Ruins Of Gomorrah
THRESHOLD OF THE USURPER, Necropolis (1998)
Necrocult Part I- The Metal War / Slavehammer / Black Funeral / The Dead Of Winter / Threshold Of The Usurper
SKELETAL SEASON, Necropolis NR032 (1999)
Shadowfiend / Dismal Wings Of Terror / Skeletal Season / Embrace Of The Dead / Prowling Death- The Demi Goddess / Cemetarian / Birmstone Fist / Wolflord
VISIONS FROM THE GODS, Necropolis NR051 CD (2000)
Soulstalker '96 / Deep In The Forest / Visions From The Gods / Dusk / Soulstalker (Original version) / Charon / Bonefire / Wolflord (Night Stalker version) / Blood Passion (Live)
NECRONEMESIS, Necropolis NR063 CD (2000)
The Incubus Breed / Slaughterstorm / In Remembrance / Necronemesis / 1666 AD / Warriors Of Iron And Rust / Deathwish / Full Metal Maelstrom / Funeral Waters / Into The Oblong Box

UTUMNO (SWEDEN)
Line-Up: Jonas Stålhammer (vocals), Staffan Johansson (guitar), Dennis Lindahl (guitar), Dan Öberg (bass), Johan Hallberg (drums)

Swedish dark Death Metal outfit UTUMNO's vocalist Jonas Ståhlhammer is also guitarist in GOD MACABRE. UTUMNO's debut album was recorded at Sunlight Studios and produced by Tomas Skogsberg.

Drummer Johan Hallberg, under the pseudonym of 'Necro-Nudist', would join arch infernal act CRANIUM.

Not to be confused with the Norwegian Black Metal UTUMNO that would become EMANCER.

Singles/EPs:
Saviour Reborn / In Misery I Dwell, Cenotaph CTR001 EP (1991)

Albums:
ACROSS THE HORIZON, Cenotaph CTR007CD (1994)
The Light Of Day / I Cross The Horizons / In Misery I Dwell / Saviour Reborn / Sunrise / Emotions Run Cold

VAAKEVANDRING
(NORWAY)
Line-Up: Ronny Hansen (vocals), Alexander Nygård (guitar), Trond Bjørnstad (bass), Morten Sigmund Magerøy (keyboards), Pål Daehlen (drums)

A self styled "Christian symphonic unblack metal band". VAAKEVANDRING ('To walk and wake the people') look and sound like a Black Metal band but lyrically are strongly evangelical. Both vocalist Ronny Hansen and keyboard player Morten Signund Magerøy have previous links to ANTESTOR.

The band was born out of the Pop act LOTHLORIEN which included guitarist Alexander Nygård, bassist Trond Bjørnstad and Magerøy. This act evolved into INERTIA but would lose their then guitarist as a result over a difference in religious opinion. Paralell to INERTIA Hansen and drummer Pål Daehlen had an act titled SIGNUM CRUSIS and with the enrollment of Magerøy this band became KORSFERD.

Bjørnstad would also join as the band became VAAKEVANDRING. In a surprise move the band's debut demo was produced by Stioan Aarstad of DIMMU BORGIR.

VAAKEVANDRING employ ANTESTOR guitarist Vermod (Lars Stokstad) for live work.

VADER (POLAND)
Line-Up: Piotr Wiwczarek (vocals / guitar), Jackie (bass), Docent (drums)

A Polish Thrash band with intense drumming and unashamed reliance on esoterica as a staple of their subject matter, VADER came together in 1986 with a line up of vocalist guitarist Peter, bassist Jackie and drummer Docent.

The band soon released their first demo tape, 'Necrolust', and this gained VADER a deal with Carnage Records. A deal was struck to subsequently distribute the 1990 demo 'Morbid Reich'. A 1991 demo featured the tracks 'The Final Massacre', 'Reign Carrion', 'Breath Of Centuries' and 'Vicious Circle'.

Upon the release of their debut album, 'The Ultimate Incantation', VADER toured Europe with BOLT-THROWER and GRAVE. Further dates in America followed with DEICIDE, SUFFOCATION and DISMEMBER.

'The Darkest Age- Live', which includes a cover of SLAYER's 'Hell Awaits', was recorded in front of a home crowd in Krakow. June 1995 found VADER out on the road in Europe once more touring alongside CRADLE OF FILTH, MALEVOLENT CREATION, OPPRESSOR, DISSECTION and SOLSTICE.

The 'Sothis' EP witnessed another cover, BLACK SABBATH's anthem 'Black Sabbath', as well as a complete rework of VADER's 1989 track 'The Wrath'.

Having added guitarist China to augment their live sound, VADER undertook a full European tour in the spring of 1996 as guests to CANNIBAL CORPSE.

Wiwczarek produced the debut album by fellow Poles DECAPITATED during 2000. VADER themselves headlined the European 'No Mercy' festivals alongside American' VITAL REMAINS, Brazilians REBAELLIUN and Germany's FLESHCRAWL.

Docent has a project band titled MOON in union with CHRIST AGONY frontman Cezar releasing two albums to date.

Docent and Mauser assembled side project DIES IRAE in 2000 for the 'Immolated' album.

Singles/EPs:
Hymn To The Ancient Ones / Sothis / De Profundis / Vision And The Voice / The Wrath / R'Lyeh / Black Sabbath, Massive MASS 001 MCD (1995) ('Sothis' EP)

Albums:
THE ULTIMATE INCANTATION, Earache (1992)
Creation / Dark Age / Vicious Circle / The Crucified Ones / Final Massacre / Testimony / Reign Carrion / Chaos / One Step To Salvation / Demon's Wind / Decapitated Saints / Breath Of Centuries
THE DARKEST AGE- LIVE '93, Arctic Serenades SERE 007 (1994)
Macbeth (intro) / Dark Age / Vicious Circle / Crucified Ones / Demon's Wind / Decapitated Saints / From Beyond (Intro) / Chaos / Reign-Carrion / Testimony / Breath Of Centuries / Omen (Outro) / Hell Awaits
DE PROFUNDIS, System Shock IRC 067 (1995)
Silent Empire / An Act Of Darkness / Blood Of Kingu / Incarnation / Sothis / Revolt / Of Moon, Blood, Dream And Me / Vision And The Voice / Reborn In Flames
FUTURE OF THE PAST, System Shock

IRC 092 (1996)
Outbreak Of Evil / Flag Of Hate / Storm Of Stress / Death Metal / Fear Of Napalm / Merciless Death / Dethroned Emperor / Silent Scream / We Are The League / IFY / Black Sabbath
BLACK TO THE BLIND, Impact IR-C-104 (1997)
Heading For Internal Darkness / The Innermost Ambience / Carnal / Fractal Light / True Names / Beast Raping / Foetus God / The Red Passage / Distant Dream / Black To The Blind
LIVE IN JAPAN, System Shock IRC 132-2 (1999)
Damien / Sothis / Distant Dream / Black To The Blind / Silent Empire / Blood Of Kings / Carnal / Red Passage / Panzerstoss / Reborn In Flames / Fractal Light / From Beyond / Crucified Ones / Foetus God / Black Sabbath / Reign In Blood / Omen / Dark Age
LITANY, (2000)
Wings / The One Made Of Dreams / Xefer / Litany / Cold Demons / The Calling / North / Forward To Die!! / A World Of Hurt / The World Made Flesh / The Final Massacre
REIGN FOREVER WORLD, Metal Blade CD 076-103182 (2001)
Reign Forever World / Frozen Paths / Privilege Of The Gods / Total Disaster / Rapid Fire / Freezing Moon / North (Live) / Forwards To Die!! (Live) / Creatures Of Light And Darkness (Live) / Carnal (Live)

VALEFOR (NORWAY)
Line-Up: Nachtotter (vocals / guitar), Darkat St Lejeune (keyboards)

The Industrial arm of Michael Ford (a.k.a. 'Baron Drakkheim Abaddon' and 'Nacttoter') of SORATH, BLACK FUNERAL, DARKNESS ENSHROUD and PSYCHONAUT.
VALEFOR employed the vocals of Shanna Lejeune for early works but by 2001 the band line up comprised of Nachtotter on vocals and keyboards, Lucifugiel on keyboards and vocalist Daucina.

Albums:
DEATH MAGICK, Death Factory (1996)
Oceans Turn Bloodred (Rise Nidhögg) / Ankon, Bearer Of The Skythe / Bubonic Death / Ritual trance / Plague, Blood And Astral Energies / Chemical Disease / Black Magick / Spells Of Darkness And Death / The Beast Within Man / The

Spheres Of Mars (Rite Of Baphomet)
INVOKATION OV FORNEUS, Dark Vinyl (1998)
Fenrir / Progression Ov Aiwass / Invocation Ov Forneus / Undead / Hadit / Caverns Of The Mind / Order Ov Domination / Pyramid Ov Sleep
THE GATE OF ANDRAS, (2001)
Empire Falls (Corpse Littering- Feast Of The Fallen) / Lilith- Samael / Angel-Serpent: Part I- God Of Fire, Part II- The Flesh Falls / Asmodeus Through The Burning Tombs / The Dead Are Speaking / Abu-Fi-Hamat (The Black Head Of Wisdom) / Izelmoth- The Shadow Of Death / Blood Spilt In The Circle Of Andras / Invocation And Defeat / We Are Descending

VALHALL (NORWAY)
Line-up: Ronny Sorkness (vocals), Geir Kolden (guitar), Robin Olsen (guitar / keyboards), Kenneth Sorkness (bass), Gribb (drums)

Drums on the Norwegian Doom outfit VALHALL's second album are performed by the ubiquitous character Fenriz of DARKTHRONE under his pseudonym of Lee Bress.
Guitarist Frode Malm would depart following the 'Moonstoned' album. New recruit was Frank Wanberg on keyboards.

Albums:
MOONSTONED, Head Not Found HNF009 (1995)
Tidal Waves / Pagan Token / Doom / Dreamer / Infinite Grieve / Come Winter / Relief / Vulture Trace Time / Moonstoned / Soul Trip
HEADING FOR MARS, Head Not Found (1997)
Intro / Arctic / Mindblaster / Mountain / Ocean / Sleeper / Childhood Memories / Livets Soyle / Past Era / Darkness Between Two Shadows / The Dream Of A Jester / Outro

VARATHRON (GREECE)
Line-up: Stephan Necroabyssious (vocals), Jim Necroslaughter (guitar), Jim Mutilator (bass), Hungry Wolfen (drums)

Greek Black Metal formation VARATHRON arose with the 1989 demo 'Procreation Of Unaltered Evil'. VARATHRON at this juncture comprised of vocalist Stephan Necroabyssious, guitarist Jim Necroslaughter, bassist Jim

Mutilator and drummer Captain Death. This was followed by a further tape two years later 'Genesis Of Apocryphal Desire' featuring guitarist Stavros and drummer Themis. VARATHON's commercial debut was the 'One Step Beyond Dreams' 7" singles on Black Vomit Records. VARATHON cut a split EP with fellow Greek Black Metal outfit NECROMANTIA during 1992. Originally on Black Power Records it was re-released by the Unisound stable with extra material from the debut single.

VARATHON's first full length album 'His Majesty At The Swamp', with new drummer Wolfen, saw the light of day in 1993. 1995 saw further line up changes with Necroabyssious and Wolfen now backed by guitarist Pyrphoros, keyboard player Adrastos. With their status increasing Unisound chose to reissue VARATHON's first demo recordings in 7" single format in 1996. A year later both demos were combined for the 'Genesis Of Apocalyptic Desire' album.

VARATHRON cut a version of MERCYFUL FATE's 'Nuns Have No Fun' during 1999. By this stage VARATHRON's line up had evolved to include keyboard player Bill ('Crazy Wizard') and bassist Kon ('Violent Warrior'). Drummer Wolfen, known to his friends as Spyros, became 'Hungry Wolfen'.

Singles/EPs:
Genesis Of An Apocryphal Desire / Descent Of A Prophetic Vision, Black Vomit (1992) ('One Step Beyond Dreams' 7" single)
Procreation Of Unaltered Evil, Unisound (1996)

Albums:
BLACK ARTS LEAD TO EVERLASTING SINS, Black Power (1992) (Split album with NECROMANTIA)
The Cult Of The Dragon / La Reine Noir / The Tressrisings Of Nyarlathothep (act I) / Outro
HIS MAJESTY AT THE SWAMP, Cyber CD8 (1993)
His Majesty At The Swamp / Son Of The Moon (Act II) / Unholy Funeral / Lustful Father / Nightly Kingdoms / Flowers Of My Youth / The River Of My Souls / The Tressrising Of Nyarlathothep (Act II)
WALPURGIS NACHT, Unisound USR 017 (1995)

Tleilaxu (The Unborn Child) / Cassiopeia's Ode / The Dark Hills / Mestigoth / Birthrise Of The Graven Image / Redeunt / Saturnia / Regna / Under The Sight Of Horus / Somewhere Beyond Seas / Sic Transit Gloria Mundi
GENESIS OF APOCALYPTIC DESIRE, Cursed Productions (1997)
Necranastasis / Dawn Of Sordid Decay / The Great Seal Of Graal / La Reine Noir / Genesis Of Apocryphal Desire / The Tressrisings Of Nyarlathothep (Act I) / Seven Endless Horizons / Journey Beyond / The Mystic Papyrus / Deep Beneath An Ancient Dominion
THE LAMENT OF GODS, Pagan (1999)
Fire Spell- Forbidden Lust / Warriors Nightmare / The World Through Ancient Eyes / Beyond The Grave / Nuns Have No Fun

VARGAVINTER (NORWAY)

Line-Up: Hughin (vocals / bass), Gavhin (guitar), Munhin (drums)

A Swedish Black Metal act formed by the duo of Hughin and Hrymr, the trio listed above were supported on record by the aforementioned Hrymr (oboe), Manstrale (spoken verses and piccolo) and one Svantit who, quite bizarrely contributed elf-like singing!!

Albums:
FROSTFÖDD, Invasion I.R. 023CD (1996)
Dimman Kring Björkö / Frostfödd / Den Lydska Örn / Älvdans / Av Vargkvinna Född / Som De Sade / Vintern Min Slayinna

VASSAGO (SWEDEN)

LORD BELIAL member Vassago issued a solo outing in 1997 sharing a split 12" single with ANTICHRIST.

Singles/EPs:
Hail War, Total War Productions (1997) (Split EP with ANTICHRIST)

Albums:
KNIGHTS FROM HELL, No Fashion (1999)
Sign Of Vassago / Total War Brings Total Death / Anal Fistfuck / Raped By The Machine / Cleansing / Thou Shalt Kill!! / Pain Believer / God Forsaken / Agent 666 / Turning The Millenium / Destroyer / The Kingdom Where I Rule Eternally / The Crying Of Evil / Satanic Slayer

(Division SS) / The Spell Of The Eastern Oracle

VED BUENS ENDE (NORWAY)
Line-Up: Fenriz (vocals), Skoll (bass), Vicotnik (guitar / harsh wails), Skoll (bass), Carl-Michael Eide (drums / laments)

Fenriz of DARKTHRONE and ISENGARD put together this side project with ULVER and ARCTURUS bassist Skoll, DØDHEIMSGARD drummer Vicotnik and ex SATYRICON drummer Carl-Michael Eide. The latter, billed as 'Aggressor', also operates in INFERNÖ and AURA NOIR.
VED BUENS ENDE, translating as 'At the end of the bow', write and play with an acknowledged disregard for musical convention. Nevertheless, their complex amalgam of sounds still manages to stay within the remit of Black Metal.
The band supported IMPALED NAZARENE for British dates.

Singles/EPs:
Those Who Caress The Pale, Ancient Lore Creations (1995) (Cassette release)

Albums:
WRITTEN IN WATERS, Misanthropy AMAZON 006 (1995)
I Sang For The Swans / You, That May Wither / It's Magic / Den Saakaldte / Carrier Of Wounds / Coiled In Wings / Autumn Leaves / Remembrance Of Things Past / To Swarm Deserted Away
THOSE WHO CARESS THE PALE, Misanthropy (1997)
A Mask In The Mirror / The Carrier Of Wounds / You That May Wither / The Plunderer / Those Who Caress The Pale / Insects Part I

VELES (POLAND)
Line-Up: Blasphemous (vocals) / Bealphares (guitar)

VELES were previously known as BELTHIL upon their formation in 1992 by the duo of vocalist Blasphemous and guitarist Bealphares. VELES recorded their first demo, 'The Triumph Of Pagan Beliefs', in 1994 utilizing members of the band LEGION as session musicians. LORD WIND and GRAVELAND's Darken features on the album 'Night On The Bare Mountain'.
After the 1996 album VELES alleged that Bealphares had died. His replacement

was Lupus of GROMOWLADNY.
Albums:
NIGHT ON THE BARE MOUNTAIN, No Colours NC 005CD (1996)
Night On The Bare Mountain (Intro) / The Winter Morning / A Dark Dream / The Final Battle / Majesty Of War / My Bloodthirst (The Horrorstorm) / Born Of Darkness / My Pagan Fatherland (Evil Power's Night) / Forest Of The Horrifying (Outro)
BLACK HATEFUL METAL- THE TRIUMPH OF PAGAN BELIEFS, No Colours NC 016CD (1998)
The Triumph Of Pagan Beliefs / The Dawn Of New Empire / Hraften / Broken Cross / The Spirit Of Ancient Europe / The Temple Of The Infernal Fire / Black Hateful Metal / Millenium Of Disgrace / After The Battle / Winds Of The Vampires / Majesty Of War / The Pact / Forgotten Time- Honoured Custom / Black Flames Spread Warfare / Battle Din / Epos

VENOM (UK)
Line-Up: Cronos (vocals / bass), Mantas (guitars), Abaddon (drums)

The Black Metal band that unwittingly inspired a plethora of imitators as part of the growing 80s extreme Metal scene in Europe and America. Newcastle trio VENOM was initially discounted for their early albums, although these records were later to be declared classics of the genre, in spite of their primitive approach. VENOM's roots lay in the Newcastle late 70's acts GUILLOTINE, ALBUM GRACIA, OBERON and DWARFSTAR. In 1978 Lant was guitarist with ALBUM GRACIA. Members from this band including vocalist Keith Ballard and drummer Kevin Robson decamped to found a new act the same year entitled DWARFSTAR. Meantime another local band GUILLOTINE, featuring guitarist Jeffrey Dunn retitled themselves VENOM in 1979. The inaugural line up of this group being Dunn, vocalist Dave Blackman, second guitarist Dave Rutherford, bassist Dean Hewitt and drummer Chris Mercaters. Both Blackman and Mercater lost their places in August of that year to former OBERON members drummer Tony Bray and singer Clive Archer. OBERON would play a further part in VENOM's later career when guitarist Eric Cook would wind up as manager of the band.
The new look VENOM, also with a fresh

bassist Alan Winston, were to pull in Lant as replacement for Rutherford in November. However, mere days before the band's debut gig in Wallsend Winston bailed out forcing Lant to take over the bassist's role. This he did by necessity plugging a bass guitar into a lead guitar amp.

By 1980 the proto VENOM had decided upon the satanic image rechristening the band members in suitable fashion. Archer became 'Jesus Christe', Lant 'Mr. Cronos', Bray 'Abbadon' and Dunn "Mantas'. A three song demo was cut in April featuring early work outs of 'Angel Dust', 'Raise The Dead' and 'Red Light Fever'. A second session, recorded for a miserly £50, laid down six more tracks with Lant taking lead vocals for 'Live Like An Angel'. Archer packed his bags soon after and the unholy triumvirate of VENOM was born.

The band adopted the position of marrying Lant's Punk influences with direct inspiration from some of the global Rock giants. In early interviews the band professed the desire to have the energy of JUDAS PRIEST with the theatrics of KISS.

Having, naturally, been signed by Neat Records VENOM debuted in 1980 with the 'In League With Satan' single and immediately came to the attention of 'Sounds' journalist Geoff Barton.

Barton's championing of the group certainly brought VENOM to the attention of the Metal loving public, although the trio had yet to play a gig.

1981 summoned the group's first album, 'Welcome To Hell', followed in 1982 by the seminal 'Black Metal' set.

VENOM's third album found the Geordie triumvirate of Metal taking huge strides forward, especially abroad, as the semi conceptual 'At War With Satan' hugely increased the band's following.

The band's first European live date came in Belgium (the group's initial live performance having ensured they would never play a club again as the event was marked by a handmade stage prop falling over and firing pyrotechnics into the audience!) where they headlined above PICTURE and ACID. It was on the continent where the band were only able to translate their mystique into material success with a series of major festival appearances and tours (including a trek through Europe in 1984 with METALLICA as the support act!) VENOM were virtually shunned by the UK audience where a succession of announced tours

were scrapped, although the 'Seventh Date Of Hell' video did arise from the group's spectacular debut at Hammersmith Odeon in London on the 'At War With Satan' tour.

Before going in to record fourth album 'Possessed', Cronos produced fellow Neat label act TYSONDOG' first album, although somewhat bizarrely he then announced to the world that it was 'shit'!

1985 began disastrously for the band. The 'Possessed' album was roundly chastised and a planned Canadian/American tour was thrown into turmoil as Mantas succumbed to glandular fever. The dates were put back and, as his health worsened, VENOM recruited AVENGER guitarist Les Cheetham and FIST guitarist Dave Irwin to fill the shoes of Mantas.

The band's New York Studio 54 show (with EXODUS and SLAYER), their most prestigious date on the tour, was less than successful as Mantas, now with restored health, was denied access to America due to passport problems.

1986 saw the departure of the guitarist following American dates with support act HIRAX. Mantas resurfaced shortly after with his own MANTAS project that issued one album, but he soon retired to concentrate on building up a martial arts centre. Cronos busied himself producing the 1986 album from WARFARE 'Mayhem Fucking Mayhem'.

Mantas was to be replaced by two guitarists, Jimmy C. and Mike H., who performed their debut live shows with VENOM touring Brazil with support act EXODUS.

This new line up recorded the lukewarm Nick Tauber / Kevin Ridley produced 'Calm Before The Storm' for RCA subsidiary Filmtrax. The album saw the band endeavouring to pursue a more finely crafted, mature approach rather than the bludgeoning ferocity of yore, but merely succeeded in alienating existing fans.

In 1988 Mantas appeared again, this time as guest guitarist on WARFARE's 'A Conflict Of Hatred' album.

Cronos quit in 1989 to form CRONOS with ex VENOM members. VENOM regrouped once more in 1989, enticing original guitarist Mantas back into the fold alongside the drumming lynchpin of Abbadon, bassist / vocalist Tony Dolan and rhythm guitarist Al Barnes.

Barnes had worked previously with Mantas on his solo album 'Winds Of Change', whilst Dolan was ex

ATOMKRAFT. This line up debuted with 'Prime Evil', once more produced by Tauber and Ridley.

VENOM took to the UK stages again in late 1989, billed under the pseudonym of SONS OF SATAN. A "secret" London Marquee gig attracted only a handful of followers, giving ample indication as to the apathy towards the band in their home country.

Their 1990 album 'Tear Your Soul Apart' featured Mantas, Abaddon and Dolan and included a bizarre cover of JUDAS PRIEST's 'Hell Bent For Leather' classic. Dolan quit, citing Abaddon's claims in the press linking VENOM with Satanism as the main reason.

In 1994 a VENOM tribute album featuring such acts as PARADISE LOST and ANATHEMA was released. Cronos also came out of the shadows, lending backing vocals to rising UK Black Metal band CRADLE OF FILTH's 'Dusk And Her Dark Embrace' album.

Meanwhile ex VENOM guitarist Mike Hickey teamed up with arch goremongers CARCASS in 1994, would later form part of CRONOS and also perform bass duties for CATHEDRAL. Latterly Hickey, now dubbed 'Mykas Lord Of Metal', operates GOATREIGN.

Following no less than three years of negotiations, the original band line up reformed in 1995, to nothing less than ecstatic European media response, to headline the Eindhoven Waldrock and Eindhoven Dynamo festivals.

During the latter event VENOM used so much pyro that one particular blast proved so powerful the band's backdrop came to rest over the drumkit midway through the set! An edited form of this show was released as the video / CD package 'The Second Coming'.

VENOM spent a large chunk of 1997 recording their ninth studio album, 'Cast In Stone', only interrupting proceedings to headline the Metal Invader Festival in Athens, Greece.

The protracted nature of the recording was to be drawn out even further when, upon nearing completion, the band actually scrapped all previous efforts, opting to re-record the entire body of work.

Upon eventual release, initial copies of 'Cast In Stone' came with recent re-recordings of VENOM classics from the early days.

VENOM made a return to America in '97 headlining the notorious Milwaukee Metalfest, but end of year European dates supported by HAMMERFALL where cancelled due to Cronos having to undergo surgery for vocal nodes.

The 2000 Charlie Bauerfiend produced VENOM album 'Resurrection' saw Abbadon, who issued a somewhat bizarre industrial solo album 'I Am Legion', replaced by Antton. The band put in two bombastic showings at European festivals prior to, in time honoured fashion, cancelling remaining dates.

Singles/EPs:

In League With Satan / Live Like An Angel (Die Like A Devil), Neat NEAT 08 (1980)

Bloodlust / In Nomine Satanas, Neat NEAT 13 (1981)

Die Hard / Acid Queen / Burning Out, Neat NEAT 27 12 (1983) (12" single)

Die Hard / Acid Queen, Neat NEAT 27 (1983) (7" single)

Warhead / Lady Lust, Neat NEAT 38 (1984) (7" single, released in three different sleeves)

Warhead / Lady Lust / The Seven Gates Of Hell, Neat 38 12 (1984) (12" single)

Manitou / Woman / Dead Of The Night, Neat NEAT 43 12 (1984) (12" single)

Manitou / Woman, Neat NEAT 43 (1984) (7" single)

Nightmare / Satanarchist / FOAD / Warhead (Live), Neat NEAT 47 12 (1985) (12" single)

Nightmare / Satanarchist, Neat NEAT 47 (1985) (7" single)

Witching Hour (Live) / Teacher's Pet (Live) / Poison (Live) / Teacher's Pet (Live), Neat NEAT 53-12 (1985) ('Hell At Hammersmith' EP)

Skool Daze / Bursting Out / The Ark / Civilized / Angel Dust / Hellbent (Live), Under One Flag MFLAG 50 (1990) ('Tear Your Soul Apart' EP)

7 Gates Of Hell / Welcome To Hell / In Nomine Satanas / Black Metal / The Evil One (New '96 track), Venom (1996) ('Venom '96' EP)

In Nomine Satanas, 2956 (1999) (Green vinyl 6" single. Russian release)

Schizo, 2934 (1999) (Brown vinyl 6" single. Russian release)

1000 Days In Sodom, 3064 (1999) (Blue vinyl 6" single. Russian release)

To Hell / Women, Leather And Hell, 3211 (1999) (Yellow vinyl 6" single. Russian release)

To Hell / Aarrrggh, 3224 (1999) (Red vinyl 6" single. Russian release)

The Other New One, 4016 (1999) (Yellow vinyl 6" single. Russian release)

Welcome To Hell, 4415 (1999) (Red

vinyl 6" single. Russian release)
Satanachist, 4418 (1999) (Green vinyl 6"
single. Russian release)
Under A Spell, 4462 (1999) (Clear vinyl
6" single. Russian release)
Muscle, 4466 (1999) (Blue vinyl 6"
single. Russian release)
Dominus Mundi, 4537 (1999) (Clear
vinyl 6" single. Russian release)
Kings Of Evil, 4542 (1999) (Green vinyl
6" single. Russian release)
Mortals, 4543 (1999) (Blue vinyl 6"
single. Russian release)

Albums:
WELCOME TO HELL, Neat NEAT 1002
(1981)
 Sons Of Satan / Welcome To Hell /
Schizo / Mayhem With Mercy / Poison /
Live Like An Angel / Witching Hour / One
Thousand Days In Sodom / Angel Dust /
In League With Satan / Red Light Fever
BLACK METAL, Neat NEAT 1005 (1982)
Black Metal / To Hell And Back / Buried
Alive / Raise The Dead / Teacher's Pet /
Leave Me In Hell / Sacrifice / Heaven's
On Fire / Countess Bathory / Don't Burn
The Witch / At War With Satan (Preview)
AT WAR WITH SATAN, Neat NEAT 1015
(1984) 48 SWEDEN, 64 UK
At War With Satan / Rip Ride / Genocide
/ Cry Wolf / Stand Up And Be Counted /
Women, Leather And Hell / Aaaaarghhhh
POSSESSED, Neat NEAT 1024 (1985)
99 UK
Moonshine / Harmony Drive / Wing And
A Prayer / Voyeur / Satanarchist /
Mystique / Possessed / Suffer Not The
Children / Hellchild / Fly Trap /
Powerdrive / Too Loud For The Crowd /
Burn This Place To The Ground
AMERICAN ASSAULT, Combat (1985)
(USA release)
Rip Ride / Bursting Out / Dead Of The
Night / The Seven Gates Of Hell (Live) /
Countess Bathory (Live) / Welcome To
Hell (Live)
CANADIAN ASSAULT, Banzai (1985)
(Canadian release)
Die Hard (Live) / Welcome To Hell (Live)
/ In Nomine Satanas (Live) / Warhead /
Woman / The Seven Gates Of Hell
FRENCH ASSAULT, Now (1985)
(French release)
Nightmare / Bloodlust / In Nomine
Satanas / Countess Bathory (Live) /
Powerdrive / Bursting Out
SCANDINAVIAN ASSAULT, Neat (1985)
Nightmare (Live) / Too Loud (For The
Crowd) (Live) / Die Hard (Live) /
Bloodlust / Powerdrive / Warhead
JAPANESE ASSAULT, VAP R 35177 25

(1985) (Japanese release)
In League With Satan / Live Like An
Angel (Die Like A Devil) / Bloodlust / In
Nomine Satanas / Die Hard / Witching
Hour (Live) / Bursting Out / Warhead /
Manitou / Dead Of The Night / The
Seven Gates Of Hell
EINE KLEINE NACHTMUSIK, Neat
NEAT 1032 (1986)
Too Loud For The Crowd / Seven Gates
Of Hell / Leave Me In Hell / Nightmare /
Countess Bathory / Die Hard / Schitzo /
In Nomine Satanas / Witching Hour /
Black Metal / The Chanting Of The
Priests / Satanarchist / Fly Trap /
Warhead / Buried Alive / Love Amongst
The Dead / Welcome To Hell / Bloodlust
OBSCENE MIRACLE, Demon APKPD
12 (1986)
FROM HELL TO THE UNKNOWN,
Rawpower (1986)
Sons Of Satan / Welcome To Hell /
Schizo / Mayhem With Mercy / Poison /
Live Like An Angel (Die Like A Devil) /
Witching Hour / 1000 Days In Sodom /
Angel Dust / In League With Satan / Red
Light Fever / Bursting Out / At War With
Satan (Introduction) / Die Hard (Live) /
Manitou / Senile Decay / Black Metal /
Possessed / The Seven Gates Of Hell
(Live) / Buried Alive / Too Loud (For The
Crowd) / Radio Interview
THE SINGLES '80- '86, Rawpower
LP024 (1986)
In League With Satan / Live Like An
Angel, Die Like A Devil / Blood Lust / In
Nomine Satanas / Die Hard / Acid
Queen / Busting Out / Warhead / Lady
Lust / Seven Gates Of Hell / Manitou /
Dead Of Night
SPEED REVOLUTION, Powerstation
941317 (1986)
GERMAN ASSAULT, Roadrunner
RR9659 (1987)
Nightmare / Black Metal / Too Loud (For
The Crowd) / Radio Interview / Witching
Hour / Powerdrive / Buried Alive
LIVE – OFFICIAL BOOTLEG, American
Phonograph (1987)
Intro / Leave Me In Hell / Countess
Bathory / Die Hard / The Seven Gates
Of Hell / Bass Solo / Buried Alive / Don't
Burn The Witch / In Nomine Satanas /
Welcome To Hell / Warhead / Stand Up
And Be Counted / Guitar Solo /
Bloodlust
CALM BEFORE THE STORM, Filmtrax
MOMENT C115 (1987)
Black Xmas / The Chanting Of The
Priests / Metal Punk / Under A Spell /
Calm Before The Storm / Fire / Krackin'
Up / Beauty And The Beast / Deadline /

Gypsy / Muscle
PRIME EVIL, Under One Flag FLAG 36 (1989)
Prime Evil / Parasite / Blackened Are The Priests / Carnivorous / Skeletal Dance / Megalomania / Insane / Harder Than Ever / Into The Fire / Scholl Daze / Live Like An Angel
TEMPLES OF ICE, Under One Flag FLAG 56 (1991)
Tribes / Even In Heaven / Trinity MCMXLV 0530 / In Memory Of (Paul Miller 1964-90) / Faerie Tale / Playtime / Acid / Arachnid / Speed King / Temples Of Ice
IN MEMORIUM, MCI VNM 1 (1991)
Angel Dust / Raise The Dead / Red Light Fever / Buried Alive / Witching Hour / At War With Satan / Warhead / Manitou / Under A Spell / Nothing Sacred / Dead Love / Welcome To Hell / Black Metal / Countess Bathory / 1000 Days In Sodom / Prime Evil / If You Wanna War / Surgery
THE WASTELANDS, Under One Flag FLAG 72 (1991)
Cursed / I'm Paralyzed / Black Legions / Riddle Of Steel / Need To Kill / Kissing The Beast / Crucified / Shadow King / Wolverine / Clarisse
ACID QUEEN, Marble Arch (1991)
Acid Queen / Dead Of Nite / Live Like An Angel (Die Like A Devil) / Die Hard / Manitou / Bloodlust / Warhead / Seven Gates Of Hell
SKELETONS IN THE CLOSET, Castle CMC 3082 (1992)
Your Intro Tape / Welcome To Hell / Dead On Arrival / Snots Shit / Black Metal / Hounds Of Hell / At War With Satan / Bitch Witch / Intro Tapes / Possessed / Sadist (Mistress Of The Whip) / Manitou / Angel Dust / Raise The Dead / Red Light Fever / Venom Station
METAL PUNK LIVE, Soundwings 111 1101-2 (1993)
Black Xmas / The Chanting Of The Priests / Metal Punk / Under A Spell / Calm Before The Storm / Fire / Crackin' Back / Beauty And The Beast / Deadline / Gypsy / Muscle
LEAVE ME IN HELL, Success 16089 (1994)
Leave Me In Hell / Black Metal / Burn This Place To The Ground / Buried Alive / Schizo / Witching Hour / Teachers Pet / Too Loud (For The Crowd) / Welcome To Hell / Satanarchist / Flytrap / Sons Of Satan / Poison / Hellchild / Angel Dust / Powerdrive
KISSING THE BEAST, (1994)
Black Metal / Die Hard / Flatline /

Welcome To Hell / In Nomine Satanas / Witching Hour / Angel Dust / Fragile Life / Bloodlust / Countess Bathory / Buried Alive / Burstin' Out
OLD, NEW, BORROWED AND BLUE, Bleeding Hearts BLEED 7 (1994)
Countess Bathory / Skeletal Dance / Speed King / Welcome To Hell / Playtime / Die Hard / Clarisse / Hell Bent For Leather / Prime Evil / Teacher's Pet / School Daze / Faerie Tale / Megalomania / Temples Of Ice / The Witching Hour
THE SECOND COMING, Hardware CMA 001 (1996)
The Seven Gates Of Hell / Die Hard / Welcome To Hell / Leave Me In Hell / Countess Bathory / Buried Alive / Don't Burn The Witch / In Nomine Satanas / Schitzo / Nightmare / Black Metal / Witching Hour
BLACK REIGN, Receiver RRCD 212 (1996)
Insane / Civilized / Die Hard / In Nomine Satanas / If You Want A War / Countess Bathory / Harder Than Ever / Welcome To Hell / Carnivorous (Live) / Angel Dust / Fragile Life / Teacher's Pet / Skool Daze/ Buried Alive / Blood Lust / Surgery / Black Metal / Flat Line / Blackened Are The Priests / Prime Evil / Bursting Out / Witching Hour
FROM HEAVEN TO THE UNKNOWN, Snapper Music SMDCD120 (1997)
Welcome To Hell / Witching Hour / Angel Dust / Red Light Fever / Black Metal / Buried Alive / Teachers Pet / Countess Bathory / Don't Burn The Witch / At War With Satan / Rip Ride / Cry Wolf / Women, Leather And Hell / Satanarchist / Possessed / Hellchild / Mystique / Too Loud (For The Crowd) / In League With Satan / Live Like Ann Angel / Bloodlust / In Nomine Satanas / Die Hard / Bursting Out / Warhead / Lady Lust / 7 Gates Of Hell / Manitou / Dead Of The Night / Dead On Arrival / Hounds Of Hell / Bitch Witch / Sadist / Black Metal / Snots Shit
CAST IN STONE, CBH Steamhammer CD 8000136 (1997)
Evil One / Raised In Hell / All Devil's Eve / Bleeding / Destroyed And Damned / Domus Mundi / Flight Of The Hydra / God's Forsaken / Mortals / Infectious / Kings Of Evil / You're All Gonna Die / Judgement Day / Swarm
VENOM CLASSICS, CBH Steamhammer CD (1997) (Free CD with 'Cast In Stone' of re-recorded 'classics')
Intro / Bloodlust / Die Hard / Acid Queen / Burstin' Out / Warhead / Ladylust / Manitou / Rip Ride / Venom

374

RESURRECTION, SPV 085 21752 (2000)
Resurrection / Vengeance / War Against Christ / All there Is Fear / Pain / Pandemonium / Loaded / Firelight / Black Fire Of Satan / Control Freak / Disbeliever / Man, Myth And Magic / Thirteen / Leviathan

VERGELMER (SWEDEN)
Line-Up: Ebboth (vocals / bass), Yngue (guitar), Nazgul (guitar / keyboards), Grimulv (drums)

Black Metallers VERGELMER include ALGAION and THE ABYSS member Mattias Kamijo in the ranks. The outfit, created by ex Death Metal band ABEMAL members guitarists Yngue Liljebäch and Mattias Kamijo (under the pseudonym Nazgul) with bassist Grimulv (real name Martin Gärdeman), debuted with a 1993 demo 'In The Dead Of Winter'. The line up was rounded off with bassist Ebboth (real name Tobias Leffler) and drummer Maunghrim.
A second demo 'Darkness Forever' followed before Maunghrim opted out. VERGELMER responded by shifting Grimulv to drums and Ebboth to bass guitar. However, with the departure of Liljebäch the band became a trio.
Liljebäch made his return in 1995 for 'The Third Winter' outing.

<u>Albums:</u>
LIGHT THE BLACK FLAME, Cacophonous (1997)
Hellstorms Over Holy Ground / Blessed By Satan / Blackened Rebirth / Her Harvest Is My Prey / At War For His Majesty / Purifying / In The Dead Of Winter / Heaven In Ruins Lay / Light The Black Flame

VESPERIAN SORROW (TX, USA)
Line-Up: Donn Donni, Chris Nunez, Walter Winkle, Michael Compton, Jerry Donohue

Self styled "purgatorical" metal from Texas.

<u>Albums:</u>
BEYOND THE CURSED ECLIPSE, Displeased (1999)
Intro / Beyond The Cursed Eclipse / Twilight Of Azrael / From An Elder Blackened Star / Alydon / Shaowlord / Windswept / Saga Of The Second Sign / Vs
VESPERIAN SORROW, Frozen Music

FM025 (2000)

VIKING CROWN (USA)
Line-Up: Killjoy (vocals), Anton Crowley (guitar / bass / drums), Opal Enthroned (keyboards)

Black Metal side project of NECROPHAGIA and RAVENOUS frontman KILLJOY, multi instrumentalist and NECROPHAGIA man 'Anton Crowley' (actually PANTERA vocalist Phil Anselmo) and keyboard player Opal Enthroned.
Anselmo also uses the 'Anton Crowley' pseudonym for his other Black Metal act CHRIST INVERSION.

<u>Albums:</u>
INNOCENCE FROM HELL, Baphomet (2000)
Intro / Asmodeus Rising / Satan Ruler Of Earth / Lust And Destruction / The Judas Goat / Unorthodox Steps Of Ritual / Blaspheme / Invocation Toward The Conjuration Of Black Souls

VILKATES (GERMANY)
Line-Up: Wolver (vocals / bass), Lord Asgaqlun (guitar), Aegir (guitar), Thyyph (drums)

East German act previously known as NUCTEMERON and including former DUNKELGRAFEN members. The band's present title VILKATES is taken from the legend of a medieval werewolf.

<u>Singles/EPs:</u>
The Heritage Of The Old Wolf, (199-) (7" picture disc single)

<u>Albums:</u>
ANGELDUST AND BLASPHEMY, Last Episode 007398-2 (1999)
Intro / Angeldust And Blasphemy / With The Eyes Of A Wolf / The Beyond / Wings Of Darkness / Total Extermination / Cycle / Vilkates / Demonworld / Ruler / Jewclan
APOCALYPTIC MILLENIUM, (2000)
Empire Of Darkness / The Way / Transijoviness / Nuclear Death / Vilkates Part II (symphony Of Lust And Pain) / Dying Flowers / Apocalyptic Millenium / Slave race

VINDSVALL (LUXEMBOURG)
Line-Up: Tyrann (vocals), Hagalaz (guitar), Might (bass), Bezerk (keyboards), Boltthorn (drums)

One of the few Black Metal bands from Luxembourg. VINDSVAL's first line up included vocalist Krig and the BLACK CIRCLE rhythm section of bassist Mogon and drummer Shadow. The demo 'Of Heathen Blood And Soil' was released before both Shadow and Mogon left. VINDSVAL resumed activity with the enlistment of German bassist Might and drummer Boltthorn of DREAMS OF NABID. VINDSVAL frontman Tyrann would guest on the 2001 AD INFERA album.

Albums:
IMPERIUM GROTESQUE, Skaldic Art (2000)
A Black Millennium Awakes / Wanterkeelt / Beholding The Glacial Empire / Farewell, Odyssey And Thew Macabre / Imperium Grotesque / Rise Of The Great Old One / Nativity Of Revenge / Retaliation / The Shadows Fade / Outroduction

VINTERLAND (SWEDEN)
Line-Up: Forn Bragman (vocals / guitar / bass), Pehr Larsson (guitar), Andreas Svensson (drums)

An atmospheric, melodic Black Metal act, VINTERLAND came into existence during 1992. At the time they went under the name of GRIMOIRES and curiously, kept their first ever demo recording to themselves. A further demo - recorded two years later - was not deemed to be good enough either. This recording has never seen the light of day.
It would appear that the third time was the charm as demo number three was mailed to No Fashion boss Tomas Nyqvist. One and a half years later Nyqvist signed the group!
Having by this time taken on the cloak of VINTERLAND, the Swedish trio recorded the debut album 'Welcome My Last Chapter' during November 1995. The recording comprised four new songs and 5 older cuts. The record was released in September 1996
Guitarist Pehr Larsson also operates in MAZE OF TORMENT.

Albums:
WELCOME MY LAST CHAPTER, No Fashion NFR017 (1996)
Our Dawn Of Glory / I'm An Other In The Night / So Far Beyond... (The Great Vastforest) / A Castle So Crystal Clear / As I Behold The Dying Sun /

Vinterskogen / Still The Night Is Awake / A Vinter Breeze / Wings Of Sorrow
VINTERSEMESTRE (NORWAY)
Line-Up: Flesh (vocals / guitar), Torso (vocals / bass), Scroll (guitar), Ril (guitar), Skk (keyboards), Mck (drums)
A Finnish Black Metal sextet who remain resolutely anonymous.
VINTERSEMESTRE translates as 'Winter Holiday'. The band's 1996 album 'Kirkkokyprpä' translates delightfully into 'Church Cock'.

Singles/EPs:
Those Tears Of Lilith / Firedance (Jää) / The Wisdom Of Usuluh (Veri) / The Darkness Of Asath (Saatana) / Silent Tongues / Abigar. MMI MMI 024 (1996) (Jääverisaatana' EP)

Albums:
KIRKKOKYPRPÄ, Autonomy APRO 028 CD (1996)
The Gathering / Opus Dei / The Darkness Of Asath / Tulivaunut / Maigist / Speak For Themselves / Human Sacrifice / Kirvesviilto / Nocturnal Witchery

VINTERSORG (NORWAY)
Line-Up: Vintersorg (vocals / guitar / bass / drums), Mattias Marklund (guitar)

VINTERSORG functioned as a one man endeavour for many years after multi instrumentalist Vintersorg split away from his former band YARGATRON in 1994. Session players for VINTERSORG's 'Till Fjalls' and 'Ödemakes Son' included keyboard player Vargher, guitarist Andreas Frank and female vocals from Cia Hedmark.
The 2000 album 'Cosmic Genesis' album saw VINTERSORG joined by guitarist Mattias Marklund. Keyboards for a live version of VINTERSORG came courtesy of ALSVARTR's Vidvandre.
Vintersorg is also lead vocalist for HAVAYOTH and has another project outing the folkloric OTYG.

Singles/EPs:
Norrland / Stilla / Norrskensdrömman / Hednaorden / Tuss Mörket, (199-) ('Hedniskhj Rtad' EP)

Albums:
TILL FJÄLLS, Napalm (1998)
Rundans / För Kung Och Fosterland / Vild Markens Förtrollande Stämmor / Till Fjälls / Urberget, Äldst Av Troven /

Hednad I Ulvermånens Tecen / Jökeln / Isjungfrun / Asatider / Fårgad Utar Nordensjäl
ÖDEMARKENSSON, Napalm NPR 072 (1999)
Når Alver Sina Runor Sjungit / Svältvinter / Under Norrskenets Fallande Ljusspel / Månskenmän / Ödemarkers Son / Trollbunden / Offerbäcken / I Den Trolska Dalens Hjärta / På Landet
COSMIC GENESIS, Napalm NPR 085 (2000)
Astral And Arcane / Algol / A Dialogue With The Stars / Cosmic Genesis / Om Regnbågen Matererialiserades / Avs Memorativa / Rainbow Demon / Natures Galleri / The Enigmatic Spirit

VITAL REMAINS (RI, USA)
Line-Up: Jeff Gruslin (vocals), Paul Flynn (guitar), Tony Lazaro (guitar), Joe Lewis (bass), Ace Alonzo (drums)

An illustrious name in Death Metal circles. Although firmly in the Death Metal camp VITAL REMAINS infuse their whole being with blasphemous content. The band's first line up for recording of the demo 'Reduced To Ashes' in 1989 comprised of vocalist Jeff Gruslin, guitarists Paul Flynn and Tony Lazaro, bass player Tom Supkow and drummer Chris Dupont. A further tape 'Excruciating Pain', with new drummer 'Ace' Alonzo, and a 7" single for French label Thrash 'Black Mass' bolstered the band's reputation and signaled a deal with British label Peaceville Records.
By the recording of 1997's 'Forever Undeground' VITAL REMAINS had trimmed down to a trio of Lazaro, bassist Joseph Lewis and drummer David Suzuki.
VITAL REMAINS were included on the 1999 tribute to JUDAS PRIEST album 'Hell Bent For Metal' covering 'You've Got Another Thing Comin'.
Vocalist Jeff Gruslin was replaced by Thorns. However, in 2000 VITAL REMAINS sacked vocalist Thorns as the remaining band members cited alleged drug abuse. VITAL REMAINS rehired Gruslin in time for European dates as part of the 'No Mercy' festival package alongside Poland's VADER, Brazil's REBAELLIUN and Germany's FLESHCRAWL.
Late 2000 found Gruslin back on the scene as part of the prominent WOLFEN SOCIETY project which included erstwhile ACHERON man Vincent

Crowley, INCANTATION's Kyle Severn and Lord Ahriman of DARK FUNERAL. The Dutch label Cyronics would re-issue the debut demo 'Reduced To Ashes' in CD format.

Singles/EPs:
Black Mass, Thrash (1991) (7" single)
Amulet Of The Conquering / , Peaceville Collectors CC 4 (1993) (Split single with MORTA SKULD)

Albums:
LET US PRAY, Peaceville CDVILE 58 (1992)
War In Paradise / Of Pure Unholiness / Ceremony Of The Seventh Circle / Uncultivated Grave / Malevolent Invocation / Isolated Magick / Cult Of The Dead / Frozen Terror / Amulet Of The Conquering
INTO COLD DARKNESS, Peaceville (1995)
Immortal Crusade / Under The Moons Fog / Crown Of The Black Hearts / Scrolls Of A Millenium Past / Into Cold Darkness / Descent Into Hell / Angels Of Blasphemy / Dethroned Emperor
FOREVER UNDERGROUND, Osmose Productions OPCD 050 (1997)
Forever Underground / Battle Ground / I am God / Farewell To The Messiah / Eastern Journey / Divine In Fire
DAWN OF THE APOCALYPSE, Osmose Productions (1999)
Intro / Black Magick Curse / Dawn Of The Apocalypse / Sanctity In Blasphemous Ruin / Came No Ray Of Light / Flag Of Victory / Behold The Throne Of Chaos / The Night Has A Thousand Eyes / Societe Des Luciferiens
REDUCED TO ASHES, Cyronics (2000)
Vital Remains / Smoldering Ritual / Morbid Death / Reduced To Ashes / More Brains / Slaughter Shack

VIU DRAKH (GERMANY)

East Germans VIU DRAKH, fronted rather oddly by Fish, started life as a Punk Hardcore unit titled TINPANALLEY but would evolve into a Black Thrash act for the self financed 'Back To The Chaos' album.

Albums:
BACK TO THE CHAOS, Karokiller (1999)
Back To The Chaos / Eyes Of Death / Downwards Again / LXXVI / Nothing To

Regret / No / Kiss The Earth / X / Amok
**TAKE NO PRISONERS, GRIND THEM
ALL AND LEAVE THIS HELL,**
Moonstorm (2000)
Black Milk / Fields Of Repulsion /
Emperors Soldiers / New Shard Disorder
/ Infra Hell / 12 Inch God / Essential
Doubts / Hate / Starfinger / Rebellion

VLAD TEPES (FRANCE)
Line-Up: Wlap Drammsleim (vocals /
guitar / drums), Vorlok Drammsleim
(vocals / bass)

Black Metal duo VLAD TEPES came to
the fore with their 1994 demo 'War
Funeral March'. A split CD with
BELKETRE ensued the following year.
A further demo was issued the same year
entitled 'Celtic Poetry' before another split
effort sharing space with TORGEIST.
The band's original demo was pressed
onto CD in 1997.

Albums:
MARCH TO THE BLACK HOLOCAUST,
Embassy Productions (1995) (Split album
with BELKETRE)
Wladimir's March / Massacre Song From
The Devastated Lands / In Holocaust To
The Natura; Darkness / Drink The Poetry
Of The Celtic Dispute / Dans Notre
Chute / Misery Fear And Storm Hunger /
Diabolical Reaps / Under The
Carpathian Poke
BLACK LEGIONS METAL, Drakkar
(1996) (Split album with TORGEIST)
Ravens Hike / Abyssic And Funeral
Symphony- An Ode To Our Ruin / In
Holocaust To The Natural Darkness /
Tepes The Unweeping / Warmoon Lord
WAR FUNERAL MARCH, Embassy
Productions (1997)
War Funeral March / From The Celtic
Moonfrost / Wallachian Tyrant /
Returning To My Old Battlegrounds /
Frozen Dead's Kingdom

VOBISCUM (AUSTRIA)
Line-Up: Arcanus (vocals), Martyr (guitar
/ bass), Daimonian (keyboards),
Dunkelfürst (drums)

VOBISCUM drummer Dunkelfürst also
has credits with SERAPH and
CLANDESTINE. Under the guise of
Count Grimthorn the man also releases
solo product under the band name
GRIMTHORN'S FOREST.

Albums:
TRAUM EWIGER FINSTERNIS, CCP
100192-2 (1998)

VOND (NORWAY)

Solo Dark Ambient releases from an ex
EMPEROR member Mortiis. The
industrious Mortiis also operates the
more familiar solo project MORTIIS as
well as FATA MORGANA and
CINTECELE DIAVOLUI. The first release
was a now extremely scarce 7" single
issued under the name HÅVAD VOND.
The debut VOND release was banned in
Germany due to the album sleeve
artwork which featured a graphic
photograph of Mortiis seemingly cutting a
girl's throat.

Albums:
SELVMORD, Nekromantik Gallery
Productions (1995)
Selvsmord / Nar Livet Tar Farrel / Reisen
Til Enny Verden / Slipp Sorgen Los
THE DARK RIVER, Shivadarshana SR
1015 (1997)
Love I Never Had / Höst II / Suicide Is
Painless / Black Hole Space Window /
The Dark River / Höst III

VONDUR (SWEDEN)
Line-Up: All (vocals), It (guitar / bass)

Side project act of ABRUPTUM and
OPTHALAMIA mentor It. Vocals are
contributed by erstwhile ABRUPTUM and
present OPTHALAMIA vocalist All. The
album title is Icelandic for 'Declaration Of
War'.
VONDUR's artwork strangely featured
the Star Wars film character Darth Vader
in an effort to convince listeners that the
band were allied to the dark force!
Both It and All were to collaborate with
HYPOCRISY men Peter Tägtgren and
Mikael Hedlund together with ex DARK
FUNERAL guitarist Blackmoon to forge
the one off 'Chaos Metal' project WAR in
1998.
1998 also saw a return for VONDUR with
'The Galactic Rock n' Roll Empire' album.
The cover artwork sported a photograph
of MÖTLEY CRÜE guitarist Mick Mars
touched up with corpse paint! Musically
the record included a bizarre cover
version of ELVIS PRESLEY's 'Love Me
Tender' and JUDAS PRIEST's 'Rocka
Rolla'.

Albums:
STRIDSYFIRLYSING, Necropolis (1995)
Kynning- (Invaldnir Et Het) / Dreptu Allur / Uppunl Vonsku / Kynning- Fjordj Riku / Fjordi Rikins Uppgangur / I Eldut og Dhrumur / Vondur / Hrafins augn er sem speglar a boini Satans Svatta Salur / Eltt Bergmal Ur Framtilinnar Dagar / Kirkjur Skola Brenna / Sigurskrift / Gud er Dainn / Ekki Krist- Opinberun 1 & II / Eg Daemi Oss til Dauda / Ekkl Nein Verdur Saklaus / Beitir Hnifar Skera Djupur / Hofdingi Satan
THE GALACTIC ROCK N' ROLL EMPIRE, Necropolis (1998)
Kill Everyone / You Don't Move Me- I Don't Give A Fuck / Rocka Rolla / Red Hot / Love Me Tender / Panzur Legions Of Vondur / The Ravens Eyes Are As Mirrors Of The Bottom Of Satan's Black Halls

VORAK (AUSTRALIA)

Neo classical Black Metal solo outing from Lord Vorak. VORAK is presently in the midst of an epic three album Wagnerian concept release. VORAK's music, lyrics and images (including Hienkel bombers in flight and quotes from Friedrich Nietzsche, Arthur Schopenhauer and Oswald Spengler) are all entrenched in Nazi rhetoric.
Album artwork is executed by another well known figure of the Australian Black Metal scene Rok of SADISTIK EXEKUTION.

Albums:
TRIUMPH OF THE WILL, Destruktïve Kommandöh DSTK7661-2CD (1996)
Blitzkrieg- Fighting Under The Rune Of Triumph / Bloodlust, Discipline, Hatred / Hail The Nuclear Beserker! / Majesty Of The War Eagle / Testimony Of Zarathustra: Weakness Is The Only Sin / Heroism And Tragedy- Ode To The Slain / Millenium Of Conquest And Sacrifice / Triumph Of The Will / Unforgotten Love / Incubus Of Melancholia / Be Mine, Sweet Countess, Or Die By My Sword / Narcosis In The Forest Of White Nothingness
RHETORIC OF THE SUPERMEN, Destruktïve Kommandöh DSTK7663-2CD (1998)
Preludium: Manifesto Of Transcendental Supremacy / Dies Irae I: Kruel And Glorious Purgation Of The Untermenschen / Fylfot Lakrimosa Et Sanguinus / Blood Reich 2000 / Austraylan Uber Volkslieder I ("One Nation, One Flag, One Anthropotypetz) / Synthetik Repenthe / Australyan Uber Volkslieder II ("One Flag, One Nation, One Anthropotypetz) / Dies Irae II: Blood Katharsis / O Du Mien Holder Abendsternz, From Tanhauser (Richard Wagner) / Elfa's Traumtz, From Lohengrin (Richard Wagner)

VORDVEN (FINLAND)
Line-Up: Mika Packalen (vocals / guitar / keyboards), Piritta Repo (vocals), Matti Kaasalainen (guitar / keyboards), Rami Suonausta (bass), Joni Virtanen (keyboards), Pekka Koponen (drums)

Prior to the 1998 album 'Towards The Frozen Stream' VORDVEN debuted with a 1996 demo entitled 'When The Wind Blew For The First Time'. However, the band's first recordings were made as a duo of vocalist / guitarist Mika Packalen and guitarist Matti Kaasalainen in 1994. For these early sessions guests bassist Rami Suontausta and drummer Tommi Rantanen were employed.
Rantanen would join NIGHTSIDE and for the 1996 demo VORDVEN pulled in drummer Pekka Koponen and keyboard player Joni Virtaren.
VORDVEN broadened their sound with the addition of female vocals courtesy of Piritta Repo in 1997. Rantanen made a return too leaving NIGHTSIDE to become VORDVEN's bassist. Another NIGHTSIDE man, drummer Beleth, was utilized on a temporary basis.

Albums:
TOWARDS THE FROZEN STREAM, No Colours NC017 (1998)
Harness To Heaven / Moonlight In The Northern Sky / Dream Of Northside / Riverdell / Aurora Borealis / Eternal Storm / When The Stormcrystal Reaches The Nightgleam / Towards The Frozen Stream
WOODLAND PASSAGES, No Colours (2000)
Heathen / Blood Never Falls / Journey Into The Realms Above / Cold Pagan Steel / Woodland Passages / … In Melancholy / Through Decades

VORPHALACK (GREECE)
Line-Up: Funeral (vocals). Than (guitar), Alex (bass / keyboards), Rotting Soul (drums)

Black Metal act VORPHALACK issued a

demo titled 'Black Sorrow For A Dead Brother' following their debut 1994 single. The band then released a split album shared with fellow Greek Metal band ZEPHYROUS in 1997.

VORPHALACK are reportedly no longer a going concern. Various members under renewed pseudonyms have created NAER MATARON together with personnel of the ORDER OF THE EBON HAND. Yet more members operate WAMPYRINACHT recording the mini album 'The Cloven Hoof'.

Singles/EPs:
Under The Sight Of The Dragon, Molon Lave (1995)

Albums:
SPLIT, Melancholy Productions (1997) (Split album with ZEPHYROUS)
Prophetic Vision Of A Cursed Domain / In Search Of Glory / Lord Of Love / Like Drawing Of An Unspeakable Act
IN MEMORY, (199-)
Angel Of Light / Four Fiery Crowns / Hymn To Satan / Morbid Rites / The Meeting

VUKODLAK (Pottsville, PA, USA)
Line-Up: Lord Akhkharu (vocals / guitar), Lord Demogorgon (guitar), Lord Sedit (bass), Hpesoj (drums)

Founded by former MASKIM XUL and BAPTISED IN BLOOD members frontrman Lord Akhkharu and bassist Lord Sedit. Ahkharu also has credits with EPITAPH whilst Sedit was once involved with TORQ III and the infamous EVIL DIVINE. The bassist's role in EVIL DIVINE was is as frontman 'J. Demonic'. VUKODLAK debuted with the 1999 demos 'Via Diabolis' and 'Eternal Devastation'.
For the album 'Blackest Autumn' the band employed the services of DIVINE RAPTURE drummer Lord Mattias. However, his commitments with his priority act led to his departure. VUKODLAK regrouped by pulling in former EVIL DIVINE, WITH IMMORTALITY and STRAIGHT HATE drummer Hpesoj and also bolstered their sound with the addition of erstwhile OLD SUFFERING guitarist Lord Demogorgon. VUKODLAK also recorded tracks for a planned split 7" single in alliance with NACHTMYSTIUM for release in 2001.
Both Akhkharu and Sedit are also members of INFERNAL HATRED, the band that evolved from ARYAN TORMENTOR. In ARYAN TORMENTOR and INFERNAL HATRED Sedit plays drums whilst Ahkharu plays bass guitar. The singer also operates LUCIFTIAS.

Albums:
BLACKEST AUTUMN, Realms Of Darkness Productions (2001)
Ol Zodameta / Burnt Horizon / Twilight / Quasb A Na / Blackest Autumn / Cryptic Passage / Blessed Be The Children

VULPECULA (Kansas City, MI, USA)

Black Metal band VULPECULA comprises of erstwhile ORDER FROM CHAOS and NEPENTHE members vocalist / bassist Chuck Keller and drummer Chris Overton.

Singles/EPs:
The Phoenix Of Creation, Eternal Darkness (1995)

Albums:
FON IMMORTALIS, Merciless (1997)
Astride The Darklands / Fons Immortalis / Down Among Them / Phoenix Of The Creation / The First Point Of Aries / Seven Legions Of Light

WALLACHIA
(NORWAY)
Line-Up: Lars Stavdal
(vocals), Eystein
Garberg (guitar),

WALLACHIA is
essentially a one man project of Lars
Stavdal, also guitarist with AMNESIA.

Singles/EPs:
Fullmane Over Fagaras / Skojld Mot
Gudslys / Arges- Riul Doamrei / Krus Den
Hellige And, (199-) ('Wallachia' EP)

Albums:
FROM BEHIND THE LIGHT, Velvet
Music International (1999)

WALLHALLA (FINLAND)
Line-Up: Ceasar T. MacLaunone (vocals /
bass), Lord Heikkenen (guitar), Eystein
Garberg (guitar), Agathon Frosteus
(drums)

WALHALLA are rooted in the fabric of the
Finnish Black Metal scene with vocalist /
bassist Ceasar T. MacLunone, guitarist
Lord Heikkenen and drummer Agathon
Frosteus all being members of
SOULGRIND and GLOOMY GRIM.
Frosteus also has credits with THY
SERPENT, NOMICON and
BARATHRUM whilst MacLaunone is
involved with NOMICON. Erstwhile
TENEBRAE member Lord Heikkenen
has a project band FIRE TRANCE 666.

Albums:
FIREREICH, (2000)
Valkyrie / Helldivision / Battlefield
Genesis / Warsong 666 / Black Cross
Burning / Martyrs Day / Horja Vs Aredia /
Winterfuhrer / War Over Hordland /
Firereich

WAR (AUSTRIA / SWEDEN)
Line-Up: Peter Tägtren, Blackmoon
(guitar), It, All, Mikael Hedlund

Deadly assemblage of VONDUR and
OPTHALMIA members It and All together
with HYPOCRISY and THE ABYSS men
Peter Tägtgren and Mikael Hedlund with
former DARK FUNERAL guitarist
Blackmoon.

Albums:
TOTAL WAR, Necropolis NR019 (1998)
Satan / I Am Elite / Total War / The Sons
Of War / Revenge / Reapers Of Stan /

Satan's Millennium
WE ARE WAR, (1999)
War / We Are War / Soldiers Of Stan /
Rapture 2 / Ave Satan / Kill God / 666 /
Infernal / Hell / Execution / Bombenhagel

WARHAMMER (GERMANY)
Line-Up: Volker Frerich (vocals), Marco
Hoffmann (guitar), Rainer Filipiak (guitar),
Frank Krynojewski (bass), Rolf Meyn
(drums)

WARHAMMER are openly blatant about
their appreciation to the cult legends
HELLHAMMER. So much so in fact that
their music is a deliberate homage to the
Swiss forefathers. The band debuted with
the demo session 'Towards The Chapter
Of Chaos'.
WARHAMMER drafted second guitarist
Rainer Filipiak for the 1999 'Deathchrist'
outing.

Singles/EPs:
Riders / Blood And Honour / Alone /
Warhammer, (199-) ('Riders' EP)

Albums:
THE WINTER OF OUR DISCONTENT,
Voices Productions (1997)
Beyond Forgiveness / Damned For
Extinction / The Shape Of The Enemy /
Warzones / Drowned In Blackness /
Devastation Of Silent Resistance /
Under The Wings Of The Cross /
Imposter Of All Times / The Void Inside
The Darkness / The Winter Of Our
Discontent / The Horror
DEATHCHRIST, Grind Syndicate Media
(1999)
This Graveyard Earth / Mankinds
Darkest Day / The Thorn Of Damnation /
Deathchrist / The Capacity Of Tragic /
Defy The Dark / The Demon's Breed /
Among The Dead / The Tempter Of
Destruction / The Realm Of Torment
THE DOOM MESSIAH, Nuclear Blast NB
603-2 (2000)
Remorseless Winter / Shadow Of The
Decapitator / Cries Of The Forsaken /
Hell Is Open… / Cruel Transcendency /
The Doom Messiah / The Serpents
Tantrum / Cruel And Dying World / In
Pain We'll Burn / The Skullcrusher

WARLOGHE (FINLAND)

Black Metal act WARLOGHE debuted
with a 1995 demo 'The Black Tower'.

Singles/EPs:
Unlighted, (1997)

Albums:
THE FIRST POSSESSION, Drakkar DKCD007 (1999)

WATAIN (SWEDEN)
Line-Up: Erik Danielsson (vocals / bass), C. Blom (guitar), K. Jonsson, Pelle Forsberg

A raw Black Metal act named after the infamous VON song. WATAIN was born when former BLOODSPILL members vocalist / bassist Erik Danielson and guitarist C. Blom forged a union with K. Jonsson and Pelle Forsberg.
WATAIN's opening demo, titled 'Go Fuck Your Jewish God', certainly put the cards on the table and before long Grim Rune Productions had picked the band up for a 7" single release.
WATAIN then signed to Drakkar Records in France for the first album 'Rabid Death Curse'. Blom would decamp following recording as the group persevered as a trio. Later live work introduced bass player T. Stjerma to the band.
A split single 'The Misanthropic Ceremonies' was released in 2001 in alliance with DIABOLICUM.

Singles/EPs:
The Essence Of Black Purity / On Horns Impaled, Grim Rune Productions (1999) (7" single)
My Fists Are Him / , Spikecult (2001) ('The Misanthropic Ceremonies' split 7" single with DIABOLICUM)

Albums:
RABID DEATH CURSE, Drakkar DKCD012 (2000)

WELTER (HOLLAND)

A solo project of Herr Krieger, otherwise known as 'Centurion' of NECROFEAST. Krieger has credits with NIDHUG and also divides his duties with Polish act MEDEAOTH.
WELTER was originally planned as a two man project together with NIDHUG vocalist / bassist Idimmu titled YSORPEL. With Idimmu's exit Krieger renamed the project WELTER for the demo 'Als Her Licht Vervalt'.
The album 'The Elder Land' includes cover versions of BLACK ART and ABSURD songs.

Albums:
THE ELDER LAND, Berzerker (2000)
Van Kust Tot Heide / Ingvian Pride / Friescre Viking / The Law Of The North-Uitgedroogd Bloed / Infinite Fire Ablaze / Bij De Sabelking / Outro- Travel Over Land And Sea / Mourning Soul

WELTMACHT (De Kalb, IL, USA)

One of JUDAS ISCARIOT, JESUS FUCKING CHRIST and SARCOPHAGUS leader Jay Andrew Harris' ('Akenaten') side concerns. WELTMACHT also includes KRIEG's Lord Imperial and SARCOPHAGUS drummer Duane Timlin under the pseudonym of Cryptic Winter.
After relocating to Germany Harris has also become bass player for Czech band MANIAC BUTCHER.

WERWOLF (AUSTRIA)
Line-Up: Hagan (vocals), Wolf (guitar / bass), Trifixion Of The Horned King (keyboards / drums)

Albums:
ZEITENWENDE – ONLY THE STRONG SURVIVE... WAR / INFERNO, Lethal LR C22 (1995)
Prelude / Warwolf / War Is King And Father Of All / The True God Lives In The Mind / Only The Strong Will Survive / On The Edge To A New Age / Under The Flag Of The Sunwheel / Eclipsed By The Moon / March Till Death

WILLOW WISP (USA)
Line-Up: Air-Rik (vocals / guitar), Toe-Knee (drums)

Albums:
THE BUILDING UP AND BREAKING DOWN OF MATTER. ACT 1, SCENE 1 OF THE EXPLOITATION THEATER, Pandemonium (1997)
Aspects Of A Mortuary / Lame / Attempting To Communicate With the Spirits / The Hurting / The Utmost / The Moon Is Rather Full, A Rape Victims Revenge / Sodomized By God / Within The Solitude Of Cemetery Soil / Carpathian Wanton / If I Committed Suicide
DELUSIONS OF GRANDEUR (A GATHERING OF HERETICS), Full Moon Productions (1999)
As They Age They Enrage / God Has Abandoned Us / The Hills Will be My Burial Shroud / Your Children Shall Take

Me As Lord / A Widow Cries… /
Copulation In The Paranormal Forest /
Bastard / Oldest Joke In The book /
Cruel, Despicable, Non Caring Breed / A
New Ice Age Approaches

WINDIR (NORWAY)
Line-Up: Valfar (vocals / guitar / bass),
Steingrim (drums)

WINDIR, a solo project of multi
instrumentalist Valfar with session
drummer Steingrim, issued two demos
'Sognerikit' and 'Det Gamle Riket' prior to
the 1997 album 'Sóknardalr'.
WINDIR session guitarist Stian Bakketeig
would later join ULCUS MOLLE.

Albums:
SÓKNARDALR, Head Not Found
HNF037CD (1997)
Sognariket Sine Krigharar / Det Some
Var Harkareid / Morket Sin Fyrste /
Sogmariket Si Herskarinne / I Ei
Krysallnatt / Rovhargare / Likbor /
Sóknardalr
ARNTOR, Head Not Found HNF048CD
(1999)
The Beginning / Arntor, A Warrior / The
Burial Mound Of King Hydres / The
Blacksmith And The Troll Of Lundamyri /
The Struggle / The Longing / Ending

WIND OF THE BLACK MOUNTAINS (USA)

WIND OF THE BLACK MOUNTAINS is a
one man project from MASOCHIST
founder member Tchort. Ejected from
MASOCHIST (as that band evolved into
SUMMON) Thchort endeavoured with his
highly praised doomy Black Metal
venture.
A bass player intended to become a
member of the band was to fall out with
Tchort and subsequently created the solo
venture BURNING WINDS.

Singles/EPs:
Force Fed Into Blasphemy / The Rise
Of Darkness, Moribund)

Albums:
SING THOU UNHOLY SERVANTS,
Moribund (1998)
Force Fed Into Blasphemy / An Autumn
Evening / Black Goat / Beautiful Sorrow /
Adversary / The Rite Of Darkness / The
Shadow / Thou Shalt Not Mourn

WINDS OF SIRIUS (FRANCE)
Line-Up: Seigneuer V. Sandragon (vocals
/ guitar), Michel Dumas (guitar), Olivier
(guitar), Cedric Ridet (bass), Fred
Puvillard (drums)

WINDS OF SIRIUS was founded by the
erstwhile AMAYON triumvirate of
frontman Lord Vincent Akhenaten
(redubbed Seigneuer V. Sandragon),
guitarist Christian Bivel and drummer
Fred Puvillard.
Upon joining with former ABYSSALS and
MUTILATED guitarist Michel Dumas and
bassist Cedric Ridet of Folkloric act
MATUTINA NOCTEM the band WINDS
OF SIRIUS was borne. However, Bivel
would soon exit.
Previous to WINDS OF SIRIUS
Akhenaton has released solo albums
billed as AKHENATON and
DAEMONIUM.

Albums:
BEYOND ALL TEMPLES AND MYTHS,
Season Of Mist (1999)
Intro / The Light Beyond / Alchemist-
Layman Temptation / The Shadow
Outside / Wise Men Keep Silent /
Everlasting / We Are Dust

WINDWALKER (SWEDEN)
Line-Up: Daniel Bryntse (vocals / guitar /
keyboards / bass / drums), Per Sandgren
(guitar / bass / mandolin)

Black Metal act WINDWALKER,
convened during 1994, is the side project
of Doom act FORLORN members Daniel
Bryntse and Per Sandgren. The original
version of WINDWALKER also included
third member Marcus Morf who was to
depart to concentrate on his other act
WYRE.
For later live work WINDWALKER
employed drummer Magnus Bjork and
bass player Tobias Fredlund. A later live
four stringer was Tobias Björklund of
WITHERED BEAUTY.
The industrious Bryntse also operates as
'Vortex' in Black Metal band MORANNON
and also shares his duties with Folk
Rockers FEBRUARI 93, Punk band
KALLT STAÄL as well as WITHERED
BEAUTY. The man also deputizes on
bass guitar for SORCERY.
Not to be confused with the contemporary
American Pop Rock act of the same
name.

Albums:
THE DANCE OF THE ELVES, Voices Of Death (1997)
Mandolin Intro / Seeker / The Song Of A Bird / ... And You Will Forget My Name / Postludium / Still Is The Night

A WINTER WITHIN (NORWAY)
Line-Up: Morloc (vocals), Sanzia (guitar), Laeturnus (bass), F. Conquer (guitar), Dominy (keyboards), S. Winter (drums)

Stavanger band A WINTER WITHIN were created in 1998 initially with a female singer although this idea was soon dropped. Founder members bassist Laeturnus and drummer S. Winter pulled in Morloc (Mikael Stokdal) of MYRIADS and MAJESTIC on lead vocals and keyboards in 1999. Later the same year Danish born ex 122 STAB WOUNDS and PANZERCHRIST guitarist F. Conquer was enrolled and then British musician Dominy took over keyboards for the 'Frostbitten' demo.
Both Laeturnus and S. winter are also employed as rhythm section for FORLORN.

Albums:
LAMENTIA, Wyvern Productions (2000)
Dying Embers / The Newborn Son / Black Orchids / Beyond The Portals Of Sleep / Gathering Of Lost Souls

WITCHBANE (GERMANY)
Line-Up: Soulreaper (vocals), Desecrator (guitar), Skullcrusher (bass), Nightstalker (drums)

WITCHBANE emerged from the departure in 1997 of vocalist Trohostpanzer from CYGNET OF DARKNESS. The remaining members, guitarist Desecrator, bassist Skullcrusher and drummer Nightstalker soldiered on renaming the band WITCHBANE.
Singer Soulreaper was drafted for the demo 'Death, Darkness And Destruction' as was temporary member Demonbreath.

Albums:
SOLDIERS OF HELL, Mascot (1999)
Sign Of Satan / Bloodsmeared / Death, Darkness And Destruction / Soldiers Of Hell / Steelgoat Domain / Dimension Warblade / Lucifer's Fellowship / The Streams Of Red / Metamorphosis / Instrumental

WITCHERY (SWEDEN)
Line-Up: Toxine (vocals), Patrick Jensen (guitar), Ricard Corpse (guitar), Sharlee D'Angelo (bass), Mique (drums)

Trad Metal merchants WITCHERY were created in 1997 from the ashes of SÉANCE and SATANIC SLAUGHTER. Both vocalist Toxine and drummer Mique had also been members of TOTAL DEATH whilst Mique had also been involved in MORGUE together with guitarist Ricard Corpse.
WITCHERY came together when SATANIC SLAUGHTER vocalist Ztephan Dark fired his entire band just days before a scheduled album recording. Undaunted the quartet stuck together to found WITCHERY enlisting MERCYFUL FATE and ILLWILL bassist Sharlee D'Angelo. The latter's priority commitments to MERCYFUL FATE meant that recording of the debut WITCHERY album was delayed until the Autumn of 1997.
The band put in their debut show in April 1998 in Copenhagen although minus Ricard who was too ill to perform.
The 1999 mini album 'Restless And Dead' comprises originals plus various covers including ACCEPT's 'Restless And Wild', BLACK SABBATH's 'Neon Knights', W.A.S.P.'s 'I Wanna Be Somebody' and JUDAS PRIEST's 'Riding On The Wind'.
WITCHERY put in a showing at the renowned German Wacken Metal festival in 1999.
Guitarist Patrick Jensen, also operates with THE HAUNTED. Toxine and Corpse also busy themselves with INFERNAL. Mique has a side project entitled RHOCA GIL.
Latterly WITCHERY have cut versions of KING DIAMOND's 'The Shrine' and the SCORPIONS 'China White' for tribute albums.

Albums:
RESTLESS AND DEAD, Necropolis NR029 (1998)
The Reaper / Witchery / Midnight At The Graveyard / The Hangman / Awaiting The Exorcist / All Evil / House Of Raining Blood / Into Purgatory / Born In The Night / Restless And Dead
WITCHBURNER, Necropolis NR034 (1999)
Fast As A Shark / I Wanna Be Somebody / Riding On The Wind / Neon Knights / The Howling / The Executioner / Witchburner

DEAD, HOT AND READY, Necropolis (2000)
Demonication / A Paler Shade Of Death / The Guillotine / Resurrection / Full Moon / The Dead And The Dance Done / Dead, Hot And Ready / The Devil's Triangle / Call Of The Coven / On A Black Horse Thru Hell...

WITCHFINDER GENERAL (UK)
Line-Up: Zeeb (vocals), Phil Cope (guitars), Rod Hawks (bass), Graham Ditchfield (drums)

Wolverhampton Black Metal band formed in 1979 by vocalist Zeeb and guitarist Phil Cope. Original members included bassist Toss McReady and drummer Steve Kinsell.
Signed to Heavy Metal Records in 1980 and released the poorly produced 'Burning A Sinner' single. The debut album was handled by producer Pete Hinton. They split with their rhythm section whilst in the studio and quickly added bassist Rod Hawks and drummer Graham Ditchfield.
The debut album attracted publicity as the sleeve featured Page Three model Joanne Latham being ritually 'executed' on a gravestone. The second album sleeve rather too predictably followed up on this theme. In recent times WITCHFINDER GENERAL have enjoyed posthumous respect from numerous death metal and doom bands.
A later WITCHFINDER GENERAL member bassist Zakk Bajjon created BAJJON, later joined LIONSHEART and would produce CRADLE OF FILTH.
With the resurgence of interest in NWoBHM across Europe it looked as though the WITCHFINDER GENERAL albums would unfortunately never be re-issued as Heavy Metal Records label boss Paul Birch is now a born again Christian and objects to the band's lyrical stance. However, after much pressure 'Death penalty' finally saw a 1996 CD release.
By 2000 Bajjon was a member of RAINMAKER 888.

Singles/EPs:
Burning A Sinner / Satan's Children, Heavy Metal HEAVY 6 (1981)
Soviet Invasion / Rabies / R.I.P., Heavy Metal HM 17 (1982)
Music / Last Chance, Heavy Metal HMPD 21 (1983)

Albums:
DEATH PENALTY, Heavy Metal HMRLP 7 (1982)
Invisible Hate / Free Country / Death Penalty / No Stayer / Witchfinder General / Burning A Sinner / RIP
FRIENDS OF HELL, Heavy Metal HMRLP 13 (1983)
Love On Smack / Last Chance / Music / Friends Of Hell / Requim For Youth / Shadowed Images / I Lost You / Quietus Reprise

WITCHFYNDE (UK)
Line-Up: Luther Beltz (vocals), Montalo (guitar), Pete Surgey (bass), Gra Scoresby (drums)

Very popular black metal act formed on Candlemass 1976 and were at the forefront of the NWoBHM movement.
The band signed to Rondolet in 1980 releasing their first single 'Give Em Hell' that year and even supporting DEF LEPPARD on tour. Mystery surrounded the band when after the release of their second album they seemingly disappeared. During this period bassist Andro Coulton left and in came Pete Surgey. They eventually emerged in 1983 with a new vocalist Luther Beltz replacing Steve Bridges and a successful single 'I'd Rather Go Wild' and a concept album 'Cloak And Dagger' to back it up.
In the summer of 1984 Surgey was replaced by former PANZA DIVISION bassist Alan Edwards. There followed another lengthy absence before their next album on yet another label with new member Ed Wolfe.
The first 10,000 copies of 'Lords Of Sin' came with a free 4 track live EP titled 'Anthems' featuring 'Give Em Hell',' Cloak And Dagger', 'Moon Magic' and 'I'd Rather Go Wild'.
The band disappeared seemingly for good in 1986. By 1995 Surgey and Beltz were members of blues covers band THE ACCELERATORS.
The band reemerged in a fashion during 1999 when press announcements were released claiming Scoresby, Beltz, Montalo and Surgey were back together as WITCHFYNDE. These reports appeared to be spurious though as it emerged Beltz had been gigging with STORMWATCH having no intention to join WITCHFYNDE.
Beltz eventually founded the LUTHAR BELTZ BAND with members of STORMWATCH and pulling off the undoubted coup of roping in ex SAXON

guitarist Graham Oliver. This outfit's first move was to cover a track for a low budget DEMON tribute album.

Beltz and Montalo did eventually team up as WITCHFYNDE with STORMWATCH bassist Dave Hewitt and ex SAVAGE and DAWNTRADER drummer Dave Lindley.

By 2000 the WITCHFYNDE story had become entangled in chaos as two bands were operating under the same name. Beltz and Hewitt were announced as playing at the German Wacken Festival as WITCHFYNDE as were Montalo, Scoresby and Surgey with fresh vocalist ex REBEL and CLOWNHOUSE singer Harry Harrison, also billed as WITCHFYNDE.

Early 2001 revealed that Luther Beltz had in fact signed to Demolition Records to release an album under the title of... WYTHCHFYNDE.

Singles/EPs:
Give 'Em Hell / Gettin' Heavy, Rondolet ROUND 1 (1980)
In The Stars / Wake Up Screaming, Rondolet ROUND 4 (1980)
I'd Rather Go Wild / Cry Wolf, Expulsion OUT 3.(1983)
Conspiracy / Scarlet Lady, Mausoleum GUTS 8404 (1984)
Cloak And Dagger (Live) / I'd Rather Go Wild (Live) / Moon Magic (Live) / Give 'Em Hell (Live), Mausoleum (1984) ('Anthems' EP)

Albums:
GIVE 'EM HELL, Rondolet ABOUT 1 (1980)
Ready To Roll / The Divine Victim / Leaving Nadir / Gettin' Heavy / Give 'Em Hell / Unto The Ages Of Ages / Pay Now, Love Later
STAGEFRIGHT, Rondolet ABOUT 2 (1981)
Stage Fright / Doing The Right Thing / Would Not Be Seen Dead In Heaven / Wake Up Screaming / Big Deal / Moon Magic / In The Stars / Trick Or Treat / Madeline
CLOAK AND DAGGER, Expulsion EXIT 5 (1983)
Welcome To The Devil's Playground / Crystal Gazing / I'd Rather Go Wild / Somewhere To Ride / Cloak And Dagger / Cry Wolf / Start Counting / Living For Memories / Rock n' Roll / Stay Away / Pra Diabolo
LORDS OF SIN / ANTHEMS, Mausoleum Records LORD 835354 (1984)

The Lord Of Sin / Stab In The Back / Heartbeat / Scarlet Lady / Blue Devils / Hall Of Mirrors / Wall Of Death / Conspiracy / Red Garters
BEST OF WITCHFYNDE, British Steel CD METAL1 (1996)
Give 'Em Hell / Unto The Age Of Ages / Ready To Roll / Leaving Nadir / Gettin' Heavy / Pay Now-Love Later / Stage Fright / Wake Up Screaming / Moon Magic / In The Stars / The Devil's Playground / I'd Rather Go Wild / Cloak And Dagger / Cry Wolf / Stay Away / Fra Diabolo

WITCH HUNT (Stafford, VA, USA)
Line-Up: Brian Straight (vocals / guitar), Seth Newton (bass), Erik Sayenga (drums)

Albums:
PROPHECIES OF A GREAT PLAGUE, Rated X XRR001 (1996)
Fragments / Confined To Illusions / Conjouring The Undivine / A World Lit Only By Fire / When All Hope Is Lost
SOULS ENSHROUDED FIRE, Rated X XRR008 (2000)
Ablaze Thy Majestic Kingdom / Under Black Celestial Skies / Enshrouded / Winds Of The Darkest Dawn / Forever Burning / As Life Fades Away / And The Sun Fell Forever / Into Definate Astral Darkness / Firestorm Of Armageddon

WITCHMASTER (POLAND)

A Retro Black Thrash band WITCHMASTER include members of the equally notorious Polish act PROFANUM.

Albums:
VIOLENCE AND BLASPHEMY, (2000)

WITCHTRAP (TURKEY)

Albums:
WITCHING BLACK, Hammer Muzik (1999)
Convent Of The Misery / Asura / Witchcraft / Dreams From Hell / The Return Of The Primewitch / Witching Black / Dark Desire / Witchtrap / Convent Of The Misery II

WITHERED BEAUTY (SWEDEN)
Line-Up: Daniel Bryntse (vocals / guitar), William Blackmon (guitar), Tobias Björklund (bass), Jonas Lindstro (drums)

A Swedish Death Black Metal band

rooted in the Death Metal act CONSPIRACY of which founder members frontman Daniel Bryntse and guitarist Magnus Björk paid their dues. Bryntse was also earlier a member of STENCH.

A brace of mid 90's demos 'Screaming From The Forest' and 'Through Silent Skies' led to a deal with the German Nuclear Blast concern. The eponymous 1997 album being produced by HYPOCRISY's Peter Tägtgren.

Following the album Björk departed and guitarist William Blackmon filled the gap. Drummer Jonas Lindstrom was also employed to take over percussion, previously handled by Bryntse.

Bryntse spreads his talents far and wide appearing as bassist in SORCERY and as a member of WINDWALKER and Doom act FORLORN. As if all this activity was not enough he operates in Black Metal act MORRAMON under the pseudonym of 'Vortex' and plays live with Punk band KALLT STAÄL.

Albums:
WITHERED BEAUTY, Nuclear Blast (1997)
Lies / Broken / Veil Of Nothing / The Worm / Through Silent Skies / Twilight Dreaming / Dying Alone / Failure / Joust / He Who Comes With The Dawn

WITHERING SURFACE (DENMARK)
Line-Up: Michael H. Anderson (vocals), Allan Tvedebrink (guitar), Heinz Schultz (guitar), Kaspar Boye-Larsen (bass), Jakob Grundel (drums)

WITHERING SURFACE were formed in Naesved during October 1994. National Danish radio voted their 1995 demo as the best demo recording of that year greatly boosting the band's profile.

The band's first commercially available recordings came with the inclusion of a track on the Serious Entertainment compilation album 'Extremity Rising Volume One'. Promoting this release WITHERING SURFACE undertook gigs with the likes of A CANOUROUS QUINTET, DAWN and INIQUITY.

The debut WITHERING SURFACE album boasts a guest appearance from IN FLAMES and HAMMERFALL man Jesper Strömblad and is produced by the DECAMERON duo of Fredrik Nordström and Alex Losbäck. Guitarist Morten Ryberg though was to lose his place to Heinz Schultz.

Shows in Germany saw support dates to NIGHT IN GALES and PURGATORY.

Albums:
SCARLET SILHOUETTES, Euphonious PHONI 007 (1997)
Scarlet Silhouettes / Beautybeast / A Lily White Sign / … And She Blossomed / Majestic Mistress / Farewell / Behind The Other Side / Pityful Emblems / Your Shadow, My Shelter
THE NUDE BALLET, (199-)
Wither / Ode For You / Dreaming Purple / Will She Defy / Black As I / Whorebride / The Last One / Nude And Humble / Dancing With Fairies / Her Valley / The Ballet

WIZZARD (FINLAND)
Line-Up: Teemu Kautonen (vocals / bass), Dan (guitar), Grobi (drums)

WIZZARD mainman Teemu Kautonen is ex DARKWOODS MY BETROTHED and NATTVINDENS GRAT. WIZZARD debuted with the demo 'I Am The King'. Although recorded in 1996 financial uncertainties with the band's German label resulted in a three year delay before the release of the debut album.

WIZZARD's early line up comprised of Kautonen, guitarist Hellboozer, second guitarist Demonos Sora of BARATHRUM and drummer Ville. After recording of the first record Wellu took over the drum position before Kautonen relocated to Germany establishing WIZZARD as an all new trio rounded off by THARGOS members guitarist Dan and drummer Grobi. By August of 1997 though the man was back in Finland laying down the sophomore 'Devilmusick' album for Spinefarm Records.

Line up for this release was Kautonen, guitarist Wilska Torquemada and drummer J. Crow. For live work another DARKWOODS MY BETROTHED man, drummer Tero, joined the fold. A package tour of Finland with BARATHRUM, HORNA and BABYLON WHORES was undertaken with JeeJee on second guitar and Torquemada switched to bass.

Further Finnish dates in April 1998 witnessed the departure of Tero and inclusion of erstwhile NIGHTWISH guitarist Samppa. With Pasi making up the numbers on drums a third album was recorded for Near Dark Productions but fiscal matters once more dogged the band and the album would be shelved. Fortunately for WIZZARD Massacre

Records sub division Gutter Records licensed the album 'Songs Of Sin And Decadence' for 2000 release. WIZZARD's 2000 EP 'Tormentor' sees a cover of JUDAS PRIEST's 'Breaking The Law'. Kautonen relocated back to Germany and also resurrected his union with Dan and Grobi for a further incarnation of WIZZARD.

Singles/EPs:
Songs Of Sin and Decadence / I Am The King / Breaking The Law / Get Slaughtered, Gutter (2000) ('Tormentor' EP)

Albums:
DEVILMUSICK, Spinefarm (1997)
Rock n' Roll (Devil's Music) / Feathers Burn, Leather Doesn't / One Way Ticket To Hell / Little Lyndsey / …Down The Pit Of Doom / Iron, Speed, Metal / Dirty As Fuck / Satan's Blues (In A Minor) / Vultures Over Golgotha / Revenge Of The Witch
WIZZARD, Nasgûl's Eyrie Productions NEP016 (1999)
Black Leather And Cold Metal / Fenris Is Loose! / Demons Blood / The Lord Of Shadows / I Am The King / Get Your Kicks On Route 666 / Possessed By Inferno / Thou Daughter Of Fire / Pestilence / Saviours Of Metal / When The Sun Goes Down / My Unholy Witch / Leather, Booze And Rock n' Roll / Hot Lead / Sabbath
SONGS OF SIN AND DECADENCE, Gutter (2000)
Sins Of A Past Life / Temple Of Eternal Evil / A Midnight Rendezvous / The Fire Of Volcanus / Angel De La Barthe / Sundown Over Lavenham / Tormentor / Nacht Der Verdammten Seele / The Left Hand Of Eternity / Harbingers Of Metal

WOLFEN SOCIETY
(SWEDEN / USA)
Line-Up: Jeff Gruslin (vocals), Lord Ahriman (guitar), Riktor Ravensbruck (guitar), Vincent Crowley (bass), Thomas Thorn (keyboards), Kyle Severn (drums)

An illustrious Black Metal project assembled in late 2000. WOLFEN SOCIETY boasted in the ranks such esteemed figures as erstwhile ACHERON man Vincent Crowley on bass, DARK FUNERAL guitarist Lord Ahriman, INCANTATION drummer Kyle Severn and VITAL REMAINS singer Jeff Gruslin. Also involved were guitarist Riktor Ravensbruck and keyboard player Thomas Thjorn of ELECTRIC HELLFIRE CLUB.

WONGRAVEN (NORWAY)
Line-Up: Wongraven (vocals / guitar / bass / keyboards), Msakn (keyboards), Hans K.K. Sörensen (drums)

'Fjeltronen' is the side project album of SATYRICON's Satyr. EMPEROR's Ihsahn aids on keyboards.

Albums:
FJELTRONEN, Moonfog FOG 006 (1995)
Del I: Del Var En Gang El Menneske / Del II: Over Odemark / Del III: Opp Under Fjellet Loner En Sang / Del IV: Tiden Er En Stenlagl Grav / Del V: Fra Fjelltronen

WYKKED WYTCH (USA)
Line-Up: Demoness Ipek (vocals), David (guitar / bass), Salvatore (keyboards), John Rae (drums)

Led by Turkish vocalist Demoness Ipek, the only surviving founder member of WYKKED WYTCH. The band's 2000 album 'Angelic Violence' was recorded in Italy and produced by Kit Woolven.

Singles/EPs:
Shallow Grave / Ripping Flesh, (1999) ('Dispelling The Myth' EP)

Albums:
SOMETHING WYKKED THIS WAY COMES, Demolition DEMCD 102 (1996)
Wytch's Sabbath / In Darkness, Let Me Dwell / Resurrection / Black Widow / Psychotic Waltz / Dripping Blood / Expect No Mercy / Requiem / Voices Are Calling
ANGELIC VIOLENCE, (2000)

WYRD (FINLAND)

Another outing from Narqath of HIN ONDE, OATH OF CIRION and VALAR.

Albums:
UNCHAINED HEATHEN WRATH, Dragonthrone DCD002 (2000)
Ravenhill / Unchained / Hel / Revenge Of The Pagan Hordes / The Old Warrior / Wotan's Heir / Wyrd

XHARATHRON
(SPAIN)

Madrid Black Metal act fronted by vocalist Goab.

Albums:
IMMEMORIAL ATLANTIC VENERATION, Reprise (1996)

YEARNING (FINLAND)
Line-Up: Juhani Palomäki (vocals / guitar / keyboards), Tero Kalliomäki (guitar), Petri Salo (bass), Toni Kostiainen (drums)

Sombre Metal act created in 1994 under an original title of FLEGETON. First product was the demo 'The Temple Of Sagal' prior to a title switch to YEARNING.
First outing for the French Holy label was the inclusion of the track 'Autumn Funeral' on the 'Holy Bible' compilation. The debut album 'With Tragedies Adorned' was recorded at Tico Tico studios in September 1996.

Albums:
WITH TRAGEDIES ADORNED, Holy (1997)
Remnants Of The Only Delight / Bleeding For Sinful Crown / Flown Away / Haze Of Despair / The Temple Of Sagal / Release / In The Hands Of Storm / Canticum
PLAINTIVE SCENES, Holy (1999)
Naiveté / Unwritten / Grey / Soliloquy / Plaintive Scenes / Soliloquy II / Eyes Of The Black Flame

YTTERBIUM (AUSTRIA)

Albums:
69, Ytterbium (2000)

YYRKOON (FRANCE)

Albums:
ONIRIC TRANSITION, Velvet Music International BP 902 (1999)
Defeat / Throne Of Complains / The Awakening / Elemental Storm / Runic Art / Last Ideal / Wind Of Decline / Onric Transitions

ZEMIAL (GREECE)

Black Metal band originally from Greece but now located in Australia. ZEMIAL had early tracks issued in bootleg form on a shared CD with MAYHEM and THOU SHALT SUFFER in 1995. The band is centred upon Eskarth The Dark One who also shares his endeavours with AGATUS.

Singles/EPs:
Sleeping Under Tarturus, Torched (1992)

Albums:
FOR THE GLORY UR, Hypervorea (1996)

ZEPHYROUS (GREECE)

Line-Up: Dreamlord (vocals), Invisible (guitar), Serpent King (bass)

Black Metal act ZEPYROUS had their 1994 demo 'Entrance And Wandering Through The Seven Zones' pressed onto CD the following year by Impure creations. The second ZEPHYROUS release was a shared album with VORPHALECK.
Following the split album drummer Emperor Of The Mourning Moon made his exit.

Albums:
ENTRANCE AND WANDERING THROUGH THE SEVEN ZONES, Impure Creations (1995)
A CARESS OF WAR AND WISDOM, Melancholy Productions (1997) (Split CD with VORPHALECK)
Ichor / The Serpent Rise / Dreamers / Entrance And Wandering On The Seven Zones / Dysangelium
ANTIQUITUIS GLORIA, (199-)
Hidden Away From The Sun / The Frozen Path Of Timeless Wisdom And Trance / The Inner Battalion Of Dagon / Everlasting Fire / Endless Abysses Of Black / Apparition Of A Haunted Dance / Darkest Dreams / Signal From The Northness Goddess / The Gifted Empire Of The Marvelous Tartarus / Sensations Lost In Time
TOWARDS, Invision Music IV003 (1999)
Embraced By The Gods Of Hunting / Confessions Of The Inmost Ruby / Shadow Path / Jesus Christ And The Pale Flowers / My Cup Of Life / Abraxas / I.F.O. / Eleusis Sacraments

ZYKLON (NORWAY)

Line-Up: Daemon (vocals), Zamoth (guitar), Destructhor (bass), Trym (drums)

A revamping of EMPEROR guitarist Samoth's (or 'Zamoth' as he is known with this project) ZYKLON B project. The second album, simply credited now to ZYKLON, had EMPEROR drummer Trym colluding with Destructor of MYRKSKOG.
Guesting on the 2000 'World Ov Worms' album is LIMBONIC ART's Daemon (Vidar Jensen), ULVER's 'Trickster G' (actually frontman Garm) and the American fetish star Persephone. Bass guitar for ZYKLON is sessioned by Cosmocrator of SOURCE OF TIDE.

Albums:
WORLD OV WORMS, Candlelight (2000)
Hammer Revelation / Deduced To Overkill / Chaos Deathcult / Storm Detonation / Zycloned / Terrordrome / Worm World / Transcendental War-Battle Between Gods

ZYKLON B (NORWAY)

ZYKLON B is the side project from EMPEROR members guitarist ZYKLON B had the man colluding with his EMPEROR colleague Ihsahn together with Frost of SATYRICON and Aldrahn of DØDHEIMSGARD.
Samoth would resurrect the outfit for a 2000 album under the less controversial banner of ZYKLON. The record had EMPEROR drummer Trym in alliance with Destructhor of MYRKSKOG and Daemon of LIMBONIC ART.

Singles/EPs:
Mental Orgasm / Bloodspoil / Warfare, Malicious (1995) ('Blood Must Be Shed' EP)

ZYKLON X (GERMANY)

Albums:
TOD UND LEBEN, Thrashback TBR 00197 (1997)
Einleitung / Zyclon B / Weise Worte / Seelenschmeid / Niha Sux / Der Mensch / Hass / Lebensfähig / Gesegnetes Land / Der Fischfreund / Nennt mich Gott / Abschied / Wiederkehr

DEATH, INCANTATION, IMPETIGO and MORBID ANGEL to the rise of Swedish Death Metal legends IN FLAMES, CARNAGE and AT THE GATES, the Death Metal of MARDUK, the Christian Death Metal of MORTIFICATION and the politically charged Noisecore of AGATHOCLES. All genres old and new are analyzed in depth with full career histories and detailed discographies.

No area of the globe has provided a safe haven and this book documents the burgeoning uprise of Death Metal bands in the Far East, Eastern Europe and South America.

Be warned - even though some of the band names are not for the faint-hearted the song titles will leave you reeling.

Paper covers, 366 pages, £14.99 in UK

THE METAL COLLECTORS SERIES

WITCHFYNDE – THE BEST OF WITCHFYNDE
CDMETAL 1

Witchfynde were part of the New Wave Of British Heavy Metal (N.W.O.B.H.M.) of the early 80's that spawned the likes of Iron Maiden, Def Leppard and Judas Priest. Witchfynde still have a great significance on the later generations of Heavy Metal artists, Metallica and Paradise Lost regularly state the band as an influence. This CD includes 16 prime cuts that features the singles, "Give Em Hell", "In The Stars" and I'd Rather Go Wild" as well as the best tracks from their rare LP's "Give Em Hell", "Stagefright" and "Cloak And Dagger". "Iron Page's" journalist Matthias Mader, an expert in the field has written the liner notes for this release on our Metal Series.
Tracklisting: Give 'Em Hell/ Unto The Ages Of The Ages / Ready To Roll / Leaving Nadir / Gettin' Heavy / Pay Now-Love Later / Stage Fright / Wake Up Screaming / Moon Magic / In The Stars / The Devil's Playground / I'd Rather Go Wild / Cloak And Dagger / Cry Wolf / Stay Away / Fra Diabolo

VARIOUS – HEAVY METAL RECORDS SINGLES COLLECTION VOL. 1
CDMETAL 3

This is a fifteen track round up of the first batch of singles released by Heavy Metal Records, the legendary Metal label of the early 80's. Again a highly collectable and expensive package when originally released, with rare and collectable tracks from, Buffalo, Dragster, Last Flight, Split Beaver, Satanic Rites and Handsome Beasts. This release appears on CD for the first time, with a full colour booklet that contains a full discography, detailed liner notes and pictures of each of the sleeves.
Tracklisting: HANDSOME BEASTS - All Riot Now / The Mark Of The Beast / Breaker / Crazy / One In A Crowd BUFFALO – Battle Torn Heroes / Women Of The Night DRAGSTER – Ambitions / Won't Bring You Back LAST FLIGHT – Dance To The Music / I'm Ready SPLIT BEAVER – Savage / Hound Of Hell SATANIC RITES – Live To Ride / Hit And Run

Also available from British Steel

THE METAL COLLECTORS SERIES

HERITAGE – REMORSE CODE
CDMETAL 4

First released by Rondelet Records in 1982 this was four piece Heritage's one and only LP and this is the first time it has ever appeared on CD. The single "Strange Place To Be" is featured on this release from one of the 'forgotten heroes' of the entire NWOBHM movement.
Tracklisting: Remorse Code / Attack Attack / Endless Flight / For Good Or Bad / Need You Today / Strange Place To Be / Slipping Away / Change Your Mood / Rudy And The Zips / A Fighting Chance / BONUS TRACKS: Misunderstood / Strange Place To Be (Single Version)

THE HANDSOME BEASTS - BEASTIALITY
CDMETAL 5

First time on CD for this legendary LP, originally issued as the first release by Wolverhampton based Heavy Metal Records. The original 9 track album has now been joined by four bonus cuts including the singles "All Riot Now" and "Sweeties" to give the definitive Handsome Beasts collection.
Tracklisting: Sweeties / David's Song / Breaker / One In A Crowd / Local Heroes / Another Day / Tearing Me Apart / High Speed / BONUS TRACKS: The Mark Of A Beast / All Riot Now / Sweeties (Single Version) / You're On Your Own

Also available from British Steel

THE METAL COLLECTORS SERIES

GASKIN – END OF THE WORLD / NO WAY OUT
CDMETAL 6

Gaskin were one of the most influential N.W.O.B.H.M. bands, to this day bands cite them as a major influence. In 1991 Lars Ulrich of Metallica included Gaskin on the "NWOBHM '79 Revisited" compilation he released. This double album on one CD features two extremely rare and collectable albums from the band. The original artwork is re-produced, with a full discography.

Tracklisting: END OF THE WORLD - Sweet Dream Maker / Victim Of The City / Despiser / Burning Alive / The Day Thou Gavest Lord Hath Ended / End Of The World / On My Way / Lonely Man / I'm No Fool / Handful of Reasons NO WAY OUT - Dirty Money / Free Man / Just Like A Movie Star / Say Your Last Word / Broken Up / Ready For Love / Come Back To Me / High Crime Zone / Queen Of Flames / No Way Out.

VARIOUS – N.W.O.B.H.M. RARITIES VOL. 2
CDMETAL 7

This album features 18 tracks from some of the finest N.W.O.B.H.M. acts of the early 80's, with nearly all of the tracks being released on CD for the first time. Included are the first two Samson singles, Stormtrooper, Xero, Paralex, The EF Band, Shiva and Janine. All the singles have a combined collectors value of over 300 (pounds). Pictures of each of the sleeves are included in the package.

Tracklisting: SAMSON – Telephone / Leavin' You STORMTROOPER – Pride Before A Fall / Still Comin' Home JANINE – Crazy On You / Candy XERO – Oh Baby / Hold On / Killer Frog PARALEX – White Lightning / Travelling Man / Black Widow SAMSON – Mr Rock 'n' Roll / Drivin' Music SHIVA – Rock Lives On / Sympathy EF BAND – Another Day Gone / Nightangel

Also available from British Steel

THE METAL COLLECTORS SERIES

SAVAGE - HYPERACTIVE
CDMETAL 10

One of the leading cult bands of the whole New Wave Of British Heavy Metal movement of the early eighties. This seminal album also includes the Mansfield based band's ultra rare three track 12" "We Got The Edge" as a bonus.
Tracklisting: We Got The Edge / Eye For An Eye / Hard On Your Heels / Blind Hunger / Gonna Tear Ya Heart Out / Stevies Vengeance / Cardiac / All Set To Sting / Keep It On Ice BONUS TRACKS Runnin' Scared / She Didn't Need You / We Got The Edge (Single Version)

VARIOUS – NEW ELECTRIC WARRIORS
CDMETAL 13

This was the first compilation album to feature bands from the N.W.O.B.H.M. Originally released 17 years ago, the album is now available for the first time on CD. Contributing bands include, Silverwing, Oxym, Buffalo and Streetfighter which was the first band to feature John Sykes of future Thin Lizzy- Whitesnake fame.
Tracklisting: TURBO - Running / BUFFALO - Battle Torn Heroes / STREETFIGHTER - She's No Angel / STORM TROOPER - Grind And Heat / TAROT - Feel The Power / BASTILLE - Hard Man / OXYM - Hot Rain / DAWN WATCHER - Firing On All Eight / VARDIS - If I Were King / SILVERWING - Rock And Roll Are Four Letter Words / RHAB STALLION - Chain Reaction / COLOSSUS - Holding Back Your Love / JEDEDIAH STRUT - Workin' Nights / WARRIOR - Still On The Outside / KOSH - The Hit / RACE AGAINST TIME - Bedtime

Also available from British Steel

THE METAL COLLECTORS SERIES

VARIOUS – N.W.O.B.H.M. RARITIES VOL. 3
CDMETAL 14

Volume three of British Steel's series collecting together many ultra rare singles releases from the late 70's - early 80's new wave of British Heavy Metal movement, none of which have ever appeared on CD before. Vol.3 includes bands such as Twisted Ace, Soldier and Jaguar, plus the very first single by Girlschool.
Tracklisting: GIRLSCHOOL - Take It All Away / It Could Be Better TWISTED ACE - I Won't Surrender / Firebird SOLDIER Sheralee / Force JAGUAR - Back Street Woman / Chasing The Dragon DENIGH - No Way / Running STATIC Voice On The Line / Stealin' SEVENTH SON - Metal To The Moon / Sound And Fury WHITE LIGHTNING - This Poison Fountain / Hypocrite DRAGONSLAYER - I Want Your Life / Satan Is Free / Broken Head

VARIOUS - ROXCALIBUR
CDMETAL 15

This legendary 14 track compilation from the 1980's is released on CD for the first time ever. All cuts are unique to this album which gathered together some of the New Wave of British heavy metal scenes rising stars and includes contributions from Black Rose, Marauder, Battleaxe and Skitzofrenik.
Tracklisting: BLACK ROSE - No Point Runnin' / Ridin' High BRANDS HATCH - Brands Hatch / No Return BATTLEAXE - Burn This Town / Battleaxe SATAN - Oppression / The Executioner MARAUDER - Battlefield / Woman Of The Night UNTER DEN LINDEN - Wings Of Night / Man At The Bottom SKITZOFRENIK - Exodus / Keep Right On

www.cherryred.co.uk

Also available from British Steel

THE METAL COLLECTORS SERIES

MYTHRA – THE DEATH AND DESTINY LP
CDMETAL 16

In their short lived career at the start of the 1980's Mythra managed to gain themselves a reputation that now sees them as one of Britain's heavy metal treasures. Cited as a 'revolutionary record' by Iron Pages' Matthias Mader this album includes tracks never released on CD format before.
Tracklisting: Paradise / England / Warrior Time / Vicious Bastard / Heaven Lies Above / At Least They Tried / The Death Of A Loved One / The Age Of Machine / Death & Destiny / Killer / Overlord / U.F.O. / Blue Acid

DRAGSTER – THE VERY BEST OF DRAGSTER
CDMETAL 17

A first time CD release for New Wave of British Heavy Metal legends Dragster. This 19 track compilation features all their fans favourites including "Bite The Bullet", "Running" and "Ambitions".
Tracklisting: So This Is England / Destiny / Heartbeat / Bite The Bullet / Ambitions / Mirror Image / Running / Here Comes The Weekend / You Win Again / Running (Version 2) / Bite The Bullet (Version 2) / Ambitions (Volume 2) / Running With The Pack / Until The Morning / Showtime / Action / I Didn't Know I Loved You / Hot legs / Hellraiser

THE METAL COLLECTORS SERIES

Available from all good record stores, plus mail-order with

VISA or MASTERCARD facilities.

Call 00 44 (0) 207 371 5844 for details.

E Mail jon@cherryred.co.uk

or

write to the mail-order department at:

Cherry Red, Unit 17, Elysium Gate West, 126-128 New King's Road,

London SW6 4LZ.

CD Prices including postage:

£9.95 in the UK, £10.45 in Europe and £10.95 for the rest of the world.

Notes

Notes

Notes

Notes

Notes

Notes

CHERRY RED BOOKS

We are always looking for interesting books to publish.
They can be either new manuscripts or re-issues of deleted books.
If you have any good ideas then please
get in touch with us.

CHERRY RED BOOKS
a division of Cherry Red Records Ltd.
Unit 17, Elysium Gate West,
126-128 New King's Road
London SW6 4LZ

E-mail: iain@cherryred.co.uk
Web: www.cherryred.co.uk